Introduction to Industrial/Organizational Psychology

Introduction to Industrial/Organizational Psychology

Ronald E. Riggio

Kravis Leadership Institute
Claremont McKenna College

Consulting Editor
Lyman W. Porter
University of California, Irvine

Third Edition

PRENTICE HALL, Upper Saddle River, New Jersey 07458

Library of Congress Cataloging-in-Publication Data

Riggio, Ronald E.
   Introduction to industrial/organizational psychology / Ronald E.
Riggio ; consulting editor, Lyman W. Porter. — 3rd ed.
      p.   cm.
   Includes bibliographical references and index.
   ISBN 0-321-05687-6
   1. Psychology, Industrial. 2. Organizational change. I. Porter,
Lyman W. II. Title III. Title: Industrial/organizational
psychology.
HF5548.8.R475   1999
158.7—dc21   99-13595
                                                    CIP

Editor-in-Chief: Nancy Roberts
Executive Editor: Bill Webber
AVP/Director of Manufacturing and Production: Barbara Kittle
Senior Managing Editor: Bonnie Biller
Assistant Managing Editor: Mary Rottino
Assistant Editor: Jennifer L. Cohen
Production Editor: Denise Phillip
Manufacturing Manager: Nick Sklitsis
Prepress and Manufacturing Buyer: Lynn Pearlman

For permission to use copyrighted material, grateful acknowledgment is made to the
copyright holders on pp. 561–564 , which are hereby made part of this copyright page.

This book was set in 11/12 Goudy by WestWords, Inc., and was printed and bound by
Courier Westford. The cover was printed by Phoenix Color Corp.

Printed in the United States of America
10   9   8   7   6   5   4   3   2

ISBN   0-321-05687-6

Prentice-Hall International (UK) Limited, London
Prentice-Hall of Australia Pty. Limited, Sydney
Prentice-Hall Canada, Inc. Toronto
Prentice-Hall Hispanoamericana, S.A., Mexico
Prentice-Hall of India Private Limited, New Delhi
Prentice-Hall of Japan, Inc. Tokyo
Pearson Education Asia Pte Ltd., Singapore
Editoria Prentice-Hall de Brasil, Ltda., Rio de Janeiro

BRIEF CONTENTS

PART ONE   INTRODUCTION

In this first section we discuss the field of industrial/organizational psychology, learn what it is, and examine its history. The second chapter is an overview of social scientific research methods, and how this methodology is used by I/O psychologists. This section sets the groundwork for what is to come.

PART TWO   PERSONNEL ISSUES

In these four chapters we will take a "tour" of personnel functions in organizations. We will examine how jobs are analyzed, how workers are recruited and selected for jobs, how workers are trained, and, finally, how workers' job performance is evaluated.

PART THREE   WORKER ISSUES

These three chapters will examine important psychological states that influence employee work behavior: the motivation to work, the satisfaction one gets from a job, and the stress that occurs because of job demands. These three states represent the vital issues of why people work and what happens to them internally because of work rewards and demands.

PART FOUR   WORK GROUP AND ORGANIZATIONAL ISSUES

In the next five chapters we will examine how workers interact in the formation of work groups and larger work organizations. The study of this interaction of workers and work groups comprises a good part of the area within I/O psychology known as organizational psychology. In reviewing organizational issues, we will start small, looking at communication between two workers, and finish big, examining how large work organizations are designed and structured.

PART FIVE   WORK TASK AND ENVIRONMENT ISSUES

In this section, we will look at the relationship between the worker and the work task. The first chapter in this section (Chapter 15) will begin by examining how the worker, characteristics of the work task (including the work tools and machinery used), and the physical work environment all interact to enable the worker to perform a job. In the last chapter (Chapter 16), we will examine how characteristics of the work environment and the conditions of work affect worker safety, well-being, and the overall quality of the working experience.

Contents

PREFACE

Introduction to Industrial/Organizational Psychology provides an inviting and comprehensive introduction to the field of industrial/organizational (I/O) psychology. Two important themes guided the writing of this textbook. First, since I/O psychology is a field with both a strong scientific base and an applied orientation, the book demonstrates the connection between psychological theory and application: Theoretical concepts are shown to lead to useful interventions. Second, this book was designed and written with the student in mind. Whenever possible, the text draws on examples and illustrations from the world of work that students understand. For instance, many work-setting examples include service industries, such as retail chains and fast food restaurants, rather than concentrating solely on traditional office or factory work settings.

Introduction to Industrial/Organizational Psychology is an introductory textbook that appeals to a wide range of students with varying academic backgrounds. It is designed for use in undergraduate survey course in I/O psychology or in psychology of work behavior courses, and is suited for courses that contain a mix of psychology majors and nonmajors. The text is appropriate for courses at four-year colleges and universities, as well as two-year community colleges. While the book is written at a level that makes the material accessible to students who are relatively new to the field of psychology, the coverage of topics is comprehensive. The inclusion of "classic" theories and research along with the latest developments and innovations makes this a thorough and challenging text for advanced psychology students as well.

What's New: The Third Edition

There has been a lot of feedback over the years from instructors, students and text reviewers, and I am grateful for their suggestions and insights. Thankfully, however, this feedback has been largely positive, and of the "it's not broke, so don't try to fix it" variety. So, most of the changes in this edition have been in response to requests to update, clarify, and add additional information on core concepts. Outdated information is gone. Although this text is technically an "introductory-level" book, it is thoroughly referenced—I venture to say that few introductory texts have as much current research information and are as well-referenced. This makes *Introduction to Industrial/Organizational Psychology* a great resource for teacher and student alike.

The major changes and additions in this edition are as follows:

- *Career Information.* Chapter 1 contains far more information on the field of I/O psychology, including information on careers, graduate training, and areas of specialization. Some of this information was in an appendix in the previous edition, but it is now "up-front" to help pique student interest.

- *Statistical Appendix.* In keeping with the introductory level of the text, higher-level statistical information has been moved from Chapter 2 to a "Statistical Appendix" at the end of that chapter. Courses that put greater emphasis on methods can easily include it, but it also serves as good later reference material for students who are not assigned it as part of the course.

- *Employee-Centered.* The traditional emphasis on "personnel" issues has been transformed to focus on "employee" issues and concerns. Thus, topics are renamed with this in mind (note changes in Chapters 3–6). There is also greater emphasis on teams and the value of the organization's human resources.

- *Thoroughly Updated.* The latest research on each key topic has been included. There are more than 250 new references. Again, students will find this an excellent resource for term papers and in their future coursework.

- *Expanded Instructor's Manual and Ancillaries.* The instructor's manual and testbank has been expanded and updated, and includes exercises and additional material. It is, by far, the best package of ancillaries in I/O psychology (I know, I married the IM coauthor).

Text Structure

Introduction to Industrial/Organizational Psychology is divided into five parts. Part One provides an introduction to the field and an overview of research methods used by I/O psychologists. Part Two covers employee and personnel issues, including separate chapters on job analysis, employee selection, employee training, and evaluating employee performance. Part Three is called "Worker Issues" and deals with processes that are worker-centered: worker motivation, job satisfaction, and stress. Part Four covers organizational topics that are group-oriented: communication, group processes, leadership, organizational power and politics, organizational structure, culture and development. Part Five deals with work environment and task issues, including the topics of human factors, work conditions, and work safety. Although human factors has, in many ways, split off from mainstream I/O psychology, this introductory-level text strives to provide breadth of coverage regarding work-related psychological topics.

Special features included in each chapter of *Introduction to Industrial/ Organizational Psychology* complement the text narrative and provide further illustrations and examples of I/O psychology in the "real world." One of these features, "Applying I/O Psychology," takes some of the theoretical and research material presented in the chapter and shows how I/O psychologists apply this knowledge to make positive changes in actual work settings. A second feature, "Up Close" (which is particularly student-oriented), provides students with practical information concerning how I/O psychology can increase understanding of everyday work situations. A third feature, "On the Cutting Edge," highlights more current areas of research or practice in I/O psychology. "Inside Tips," found at the beginning of each chapter, is designed to connect chapters and help students see the "big picture" of the field of I/O psychology, as well as to provide specific study tips.

The chapters are designed to facilitate learning. Each chapter begins with an outline of the topics and ends with a chapter summary and a series of study questions/exercises that help students review and think about the chapter material. "Stop and Review" questions are strategically placed in the margins. These questions are designed to allow the student to "self-test" whether she or he has retained important material just read or studied. A glossary of key terms also appears throughout the chapters, with a more complete alphabetical glossary at the end of the book.

The text is complemented by an instructor's resource book prepared by Heidi Riggio and me. We have worked hard to make this ancillary package the best available. It includes detailed outlines, suggestions for lectures, discussion questions, in-class exercises, audiovisual resources, transparency masters, and other special features. Finally, Susan Murphy and I have worked with Prentice-Hall to produce a book of readings. *Readings in I/O Psychology* is a compilation of classic and cutting-edge articles from core I/O psychology publications. It can be used as a supplementary book of readings, since it follows the general structure of the text (or it is a useful resource for an advanced I/O course).

Acknowledgments

I would like to thank the many adopters of the previous editions of the text. Many of you have provided important feedback that have helped in revisions. I would also like to thank the many reviewers whose valuable input helped shaped the three editions of the text. They are:

Christopher A. Capuano, Fairleigh Dickinson University; Caran Colvin, San Francisco State University; Michael Coovert, University of South Florida; Chris Cozby, California State University, Fullerton; Jack Croxton, State University of New York at Fredonia; Diane Davis, Oakton Community College; George M. Diekhoff, Midwestern State University; Cheryl Drout, State University of New York at Fredonia; Juanita V. Field, Plymouth State College; Kevin Ford, University of Michigan; Harold W. Goldstein, Bowling

Green State University; Jan Halpert, DePaul University; Scott Highhouse, Indiana University-Purdue University, Indianapolis; Allen Huffcut, Bradley University; Douglas Johnson, University of Arkansas at Little Rock; Patrick Knight, Kansas State University; Janet Kottke, California State University, San Bernadino; Diane Krum, College of Lake County; Thomas Lee, University of Washington; Andrea Markowitz, University of Baltimore; Michael McCall, Ithica College; Frederick R. Mitchell, Harford Community College; Clay Moore, Oakton Community College; Robert Ostermann, Fairleigh Dickinson University; Paul Elliot Spector, University of South Florida, Tampa; Christopher Taylor, Western Washington University; Wanda A. Trahan, University of Wisconsin, Oshkosh; Robert Vance, Ohio State University; Peter Villanova, Northern Illinois University; Maxine Warnath, Western Oregon State College; Matthew Westra, Longview Community College; Sheldon Zedeck, University of California, Berkeley.

I welcome all comments, criticisms, and suggestions. Please contact me at:

Ron Riggio, Ph.D.
Kravis Leadership Institute
Claremont McKenna College
850 Columbia Avenue
Claremont, CA 91711
e-mail: ronald_riggio@mckenna.edu

A special thanks to Heidi for her many contributions to the text (and to my life), and a thanks also to Becky Pascal and Barbara Chamberlin.

To the Student (Please don't skip this. It will help.)

This book was written for you. When I decided to write the first edition of this text in 1987, I did so because my students complained about the texts I had been using. I was not happy with them either. They simply weren't accessible. They were too technical and not "student friendly." So, when I wrote this book (and subsequent editions), I have tried to keep my students in mind every step of the way. I have tried to keep the book current, readable, and relevant to students' current and future working lives. There are special features, such as the "Stop and Review" questions that were created to help you determine if you are retaining the material you are reading and studying.

This text is set up to cover the broad-ranging field of I/O psychology, and I've tried to keep it interesting and lively. In addition, the text is designed, not only to maximize learning, but to be a resource book for continued explorations of the field of I/O psychology. For instance, there is career and educational information about the field, and the book is very thoroughly referenced. Although some students may find it distracting to have points referenced with ("Author, 1998)" throughout, these references will be extremely useful in finding starting points for term papers or future exploration. I hope that you will find this text an important, permanent addition to your personal library. It is a book that can be used in future scholarly work and you will find it a useful reference in your later career.

I would like to thank the student readers of previous editions for their valuable input, suggestions, and comments about the text. Please let me hear from you, as well.

How to Read and Study this Book

This book is set up to maximize your learning about industrial/organizational psychology. Key terms are set in boldface type when they are first discussed, and brief definitions of these terms appear in the adjacent margins (longer definitions are at the end in a glossary). You should look over the key terms before you begin reading a chapter and then alert yourself to them as you read. As you move along you can test yourself by using the margin definitions. Of course, the key terms deal only with major points in each chapter for there is much more to mastering the material. Not only should you be able to define important terms and concepts, but you should also know how they *apply* to work behavior. As you learn the important points made throughout the book, stop occasionally and ask yourself such questions as, "How does this apply to the working world that I know?" "Have I seen examples of this concept before?" "How can the material that I am learning be applied in my own working life?" "How can this new information help me to see work and work behavior in a new and different way?"

Also located in the margins are brief "Stop and Review" questions. Their purpose is to stop you at certain points in your reading/studying, so that you can go back and review the material just covered. Often, students find that they get caught up in the reading, and they forget to retain or "encode" the material for later recall. The review questions are intended to help you check if you are retaining important pieces of information.

Three other chapter features are also set off from the text. The first, "Applying I/O Psychology," deals with specific applications of I/O psychology theories or concepts. The "Up Close" feature offers helpful research-based information that can futher your understanding of your past, present, or future world of work. These usually take a "how-to" approach to some common issue or problem at work. Finally, "On the Cutting Edge" offers some latest developments in the field.

At the beginning of each chapter is another learning aid called "Inside Tips." This aid will help you understand how the various chapters and topic areas fit together. They may also offer suggestions on how to study the information in the chapter.

At the end of each chapter is a brief summary of the central concepts. There are also study questions and exercises designed to make you think a little bit more about the topics presented and to review and apply what you have learned. Finally, there are suggestions for additional reading. These usually include at least one reference book related to the general theme of the chapter (useful as a starting point for research papers), and a couple of topical readings—books or journal review articles on a specific topic. Welcome to I/O psychology.

Ron Riggio

INTRODUCTION: DEFINITIONS AND HISTORY

UNDERSTANDING INDUSTRIAL/ORGANIZATIONAL PSYCHOLOGY

INSIDE TIPS

This first chapter is intended to define I/O psychology and to give you a feel for what the field is all about and what I/O psychologists do. The examples drawn from the early history of I/O psychology and the discussion of current and future trends show how far the field has progressed in a relatively brief period.

Since industrial/organizational psychology is so broad in its scope, it is not easy to gain a good understanding of the entire field by simply learning definitions or studying some of its historical roots; to actually comprehend the scope of I/O psychology you need to get through this entire textbook. Each chapter, from Chapters 3 through 16, presents a general topic and several specialties that I/O psychologists study. As you go through the book, step back and try to see how the various topics fit together. You will then begin to find the threads that hold the field of I/O psychology together.

Like it or not, you and I will spend a big part of our waking lives working. Not only does work take up a large chunk of the day, but it also often governs where we live, how we live, and the kinds of people with whom we associate.

It makes sense, then, that we should want to learn more about the world of work and our own work behavior.

Have you ever wondered what motivates people to work, what makes someone a good manager or leader, or why some people are competent, loyal workers, while others are untrustworthy and unreliable? Have you ever considered the ways a particular job might be redesigned to make it more efficient or the processes by which large organizations make decisions? Have you noticed that work can sometimes be a great source of satisfaction, but it can also be terribly stressful at times? All these and other questions and issues have been studied by industrial/organizational psychologists.

In this chapter, we will define the field of industrial/organizational psychology, look at some of the specialty areas within the discipline, and learn a bit about what industrial/organizational psychologists do. We will also look briefly at the history of industrial/organizational psychology, focusing on some of the important early developments in the field. Finally, we will consider industrial/organizational psychology today to see how the field is progressing and we will examine some of the important trends now and for the near future.

What Is Industrial/Organizational Psychology?

psychology
the study of behavior and mental processes

Psychology is the scientific study of behavior and mental processes. Psychologists use systematic scientific methods in an effort to understand more about the hows and whys of behavior and human thought processes. Within the broad field of psychology, there are many specialty areas, each of which focuses on a different aspect of behavior. For instance, developmental psychology focuses on developmental behavior over the lifespan, abnormal psychology studies abnormal and psychopathological behavior, while social psychology studies human social behavior.

industrial/organizational (I/O) psychology
the branch of psychology that is concerned with the study of behavior in work settings and the application of psychology principles to change work behavior

Industrial/organizational (I/O) psychology is that specialty area within the broad field of psychology that studies human behavior in work settings. As you might imagine, the study of human behavior in work settings is a large undertaking. Most jobs are quite complicated, requiring the use of a wide range of motor and mental skills. Work organizations are often large and complex entities made up of hundreds or even thousands of workers who must interact and coordinate activities in order to produce some product or service.

Some I/O psychologists study the basic personnel functions within organizations, such as the way workers are recruited and selected, how employees are trained and developed, and the measurement of employee job performance. Other I/O psychologists study the psychological processes underlying work behavior, such as the motivation to work, and worker feelings of job satisfaction and stress. Still other I/O psychologists focus on group processes in the workplace, including the relationships between workplace supervisors and subordinates, and how groups of workers coordinate to get

In this raft-building exercise for executives, communication and leadership—two topics studied in industrial/organizational psychology—make one group more successful than the other.

the job done. Finally, there are I/O psychologists who study the conditions of work, including the systems used to perform work, and how the physical and psychological environment affects worker behavior. The structure of this textbook will parallel these various areas of subspecialization in I/O psychology.

The Science and Practice of Industrial/Organizational Psychology

I/O psychology has two objectives: first, to conduct research in an effort to increase our knowledge and understanding of human work behavior; second, to apply that knowledge to improve work behavior, the work environment, and the psychological conditions of workers. Thus, I/O psychologists are trained to be both scientists and practitioners, in what is referred to as the *scientist-practitioner model*. Although some I/O psychologists may operate primarily as either scientists or practitioners, most I/O psychologists believe that the best practitioners are strongly based in the science of I/O psychology (Katzell & Austin, 1992).

The scientific objective of I/O psychology involves the study and understanding of all aspects of behavior at work. As scientists, I/O psychologists conduct research, and publish the results of these efforts in professional journals such as those listed in Table 1.1. We will discuss the scientific objective in great depth in Chapter 2.

It is important to realize, however, that the study of work behavior is a multidisciplinary, cooperative venture. Industrial/organizational psychologists are not the only professionals who study work behavior. Researchers in the fields of management, sociology, political science, organizational communication, economics, and several other social sciences contribute to

TABLE 1.1

Journals Publishing Research in Industrial/Organizational Psychology and Related Areas

Academy of Management Journal
Academy of Management Review
Administrative Science Quarterly
Annual Review of Psychology
Applied Ergonomics
Applied Psychological Measurement
Ergonomics
Human Factors
Human Relations
The Industrial-Organizational Psychologist
International Review of I/O Psychology
Journal of Applied Psychology
Journal of Applied Social Psychology
Journal of Business and Psychology
Journal of Business Research
Journal of Management
Journal of Occupational and Organizational Psychology
Journal of Organizational Behavior
Leadership Quarterly
Organization Science
Organizational Behavior and Human Decision Processes
Organizational Dynamics
Personnel
Personnel Psychology
Training and Development Journal
Work & Stress

what we know and understand about the worker and work organizations. Because this research takes place on many fronts, I/O psychologists need to be aware of recent developments in other fields. A quick look at the titles of journals that publish research of interest to I/O psychologists illustrates the multidisciplinary nature of the study of work behavior, including such terms as "management," "business," "personnel" and "ergonomics" (see Table 1.1).

The multidisciplinary nature of the study of work behavior may be illustrated by an issue that was of utmost concern to many U.S. businesses during the 1980s: the ability of Japanese companies to outproduce (in terms of both quantity and quality) U.S. manufacturers of such products as automobiles, high-tech electronic equipment, and steel. In studying this issue, a psychologist might focus on differences between the workers or between the work systems of the two countries. An economist might concentrate on the fact that Japan puts a greater proportion of its financial and human resources into these particular industries than does the United States. A political scientist might examine the politics involved, whereas a management researcher might look at differences in management philosophy and style between the two countries. In reality, all of these factors were probably involved, and each approach is valid (Zussman, 1983). Many work issues are similarly extremely complex and need to be examined from a variety of perspectives. Most important, we need to keep an open mind and stay in touch with what other disciplines are doing if we are going to truly understand the working world and human work behavior.

The applied objective of I/O psychology involves the application of psychological principles, and of knowledge gleaned from psychological research, to work behavior. As practitioners, I/O psychologists may be called on to deal with specific work-related problems or issues. For example, an I/O psychologist might evaluate a personnel testing program, or conduct an employee attitude survey or some type of employee training program. More and more, however, I/O psychologists are assisting organizations at a deeper, more global level (London & Moses, 1990).

UP CLOSE

What Does an I/O Psychologist *Really* Do?

One of the most common questions asked by students in I/O psychology courses is, "What does an I/O psychologist do, *really*?" The answer to this question is not simple for a couple of reasons. First, many undergraduate students and laypersons have not had much exposure to I/O psychologists either face-to-face or in the media. Unlike clinical psychologists, who are frequently depicted in films, interviewed on news shows, and stereotyped in cartoons and on TV, most people have never seen an I/O psychologist. A second and more important reason why it is difficult to understand what I/O psychologists do is because I/O psychologists do so many different kinds of things. I/O psychology is a broad field encompassing a large number of specialty areas, many of which are quite unrelated to one another. Consequently, it is next to impossible to talk about a "typical" I/O psychologist.

In addition to performing a variety of jobs and tasks, I/O psychologist researchers and practitioners (Ph.D.-level) are employed in a variety of settings, with a little more than one-third employed in colleges and universities, about one-third working in research or consulting firms, about 20 percent working for businesses and industries, and about 10 percent employed in federal, state, or local government (Balzer & Howard, 1994).

I/O psychologists work for a variety of major U.S. and international corporations, including Dow Chemical, Ford Motor Company, IBM, Toyota, Disney, Standard Oil, Xerox Corporation, Unisys, United Airlines, and Pepsi. They can hold job titles such as Director of Human Resources, Personnel Research Psychologist, Vice President of Employee Development, Manager of Employee Relations, Senior Employment Specialist, Director

UP CLOSE (*continued*)

of Human Factors Department, Testing Specialist, Quality Performance Manager, Consultant, and Staff Industrial Psychologist.

To help you better understand what I/O psychologists do, as well as help you understand the diverse areas of specialization within I/O psychology, let's look at some brief profiles of actual I/O psychologists:

Dr. M is an I/O psychologist working for a large aerospace firm. Her main area of expertise is sophisticated robot systems, and she has helped design and test several sophisticated robotlike systems for use in outer space. Her latest project involves working on the development of a proposed orbiting space station in which much of the construction is done by robots. Dr. M maintains that her training in research methods, which allows her to approach work problems systematically, was the most valuable part of her academic education.

Dr. C received his Ph.D. in I/O psychology in the early 1970s. His first job was conducting research for the General Telephone and Electronics Laboratories on the organizational processes in some of the company's operational units, including assessing job satisfaction, facilitating communication, and helping to resolve conflicts. Some years later, Dr. C joined a large consulting firm, and he currently is employed by an international consulting company where he conducts survey feedback and other organizational development programs for a variety of businesses and organizations.

Dr. H is an I/O psychologist who is in the United States Navy. His responsibilities include developing and researching placement systems for certain Navy personnel. Dr. H is active in the American Psychological Association's divisions of I/O Psychology (Division 14) and Military Psychology (Division 19), and regularly reports his research at national and regional professional conferences. Much of his work involves personnel selection within the military—trying to fit new recruits to the types of positions for which they are best suited.

Dr. R is an I/O psychologist who owns a private consulting practice in a small Midwestern city. Before becoming an independent consultant, Dr. R worked for a large consulting firm in a metropolitan area, where he conducted job analyses and ran training seminars for businesses. His decision to move to a less urban area was primarily responsible for his decision to start an independent practice. Dr. R specializes in personnel selection, job analysis, and the design of training and development programs, although he occasionally engages in other activities such as conducting attitude and marketing surveys and serving as an expert witness in labor-related legal cases. In a sense, he has had to become an industrial/organizational "jack-of-all-trades," because he is one of the few I/O psychologists in his region. Dr. R claims that the most valuable training he received was in statistics, psychology, and the business courses that he took after receiving his Ph.D., so that he could become more knowledgeable about various business operations and learn business terminology.

Ms. O received a master's degree in industrial/organizational psy-

UP CLOSE (continued)

chology just a few years ago. She is an assistant director of marketing research for a national chain of fast food restaurants. Her duties include researching the sites for new restaurants, and designing and organizing customer satisfaction surveys. Ms. O also teaches I/O psychology and marketing courses at a local junior college.

Dr. P, an I/O psychologist, is a professor in the school of management in a large state university. He previously held academic positions in university psychology departments. Dr. P is quite well-known and respected for his research in I/O psychology. In addition to his research and teaching, Dr. P has served as a consultant for several large corporations, including many Fortune 500 companies.

Mr. K, who has a master's degree in organizational psychology, is the director of human resources for a biomedical company, which means that he is responsible for the administration of all facets of human resources for his organization. Mr. K oversees payroll, benefits, compensation, and personnel activities such as the development of job descriptions, employee selection, and personnel training. He also has an active internship program that uses undergraduate and graduate students as interns who help set up special human resource programs for his employees.

After a successful career in the finance industry, Dr. A went back to graduate school and received her Ph.D. in industrial/organizational psychology. She has worked in the human resources department at AT&T and has published books and research articles on a variety of topics in I/O psychology. She is currently president of a consulting organization and is quite active in research and professional affairs in the field.

The Roots and Early History of Industrial/Organizational Psychology

In order to understand the impact that I/O psychology has had on the world of work, it is important to know a little bit about the history of the field. We will examine historical periods in I/O psychology's past, and focus on a significant event or important phenomenon in each time period. We will later look at the present and future of I/O psychology.

THE BEGINNINGS

Around the turn of the century, when the field of psychology was still in its infancy, a few early psychologists dabbled in the study of work behavior. For example, Hugo Munsterberg was an experimental psychologist who became interested in the design of work and personnel selection for jobs such

STOP AND REVIEW

Describe in detail the two objectives of I/O psychology.

time-and-motion studies *procedures in which work tasks are broken down into simple component movements and the movements timed to develop a more efficient method for performing the tasks*

scientific management *begun by Frederick Taylor, a method of using scientific principles to improve the efficiency and productivity of jobs*

Frederick W. Taylor was the founder of the scientific management movement.

Hugo Munsterberg was an early I/O psychologist.

as streetcar operator (Munsterberg, 1913). Another experimental psychologist who pioneered the field of industrial psychology (the broader label, "industrial/organizational psychology," was not used extensively until the 1970s) was Walter Dill Scott, who was interested in studying salespersons and the psychology of advertising (Scott, 1908).

Another early spark that helped ignite the field of I/O psychology was provided not by a psychologist, but by an engineer named Frederick W. Taylor. Taylor believed that scientific principles could be applied to the study of work behavior to help increase worker efficiency and productivity. He felt that there was "one best method" for performing a particular job. By breaking the job down scientifically into measurable component movements and recording the time needed to perform each movement, Taylor believed that he could develop the fastest, most efficient way of performing any task. He was quite successful in applying his methods, which became known as **time-and-motion studies**. These time-and-motion procedures often doubled, tripled, and even quadrupled laborer output! Taylor's system for applying scientific principles to increase work efficiency and productivity eventually became known as **scientific management**. In addition to applying time-and-motion procedures, Taylor also incorporated into his system of scientific management other considerations, such as selection of workers based on abilities and the use of proper tools (Taylor, 1911).

Taylor and his followers, including the husband-and-wife team of Frank and Lillian Gilbreth (Lillian Gilbreth was one of the earliest women I/O psychologists), implemented the principles of scientific management and revolutionized several physical labor jobs by making the accepted work procedures more efficient and productive (Gilbreth, 1916). For example, scientific management principles and procedures such as time-and-motion studies greatly improved the efficiency of a wide variety of typical types of jobs, including cabinetmaking, clerical filing, lumber sawing, and the making of reinforced concrete slabs (increased from 80 to 425 slabs per day!) (Lowry, Maynard, & Stegemerten, 1940).

Unfortunately, Taylor's philosophy was quite narrow and limited. In his day many jobs involved manual labor and were thus easily broken down and made more efficient through the application of principles of scientific management. Today jobs are much more complex, often demanding sophisticated problem-solving skills or the use of creative thinking. Fewer and fewer people engage in physical labor. Many of these "higher-level" tasks are not amenable to time-and-motion studies. In other words, there is probably not one best method for creating computer software, developing an advertising campaign, or managing people.

It is important to emphasize that scientific management and I/O psychology are not directly connected, although the principles of scientific management did have an influence on the development of I/O psychology. While work efficiency and increased productivity are certainly important to I/O psychologists, I/O psychology looks beyond efficiency to examine the impact of work procedures and conditions on the working person.

World War I and the 1920s

At the outbreak of World War I, Robert Yerkes, who was president of the American Psychological Association, and a group of psychologists worked with the U.S. Army to create intelligence tests for the placement of Army recruits. The Army Alpha and Beta tests represented the first mass testing efforts, and set the stage for future testing efforts. Even today, employee testing and selection is an important area of I/O psychology. Following World War I, psychologists began to be involved in the screening and placement of personnel in industry. Throughout the 1920s, while the U.S. was experiencing tremendous industrial growth, industrial psychology began to take hold: The first doctoral degree in industrial psychology was awarded in 1921, and psychologists worked directly with industries as consultants and researchers (Katzell & Austin, 1992).

The Great Depression Years and World War II

As the U.S. economy slumped during the 1930s, there was less opportunity for industrial psychologists to work with industries and businesses. While industrial psychology continued to grow at a slower pace, an important development came out of this period from a group of Harvard psychologists who were conducting a series of experiments at a manufacturing plant of the Western Electric Company, in Hawthorne, Illinois. Researcher Elton Mayo and his colleagues wanted to study the effects of the physical work environment on worker productivity.

In the most famous of the experiments, Mayo explored the effects of lighting on worker productivity. Focusing on a group of women who were assembling electrical relay-switching devices, he systematically varied the level of illumination in the room. He expected to be able to determine the optimal level of lighting for performing the task. However, the results were surprising and dramatically changed psychologists' view of the worker from then on. No matter what level the lighting was set at, productivity increased! When lighting was increased, worker output went up. Further increase to very bright illumination resulted in further improvement. Turning the lights down (even to such low levels that it appeared that the women were working in moonlight) also led to increases in productivity. There was a steady increase in workers' output following *any* change in lighting. In other studies, Mayo systematically varied the length and timing of work breaks. Longer breaks, shorter breaks, more or fewer breaks, all resulted in a steady increase in worker output (Mayo, 1933).

Mayo knew that every change in the work environment could not possibly be causing the steady rises in worker productivity. Something else had to be affecting output. Upon closer examination, he concluded that the workers were being affected not by the changes in the physical environment but by the simple fact that they knew they were being observed. According to Mayo,

Workers in the original Hawthorne studies.

Hawthorne effect
changes in behavior occurring as a function of participants' knowledge that they are being observed and their expectations concerning their role as research participants

these workers believed that the studies were being conducted in an effort to improve work procedures, and their positive expectations, coupled with their knowledge of the observations, determined their consistent increases in productivity, a phenomenon that has been labeled the **Hawthorne effect**. Although in the first example discovered by Mayo the "Hawthorne effect" was positive, resulting in increased productivity, this is not always the case. In another of his studies, work group productivity *fell* following the introduction of changes in the work environment. Because these workers believed that the results of the studies would lead to more demanding production quotas, they restricted output whenever they were being observed, thus producing a "negative" Hawthorne effect (Roethlisberger & Dickson, 1939).

Although researchers have noted a number of serious flaws in the methods Mayo used to conduct the Hawthorne experiments (see Chapter 2), the general conclusions reached by Mayo and his colleagues resulted in the development of the **human relations movement**, which recognized the importance of social factors and something called "worker morale" in influencing work productivity. In fact, this movement stated that a harmonious work environment, with good interpersonal relationships among coworkers, will be a productive work environment, particularly when the work itself is boring or monotonous. According to Mayo, workers in repetitive or low-level positions—jobs that do not themselves provide satisfaction—will turn to the social environment of the work setting for motivation.

human relations movement
a movement based on the studies of Elton Mayo that emphasizes the importance of social factors in influencing work performance

World War II also contributed greatly to the growth of I/O psychology. First, the tremendous need for state-of-the-art machinery, and the increasing complexity of that machinery, was an important impetus for human factors psychology. Second, I/O psychologists were called on to improve selection and placement of military personnel, continuing the work that psychologists had begun during World War I.

The Army General Classification Test, a group-administered pencil-and-paper test, was developed to separate recruits into categories based on

A sign reminds a textile worker that he can shut down the line if he spots a defect. Such emphasis on employee decisionmaking stems from the human relations movement.

their abilities to learn military duties and responsibilities. Screening tests were also created to select candidates for officer training. In addition, psychologists helped the United States Office of Strategic Services (OSS) develop intensive assessment strategies for selecting candidates for dangerous espionage positions. Some of these techniques included "hands-on" situational tests in which candidates had to perform some tasks under difficult and near impossible conditions. The aim was to assess their ability to deal with stressful and frustrating circumstances, which is very important for soldiers involved in military espionage.

THE POST-WAR YEARS AND THE MODERN ERA

It was after World War II that I/O psychology truly began to blossom and specialty areas began to emerge. A distinct focus on personnel issues, such as testing, selection, and the evaluation of employees, was helped in part by the publication of a new journal, *Personnel Psychology*, in 1948. During the Cold War years of the 1950s and 1960s the growth of the defense industry further spurred the development of a specialty area called engineering psychology (today referred to as human factors psychology, or ergonomics). Engineering psychologists were called in to help design control systems that were both sensible and easy to operate. In addition, the contributions of sociologists and social psychologists who began studying and performing extensive research in work organizations helped create a subspecialty area of organizational psychology.

The 1960s through the early 1990s was a time when research and practice in industrial/organizational psychology flourished. Many of the topics currently associated with I/O psychology were developed and explored in depth during this period, particularly topics such as motivation and goal setting, job attitudes, organizational stress, group processes, organizational power and politics, and organizational development. We will examine a great deal of this work throughout this book.

One historical event during this time period that had a major impact on I/O psychology was civil rights legislation. One portion of the sweeping Civil Rights Act of 1964, Title VII, banned discrimination in employment practices. Designed to protect underrepresented groups, such as ethnic minorities, from being unfairly discriminated against in work-related decisions, this legislation forced organizations to take a closer look at the ways people were selected for jobs. Particular attention was given to the fairness of employment selection tests and personnel decisions such as promotions and firings. Subsequent civil rights legislation protected other groups from discrimination, including older people (Age Discrimination in Employment Act, 1967 and 1978), and people with disabilities (Americans with Disabilities Act, 1990). As a result, I/O psychologists have played an important part in helping to establish and implement fair employment standards. We will discuss these matters further in Part II.

STOP AND REVIEW

Name three pre-World War II events that had a significant impact on I/O psychology.

Industrial/Organizational Psychology Today and in the Future

Today, industrial/organizational psychology is one of the fastest growing areas of psychology. I/O psychologists are in the forefront of those professionals who are satisfying the huge demand for information leading to greater understanding of the worker, the work environment, and work behavior. They are involved in nearly every aspect of business and industry, and as we will see, the range of topics they research and the varieties of tasks they perform are extensive.

APPLYING I/O PSYCHOLOGY

Exploring Training and Careers in Industrial/Organizational Psychology

The usual professional degree in industrial/organizational psychology, as in all areas of psychology, is the doctorate (Ph.D.). However, a growing number of programs offer master's degrees in psychology with an emphasis in I/O psychology, and a handful of college programs even offer a bachelor's degree with a major in I/O psychology (Koppes, 1991). The master's degree (M.A. or M.S.) can also qualify one as a prac-

APPLYING I/O PSYCHOLOGY (*continued*)

titioner of psychology, although licensing requirements may vary from state to state. In recent years, the employment picture for I/O psychologists, particularly those with a Ph.D., has been very good, with salaries among the highest in the field of psychology.

To explore graduate training in I/O psychology:

- Talk to your psychology advisor in depth about the process of applying to graduate programs, including the alternatives available, the requirements for admission, the deadlines, letters of recommendations, and the like.
- Find out additional information about graduate programs and the application process by contacting the following professional organizations:
  - The American Psychological Association (APA) is the largest professional organization for psychologists. They maintain a website (www.apa. org) with detailed, step-by-step information for exploring and applying to graduate programs (including a "Guide to Getting into Graduate School").
  - The Society for Industrial and Organizational Psychology, Inc. (SIOP) is the professional organization for I/O psychologists. They maintain a website (www.siop.org), and have detailed information available about I/O psychology graduate programs at both the Ph.D. and master's levels.
  - The American Psychological Society has some relevant information about scientific

careers in psychology (www. psychologicalscience.org).

To explore a possible career in industrial/organizational psychology:

- Go to your university's career guidance office and to the psychology department advisor to find out what information is available on careers in I/O psychology.
- Both APA and SIOP have career information available at their respective websites.
- Arrange a short "information interview" with a practicing I/O psychologist in your area. Ask for a few minutes of the professional's time to find out firsthand what she or he does for a living. You might talk to several such professionals, since individuals' job duties can vary greatly. Again, the career guidance office may be able to help you locate practicing I/O psychologists.
- Read beyond the textbook. Examine some of the suggested readings at the end of each chapter. Go to the library and scan through some of the journals that publish research in I/O psychology. (There is a list of these journals in Table 1.1).

Regardless of whether you choose a career in I/O psychology, the topics studied by I/O psychologists pertain to just about any job in any work setting. A knowledge of principles of industrial/organizational psychology can help facilitate understanding of human behavior and organizational processes occurring in the work place.

Note: All 3 professional organizations offer student affiliate memberships that you can join to receive regular mailings.

While the work of I/O psychologists has helped improve behavior at work, other developments in the working world and in the world at large have in turn influenced the field of I/O psychology. We will examine four key trends in the world of work that are important today and in the future of I/O psychology.

First trend: The changing nature of work

Jobs and organizations are rapidly changing and evolving. Many jobs are becoming increasingly complex due to technological advancements, and they are more demanding, requiring workers to process more and more information and to make more decisions (Ones & Viswesvaran, 1998). In addition, organizations worldwide are reducing their workforces. **Organizational downsizing** is a strategy of reducing an organization's workforce to improve organizational efficiency, productivity, and/or competitiveness (Freeman & Cameron, 1993). Organizations are downsizing because of technological advancements such as robotic and computer-assisted manufacturing that eliminates workers' jobs because of increased efficiency in jobs and the elimination of overlapping worker functions, and a general reduction in middle-level managers (Murphy, 1998). Downsizing requires organizations to "do more with less" in order to survive—including the fact that fewer workers are doing more work (DeWitt, 1993; Greenhalgh, Lawrence, & Sutton, 1988; Sutton & D'Aunno, 1989).

Organizations are becoming flatter, with fewer levels in the hierarchy, and they are being broken up into smaller subunits with greater emphasis on work teams. With telecommuting, advanced communication systems, and sophisticated computer networking, people can work in almost any location, with team members who are quite remote. This will have important implications for how work is done, and I/O psychologists will be very involved in helping workers adapt to technological and structural changes (Craiger, 1997). In addition, I/O psychologists will assist organizations in redesigning jobs for greater efficiency, in creating new and more flexible organizational structures and work teams, and in helping workers deal with stresses that result from all of the changes.

Second trend: Expanding focus on human resources

The increasing concern with the management and maintenance of an organization's human resources that began with Mayo and the human relations movement continues to be important. Organizations have become more and more concerned about and responsive to the needs of workers. This will be even more important in the future.

The past few years have seen a tight labor market for truly skilled workers. This means that organizations will have to compete ferociously to attract and keep the best workers (May, 1998). Greater emphasis will need to be given to such areas as employee recruitment and selection procedures. Companies will also have to offer more enticing benefit programs to attract

organizational downsizing
a strategy of reducing an organization's workforce to improve organizational efficiency and/or competitiveness

and retain the best workers. In addition, continuing advancements in work technology and the ever-increasing body of knowledge needed by workers to perform their jobs mean that older workers will have to be retrained often to remain contributing members of the workforce. All of this suggests the need for greater focus on personnel issues, such as recruiting, screening, and testing potential workers, and on employee training, development, and compensation programs, all of which are specialties of I/O psychologists.

While the skilled labor force is dwindling, the number of low-skilled jobs in the service industry is growing, as is the population of low and unskilled workers. A human resources challenge for the future is to help provide meaningful and rewarding work experiences in these positions, and to help transition workers from the unskilled to the skilled labor force.

Finally, research in I/O psychology is beginning to focus more broadly, seeing the worker as a "whole person" rather than just a working being. I/O psychology is looking more and more at individual development, addressing topics such as the processes by which workers cope with stress and adapt to changes, and understanding the role of emotions in the workplace (Vandaveer, 1998). I/O psychology has also recognized the "overlap" between employees' work life and home life—that issues at home can spill over into the workplace, and vice versa.

Third trend: Increasing diversity of the workforce

The increasing number of women and ethnic minorities entering the organizational workforce has led to greater and greater workplace diversity. This diversity will increase in the future. For example, women make up two-thirds of all entering workers in the labor market, while about one-third of all entering workers are members of ethnic minorities. By the year 2010, white males—the current majority of the U.S. workforce—will constitute less than forty percent of the workforce of the future (APS, 1993; Loden & Rosener, 1991; Williams & O'Reilly, 1998). Moreover, the diversity of cultures in workplaces will also increase as workers become more internationally mobile. Existing workforces will consist of members from a greater number and variety of cultures.

While increased diversity presents challenges to organizations and managers, this increased workforce diversity also represents a tremendous strength and opportunity. An obvious advantage of increased workforce diversity is the opportunity for different viewpoints and perspectives that will lead to organizational creativity and innovation (Harrison, Price, & Bell, 1998; Milliken & Martins, 1996). Increased workforce diversity can also help an organization in understanding and reaching new markets for products or services. An organization's commitment to diversity can also help in recruiting and retaining the best workers. For instance, cutting-edge companies that value workforce diversity not only attract the most qualified workers, but the valuing of diversity permeates the entire organizational culture, leading to reduced organizational conflict, greater cooperation among workers, and increased flexibility and innovation (Jackson, 1994; Loden & Rosener, 1991).

The increasing diversity of the workforce is an important trend for the future.

Industrial/organizational psychologists will have to assist organizations in dealing with the challenges increasing diversity will bring. While diversity has benefits, demographic and cultural differences can, if not carefully managed, create great difficulties in the functioning of work teams—increasing destructive conflict, inhibiting team cooperation, and impeding performance (Chen, Chen, & Meindl, 1998; Lau & Murnighan, 1998; Williams & O'Reilly, 1998). The key to dealing successfully with diversity will involve getting beyond the "surface" issues that divide people, and getting at the "deeper" benefits that diversity brings (Harrison et al., 1998; Hartel, 1998).

Fourth trend: Increasing globalization of business

In recent years, there has been a rapid, continuing shift toward a more global economy. Businesses and industries in the U.S. and other Western nations are focusing more and more on the global marketplace. Companies that were formerly concerned only with domestic markets and competition must now consider the international picture. As more and more organizations go international, there is an increasing need for workers to be trained for working in or with organizations located in other countries (Adler, 1991; Earley, 1987; Earley & Singh, 1995; Rothwell, 1992). The successful executive or manager of the future must be globally aware, knowledgeable and respectful of other cultures, and capable of working with people from a wide variety of backgrounds.

Describe three current and future trends in I/O psychology.

Summary

Industrial/organizational psychology is the branch of psychology that deals with the study of work behavior. I/O psychologists are concerned with both the science and practice of industrial/organizational psychology. The scientific goal is to increase our knowledge and understanding of work behavior, while the practical goal is to use that knowledge to improve the psychological well-being of workers. The study of work behavior is a multidisciplinary, cooperative venture. Because I/O psychologists are not the only professionals who study work behavior, they combine their research with that of other social sciences.

Important historical contributions that led to the development of the field of I/O psychology include the work of Frederick Taylor, who founded the school of *scientific management*, which held that work behavior could be studied by systematically breaking down a job into its components and recording the time needed to perform each. The application of such *time-and-motion studies* increased the efficiency of many manual labor jobs. During both World War I and World War II, psychologists became involved in the psychological testing of military recruits to determine work assignments. This first large-scale testing program was the beginning of formalized personnel testing, which is still an important part of I/O psychology. Elton

Mayo and his *human relations movement* emphasized the role that social factors play in determining worker behavior. Through a series of studies he demonstrated the importance of worker morale or satisfaction in determining performance. Mayo also discovered the *Hawthorne effect,* or the notion that subjects' behavior could be affected by the mere fact that they knew they were being observed and by the expectations they associated with being subjects in an experiment. Following World War II, there was tremendous growth and specialization in I/O psychology, including specialties within the field that focus on how work groups and organizations function, and on how technology and workers interface.

Today, industrial/organizational psychology is a rapidly growing field. Several important trends present challenges to I/O psychology and represent cutting-edge areas of research in the field. These include: the changing nature of work, and the rapidly expanding nature of jobs, partly caused by a reduction in workforce due to *organizational downsizing* for efficiency; an expanding focus on human resources; increasing diversity in the workforce that presents both challenges and opportunities; and the increasing globalization of business.

Study Questions and Exercises

1. Although I/O psychology is a distinct specialty area in the larger field of psychology, consider how the topics studied by I/O psychologists might benefit from other psychology specialty areas. For example, what contributions have social psychology, educational psychology, cognitive psychology, and other areas made to I/O psychology?

2. Consider the historical advancements made by scientific management, human relations, and the army's intelligence testing programs. How have each of these influenced what we know about work and about workers today?

3. Consider the important trends in I/O psychology today. Are there any ways that these trends have affected or will affect your life as a worker?

4. Imagine that you chose a career path in I/O psychology. What research questions or practice issues interest you? How might these interests affect your choice of training in I/O psychology, and the job title you might hold?

Suggested Readings

Dunnette, M.D., Hough, L.M., and Associates (1990–94). *The handbook of industrial/organizational psychology* (2nd ed.). Palo Alto, CA: Consulting Psychologists Press. *The classic "encyclopedia" for the field, in its revised edition. These four comprehensive volumes contain everything you wanted to know about I/O psychology, and more.*

Howard, A. (Ed.). (1995). *The changing nature of work.* San Francisco: Jossey-Bass. *This edited book contains articles that focus on the future of work and how jobs and the workplace are changing. This book is part of a series in I/O psychology sponsored by SIOP (see below).*

Katzell, R.A., & Austin, J.T. (1992). From then to now: The development of industrial-organizational psychology in the United States. *Journal of Applied Psychology, 77, 803–35. Published for the one hundredth anniversary of the American Psychological Association (APA), this is a comprehensive and detailed history of I/O psychology in the United States.*

Society for Industrial and Organizational Psychology, Inc. (SIOP), Division 14 of the American Psychological Association. *The Industrial-Organizational Psychologist. The official newsletter of the largest U.S. organization of I/O psychologists. Although it is actually SIOP's newsletter, it looks more like a journal and contains current information about the field, timely articles, and reviews, as well as job announcements.*

CHAPTER TWO

RESEARCH METHODS IN INDUSTRIAL/ORGANIZATIONAL PSYCHOLOGY

CHAPTER OUTLINE

UNDERSTANDING THE BASICS OF RESEARCH METHODS AND DESIGN

INSIDE TIPS

This chapter presents a general overview of selected research methods topics and their use in I/O psychology. Although it is intended to be a general introduction to research methods, some of the material can be quite complicated, particularly if you have not had a course that has introduced you to these concepts. If this is the case, you might want to devote some extra time to this chapter and consider looking at an introductory research methods textbook, such as the one listed in the Suggested Readings.

Many of the concepts discussed in this chapter will be used throughout the book when presenting and discussing theories, interpreting research results, and studying the effectiveness of various interventions used by I/O practitioners. Because this chapter introduces a number of important terms, you should plan to spend some time studying their definitions and understanding how they are used. In summary, this is an important chapter that serves as a foundation for what is to come.

Imagine that you want to find the answer to a work-related question such as what qualities make a person an effective manager. How would you go about answering this question? You might ask people you know, but what if you get conflicting answers? Your father might say that a good manager must have a thorough knowledge of the task and of work procedures. A friend might believe that the most important quality is skill in relating to people. Your boss might answer that the situation determines which type of manager works best. Three people, three answers. Who is correct?

You might then try another strategy: observing some good managers to see for yourself which qualities make someone an effective work group leader. But how do you know who is a "good" manager? Moreover, how will you determine which characteristics make the good manager effective? The only sound procedure for answering the question of what makes a good manager is to use systematic, scientific research methods.

How would you approach the problem in a more systematic, scientific fashion? First, to determine the most important characteristics of a successful work group manager, you would need to define "success." Is a successful manager one who leads a productive work group, one who is well-liked and respected by subordinates, or one who leads a work group that is both productive *and* satisfied? Once you have defined your criteria for managerial success, the next step is to figure out how you will measure such success. It is important that the measurement be accurate and precise so that a clear distinction between truly successful and unsuccessful managers can be made. Next, you must isolate the specific characteristics that are believed to be related to success as a work group manager. From your experience or reading you may have some informed ideas about the kinds of knowledge, abilities, or personality that make a successful manager, but you must test these ideas in some systematic fashion. This is the purpose of research methods in psychology. Research methodology is a set of procedures that allows us to investigate the hows and whys of human behavior and to predict when certain behavior will and will not occur.

In this chapter we will study the basic social scientific research methods used by I/O psychologists to study work behavior. We will learn why the research process is important for industrial/organizational psychology and examine the goals of social science research methods. We will review the step-by-step procedures used in social science research and conclude with a discussion of how research results are interpreted and applied to increase our understanding of actual work behavior.

Social Scientific Research Methods

One of the prime purposes of the social scientific research methods used by I/O psychologists is to enable the researcher to step back from any personal feelings or biases in order to study a specific issue objectively. **Objectivity** is the overriding theme of scientific research methods in general, and of social science research methods in particular. It is this objectivity, accomplished via the social scientific process, that distinguishes how a social scientist approaches a work-related problem or issue and how a nonscientist practitioner might approach the same problem or issue. Research methodology is simply a system of guidelines and procedures designed to assist the researcher in obtaining a more accurate and unbiased analysis of the problem at hand. Similarly, statistical analysis is nothing more or less than procedures for testing the repeated objective observations that a researcher has collected.

objectivity
the unbiased approach to observation and interpretations of behavior

GOALS OF SOCIAL SCIENTIFIC RESEARCH METHODS

Since I/O psychology is a science, it shares the same basic goals of any science: to *describe*, *explain*, and *predict* phenomena (Kaplan, 1964). Because I/O psychology is the science of behavior at work, its goals are to describe, explain, and predict work behavior. For example, an I/O psychologist might attempt to satisfy the first goal by describing the production levels of a company, the rates of employee absenteeism and turnover, and the number and type of interactions between supervisors and workers for the purpose of arriving at a more accurate picture of the organization under study. The goal of explaining phenomena is achieved when the I/O psychologist attempts to discover why certain work behaviors occur. Finding out that a company's employee turnover rates are high because of employee dissatisfaction with the levels of pay and benefits would be one example. The goal of prediction would be addressed when a researcher attempts to use the scores from certain psychological tests to predict which employee would be the best candidate for a management position, or when a researcher uses a theory of motivation to predict how employees will respond to different types of incentive programs.

I/O psychology is also an applied science and therefore has the additional goal of attempting to *control* or *alter* behavior to obtain desired outcomes. Using the results of previous research, an I/O psychologist can attempt to alter some aspect of work behavior. For example, there is some evidence of a connection between employee participation in organizational decision making and levels of job satisfaction (Argyris, 1964; Locke & Schweiger, 1979). Knowing this, an I/O psychologist might implement a program of increased employee participation in company policy decision making in an effort to improve levels of employee job satisfaction.

FIGURE 2.1

Steps in the Research Process

STEPS IN THE RESEARCH PROCESS

The process of conducting research typically follows a series of steps (see Figure 2.1). The first step is the formulation of a problem or issue for study. The second step is the generation of hypotheses. The third step is designing the research, which includes selecting the appropriate research method or design. The fourth step is the actual collection of data, which is governed by the particular research design used. The fifth step involves analyses of the collected data. This leads to the final step, which involves the interpretation of results and the drawing of conclusions based on the results.

Formulation of the problem or issue

The first step in conducting research is to specify the problem or issue to be studied. Sometimes, a researcher develops an issue because of his or her interests in a particular area. For example, an I/O psychologist might be interested in the relationships between worker job satisfaction and employee loyalty to the organization, or between worker productivity and the length of time employees stay with a particular organization. Often, the selection of a research problem is influenced by previous research. On the other hand, the practicing I/O psychologist-consultant may be provided with an issue by a client company that has a particular problem that needs to be alleviated, such as an extraordinarily high level of employee absenteeism.

Generation of hypotheses

variables
the elements measured in research investigations

hypotheses
statements about the supposed relationships between or among variables

theory/model
the organization of beliefs into a representation of the factors that affect behavior

The next step in the research process involves taking those elements that the researcher intends to measure, known as **variables**, and generating statements concerning the supposed relationships between or among variables. These statements are known as **hypotheses**. In the examples of research issues given above, job satisfaction, worker productivity, employee loyalty, employment tenure, and absenteeism are all variables. The hypotheses will later be tested through the analysis of the collected, systematic observations of variables, better known as the collection and analysis of research data.

By testing hypotheses through the collection of systematic observations of behavior, a researcher may eventually develop a **theory** or **model**, which is an organization of beliefs that enables us to understand behavior more completely. In social science, models are representations of the complexity of factors that affect behavior. In I/O psychology, models are representations of the factors that affect *work* behavior.

TABLE 2.1

Examples of Hypotheses in I/O Psychology Research

- Greater employee participation in organizational decision making is related to higher levels of job satisfaction (Locke & Schweiger, 1978).
- Use of tests of mechanical ability increases the effectiveness of selecting employees for mechanical and engineering positions (Muchinsky, 1993).
- Applicants who are characterized by a higher degree of conscientiousness will exhibit higher levels of job performance (Barrick & Mount, 1991).
- Commitment to a work organization will decrease as the perceived chances of finding a job with another company increase (Bateman & Strasser, 1984).
- As employee age increases, voluntary absenteeism decreases (Hackett, 1990).
- Increasing employees' sense of control over the work environment is related to reductions in work stress (Jackson, 1983).

We have all seen architects' cardboard and plaster models of buildings and the plastic models of aircraft that can be purchased in hobby shops. These are *concrete* models that represent the physical appearance of the actual building or aircraft. The models used in I/O psychology research are *abstract* representations of the factors influencing work behavior. Developing a theory and diagramming that theory are convenient ways to organize our thinking and our understanding of complex behavioral processes.

Many people who do not have an understanding of scientific research methodology have misconceptions about theories. Either they believe that theories represent the personal views of scientists, or they believe that theories represent proven facts. Neither is wholly true. Theories are important because they help us to represent the complex and often intangible forces that influence human behavior. By using a theory as a guide, I/O psychologists can develop strategies for conducting research to find support for, or disprove, the theory. A theory is the starting point for understanding and influencing behavior, and theories can be used as guides to improve the work world for all concerned.

Although I/O psychologists use research models to guide their investigations, models of human work behavior are also the *products* of research. The researcher may use an existing theory or model to develop certain hypotheses about aspects of work behavior and then test those hypotheses through research. These results may then be used to refine the model or to create a new, "improved" model.

Selecting the research design

Once hypotheses are generated, the researcher chooses a research design that will guide the investigation. The type of design selected depends on such things as the research setting, and the degree of control that the researcher has over the research setting. For instance, a researcher may decide that she will conduct a study of workers' task performance by observing workers in the actual work setting during normal working hours, in order to make the setting as "natural" as possible. Alternatively, the researcher may decide instead that it would be less disruptive to bring workers into a laboratory room where the work tasks could be simulated. Different settings may require different research designs.

The researcher may also be constrained in the selection of a research design by the amount of control the researcher has over the work setting and the workers. The company may not allow the researcher to interfere with normal work activities, forcing the researcher to use observational measurement of behavior, or to use existing data that the organization has already collected. We shall discuss specific research designs shortly.

Collection of data

The next step in the research process involves the testing of hypotheses through data collection. The collection of data is governed by the particular research design used. However, an important concern in data collection is **sampling**, or selecting a representative group from a larger population for study. In most research, it is impossible to investigate *all* members of a particular population. For example, in preelection polls of preferences, all potential voters cannot be surveyed. Instead a sample is selected, and the results obtained from this subgroup are generalized to the larger population. The process of selection must follow strict guidelines in order to ensure that the sample is indeed representative of the larger population from which it is drawn. Two such sampling techniques are random sampling and stratified sampling.

With **random sampling**, research participants are chosen from a specified population in such a way that each individual has an equal probability of being selected. For example, to choose a random sample of twenty workers from a large company of two hundred workers, we would begin with a list of all workers, and using a table of random numbers or a computer program that generates random numbers, randomly select twenty workers. The concept of sampling also applies to studying behaviors from certain individuals or groups of individuals. For example, if we wanted a random sampling of a particular employee's typical work behavior, we might study different, random five-minute time periods throughout a typical work day or week.

Stratified sampling begins with the designation of important variables that divide a population into subgroups, or strata. For example, we might want to consider male and female employees and management and nonmanagement personnel as different strata. We then randomly select a specified number of employees in such a way that our research sample mirrors the actual breakdown of these groups in the total population. For example, assume that 40 percent of the individuals in our total worker population are female and 60 percent are male, while 25 percent are management and 75 percent are nonmanagement. We would want to choose a sample that represented these percentages. Forty percent of the individuals in our selected sample

sampling
the selection of a representative group from a larger population for study

random sampling
the selection of research participants from a population so that each individual has an equal probability of being chosen

stratified sampling
the selection of research participants based on categories that represent important distinguishing characteristics of a population

should be female and 25 percent should be management personnel. We may also want to ensure that the percentages of male and female managers and nonmanagers in our sample are representative of the larger population.

Both of these sampling techniques help ensure that the sample is representative of the population from which it is drawn. The random selection procedure also protects against any sorts of biases in the choice of participants for study.

Analyses of research data

Once data are gathered, they are subjected to some form of analysis for interpretation. Most often, this involves *statistical* analyses of the data, although data can be analyzed using nonstatistical, *qualitative* data analysis techniques. Statistical analysis of data requires that the research observations be quantified in some way. Statistics are simply tools used by the researcher to help make sense out of the observations that have been collected. Some statistical analyses are very simple and are used to help describe and classify the data. Other statistical techniques are quite complex and help the researcher make detailed inferences. For example, some statistics allow the researcher to determine the causes of certain observed outcomes. A brief discussion of certain statistical analysis techniques is presented in an appendix at the end of this chapter.

A researcher who studied management styles in a garment factory would need to be cautious in interpreting data. Would the same kind of supervision produce the same results in a retail store? in a law firm?

Interpretation of research results

The final step in the research process is interpretation of the results. Here the researcher draws conclusions about the meaning of the findings and their relevance to actual work behavior as well as their possible limitations. For example, imagine that a researcher decides to study the effects on work group productivity of two managerial styles: a *directive* style, whereby the manager closely supervises workers, telling them what they should be doing and how they should be doing it, and a *nondirective* style, whereby the manager allows the workers a great deal of freedom in deciding how they will get the work task done. The researcher conducts the study on groups of directive and nondirective front-line managers who are employed at several factories that manufacture jet aircraft parts. By collecting and analyzing data, the researcher concludes that directive managers lead more productive groups. However, the researcher might want to set some limits for the use of these findings. The researcher might caution that these results may only apply to managers who are supervising factory work groups and might not pertain to managers of service organizations, such as hospitals or restaurants, or to managers of salespersons. The researcher might also mention that although a directive management style appears to be related to productivity, it is not known whether it is related to other important variables, such as employee satisfaction or work quality.

In the next few sections we will examine in depth some of the steps in the research process. First, we will examine the various research designs used to govern the collection of research data. Second, we will briefly discuss how research variables are measured. Next, we will discuss some of the problems and limitations of conducting research in I/O psychology and will consider the ways that research results and theories can be applied to the practice of I/O psychology. Finally, we will discuss rules of conduct for researchers who are studying people and their work behavior. Research methods are obviously important to practicing I/O psychologists. See the Up Close feature to learn how a knowledge of research methods can help you in your working life.

UP CLOSE

How to Use Research Methods in Your Own Life

While a thorough knowledge of social science research methods is critical for an I/O psychologist, how might this knowledge apply to the life of the typical working person?

Perhaps the greatest value of social science research methods is that the general principles of trying to take an objective (unbiased) perspective, using caution concerning cause-and-effect interpretations, and basing interpretations on repeated observations can be extremely useful as guidelines for decision making. Rather than basing important work-related decisions on hunches, previous experience, or personal preferences, approach the problems as a scientist would. Step back from your own biases. Try to collect some objective data to clarify the problems, and base your decisions on the data.

For example, a student approached me about her part-time job, which had been a source of grief to her and to others who worked with her at the customer service desk of a large department store. The problem was that the manager never seemed to schedule hours in a way that satisfied all of the employees. Some employees seemed to get the "better" hours, while others were complaining that they consistently had to work the "bad" shifts. The student believed that she had the perfect solution: The employees would all submit their ideal work schedules and possible alternatives, and the manager would arrange them in a way that was satisfactory to everyone.

I suggested that rather than assuming that she had reached a workable solution, she should go back and approach the problem from a research perspective. First, I recommended that she determine the magnitude and scope of the problem. She developed a brief survey that she gave to all of the department employees, asking about their satisfaction with the current work scheduling. The results indicated that the majority of the workers did indeed have difficulties with the scheduling. She next approached the manager to see whether she would be open to suggestions for change, which she was. Rather than relying on just her solution, the student then solicited suggestions for dealing with the difficulties from all of the employees. When a new strategy was eventually selected (they did try a variation of her suggestion), it was implemented on a trial basis, with careful assessment of its effects on employee attitudes and on difficulties related to scheduling conflicts. By following this systematic method of relying on

UP CLOSE (*continued*)

data, the workers were thus able to improve their situation.

A sound background in research methods can also assist in the evaluation of new work techniques or management strategies. Whenever you hear of some revolutionary strategy for increasing work performance or efficiency, do what a good social scientist would do: Go directly to the primary source. Find out what research evidence (if any) supports the technique, and read those reports with a critical eye. See if there are serious flaws in the ways that the technique was tested, flaws which might make you doubt whether it really works.

STOP AND REVIEW

Describe the six steps in the research process.

Major Research Designs

When testing theories and collecting data, researchers typically follow one of two types of general research designs: the experimental method or the correlational method. We will look at each of these general research designs. Another method of conducting research is called *meta-analysis*. This is a method that allows researchers to "combine" results from different studies. Finally, researchers will occasionally conduct an in-depth, descriptive investigation of a particular issue, which is known as a case study. Each of these research designs will be explored.

THE EXPERIMENTAL METHOD

The **experimental method** is most commonly associated with research conducted in a laboratory, although it can also be applied in an actual work setting, in which case it is known as a field experiment. The experimental method is designed to give the researcher a very high degree of control over the research setting. You can imagine that in a laboratory experiment, the researcher has a great deal of control, which is a major advantage of conducting research in a laboratory. In a field experiment, the researcher typically has less control than in the laboratory, but the researcher must still maintain strong control over the situation in a field experiment in order to draw strong conclusions.

In the experimental method, the researcher systematically manipulates levels of one variable, called the **independent variable**, and measures its effect on another variable, called the **dependent variable**. The dependent variable is the outcome variable, or the behavior that is of primary interest to the investigator. In the experimental method, other variables in the setting are presumed to be held constant. That is, no elements except the independent variable are allowed to vary. Therefore, any change in the dependent variable is presumed to have been caused by the independent

experimental method
a research design characterized by a high degree of control over the research setting to allow for the determination of cause-and-effect relationships among variables

independent variable
in the experimental method, the variable that is manipulated by the researcher

dependent variable
in the experimental method, the variable that is acted upon by the independent variable; the outcome variable

variable. The primary advantage of the experimental method is that it allows us to determine cause-and-effect relationships among variables.

To determine whether the manipulation of an independent variable produces any significant change in a dependent variable, researchers following the experimental method usually compare the results of two groups of participants. One group, called the experimental group, or **treatment group**, is subjected to the change in the independent variable. The second group, called the **control group**, receives no change. In other words, the second group is not subjected to the treatment. This comparison of treatment and control groups allows the researcher to determine the magnitude of the effect produced by the manipulation of the independent variable (the treatment). Measuring the dependent variable of the control group allows the researcher to rule out any normal fluctuations that might have occurred naturally in the absence of the treatment. The comparison of treatment and control groups gives the researcher greater confidence that the treatment was (or was not) effective.

For example, imagine that a researcher wants to test the effectiveness of a new training program for sales skills. A number of salespersons are randomly assigned to the treatment group and attend the training session. Other salespersons are randomly assigned to the control group and do not receive the training content. (In a good experimental design the control group should also attend "a session," but one that does not have the training content; this allows the researcher to control for any effects that may result from participants simply attending a program). A comparison of the two groups' subsequent sales records allows the researcher to determine the effectiveness of the program. In this case, the independent variable is whether the salespersons did or did not receive the training content; the dependent variable would be the amount of sales. It is also possible to expand the experimental method to include a number of different treatment groups—for example, different types of sales training programs—and to compare the effectiveness of these various treatments with one another and with a control group. Of course, the experimental method is not used only for comparing treatment and control groups. Any variable that can be broken into distinct categories or levels can serve as an independent variable in an experimental design. For instance, we might examine differences between male and female workers, or among "high," "medium" and "low" producing workers (as determined by productivity measures).

Aside from the specified independent variables, other variables that may be affecting the dependent variable are termed **extraneous variables**. It is these variables that increase the difficulty of conducting research, because they can be any factors other than the independent variables that influence the dependent variable. Consider, for example, the Hawthorne studies discussed in Chapter 1. In these studies of the influence of lighting and other work conditions on assembly line productivity (the independent variables), the attention paid to the workers by the researchers was an extraneous variable that affected productivity (the dependent variable).

---

treatment group
the group in an experimental investigation that is subjected to the change in the independent variable

control group
a comparison group in an experimental investigation that receives no treatment

extraneous variables
variables other than the independent variable that may influence the dependent variable

The key to the success of the experimental method is to hold all extraneous variables constant, but this is much easier to do in a laboratory setting than in an actual work setting. Sometimes extraneous variables result from systematic differences in the individuals being studied. For example, if participants are given the opportunity to volunteer to participate in a particular treatment group (with the nonvolunteers serving as a control group), there may be some motivational differences in the treatment volunteers that might act as a moderating or confounding variable, thus affecting the results. That is, participants in the treatment group might be more energetic and "helpful" than those in the control group, and it would thus be impossible to tell whether any differences between the two groups resulted from the treatment or from these inherent motivational differences. Many potential extraneous variables can be controlled through the **random assignment** of participants to the experimental and control groups. Random assignment ensures that any motivational differences or other individual characteristics show up in equivalent proportions in both groups. In other words, assigning participants randomly to treatment and control groups serves to control for the effects of extraneous variables.

random assignment
a method of assigning subjects to groups by chance to control for the effects of extraneous variables

One of the major drawbacks of the experimental method is its artificiality. A researcher who controls the experimental setting may create a situation that is quite different from the actual work setting. There may thus be some concern about whether the results will apply or generalize to real settings. In field experiments, there is less concern about the generalizability of findings, since the participants and the setting are usually representative of those that can be affected by the results. However, any time that a researcher creates an experimental situation, he or she runs the risk of generating artificial conditions that would not exist in the usual work setting.

Two examples of the experimental method: A laboratory and a field experiment

A recent study was designed to determine which of two decision-making styles was most effective when individuals were working under high stress conditions (Johnston, Driskell, & Salas, 1997). In this laboratory experiment, 90 U.S. Navy enlisted personnel volunteered and were required to take part in a simulation, where they would be working as a ship's radar screen operator. The participants were randomly assigned to one of two training groups. The first group learned a "vigilant" decision-making style. Vigilant decision making is where the decision maker scans and considers all information in an orderly, sequential fashion, taking into account all information, and reviewing all alternatives before making a decision. Participants in the second group were trained in "hypervigilant" decision making. In hypervigilant decision making, the decision maker scans only the information that is needed in a particular circumstance, and scanning of information does not follow a systematic, ordered sequence. The type of training participants received constituted the independent variable. Stress was created by having distracting radio communications played, and by an experimenter who told the participants to "hurry up" and "perform better" at regular intervals.

The participants were seated at a computer screen that presented a simulation of a ship's radar screen that systematically presented images representing approaching ships, submarines, and aircraft. Participants had to identify each object, determine if it was a "friendly" or enemy craft, and engage the enemy crafts. The dependent variable in this study consisted of the number of objects that were correctly identified and dealt with appropriately. The results of the study confirmed the researchers' hypothesis that hypervigilant decision making was best under high stress conditions, primarily because it is quicker, more efficient, and provides less of a cognitive "load" on the radar operator.

Our second example of the experimental method is a field experiment designed to test the effects on safe driving behavior of worker participation in setting safety-related goals (Ludwig & Geller, 1997). The study participants were 324 college-aged pizza deliverers from three pizza stores. Pizza deliverers were randomly assigned to one of two types of safety meetings. In one condition, driving-related safety goals were set by store managers. In the other condition, the deliverers participated in setting their driving safety goals. The type of goal setting constituted the independent variable. At certain intervals, the managers observed specific safety behaviors as the drivers exited the stores' parking lots and headed down the road on their deliveries. Specifically, the managers recorded whether or not the drivers wore their safety belts, used their turn signals when turning onto the highway, and came to a complete stop before proceeding through an intersection. Combined, the incidence of these safe driving behaviors constituted the study's dependent variable.

The results showed that both groups, those who helped set their own safety goals and those whose goals were set by managers, engaged in safer driving behaviors during the time period when their managers were watching. The researchers, however, were interested in the long-term effects of the different goal-setting practices. Therefore, unbeknownst to the drivers, hidden observers continued to record the drivers' safe driving practices for several additional months. Those drivers who had participated in the setting of safety goals showed significantly higher levels of safe driving behaviors than did drivers whose goals were set for them, months later when the drivers did not know that they were being observed.

Although both of these studies are fairly well-designed and executed, and produced some useful knowledge, both have limitations. The laboratory investigation used navy enlisted personnel, not actual ship radar operators, which raises the question of whether the results would generalize to actual radar operators, or to other similar workers, such as air traffic controllers. As presented, the dependent variables in the studies are fairly limited. (Both studies were presented in simplified format. Additional variables were measured in each.) For example, while the safety study found that drivers increased seat belt usage and the use of their turn signals, we don't know if other driving behaviors (e.g., speeding) were affected. While the results of studies such as these may answer some questions, additional questions might arise. For example, from the results of these experiments, we still don't know for sure why one particular decision-making style was better, or exactly why setting your own safety goals has longer-lasting effects on safe driving.

This is the research process. Results of one study may stimulate subsequent research in the same area. Scientific research builds on the results of previous studies, adding and refining, to increase our knowledge of the behavior in question.

THE CORRELATIONAL METHOD

The second major method for data collection, the **correlational method** (also referred to as the *observational* method), looks at the relationships between or among variables as they occur naturally. When the correlational method is used, in contrast to the experimental method, there is no manipulation of variables by the experimenter. A researcher simply measures two or more variables and then examines their statistical relationship to one another. Because the correlational method does not involve the manipulation of independent variables, distinctions between independent and dependent variables are not nearly as important as they are in the experimental method. Since the correlational method does not require the rigid control over variables associated with the experimental method, it is easy to use in actual work settings. A great deal of the research on work behavior thus uses the correlational method. The major drawback of this method is that we cannot determine cause-and-effect relationships. The most common problem is the tendency of people to try to make causal statements from correlations, which leads to many misconceptions and faulty interpretations of data. Many students of statistics quickly learn that correlation does not necessarily imply causality.

Considerable caution must be exercised when interpreting the results of correlational research. For example, suppose that a researcher finds a relationship between workers' attitudes about their employer and the amount of money they invest in a company stock program. Employees with very positive attitudes tend to use a greater portion of their income to purchase stock. It could be that their favorable attitudes cause them to demonstrate their support for (and faith in) the company by buying stock, but the cause-and-effect relationship could also go the other way: Employees who purchase stock at bargain prices may develop more positive attitudes about the company because they now have an investment in it. On the other hand, a third variable (an extraneous variable), such as the length of time employees have worked for the company, may actually be the cause of the observed correlation between employee attitudes and stock purchases. Employees with a long tenure may generally have more favorable attitudes about the company than newcomers (over time those with negative attitudes usually leave the organization). These employees are also older and may be able to

correlational method
a research design that examines the relationship among or between variables as they naturally occur

invest a larger proportion of their incomes in stock options than younger workers, who may be raising families and purchasing first homes. Length of time on the job may thus influence both of the other two variables. The simple correlation between employee attitudes and stock purchases therefore does not lead us to any firm cause-and-effect conclusions.

Two examples of the correlational method

Two researchers studied the ability of certain tests and other assessment methods to predict future managerial success. The participants were more than 1,000 entry-level women managers, all of whom took part in a two-day testing program at an assessment center. The assessment techniques included an interview, some standardized tests, and several scored exercises. (We will discuss assessment centers and employee assessment techniques in Chapter 4.) At the end of the assessment, each woman was rated on a four-point scale of "middle-management potential," with end points ranging from *not acceptable* to *more than acceptable*. Seven years later, measures of the women's "management progress" were obtained. Results indicated "a sizable correlation between predictions made by the assessment staff and subsequent progress seven years later" (Ritchie & Moses, 1983, p. 229).

In a study of secretaries and managers in seven German companies, researchers examined the relationship between the time it took for these office workers to deal with computer errors and the workers' "negative emotional reactions," such as voicing frustration, or outbursts of anger (Brodbeck, Zapf, Prumper, & Frese, 1993). This study was an *observational field study* because the researchers observed the workers as they went through their normal daily routine at work. The observers merely recorded the errors workers made while working at computers, noted the time that it took workers to deal with the computer errors, and noted their emotional reactions. As you might expect, there was a significant positive relationship (a positive correlation) between the length of time workers spent trying to solve computer errors and their reactions of frustration and anger. In other words, the more time spent trying to solve computer errors, the more angry and frustrated workers became.

As mentioned, each of the methods, experimental and correlational, has its own strengths and weaknesses. Sometimes researchers might use both methods in a large-scale investigation. Although the experimental method is most commonly associated with laboratory studies, and correlational research is most often associated with field research, either method can be used in either setting. The key to using the experimental method in a field investigation is gaining control over the environment by manipulating levels of the independent variable and holding extraneous variables constant. Because the correlational method looks at the relationships among variables as they naturally exist, a correlational design may often be easier to implement, particularly in actual work settings, as the study of German office workers demonstrates.

META-ANALYSIS

As we have seen, the results of a single research study provide some answers, but often raise other questions. Moreover, different research investigations of the same topic or issue may reach inconsistent, and sometimes totally contradictory, conclusions. For example, one study may find strong support for a given hypothesis, a second may find only weak support, and a third study may have results that are opposite those of the first study. Students who are just beginning to explore research in I/O psychology or other social sciences seem to get particularly frustrated by such inconsistencies. How can any conclusions be drawn from the varying and often conflicting results of several independent research investigations?

The answer is found in a methodological technique called **meta-analysis**, which allows the results of a number of studies to be combined and analyzed together to draw a summary conclusion (Rosenthal, 1991; Wolf, 1986). Meta-analyses are usually conducted when there are 20 or more separate studies of a given hypothesis or topic. Meta-analysis may be used for several purposes, including summarizing the relationship between variables examined in each of a set of studies, and determining other factors that are associated with increases or decreases in the magnitude of relationships between variables of interest (these "other factors" are often referred to as moderating variables). Although it depends on the research question and the types of studies and their specific research designs, meta-analysis will typically use an indicator of *effect size* from each examined study. **Effect size** refers to an estimate of the magnitude of the relationship between any variable X and any variable Y (in a correlational design), or the size of the effect of an independent variable on a dependent variable (in an experimental design). One measure of effect size is the correlation coefficient, which is provided in many studies to describe relationships between variables (see the Statistical Appendix for more information on correlation coefficients).

Meta-analysis is used to compare and combine data from all of the examined studies, taking into account the effect sizes and the number of participants in each of the independent studies. Typically, meta-analytic techniques yield a summary statistic which tells us something about the overall relationship between the variables examined in each of the studies, and whether the results from the independent studies are significantly different from each other in meaningful ways. For example, different studies examining the relationship between job satisfaction and employee absenteeism have produced different results, with some studies reporting higher levels of job satisfaction associated with lower rates of absenteeism (e.g., Ostroff, 1993a), and others reporting no association between the two factors (Ilgen & Hollenback, 1977; see Chapter 8 for more information). Meta-analytic procedures may suggest that different studies yield different results because each uses a different measure of absenteeism or job satisfaction, or because the participants in studies were different. Meta-analyses have been used to summarize the research results from

meta-analysis
a technique that allows results from several different research studies to be combined and summarized

effect size
an estimate of the magnitude of a relationship or effect found in a research investigation

Describe and contrast the experimental and correlational methods.

many studies of the absenteeism-job satisfaction relationship, and have found that the two factors are indeed related—low satisfaction is related to higher rates of absenteeism—but the relationship is not very strong (e.g., Scott & Taylor, 1985).

Meta-analytic studies have become quite popular, particularly in I/O psychology and other fields studying work behavior (Steiner, Lane, Dobbins, Schnur, & McConnell, 1991). These analyses have addressed such issues as the effectiveness of employment tests, college grade point average, and other measures in predicting job performance (Hunter & Hunter, 1984; Roth, BeVier, Switzer, & Schippman, 1996), the relationship between job satisfaction and turnover (Carsten & Spector, 1987), the effectiveness of managerial training programs (Burke & Day, 1986), and the validity of certain leadership theories (Gerstner & Day, 1997; Strube & Garcia, 1981).

One meta-analysis examined the relationship between employee absenteeism and work performance, and confirmed the widely held view that frequently absent employees tend to be poorer work performers as measured by performance appraisals (Bycio, 1992). In a more recent meta-analysis, of 55 studies investigating the relationship between workers' personalities, positive job attitudes, and organizational citizenship behaviors—pro-company behaviors by employees—it was found that positive job attitudes were a better predictor of organizational citizenship behaviors than were workers' personalities (Organ & Ryan, 1995).

THE CASE STUDY METHOD

We have stated that there are difficulties in conducting controlled research in actual work settings. Often a researcher or scientist-practitioner will have the opportunity to conduct research in a business or industry, but will find it impossible to follow either the experimental or the correlational method. The study may involve a one-time-only assessment of behavior, or the application of an intervention to only a single group, department, or organization. Such research is known as a **case study**. The results of a single case study, even if the study involves the application of some highly researched intervention strategy, do not allow us to draw any firm conclusions. A case study is really little more than a descriptive investigation. We are unable to test hypotheses or to determine cause-and-effect relationships from a case study because it is like conducting research with only one participant. What may have seemed to work in this one instance may not work in a second or third case. However, this does not mean that the case study method is not valuable, and in fact, many exploratory studies follow this method. Case studies can provide rich, descriptive information about certain work behaviors and situations. In some topic areas, where it has been impossible to conduct controlled experimental studies, the results of case studies may be the only evidence that exists. Moreover, such results might inspire the development of hypotheses that will later be tested with experimental or correlational studies (Dunnette, 1990).

case study
a research investigation involving a one-time assessment of behavior

In one example of the case study method, a psychologist found that company picnics, games, and other social activities increased employee's loyalty to the organization.

Measurement of Variables

One of the more difficult aspects of research is the measurement of variables. A variable must be **operationalized**, that is, brought down from the abstract level to a more concrete level and clearly defined so that it can be measured or manipulated. In the first example of the correlational method outlined above, the variable "middle-management potential" was operationalized as a rating on a four-point scale. In the experimental study of pizza delivery drivers, "safe driving behavior" was operationalized as wearing a seat belt, using a turn signal, and coming to a full stop at an intersection. Both variables could be considered as operational definitions of the more general variable of "performance".

During the process of operationalizing a variable, a particular technique for measuring the variable is usually selected. We will examine two of the variety of techniques used to measure variables in I/O psychology: observational techniques and self-report techniques.

operationalized
clearly defining a research variable so that it can be measured

OBSERVATIONAL TECHNIQUES

One procedure for measuring research variables is through direct, systematic observation. This involves the researchers themselves recording certain behaviors that they have defined as the operationalized variables. For example, a researcher might consider the number of items manufactured as a measure of productivity or may look for certain defined supervisory behaviors, such as demonstrating work techniques to subordinates, giving direct orders, and setting specific work quotas, to assess whether a manager has a "task-oriented" supervisory style.

The measurement of variables through direct observation can be either obtrusive or unobtrusive. With **obtrusive observation** the researcher is visible to the persons being observed. The primary disadvantage of this technique is that the participants may behave differently because they know that they are a part of a research investigation. This is exactly what happened in the original Hawthorne experiments. Researchers engaging in obtrusive observation must always consider how their presence will affect participants' behavior, and thus the results of the study.

Unobtrusive observation also involves direct observation of behavior, but in this case participants are unaware of the researcher's presence and do not know that their behavior is being studied. The primary advantage of unobtrusive observation is that the researcher can be fairly confident that the recorded behavior is typical. The major drawback to unobtrusive observation lies in ethical concerns about protecting the privacy of the participants.

SELF-REPORT TECHNIQUES

Direct observational measurement techniques are often costly and difficult to obtain, requiring the assistance of trained observers. More commonly, researchers measure variables through **self-report techniques**, which include a variety of methods for assessing behavior from the responses of the research participants themselves. One of the most popular self-report techniques is surveys. **Surveys** can be used to measure any number of aspects of the work situation, including workers' attitudes about their jobs, their perceptions of the amount and quality of the work they perform, and the specific problems they encounter on the job. Most typically, surveys take the form of pencil-and-paper measures that the participants can complete either in a group session or on their own time. However, surveys can also involve face-to-face or telephone interviews.

The most obvious problem with surveys is the possibility of distortion or bias of responses (either intentional or unintentional). If the survey is not conducted in a way that protects respondents' anonymity, particularly when it deals with sensitive issues or problems, workers may feel that their answers can be traced back to them and possibly result in retribution by management. In these cases, workers may temper their responses and give "socially desirable" answers to survey questions.

Self-report techniques are also used in I/O psychology research to assess workers' personalities, occupational interests, and management or supervisory style; to obtain evaluations of job candidates; or to elicit supervisors' ratings of worker performance. Compared to observational techniques, self-

obtrusive observation
research observation in which the presence of the observer is known to the participants

unobtrusive observation
research observation in which the presence of the observer is not known to the participants

self-report techniques
measurement methods relying on research participants' reports of their own behavior or attitudes

surveys
a common self-report measure in which participants are asked to report on their attitudes, beliefs, and/or behaviors

reports allow the researcher to collect massive amounts of data relatively inexpensively. However, developing sound self-report tools and interpreting the results are not easy tasks, and require thorough knowledge of measurement theory as well as research methods and statistics. Many I/O psychologist researchers and practitioners use self-report measures extensively in their work.

MEASURING WORK OUTCOMES: THE BOTTOM LINE

There are a tremendous number of potential independent variables in I/O psychology research. I/O psychologists have examined how characteristics of workers such as personality, attitudes, and education affect work behavior. As we saw in Chapter 1, factors in the physical and social work environment can be manipulated to see how they affect worker performance and satisfaction. Other variables, such as the amount and frequency of compensation, styles of supervision, work schedules, and incentive programs, also serve as independent variables in research on work behavior.

There are also many dependent variables studied in I/O research. However, a great deal of research in I/O psychology focus on dependent variables such as productivity, work quality, employee turnover, employee absenteeism, and employee satisfaction. These key dependent variables represent work outcomes—what often translates to the "bottom line" in work organizations. Most commonly, changes in these important variables result in financial losses or gains for businesses.

Of these important dependent variables, the first two, work productivity and quality, are usually theoretically linked, because a company's goals should be to produce as much as possible while ensuring that the output is of high quality. However, although these variables are linked, they are typically considered separately by many businesses. In fact, in many manufacturing plants the departments responsible for production volume and for quality control are often separate.

On the surface, it may seem that the measurement of a variable like productivity is relatively simple and accurate. This may be true if the task involves production of concrete objects, such as the number of hamburgers sold or the number of books printed. However, for companies that deal with more abstract products, such as services, information, or ideas, the measurement of productivity is not as easy nor as precise.

The accurate measurement of quality is often more difficult (Hoffman, Nathan, & Holden, 1991). For example, in a department store, productivity may be assessed by the dollar amount of sales, which is a fairly reasonable and simple assessment. However, the quality of the salespersons' performance might involve factors such as the friendliness, courteousness, and promptness of their service, which are usually more difficult to measure. Similarly, a writer's productivity might be defined as the number of books or articles the author produced (a straightforward assessment), while the quality of the writing may be more difficult to measure. Thus, quality is often quite difficult to define operationally. We will deal with the measurement of worker productivity and worker performance in more detail in upcoming chapters, particularly in Chapter 3 and Chapter 6.

Although they are distinct variables, employee absenteeism, turnover, and satisfaction are also theoretically tied to one another (Vroom, 1964). In Chapter 1 we saw that Mayo believed that there was a strong relationship between employee satisfaction and productivity. However, this is not always the case; the happy worker is not necessarily the productive worker. There may, however, be a relationship between employee satisfaction and a tendency to show up for work and stay with the job. Specifically, it is thought that higher satisfaction leads to lower absenteeism and turnover. However, these long-standing notions about the interrelatedness of job satisfaction, absenteeism, and turnover have come under question, primarily because of problems in the accurate measurement of absenteeism and turnover (see Hollenbeck & Williams, 1986; Porter & Steers, 1973; Tharenou, 1993). Some forms of absenteeism and turnover are inevitable, due to circumstances beyond the employees' control, such as severe illness or a move dictated by a spouse's job transfer. These types of absenteeism and turnover are not likely to be affected by job satisfaction, whereas voluntary absenteeism—playing "hooky" from work—may be caused by low levels of job satisfaction. We will discuss this issue in detail in Chapter 8.

In any case, the interrelationships between job satisfaction, absenteeism, and turnover are important. If negative relationships do indeed exist between employee satisfaction and rates of absenteeism and turnover (they are negative relationships because *higher* satisfaction would be associated with *lower* absenteeism and *lower* turnover), it is important that companies strive to keep workers satisfied. Happy workers may be less likely to be absent from their jobs voluntarily or to look for work elsewhere. Reduced rates of absenteeism and turnover can translate into tremendous savings for the company.

Turnover and absenteeism can be measured fairly easily, but the assessment of worker satisfaction is much less precise, since attitudes about a wide range of elements in the work environment must be considered. We will deal more deeply with this point in Chapter 8.

Although these key variables are most commonly considered dependent variables, this does not preclude the possibility that any one of them could be used as an independent variable. For example, we might classify workers into those who are "good attenders" with very few absences, and "poor attenders," who have regular absences. We could then see whether there are differences in the good and poor attenders' performance levels or in their attitudes about their jobs. However, certain variables, such as productivity, absenteeism, and turnover, represent the bottom-line variables that translate into profits or losses for the company, while job satisfaction tends to be the bottom-line variable for the employee. These bottom-line variables are most often considered dependent variables.

Interpreting and Using Research Results

When a researcher conducts a study and obtains research results, it is the researcher's task to make sense out of the results. To interpret research data accurately, an I/O psychologist must be very knowledgeable about methods of data collection and statistical analysis, and be aware of potential research problems and the strengths and limitations of the methods that have been used.

When interpreting results, it is important to consider the limitations of the findings. Of particular concern is the **external validity** of the research results, that is, whether the results obtained will generalize to other work settings. In other words, how well do the findings apply to other workers, jobs, and/or environments? For example, say that the results of research on patterns of interactions in workers in an insurance claims office indicate a significant positive relationship between the amount of supervisor-subordinate contact and worker productivity: As supervisors and subordinates interact more, more work is completed. Can these results be generalized to other settings? Maybe, maybe not. These findings might be particular to these workers, related to their specific characteristics. The participants may be the kind of workers who need a lot of supervision to keep them on task. Other groups of workers might view interactions with supervisors negatively, and the resulting dissatisfaction might lead to a restriction of output. Alternatively, the results might be specific to the type of tasks in which workers are engaged. Because insurance claims often need to be approved by supervisors, a subordinate must interact with the supervisor to complete the job. Therefore, increased supervisor-subordinate contact may be a sign of increased efficiency. For assembly line workers, however, supervisor-subordinate interactions might be a distraction that reduces productivity, or they might have little effect on output. To know whether research results will generalize to a variety of work settings, results must be replicated with different groups of workers in different work settings. Eventually, further research may discover the moderating variables that determine when and where supervisor-subordinate contacts have beneficial effects on work productivity.

External validity is especially important for research conducted under tightly controlled circumstances, such as a laboratory investigation, where the conditions of the research setting may not be very similar to actual work conditions. One solution is to combine the strength of experimental research—well-controlled conditions—with the advantage of real-world conditions by conducting experimental research in actual work settings.

So far, we have been discussing only one objective of research in I/O psychology: the scientific objective of conducting research to understand work behavior more completely. As you recall, in Chapter 1 we mentioned that there are two goals in industrial/organizational psychology: the scientific and the practical, whereby new knowledge is applied toward improving

external validity
whether research results obtained in one setting will apply to another setting

List the five common work
outcomes that are often
measured in I/O psychology.

work conditions and outcomes. While some research in I/O psychology is conducted merely to increase the base of knowledge about work behavior, and some I/O practitioners (and practicing managers) use strategies to affect work behavior that are based on hunches or intuition rather than on sound research evidence, the two facets of I/O psychology should work together. To be effective, the applications used by I/O practitioners to improve work behavior must be built on a strong foundation of research. Through sound research and the testing of hypotheses and theories, better applications develop. Moreover, the effectiveness of applications can be demonstrated conclusively only through additional evaluation and research (see Applying I/O Psychology).

APPLYING I/O PSYCHOLOGY

The Hawthorne Effect: A Case Study in Flawed Research Methods

The initial Hawthorne studies clearly followed the experimental method because Mayo and his colleagues manipulated levels of lighting and the duration of work breaks. Furthermore, since the studies were conducted in the actual work setting, they were also field experiments. The result, particularly the discovery of the Hawthorne effect, is a classic in the field of I/O psychology. In fact, this effect is studied in other areas of psychology and social science.

While the original Hawthorne studies were set up in the experimental method, the discovery of the Hawthorne effect actually resulted from a breakdown in research procedures. The changes observed in the dependent variable (productivity) were caused not by the independent variable (lighting), but by an extraneous variable that was not controlled by the researchers: the attention the workers received from the observers. While Mayo and his colleagues eventually became aware of this unanticipated variable, which led to the discovery of the Hawthorne effect,

there were other methodological problems in the design and implementation of the studies.

In the 1970s, researchers reexamined the data from the original Hawthorne experiments, combing through the records and diaries kept by Mayo and his colleagues. These investigators found a series of very serious methodological problems which cast doubt on the original conclusions drawn from the Hawthorne studies. These reanalyses indicated difficulties with the number of participants (one of the studies used only five participants), the experimenters' "contamination" of the participant population (two of the five participants were replaced because they were not working hard enough), the lack of control or comparison groups, and the absence of appropriate statistical analyses of data (Franke & Kaul, 1978; Parsons, 1974). The I/O psychologist Parsons discovered not only serious flaws in the published reports of the Hawthorne experiments but also a number of extraneous variables

APPLYING I/O PSYCHOLOGY (*continued*)

that were not considered, further confounding the conclusions. For example:

> [U]nlike the big open floor of the relay assembly department, the test room was separate, smaller, and quieter . . . and the supervisors were friendly, tolerant observers, not the usual authoritarian foremen . . . Back in their relay-assembly department, the women had been paid a fixed hourly wage plus a collective piecework rate based on the department's total output. In the test room, the collective piecework rate was based on the output of only the five workers, so that individual performance had a much more significant impact on weekly pay. The monetary reward for increased individual effort thus became much more evident and perhaps more effective than in the department setting. (Rice, 1982, pp. 70–74).

All in all, there are significant flaws in the research design and execution of the Hawthorne experiments. Of course this does not mean that a Hawthorne effect cannot exist, since we do know that the presence of others can affect behavior. What it does mean is that the original Hawthorne studies were too methodologically muddled to enable researchers to draw any firm conclusions from them. On one hand, we must forgive Mayo and his associates on some of these issues because their studies were conducted before many advancements in research methodology and design were made. On the other hand, some of the errors in data collection were obvious. In many ways, the Hawthorne studies illustrate some of the difficulties of conducting research and the dangers of drawing conclusions based on flawed research methods. The moral is that conducting research is a complex but important endeavor. Researchers and users of research must display caution in both the application of methods and the interpretation of results in order to avoid errors and misinformation.

ON THE CUTTING EDGE

Multivariate Research in I/O Psychology

The examples of research designs in this chapter are relatively simple designs, or were presented in a simplified format. State-of-the-art research in I/O psychology, and in most social science disciplines, uses rather complex and sophisticated designs that examine the relationships among numerous variables. Indeed, such complex, *multivariate* designs have become the rule rather than the exception.

The purpose of complex, multivariate research designs is to capture the complexity of "real world" behavior—an issue which is particularly important when the study focuses on the complex behavior of

ON THE CUTTING EDGE *(continued)*

workers in organizations. For example, if a researcher is interested in examining the causes of employee turnover, there are a number of different variables that could influence the behavior of leaving a job. For instance, a worker may quit because of job dissatisfaction, or because of a better offer from another company, or because the worker's spouse received a job transfer to another state. Characteristics of the worker himself or herself may also contribute to turnover decisions. In other words, the worker may simply have a habit of changing jobs every few years, or the worker may quit because of a burning desire to go back to school and learn some new job skills. Unfortunately, simple experimental or correlational designs, like the ones presented in this chapter, do not do a good job of examining such complex interrelationships among variables. Modern statistical analysis techniques, however, allow a researcher to look at the complex interactions of many variables.

One complex statistical technique that allows researchers to examine "simultaneously" the complex interactions among many variables is referred to as *structural equation modeling*, or *covariance structure modeling* (see Coovert, Penner, & MacCallum, 1990, for an overview). A structural equation model for the relationships among job satisfaction, intention to leave a job, actual turnover, and other relevant variables, is presented in Figure 2.2.

As can be seen, this model contains a total of four variables. The first two variables in the model, current job dissatisfaction and the worker's tendency to change jobs, are hypothesized to affect the worker's intention to leave the current job. If the worker has a strong intention to leave the current job, this might stimulate seeking out alternative jobs (a behavior that is not represented in the model), and thus lead to actual turnover behavior. In structural equation modeling, the

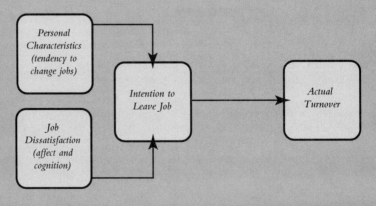

FIGURE 2.2

A Structural Equation Model for Employee Turnover

ON THE CUTTING EDGE (*continued*)

researcher obtains measures of these variables, and then uses that collected data to test whether the hypothesized relationships (represented in the figure as directional arrows) do indeed explain, or "fit," the data. In actual analyses, the relationships are usually even more complex than those depicted in Figure 2.5. In structural equation modeling, the "goodness of fit" of the model is represented by a statistical outcome.

Structural equation modeling represents a "cutting-edge" research tool used by I/O psychologists and other social science researchers. If you examine recent research published in I/O psychology, you will likely find several examples of structural equation modeling and related statistical techniques.

Summary

The goals of I/O psychology are to describe, explain, predict and then alter work behavior. Research methods are important tools for I/O psychologists because they provide a systematic means for investigating and changing work behavior. *Objectivity* is the overriding theme of the social scientific method used to study work behavior.

The first step in conducting research involves the formulation of the problem or issue. The second step is the generation of *hypotheses*, which are simply statements about the supposed relationships among variables. It is through the systematic collection of observations of behavior that a researcher may develop a set of hypotheses into a more general *theory*, or *model*, which are ways of representing the complex relationships among a number of variables related to actual work behavior. The third step in conducting research is choosing a particular design to guide the actual collection of data (the fourth step). The data collection stage includes sampling, the methods by which participants are selected for study. The final steps in the process are the analyses of research data and the interpretation of research results.

Two basic types of research designs are used by I/O psychologists. In the *experimental method*, the researcher manipulates one variable, labeled the *independent variable*, and measures its effect on the *dependent variable*. In an experimental design, any change in the dependent variable is presumed to be caused by the manipulation of the independent variable. Typically, the experimental method involves the use of a *treatment group* and a *control group*. The treatment group is subjected to the manipulation of the independent variable, while the control group serves as a comparison by not receiving the treatment. Variables that are not of principal concern to the researchers, but which may affect the results of the research, are termed *extraneous variables*. In the experimental method, the researcher attempts to control for extraneous variables through the *random assignment* of participants to the treatment and control groups, in order to ensure that any extraneous variables will be distributed evenly between the groups. The strength of the experimental method is the high level of control that the researcher has over the setting, which allows the investigator to determine cause-and-effect relationships. The weakness of the method is that the controlled conditions may be artificial and may not generalize to actual, uncontrolled work settings. The other type of research method, the *correlational method* (sometimes called the observational method), looks at the relationships among measured variables as they naturally occur, without the intervention of the experimenter and without strict experimental controls. The strength of this design is that it may be more easily conducted in actual settings. However, the correlational method does not allow the specification of cause-and-effect relationships.

Meta-analysis is a method that allows the results of a number of studies to be combined and analyzed together to draw an overall summary or conclusion. Meta-analysis may also be used to determine if the results of different studies of the same factors are significantly different from each other.

The *case study* is a commonly used descriptive investigation that lacks the controls and repeated observations of the experimental and correlational methodologies. The case study can provide important information, but does not allow the testing of hypotheses.

An important part of the research process involves the measurement of variables. The term *operationalization* refers to the process of defining variables so that they can be measured for research purposes. A variety of measurement techniques are used by I/O psychology researchers. Researchers may measure variables through the direct *obtrusive* or *unobtrusive* observation of behavior. In obtrusive observation, the researcher is visible to the research participants, who know that they are being studied. Unobtrusive observation involves observing participants' behavior without their knowledge. Another measurement strategy is *self-report techniques*, which yield information about participants' behavior from their own reports. One of the most widely used self-report techniques is the *survey*.

When interpreting research results, attention must be given to the *external validity* of the findings, that is, whether they will generalize to other settings. A critical concern to I/O psychologists is the interrelation of the science and practice of industrial/organizational psychology.

Study Questions and Exercises

1. Consider the steps in the research process. What are some of the major problems that are likely to be encountered at each step in the research process?

2. What are the strengths and weaknesses of the experimental and the correlational methods? Under what circumstances would you use each?

3. Consider the various measurement techniques used by I/O psychologists. Why are many of the variables used in I/O psychology difficult to measure?

4. Choose some aspect of work behavior and develop a research hypothesis. Now try to design a study that would test the hypothesis. Consider what your variables are and how you will operationalize them. Choose a research design for the collection of data. Consider who your participants will be and how they will be selected. How might the hypothesis be tested statistically?

Suggested Readings

Aron, A., & Aron, E. (1999). *Statistics for psychology* (2nd ed.). Englewood Cliffs, NJ: Prentice-Hall. *This straightforward text examines basic methods students in the social and behavioral sciences need to analyze data and test hypotheses.*

Cozby, P.C. (1997). *Methods in behavioral research* (6th ed.). Mountain View, CA: Mayfield Publishing. *An excellent and very readable introduction to research methods.*

Miner, J.B. (1983). The unpaved road from theory: Over the mountains to application. In R.H. Kilmann, K.W. Thomas, D.P. Slevin, R. Nath, & S.L. Jerrell (Eds.), *Producing useful knowledge in organizations* (pp. 37–68). New York: Praeger. *This interesting chapter compares well-known theories from I/O psychology, and evaluates them in terms of both how sound they are and their usefulness in actual work settings.*

Appendix: Statistical Analyses of Research Data

While a comprehensive treatment of research methods and statistics is beyond the scope of this text, it is important to emphasize that the science and practice of industrial/organizational psychology require a thorough knowledge of research methods and statistics, and some experience using them. More important for our present concerns, it is impossible to gain a true understanding of the methods used by I/O psychologists without some discussion of the statistical analyses of research data.

As mentioned earlier in this chapter, research methods are merely procedures or tools used by I/O psychologists to study work behavior. Statistics, which are arithmetical procedures designed to help summarize and interpret data, are also important research tools. The results of statistical analyses help us to understand relationships between or among variables. In any research investigation there are two main questions: a) Is there a statistically significant relationship between or among the variables of interest; and b) What is the strength of that relationship? For example, does the independent variable have a strong, moderate, or weak effect on the dependent variable (i.e., what is the effect size?)? Statistics provide the answers to these questions.

There are many types of statistical analyses, and which is most appropriate in a given study depends on such factors as the variables of interest, the way these variables are measured, the design of the study, and the research questions. Concerning the measurement of variables, it is important to point out that variables can be described as being *quantitative* or *qualitative* in nature. **Quantitative data** (also known as *measurement data*) refers to a numerical representation of a variable, such as an individual's weight provided by a scale, a score on a cognitive ability test, a student's grade point average, and so on. In all cases, some sort of measurement instrument has been used to measure some quantity. **Qualitative data** (also referred to as *categorical* or *frequency* data) refers to numbers that are used as labels to categorize people or things; the data provide frequencies for each category. When data collection involves methods like discussion or focus groups, for example, the data is likely to be qualitative and expressed in such statements as, "Twelve people were categorized as 'highly favorable' to changes in work schedules, twenty as 'moderately favorable,' and nine as 'not favorable.'" Here, we are categorizing participants into groups and the data represent the frequency of each category. In contrast, if instead of categorizing participants into high, moderate, and low favorability, we assigned each of them a score based on some continuous scale of favorability (scale from 1 to 12), the data would be measurement data, consisting of scores for each participant on that variable. Independent variables are often qualitative, involving categories, although they may also involve quantitative measurement, whereas dependent variables are generally quantitative. Different types of statistical techniques are used to analyze quantitative and qualitative data. Because they tend to be more frequently used in I/O psychology, our discussion will focus on procedures used to analyze quantitative, or measurement, data.

We will discuss two types of statistics: *descriptive statistics*, used to summarize recorded observations of behavior, and *inferential statistics*, used to test hypotheses about research data.

Descriptive Statistics

The simplest way to represent research data is to use **descriptive statistics**, which describe data in ways that give the researcher a general idea of the results. Suppose we have collected data on the job performance ratings of sixty employees. The rating scale ranges from 1 to 9, with 9 representing outstanding performance. As you can see in Table A.1, it is difficult to make sense out of the raw data. A **frequency distribution**, which is a descriptive statistical technique that presents data in a useful format, arranges the performance scores by category, so that we can see at a glance how many employees received each numerical rating. The frequency distribution in Figure A.1 is in the form of a bar graph or histogram.

Other important descriptive statistics include **measures of central tendency** and **variability**. Measures of central tendency present the center

---

quantitative (measurement) data
data that measure some numerical quantity

qualitative (categorical or frequency) data
data that measure some category or measurement quality

descriptive statistics
arithmetical formulas for summarizing and describing research data

frequency distribution
a descriptive statistical technique that arranges scores by categories

measures of central tendency
present the center point in a distribution of scores

variability
estimates the distribution of scores around the middle or average score

TABLE A.1

Performance Rating Scores of 60 Employees

Employee	Score	Employee	Score	Employee	Score
Adams	5	Alva	6	Ang	6
Bates	4	Bender	1	Berra	7
Brown	6	Cadiz	5	Camus	8
Chow	7	Cisneros	4	Crow	5
Davis	8	Dawes	7	DeRios	4
Driver	4	Dudley	6	Evans	6
Ewing	5	Exner	4	Fang	2
Farris	3	Fernal	5	Ford	9
Frank	5	Gant	3	Ghent	5
Gower	3	Grant	6	Gwynne	2
Hall	6	Hawkes	7	Horner	4
Hull	4	Hu	8	Jacobs	6
Justin	3	Kee	5	Kubiak	9
Lang	5	Lantz	7	Leong	5
Mayes	5	Mertz	3	Mio	4
Murphy	4	Nauls	5	Page	5
Pierce	2	Rabago	6	Richards	3
Sherrod	7	Simpson	8	Suls	6
Taylor	3	Tucker	2	Tran	4
Woll	5	Young	6	Zapf	5

FIGURE A.1

Frequency Distribution (Histogram) of Employee Performance Rating Scores

mean
a measure of central tendency; also known as the average

median
a measure of central tendency; the midpoint of a distribution of scores

standard deviation
a measure of variability of scores in a frequency distribution

point of a distribution of scores. This is useful in summarizing the distribution in terms of the middle or average score. The most common measure of central tendency is the **mean**, or average, which is calculated by adding all of the scores and dividing by the number of scores. In our performance data, the sum of the scores is 303, and the number of scores is 60. Therefore, the mean of our frequency distribution is 5.05. Another measure of central tendency is the **median**, or the midpoint of the distribution, such that 50 percent of the scores (in this example, 50 percent would be 30 of the 60 scores) fall below the median, and 50 percent fall above the median. In this distribution of scores, the median is in the center rating category of 5.

Measures of variability show how scores are dispersed in a frequency distribution. If scores are widely dispersed across a large number of categories, variability will be high. If scores are closely clustered in a few categories, variability will be low. The most commonly used measure of distribution variability is the **standard deviation**. In a frequency distribution, the standard deviation indicates how closely the scores spread out around the mean. The more widely dispersed the scores, the greater the standard deviation. The more closely bunched the scores, the smaller the standard deviation. For example, imagine that two managers each rate 15 subordinates on a five-point performance scale, and the mean (average) ratings given by each manager are the same: 2.8 on the five-point scale. However, manager A's ratings have a large standard deviation, while manager B's ratings have a very small standard deviation. What does this tell you? It means that manager A gave more varied ratings of subordinate performance than did manager B, because the standard deviation represents the *variance* of the distribution of scores. In contrast, manager B gave similar ratings for all 15 subordinates, such that all the ratings are close in numerical value to the average and do not vary across a wide numerical range. Both the mean and the standard deviation are important to more sophisticated inferential statistics.

Inferential Statistics

inferential statistics
statistical techniques used for analyzing data to test hypotheses

statistical significance
the probability of a particular result occurring by chance, used to determine the meaning of research outcomes

While descriptive statistics are helpful in representing and organizing data, **inferential statistics** are used to test hypotheses. For example, assume that we wanted to test the hypothesis that a certain safety program effectively reduced rates of industrial accidents. One group of workers is subjected to the safety program, while another (the control group) is not. Accident rates before and after the program are then measured. Inferential statistics would tell us whether or not differences in accident rates between the two groups were meaningful. Depending on the research design, different sorts of inferential statistics will typically be used.

When inferential statistics are used to analyze data, we are concerned about whether a result is meaningful, or statistically significant. The concept of **statistical significance** is based on theories of probability. A research result is statistically significant if its probability of occurrence by chance is very low. Typically, a research result is statistically significant if its probability of occurrence by chance is less than 5 out of 100 (in research terminology, the probability, or p, is less than .05; $p < .05$). For example, say we find that a group of telephone salespersons who have undergone training in sales techniques have average (mean) sales of 250 units per month, while salespersons who did not receive the training have mean sales of 242 units. Based on the difference in the two means and the variability (standard deviations) of the two groups, a statistical test will determine whether the difference in the two groups is statistically significant (and thus if the training program actually increases sales).

The concept of the **normal distribution** of variables is also important for the use of inferential statistics. It is assumed that many psychological variables, especially human characteristics such as intelligence, motivation, or personality constructs, are normally distributed. That is, scores on these variables in the general population are presumed to vary along a continuum, with the greatest proportion clustering around the midpoint and proportions dropping off toward the endpoints of the continuum. A normal distribution of scores is symbolized visually by the **bell-shaped curve**. The bell-shaped curve, or normal distribution, is a representative distribution of known mathematical properties that can be used as a standard for statistical analyses. The mathematical properties of the normal distribution are represented in Figure A.2. The exact midpoint score, or median, of the normal distribution is the same as its mean. In a normal distribution, 50 percent of the scores lie above the midpoint and 50 percent below. The normal distribution is also divided in terms of standard deviations from the midpoint. In a normal distribution, approximately 68 percent of all scores lie within one standard deviation above or below the midpoint or mean. Approximately 95 percent of all scores in a normal distribution lie within two standard deviations above or below the mid-point. Now that you know the properties

normal distribution (bell-shaped curve) *a distribution of scores along a continuum with known properties*

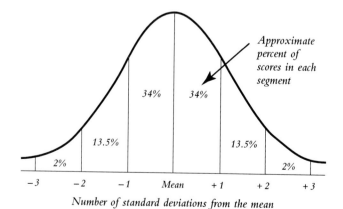

Approximate percent of scores in each segment

FIGURE A.2

A Normal Distribution

of the bell-shaped, or normal, curve, go back to the frequency distribution in Figure A.1. You should notice that this distribution closely approximates the bell-shaped, normal distribution.

Statistical Analysis of Experimental Method Data

As mentioned, depending on the research design, different inferential statistics may be used to analyze data. Typically, one set of statistical techniques is used to test hypotheses from data collected in experimental methods, and another set is used to analyze data from correlational research.

The simplest type of experimental design would have a treatment group, a control group, and a single dependent variable. Whether or not a group receives the treatment represents levels of the independent variable. The most common statistical technique for this type of study is the **t-test**, which examines the difference between the means on the dependent variable for the two groups, taking into account the variability of scores in each group. In the example of trained and untrained salespersons used above, a t-test would determine whether the difference in the two means (250 units versus 242 units) is statistically significant, that is, *not* due to chance fluctuations. If the difference is significant, the researcher may conclude that the training program did have a positive effect on sales.

When an experimental design has three or more groups, a statistical method called *analysis of variance*, or ANOVA, is often used. Analysis of variance looks at differences among more than two groups on a single dependent variable. For example, if we wanted to examine differences in sales performance between a group of salespersons exposed to two weeks of "sales influence tactic training," a group exposed to two days of training, and a group with no training, analysis of variance would be the appropriate technique. In this instance, we still have one dependent variable and one independent variable as in the two-group case; however, the independent variable has three, rather than two, levels. Whenever a research design involves a single independent variable with more than two levels and one dependent variable, the typical statistical technique is referred to as a *one-way analysis of variance* (it is called a "one-way" because there is a single independent variable). The one-way ANOVA would tell us whether our three groups differed in any meaningful way in sales performance.

When a research design involves more than one independent variable, which is very common, the technique that is typically used is the *factorial analysis of variance*. For example, we may wish to examine the effect of the three levels of our influence training program on sales performance for a group of salespersons that receives a sales commission compared to one that does not. This design involves a single dependent variable (sales performance), and two independent variables, one with three levels (training) and one with two levels (commission vs. no commission). The number of different groups in a research study is determined by the number of independent variables and their levels. In this case, our design would result in six

t-test
a statistical test for examining the difference between the means of two groups

How would a researcher use descriptive and inferential statistics?

groups of salespersons ($2 \times 3 = 6$), and the analysis would involve a 2×3 factorial analysis of variance.

There is a major advantage to examining more than one independent variable in a research study, and it involves the types of effects that may be detected. Suppose that in our study we find that influence tactic sales training significantly increases sales performance. This change in the dependent variable due to the independent variable of training is called a *main effect*. Similarly, we may find a main effect of the sales commission variable, such that salespersons who receive a commission have significantly higher sales performance than those who do not. This type of effect could be detected if we were examining either independent variable alone. However, by examining both independent variables at the same time, we may detect a different type of effect called an *interaction*. Two variables are said to interact when the effect of one independent variable on the dependent variable differs depending on the level of the second independent variable. In our study, an interaction between influence tactic sales training and sales commission would be indicated if our training program only increased the sales performance of salespersons who received a commission, and did not affect the performance of salespersons who did not receive commissions.

An even more sophisticated technique, *multivariate analysis of variance* (MANOVA), examines data from multiple groups with multiple dependent variables. The logic of MANOVA is similar to that of ANOVA, but there is more than one dependent variable investigated at a time. For instance, we may want to investigate the effects of training or receiving a sales commission (or both) on sales performance and worker job satisfaction. MANOVA procedures would tell us about differences between our groups on each of these dependent variables. Understanding how these complex statistical techniques work and how they are calculated is not important for our discussion. These terms are presented only to familiarize you with some of the statistics that you might encounter in research reports in I/O psychology or in other types of social science research, and to increase your understanding of the purposes of such procedures.

Statistical Analysis of Correlational Method Data

When a research design is correlational, a different set of statistical techniques is usually used to test hypotheses about presumed relationships among variables. As mentioned, the distinction between independent and dependent variables in a correlational design is not as important as in the experimental method. In a correlational design, the independent variable is usually called the predictor, and the dependent variable is often referred to as the criterion. In a simple correlational design with two variables, the usual statistical analysis technique is the **correlation coefficient**, which measures the strength of the relationship between the predictor and the criterion. The correlation coefficient ranges from $+1.00$ to -1.00. The closer the coefficient is to either $+1.00$ or -1.00, the stronger the relationship between the

correlation coefficient
a statistical technique used to determine the strength of a relationship between two variables

two variables. The closer the correlation coefficient is to zero, the weaker the relationship. A positive correlation coefficient means that there is a positive relationship between the two variables, where an increase in one variable is associated with an increase in the other variable.

Assume that a researcher studying the relationship between the commuting distance of workers and work tardiness obtains a positive correlation coefficient of .75. This figure indicates that the greater the commuting distance of employees, the greater the likelihood that they will be late for work. A negative correlation coefficient indicates a negative relationship: An increase in one variable is associated with a decrease in the other. For example, a researcher studying workers who cut out patterns in a clothing factory hypothesizes that there is a relationship between workers' job experience and the amount of waste produced. Statistical analysis indicates a negative correlation coefficient of −.68: The more experience workers have, the less waste they produce. A correlation coefficient of zero indicates that there is no relationship between the two variables. For example, a researcher measuring the relationship between the age of factory workers and their job performance finds a correlation coefficient of approximately .00, which shows that there is no relationship between age and performance. (These relationships are presented graphically in Figure A.3.)

While the simple correlation coefficient is used to examine the relationship between two variables in a correlational study, the *multiple regression* technique allows a researcher to assess the relationship between a single criterion and multiple predictors. Multiple regression would allow a researcher to examine how well several variables, in combination, predict levels of an outcome variable. For example, a personnel researcher might be interested in how educational level, years of experience, and scores on an aptitude test predict the job performance of new employees. With multiple regression, the researcher could analyze the separate and combined predictive strength of the three variables in predicting performance. Again, a detailed understanding of multiple regression is far beyond the scope of this text, although we will discuss the use of multiple regression in personnel selection in Chapter 4.

Another statistical method that is often used in correlational designs is *factor analysis*, which shows how variables cluster to form meaningful "factors." Factor analysis is useful when a researcher has measured many variables, and wants to examine the underlying structure of the variables, or combine related variables to reduce their number for later analysis. For example, using this technique, a researcher measuring workers' satisfaction with their supervisors, salary, benefits, and working conditions finds that two of these variables, satisfaction with salary and benefits, cluster to form a single factor that the researcher calls "satisfaction with compensation." The other two variables, supervisors and working conditions, form a single factor that the researcher labels "satisfaction with the work environment." If you read literature in I/O psychology or related social sciences you may see examples of the use of factor analysis.

STOP AND REVIEW

Describe a statistical test that would be used in an experimental research design and one that would be used in a correlational research design.

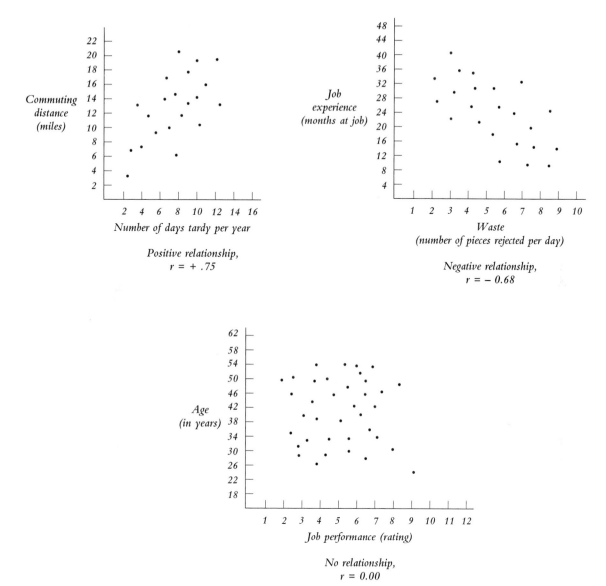

FIGURE A.3

Plots of Scores for Positive, Negative, and Zero Correlations

Appendix Summary

Statistics are research tools used to analyze research data. *Descriptive statistics* are ways of representing data to assist interpretation. One such statistic is the *frequency distribution*. The *mean* and *median* are measures of central tendency in a distribution, and the *standard deviation* is an indicator of distribution variability. *Inferential statistics* are used to test hypotheses. The concept of *statistical significance* is used to determine whether a statistical test of a hypothesis produced a meaningful result. The concept of the *normal distribution* provides a standard for statistical analyses. Different inferential statistics are typically used to analyze data from different research designs. For example, a *t-test* is used to examine the difference between two groups on some dependent variable. *Analysis of variance (ANOVA)* is used for statistical analyses when there are more than two groups, and a *multivariate analysis of variance (MANOVA)* is used when there is more than one dependent variable. Statistical analyses of correlational method data rely on the *correlation coefficient*, a statistic that measures the strength and direction of a relationship between two variables.

JOB ANALYSIS

JOB ANALYSIS: ESTABLISHING A FOUNDATION FOR PERSONNEL PSYCHOLOGY

INSIDE TIPS

The topic of this chapter, job analysis, is the foundation of nearly all personnel activities. To appraise employee performance, hire the right person for a job, train someone to perform a job, or change or redesign a job, we need to know exactly what the job is. This is the purpose of job analysis. Many of the topics we will discuss in the next several chapters rest on this foundation. For example, when we discuss the recruitment, screening, and selection of applicants for a job, we determine what knowledge, skills, abilities, and other characteristics (KSAOs) are required to perform the job before we hire someone. When we discuss evaluating job performance, we need to know what the job consists of before we can tell if someone is doing it well or poorly.

In addition, the analysis of jobs draws heavily on the research methods and measurement issues studied in Chapter 2. In job analysis, we strive to be as objective and precise as possible. Measurement methods and techniques of observing and recording data are critical issues in analyzing jobs.

The topic of job analysis also relates to some of the issues discussed in Chapter 1. For example, when Taylor was applying time-and-motion methods to the study of a job, he was in effect conducting a job analysis. Additionally, one of the job analysis methods we will discuss in this chapter examines the specific processes by which a job gets done. These are the same types of processes Taylor studied in his scientific management methods. Making connections such as these will help you to see how the various topics that we will be discussing fit together.

In the next four chapters, we will be examining the specialty of industrial/organizational psychology referred to as personnel psychology. **Personnel psychology** is concerned with the creation, care and maintenance of a work force, which includes the recruitment, placement, training, and development of workers; the measurement and evaluation of their performance; and concern with worker productivity and satisfaction. In short, the goal of personnel psychology is to take care of an organization's human resources (the organization's personnel).

In the past, the personnel department of a traditional organization was primarily a clerical unit, responsible for maintaining employee records—tabulating attendance, handling payroll, and keeping retirement records. Personnel departments were not very high in organizational status and were not considered very important. In modern times, this has changed, for as work organizations have become more complex, the importance and scope of personnel departments, and personnel psychology, have expanded. Today, the personnel department is typically known as the *human resources department*, which indicates a more global concern with all aspects of the company's most valuable assets: its human workers. Personnel psychologists are involved in personnel activities such as employee recruitment and selection, the measurement of employee performance and the establishment of good performance review procedures, the development of employee training and development programs, and the formulation of criteria for promotion, firing, and disciplinary action. They may also establish effective programs for employee compensation and benefits, create incentive programs, and design and implement programs to protect employee health and well-being.

personnel psychology
the specialty area of I/O psychology focusing on an organization's human resources

Job Analysis

One of the most basic personnel functions is **job analysis,** or the systematic study of the tasks, duties, and responsibilities of a job and the knowledge, skills, and abilities needed to perform it. Job analysis is the starting point for nearly all personnel functions, and job analysis is critically important for developing the means for assessing personnel (Wheaton & Whetzel, 1997). Before a worker can be hired or trained and before a worker's performance can be evaluated, it is critical to understand exactly what the worker's job entails. Such analyses should also be conducted on a periodic basis, in order to ensure that the information on jobs is up-to-date. In other words, it needs to reflect the work actually being performed. For example, as time goes by, a secretary in a small organization might assume additional tasks and responsibilities that did not exist earlier. If the company has to replace the secre-

job analysis
the systematic study of the tasks, duties, and responsibilities of a job and the qualities needed to perform it

tary, but does not have an up-to-date job analysis for the position, it is doubtful that the company would be able to hire an individual with all of the knowledge, skills, abilities, and other characteristics needed to perform the job as it currently exists.

Since most jobs consist of a variety of tasks and duties, gaining a full understanding of a job is not always easy. Therefore, job analysis methods need to be comprehensive and precise. Indeed, large organizations have specialists whose primary responsibilities are to analyze the various jobs in the company and develop extensive and current descriptions for each.

Jobs are complex things. Most jobs require workers to possess certain types of knowledge and skills in order to perform a variety of different tasks. Workers may need to operate complex machinery to perform their jobs, or they might need to possess a great deal of information about a particular product or service. Jobs might also require workers to interact effectively with different types of people. Or, a single job might require a worker to possess all of these important skills and knowledge. As jobs become more and more complex, the need for effective and comprehensive job analyses becomes increasingly important.

In order to perform a good job analysis, the job analyst must be well-trained in the basic research methods we discussed in Chapter 2. Job analysis typically involves the objective measurement of work behavior performed by actual workers. Therefore, a job analyst must be expert in objective measurement techniques in order to perform an accurate job analysis. In fact, a review of research on job analysis suggests that experience and training in job analysis methods are critical for effective job analysis (Landy, 1993).

A job analysis leads directly to the development of several other important personnel "products": a job description, a job specification, a job evaluation, and performance criteria. A **job description** is a detailed accounting of the tasks, procedures, and responsibilities required of the worker; the machines, tools, and equipment used to perform the job; and the job output (end product or service). Workers are most familiar with job descriptions. Often new workers are provided with descriptions of their jobs during initial orientation and training. Or, human resources departments may make job descriptions for various jobs accessible to employees. Sometimes you can see job descriptions posted on bulletin boards as part of announcements for company job openings.

A job analysis also leads to a **job specification**, which provides information about the human characteristics required to perform the job, such as physical and personal traits, work experience, and education. Usually, job specifications give the minimum acceptable qualifications that an employee needs to perform a given job. Sample job descriptions and job specifications are presented in Table 3.1. A third personnel "product," **job evaluation**, is the assessment of the relative value or worth of a job to an organization in order to determine appropriate compensation, or wages. We will discuss job evaluation in much more depth later in this chapter.

job description
a detailed description of job tasks, procedures, and responsibilities; the tools and equipment used; and the end product or service

job specification
a statement of the human characteristics required to perform a job

job evaluation
an assessment of the relative value of a job to determine appropriate compensation

TABLE 3.1

Examples of a Job Description and a Job Specification

Partial job description from a government contractor for the job:
Engine Lathe Operator—First Class

Job summary: Sets up and operates an engine lathe to turn small airplane fittings from brass or steel bar stock or from unfinished aluminum or magnesium alloy castings, finishing fitting down to specified close tolerances.

Work performed: (1) Sets up lathe; carefully examines blueprints to determine the dimensions of the part to be machined, using shop mechanics to calculate any dimensions not given directly on the print or to calculate machine settings. (2) Sets up lathe to turn stock held in chuck; attaches to lathe the accessories such as chuck and tool holder necessary to perform the machining, threading and locking the chuck and the head stock spindle and setting.

Job specification for Engine Lathe Operator—First Class

Minimum two years experience operating engine lathe; experience working with small airplane fittings. Must possess a high school diploma and receive passing score on tests of shop mechanics and blueprint reading. Must be a U.S. citizen, with no criminal record, eligible for security clearance to work on government contracts. [Note that this particular job description is from a company that contracts with the federal government. Private industry cannot demand U.S. citizenship or a high school diploma (unless a diploma actually predicts job performance)]

Source: Job description from E.J. McCormick, *Job Analysis: Methods and Applications* (New York: AMACOM, 1979), p. 63.

Finally, a job analysis helps outline performance criteria, which are the means for appraising worker success in performing a job. Performance criteria and performance appraisals will be the topics of Chapter 6.

These products of job analysis are important because they provide the detailed information needed for other personnel activities, such as planning, recruitment and selection programs, and performance appraisal systems (see Figure 3.1). Job analyses and their products are also valuable because of recent legal decisions that make organizations more responsible for personnel actions as part of the movement toward greater legal rights for the worker. Foremost among these laws are those concerned with equal employment opportunities for disadvantaged and minority workers. Employers can no longer make hasty or arbitrary decisions regarding the hiring, firing, or promotion of workers. Certain personnel actions, such as decisions to hire or promote, must be made on the basis of a thorough job analysis. Personnel decisions that are not so made are difficult to defend in court. Sometimes a job analysis and a job description are not enough. Courts have also questioned the *quality*

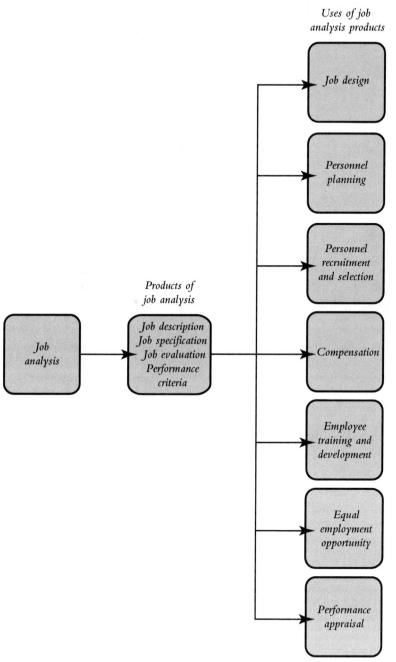

Uses of job
analysis products

Products of
job analysis

Job analysis

Job description
Job specification
Job evaluation
Performance
criteria

Job design

Personnel
planning

Personnel
recruitment
and selection

Compensation

Employee
training and
development

Equal
employment
opportunity

Performance
appraisal

FIGURE 3.1

Links Between Job Analysis and Personnel Functions
Source: Based on J.V. Ghorpade, *Job Analysis: A Handbook for the Human Resource Director.*
Englewood Cliffs, NJ: Prentice-Hall, 1988, p. 6.

of job descriptions and the methods used in job analysis by many companies (Ghorpade, 1988). The passage of the Americans with Disabilities Act (ADA) in 1990 requires that employers make "reasonable accommodations" so that people with physical, mental, or learning disabilities can perform their jobs. This means that job analysts must sometimes be concerned with analyzing jobs specifically with disabled workers in mind, in order to make accommodations so that those workers can perform the jobs (we will discuss the ADA in more depth later).

The Americans with Disabilities Act (ADA) requires that employers make reasonable accommodations so that disabled workers can perform their jobs.

List and define three products of a job analysis.

UP CLOSE

What is Your Job Description?

Companies are not required by law to have job descriptions. As a result, some workers have never seen a job description for their jobs. Whether or not you have read a formal job description, the process of organizing the information required to write such a description will help you to better understand the process as well as the product.

Consider the job you currently hold, one you held in the past, or the "job" of student if you have never had a job. The following list of common elements in job descriptions (Cascio, 1987), can be used to get an idea of what a job description for the job you have in mind would look like.

1. *Job title.*
2. *Job activities and procedures*—Describe activities and tasks performed; include descriptions of material and machinery used and the nature of supervision given or received (e.g., expected to complete work alone, receive constant supervision, etc.).
3. *Working conditions and the physical environment*—Describe the location (indoor/outdoor), the environmental conditions (e.g., temperature), and any hazardous conditions.
4. *Social environment*—Include the number of people in the work group and the amount of social interaction the job requires.
5. *Conditions of employment*—Describe the hours of work, wages, benefits, opportunities for promotion, etc.

You can see how important the information provided here would be if you were to be assigned the task of hiring someone to fill the position you described. Such a job description would help to focus on the elements of the job that are important in selecting a qualified person.

While job descriptions are an important source of information, they are only one product of a thorough job analysis. Therefore, Cascio cautions against organizations' tendencies to overrely on job descriptions as a source of information about jobs. In addition, an accurate and thorough job description cannot be developed unless the job has been thoroughly analyzed.

Job Analysis Methods

There are a variety of methods and procedures for conducting a job analysis, including observational techniques, examination of existing data on jobs, interview techniques, and surveys. Each method will yield a different type of information, and each has its own strengths and weaknesses. In certain methods, such as interviewing, the data may be obtained from a variety of sources, such as the job incumbent (the person currently holding the job), supervisory personnel, or outside experts. Moreover, different job analysis methods are often used in combination to produce a detailed and accurate description of a certain job (Levine, Ash, & Bennett, 1980).

Observations

Observational methods of job analysis are those in which trained job analysts gather information about a particular job. To do this the analyst usually observes the job incumbent at work for a period of time. More recently, job analysts are making use of video cameras to record work behavior for more detailed analysis. Typically in observational analysis, the observer takes detailed notes on the exact tasks and duties performed. However, to make accurate observations, the job analyst must know what to look for. For example, a subtle or quick movement, but one that is important to the job, might go unnoticed. Also, if the job is highly technical or complex, the analyst may not be able to observe some of its critical aspects, such as thinking or decision making. Observational techniques usually work best with jobs

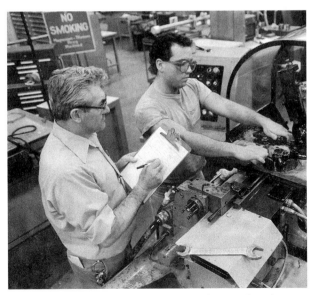

This job analyst uses observational methods to analyze this machinist's job.

involving manual operations, repetitive tasks, or other easily seen activities. For example, describing the tasks and duties of a sewing machine operator is much simpler than describing the job of a computer programmer, since much of the computer programmer's job involves cognitive processes.

With observational techniques, it is important that the times selected for observation are representative of the worker's routine, especially if the job requires that the worker be engaged in different tasks during different times of the day, week, or year. For example, an accounting clerk may deal with payroll vouchers on Thursdays, may spend most of Fridays updating sales figures, and may be almost completely occupied with preparing a company's tax records during the month of January.

One concern regarding observational methods is whether the presence of the observer in some way influences workers' performance. There is always the chance that workers will perform their jobs differently simply because they know that they are being watched (recall the Hawthorne effect discussed in Chapter 1).

Participation

In some instances, a job analyst may want to actually perform a particular job or job operation in order to get a firsthand understanding of how the job is performed. For example, several years ago, I was involved in conducting a job analysis of workers performing delicate microassembly operations. These microassemblers were working with fitting together extremely tiny electrical components. The only way to gain a true understanding of (and appreciation for) the fine hand-eye coordination required to perform the job was to attempt the task myself.

Existing data

Most large, established organizations usually have some information or records that can be used in the job analysis, such as a previous job analysis for the position or an analysis of a related job. Such data might also be borrowed from another organization that has conducted analyses of similar jobs. Human resources professionals often exchange such information with professionals at other organizations. Existing data should always be checked to make sure it conforms to the job as it is currently being performed, and also to determine if the existing data accounts for the inclusion of new technology in the job.

Interviews

Interviews are another method of job analysis. They can be open-ended ("Tell me all about what you do on the job"), or they can involve structured or standardized questions. Since any one source of information can be biased, the job analyst may want to get more than one perspective by interviewing the job incumbent, the incumbent's supervisor, and, if the job is a supervisory one, the incumbent's subordinates. The job analyst might also interview several job incumbents within a single organization in order to get a more reliable representation of the job and to see whether various people holding the same job title in a company actually perform similar tasks.

Surveys

Survey methods of job analysis usually involve the administration of a pencil-and-paper questionnaire that the respondent completes and returns to the job analyst. Surveys can consist of open-ended questions ("What abilities or skills are required to perform this job?"), closed-ended questions ("Which of the following classifications best fits your position? a. supervisory, b. technical, c. line, d. clerical"), or checklists ("Check all of the following tasks that you perform in your job").

The survey method has two advantages over the interview method. First, the survey allows the collection of information from a number of workers simultaneously. This can be helpful and very cost-effective when the analyst needs to study several positions. Second, since the survey can be anonymous, there may be less distortion or withholding of information than in a face-to-face interview. One of the drawbacks of the survey, however, is that the information obtained is limited by the questions asked. Unlike an interview, a survey cannot probe for additional information or for clarification of a response.

Often in conducting job analyses, job incumbents or knowledgeable supervisors of job incumbents are referred to as "subject matter experts" (or SMEs). Subject matter experts can provide job analysis information via interviews, or through survey methods.

Job diaries

Another method for job analysis is to have job incumbents record their daily activities in a diary. An advantage of the job diary is that it provides a detailed, hour-by-hour, day-by-day account of the worker's job. One difficulty of diary methods, however, is that it is quite time-consuming, both for the worker who is keeping the diary and for the job analyst who has the task of analyzing the large amount of information contained in the diary.

An important concern in all of the above methods of job analysis is potential errors and inaccuracies that occur simply because job analysts, job incumbents, and subject matter experts are all human beings. In a recent review, Morgeson and Campion (1997) outlined 16 potential sources of inaccuracy in job analysis, ranging from mere carelessness and poor job analyst training to biases such as overestimating or underestimating the importance of certain tasks and jobs to information overload stemming from the complexity of some jobs. As you recall from our discussion of research methods, an important theme for I/O psychologists is to take steps to ensure that proper methods are used in all sorts of organizational analyses. Nowhere is this more important than in conducting job analyses.

APPLYING I/O PSYCHOLOGY

A Detailed Job Analysis of Real Estate Agents

In one project, the State of California hired an industrial/organizational psychologist to undertake a detailed job analysis of real estate salespersons and brokers (Buckly, 1993). The state wanted to understand the real estate professional's job better in order to improve the existing state licensing exam for real estate agents/brokers.

The I/O psychologist began by surveying nearly 1,000 real estate salespersons and brokers, asking them about the activities they engaged in and the knowledge they needed to perform their jobs. The results of this job analysis indicated that real estate salespersons typically engaged in the following activities:

1. *Locating and listing property*— Includes inspecting the property, performing a market analysis, and suggesting a price range for the property.
2. *Marketing property*—Includes promoting the property through advertising; finding prospective buyers; showing and describing features of the property to prospective buyers.
3. *Negotiating sales contracts*— Includes preparing and presenting offers and counteroffers and negotiating deals.

4. *Assisting with transfer of property*— Includes arranging for escrow; assisting the buyer to find financing; coordinating with inspectors, appraisers, and the escrow and title companies; and reviewing closing documents with clients.
5. *Maintaining professional image*— Includes staying informed about changes in real estate laws and staying informed about market trends and the community.

In addition to the above activities, real estate salespersons had to demonstrate knowledge of:

- Types of properties and ownerships (i.e., leases, common interest properties)
- Land use controls and regulations (zoning, property taxes, building codes, etc.)
- Market value and market analysis
- Property financing and financing regulations
- Contracts
- Transfer of property rules and laws

The result of this project was that the I/O psychologist recommended that the state change the licensing examination test items in order to better reflect the job as described by real estate salesperson job incumbents.

Specific Job Analysis Techniques

In addition to these various *general* methods for conducting job analyses, there are also a number of *specific*, standardized analysis techniques. These techniques have not only been widely used but have also generated a considerable amount of research on their effectiveness. We will consider four of these specific techniques: the job elements method, functional job analysis, the Position Analysis Questionnaire, and the critical incidents technique.

Job Elements Method

The **job elements method** of job analysis looks at the basic knowledge, skills, abilities, or other characteristics—KSAOs—that are required to perform a particular job (Primoff, 1975). These KSAOs constitute the basic job elements.

In the job elements method the job analyst relies on "experts" (subject matter experts, or SMEs) who are informed about the job in order to identify the job elements (KSAOs) required for a given job. The experts then rate or rank the different elements in terms of their importance for performing the job. The job elements method is "person-oriented" in that it focuses on the characteristics of the individual who is performing the job.

job elements method
a job analysis method that analyzes jobs in terms of the knowldege, skills, abilities, and other characteristics (KSAOs) required to perform the jobs

Functional Job Analysis

Functional job analysis (FJA) has been used extensively by organizations in both the public and private sectors (Fine & Getkate, 1995; Fine & Wiley, 1971). It was developed in part to assist the United States Department of Labor in the construction of a comprehensive job classification system and to help create the **Dictionary of Occupational Titles** (*DOT*) (U.S. Department of Labor, 1991), a reference guide that classifies and gives general descriptions for over 40,000 different jobs. If it seems unimaginable that over 40,000 different jobs exist, you should know that the jobs contained in the *DOT* include: Rag Sorter, Human Projectile, Egg Smeller, Lump Receiver, Bone Crusher, Bung Dropper, Loose End Finder, Germ Drier, and Side Splitter (Booth, 1992). [Readers interested in any of these jobs should consult the *DOT* for more detailed information].

The *DOT* classifies each job using a nine-digit code that represents the job classification and gives an idea of the level of work functioning that the job requires. The first three digits of the code simply indicate the occupational code, job title, and type of industry or "industry designation"; the last three digits serve as an alphabetical ordering of jobs within the same occupational grouping. It is the second three digits that are important for describing the type of work involved in a particular job. These digits represent the job's typical interaction with data, people, and things. *Data* is information, knowledge, and conceptions. Jobs are evaluated with an eye to the amount and type of interaction the person performing the job has with data—numbers, words, symbols, and other abstract elements. *People* refers to the amount of contact with others that a job requires. These people can be coworkers, supervisors, customers or others. *Things* refers to the worker's interaction with inanimate objects such as tools, machines, equipment, and tangible work products. Although FJA originally led to the development of the *DOT*, today it uses the *DOT* descriptions as a starting point for more detailed descriptions.

functional job analysis (FJA)
a structured job analysis technique that examines the sequence of tasks in a job and the processes by which they are completed

Dictionary of Occupational Titles (DOT)
a reference guide that classifies and describes over 40,000 jobs

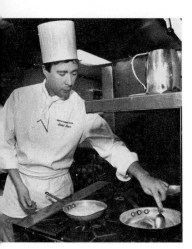

According to functional job analysis, the job of restaurant cook involves compiling data, speaking to people, and doing precision work with things.

Functional job analysis begins by examining what gets done—the sequence of tasks that must be completed—and how it gets done—the processes by which the worker completes the tasks. According to FJA, all jobs require workers to interact with the three components of data, people, and things. Within each of these categories there is a hierarchy of work functions which ranges from the most involved and complex functions (given the numerical value of "0") to the least involved and least complex (the highest digit in the category; see Table 3.2). These digits are used to classify the functions of specific jobs in the *DOT*. For example, in our sample *DOT* entries in Table 3.3, the job of industrial/organizational psychologist has the numerical code 045.107–030. The three middle digits, 107, refer to the three components of job functions. The 1 means that the job of I/O psychologist requires "coordinating" data. The 0 indicates that I/O psychologists are involved in "mentoring" people, and the 7 shows that their job requires "handling" things. For the occupation of job analyst, the important digits are 267, meaning that the job involves "analyzing" data, "speaking" to people, and "handling" things. The fun house operator's code of 665 means that job involves "comparing" data, "speaking and signalling" to patrons, and "tending" machinery.

In using functional job analysis, the job analyst begins with the general job description provided by the *DOT*. The analyst will then use interviewing and/or observational techniques to conduct a more detailed study of a certain job. FJA is especially helpful when the job analyst must create job descriptions for a large number of positions. It is also quite popular because it is cost-effective and because it uses job descriptions based on the *DOT*, which are often considered satisfactory by federal employment enforcement agencies (Mathis & Jackson, 1985). FJA has also proven useful in research

TABLE 3.2

Hierarchy of Work Functions Used in Functional Job Analysis

Data (4th digit)	People (5th digit)	Things (6th digit)
0 Synthesizing	0 Mentoring	0 Setting up
1 Coordinating	1 Negotiating	1 Precision working
2 Analyzing	2 Instructing	2 Operating-controlling
3 Compiling	3 Supervising	3 Driving-operating
4 Computing	4 Diverting	4 Manipulating
5 Copying	5 Persuading	5 Tending
6 Comparing	6 Speaking, Signaling	6 Feeding, Off bearing
	7 Serving	7 Handling
	8 Taking instruction, helping	

Source: U.S. Department of Labor, *Dictionary of Occupational Titles*, Rev. 4th ed. (Washington, DC: Government Printing Office, 1991).

TABLE 3.3

Sample Entries from the Dictionary of Occupational Titles

Job: 045.107–030 Psychologist, Industrial-Organizational

Develops and applies psychological techniques to personnel administration, management and marketing problems: Observes details of work and interviews workers and supervisors to establish physical, mental, educational, and other job requirements. Develops interview techniques, rating scales, and psychological tests to assess skills, abilities, aptitudes, and interests as aids in selection, placement, and promotion. Organizes training programs, applying principles of learning and individual differences, and evaluates and measures effectiveness of training methods by statistical analysis of production rate, reduction of accidents, absenteeism, and turnover. Counsels workers to improve job and personal adjustments. Conducts research studies of organizational structure, communication systems, group interactions, and motivational systems, and recommends changes to improve efficiency and effectiveness of individuals, organizational limits, and organization. Investigates problems related to physical environment of work, such as illumination, noise, temperature, and ventilation, and recommends changes to increase efficiency and decrease accident rate. Conducts surveys and research studies to ascertain nature of effective supervision and leadership and to analyze factors affecting morale and motivation. . . . May adapt machinery, equipment, workspace, and environment to human use. . . .

Job: 166.267–018 Job Analyst

Collects, analyzes, and prepares occupational information to facilitate personnel, administration, and management functions of organization: Consults with management to determine type, scope, and purpose of study. Studies current organizational occupational data and compiles distribution reports, organization and flow charts, and other background information. Observes jobs and interviews workers and supervisory personnel to determine job and worker requirements. Analyzes occupational data, such as physical, mental, and training requirements of jobs and workers and develops written summaries, such as job descriptions, job specifications, and lines of career movement. Utilizes developed occupational data to evaluate or improve methods and techniques for recruiting, selecting, promoting, evaluating, and training workers . . .

Job: 342.665–010 Fun-House Operator

Tends one or several pieces of automatic equipment designed to amuse, excite, or mystify patrons of fun house in amusement park: Switches on device that automatically blows blasts of air under women's skirts. Starts revolving turntables, conveyor belt, drum or similar device. Ejects rowdy persons from establishment. Observes equipment for efficient operation and repairs minor breakdowns in equipment.

How to interpret the DOT code

The first three digits indicate the occupational code, title, and industry designations. The next three digits represent the job's typical interaction with data, people, and things (see Table 3.2). The final three digits denote an alphabetical ordering of jobs within the same occupational grouping.

Source: U.S. Department of Labor, *Dictionary of Occupational Titles,* Rev. 4th ed. (Washington, DC: Government Printing Office, 1991).

designed to gain insight into how workers are performing their jobs. For instance, in a study of over 200 nursing assistants in nursing homes, functional job analysis discovered that nursing assistants were spending too little time dealing with the *people* aspects of their jobs (e.g., giving attention to elderly residents), and a disproportionately large amount of time dealing with *data* (e.g., reports) and *things*, such as changing bedding (Brannon, Streit, & Smyer, 1992).

Position Analysis Questionnaire

Position Analysis Questionnaire (PAQ)
a job analysis technique that uses a structured questionnaire to analyze jobs according to 187 job statements, grouped into 6 categories

Define the three dimensions used in Functional Job Analysis.

One of the most widely researched job analysis instruments is the **Position Analysis Questionnaire (PAQ)** (McCormick, Jeanneret, & Mecham, 1969), which is a structured questionnaire that analyzes various jobs in terms of 187 job elements that are arranged into six categories, or divisions, as follows:

Information input—Where and how the worker obtains the information needed to perform the job. For example, a newspaper reporter may be required to use published, written materials as well as interviews with informants to write a news story. A clothing inspector's information input may involve fine visual discriminations of garment seams.

Mental processes—The kinds of thinking, reasoning, and decision making required to perform the job. For example, an air traffic controller must make many decisions about when it is safe for jets to land and take off.

Work output—The tasks the worker must perform and the tools or machines needed. For example, a word processor must enter text using keyboard devices.

Relationships with other persons—The kinds of relationships and contacts with others required to do the job. For example, a teacher instructs others, and a store clerk has contact with customers by providing information and ringing up purchases.

Job context—The physical and/or social contexts in which the work is performed. Examples of job context elements would be working under high temperatures or dealing with many conflict situations.

Other job characteristics—Other relevant activities, conditions, or characteristics necessary to do the job.

Each of these job elements is individually rated using six categories: extent of use, importance to the job, amount of time, applicability, possibility of occurrence, and a special code for miscellaneous job elements. The standard elements are rated on a scale from 1, for minor applicability, to 5, for extreme applicability. There is an additional rating for "does not apply" (McCormick, 1979). A sample page from the PAQ is shown in Figure 3.2.

The PAQ results produce a very detailed profile of a particular job that can be used to compare jobs within a company or similar positions in different organizations. Because the PAQ is a standardized instrument, two analysts surveying the same job should come up with very similar profiles. This might not be the case with interview techniques, where the line of

INFORMATION INPUT

    1. INFORMATION INPUT

    1.1 Sources of Job Information

Rate each of the following items in terms of the
extent to which it is used by the worker as a
source of information in performing his job.

Code	Extent of Use (U)
N	Does not apply
1	Nominal/very infrequent
2	Occasional
3	Moderate
4	Considerable
5	Very substantial

1   _____   Written materials (books, reports, office notes, articles, job instructions, signs, etc.).

2   _____   Quantitative materials (materials which deal with quantities or amounts, such as graphs, accounts, specifications, tables of numbers, etc.).

3   _____   Pictorial materials (pictures or picturelike materials used as *sources* of information, for example, drawings, blueprints, diagrams, maps, tracings, photographic films, x-ray films, TV pictures, etc.).

4   _____   Patterns/related devices (templates, stencils, patterns, etc., used as *sources* of information when *observed* during use; do *not* include here materials described in item 3 above).

5   _____   Visual displays (dials, gauges, signal lights, radarscopes, speedometers, clocks, etc.).

6   _____   Measuring devices (rulers, calipers, tire pressure gauges, scales, thickness gauges, pipettes, thermometers, protractors, etc., used to obtain visual information about physical measurements; do *not* include here devices described in item 5 above).

7   _____   Mechanical devices (tools, equipment, machinery, and other mechanical devices which are *sources* of information when observed during use or operation).

8   _____   Materials in process (parts, materials, objects, etc., which are *sources* of information when being modified, worked on, or otherwise processed, such as bread dough being mixed, workpiece being turned in a lathe, fabric being cut, shoe being resoled, etc.).

9   _____   Materials *not* in process (parts, materials, objects, etc., not in the process of being changed or modified, which are sources of information when being inspected, handled, packaged, distributed, or selected, etc., such as items or materials in inventory, storage, or distribution channels, items being inspected, etc.).

10   _____   Features of nature (landscapes, fields, geological samples, vegetation, cloud formations, and other features of nature which are observed or inspected to provide information).

11   _____   Constructed features of environment (structures, buildings, dams, highways, bridges, docks, railroads, and other "man made" or altered aspects of the indoor or outdoor environment which are *observed* or *inspected* to provide job information; do not consider equipment, machines, etc., that an individual uses in work, as covered by item 7).

FIGURE 3.2

Sample Page from the Position Analysis Questionnaire (PAQ).
Source: E.J. McCormick, P.R. Jeanneret, and R.C. Mecham, *Position Analysis Questionnaire* (West Lafayette, IN: Occupational Research Center, Purdue University, 1969), p. 4.

questioning and interpersonal skills specific to the interviewer could greatly affect the job profile.

Research Using the PAQ

As mentioned, the PAQ is one of the most widely used and thoroughly researched methods of job analysis (Hyland & Muchinsky, 1991; Peterson & Jeanneret, 1997). For example, the PAQ has been used to identify similarities between different classes of jobs, and of similar classes of jobs in different organizations. The PAQ has also been used to provide information on the feasibility, cost, and time required to retrain workers for new positions (Kraiger, 1991). This latter information is valuable to employers who wish to retrain laid-off workers, to cross-train workers for other positions, or when there is a dramatic change in a worker's current job due to new technology or organizational restructuring.

The PAQ has also been used to assess the validity of a theory of how people choose vocations (Hyland & Muchinsky, 1991). More specifically, in this study, the PAQ was used to identify the type of work performed within six major types of vocations. In another interesting study, the PAQ was used to analyze the job of homemaker. It was found that a homemaker's job is most similar to the jobs of police officer, firefighter, and airport maintenance chief (Arvey & Begalla, 1975).

Research indicates that the PAQ is more accurate when positions are rated by expert job analysts than by other raters, such as job incumbents (Harvey & Lozado-Larsen, 1988). Evidence indicates that this result may be attributable to differences in verbal ability rather than expertise (Harvey, Hakel, Friedman, & Cornelius, 1988). In other words, perhaps expert job analysts have higher verbal skills than do job incumbents.

CRITICAL INCIDENTS TECHNIQUE

critical incidents technique (CIT)
a job analysis technique that relies on instances of especially successful or unsuccessful job performance

The **critical incidents technique (CIT)** of job analysis records the specific worker behaviors that have led to particularly successful or unsuccessful job performance (Flanagan, 1954). For example, some critical incidents for the job of clerk typist might include: "Produces a manuscript with good margins, making it look like a typeset document"; "Notices an item in a letter or report that doesn't appear to be right, checks it, and corrects it"; "Misfiles charts, letters, etc., on a regular basis"; and "When in doubt, uses a dictionary to check the spelling of a word." All of these behaviors presumably contribute to the success or failure of the clerk typist. Research indicates that information is best provided by experts on the job (Mullins & Kimbrough, 1988). Therefore, information on such incidents are obtained by questioning, either through interviews or questionnaires, job incumbents, job supervisors, or other knowledgeable individuals. Through the collection of hundreds of critical incidents, the job analyst can arrive at a very good picture of what a particular job—and its successful performance—are all about. An example of a critical incidents interview form is presented in Figure 3.3.

The real value of the CIT is in helping to determine the particular knowledge, skills, and abilities that a worker needs to perform a job successfully. For example, from the critical incidents given for the clerk typist position we know that the successful typist will need to know how to file, use a dictionary, check basic grammar and sentence structure, and set up a typed manuscript page. The CIT technique is also useful in developing appraisal systems for certain jobs, by helping to identify the critical components of successful performance.

The following is an example of an interview question designed to elicit critical incidents for a particular job. This question focuses on an incident where a subordinate was behaving in a "helpful" way. Another question might try to elicit when workers are not being helpful; in other words, when they may be hurting group productivity.

"Think of the last time you saw one of your subordinates do something that was very helpful to your group in meeting their production schedule." (Pause until the respondent has such an incident in mind.) "Did the subordinate's action result in an increase in production of as much as one percent for that day?–or some similar period?"
(If the answer is "no", say) "I wonder if you could think of the last time that someone did something that did have this much of an effect in increasing production." (When respondent indicates he/she has such a situation in mind, say) "What were the general circumstances leading up to this incident?"

"Tell me exactly what this person did that was so helpful at that time."
"Why was this so helpful in getting your group's job done?"
"When did this incident happen?"
"What was this person's job?"
"How long has the person been on this job?"

Another example of a question designed to elicit critical incidents may be as simple and general as, "Think of the best (worst) subordinate you have known. Tell me about a time that shows why this person was the best (worst)."

FIGURE 3.3

Critical Incidents Interview Form
Source: Adapted from J.C. Flanagan, "The Critical Incidents Technique," *Psychological Bulletin,* 51 (1954), p. 342.

COMPARING THE DIFFERENT JOB ANALYSIS TECHNIQUES

Several comparison studies of the various job analysis techniques have been conducted. A series of investigations by Levine and his associates (Levine, Ash, & Bennett, 1980; Levine, Ash, Hall, & Sistrunk, 1983) compared various techniques in terms of their accuracy, level of detail, and cost effectiveness. They found that functional job analysis, the critical incidents technique, and the Position Analysis Questionnaire were all reasonably effective job analysis methods. While FJA and the CIT provided detailed, comprehensive types of analyses, the PAQ yielded more limited information, probably because it uses the same general instrument to analyze all types of jobs. The FJA and CIT, by contrast, are tailored to analyze specific jobs, and CIT is particularly suited to analyzing complex jobs (Anderson & Wilson, 1997). However, the PAQ was found to be more cost-effective and easier to use than the other methods.

Regardless of the specific instrument used, when job analysis is used to compare different types of jobs, the job analyst must use caution in the interpretation of numerical scale values. For example, both a marketing director and a head janitor could conceivably be rated on the behavior of "negotiation with others" as the same value on a rating scale. Even though these jobs may be similar in the amount of time spent in negotiations, it would be erroneous to conclude that the negotiations have equal weight, that they are equally demanding, or that they require an equal level of skill. One suggested solution to this problem is to rate the "relative importance" (RI) of tasks, including the RI between jobs, the RI within similar jobs, and also to evaluate the tasks "qualitatively", rather than relying solely on quantitative evaluation (Harvey, 1991).

Overall, no one method or technique of job analysis has emerged as superior to all others. It may be that a trained analyst could conduct very good job analyses using any of several methods (Muchinsky, 1987). Obviously, a combination of methods should lead to a more detailed, more reliable, and "better" analysis than the use of any one technique alone.

Job Analysis and the ADA

In 1990, passage of the Americans with Disabilities Act (ADA) presented a new challenge to job analysts. Title I of the ADA stated that "in employment matters it is illegal to discriminate against a qualified person with a disability: Such an individual is one who can perform the essential functions of a job with or without reasonable accommodation." Implementation of the ADA also requires that employers prevent employment discrimination against disabled persons, and they must also make reasonable accommodations that will allow disabled persons to perform essential job duties. For example, an employer may need to construct a different type of work station for an employee in a wheelchair.

While the ADA does not require employers to conduct formal job analyses (Esposito, 1992), you might imagine the difficulties involved in trying to adapt or alter a job for a disabled employee without having conducted a thorough analysis of it. Moreover, compliance with the ADA requires employers to understand the "essential elements" (i.e., functions), or content of a job (Greenlaw & Kohl, 1993). It is imperative that requirements for a particular job be reviewed and updated. For example, an old job specification for a warehouse stocker might require heavy lifting, yet since the position involves operating a forklift, there may be little or no manual lifting required. Therefore, a person with a serious disability might be able to perform this job without difficulty. Likewise, as more and more tasks become computerized, job analyses need to be kept up to date so that they reflect the impact of computerization on job content and requirements.

Only through job analysis can essential job elements and job requirements be determined. It is these elements and requirements that need to be considered when interviewing, hiring, and training workers with disabilities. Due to legislative actions such as the ADA, job analysis is becoming more complex, more challenging, and more critical to job analysts, employers, and personnel psychologists.

Job Evaluation and Comparable Worth

As mentioned at the beginning of the chapter, one of the products of a job analysis is a *job evaluation*, which is the process of assessing the relative value of jobs to determine appropriate compensation. That is, the wages paid for a particular job should be related to the knowledge, skills, abilities, and other characteristics it requires. However, a number of other variables, such as the supply of potential workers, the perceived value of the job to the company, and the job's history, can also influence its rate of compensation.

Detailed job evaluations typically examine jobs on a number of dimensions called **compensable factors**. Examples of compensable factors might be the physical demands of a job, the amount of training or experience required, the working conditions associated with the job, and the amount of responsibility the job carries. Each job may be given a score or weighting on each factor. The summed total of the weighted compensable factors indicates the value of the job, which is then translated into the dollar amount of compensation. Table 3.4 presents two examples of this point system of job evaluation. According to these examples, the job of turret lathe programmer/operator receives a slightly higher point total than the forklift operator position. Therefore, the turret operator should receive a higher rate of compensation. Bear in mind that a compensable factors analysis of a job determines rates of compensation based solely on the training, responsibility, and conditions associated with a job. It does not take into account market conditions, such as the supply and demand for workers for a certain job. Therefore, because these market factors are not considered, a compensable factors analysis would show that a brain surgeon should be paid more than a major league left-handed relief pitcher. Market factors, including the scarcity of big league pitchers (and left handers in particular), are what cause the average pitcher's salary to be much higher than the surgeon's.

For decades, the issue of how jobs are compensated has been a source of controversy. Specifically, there has been a great deal of concern over discrimination in compensation, particularly wage discrepancies for men and women. Two pieces of federal legislation address this issue. The Equal Pay Act of 1963 mandates that men and women performing equal work receive equal pay. Further, a U.S. Supreme Court ruling made defense of pay differentials by employers more difficult than it has been in the past (Greenlau & Kohl, 1992). Title VII of the Civil Rights Act of 1964 prohibits discrimination in employment practices based on race, color, religion, *sex*, and national origin. In spite of these laws, however, there is considerable evidence that women receive lower wages than men performing the same or equivalent work (Treiman & Hartmann, 1981). In fact, although the most recent research shows that pay for women is catching up to the wages paid men, these gains are slow in coming. The best estimates are that women, on the average, are only paid about 70 percent of the wages paid to men for comparable work (Sorensen, 1994).

compensable factors
the job elements that are used to determine appropriate compensation for a job

Explain the Americans with Disabilities Act (ADA).

TABLE 3.4

Two Job Evaluations Using a Point System

Job Name: Turret Lathe Programmer/Operator

Compensable Factors	Substantiating Data	Points
Education	Must read work orders, use shop mathematics, use precision measuring instruments and gauges. Equivalent to 2–3 years applied trades training.	42
Experience	Over 4 years, up to and including 5 years.	88
Initiative and ingenuity	Plan and perform machine programming and operations. Requires considerable judgment to program, operate, and adjust machinery.	56
Physical demand	Light physical effort. Occasionally lifts or moves average-weight material.	20
Mental demand	Concentrated mental attention required.	20
Responsibility for equipment and materials	Careless, negligent, or improper performance could damage tools, equipment, or product.	35
Responsibility for safety of others	Improper performance of work may cause others hand, foot, or eye injury.	15
Responsibility for work of others	Responsible for 1 or 2 persons 50% or more of time.	10
Working conditions	Good. Exposed to office and shop conditions that are not disagreeable.	20
Hazards	Accidents may cause injury to hand, foot, or eye.	15
	Total points =	321

Job Name: Forklift Operator

Compensable Factors	Substantiating Data	Points
Education	Must read work orders, use simple mathematics. Grammar school education desirable.	32
Experience	Must learn to operate forklift and hand truck. Two to three weeks on-the-job training.	48
Initiative and ingenuity	Some variety on the job. Uses some discretion in keeping product in order.	38
Physical demand	On feet most of day when not driving forklift. Pushes empty and full pallets with hand truck. Some lifting of heavy boxes.	30
Mental demand	Concentrated mental attention required.	20
Responsibility for equipment and materials	Careless, negligent, or improper performance could damage tools, equipment, or product.	35
Responsibility for safety of others	Improper performance of work may cause serious injury to others.	25
Responsibility for work of others	None.	0
Working conditions	In freezer (0°C) for a total of 2–3 hours per day.	38
Hazards	Accidents may cause serious injury.	25
	Total points =	291

Sources: F.J. Landy, *Psychology of Work Behavior*, 3rd ed. (Homewood, IL: Dorsey, 1985), p. 158. M.L. Rock, *Handbook of Wage and Salary Administration* (New York: McGraw-Hill, 1984), p. 136.

Women workers have made some small advances in the wages "gender gap" since this cartoon came out.

Two issues bear directly on the "gender gap" in wages. The first concerns access to higher-paying jobs (Wittig & Berman, 1992). Traditionally, many such jobs were primarily held by men, but throughout the 1960s and 1970s, the women's rights movement helped increase the access of women to these positions. However, while women are now found in nearly every type of job, there is still considerable sex stereotyping of jobs, which means that many relatively high-paying jobs and professions are still filled mainly by men. For example, men are found in large numbers in skilled craft jobs that receive higher wages than clerical jobs, which are filled mainly by women.

The second issue deals with the fact that women are often paid far less than men for performing equivalent tasks. In the 1980s, this gender-based pay disparity gave birth to the concept of **comparable worth**, or equal pay for equal work. For example, the job of personnel clerk, a traditionally "female" job, and the position of records manager in the production department, a job usually filled by men, both require workers to perform similar tasks, such as keeping records and managing data files. Because of the similarity in duties, both positions should be paid equal wages. However, the job of records manager typically pays higher wages than the position of personnel clerk.

Because of its focus on evaluating the worth of work tasks, the issue of comparable worth is tied to the ability of organizations to conduct valid and fair job evaluations, which should reveal instances of equal jobs receiving unequal compensation. However, opponents of the comparable worth

comparable worth
the notion that jobs that require equivalent KSAOs should be compensated equally

What is a compensable factors analysis?

exceptioning
the practice of ignoring pay discrepancies between particular jobs possessing equivalent duties and responsibilities

movement argue that job evaluation methods may be inaccurate because they do not account for factors like the oversupply of female applicants for certain jobs, such as teachers and airline attendants, the lower levels of education and work experience of women relative to men, and women's preferences for certain types of "safe" jobs with "pleasant working conditions." Advocates of the comparable worth movement argue that even these factors do not account for the considerable disparity in pay for men and women (Judd & Gomez-Mejia, 1987; Pinzler & Ellis, 1989; Thacker, 1995).

For a number of reasons, women are simply not paid the same wages for the same level of work. One argument is that society does not value the type of work required by many jobs that are filled primarily by women, such as secretarial, clerical, teaching, and nursing positions. Alternatively, certain jobs that are filled primarily by men may be compensated at higher levels because more value is ascribed to them (Sorensen, 1994).

Another reason for gender-based pay disparity is the practice of **exceptioning**, whereby a job evaluation reveals that two jobs, with equivalent duties and responsibilities, receive very different rates of pay, yet no steps are taken to rectify the inequality. In other words, an "exception" is made because it is too costly or too difficult to raise the wages of the lower-paid job. An example of exceptioning is the pay rates for physicians and nurses. The average salary of a physician is three to five times that of a nurse, yet the two jobs have many comparable duties and responsibilities. Although the imbalance in salaries is known to exist, hospitals are financially unable to pay nurses what they are worth, so an exception is made.

The issue of comparable worth has been hotly debated by both business and government officials. Certain cases of sex discrimination in employee compensation have reached the courts, highlighting the issue of comparable worth. For example, in *AFSCME* v. *State of Washington* (1983), a job evaluation of state employee positions found that women's job classes were paid approximately 20 percent less than comparable men's classes. It was recommended that women state employees should be paid an additional $38 million annually. Because the state of Washington did not act on the recommendation, the women employees' union sued. The court ruled that the state was discriminating against its women employees and awarded them nearly $1 billion.

If the comparable worth movement goes forward and the government decides to take steps to correct pay inequalities, the impact on workers and work organizations will be tremendous. First, job evaluations will have to be conducted for nearly all jobs in the country—a staggering and expensive task. Second, since it is unlikely that workers and unions will allow the wages of higher-paid workers to be cut, the salaries of the lower-paid workers will have to be raised—also an enormous expense. Regardless of what takes place in the next few years, the issue of comparable worth has focused greater attention on job evaluations and job evaluation procedures. It is thus likely that greater attention will be given to improving such procedures in the near future (Lowe & Wittig, 1989; Risher, 1984).

ON THE CUTTING EDGE

Breaking the Glass Ceiling: Eliminating Gender and Ethnic Inequities in the Workplace

The term **glass ceiling** typically refers to the limitations placed on women and ethnic minorities that prevent them from advancing into top management positions. While discrimination in employment practices is illegal, biases and stereotypes still influence decisions as to who is and who is not qualified to hold a position (Fagenson & Jackson, 1993). For example, one common stereotype holds that women have a management style that is different (and therefore less effective) than men, although studies have shown no substantial differences in the styles of male and female managers (Lester, 1993).

Although some recent studies indicate that women are making some small gains in achieving equality in pay and level of positions (Lissy, 1993; Mason, 1993), other studies indicate that there is still a wide gender gap in top-level positions. For example, one study concluded that only about 3 percent of top management personnel are women (Lester, 1993). Another study found significantly fewer females among the top ranks of university professors (Fisher, Motowidlo, & Werner, 1993). In a study of 799 non-profit foundations, it was found that the percentage of high-level female executives had increased from 26 percent to 43 percent from 1982 to 1992; however, in 1992, only 5.7 percent of these top positions were held by ethnic minorities (Zehr, 1993). Rather than simply being shut out of promotion to top-level positions, there is evidence that the career progression of women and ethnic minorities is slower than that of white males,

so that it takes longer to get to the top (Powell & Butterfield, 1994, 1997).

Sadly, the glass ceiling seems to be a worldwide phenomenon. Women represent less than 10 percent of senior management in all industrialized countries, ranging from a high of 8 percent in Belgium to a low of 0.3 percent in Japan (Adler, 1993). In a study of workers in the U.S., United Kingdom, Africa, Australia, and Papua New Guinea, glass ceilings existed for all "nondominant" groups in the companies surveyed. The "nondominant" groups varied from country to country, but in each case members of these groups were underutilized, were underrepresented in high-level positions, and followed different career paths than members of the dominant group (Stamp, 1990).

What can be done to break the glass ceiling? First, in the U.S., the Civil Rights Act of 1991 created a Glass Ceiling Commission, and gave women the right to sue on the basis of discrimination (Tavakolian, 1993). The U.S. Office of Federal Contract Compliance Programs (OFCCP) also began examining the recruitment and promotion policies at upper management levels, focusing on possible discrimination against women in upper-level positions (Brown, 1991). Such laws and attention from federal governments will obviously help protect women and minorities from blatant discrimination. However, much of the "gender gap" may not result from blatant discrimination, but from the devaluing of certain occupations, such as teaching or nursing—occupations that are dominated by women (Sorensen, 1994).

glass ceiling
limitations placed on women and minorities preventing them from advancing into top-level positions in organizations

STOP AND REVIEW

What two issues are involved in the wage gender gap?

Summary

Job analysis is the systematic study of a job's tasks, duties, and responsibilities, and the knowledge, skills, and abilities needed to perform the job. The job analysis, which is the important starting point for many personnel functions, yields several products: *a job description*, which is a detailed accounting of job tasks, procedures, responsibilities, and output; a *job specification*, which consists of information about the physical, educational, and experiential qualities required to perform the job; a *job evaluation*, which is an assessment of the relative value of jobs for determining compensation; and performance criteria, which serve as a basis for appraising successful job performance.

Job analysis methods include observation, the use of existing data, interviews, and surveys. One structured job analysis technique is the *job elements approach*, a broad approach to job analysis that focuses on the knowledge, skills, abilities and other characteristics (KSAOs) required to perform a particular job. *Functional job analysis (FJA)* is a method that has been used to classify jobs in terms of the worker's interaction with data, people, and things. FJA uses the *Dictionary of Occupational Titles (DOT)*, a reference book listing general job descriptions for thousands of jobs, and examines the sequence of tasks required to complete the job as well as the process by which the job is completed. Another structured job analysis technique, the *Position Analysis Questionnaire (PAQ)*, uses a questionnaire that analyzes jobs in terms of 187 job elements arranged into 6 categories. Finally, the *critical incidents technique* of job analysis involves the collection of particularly successful or unsuccessful instances of job performance. Through the collection of hundreds of these incidents, a very detailed profile of a job emerges. Research has determined that all of these specific, standardized methods are effective.

Job analysis yields a job evaluation, or an assessment of the relative value of jobs used to determine appropriate compensation. These evaluations usually examine jobs on dimensions that are called *compensable factors*, which are given values that signify the relative worth of the job and translate into levels of compensation.

A current topic in the area of job evaluation concerns the "gender gap" in wages. Evidence indicates that women are paid far less than men for comparable work. This inequity has recently given rise to the *comparable worth* movement, which argues for equal pay for equal work. This issue is controversial because of the difficulty and costs of making compensation for comparable jobs equitable. Research has also suggested that women and ethnic minorities are affected by a *glass ceiling*, which creates difficulties for members of minority groups in rising to the highest-level positions in organizations.

Study Questions and Exercises

1. Consider each of the products of a job analysis. How do these products affect other organizational outcomes?

2. Compare and contrast the four specific, structured methods of job analysis: functional job analysis, the job elements approach, the *Position Analysis Questionnaire*, and the critical incidents technique. Make a table listing their respective strengths and weaknesses.

3. Consider your current job, or a job that you or a friend held in the past. How would you begin to conduct a job analysis of that position? What methods would you use? What are the important components of the job?

4. List some of the reasons why women are paid less for comparable work performed by men. Think of some stereotypically "female" jobs and comparable jobs that are stereotypically held by men. Are there inequities in compensation between the "male" and "female" jobs? Why or why not?

Suggested Readings

Fine, S.A., & Getkate, M. (1995). *Benchmark tasks for job analysis: A guide for Functional Job Analysis (FJA) scales.* Hillsdale, NJ: Lawrence Erlbaum Associates. *This is an easy-to-understand, very detailed guide for constructing and using job descriptions for the practicing HR manager. One chapter is called, "One Hundred Thirty-Two Major Management Uses for the Job Description."*

Harvey, R.J. (1991). Job analysis. In M.D. Dunnette & L.M. Hough (Eds.), *Handbook of industrial and organizational psychology,* (2nd ed., Vol. 2, pp. 71–163). Palo Alto, CA: Consulting Psychologists Press. *A comprehensive review of research in all areas of job analysis.*

Sorensen, E. (1994). *Comparable worth: Is it a worthy policy?* Princeton, NJ: Princeton University Press. *This scholarly, but straightforward book discusses most of the key issues related to comparable worth, with good analyses of available data on employment of men and women.*

EMPLOYEE SELECTION

INSIDE TIPS

UNDERSTANDING EMPLOYMENT ISSUES AND PROCESSES

In this chapter, we continue to build on some of the topics and concepts introduced in the two previous chapters. Employee screening, testing, and selection processes are strongly grounded in research and measurement issues. For example, in our discussion of screening and testing methods, we investigate the important measurement issues of reliability and validity. This continues the discussion of methods begun in Chapter 2. The employment processes discussed in this chapter are also built on a foundation of job analysis, which was presented in Chapter 3.

A study hint for organizing and understanding the many screening and testing procedures presented in this chapter is to consider those processes in the context of some of the methodological issues discussed previously. In other words, much of the strength or weakness of any particular employment method or process is determined by its ability to predict important work outcomes, which is usually defined as "job performance." The ability to predict future employee performance accurately from the results of employment tests or from other employee screening procedures is critical. However, other important considerations for screening methods concern their cost and ease of use, or in other words, their utility. Hiring interviews, for example, are considered to be relatively easy to use, while testing programs are thought (rightly or wrongly) to be costly and difficult to implement.

When considering the steps in the employee selection process it is important to note the influence exerted by federal legislation and court decisions. Federal guidelines developed to prevent employment discrimination have, in a sense, forced employers to take a hard look at the quality of the methods used to recruit, screen, and select employees. This has led to the greater involvement of I/O psychologists in the development of more accurate and fairer employee screening and selection procedures. For instance, I/O psychologists play a major role in designing and validating employment tests.

Since employee issues deal with the care and nurturing of an organization's human resources and since psychology often has a similar concern with human potential, there is a natural link between psychology and personnel work. As a result, many students trained in psychology and other social sciences are drawn to careers in human resources. The use of psychological testing, interviewing procedures, and measurement issues in general also help to connect the two fields.

In the previous chapter (Chapter 3), we saw how job analysis is the basic foundation of personnel psychology. Job analysis leads to a thorough understanding of jobs. Once we have a good understanding of the various jobs within an organization, we are better able to find persons who can fill those jobs, and who can excel at performing them. We will look now at how organizations find and hire persons to perform jobs.

Organizations spend a tremendous amount of time, money, and energy trying to recruit and select a qualified, capable, and productive workforce. Although there are always significant numbers of unemployed workers in the population, the market for truly skilled workers is tight. Organizations continue to compete with one another for the most skilled and productive employees. More and more, companies are realizing the importance of developing comprehensive programs for employee recruitment, screening, and selection. Moreover, they are beginning to understand that the costs of hiring the wrong types of workers greatly outweigh the investment of developing good recruitment and screening programs. Depending on the job level, the costs of recruiting, selecting, training, and then releasing a single employee can range from a few thousand dollars to several hundreds of thousands of dollars (Wanous, 1992).

In this chapter, we will follow the progression of personnel functions involved in the recruitment, selection, and placement of workers. We will begin with an examination of employee recruitment and then look at the procedures for screening and evaluating job applicants, including hiring interviews and standardized tests. Finally, we will discuss how employers use the information obtained from job applicants to make their selection decisions and to place workers in appropriate jobs. But first, we must examine a model that will help us understand the process of recruiting, screening, and selecting people for jobs.

A Model for Employee Selection

criteria
*measures of job success
typically related to
performance*

The model for recruiting and hiring effective and productive workers is actually quite simple. It consists of two categories of variables: criteria and predictors. **Criteria** (or the singular, *criterion*) are measures of success. The most common way to think of success on the job is in terms of *performance criteria*. A performance criterion for a telephone installer may be the number of units installed. For a salesperson, dollar sales figures may be a performance criterion (we will discuss performance criteria in more depth in Chapter 6). Yet, when it comes to hiring good employees, we may want to go beyond these rather simple and straightforward performance criteria. The general criterion of "success" for an employee may be a constellation of many factors, including: performance, loyalty and commitment to the organization, a good work attendance record, ability to get along with supervisors and coworkers, and ability to learn and grow on the job. Thus, for the purpose of hiring workers, we might want to think of "success on the job" as the *ultimate criterion*—a criterion we aspire to measure, but something that we may never actually be able to capture with our limited measurement capabilities.

predictors
*variables about applicants
that are related to (predictive
of) the criteria*

Predictors are any pieces of information that we are able to measure about job applicants that are related to (predictive of) the criterion. In employee selection, we measure predictors, such as job-related knowledge and expertise, education, and skills, in an effort to predict who will be successful in a given job. Figure 4.1 illustrates this model for employee selection. Through evaluation of resumes and hiring interview performance, and from the results of employment tests, applicants are measured on a number of predictors. These predictor variables are then used to select applicants for jobs. Evaluation of the success of an employee selection program involves demonstrating that the predictors do indeed predict the criterion of success on the job (see Smith, 1994).

Steps in the Employee Selection Process

In order to understand how organizations select employees for jobs, we will look at each of the steps in the process, from the recruitment of applicants, to the various employee screening and testing procedures, to selection decisions and placement of employees in appropriate jobs. Throughout this rather lengthy discussion, bear in mind that the goal is straightforward—to try to gather information that will predict who, from the pool of applicants, will be the "best" employees.

Employee Recruitment

employee recruitment
*the process by which
companies attract qualified
applicants*

Employee recruitment is the process by which organizations attract potential workers to apply for jobs. Greater numbers of organizations are developing strategic programs for recruitment. The starting point for a good

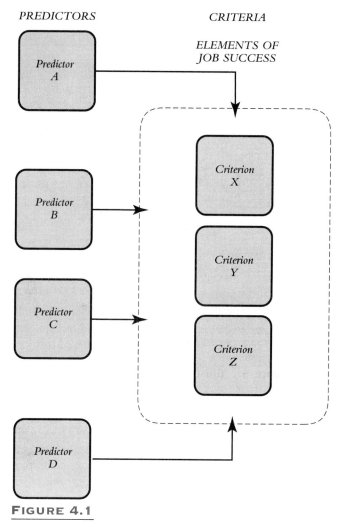

FIGURE 4.1

A Model for Employee Selection.

recruitment program is an understanding of the job and what kinds of worker characteristics are required to perform the job. Here, the recruiter relies on the products of job analysis—job descriptions and job specifications (see Chapter 3).

One of the primary objectives of a successful program is to attract a large pool of qualified applicants. There is a wide variety of recruitment techniques and tactics. Those most familiar to college students are the on-campus recruitment programs conducted by large organizations and the traditional advertisement of job openings in newspapers or trade magazines.

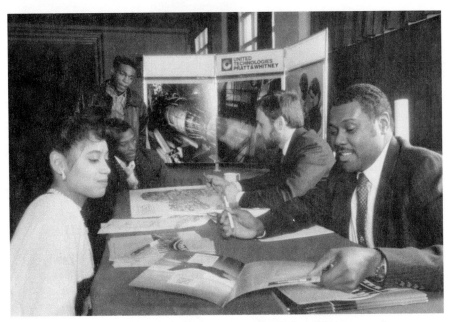

On-campus recruitment programs help major companies find qualified new employees.

Other methods include various media advertising, such as job advertisements on television, radio, the Internet, or billboards; the use of employment agencies; and referrals by current employees.

Research has assessed the effectiveness of the various recruitment methods by examining both the quality of newly hired workers and the rate of turnover in new workers. There is evidence that employee referrals and applicant-initiated contacts (that is, "walk-ins") yield higher quality workers and workers who are more likely to remain with the company than newspaper ads or employment agency placement (Breaugh, 1981; Decker & Cornelius, 1979; Saks, 1994; Taylor & Schmidt, 1983). However, since different methods of recruitment will reach different types of workers, the success of any particular tactic may depend on the sort of job opening and the ability of the method to reach the "right" group of potential job applicants (Swaroff, Barclay, & Bass, 1985; Vecchio, 1995; Williams, Labig, & Stone, 1993). For example, it is commonly thought that potential employees for higher-level management positions are recruited through word of mouth or employment agencies, but rarely through newspaper ads, which are considered more appropriate for lower-level jobs. In one study of the recruitment processes in small businesses in Great Britain, it was found that the majority of job applicants were either referred by employment agencies, career services offices, or by current employees, with only about 25 percent of applicants responding to job advertisements (Bartram, Lindley, Marshall, & Foster, 1995).

Recruitment is a two-way process: While the recruiting organization is attempting to attract and later evaluate prospective employees, job applicants are evaluating various potential employers (Turban, Forret, & Hendrickson, 1998). There is considerable evidence that the characteristics of an organization's recruitment program and of recruiters can influence applicants' decisions to accept or reject offers of employment (Maurer, Howe, & Lee, 1992; Rynes, 1993; Stevens, 1997; Taylor & Bergmann, 1987). In other words, it is important for organizations to make a favorable impression on a prospective employee in order to encourage the individual to want to take the job offer.

In their efforts to attract applicants, however, many companies will "oversell" a particular job or their organization. Advertisements may say that "this is a great place to work," or that the position is "challenging" and offers "tremendous potential for advancement." This is not a problem if such statements are true, but if the job and the organization are presented in a misleading, overly positive manner, the strategy will eventually backfire. Although the recruitment process may attract applicants, the new employees will quickly discover that they were fooled, and may look for work elsewhere or become dissatisfied and unmotivated. An important factor in the recruitment process that may help alleviate potential misperceptions is the **realistic job preview (RJP)**, which is an accurate description of the duties and responsibilities of a particular job. Realistic job previews can take the form of an oral presentation from a recruiter, supervisor, or job incumbent; a visit to the job site; or a discussion in a brochure, manual, or videotape (Colarelli, 1984; Wanous, 1989). However, research indicates that face-to-face RJPs may be more effective than written ones (Saks & Cronshaw, 1990).

realistic job preview (RJP)
an accurate presentation of the prospective job and organization made to applicants

Research has also shown that realistic job previews are important in increasing job commitment and satisfaction, and in decreasing initial turnover of new employees (McEvoy & Cascio, 1985; Premack & Wanous, 1985). Some of the positive effects of RJPs are caused by the applicant's process of self-selection. Presented with a realistic view of what the job will be like, the applicant can make an informed decision about whether the job is appropriate. RJPs may also be effective because they lower unrealistically high expectations about the job and may provide an applicant with information that will later be useful in dealing with work-related problems and stress (Porter & Steers, 1973; Wanous, 1992). The implementation of realistic job previews often requires recruiting more applicants for job openings, because a greater proportion of applicants presented with the RJP will decline the job offer than when no preview is given. However, the usual result is a better match between the position and the worker hired, and a more satisfied new worker.

Another important goal for any recruitment program is to avoid intentional or unintentional discrimination against underrepresented groups, such as women, ethnic minorities, the elderly, and the disabled. Employment discrimination against any of the above groups, intentional or unintentional, is illegal. In order to avoid unintentional discrimination, employers should take steps to attract applicants from underrepresented groups in proportion to their numbers in the population from which the company's workforce is drawn. In other words, if a company is in an area where the population within a 10- to 20-mile radius is 40 percent white, 30 percent African-American, 10 percent Asian-American, and 10 percent Hispanic, the recruitment program should draw applicants in roughly those proportions in order to avoid unintentionally discriminating against any group. We will discuss the topics of employment discrimination, equal employment opportunity and affirmative action later in this chapter.

Employee Screening

employee screening
the process of reviewing information about job applicants used to select workers

Employee screening is the process of reviewing information about job applicants to select individuals for jobs. A wide variety of data sources, such as resumes, job applications, letters of recommendation, employment tests, and hiring interviews, can be used in screening and selecting potential employees. If you have ever applied for a job, you have had firsthand experience with some of these. We will consider all of these screening methods in this section, except for employment tests. Because of the variety and complexity of tests used in employee screening and selection, we will consider employment testing and hiring interviews in a separate section.

List three goals of an employee recruitment program.

EVALUATION OF WRITTEN MATERIALS

The first step in the screening process involves the evaluation of written materials, such as applications and resumes. Usually, standard application forms are used for screening lower-level positions in an organization, with resumes used to provide biographical data and other background information for higher-level jobs, although many companies require all applicants to complete an application form. The main purpose of the application and resume is to collect biographical information such as education, work experience, and outstanding work or school accomplishments. Such data are believed to be among the best predictors of future job performance (Feldman & Klich, 1991; Knouse, 1994; Owens, 1976). It is important to mention, however, that first impressions play a big role in selection decisions. Since written materials are usually the first contact a potential employer has with a job candidate, the impressions of an applicant's credentials received from a resume or application are very important. In fact, research has shown that impressions of qualifications from written applications influenced impressions of applicants in their subsequent interviews (Macan & Dipboye, 1994).

Most companies use a standard application form (see the sample application form in Figure 4.2). As with all employment screening devices, the application form should collect only information that has been determined to be job-related. Questions that are not job-related, and especially those that may lead to job discrimination, such as inquiries about age, ethnic

FIGURE 4.2

A Sample Application Form.

background, religious affiliation, marital status, or finances, should not be included.

From the employer's perspective, the difficulty with application forms is in evaluating and interpreting the information obtained to determine the most qualified applicants. For example, it may be difficult to choose between an applicant with little education but ample work experience and an educated person with no work experience.

weighted application forms
forms that assign different weights to the various pieces of information provided on a job application

There have been attempts to quantify the biographical information obtained from application forms through the use of either weighted application forms or biographical information blanks (BIBs). **Weighted application forms** assign different weights to each bit of information on the form. The weights are determined through detailed research, conducted by the organization, to determine the relationship between specific bits of biographical data, often referred to as *biodata*, and criteria of success on the job (Cascio, 1987; Mael, 1991). We will discuss the use of biodata in more detail in the section on employment tests.

REFERENCES AND LETTERS OF RECOMMENDATION

Two other sources of information used in employee screening and selection are references and letters of recommendation. Unfortunately, very little research has examined their validity as selection tools (Muchinsky, 1979). Typically, reference checks and letters of recommendation can provide four types of information: (1) employment and educational history, (2) evaluations of the applicant's character, (3) evaluations of the applicant's job performance, and (4) the recommender's willingness to rehire the applicant (Cascio, 1987).

For a couple of reasons, the use of references and letters of recommendation in applicant screening is on the decline. First, since applicants can usually choose their own sources for references and recommendations, it is unlikely that they will supply the names of persons who will give bad recommendations. Therefore, letters of recommendation tend to be distorted in a very positive direction, so positive that they may be useless in distinguishing among applicants. Second, because of recent litigation against individuals and former employers who provide negative recommendations, many companies are refusing to provide any kind of reference for former employees except for dates of employment. The net result is that many organizations are simply foregoing the use of reference checks and letters of recommendation.

Letters of recommendation are still widely used, however, in applications to graduate schools. In many graduate programs steps have been taken to improve the effectiveness of these letters as a screening and selection tool by including forms that ask the recommender to rate the applicant on a variety of dimensions, such as academic ability, motivation/drive, oral and written communication skills, and initiative. These rating forms often use graphic rating scales to help quantify the recommendation for comparison with other applicants. They also attempt to improve the accuracy of the reference by protecting the recommender from possible retaliation by having the applicants waive their rights to see the letter of reference.

EMPLOYMENT TESTING

After the evaluation of the biographical information available from resumes, application forms, or other sources, the next step in comprehensive employee screening programs is employment testing. As we saw in Chapter 1, the history of personnel testing in I/O psychology goes back to World War I, when intelligence testing of armed forces recruits was used for employee placement. Today, the use of tests for employment screening and placement has expanded greatly. A considerable percentage of large companies and most government agencies routinely use some form of employment tests to measure a wide range of characteristics that are predictive of successful job performance. For example, some tests measure specific skills or abilities required by a job, while others assess more general cognitive skills as a means of determining if one has the aptitude believed to be needed for the successful performance of a certain job. Still other tests measure personality dimensions that are believed to be important for particular occupations. Before we discuss specific types of screening tests, however, it is important to consider some issues and guidelines for the development and use of tests and other screening methods.

CONSIDERATIONS IN THE DEVELOPMENT AND USE OF EMPLOYEE SCREENING AND TESTING METHODS

Any type of measurement instrument used in industrial/organizational psychology, including those used in employee screening and selection, must meet certain measurement standards. Two critically important concepts in measurement are reliability and validity. **Reliability** refers to the stability of a measure over time or the consistency of the measure. For example, if we administer a test to a job applicant, we would expect to get essentially the same score on the test if it is taken at two different points of time (and the applicant did not do anything to improve test performance in between). Reliability also refers to the agreement between two or more assessments made of the same event or behavior, such as when two interviewers independently evaluate the appropriateness of a job candidate for a particular position.

reliability
the consistency of a measurement instrument or its stability over time

Validity refers to the accuracy of a measure—whether the instrument or method measures the variable that it is supposed to measure. For example, in employee screening, validity refers to whether a score on an employment test, a judgment made from a hiring interview, or a conclusion drawn from the review of information from a job application does indeed lead to a representative evaluation of an applicant's qualifications for a job.

validity
a concept referring to the accuracy of a measurement instrument

All predictors used in employee selection, whether they be evaluations of application materials, employment tests, or judgments made in hiring interviews, must be reliable and valid. Standardized and commercially available psychological tests have typically demonstrated high levels of reliability and validity for use in certain circumstances. However, even with widely used standardized tests, it is critical that their ability to predict job success be established for the particular positions in question. It is especially necessary to assure the reliability and validity of nonstandardized screening methods, such as a weighted application form or a test constructed for a specific job.

There are a variety of methods for establishing the reliability of a screening instrument. One technique is **test-retest reliability**. Here, a particular test or other measurement instrument is administered to the same individual at two different times, usually involving a one- to two-week interval between testing sessions. Scores on the first test are then correlated with those on the second test. If the correlation is high (a correlation coefficient approaching +1.0), reliability is established. Of course the assumption is made that nothing has happened during the administration of the two tests that would cause the scores to change drastically.

A second means of determining the reliability of an employment screening measure is the **parallel forms** method. Here two equivalent tests are constructed, each of which presumably measures the same construct but using different items or questions. Test-takers are administered both forms of the instrument. Reliability is established if the correlation between the two scores is high. Of course the major drawbacks to this method are the time and difficulty involved in creating two equivalent tests.

Another way to establish the reliability of a test instrument is by estimating its **internal consistency**. If a test is reliable, each item should measure the same general construct, and thus performance on one item should be consistent with performance on all other items. Two specific methods are used to determine internal consistency. The first is to divide the test items into two equal parts and correlate the summed score on the first half of the items with that on the second half. This is referred to as *split-half reliability*. A second method, which involves numerous calculations, is to determine the average intercorrelation among all items of the test. The resulting coefficient is an estimate of the test's internal consistency.

Although there are many ways to determine test validity, the two forms of validity that are most important for the development and use of employment screening tests are content validity and criterion-related validity.

Content validity is the ability of the content of the measurement instrument (that is, the test items) to measure adequately the knowledge, skills, abilities, and other characteristics necessary to perform a job. Typically, content validity is established by having experts such as job incumbents or supervisors judge the appropriateness of the test items, taking into account information from the job analysis (Hughes & Prien, 1989). Ideally, the experts should determine that the test content does indeed represent the job content. Content validity is especially important for organizations constructing their own screening tests for specific jobs.

Criterion-related validity is established by determining the relationship between the test score and some criterion of job success, which is most often

test-retest reliability
a method of determining the reliability of a measurement instrument by administering the same measure to the same people at two different times and then correlating the scores

parallel forms
a method of establishing the reliability of a measurement instrument by correlating scores on two different but equivalent versions of the same instrument

internal consistency
a common method of establishing a measurement instrument's reliability by examining how the various items of the instrument intercorrelate

content validity
the ability of the items in a measurement instrument to measure adequately the various characteristics needed to perform a job

criterion-related validity
the accuracy of a measurement instrument in determining the relationship between scores on the instrument and some criterion of job success

an indicator of job performance, such as a measure of work output or quality. There are two approaches to determining criterion-related validity. The first is the *follow-up method* (often called *predictive validity*). Here, the screening test is administered to applicants without interpreting the scores and without using them to select among applicants. Once the applicants become employees, criterion measures such as job performance assessments are collected. If the test instrument is valid, the test scores should correlate positively with the criterion measure. Once the validity of the instrument is established, test scores are used to select the highest scoring applicants for jobs. The obvious advantage of the predictive validity method is that it demonstrates how scores on the screening instrument actually relate to future job performance. The major drawback to this approach is the time that it takes to establish validity. During this validation period applicants are tested, but are not hired based on their test scores.

In the second approach, known as the *present-employee method* (also termed *concurrent validity*), the test is given to current employees, and their scores are correlated with some criterion of their current performance. Again, a positive relationship between test scores and criterion scores establishes validity. Once validity is established, a comparison of applicants' test scores with the incumbents' scores is used to select the most qualified applicants. While the concurrent validity method leads to a quicker estimate of validity, it may not be as accurate an assessment of criterion-related validity as the predictive method, since the job incumbents represent a select group, and their test performance is likely to be high, with a restricted range of scores. In other words, there are no test scores for the "poor" job performers, such as workers who were fired or quit their jobs, or applicants who were not chosen for jobs.

TYPES OF EMPLOYEE SCREENING TESTS

The majority of employee screening and selection instruments are standardized, published tests that have been subjected to research aimed at demonstrating their validity and reliability. Most also contain information to insure that they are administered, scored, and interpreted in a uniform manner. The alternative to the use of standardized tests is for the organization to construct a test for a particular job or class of jobs, and conduct its own studies of the test's reliability and validity. However, because this is a costly and time-consuming procedure, most employers use standardized screening tests.

Test formats

Test formats, or the ways in which tests are administered, can vary greatly. Several distinctions are important when categorizing employment tests.

Individual versus group tests—Individual tests are administered to only one person at a time. In individual tests, the test administrator is usually more involved than in group tests. Typically, tests that require some kind of sophisticated apparatus, such as a driving simulator, or tests that require

Some employment tests involve sophisticated technology, such as this flight simulator used to train and test airline pilots.

constant supervision are administered individually, as are certain intelligence and personality tests. Group tests are designed to be given simultaneously to more than one person, with the administrator usually serving as only a test monitor. The obvious advantage to group tests is the reduced cost for administrator time.

Speed versus power tests—Speed tests have a fixed time limit. An important focus of a speed test is the number of items completed in the time period provided. A typing test and many of the scholastic achievement tests are examples of speed tests. A power test allows the test taker sufficient time to complete all items. Typically, power tests have difficult items, with a focus on the percentage of items answered correctly.

Paper-and-pencil versus performance tests—Paper-and-pencil tests require some form of written reply, either in a forced choice or open-ended, "essay" format. Many employee screening tests, and nearly all tests in schools, are of a paper-and-pencil format. Performance tests, such as typing tests and tests of manual dexterity or grip strength, usually involve the manipulation of physical objects.

While the format of an employment test is significant, the most important way of classifying the instruments is in terms of the characteristics or attributes they measure such as biographical information (biodata instruments), cognitive abilities, mechanical abilities, motor and sensory abilities, job skills and knowledge, or personality traits (see Table 4.1 for examples of these various tests)

STOP AND REVIEW

What are three methods of validation that are important for employee screening tests?

TABLE 4.1

Some Standardized Tests Used in Employee Screening and Selection

Cognitive Ability Tests

Comprehensive Ability Battery (Hakstian & Cattell, 1975–82): Features 20 tests, each designed to measure a single primary cognitive ability, many of which are important in industrial settings. Among the tests are those assessing verbal ability, numerical ability, clerical speed and accuracy, and ability to organize and produce ideas, as well as several memory scales.

Wonderlic Personnel Test (Wonderlic, 1983): A 50-item pencil-and-paper test measuring level of mental ability for employment.

Wechsler Adult Intelligence Scale-Revised or *WAIS-R* (Wechsler, 1981): A comprehensive group of 11 subtests measuring general levels of intellectual functioning. The WAIS-R is administered individually and takes more than an hour to complete. One of the most widely used intelligence tests.

Mechanical Ability Tests

Bennett Mechanical Comprehension Test (Bennett, 1980): A 68-item pencil-and-paper test of ability to understand physical and mechanical principles in practical situations. Can be group administered; comes in two equivalent forms.

Mechanical Ability Test (Morrisby, 1955): A 35-item multiple-choice instrument that measures natural mechanical aptitude. Used to predict potential in engineering, assembly work, carpentry, and building trades.

Motor and Sensory Ability Tests

Hand-Tool Dexterity Test (Bennett, 1981): Using a wooden frame, wrenches, and screwdrivers, the test taker takes apart 12 bolts in a prescribed sequence and reassembles them in another position. This speed test measures manipulative skills important in factory jobs and in jobs servicing mechanical equipment and automobiles.

O'Connor Finger Dexterity Test (O'Connor, 1977): A timed performance test measuring fine motor dexterity needed for fine assembly work and other jobs requiring manipulation of small objects. Test taker is given a board with symmetrical rows of holes and a cup of pins. The task is to place three pins in each hole as quickly as possible.

Job Skills and Knowledge Tests

Minnesota Clerical Assessment Battery or *MCAB* (Vale & Prestwood, 1987): A self-administered battery of six subtests measuring the skills and knowledge necessary for clerical and secretarial work. Testing is completely computer-administered. Included are tests of typing, proofreading, filing, business vocabulary, business math, and clerical knowledge.

Purdue Blueprint Reading Test (Owen & Arnold, 1988): A multiple-choice test assessing the ability to read standard blueprints.

Judd Tests of Software Skills (Simmons, 1993): Measures proficiency in DOS, word processing, and spreadsheet use.

TABLE 4.1

Some Standardized Tests Used in Employee Screening and Selection (Continued)

Personality Tests

California Psychological Inventory or *CPI* (Gough, 1987): A 480-item pencil-and-paper inventory of 20 personality dimensions. Has been used in selecting managers, sales personnel, and leadership positions.

Hogan Personnel Selection Series (Hogan & Hogan, 1985): This pencil-and-paper test assesses personality dimensions of applicants and compares their profiles to patterns of successful job incumbents in clerical, sales, and managerial positions. Consists of four inventories: the prospective employee potential inventory, the clerical potential inventory, the sales potential inventory, and the managerial potential inventory.

Sixteen Personality Factors Questionnaire or *16 PF* (Cattell, 1986): Similar to the CPI, this test measures 16 basic personality dimensions, some of which are related to successful job performance in certain positions. This general personality inventory has been used extensively in employee screening and selection.

Revised NEO Personality Inventory or *NEO-PI-R* (Costa & McCrae, 1992). An increasingly popular personality inventory used in employee screening and selection. This inventory measures the five "core" personality constructs of Neuroticism (N), Extraversion (E), Openness (O), Agreeableness (A), and Conscientiousness (C).

BIODATA INSTRUMENTS

biodata
background information and personal characteristics that can be used in employee selection

As mentioned earlier, **biodata** refers to background information and personal characteristics that can be used in a systematic fashion to select employees. Developing biodata instruments typically involves taking information that would appear on application forms and other items about background, personal interests, and behavior, and using that information to develop a form of forced-choice employment test. Along with items designed to measure basic biographical information, such as education and work history, the biodata instrument might also involve questions of a more personal nature, probing the applicant's attitudes, values, likes, and dislikes (Owens, 1976; Stokes, Mumford, & Owens, 1994). Biodata instruments are unlike the other test instruments we will discuss, because there are no standardized biodata instruments. Instead, biodata instruments take a great deal of research to develop and validate. Because biodata instruments are typically designed to screen applicants for one specific job, they are most likely to be used only for higher-level positions. Research indicates that biodata instruments can be effective screening and placement tools (Bliesener, 1996; Rothstein, Schmidt, Erwin, Owens, & Sparks, 1990). Comprehensive biodata instruments can give a very detailed description and classification of an applicant's behavioral history—a very good predictor of future behavior (sample biodata items are given in Figure 4.3). One potential problem in

How successful were your teachers in arousing your academic interests?
   a. Extremely successful
   b. Very successful
   c. Somewhat successful
   d. Not at all successful

What is your usual state of health?
   a. Never ill
   b. Never seriously ill
   c. About average
   d. Feel poorly from time to time
   e. Often feel "under the weather"

On the average, how many hours of homework did you do a week in high school?
   a. 20 or more
   b. 10–20
   c. 5–10
   d. Less than 5

Which one of the following seems most important to you?
   a. A pleasant home and family life
   b. A challenging and exciting job
   c. Getting ahead in the world
   d. Being active and accepted in community affairs
   e. Making the most of your particular ability

Do you generally do your best:
   a. At whatever job you are doing
   b. Only in what you are interested
   c. Only when it is demanded of you

FIGURE 4.3

Sample Biodata Items.

the use of biodata instruments concerns the personal nature of many of the questions and the possibility of unintentional discrimination against minority groups because of items regarding age, financial circumstances, and the like. Thus, biodata instruments should only be developed and administered by professionals trained in test use and validation.

Cognitive ability tests

Tests of cognitive ability range from tests of general intellectual ability to tests of specific cognitive skills. Group-administered, pencil-and-paper tests of general intelligence have been used in employee screening for some time. Two such widely used older instruments are the Otis Self-Administering Test of Mental Ability (Otis, 1929) and the Wonderlic Personnel Test (Wonderlic, 1945, 1983). Both are fairly short and assess basic verbal and numerical abilities. Designed to measure the ability to learn simple jobs, to follow instructions, and to solve work-related problems and difficulties, these tests are used to screen applicants for positions as office clerks, assembly workers, machine operators, and certain front-line supervisors.

One criticism of using general intelligence tests for employee selection is that they measure cognitive abilities that are *too* general to be effective predictors of specific job-related cognitive skills. However, research indicates that such general tests are reasonably good predictors of job performance (Barrett & Depinet, 1991; Gottfredson, 1986; Hunter & Hunter, 1984). In fact, it has been argued that general intelligence is the most consistent predictor of performance, across all types and categories of jobs (Schmidt & Ones, 1992; Thorndike, 1986).

Historically, there has been some reluctance on the part of employers to use general intelligence tests for screening job applicants. Because there is some evidence that scores on some general intelligence tests may favor the economically and educationally advantaged, there are fears that general intelligence tests might discriminate against certain ethnic minorities, who tend to be overrepresented among the economically disadvantaged. It has been argued that general intelligence tests may underestimate the intellectual abilities and potentials of members of certain ethnic minorities. More recently, it has been suggested that cognitive test performance may be affected by ethnic differences in test-taking motivation, such that members of ethnic minority groups may have less positive expectations and more aversion to taking tests than members of the white majority group (Chan, Schmitt, DeShon, Clause, & Delbridge, 1997). In certain instances, this may lead to unfair discrimination in employee selection, a concern we will discuss in the section on legal issues later in this chapter.

Mechanical ability tests

Standardized tests have also been developed to measure abilities in identifying, recognizing, and applying mechanical principles. These tests are particularly effective in screening applicants for positions that require operating or repairing machinery, for construction jobs, and for certain engineering positions. The Bennett Mechanical Comprehension Test, or BMCT (Bennett, 1980), is one such commonly used instrument. The BMCT consists of 68 items, each of which requires the application of a physical law or a mechanical operation (for examples, see Figure 4.4). One study using the BMCT and several other instruments determined that the BMCT was the best single predictor of job performance for a group of employees manufacturing electromechanical components (Muchinsky, 1993).

Motor and sensory ability tests

A number of tests measure specific motor skills or sensory abilities. Tests such as the Crawford Small Parts Dexterity Test (Crawford, 1981) and the Purdue Pegboard (Tiffin, 1968) are timed performance instruments (speed tests) that require the manipulation of small parts in order to measure the fine motor dexterity in hands and fingers required in jobs such as assembling

Which room has more of an echo?

Which would be better shears for cutting metal?

Which man carries more weight?
(if equal, mark C).

Which letter shows the seat where
a passenger will get the smoothest ride?

FIGURE 4.4

Sample Items from the Bennett Test of Mechanical Comprehension
Source: G.K. Bennett, *Test of Mechanical Comprehension* (New York: Psychological Corporation, 1940).

computer components and soldering electrical equipment. For example, the Crawford test uses boards with small holes into which tiny pins must be placed using a pair of tweezers. The second part of the test requires screwing small screws into threaded holes with a screwdriver.

Sensory ability tests include tests of hearing, visual acuity, and perceptual discrimination. The most common test of visual acuity is the Snellen Eye Chart, which consists of rows of letters that become increasingly smaller. Various electronic instruments are used to measure hearing acuity. No doubt you have taken one or more of these in school or in a doctor's office. In employment settings, they are used in basic screening for positions such as inspectors or bus drivers that require fine audio or visual discrimination.

Job skills and knowledge tests

Various standardized tests also assess specific job skills or domains of job knowledge. Examples of job skill tests for clerical workers would be a standardized typing test or tests of other specific clerical skills such as proofreading, alphabetical filing, or correction of spelling or grammatical errors, as well as the use of software. For example, the Judd Tests (Simmons, 1993), are a series of tests designed to assess competency in several areas of computer competence, including word processing, spreadsheet programs, and database management.

work samples
used in job skill tests to measure applicants' abilities to perform brief examples of important job tasks

A special sort of job skill test involves the use of **work samples**, which measure applicants' abilities to perform brief examples of some of the critical tasks that the job requires. The sample tasks are constructed as tests, administered under standard testing conditions, and scored on some predetermined scale. Their obvious advantage is that they are clearly job-related. A drawback is that work samples are usually rather expensive to develop and take a great deal of time to administer.

One example of a work sample test was developed for applicants for the job of concession stand attendant at a city park's snack bar. The test required applicants to use the cash register, make change, fill out a report, page someone over a loudspeaker, and react to an "irate customer" who was arguing about receiving the wrong change. In addition to being an effective screening device, this work sample also served as a realistic job preview, providing applicants with a good idea of what the job was all about (Cascio & Phillips, 1979).

Job knowledge tests are instruments that assess specific types of knowledge required to perform certain jobs. For example, a job knowledge test for nurses or paramedics might contain questions asking about appropriate emergency medical procedures. A job knowledge test for a computer operator might ask about certain computer operating systems and procedures.

Personality tests

personality tests
instruments that measure psychological characteristics of individuals

Personality tests are designed to measure certain psychological characteristics of workers. A wide variety of these tests are used in employee screening and selection in an attempt to match the personality characteristics of job applicants with those of workers who have performed the job successfully in the past. During the 1960s and 1970s there was some controversy over the use of such tests because of evidence that the connection between general personality dimensions and the performance of specific work tasks was not very strong or direct (Ghiselli, 1973; Guion & Gottier, 1965). However, more recent meta-analytic reviews of research suggest that certain work-related personality characteristics can be quite good predictors of job performance, particularly when the personality dimensions assessed are derived from a thorough analysis of the requirements for the job (Robertson & Kinder, 1993; Tett, Jackson, & Rothstein, 1991).

General personality inventories, such as the Minnesota Multiphasic Personality Inventory or MMPI (Hathaway & McKinley, 1970), are also used to screen out applicants who possess some psychopathology that might hinder the performance of sensitive jobs, such as police officer, airline pilot, or nuclear power plant operator. However, most of the time, personality tests are used to assess the "normal" characteristics that are deemed to be important for the performance of certain jobs. For example, personality dimensions such as achievement motivation or persistence might be used to screen applicants for positions in sales jobs, and tests for traits of responsibility and service orientation may be administered to applicants for bank teller positions.

In the past two decades, there has been a trend toward developing personality tests that more specifically measure job-relevant aspects of personality. For example, Gough (1984, 1985) has derived work orientation and managerial potential scales from the California Psychological Inventory (CPI), a general personality inventory that measures 20 personality dimensions (Gough, 1987) (see Figure 4.5). The work orientation scale of the CPI is a predictor of employee performance across positions, while the managerial potential scale is used in screening and selecting candidates for management

---

If you agree with a statement, or feel that it is true about you, answer TRUE.
If you disagree with a statement, or feel that it is not true about you, answer FALSE.

TRUE   FALSE

People often expect too much of me.
The idea of doing research appeals to me.
It is hard for me just to sit still and relax.
I enjoy hearing lectures on world affairs.
I read at least ten books a year.
I like parties and socials.

FIGURE 4.5

Sample Items from the California Psychological Inventory. *Note:* This is not a "mini-test". It is simply an illustrative sample. Reproduced by special permission of the Publisher, Consulting Psychologists Press, Inc., Palo Alto, CA 94303 from the *California Psychological Inventory–Form 434* by Harrison G. Gough. Copyright 1987 by Consulting Psychologists Press Inc. All rights reserved. Further reproduction is prohibited without the Publisher's written consent.

and supervisory positions. Hogan and Hogan (1985) and others have developed a series of personality scales to measure personality characteristics predictive of employee success in general job categories such as sales, management, and clerical work.

Recent research examining the use of personality tests in employee screening has found that certain personality characteristics, such as "conscientiousness" and "dependability," are good predictors of both job performance and work attendance (Barrick & Mount, 1991; Barrick, Mount, & Strauss, 1994). In addition, the personality traits of "dominance" and "extraversion" are good predictors of success as a manager (Barrick & Mount, 1993; Megargee & Carbonell, 1988). We will examine the role that personality variables play in contributing to managerial performance more fully in Chapter 12, when we discuss leadership.

Honesty and integrity tests

polygraphs

instruments that measure physiological reactions presumed to accompany deception; also known as lie detectors

In the past, **polygraphs**, or lie detectors—instruments designed to measure physiological reactions presumably associated with lying such as respiration, blood pressure, or perspiration—were used in employee selection. Most often polygraphs were used to screen out "dishonest" applicants for positions in which they would have to handle cash or expensive merchandise, although they have also been used by a wide number of organizations to screen and select employees for almost any position. Research, much of it conducted by industrial/organizational psychologists, called into question the validity of polygraphs. A major problem concerned the rate of "false positive" errors, or innocent persons who are incorrectly scored as lying. Because of this questionable validity and the potential harm that invalid results could cause innocent people, the federal government passed legislation in 1988 which severely restricted the use of polygraphs in general employment screening. However, polygraphs are still allowed for the testing of employees about specific incidents, such as thefts, and for screening applicants for public health and safety jobs and for sensitive government positions (Camara, 1988).

integrity tests

measures of honest or dishonest attitudes and/or behaviors

Since the establishment of restrictions on the use of polygraphs, many employers have turned to using pencil-and-paper measures of honesty, referred to as **integrity tests**. Typically, these tests ask about past honest/dishonest behavior or about attitudes condoning dishonest behavior. Typical questions might ask, "What is the total value of cash and merchandise you have taken from your employer in the past year?" or "An employer who pays people poorly has it coming when employees steal. Do you agree or disagree with this statement?" One obvious problem with these tests is the possibility of faking the results and thus "beating" the test, although some of the instruments do include scales to measure if the respondents are distorting their responses (Ryan & Sackett, 1987). Despite the fact that only a very few individuals would be knowledgeable enough about integrity tests to be able to beat them, this can still cause a problem, since persons motivated to try to beat the test are most likely to be those who have something important to hide. Like polygraphs, these tests also raise the important issue of "false positives," or honest persons who are judged to be dishonest by the instruments (Murphy, 1993). On the other hand, meta-analyses of validity studies of integrity tests indicate that they are somewhat valid predictors of employee dishonesty and "counterproductive behaviors," such as chronic tardiness, taking extended work breaks and "goldbricking" (ignoring or passing off assigned work tasks) (Murphy, 1993; Ones, Viswesvaran, & Schmidt, 1993). More recently, it was determined that integrity tests also predict productive employee behaviors, although it is acknowledged that some of the relationship between integrity and productivity is due to the fact that integrity overlaps with work-related personality constructs such as conscientiousness and emotional stability (Sackett & Wanek, 1996).

ON THE CUTTING EDGE

The Future of Employment Testing: "Smart" Tests and Performance-based Simulations

As in all areas of work life, computer technology has revolutionized employment testing. More and more, companies are turning to the use of computer-based testing (CBT) to administer pencil-and-paper employment tests (Burke, 1992). In CBT, applicants complete the test instruments using a computer terminal. The computer can then immediately score the tests, record the results in its databanks, and provide the test taker with feedback if appropriate. Research on CBT indicates that it is a practical and cost-effective alternative to traditional testing (Schmitt, Gilliland, Landis, & Devine, 1993). Moreover, meta-analytic research has shown that for most uses, there are no significant differences in test results between tests administered in computerized versus pencil-and-paper format (Mead & Drasgow, 1993).

An even more recent testing development is the use of computer-adaptive testing (CAT). In computer-adaptive tests (often referred to as "smart" tests), the computer program "adjusts" the difficulty of test items to the level of the person being tested. For example, if a test taker misses several questions, the computer will adjust the level of test difficulty by asking easier questions. If the test taker is getting several answers correct, the computer will present more difficult questions. CAT is typically only used with knowledge-based tests where there are right and wrong answers. Computer-adaptive testing is usually quicker and more efficient than traditional testing because by adjusting the test's difficulty to fit the test taker, the computer can get an accurate assessment using fewer questions. You may soon encounter a CAT program since many of the standardized graduate school entrance exams are now available in CAT form.

Traditional employment tests, whether they be on paper or computer administered, are limited by the fact that they present only written information. A novel approach

Much employment testing today is computer administered.

ON THE CUTTING EDGE(*continued*)

to testing makes use of interactive video-computer technology. In interactive video testing, an applicant views a videotaped example of a simulated work setting. The video scene usually presents a realistic, work-related problem situation. The applicant is then asked to respond with an appropriate solution. In effect, through video-computer technology, the applicant is "transported" into the work situation and required to "perform" work-related tasks. In addition to testing an applicant's work-related knowledge and decision making, such interactive testing provides applicants with a realistic job preview of the job. The major drawback to interactive computer-video testing is the cost of development of such testing programs. However, with the rapid advancements in computer technology, and in testing generally, interactive testing should become more common in the near future.

Other employee screening tests

In addition to the categories of employee tests we have discussed, there are other types of tests that do not fit neatly into any of the categories. For example, many employers screen applicants for drug use, usually through analysis of urine samples. Unfortunately, current laboratory tests are not 100 percent accurate. Interestingly, the problem with drug testing is unlike the problem with polygraphs, since drug testing inaccuracies are more likely to be false *negatives*—failing to detect the presence of drugs—rather than false positives (Normand, Salyards, & Mahoney, 1990). Unlike the polygraph, however, today there are few restrictions on drug testing in work settings. Moreover, such testing is on the rise, with estimates ranging from more than 60 percent to as high as 87 percent of U.S. companies conducting some sort of drug testing (Harris & Heft, 1992; *Wall Street Journal*, 1993). More recently, pencil-and-paper tests have been developed to screen employees who have attitudes that are related to drug use (Marcoulides, Mills, & Unterbrink, 1993).

A very questionable screening "test" is handwriting analysis, or *graphology*. In graphology, a person trained in handwriting analysis makes judgments about an applicant's job potential by examining the personality characteristics that are supposedly revealed in the shape, size, and slant of the letters in a sample of handwriting. Although used by some companies to screen applicants, the validity of handwriting analysis in assessing performance potential is highly questionable (Ben-Shakhar, Bar-Hillel, Bilu, Ben-Abba, & Flug, 1986; Bushnell, 1996; Driver, Buckley, & Frink, 1996).

THE EFFECTIVENESS OF EMPLOYEE SCREENING TESTS

The effectiveness of using standardized tests for screening potential employees remains a controversial issue. Critics of testing cite the low validity coefficients (approximately .20) of certain employment tests. (As the model at the beginning of the chapter illustrates, the validity coefficient is the correlation coefficient between the predictor, or the test score, and the criterion, usually a measure of subsequent job performance). However, supporters believe that a comparison of all screening methods—tests, biographical information, and hiring interviews—across the full spectrum of jobs reveals that employment tests are the best predictors of job performance (Hunter & Hunter, 1984). Obviously, the ability of a test to predict performance in a specific job depends on how well it can capture and measure the particular skills, knowledge, or abilities required. For example, tests of word processing and other clerical skills are good predictors of success in secretarial positions because they do a good job of assessing the skills and knowledge needed to be a successful secretary.

The most effective use of screening tests occurs when a number of instruments are used in combination to predict effective job performance. Because most jobs are complex, involving a wide range of tasks, it is unlikely that successful performance is due to just one particular type of knowledge or skill. Therefore, any single test will only be able to predict one aspect of a total job. Employment screening tests are usually grouped together into a **test battery**. Scores on the various tests in the battery are used in combination to help select the best possible candidates for the job (see Ackerman & Kanfer, 1993).

We have seen that standardized tests can be reliable and valid screening devices for many jobs. However, two important issues regarding this use of tests must be considered: validity generalization and test utility. The **validity generalization** of a screening test refers to its validity in predicting performance in a job or setting different from the one in which the test was validated. For example, a standardized test of managerial potential is found to be valid in selecting successful managers in a manufacturing industry. If the test is also helpful in choosing managers in a service organization, its validity has generalized from one organization to another. Similarly, validity generalization would exist if a test of clerical abilities is successful in selecting applicants for both secretarial and receptionist positions. Of course, the more similar the jobs and organizations involved in the validity studies are to the jobs and organizations that subsequently use the screening tests, the more likely it is that validity will generalize from one situation to another.

High validity generalization of a standardized test will greatly increase its usefulness—and reduce the work load of I/O psychologists because the instrument may not need to be validated for use with each and every position and organization. Some I/O psychologists, such as Schmidt and his colleagues, argue that the validity generalization of most standardized employee screening procedures is quite high, which means that they can be used successfully in a variety of employment settings and job classifications (Schmidt & Hunter, 1977, 1981; Schmidt, Hunter, Outerbridge, & Trattner, 1986;

test battery
a combination of employment tests used to increase the ability to predict future job performance

validity generalization
the ability of a screening instrument to predict performance in a job or setting different from the one in which the test was validated

Schmidt, Law, Hunter, Rothstein, Pearlman, & McDaniel, 1993). At the other extreme is the view that the ability of tests to predict future job success is situation-specific, and validity should be established for each use of a screening instrument. Although few I/O psychologists believe that the validity of test instruments is completely situation-specific, there is some disagreement over how well their validity generalizes.

test utility
the value of a screening test in determining important outcomes, such as dollars gained by the company through its use

Test utility is the value of a screening test in helping to affect important organizational outcomes. In other words, test utility determines the success of a test in terms of dollars gained by the company through the increased performance and productivity of workers selected based on test scores. For example, in one organization a valid screening test was used to select applicants for 600 jobs as computer programmers (Schmidt, Hunter, McKenzie, & Muldrow, 1979). The estimated money gained in one year from the increased speed and efficiency of the chosen workers was more than $97 million. The initial cost of the screening tests was only ten dollars per applicant, a very good return on investment.

All in all, utility analyses of standardized employee testing programs indicate that such tests are usually cost effective. Hunter and Schmidt (1982) go as far as to estimate that the U.S. gross national product would be increased by tens of billions of dollars per year if improved employee screening and selection procedures, including screening tests, were routinely implemented. Utility analyses allow the employer to determine the financial gains of a testing program and then compare them to the costs of developing and implementing the program.

Another important issue in testing is the importance of ethics in the administration and use of employment testing, including the protection of the privacy of persons being tested. I/O psychologists are very concerned about ethical issues in testing. In fact, the Society for Industrial and Organizational Psychology will soon be publishing the fourth edition of its *Principles for the Validation and Use of Personnel Selection Procedures*. This publication outlines important ethical concerns for employment testing

Define five categories of employment tests.

ASSESSMENT CENTERS

assessment center
a detailed, structured evaluation of job applicants using a variety of instruments and techniques

One of the most detailed forms of employment screening and selection takes place in an **assessment center**, which offers a detailed, structured evaluation of applicants on a wide range of job-related knowledge, skills, and abilities. Specific managerial skills and characteristics an assessment center attempts to measure include oral and written communication skills, behavioral flexibility, creativity, tolerance of uncertainty, and skills in organization, planning, and decision making. Because a variety of instruments are used to assess participants, the assessment center makes use of large test batteries. The assessment center approach was developed during World War II by the United States Office of Strategic Services (the forerunner of the CIA) for the selection of spies. Today, they are used primarily to select managers (although see Applying I/O Psychology).

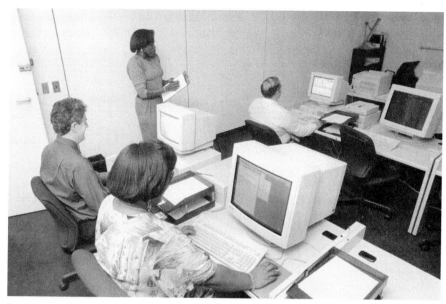

In this assessment center, applicants are assessed as they play the role of a marketing manager—writing memos, answering e-mail messages, making decisions—as part of a computerized in-basket exercise.

In assessment centers, applicants are evaluated on a number of job-related variables using a variety of techniques, such as personality and ability tests, that are considered to be valid predictors of managerial success. Applicants also take part in a number of **situational exercises**, which are attempts to approximate certain aspects of the managerial job. These exercises are related to work samples, except that they are approximations rather than actual examples of work tasks (see Howard, 1997; Streufert, Pogash, & Piasecki, 1988). One popular situational exercise is the *in-basket test* (Fredericksen, 1962), which requires the applicant to deal with a stack of memos, letters, and other materials that have supposedly collected in the "in-basket" of a manager. The applicant is given some background information about the job and then must actually take care of the work in the in-basket by answering correspondence, preparing agenda for meetings, making decisions, and the like. A group of observers considers how each applicant deals with the various tasks and assigns a performance score. Despite the obvious "face validity" of the in-basket exercise, some research has been critical of the in-basket exercise as a selection tool (Schippman, Prien, & Katz, 1990). Much of the criticism, however, deals with the fact that in-basket exercises are difficult to score and interpret because they are attempting to assess a variety of complex skills and knowledge bases.

Another situational exercise is the leaderless group discussion (Bass, 1954). Here, applicants are put together in a small group to discuss some

situational exercise
assessment tools that require the performance of tasks that approximate actual work tasks

work-related topic. The goal is to see how each applicant handles the situation and who emerges as a discussion leader. Again, trained observers rate each applicant's performance.

APPLYING I/O PSYCHOLOGY

The Use of Assessment Center Methodology for Assessing Employability of College Graduates

Since the early 1990s, the use of assessment centers and assessment center methods has grown. There has been an increase in the use of assessment centers in managerial selection, and assessment centers are also being used as a means of training and "brushing up" managers' skills (Hollenback, 1990). Even more recently, assessment center methods are being expanded to facilitate screening and orientation of entry-level employees. In colleges and universities, assessment center methodologies are being used to evaluate new students, or in outcome evaluation—measuring the managerial skills and potential "employability" of students as they graduate.

For instance, in one university's master's-level program in industrial/organizational psychology, first-year master's students are put through an assessment center evaluation, with second-year master's students serving as evaluators (Kottke & Schultz, 1997). This not only allows for an assessment of student skills, but provides students with direct, hands-on experience with assessment. In another project, all graduates of a state university's business school underwent a "mini" assessment center, including completing a computerized in-basket test that assesses both managerial skills and skills in operating computer systems, and participation in a leaderless group discussion, mock

hiring interview, and formal presentation (Riggio, Aguirre, Mayes, Belloli, & Kubiak, 1997). The goal was to evaluate the "managerial potential" of business school graduates, and to track them during their early careers as a way of determining if the knowledge and skills measured in the assessment center are indeed predictive of future career success.

Why the surge of interest in assessment centers? There are several reasons. First, the assessment center methodology makes sense. It offers a detailed, multimodal assessment of a wide range of knowledge, skills, abilities, and psychological characteristics. This is the test battery approach we discussed earlier. Second, much of the measurement in assessment centers is "performance-based," and there is a trend in assessment away from pencil-and-paper assessment and towards more behavior- or performance-based assessment. Third, assessment centers are easier to conduct today. With computer and videotape technology, it is easy to conduct an assessment center and store the participants' performance data for later, more convenient, evaluation. Finally, evidence indicates that assessment centers serve a dual purpose by assessing participants and also helping them to develop managerial skills by undergoing the assessment center exercises (Englebrecht & Fischer, 1995; Howard, 1997).

Instructions:

You are now Mr. C. D. Evans, Plant Superintendent of the East District in Division A of the Green Area of the Eastern Telephone Company. You have just arrived in your new job. Mr. I. W. Prior, your predecessor, died suddenly of a heart attack last Wednesday, March 28. You were notified Friday at 4 P.M. of your new appointment, but you could not get here until today, Sunday, April 1.

Today is your first day on your new job and here is what your secretary has left for you. Since it is Sunday, no one else is around and you cannot reach anyone on the telephone. You must leave in exactly three hours to catch a plane for an important meeting connected with your previous assignment . . . In the large envelope in front of you, you will find three packets. One contains an organization chart, a map of the district and the division, a copy of the management guide, and a copy of the union contract. The second packet contains the materials your secretary has left on your desk for your attention. These materials include letters, reports, memoranda, etc. Your secretary has attached materials from the files to some of the documents. The third packet contains . . . office forms, memo pads, pencils, and paper. You can use these materials to write letters, memos, notes to yourself, etc. (Bray, Campbell, & Grant, 1974, pp. 24-25)

The second packet on the hypothetical desk contained twenty-five problems that the participants had to address.

FIGURE 4.6

Example of an Assessment Center In-basket Exercise

The result of testing at the assessment center is a very detailed profile of each applicant, as well as some index of how a particular applicant rated in comparison to others. While research has indicated that assessment centers are relatively good predictors of managerial success (Gaugler, Rosenthal, Thornton, & Bentson, 1987; Schmitt, Gooding, Noe, & Kirsch, 1984; Tziner, Ronen, & Hacohen, 1993), the reasons why assessment centers work are less clear (Kleinmann, 1993; Klimoski & Brickner, 1987). Of course, the major drawback is the huge investment of time and resources they require, which is the major reason that assessment centers are usually only used by larger organizations and for the selection of candidates for higher-level management positions. However, recent innovations using videotape and computerized assessment of participants has led to a recent renewal of interest in assessment centers, both in managerial selection and in other forms of evaluation (see Applying I/O Psychology).

HIRING INTERVIEWS

To obtain almost any job in the United States, an applicant must go through at least one hiring interview, which is the most widely used employee screening and selection device. Despite its widespread use, however, the hiring interview, as it is conducted in most work settings, is unfortunately not one of

The hiring interview should maintain high standards of measurement, the same as other screening methods

the most reliable and valid methods of screening and selection. While most reviews of the research seem to come to the conclusion that interviews are not a very effective means for selecting people for jobs (Arvey & Campion, 1982; Hunter & Hunter, 1984; Schmitt, 1976), more recent reviews are showing that interviews may have some validity as a selection tool, if conducted properly (Harris, 1989; Huffcutt & Arthur, 1994). Part of the problem with the validity of interviews is that many interviews are conducted haphazardly, with little structure to them (Wright, Lichtenfels, & Pursell, 1989). You may have experienced one of these poor interviews that seemed to be nothing more than a casual conversation, or you may have been involved in a job interview in which the interviewer did nearly all of the talking. While you might have learned a lot about the company, the interviewer learned little about your experience and qualifications. In these cases it is obvious that little concern has been given to the fact that, just like a psychological test, the hiring interview is actually a measurement tool and employment decisions derived from interviews should be held to the same standards of reliability, validity, and predictability as tests (Dipboye, 1989).

A number of variations on the traditional interview format have been developed to try to improve the effectiveness of interviews as a selection tool. One variation is the *situational interview,* which asks interviewees how they would deal with specific job-related, hypothetical situations (Latham, Saari, Pursell, & Campion, 1980; Motowidlo, Dunnette, & Carter, 1990). Another variation has been referred to as the *behavior description interview* (Janz, 1982) or *structured behavioral interview,* which asks interviewees to draw on past job incidents and behaviors in order to deal with hypothetical future work situations (Motowidlo, Carter, Dunnette, Tippins, Werner, Burnett, & Vaughan, 1992). Research has shown that the additional structure and focusing provided by these variations to traditional interviews are effective in improving the success of hiring interviews as selection devices (Maurer & Faye, 1988; Weekley & Gier, 1987).

Because of its popularity, the hiring interview will likely continue to be a central component of employee selection in spite of concerns over its validity. For interviews to be effective, however, greater concern must be given to their structure and conduct. Industrial/organizational psychologists have done extensive research on the hiring interview. One of the outcomes of this research is the development of methods to help make the interview a more effective selection tool (see Up Close).

When used correctly as part of an employee screening and selection program, the hiring interview should have three major objectives. First, the interview should be used to help fill in gaps in the information obtained from the applicant's resume and application form, and to measure the kinds of factors that are only available in a face-to-face encounter, such as appearance and oral communication skills. Second, the hiring interview should provide applicants with realistic job previews, which help them decide whether they really want the job and offer an initial orientation to the organization

UP CLOSE

How to Conduct More Effective Hiring Interviews

A great deal of research indicates that typical hiring interviews, although widely used, are not always effective predictors of job performance. There are, however, ways to improve their reliability and validity, some of which are outlined here:

Use structured interviews. Structured interviewing, in which the same basic questions are asked of all applicants, is nearly always more effective than unstructured interviewing, because it allows for comparisons among applicants (Arvey & Campion, 1982; Dipboye, 1994; Wiesner & Cronshaw, 1988). The use of structured questions also helps prevent the interview from wandering off course and assists in keeping interview lengths consistent.

Make sure that interview questions are job-related. Interview questions must be developed from a detailed job analysis to ensure that they are job-related (Goodale, 1989). Some researchers have developed situational interview questions (Latham, Saari, Pursell, & Campion, 1980), which are derived from critical incidents job analysis techniques that ask applicants how they would behave in a given job situation. Evidence indicates that situational interviews predict job success more accurately than the traditional interview format (Latham & Saari, 1984; Latham, 1989).

Provide for some rating or scoring of applicant responses. To interpret the applicant responses objectively, it is important to develop some scoring system (Goodale, 1989; Graves & Karren, 1996). Experts could determine beforehand what would characterize good and poor answers. Another approach is to develop a scale for rating the quality of the responses. It may also be beneficial to make some record of responses to review later and to substantiate employment decisions. Huffcutt and Arthur (1994) emphasize that it is important that interviewers have *both* structured interview questions and structured criteria (e.g., rating scales) for evaluating applicants.

Use trained interviewers. Although the research on whether interviewer training improves the quality of hiring interview decisions is somewhat inconclusive (Howard & Ferris, 1996; Vance, Kuhnert, & Farr, 1978; Wexley, Sanders, & Yukl, 1973), it is reasonable to assume that trained interviewers will function better than untrained ones. There is also some evidence that interviewers may get better with experience (Arvey, Miller, Gould, & Burch, 1987). Interviewers can be instructed in proper procedures and techniques and trained to try to avoid systematic biases (Howard & Dailey, 1979). Because of the public relations function of hiring interviews (the interviewer is representing the organization to a segment of the public), it is also probably a good idea to have all interviewers undergo some training (Stevens, 1998).

Consider using panel or multiple interviews. Because of personal idiosyncrasies, any one interviewer's judgment of an applicant may be inaccurate. One way to increase interview reliability is to have a group of evaluators assembled in a panel (Arvey & Campion, 1982; Roth &

Campion, 1992). While panel interviews may improve reliability, they may still have validity problems if all interviewers are incorrect in their interpretations or share some biases or stereotypes. Also, the use of panel interviews is costly. Using multiple (separate) interviews is another way to increase the reliability of judgments made in hiring interviews (Conway, Jako, & Goodman, 1995).

Use the interview time efficiently. Many times, interviewers waste much of the time asking for information that was already obtained from the application form and resume. In one study it was found that previewing the applicant's written materials yielded more information in the hiring interview (Dipboye, Fontenelle, & Garner, 1984). However, information obtained from the written materials should not be allowed to bias the processing of information received during the interview (Dipboye, 1982).

One study used a highly structured interview with many of the above properties, including questions based on job analysis, consistent questions and structure for all interviews, rating scales with examples

and illustrations to assist in scoring answers, and an interview panel. The results indicated high agreement on decisions made by different interviewers on the same applicants, indicating good reliability of interview evaluations and good prediction of subsequent job performance of applicants hired for entry-level positions in a paper mill (Campion, Pursell, & Brown, 1988).

It is interesting to note that in a recent review of court cases involving allegations of discrimination in hiring, judges also valued good measurement properties in hiring interviews—ruling more favorably for the organization if the interviews were objective, job-related, structured, and based on multiple interviewers' evaluations (Williamson, Campion, Malos, Roehling, & Campion, 1997).

Monitor the effectiveness of interviews. A hiring interview needs to meet the same standards as any screening instrument, such as an employment test. Therefore, it is very important to collect data on the effectiveness of hiring interview procedures to ensure that the interview process is indeed working (Graves & Karren, 1996).

(Rynes, 1989). Finally, since the hiring interview is one way that an organization interacts directly with a portion of the general public, it can serve an important public relations function for the company (Cascio, 1987).

As mentioned, there are serious concerns about the accuracy of judgments made from hiring interviews. Why is this so? Unlike screening tests or application forms, which ask for specific, quantifiable information, hiring interviews are typically more freewheeling affairs. Interviewers may ask completely different questions of different applicants, which makes it very

"WHOEVER YOU ARE, YOU'RE HIRED."

One problem with hiring interviews is the tendency for interviewers to make snap decisions based on first impressions or limited information.

difficult to compare responses. Although hiring interviews are supposed to be opportunities for gathering information about the applicant, at times the interviewer may do the majority of the talking. These interviews certainly yield very little information about the applicant and probably no valid assessment of the person's qualifications.

The reliability of interviewer judgments is also problematic. Different interviewers may arrive at completely different evaluations of the same applicant, even when evaluating the same interview (Arvey & Campion, 1982; Riggio & Throckmorton, 1987). Also, because of nervousness, fatigue, or some other reason, the same applicant might not perform as well in one interview as in another, which further contributes to low reliability.

snap judgment
arriving at a premature,
early overall evaluation of
an applicant in a hiring
interview

Perhaps the greatest source of problems affecting hiring interview validity is interviewer biases. Interviewers may allow factors such as an applicant's gender, race, physical disability, physical attractiveness, appearance, or assertiveness to influence their judgments (Forsythe, Drake, & Cox, 1985; Gallois, Callan, & Palmer, 1992; Heilman & Saruwatari, 1979; Van Vianen & Van Schie, 1995; Wright & Multon, 1995). There may also be a tendency for an interviewer to make a **snap judgment**, arriving at an overall evaluation of the applicant in the first few moments of the interview. The interviewer may then spend the remainder of the time trying to confirm that first impression, selectively attending to only the information that is consistent with the initial evaluation. Another potential source of bias is the *contrast effect*, which can occur after the interview of a particularly good or bad applicant. All subsequent applicants may then be evaluated either very negatively or very positively in contrast to this person.

In general, the hiring interview often fails to predict job success accurately because of a mismatch between the selection instrument and the information it obtains, and the requirements of most jobs. Receiving a positive evaluation in an interview is related to applicants' abilities to present themselves in a positive manner and to carry on a one-on-one conversation (Guion & Gibson, 1988; Hanson & Balestreri-Spero, 1985; Kacmar, Delery, & Ferris, 1992). In other words, evaluations of interviewees may be strongly affected by their level of communication or social skills. Therefore, for some jobs, such as those that involve primarily technical skills, performance in the interview is in no way related to performance on the job, because the types of skills required to do well in the interview are not the same as those required in the job. More recently, researchers have found a relationship between general cognitive ability and interview performance—suggesting that more intellectually gifted persons receive more positive interview evaluations (Huffcutt, Roth, & McDaniel, 1996). Of course, this may not be a problem since cognitive ability is a good predictor of job performance (Hunter & Hunter, 1984).

Employee Selection and Placement

employee selection
the process of choosing
applicants for employment

Employee selection is the actual process of choosing people for employment from a pool of applicants. In employee selection, all of the information gained from screening procedures, such as application forms, resumes, test scores, and hiring interview evaluations, is combined in some manner to make actual selection decisions.

Name and define four
potential biases in hiring
interviews.

MAKING EMPLOYEE SELECTION DECISIONS

Once employers have gathered information about job applicants, they can combine that information in various ways to make selection decisions. All too often such choices are made subjectively, using what is often referred to as the clinical approach. In this approach, a decision maker simply combines the sources of information in whatever fashion seems appropriate to obtain some general impression about applicants. Based on experience and beliefs about which types of information are more or less important, a decision is made. Although some good selection decisions may be made by experienced decision makers, subjective, clinical decisions are error-prone and often inaccurate (see Meehl, 1954). The alternative is to use a statistical decision-making model, which combines information for the selection of applicants in an objective, predetermined fashion. Each piece of information about job applicants is given some optimal weight that indicates its strength in predicting future job performance. It makes sense that an objective decision-making model will be superior to clinical decisions, since human beings, in most cases, are incapable of accurately processing all of the information gathered from a number of job applicants. Statistical models are able to process all of this information without human limitations.

One statistical approach to personnel decision making is the **multiple regression model**, an extension of the correlation coefficient (see Chapter 2 Statistical Appendix). As you recall, the correlation coefficient examines the strength of a relationship between a single predictor, such as a test score, and a criterion, such as a measure of job performance. However, rather than having only one predictor of job performance, as in the correlation coefficient or bivariate regression model, multiple regression analysis uses several predictors. Typically, this approach combines the various predictors in an additive, linear fashion. In employee selection, this means that the ability of each of the predictors to predict job performance can be added together and that there is a linear relationship between the predictors and the criterion; higher scores on the predictors will lead to higher scores on the criterion. While the statistical assumptions and calculations on which the multiple regression model is based are beyond the scope of this text, the result is an equation that uses the various types of screening information in combination.

The multiple regression model is a compensatory type of model, which means that high scores on one predictor can compensate for low scores on another. This is both a strength and a weakness of the regression approach. For example, an applicant's lack of previous job-related experience can be compensated for by test scores that show great potential for mastering the job. However, in other situations this may be problematic. Take, for example, the screening of applicants for a job as an inspector of microcircuitry, a position that requires the visual inspection of very tiny computer circuits under a microscope. From her scores on a test of cognitive ability, an applicant might show great potential for performing the job. However, the applicant might have an uncorrectable visual problem that leads her to score poorly on a test of visual acuity. Here, the compensatory regression model would not lead to a good prediction, for the visual problem would mean that the applicant would fail, regardless of her potential for handling the cognitive aspects of the job.

A second type of selection strategy, one that is not compensatory, is the **multiple cutoff model**, which uses a minimum cutoff score on each of the

multiple regression model
an employee selection method that combines separate predictors of job success in a statistical procedure

multiple cutoff model
an employee selection method using a minimum cutoff score on each of the various predictors of job performance

predictors. An applicant must obtain a score above the cutoff on each of the predictors to be hired. Scoring below the cutoff on any one predictor automatically disqualifies the applicant, regardless of the scores on the other screening variables. For example, a school district may decide to hire only those probationary high school teachers who have completed a specified number of graduate units and who have scored above the cutoff on a national teacher's examination. The main advantage of the multiple cutoff strategy is that it insures that all eligible applicants have some minimal amount of ability on all dimensions that are believed to be predictive of job success.

Cutoff scores are most commonly used in public sector organizations that give employment tests to large numbers of applicants (Truxillo, Donahue, & Sulzer, 1996). The setting of cutoff scores is an important and often controversial decision, because of the legal issues involved. Particular care needs to be taken by I/O psychologists to set cutoff scores that distinguish the best candidates for jobs, but cutoffs that do not unfairly discriminate against members of certain ethnic minority groups, women, or older workers (see Cascio, Alexander, & Barrett, 1988).

The multiple regression and multiple cutoff methods can be used in combination. If this is done, applicants would be eligible for hire only if their regression scores are high and if they are above the cutoff score on each of the predictor dimensions. Of course, using both strategies at the same time greatly restricts the number of eligible applicants, so they are used together only when the pool of applicants is very large.

multiple hurdle model
an employee selection strategy that requires that an acceptance or rejection decision be made at each of several stages in a screening process

Another type of selection decision-making method is the **multiple hurdle model**. This strategy uses an ordered sequence of screening devices. At each stage in the sequence, a decision is made either to reject an applicant or to allow the applicant to proceed to the next stage. An example of the multiple hurdle model used for hiring police officers is presented in Figure 4.7. In this example, the first stage or hurdle is receiving a passing score on a civil service exam. If a passing score is obtained, the applicant's application blank is evaluated. An applicant who does not pass the exam is no longer considered for the job. Typically, all applicants who pass all the hurdles are then selected for jobs.

One advantage of the multiple hurdle strategy is that unqualified persons do not have to go through the entire evaluation program before they are rejected. Also, because evaluation takes place at many times on many levels, the employer can be quite confident that the applicants who are selected do indeed have the potential to be successful on the job. Because multiple hurdle selection programs are expensive and time-consuming, they are usually only used for jobs that are central to the operation of the organization.

EMPLOYEE PLACEMENT

employee placement
the process of assigning workers to appropriate jobs

While employee selection deals with how people are hired for jobs, **employee placement** is the process of deciding to which job hired workers should be assigned. Employee placement typically only takes place when there are two or

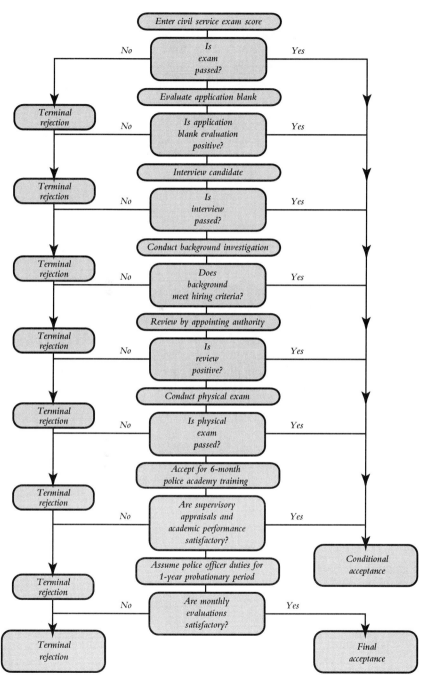

FIGURE 4.7

Multiple Hurdle Model for Policy Officer Selection.
Source: W.E. Cascio. *Appied Psychology in Personnel Management* (Englewood Cliffs, NJ: Prentice-Hall. 1987, p. 282).

Define and give examples of four employee selection methods.

more openings that a newly hired worker could fill. Placement also becomes important when large organizations close departments or offices, and the company does not want to lay off the workers from the closed sites, but instead wants to reassign these workers to other positions within the organization. While placement is a different personnel function, many of the methods used in placement are the same as those used in employee selection. The main difference is that in placement the worker has already been hired. Therefore, the personnel specialist's job is to find the best possible "fit" between the worker's attributes (KSAOs) and the requirements of the job openings.

EQUAL EMPLOYMENT OPPORTUNITY IN EMPLOYEE SELECTION AND PLACEMENT

In 1964 the Civil Rights Act was passed. A section of this major piece of federal legislation, Title VII, was intended to protect against discrimination in employment on the basis of race, ethnic background, gender, or religious preference. Additional laws have since helped protect against age discrimination and discrimination against disabled persons (see Table 4.2). This antidiscrimination legislation has led to massive changes in personnel procedures and decision making.

As a result of the Civil Rights Act, a federal agency, the **Equal Employment Opportunity Commission (EEOC),** was created to ensure that employers' employee selection and placement procedures complied with the antidiscrimination laws. In the 1970s the EEOC developed the *Uniform Guidelines on Employee Selection Procedures* (1974, 1978), which serve as the standards for complying with antidiscrimination laws. Three concepts are important for understanding the *Guidelines* and their impact on employee selection procedures.

The first of these concepts is the notion of **protected groups**, which include women, African Americans, Native Americans, Asian Americans, and Latinos. Employers must keep separate personnel records, including information on all actions such as recruitment, selection, promotions, and firings, for each of these groups and for whites. If some action is found to discriminate against one or more of these groups, the second concept, *adverse impact*, comes into play. **Adverse impact** refers to discrimination, either intentional or unintentional, against a protected group by some personnel action by an employer. For instance, the *Guidelines* state that if any personnel decision causes a disproportionate percentage of people in a particular group to be hired in comparison to another group, adverse impact exists. The *Guidelines* led to the establishment of the *four-fifths rule*, which states that a hiring procedure has adverse impact when the selection rate for any protected group is 4/5, or 80 percent, of the group with the highest hiring rate. If the four-fifths rule demonstrates adverse impact, the employer must show that the hiring procedures used are valid. In a classic legal decision, *Griggs v. Duke Power Company* (1971), the Supreme Court ruled that the burden of proof on whether an employment selection test is fair rests with the employer. This

Equal Employment Opportunity Commission (EEOC)
the federal agency created to protect against discrimination in employment

protected groups
groups including women and certain ethnic and racial minorities that have been identified as previous targets of employment discrimination

adverse impact
discrimination against a protected group by an employer's personnel actions

means that it is up to employers to show that their screening tests and other selection methods are valid indicators of future job performance. The Civil Rights Act of 1991 reaffirmed the *Griggs* v. *Duke* concepts. Therefore, it is wise for organizations to validate any and all of their employee screening instruments to ensure against possible instances of discrimination.

The final important concept from the *Guidelines* is **affirmative action**, the voluntary development of organizational policies that attempt to ensure that

affirmative action
the voluntary development of policies that try to ensure that jobs are made available to qualified individuals regardless of sex, age, or ethnic background

TABLE 4.2

Federal Laws and Key Court Cases Affecting Employment

Civil Rights Act of 1964

Protects against employment discrimination on the basis of "race, color, religion, sex, or national origin." Led to the establishment of the Equal Employment Opportunity Commission (EEOC), the federal body that enforces the law.

Age Discrimination in Employment Act (passed in 1967, amended in 1978)

Protects against employment discrimination on the basis of age. Specifically targeted toward workers between 40 and 70 years of age.

Griggs v. Duke Power Company (1971)

This Supreme Court ruling said that if hiring procedures led to adverse impact, the employer has the burden of proof to show that the hiring procedures are valid.

Albermarle Paper Company v. Moody (1975)

A Supreme Court ruling that required employers to adhere to the *Uniform Guidelines*, including demonstrating that selection procedures are valid.

EEOC Uniform Guidelines (1974, 1978)

Established rules for fair employment practices. Established the notion of adverse impact and the four-fifths rule.

Americans with Disabilities Act (1990)

Protects against employment discrimination for qualified individuals with a physical or mental disability. Says that employers must provide "reasonable accommodations" to help the individual perform the job.

Civil Rights Act of 1991

Upheld the concepts set forth in *Griggs* v. *Duke* and allows workers who claim discrimination to have a jury trial and seek both compensatory and punitive damages against employers.

Family and Medical Leave Act of 1993

Allows employees in organizations of 50 or more workers to take up to 12 weeks of unpaid leave each year for family or medical reasons.

jobs are made available to qualified persons regardless of sex, age, or ethnic background. In general, affirmative action programs will hire or promote a member of a protected group over an individual from the majority group if the two are determined to be equally qualified. However, if the protected group member is less qualified than a majority group applicant—usually a white male—the organization is under no obligation to hire the less qualified applicant. Affirmative action programs typically deal with all personnel functions, including recruitment, screening, selection, job placements, and promotions.

TESTING DISABLED JOB APPLICANTS

As you might imagine, a physical disability might unfairly impair a job applicant's performance on a employee screening test. Yet, the disability may not hinder the individual's ability to do the job. Therefore, personnel specialists must offer reasonable accommodations so that an applicant's disability does not interfere with test performance. For instance, a vision-impaired applicant may need to be presented with a large-print version of a pencil-and-paper test, or if vision is severely impaired, an audio test may need to be administered. Any written test might be inappropriate for testing a dyslexic applicant. A difficulty then arises in comparing the test results of the disabled applicant, who received a different version of the test, or who was administered the test in a different format, with applicants completing the regular version of the test (Ingate, 1992). An even more fundamental issue is determining if an applicant even has a disability, since it is illegal to ask applicants about disabilities.

The passage of the Americans with Disabilities Act (ADA) has sparked a great deal of debate about whether or not disabled applicants whose disability interferes with test taking should or should not be tested (Arnold & Thiemann, 1992). It seems the solution lies not in the test scores themselves, but in the judicious interpretation of the scores (Ingate, 1992).

Define and discuss the concepts of protected groups, adverse impact, and affirmative action.

Summary

Employee recruitment is the process of attracting potential workers to apply for jobs. There are a variety of employee recruitment methods, such as advertisements, college recruitment programs, employment agencies, and employee referrals. An important element of the recruitment process is presenting applicants with an accurate picture of the job through the use of *realistic job previews (RJPs)*, which help increase satisfaction and decrease turnover of new employees.

Employee screening is the process of reviewing information about job applicants to select individuals for jobs. The first step is the evaluation of written materials such as applications and resumes. Basic background information can be translated into numerical values to compare the qualifications of applicants through the use of *weighted application forms* or *biographical information blanks (BIBs)*. Employee screening also involves methods, such as references and letters of recommendation. However, the use of these methods is on the decline because they tend to be overly positive and are often uninformative.

The second step in screening is employee testing, which typically uses standardized instruments to measure characteristics that are predictive of job performance. Any screening test or method must demonstrate that it is a reliable and valid predictor of job performance. Three methods for establishing reliability are *test-retest reliability*, *parallel forms*, and *internal consistency*. The two forms of validity that are most important for the development and use of screening tests are *content validity*, or whether the test content adequately measures the knowledge, skills, and abilities required by the job, and *criterion-related validity*, or the relationship between screening test scores and some criterion of job success.

Employee screening tests vary greatly both in their format and in the characteristics that they measure. Categories of such tests include cognitive ability tests, mechanical ability tests, motor and sensory ability tests, job skills and knowledge tests, personality tests, and miscellaneous instruments such as *polygraphs*. For the most part, the standardized tests are among the best predictors of job performance. Often they are used in combination—in *test batteries*—to help select the best qualified candidates. An important issue regarding the effectiveness of employee screening tests is *validity generalization*, or a test's ability to predict job performance in settings different from the one in which it was validated. Another concern is *test utility*, an estimate of the dollars gained in increased productivity and efficiency because of the use of screening tests. *Assessment centers* use the test battery approach to offer a detailed, structured assessment of applicants' employment potential, most often for high-level managerial positions.

Employment screening for most jobs includes at least one *hiring interview*. Just like any other selection method, the interview is a measurement tool. Unfortunately, research indicates that the hiring interview, as it is typically used, generally has low levels of reliability and validity. Used correctly, the interview should help supply information that cannot be obtained from applications, resumes, or tests, and should present the applicant with a realistic job preview. However, most interviews are not conducted with this in mind. One of the greatest sources of problems with hiring interviews stems from interviewer biases.

Once the screening information has been obtained, a selection decision must be made. All too often, subjective decision-making processes are used. Statistical models of decision making include the *multiple regression model*, an approach that allows predictors to be combined statistically; the *multiple cutoff* strategy, a method of setting minimum cutoff scores for each predictor; and the *multiple hurdle* approach, a stringent method that uses an ordered sequence of screening devices.

Regardless of the screening and selection procedures used, an overriding concern in all personnel decisions is to protect against discrimination in employment. The federal *Equal Employment Opportunity Commission*

(EEOC) has established guidelines to prevent discrimination against ethnic minorities and other *protected groups*. To take preventive steps to avoid employment discrimination, many organizations have adopted *affirmative action* plans to ensure that jobs are made available to members of protected groups.

Study Questions and Exercises

1. What are the various steps in the employee screening process? Consider the strengths and weaknesses of each. For example, what types of information are obtained about applicants at each step? What are some of the dangers or difficulties associated with each stage?

2. Imagine that you are the human resources director for a large company. Design an employee recruitment, screening, and selection program for your lower-level employees. What elements would you include and why? Design a similar program for recruiting and selecting employees for upper-level management positions. What elements would be included in this program? Why?

3. In what ways has antidiscrimination legislation affected how personnel professionals recruit, screen, and select people for jobs? List some ways that employers can try to avoid discrimination in personnel decision making.

4. Consider the last job that you applied for. What kinds of screening procedures did you encounter? What were their strengths and weaknesses? How could they have been improved?

5. Consider the different employee selection methods: multiple regression, multiple cutoff, and multiple hurdle. For each, develop a list of jobs or occupations that would probably require that particular method.

6. It is clear that in much of the hiring that takes place, subjective evaluations of applicants are often the basis for the decisions. Why is this the case? What are some reasons that more objective—and more valid—hiring procedures are often ignored by employers?

Suggested Readings

Arvey, R.D. (1979). *Fairness in selecting employees.* Reading, MA: Addison-Wesley. *Although somewhat dated, this book is a good reference for issues related to discrimination in employee selection. It also offers good coverage of research on the strengths and weaknesses of different selection methods.*

Cook, M. (1988). *Personnel selection and productivity.* Chichester, England: John Wiley & Sons. *An overview of issues in employee selection that includes chapters on nearly every type of screening and selection method. Written by a British psychologist in an informal, interesting style.*

Eder, R.W., & Ferris, G.R. (eds.) (1989). *The employment interview: Theory, research, and practice.* Newbury Park, CA: Sage. *A series of papers dealing with nearly every aspect of work on hiring interviews.*

Personnel and *Personnel Journal*. These journals have many informative and readable articles discussing issues related to recruitment, screening, and selection.

Schuler, H., Farr, J.L., & Smith, M. (eds.) (1993). *Personnel selection and assessment: Individual and organizational perspectives*. Hillsdale, NJ: Lawrence Erlbaum Publishers. A scholarly, informative series of articles dealing primarily with employee selection, but also touching on issues in job analysis (Chapter 3), and performance assessment (Chapter 6).

Society for Industrial and Organizational Psychology. (1987). *Principles for the validation and use of personnel selection procedures* (3rd ed.). College Park, MD: Society for Industrial and Organizational Psychology. *This handbook is a statement of the principles, adopted by the Society for Industrial and Organizational Psychology, of "good practice in the choice, development, evaluation) and use of personnel selection procedures."*

CHAPTER FIVE

EMPLOYEE TRAINING AND DEVELOPMENT

CHAPTER OUTLINE

INSIDE TIPS

LINKS BETWEEN LEARNING THEORIES AND TRAINING METHODS

This chapter on employee training has two general objectives. The first is to present the basic theories and processes of learning, with a focus on how workers learn about their jobs. The second goal is to discuss the procedures used in the design, implementation, and evaluation of employee training programs. Together these two objectives represent the theory and practice of employee training, respectively. In studying this chapter, try to bear in mind the links between learning theories and training methods.

We will also touch on topics that were introduced in several of the earlier chapters. We return to methodological issues (particularly experimental design issues) when considering the evaluation of training programs. The section on assessing training needs is in some ways related to the discussion of job analysis procedures in Chapter 3, except that now we are assessing what knowledge, skills, abilities, and other characteristics (KSAOs) workers need to perform their jobs rather than analyzing the jobs themselves. Because training relates to many personnel decisions, the same kinds of legal concerns regarding equal employment opportunity that we looked at in Chapter 4 are relevant here too. It is important to consider how employee training ties in with the other personnel and employee issues studied previously, and with those employee issues we will look at in the next chapter.

Once an applicant has gone through the often arduous process of screening and has actually been selected for a job, that person must next undergo some sort of employee orientation and training.

Employee training is a planned effort by an organization to facilitate employees' learning, retention, and transfer of job-related behavior. In most organizations that offer training, training is not limited to new employees, as various types of training and development programs are offered at all stages of an employee's career.

In this chapter we will begin by examining areas of employee training. We will also examine the fundamentals of the learning process and how learning applies to employee training and development. We will then look at factors that affect the success of training programs. Next, we will look at how employee training needs are assessed and study general training methods. Finally, we will examine how training programs are evaluated.

employee training
planned organizational efforts to help employees learn job-related knowledge, skills, and other characteristics

Areas of Employee Training

Training, like learning, is a lifelong process. Organizations are beginning to see value in considering and providing for the wide variety of training needs of workers. We will briefly examine some of these specific focuses of employee training and development programs.

New employee orientation and training

Orientation programs are typically designed to introduce employees to the organization and its goals, philosophy, policies, and procedures. They can also acquaint workers with both the physical structure and the personnel structure of the organization, such as the chain of supervisory command and the various relevant departments and divisions. During orientation new employees also learn about compensation, benefits, and safety rules and procedures. In short, initial training should provide enough information so that new employees can quickly become productive members of the organization's workforce. In fact, there is some evidence that when it comes to employee orientation and early training, more is better (Saks, 1996). An additional function of an orientation program is to help newcomers deal with the stresses of adjusting to a new work environment (Wanous, 1993; Waung, 1995).

Although new employee orientation and training are a large part of most organizations' training programs, many do not give sufficient attention or resources to this area despite its very important role in creating a productive and dedicated workforce. In fact, research shows that new workers are often eager and willing to learn (Morrison, 1993). Moreover, evidence suggests that employees receiving adequate initial training are more satisfied and less likely to quit during the first six months of a job than workers who receive little initial training (Wanous, Poland, Premack, & Davis, 1992; Wanous, Stumpf, & Bedrosian, 1979).

Retraining and continuing education programs

Considerable evidence indicates that a certain amount of the knowledge and skills of workers either erodes or becomes obsolete during their work careers (London & Bassman, 1989). To maintain workers' proficiencies, organizations must encourage and support basic "refresher courses" as well as continuing education programs that provide workers with new information. With rapid technological advancements, it is critical that the skills and knowledge of persons employed in jobs that require the use of advanced technology be constantly updated.

Certain professionals, particularly those in licensed health care professions such as medicine, dentistry, and clinical psychology, require some form of continuing education to continue to work in the field. Other professionals, such as managers, lawyers, engineers, and architects, are also increasingly encouraged to participate in continuing education programs.

Retirement planning and preparation

In recent years, the training departments of many organizations have begun offering employees assistance in planning and preparing for retirement. Seminars are offered on such topics as making the retirement decision, retirement plans and options, investment and money management, and services and opportunities for retirees and seniors. More general programs aimed at helping retirees adjust to a nonworking lifestyle are also offered. This increase in preretirement training programs reflects a general trend toward more employee training and greater concern for employees' pre- and postretirement welfare.

Employee career development

Organizations are becoming more and more aware of the need for greater attention to the development and planning of employees' careers. Helping workers plan their careers can help lead to a more productive, more satisfied, and more loyal workforce (Hall & Hall, 1976; Krau, 1981; Noe, 1996). Many organizations are developing formal career development systems, which benefit all parties involved, including workers, managers, and the organization (see Table 5.1).

Career development systems typically offer a variety of programs, including career counseling, courses in career planning, and workshops that

TABLE 5.1

Benefits Of A Career Development System

For Managers/Supervisors	For Employees	For the Organization
Increased skill in managing own careers	Helpful assistance with career decisions and changes	Better use of employee skills
Greater retention of valued employees	Enrichment of present job and increased job satisfaction	Increased loyalty
Better communication be-tween manager and employee	Better communication between employee and manager	Dissemination of infor-mation at all organiza-tional levels
More realistic staff and devel-opment planning	More realistic goals and expec-tations	Better communication within organization as a whole
Productive performance ap-praisal discussions	Better feedback on performance	Greater retention of valued employees
Increased understanding of the organization	Current information about the organization and future trends	Expanded public image as a people-developing organization
Enhanced reputation as a people developer	Greater sense of personal re-sponsibility for managing career	Increased effectiveness of personnel systems and procedures
Employee motivation for ac-cepting new responsibilities		Clarification of organi-zation goals
Build talent inventory for spe-cial projects		
Clarification of fit between organizational and individual goals		

Source: Z.B. Leibowitz, C. Farren, and B.I. Kaye. *Designing Career Development Systems*, (San Francisco: Jossey-Bass, 1986), p. 7.

provide tools and techniques for helping employees manage their careers. For example, career counseling programs might help individuals set career goals and develop a plan for getting the type of training and education nec-essary to meet those goals. They may also assist in finding jobs for employees who are about to be laid off.

Training workers for international business

The increasing globalization of business means that workers may be required to interface with representatives of organizations based in other nations. In some cases, workers may work for a foreign-based company, or they may spend some time working in a host country. Working in another culture requires special training (Tung, 1997). There are many important objectives for programs to train employees for work in international settings. Some of the skills required for working in another culture include foreign language skills, knowledge of the host country's general culture, and knowledge of the country's specific business culture and work rules (Ronen, 1989). One international training program preparing U.S. government employees for work in Japan found that this sort of training was quite effective in preparing its employees for work in a different culture (Harrison, 1992).

Fundamental Issues in Employee Training

Before we examine the specifics of training programs and methods, and their role in influencing important organizational outcomes such as improved productivity or quality, we must first have some fundamental understanding of basic learning processes.

learning
a relatively permanent change in behavior, behavior potential, or cognitive structures that occurs as a result of experience

   Learning is a relatively permanent change in behavior, in the potential to change behaviors, or in cognitive structures, that takes place as a result of experience. Learning thus typically occurs as an interchange between the person and the environment. Through our daily experiences, both on and off the job, we learn new skills, sharpen existing skills, and add to our accumulated knowledge bank. Yet learning is selective, and we do not learn everything to which we are exposed. Exactly when, how, and why we learn are difficult and complex questions to answer.

THEORIES OF LEARNING

To understand the fundamentals of learning more fully, we will briefly consider several basic theories of learning: classical conditioning, operant conditioning, modeling, and cognitive learning theories. Each presents a different view of how learning can take place.

classical conditioning
learning that takes place when two events are experienced together in space and time and become associated with each other

   Classical conditioning, also referred to as *respondent* or *Pavlovian conditioning*, occurs when two events, experienced together in space and time, become associated with each other. Classical conditioning is a passive form of learning because it occurs naturally, with little effort from the learner. It begins with a stimulus, termed the unconditioned stimulus (or UCS), which is something in the environment that automatically creates an unconditioned response (or UCR) in the individual or organism. For example, an employee who received a prestigious performance award from the company's CEO at the firm's end-of-the-year celebration might get a warm, positive feeling upon receiving the award. This feeling is a natural, unconditioned (or unlearned) response (UCR) to receiving the award (UCS). Because the employee received the award from the CEO, she may come to associate that positive feeling with the CEO. Thus, the original unconditioned response becomes a conditioned response (CR) to a stimulus that would not normally elicit the response. In other words, the CEO has become a conditioned stimulus (CS), which through learning has acquired the capacity to elicit the unconditioned response. Now, when the employee passes the CEO in the hall, she gets a warm, positive feeling.

Classical conditioning, although important, only deals with a limited range of learning and for the most part has very few applications in the work world. However, there are some instances where classical conditioning may be relevant. For instance, in some police training procedures, recruits are conditioned to be alert and apprehensive to certain seemingly harmless behaviors that might be life-threatening in actual police work. For example, in a role-played encounter a trainer may blow a whistle to startle a police cadet in order to condition the trainee to be wary of such behaviors as a car passenger reaching under a seat in a routine traffic stop, which is a signal that the person may be reaching for a weapon. Classical conditioning illustrates simple, reflexive learning processes that occur naturally, without much thought on the part of the learner.

The second type of learning, **operant conditioning**, deals with a more voluntary learning of behavior. Operant conditioning begins with the individual's behavior, called the *operant*, which is followed by some *consequence*, or an environmental event that follows the performance of a particular behavior. Consequences that strengthen a tendency to respond are termed *reinforcers*. Consequences that weaken a tendency to respond are *punishments*. When a positive consequence follows some behavior, it is more likely that the behavior will be exhibited again (a *positive reinforcer*, or *reward*). A punishment following the performance of a behavior makes it less likely that the behavior will be repeated. Through the rewarding of desirable behaviors and the punishing of undesirable behaviors, a great deal of human learning takes place.

operant conditioning
a learning process in which behaviors are followed by reinforcing or punishing consequences

The workplace offers a variety of positive reinforcers, such as pay raises, and recognition or praise from supervisors or coworkers, to encourage the learning of desirable behaviors. Moreover, to ensure that employees continue to develop their skills, other rewards are offered, including promotions, awards, and more interesting and challenging assignments. Conversely, a variety of negative consequences, such as reprimands and demotions, can help eliminate undesirable behavior at work.

A third type of basic learning is termed **modeling**, which is imitative learning that occurs through observing and reproducing another person's actions. For example, an employee may learn to operate a piece of machinery or a computer program by watching a supervisor work with the equipment. The concept of modeling and the processes involved are included in Bandura's (1977) **social learning theory**, which holds that four important processes are necessary if learning is to occur. The first process is *attention*. To imitate a particular behavior, attention must be focused on the behavior. A number of factors will increase the probability that a potential learner will attend to another's behavior. For example, people are more likely to pay attention to and imitate the behavior of persons who are of higher status, such as supervisors, or who are otherwise respected, such as particularly talented or knowledgeable coworkers. The second process is *retention*. To be modeled,

modeling
learning that occurs through the observation and imitation of the behavior of others

social learning theory
learning theory that emphasizes the observational learning of behavior.

People may pay more attention to and model the behavior of those in authority.

cognitive theories
learning theories that emphasize that humans are information processors

behavior must somehow be processed and recorded in memory, either by forming a mental picture or a step-by-step verbal description. For example, a secretary watching someone demonstrate a fax machine might retain the operating instructions verbally: "First, he loaded the pages face down. Then he dialed the number on the keypad. Then he hit the 'start' button." A third process is the learner's capacity for *motor reproduction* of the behavior. In other words, to learn through modeling, one must have the physical abilities and skill to imitate the exact movements of the model. For example, most of us would be unable to do a good job of imitating the drawing of a talented artist or the swing of a professional golfer merely because we watched their movements unless we also possessed some specific artistic or athletic skills and some previous motor experience with the behavior. A final process that affects imitative learning is *motivation:* There must be some reason for learning the observed behavior. For example, you might be more strongly motivated to pay attention to and learn about the various tasks required to perform your boss's job if you aspire to hold the position yourself one day.

In addition to the above learning models, more recently a number of **cognitive theories** of human learning have been developed and applied to personnel training (Howell & Cooke, 1989; Tannenbaum & Yukl, 1992). These cognitive approaches to training emphasize that human workers are, in effect, information processors. Cognitive models of learning are focused on how new information is stored and retrieved, and how the information is used to produce work behavior. Cognitive models are particularly useful in understanding complex thinking processes, such as how workers can go beyond learned information and come up with novel and creative solutions or ideas. Cognitive models of learning and information processing are also important in understanding how workers make decisions, and how they learn to operate complex machinery or work systems. We will look at these topics in Chapter 15 when we examine another area of I/O psychology—human factors.

The operant and classical conditioning models of learning focus exclusively on the stimulus-response relationship, whereas social learning theory and cognitive theories emphasize the role of cognitive processes in learning and consider the fact that people think about their actions and can consciously monitor and regulate their behavior. We use our experiences to decide on a plan for future behavior. We can learn to improve our performance by comparing our behavior with the results of our own previous performances or those of others. While operant conditioning views learning as taking place through a simple process of worker behavior and subsequent environmental consequences, social learning and cognitive theories assert that work behavior can be best understood in terms of an interaction and a reciprocal cause-and-effect relationship among the individual, the behavior, and the work environment (Davis & Luthans, 1980; Tannenbaum & Yukl, 1992).

Each of these learning approaches offers a different way of understanding how learning takes place and somewhat different implications for encouraging learning in the workplace. Sometimes training programs rely heavily on one theoretical approach. For example, a program designed to teach assembly workers to pay closer attention to product quality may apply operant conditioning principles by offering a cash reward to those who reduce the percentage of rejects they produce. Relying on social learning theory, a new employee training program may simply show videotapes of models performing complex work tasks. However, many effective training programs combine theories, using paired associations, combinations of rewards and punishments, and modeling and cognitive techniques.

STOP AND REVIEW

List and describe three learning theories that are relevant to employee training.

KEY ISSUES IN THE SUCCESS OF TRAINING PROGRAMS

In order for learning to translate into positive changes in work performance, a number of key issues should be considered when implementing a personnel training program. For example, we must take care to see that learning achieved during the training sessions actually transfers to new behaviors at the worksite. We also need to consider the trainees' willingness and readiness to learn. In addition, we need to look at the structure of the training program in terms of when, where, and how training will take place. Let's look more closely at these key training issues.

Transfer of training

An important concern is the **transfer of training** (Baldwin & Ford, 1988). How well does learning transfer from the training situation to the actual work environment? Since training transfer is influenced by the degree of similarity between the training tasks and the actual job tasks, the most useful training programs directly address the actual tasks that are performed on the job. Positive transfer of learned tasks has been found to be maximized when there are identical stimulus and response elements found in the training and in job situations (Wexley & McCellin, 1987). Transfer of training will also be more likely if the work environment supports the new behaviors that are learned, and if the work environment allows the trainee opportunity to use those newly learned behaviors (Ford, Quinones, Sego, & Sorra, 1992; Tracey, Tannenbaum, & Kavanagh, 1995).

Setting training goals, and receiving feedback and reinforcement for achieving training goals, also positively impact training transfer (Winters & Latham, 1996). One study found that when trainees set goals for implementing the training strategies, and feedback was given concerning the achievement of those goals, the trained behaviors tended to stay in place (Wexley & Baldwin, 1986). Without feedback and reinforcement, learned skills or procedures may deteriorate as workers forget some of their important elements, pick up bad habits that interfere with their application, or lapse into using old work strategies (Marx, 1982). Thus, concern should be given to the *maintenance* of newly learned work behaviors. It is important that workers see the connection between the learning of new behaviors and how the use of the new learning will enhance their working lives. "Brush-up" or reminder training sessions should follow a few months down the line. In short, training should take place on a regular basis, should be thorough,

transfer of training concept dealing with whether training is actually applied in the work setting and should continue throughout an employee's career. For effective transfer and maintenance of learning, employees must see that learning new work skills helps them to be better, more productive workers, which in turn can lead to promotions and other forms of career advancement.

Trainee readiness

trainee readiness
the individual's potential for
successful training

A second consideration is what could be termed **trainee readiness**. A great deal of research indicates that positive employee attitudes toward training programs are critical for training success (Noe, 1986; Warr & Bunce, 1995; Webster & Martocchio, 1993). Is the trainee prepared to learn? Does the trainee feel the need for training and see the usefulness of the material that will be learned? Trainee ability, or "trainability," is another important factor to consider (Kanfer & Ackerman, 1989). For example, does the employee possess the basic prerequisites to be a good candidate for learning these new behaviors? In other words, does the trainee have the aptitude to learn? Finally, if a training program is going to be successful, we must consider the trainee's motivation. If an individual has no desire to learn new tasks and to take on new responsibilities, it is unlikely that much learning will take place (Baldwin, Magjuka, & Loher, 1991). Or, if a trainee feels unable to master the material—if he or she feels the material is "beyond reach"—learning will be adversely affected (Mathieu, Martineau, & Tannenbaum, 1993). Moreover, research has indicated that giving employees a realistic preview of what the training program is about, and providing them with the personal and career-related benefits, have positive effects on both trainee reactions to the program and their learning (Martocchio, 1993; Smith-Jentsch, Jentsch, Payne, & Salas, 1996; Webster & Martocchio, 1995).

Training program structure

A third issue concerns the *structure* of the training program. When and how often does training take place? How long are the training sessions? How much opportunity is there for trainees to practice or apply what they have learned? How much guidance and individual attention does each trainee receive?

The bulk of research evidence does indeed support the old adage that "practice makes perfect." In fact, evidence indicates that practice should continue to the point of *overlearning*, or where practice continues even after the trainee has established that the material has been learned (Driskell, Willis, & Copper, 1992; McGeehee & Thayer, 1961). Should the practice be continuous, in what is called *massed* practice, or should practice sessions be *spaced* over time? Nearly all evidence supports spaced over massed practice, particularly if the practice involves retrieval type learning (such as a recall test) rather than recognition learning (Schmidt & Bjork, 1992). Students are probably familar with this. Studying course material in continuous, spaced sessions over the semester beats intense, last-minute "cramming" nearly every time!

Training research has also looked at whether it is better to segment the material into parts, in what is called *part learning*, or present the material as a whole (*whole learning*). The research evidence suggests that whole learning is better than part learning, particularly when the trainees have high levels of cognitive abilities (Adams, 1987). For example, teaching a worker to operate a bulldozer would be more successful if presented as a whole task, such as learning to manipulate the controls that both drive the vehicle and operate the shovel, as opposed to learning the two tasks separately, particularly since operating a bulldozer requires driving while controlling the shovel simultaneously.

Another critical element is providing trainees with *feedback* about learning accomplishments. To be effective, feedback must be immediate rather than delayed. More feedback is generally better, although there is a point where too much feedback may only serve to overload and confuse trainees. Finally, research has shown that positive feedback—information about what a trainee has done right—is more effective than negative feedback, which focuses on what the trainee has done wrong (Martocchio & Webster, 1992).

Finally, evidence indicates that to be effective, training programs should be highly structured in order to increase the meaningfulness of the material to be learned (Fantuzzo, Riggio, Connelly & Dimeff, 1989; Wexley & Latham, 1991). Adding structure to training programs may involve presenting a general overview of the material to trainees before actual training begins, and imposing a logical or orderly sequence on the presentation of the training material.

COMMON PROBLEMS IN EMPLOYEE TRAINING PROGRAMS

Estimates of the cost of personnel training in the United States alone range from the tens of billions to the hundreds of billions of dollars per year. Yet, one problem with many personnel training programs is that although organizations make a major commitment to training in terms of time, money, and other resources, training programs are not as effective as they could be, partly because they do not adequately follow theoretical models of learning. Another problem is that employee training programs in some companies are not well-organized. Perhaps you have even experienced such "haphazard" training in one of your own jobs, where you received little formal training and were expected to learn "on-the-job" with little guidance. Or, you may have heard of workers who attend training sessions that seem to have little relevance to the jobs the workers perform (see Up Close).

UP CLOSE

Why Do Some Organizations Give So Little Attention to New Employee Orientation and Training?

Traditionally, some organizations have tended to throw new employees into a work situation with only minimal training and orientation, assuming that they will learn the job by observing and doing (Dipboye, 1997). In these instances, there appears to be a strong belief that the really good workers will distinguish themselves by their ability to adapt and survive.

███   UP CLOSE (*continued*)

One reason for this "sink-or-swim" treatment of new employees is that employee training and orientation have not been very high priorities for many organizations, particularly smaller businesses and relatively new companies. These organizations are so preoccupied with basic survival—maintaining productivity rates and keeping the size and quality of the workforce constant—that training (along with other personnel considerations, such as a program of regular performance appraisals) is put on the back shelf. When conditions stabilize and the company has grown or matured, these personnel functions may be given greater emphasis.

Another reason for the absence of new employee training programs is the lack of assessment of training needs (Dipboye, 1997). Many organizations are simply unaware of what new employees need (and want) to know. Those who know the most about new employee training needs are probably the front-line supervisors, who observe firsthand the skill and knowledge deficiencies of new workers. For some reason, however, these training needs are not communicated to the upper-level decision makers. Of course it may not be help-

ful to ask the new workers about their needs, since because they are new they are usually unaware of their training requirements. New workers may also not readily admit to certain skill or knowledge deficiencies in an effort to appear that they are indeed competent. A related problem arises when there is no sound evaluation of existing training programs, for it is unlikely that additional resources will be allocated unless the benefits of such programs have been demonstrated. Finally, inadequate training and orientation may be rooted in the belief that the best way for new workers to learn is by doing. While on-the-job training can be effective, organizations need to consider its costs for new employees, such as reduced levels of production and potential damage to the product, equipment, or the workers. For instance, at IBM's higher-end computer manufacturing plant it is estimated that a poorly trained assembly worker's mistake while constructing an expensive computer system can cost between $10,000 and $100,000 worth of damage (DeAngelis, 1994). Unregulated on-the-job training may also cause workers to learn poor work habits rather than the proper ones.

List and define four key issues that are important in determining the success of training programs.

A Model for Successful Training Programs

Theories and principles of learning should be taken into account in the design and implementation of any good employee training program. In addition, to be successful, training programs need to follow a structured, step-by-step model (see Figure 5.1). A successful training program should begin by *assessing training needs.* In other words, the organization must first have some idea of what workers need to know to perform their jobs.

The next step is *establishing training objectives*—goals for what the training is supposed to accomplish. Training objectives need to be specific and related to measurable outcomes, since training objectives are used both to set a course for the training program, and to help later in determining if the training was indeed successful (Goldstein, 1993).

The next step in the training program involves the *development and testing of training materials*. A variety of factors must be taken into account in developing training materials, such as the trainees' educational and skill level, whether the training material focuses on the areas that are directly related to successful job performance, and what training methods will provide the best cost-benefit trade-off. It is also important that training materials be thoroughly tested before they are put into regular use.

The actual *implementation of the training program* is the next step in the training model. Important considerations in implementing the training program include: when and how often the training will take place, who will conduct the training, the assignment of trainees to sessions, and where the training will be conducted.

The final step is the *evaluation of the training program* in order to determine if the training was effective. This step involves a detailed analysis of whether training objectives were met and whether the training translates into trainees using the newly learned behaviors on the job.

Let's look more closely at some of the issues related to successful personnel training programs, starting with a discussion of training needs assessment.

ASSESSING TRAINING NEEDS

A successful training program should begin by *assessing training needs*. In other words, the organization must have some idea of what workers need to know to perform their jobs. Typically, an assessment of training needs should include analyses on many levels: the organizational level (the needs and goals of the organization), the task level (the requirements for performing the task), and the person level (the skills and knowledge required to do the job). An additional analysis can be done at the demographic level (determining training needs for specific demographic groups).

Organizational analysis

The organizational level of needs analysis considers issues such as the long- and short-term organizational goals and their implications for training, available training resources, and the general climate for training (that is, the workers' and supervisors' commitment to participation in the training program). In addition, organizational analysis considers training needs that are the result of internal and external factors affecting the organization. For example, the introduction of a new manufacturing system and technology would require the organization to plan the kinds of technical skills, managerial skills, and support that workers will need to use the new machines and process (Kozlowski & Salas, 1997). Similarly, a sales organization's decision

FIGURE 5.1

A Model for Successful Employee Training Programs.

to provide greater emphasis on customer service might require the development of new training programs. In an organizational analysis, a strategy for assessing training climate might involve surveying employees regarding their perceptions of training needs and their attitudes toward participation in training programs. The organizational level of needs analysis would also want to determine whether managers' expectations regarding training needs were consistent with organizational goals.

Task analysis

The task level of analysis is concerned with the knowledge, skills, and abilities and other characteristics (KSAOs) that a worker requires to perform a specific job effectively. The starting point for obtaining this information is the job description derived from a detailed job analysis. (As you may recall from Chapter 3, a job analysis is the starting point for just about any personnel operation.) The next and most difficult step involves translating the specific task requirements of the job into the basic components of knowledge and skill that can be incorporated into a training program. For example, a job as department store assistant manager might require the worker to handle customer complaints effectively. However, it may be difficult to determine the specific skills required to perform this task in order to train prospective employees.

Person analysis

The person analysis of employee training needs examines the current capabilities of the workers themselves to determine who needs what sort of training. Person analysis usually relies on worker deficiencies outlined in performance appraisals for incumbent workers, and information derived from employee selection data, such as screening tests for new workers (we will discuss performance appraisals in the next chapter). Another important source of information is job incumbents' self-assessments of training needs (Ford & Noe, 1987), which may also help build employee commitment to the training program.

The use of the three levels of training needs analysis—task, organizational, and person analysis—can help determine which workers need training in which areas and provide information to guide the development of specific training techniques. It has been argued that effective training programs should be based on analysis of training needs on many levels, rather than simply focusing on one level of analysis (Ostroff & Ford, 1989). In addition, the organization must consider the impact of a proposed training program in terms of both the potential benefits, such as increased efficiency and productivity, and the potential costs of the program itself.

Demographic analysis

It has been suggested that training needs analysis may have to be conducted on a fourth level, *demographic* analysis (Latham, 1988). A demographic analysis involves determining the specific training needs of various demographic groups, such as women and men, certain ethnic minorities, and workers of different age brackets. For example, a study of the perceived training needs of workers 40 years of age and older found that the younger workers (aged 40 to 49) believed that they needed training in management skills and the middle-aged group (aged 50 to 59) preferred training in technological skills, while the oldest group (60 years and older) showed little interest in any type of training, perhaps because they felt that they had little to gain from additional training (Tucker, 1985). Another study looking at management training needs found that male and female managers were perceived as needing training in different types of communication skills. Women managers were perceived by upper-level management as requiring training in assertiveness, confidence building, public speaking, and dealing with males, whereas male manager training needs were identified as listening, verbal skills, nonverbal communication, empathy, and sensitivity (Berryman-Fink, 1985). (It is important to emphasize, however, that these training needs were the *perceptions* of upper-level managers—perceptions that might have been affected by gender stereotypes of female and male managers. They may not have reflected *actual* training needs.) We will discuss training for special groups later in the chapter.

ESTABLISHING TRAINING OBJECTIVES

The second step in a successful training program is *establishing training objectives*. As mentioned earlier, it is important that objectives be specific and that they be associated with measurable outcomes. Training objectives should specify what the trainee should be able to accomplish on completion of the training program (Goldstein, 1993). For example, objectives for a training program for cashiers might be that the trainee will be able to operate the cash register, maintain the cash register, and make change upon completion of training.

Training objectives are important in guiding the design of the training program and the selection of training techniques and strategies. Moreover, the emphasis on establishing training objectives that are specific and measurable is particularly important in eventually evaluating the effectiveness of the training program (Kraiger, Ford, & Salas, 1993; Kraiger & Jung, 1997).

Older employees may have different training needs than younger employees.

DEVELOPING AND TESTING TRAINING MATERIALS: EMPLOYEE TRAINING METHODS

The next step in our employee training model involves *developing and testing the training materials*. There are a wide variety of employee training methods ranging from the relatively simple and straightforward to the fairly complex and sophisticated, although all involve the basic principles and fundamental issues of learning discussed earlier. In actual practice, most comprehensive training programs utilize a combination of several training methods and techniques.

It is important to pilot test the training materials, perhaps by using a group of workers who can provide their reactions to the materials and the program. This process leads to a refinement of the training materials and improvement in the program. Let's look at some of the more common training materials and methods.

Employee training methods can be grouped into two broad categories: the on-site methods, or those conducted on the job site, and the off-site methods, or those conducted away from the actual workplace.

On-site methods

On-site training methods may be further divided into several categories, including on-the-job training, apprenticeship, vestibule training, and job rotation.

On-the-job training—One of the oldest and most widely used training methods, **on-the-job training** consists simply of putting an inexperienced worker in the workplace and having a more experienced worker teach that person about the job. This technique thus relies on principles of modeling, with the experienced worker serving as the role model. Also, because actual hands-on learning is involved, the worker can receive immediate feedback, be reinforced for successful efforts, and have a chance to learn how to correct errors.

The popularity of on-the-job training is obvious since it requires little preparation and few costs to the organization, aside from the time invested by the experienced worker. Moreover, because the trainee is actually working while learning, certain small levels of output offset the costs of the supervising worker's time. However, problems occur when the organization neglects to consider the abilities and motivations of the experienced workers who serve as trainers. If these trainers do not see the personal benefits of serving as trainers (especially when there are no obvious benefits!), they will not be motivated to do a good job. Also, being a good trainer requires certain qualities, such as patience and an ability to communicate. If the trainer lacks these characteristics, this can interfere with trainees' learning. Problems can also arise if the trainer does not know or follow proper work procedures. In this case, the trainer may teach the new worker wrong or inefficient methods.

On-the-job training is best used when the trainers have been carefully selected because of their ability to teach and when they have received systematic training to help them be more effective. Trainers should also receive some type of reward or recognition for performing their training duties. Finally, the organization must accept the fact that during the on-the-job training period, production rates will suffer. It is impossible to expect the trainer-trainee team to do a good job of training while simultaneously maintaining high output rates. It has been suggested that to be effective, on-the-job training should be used with other training methods, including off-site methods such as seminars and programmed instruction (Wexley & Latham, 1991).

on-the-job training
an employee training method of placing a worker in the workplace to learn firsthand about a job

Apprenticeship—Skilled trade professions, such as carpentry, printing, masonry, and plumbing, use a very old type of training program called **apprenticeship**. A typical apprenticeship can last for several years and usually combines some supervised on-the-job training experience (usually at least 2,000 hours) with classroom instruction. The on-the-job experience allows the apprentice to learn the mechanics of the profession, while the classroom training usually teaches specific cognitive skills and rules and regulations associated with the profession. For example, an apprentice in the housing construction industry will learn the mechanical skills of building a house while on the job and will learn about building codes and how to read blueprints in the classroom. The obvious advantage of apprenticeship programs is the detailed and long-term nature of the learning process. However, there have been charges from civil rights groups that apprentices are disproportionately chosen from majority groups and that women and members of ethnic minorities have been selectively omitted. In recent years, however, affirmative action programs in many apprenticed professions have attempted to rectify these problems (Carnevale, Gainer, & Villet, 1990; Wexley & Yukl, 1984).

It is important to mention that the term "apprenticeship" has been used to describe a number of training programs that are quite different from traditional, formal apprenticeship. These informal "apprenticeships" might be better labeled as "mentorships," since they typically do not have the strict combination of hands-on learning and classroom training required by formal apprenticeships. We will discuss mentoring a bit later when we look at the use of mentoring in managerial training.

Vestibule training—**Vestibule training** is another on-site training method. This method uses a separate training area adjacent to the actual work area to simulate that setting, complete with comparable tools and equipment. In vestibule training, professional trainers teach the new workers all aspects of the job, allowing them hands-on experience in the work simulation area. The main advantage of vestibule training is that there is no disruption of actual production, since trainers rather than experienced workers provide instruction and the novice workers are not in the actual work setting. The major drawback to this method is its costs in terms of the trainers, space, and equipment needed. In recent years, some large supermarkets have set up vestibule training areas at closed check-out stations to teach prospective checkers how to operate laser scanners and cash registers to ring up goods. Vestibule training is used to eliminate the delays to customers that inevitably occur when using on-the-job training.

Job rotation—A final on-site training method is **job rotation,** in which workers are rotated among a variety of jobs, spending a certain length of time (usually several weeks to two months) at each. The basic premise behind job rotation is to expose workers to as many areas of the organization as possible so that they can gain a good knowledge of its workings and how the various jobs and departments fit together. Job rotation can also be beneficial to the organization because of "cross-training" of workers. Thus, if a worker is absent

apprenticeship
a training technique, usually lasting several years, that combines on-the-job experience with classroom instruction

Skilled trades such as carpentry typically require formal apprenticeships.

vestibule training
training that uses a separate area adjacent to the work area to simulate the actual work setting

job rotation
a method of rotating workers among a variety of jobs to increase their breadth of knowledge

or quits, another worker has already been trained to perform the job. Most commonly, job rotation is used to help entry-level management personnel find the positions for which they are best suited. It can also be used to groom managers for higher-level positions, presumably making them more effective by enabling them to see the organization from a variety of perspectives. Research has shown that job rotation not only increases learning, but it also has positive effects on employees' career progression and development (Campion, Cheraskin, & Stevens, 1994). Job rotation has also been used in various team approaches to work task design to increase worker flexibility, eliminate boredom, and to increase worker job satisfaction and commitment to the organization (Wexley & Latham, 1991).

It is important to mention, however, that job rotation does not consist of simply moving workers from task to task with little or no preparation. A careful analysis of training needs should be done for each position to which a worker is rotated. It is also important to orient and train the worker adequately on each task. Finally, an evaluation should be done of the worker's performance at each task, and the effectiveness of the overall job rotation training experience should be conducted.

Off-site methods

Training that takes place in a setting other than the actual workplace uses off-site methods. Because of the greater flexibility and control over the situation they afford, off-site methods are more varied and diverse than the on-site techniques. We will consider several off-site methods: seminars, audiovisual instruction, behavior modeling training, simulation techniques, programmed instruction, and computer assisted instruction.

Seminars—A very common method of employee training, and one that is very familiar to students, is the **seminar**, which typically involves some expert providing job-related information orally in a classroomlike setting. Although this method of training allows a large number of workers to be trained simultaneously at relatively low cost, it has some drawbacks. First, because the seminar is primarily a one-way form of communication, employees may not become highly involved in the learning process. Also, it is unclear whether workers will be able to translate the information they receive from seminars into actual performance of work behaviors. Finally, the seminar method is often only as good as the presenter. A training program presented by a speaker who is unprepared and speaks in a monotone is unlikely to lead to any significant learning. In fact, one early study found that the seminar was one of the least effective of various employee training methods (Carroll, Paine, & Ivancevich, 1972). On a more positive note, however, seminar methods of instruction have been shown to be an effective learning strategy, particularly when used with more educated workers, such as when seminars are used in managerial training (Burke & Day, 1986). Of course, seminars can be made even more effective if the lecture presentation is combined with question-and-answer periods or audience discussion, to encourage a more "active" learning process.

seminar

a common training method in which an expert provides job-related information in a classroomlike setting

At an insurance company's training facility, claims adjusters are given audiovisual instruction as well as hands-on experience.

Audiovisual instruction—**Audiovisual instruction** uses films, slide presentations, videotapes, and closed-circuit television to train workers. In effect, audiovisual instruction is a seminar provided in a different format. Increased access to advanced audiovisual technology means that just about any size organization can afford the equipment needed to create and/or present such training programs. Although there may be some fairly large initial costs, the audiovisual method can be even more cost-effective than traditional seminar techniques if large numbers of employees are going to be trained.

As in seminars, the quality of audiovisual instruction determines its effectiveness as a training tool. In many instances, a film or slide show can be more entertaining than a seminar and may do a better job of attracting the audience's attention. An obvious problem occurs, however, when the informational content is sacrificed for entertainment value.

Audiovisual presentations are especially effective when the information is presented visually rather than verbally. A few minutes of videotape can visually demonstrate manual operations (with instant replay, stop action, or slow motion) or can expose workers to a number of different locations and settings, both of which would be impossible in a seminar presentation. Moreover, recorded audiovisual programs can ensure uniformity of training by exposing all workers to the same information. For example, one large printing and publishing company has prepared an audio-slide presentation

audiovisual instruction
the use of films, videotapes, and other electronic media to convey training material

to give groups of new employees information about company policies, procedures, and employee rights and benefits in a thorough, graphic, and cost-effective manner.

Behavior modeling training—Another employee training technique is **behavior modeling training** (Decker & Nathan, 1985; Goldstein & Sorcher, 1974). In behavior modeling training, which is based on social learning theory, trainees are exposed to videotaped or live role models displaying both appropriate and inappropriate work behaviors as well as their successful or unsuccessful outcomes. Trainees are then allowed an opportunity to try to replicate and practice the positive work behaviors. Research indicates that behavior modeling training, if used correctly, can effectively improve employee job performance (Decker, 1982; Mann & Decker, 1984; Meyer & Raich, 1983). Behavior modeling training was also shown to be effective in computer software training (Gist, Schwoerer, & Rosen, 1989). In another interesting study, behavior modeling training was found to be more effective than either seminars or programmed instruction (see below) in training computer operators (Simon & Werner, 1996).

Simulation techniques—**Simulation** training is a method of replicating job conditions to instruct employees in proper work operations without actually putting them in the job setting. Jet pilots, astronauts, and nuclear power plant operators are all subjected to intensive simulation training before they are allowed to control the complex and dangerous machinery that they will operate on the job. Simulation training allows the worker hours of practice under conditions that are quite similar to the actual work setting, without allowing the possibility of damaging the equipment, the product, the environment, or themselves.

Most commonly, simulation training uses replications of complex machinery or equipment, such as jet cockpit flight simulators or mock-ups of the control panels used by nuclear power plant operators. Other simulations may be designed to give trainees exposure to what would normally be very hazardous working conditions. For example, a Southern California police department has constructed a mock city (complete with a bank and a convenience store!) for use in training police personnel in simulated emergency conditions. Police trainees attempt to foil simulated robbery attempts and rescue hostages from terrorists using the mock city and blank ammunition. According to the police authorities, the realism of this simulation has led to better preparation of new officers in dealing with actual life-threatening situations. As you can imagine, simulation training is often very expensive. However, the chance for hands-on experience, immediate feedback, and repeated practice make it a very effective technique.

Programmed instruction—**Programmed instruction** involves the use of self-paced individualized training. Each trainee is provided with materials (usually a printed booklet) to learn and then a series of questions that test how much learning has taken place. When test answers are substantially correct, the trainee is instructed to move on to the next unit. If the questions are answered incorrectly, some review of the previous unit is required.

---

behavior modeling training
a training method that exposes trainees to role models performing appropriate and inappropriate work behaviors and their outcomes and then allows trainees to practice modeling the appropriate behaviors

simulation
training that replicates job conditions without placing the trainee in the actual work setting

programmed instruction
self-paced individualized training in which trainees are provided with training materials and can test how much they have learned

Most of the student study guides that accompany college textbooks are examples of programmed instruction.

Programmed instruction draws on principles of reinforcement, with correct answers being either extrinsically (e.g., "Good job! Go on to the next section.") or intrinsically reinforced (i.e., the self-satisfaction that you learned the material). The benefits of programmed instruction are that it is efficient, since individuals proceed at their own paces, and that it provides immediate feedback. In addition, programmed instruction is a very "active," involved form of learning. Furthermore, although the development of such programs is time-consuming, the initial cost diminishes greatly over time if large numbers of employees are trained. A problem can arise, however, in keeping the programs up-to-date, especially in fields where there are rapid changes in technology or in the types of products produced or services performed, requiring that new instruction programs must be continually created.

Computer assisted instruction (CAI)—A more modern approach to individualized employee training is **computer assisted instruction (CAI)**. The tremendous power, flexibility, and the recent affordability of powerful computing systems have led to an increase in computer-assisted instruction. Although CAI is actually a form of programmed instruction, CAI systems offer the flexibility to change and update the instructional programs continually. CAI also allows for immediate testing of the trainee's learning because the computer can ask questions and instantly score the correctness of responses, automatically returning the trainee to the earlier lesson if the answers are incorrect, and presenting the next unit when the answers are correct (recall the computer-adaptive testing discussed in the previous chapter, Chapter 4). The computer can also generate detailed data on each trainee's performance across all of the lessons. CAI thus offers all of the advantages of programmed instruction, although the initial costs are even greater because of the need for computer hardware and costly software. Another advantage of CAI is that most people find interaction with the computer enjoyable (more enjoyable than working with a printed booklet), although some individuals may have some initial apprehension (Goldstein, 1986; Wexley & Latham, 1981).

A recent development in CAI is computerized, interactive videodisk programs that combine audiovisual techniques, programmed instruction, and simulation techniques. With these programs, a trainee may be presented with a videotape of a work situation. The computer then asks questions about which course of action the trainee would like to take. The response is then used to choose the next videotape segment, where the trainee can see the results of the choice played out on videotape. One such program, used for management training, exposes the trainee to a variety of difficult interpersonal and decision-making situations. Through the eye of the video camera, the trainee is brought into a simulated work situation with actors portraying the roles of coworkers. In one setting, the trainee might need to deal with a subordinate who is angry about having been given a negative performance appraisal. In another situation, the trainee may be asked to play the role of leader of a decision-making group and choose one of four possible courses of action. Choosing the correct management strategies leads to a positive outcome. If an incorrect choice is made, the trainee will view the disastrous results played out by the actors in the subsequent scene. Similar interactive videodisk training programs have been developed to teach medical students diagnosis of illness and treatment decisions.

Special management training methods

Because managers are considered to play such a central role in administrative functions, coordinating organizational activities and motivating workers, and because managerial skills are abstract and difficult to learn, a large share of training resources go into the training and development of managers. In fact, a variety of special techniques are used almost exclusively in management training.

problem-solving case study
a management training technique that presents a real or hypothetical organizational problem that trainees attempt to solve

One common and very popular management training technique is the **problem-solving case study**, which presents trainees with a written description of a real or hypothetical organizational problem. Each trainee is allowed time to study the case individually and come up with a solution. The trainees then meet in small groups to present and critique their solutions and discuss the problem further. One purpose of such studies is to show trainees that there are no single or easy solutions to complex problems (Berger, 1983). Another goal is to help trainees develop skills in diagnosing and dealing with organizational problems. Although the problem-solving case study is a popular management training method, some doubt its effectiveness (Argyris, 1980; Campbell, Dunnette, Lawler, & Weick, 1970), specifically whether the learning from the hypothetical situation transfers well to actual management situations.

role playing
a management training exercise that requires trainees to act out problem situations that often occur at work

An extension of this method is to have trainees engage in **role playing** a certain management situation. For example, in a role-playing exercise to develop managers' abilities to handle difficult interpersonal situations, a trainer may play a subordinate who has chronic performance problems. The trainee plays the manager, and the trainer may later offer feedback concerning how the situation was handled. In role playing the basic idea is that trainees will become more involved in a problem situation if they act it out. Sometimes, participants will reverse roles to gain a different perspective on the problem situation. A beneficial side effect of role playing may be that management trainees simultaneously learn to develop their presentational and communication skills.

management games
a management training technique using scaled-down enactments of the operations and managements of organizations.

Another management training technique is **management games**, which are usually scaled-down enactments of the management of organizations. They are in many ways similar to some of the more complicated board games that people play at home. In certain management games, participants are presented with a hypothetical organization, budget, and other resources. Various rules and procedures govern the game play. The goal is to make management decisions that will maximize the organization's outcomes, usually expressed in terms of profits. Participants may play either in groups, forming management teams to compete against other teams, or against one another individually. As with case studies, the difficulty is in generalizing learning from the game situation to the actual work setting. Also, participants may become so caught up in the game that they do not comprehend the management principles that are being taught. A review of research on management games, however, indicates that they are an effective management training technique, and predicts that the use of management games in training will increase in the future (Keys & Wolfe, 1990).

One example of a management game is called the "Organization Game" (Miles & Randolph, 1985), which involves an imaginary organization composed of four divisions, with each division containing one or more basic operating units. Each operating unit is responsible for certain organizational tasks (see Figure 5.2). There are three operating units that are responsible for production, with other units responsible for accounting, information processing and organizational communication, management consultation, and human resources. Before play in the Organization Game begins, eight players are chosen to serve as the supervisors for each of the eight operating units. These unit heads in turn are responsible for staffing their respective units, choosing their staff from among the remaining players. The main objectives for each player in the Organization Game are to achieve personal goals, to aid the assigned unit in achieving its operating goals, and to help the organization as a whole be successful. Player-employees can be transferred to other units or terminated, or they can ban together and organize a strike. Participating in complex simulations like the Organization Game may help potential managers to understand the complicated structure and various functions of organizations, as well as help them become more effective in dealing with employees.

Another management training technique is the **conference**, or *group discussion*. Conferences usually involve a very unstructured type of training in which participants are brought together to share ideas and information and solve some shared management problems. The basic goal of conferences is for practicing managers to learn effective management techniques that have been used by other managers. Their main advantage is that they encourage individual participation in the learning process. As mentioned, full-scale training programs usually include a number of training methods. This is particularly true in management training, in which trainees may attend workshops lasting several days, with participants exposed to training in a variety of areas, including problem solving, decision making, and interpersonal skills, using a number of techniques.

An increasingly popular training program for new managers that combines elements of on-the-job training and a sort of informal "apprenticeship" is **mentoring**, a process by which an inexperienced worker develops a relationship with an experienced worker to promote the former's career development. Much of the learning that takes place in these relationships involves the protégé attempting to imitate the mentor's work and interpersonal style. Modeling thus appears to be one key learning process in

conference
an unstructured management training technique in which participants share ideas, information, and problems; also called a group discussion

mentoring
a training program in which an inexperienced worker develops a relationship with an experienced worker who serves as an advisor

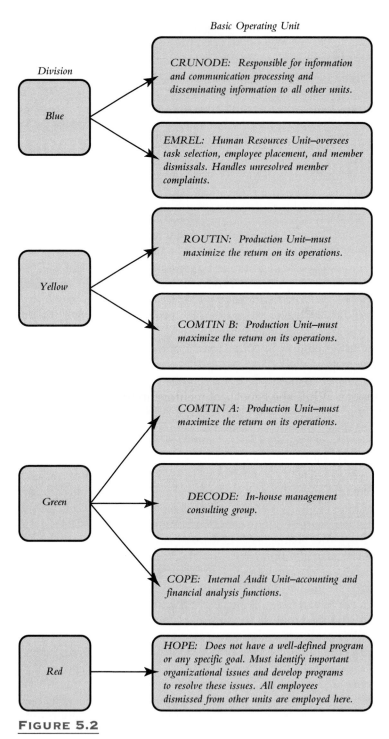

FIGURE 5.2

Operating Units for the Management Simulation Called the Organization Game.

mentoring. Mentoring among managers in large organizations is becoming more and more common as young, inexperienced workers typically look to older, more experienced workers to help them to "learn the ropes" of the job (Kram & Hall, 1989). It has even been suggested that women executives will have difficulty moving up the corporate ladder unless they receive some mentoring from higher ups (Ragins, 1989).

Since its appearance as a formal training strategy in the late 1970s (Roche, 1979), there has been extensive research, as well as popular interest, in mentoring as a management training and development technique. While early research on mentoring touted its many benefits, more recent research has discovered that for mentoring to be effective a number of variables must be considered. For example, research shows that while protégés receive support and encouragement from mentors, mentors are not necessarily helpful in influencing protégé career advancement (Noe, 1988; Ostroff & Kozlowski, 1993). Research has also indicated that a number of factors may influence workers' willingness to serve as mentors. For instance, managers are more willing to mentor newer workers if those workers show greater promise and if they are more similar to the mentor in terms of factors such as educational background (Burke, McKeen, & McKenna, 1993; Olian, Carroll, & Giannantonio, 1993). Gender may also play a part in willingness to mentor (Ragins & Cotton, 1993), with women less likely than men to volunteer as mentors, particularly if the protégé is a man.

Mentoring as a management development technique is quite popular in organizations today. While the benefits of mentorship to protégés are obvious, there are also some payoffs for the mentor and for the organization (Fagenson, 1989). The mentor, who may be at a midlife career standstill, may become energized by the chance to assist in the development of an eager young worker's career. The organization also benefits, since mentoring leads to a more well-trained and satisfied young workforce. On the other hand, mentors may find mentoring time-consuming and burdensome (Ragins, 1989; Ragins & Scandura, 1993). Protégés may also react negatively if they feel "forced" into participating in mentorship programs (Chao, Walz, & Gardner, 1992; Gunn, 1995).

Give three examples each of off-site and on-site employee training methods.

IMPLEMENTATION OF THE TRAINING PROGRAM

Once the training materials and methods have been selected and pilot tested, the next step in the training model is the implementation of the training program. When implementing the training program, factors such as trainee readiness, trainee expectations, and the climate for training—whether the employees and the organization feel positively about the training and encourage it—need to be considered. It is also important to provide trainees with a "rationale" for training—to let them know how the training will benefit them and the organization (Quinones, 1997). As training progresses, it is important that trainees be given feedback about their learning and opportunities to practice newly learned techniques or behaviors.

EVALUATION OF THE TRAINING PROGRAM

A crucial component of any employee training program is the evaluation of training effectiveness, for there is no use in investing money and resources in training programs unless they do indeed work. In spite of its importance, however, relatively few programs are actually subjected to rigorous evaluation (Goldstein, 1993).

The evaluation of a training program should first outline the criteria that indicate the program's success and develop the means for measuring these criteria. One framework suggests that there are four types of criteria for evaluating a program's effectiveness (Kirkpatrick, 1959–60; Latham & Saari, 1979):

1. *Reaction criteria*—measures of the impressions of trainees, including their assessments of the program's value, the amount of learning they received, and their enjoyment of the program. Reaction criteria are usually assessed via training evaluation rating surveys given to trainees immediately after training sessions or workshops. It is important to note that reaction criteria do not measure whether any learning has taken place. Rather, they assess trainees' opinions about the training and their learning.

2. *Learning criteria*—measures of the amount of learning that has taken place. Typically, these take the form of some sort of tests assessing the amount of information retained from the program.

3. *Behavioral criteria*—measures of the amount of newly learned skills displayed once the trainee has returned to the job. Observational methods of measurement are typically used to assess behavioral criteria, with supervisors recording the use of newly learned behaviors.

4. *Results criteria*—measures the outcomes that are important to the organization, such as increased trainee work output as expressed by production rates, dollar sales figures, or quality of work. Using the results criteria, a cost-benefit analysis can be performed by comparing the costs of the program to the dollar value of the results. This is usually the most important evaluation of a program's effectiveness. However, it is sometimes difficult to translate training outcomes into dollars and cents. For example, if one of the goals is to improve employee attitudes, it may be very hard to place a dollar value on such results.

The important question in the evaluation of programs is whether any measured changes in criteria are indeed the result of training. The methods used in the proper evaluation of a training program are those used to determine the effectiveness of any other type of program introduced into an organization. For a formal evaluation to demonstrate conclusively that training has caused certain outcomes, it should be based on experimental designs. Unfortunately, many evaluations use what might be called "preexperimental designs," which do not allow for proper assessments (Campbell & Stanley, 1963). One example, the **posttest only design**, simply measures criteria

posttest only design
a program evaluation that simply measures training success criterion following completion of the training program

following the completion of a training program. However, this does not tell us anything conclusive about its effectiveness because we have no basis for any sort of comparison.

A **pretest-posttest design**—measuring behavior before and after training—is also an inadequate experimental design. Although this approach compares the criterion measures collected before and after the training program, we cannot be sure that the differences from pretest to posttest were due to the program. Consider the example of a training program designed to teach bank tellers to be more friendly and attentive to customer needs. With a simple pretest-posttest evaluation we can never be sure that later observed increases in the quality of customer service were due to training or to other factors, such as a recent pay raise or change in management. Although these limited designs do not allow us to draw clear conclusions, even such limited evaluations are better than no evaluation at all (Sackett & Mullen, 1993).

To be sure of the effectiveness of a training program, one should apply a more sophisticated, true experimental design that uses at least one treatment group, which receives the training, and one control group, which does not undergo any training. The simplest and most common experimental design for evaluation research uses one training group and one control group, both of which are measured before and after the program. To ensure that there are no unexpected differences in members of the training and control groups, employees are randomly assigned to the two groups. The pretest and posttest scores are then compared. This experimental design makes it clear that any positive changes in the criterion measures of the training group, relative to the control group, are most likely due to the training program.

A more sophisticated experimental design is the **Solomon four-group design** (Solomon, 1949). This method of evaluation uses four groups, two that are trained and two that are not. In the Solomon design, two of the groups are identical to those in the basic experimental design mentioned above. That is, one training group and one control group are measured both before and after the training program. However, the additional training and control groups are measured only *after* the program, which is intended to help rule out the fact that administering a pretraining measure might sensitize employees to what the program is designed to do and might thus produce certain changes in the criterion measures that occur without the benefit of training. For example, if our bank tellers are given a pretraining test of their customer service knowledge, they might realize that management is very interested in this issue, which might cause all tellers to give greater attention to customers, regardless of whether they later receive customer service training. Although the Solomon four-group design is an effective design for evaluating training programs, it is underused, primarily because of the large number of participants and groups required (Braver & Braver, 1988). Figure 5.3 summarizes the various evaluation designs.

A comprehensive evaluation of a training program must be well-designed and executed to ensure that the training is indeed effective. This

pretest-posttest design
a design for evaluating a training program that makes comparisons of criterion measures collected before and after the introduction of the program

Solomon four-group design
a method of program evaluation using two treatment groups and two control groups

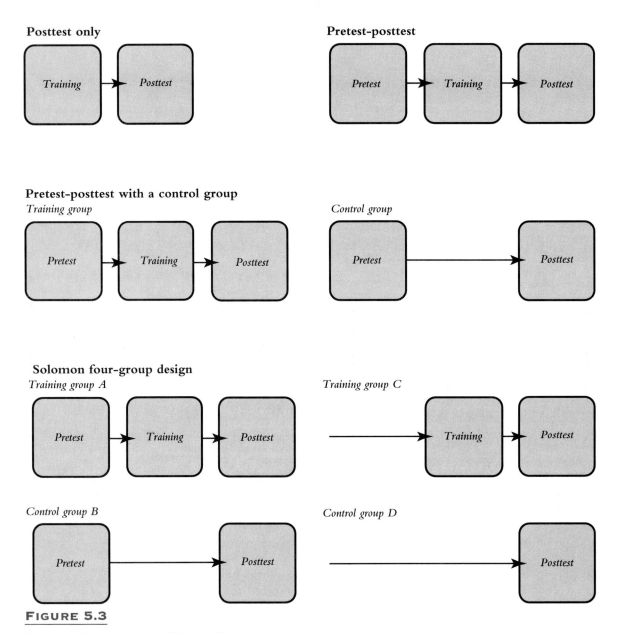

FIGURE 5.3

Four Methods for Evaluation of Training Programs.

means careful consideration must be given to the selection and measurement of criteria, an experimental design with adequate control groups must be used, and the costs versus benefits of the program must be assessed (see, e.g., Arvey, Maxwell, & Salas, 1992).

An obvious problem in evaluating the effectiveness of training programs is the inability to use a true experimental design due to constraints imposed by the particular work organizations. But there is another alternative—what are called *quasi-experimental designs* (Campbell & Stanley, 1963; Cook, Campbell, & Peracchio, 1991). Quasi-experiments are approximations of experimental designs. One example is the *nonequivalent control group design*. This design is typically used when it is impossible to assign trainees randomly to experimental and control groups. A nonequivalent control group might consist of similar employees from another company location that is not undergoing the new training program. The training and control group are "nonequivalent" because they may differ systematically on variables, such as experience, previous training, supervisory methods, or any other factor that would be controlled for via random assignment in a true experimental design.

Diversity and Equal Employment Opportunity Issues in Employee Training

There is no doubt about it, the workforce in the U.S., and in many other nations, is becoming more and more diverse. Increased participation of women, ethnic minorities, and people with disabilities in the workforce requires some concern on the part of organizations to assist workers in dealing with this diversity. More and more companies are sponsoring programs to promote awareness of cultural diversity and to facilitate intercultural relationships on the job. For example, glass products manufacturer Corning, Inc., has implemented regular "race and gender awareness" training programs (Hall & Parker, 1993). The Hong Kong Bank and the Bank of Montreal have longstanding training programs to deal with issues related to gender, racial, and cultural diversity (Tung, 1997).

Another topical training issue involves increasing awareness of sexual harassment in the workplace. Highly publicized cases of sexual harassment in corporations (Boeing Aircraft, Mitsubishi), in the government (the confirmation hearings for Supreme Court Justice Clarence Thomas; allegations against former Oregon Senator Robert Packwood and President Bill Clinton), and in the military (the U.S. Navy's Tailhook incident) have brought this issue to the public's attention. Research evidence suggests that sexual harassment in the workplace is both widespread, and is affected by the organizational culture and climate (Fitzgerald, Drasgow, Hulin, Gelfland, & Magley, 1997). As a result, a majority of U.S. companies have developed training programs designed to reduce sexual harassment in the workplace. Many of these programs focus on increasing awareness of harassing behavior (e.g., Blakely, Blakely, & Moorman, 1998) and trying to

Training requirements should not exclude employees on the basis of gender or ethnicity.

neutralize situations and "cultures" that promote or allow sexual harassment. Nevertheless, despite the increase in the number of these programs, there has been little sound evaluation research exploring their effectiveness (Lengnick-Hall, 1995). In sum, training programs for special groups, or for special organizational needs, are likely to become more and more commonplace in the future.

Because training is linked to job performance and can lead to personnel actions such as pay increases, promotions, and terminations, several equal employment opportunity concerns are related to personnel training (Russell, 1984). One such issue deals with educational or training prerequisites for certain jobs. Because members of underprivileged groups are likely to have less education and formal job training than members of more privileged groups, setting certain levels of education or training as job prerequisites may be considered discriminatory. As mentioned in Chapter 4, equal employment opportunity legislation protects against discrimination against specific groups in providing access to jobs. If access to some jobs requires certain training, employers must take steps to guard against any discrimination in this area by providing remedial education or training for groups of workers who lack the educational prerequisites. For example, some employers are supporting agencies that will train chronically unemployed or underemployed individuals in basic job skills either by making financial contributions or by hiring persons who have undergone the training.

The methods used in employee training programs may also create instances of potential discrimination. For example, the lectures offered in many seminar programs may lead to different rates of learning in different groups of trainees. If certain underprivileged groups lack the education needed to process the information and to perform well on any examinations administered, using the results of such training classes to screen or place workers can lead to unintentional discrimination. A similar case occurs in training courses that require certain strenuous activities, such as lifting and carrying heavy materials, in which women may be at some disadvantage. One example was a training course for firefighters that demanded that trainees lift and carry a 150-pound dummy over their shoulders for several yards or down a flight of stairs to simulate carrying an unconscious person from a burning building. A question arose as to whether this part of the course discriminated against women. Critics stated that firefighters rarely carried a person out of a burning building, and that the ability to do this was not a critical requirement for adequate performance of their job. Because of the possibility of discrimination and because the fire department could not prove that this was a necessary skill for the position, the training task was eliminated.

Similarly, organizations that require workers to attend and complete some type of training program to gain a position or a promotion must demonstrate that completion of the program is predictive of success in the jobs that trainees will be holding. If not, there is the possibility that certain disadvantaged groups of trainees may not do as well in the program because of unfamiliarity with the training procedures and format. In other words, because of their lack of experience with the classroom situation, they may not learn as well as members of the majority group, which can lead to discrimination. For example, if being promoted to a front-line supervisory position in a factory requires attending classes in supervisory skills and passing an examination to complete the course, the organization must prove that completion of the training is related to later success as a supervisor and that the program itself does not discriminate in terms of ability to pass the course. In these cases, the training program is just like any other selection tool. It must be shown to be valid, fair, and job-related.

Illustrate the four types of criteria for evaluating employee training programs.

ON THE CUTTING EDGE

Organizational Learning: Setting a Companywide Climate for Enhanced Learning

In recent years, there has been increasing attention given to setting an organizationwide "climate" to encourage learning and innovation in the workplace (Dodgson, 1993; Quinones, 1997). Many theorists are talking about what are called "learning organizations" (Garvin, 1993; Schein, 1993). Examples of organizations that have been successful in creating a positive learning climate range from Xerox to Home Depot to the San Diego Zoo (McGill & Slocum, 1993).

One model states that learning organizations are skilled at several learning activities, including: systematic problem solving, experimentation with new approaches, ability to learn from the past experiences of the organization and from the experiences of other organizations, and the ability to transfer knowledge quickly throughout the organization (Garvin, 1993).

Most of the models of learning organizations treat companies as learning entities, and all models follow the basic approach used in all areas of organizational training, including a strong emphasis on objective evaluation of learning outcomes. In a sense, the notion of learning organizations is similar to another approach that focuses on improving an organization's ability to change and adapt: the area known as organizational development, a topic that we will discuss in detail in Chapter 14.

Summary

Employee training is a planned effort by an organization to facilitate the learning, retention, and transfer of job-related behavior. Training is not limited to new employees, but often involves various types of training and development programs offered throughout an employee's career. Specific areas of employee training include: new employee orientation, employee retraining and continuing education, retirement planning and career development, and worker training for international business.

An understanding of learning theories is fundamental in the design of employee training programs. Basic *learning* theories describe how learning takes place in employee training: *classical conditioning*, which involves the paired association of two events; *operant conditioning*, which is learning that occurs as a result of reinforcement or punishment for specific behaviors; *modeling*, which is imitative learning; and *cognitive theories* of learning, which emphasize humans as information processors. The concept of modeling is expressed in *social learning theory*, which holds that for learning to take place, attention must first be focused on a model's behavior and there must be some retention and motor reproduction of the behavior, as well as some motivation for performing the behavior.

If training programs are to be successful, a number of key issues will impact their effectiveness. For example, *transfer of training*, or how the learning translates into use of the newly learned behaviors, and the job characteristics of the trainees, such as *trainee readiness*, must be taken into account. Finally, concern must be given to how training programs are structured and how they are conducted.

The first step in a successful employee training program is assessing training needs, which occurs on several levels. *Organizational analysis* considers the organization's goals, resources, and the climate for training; *task analysis* evaluates the specific knowledge, skills, and abilities that a job requires; and *person analysis* examines the capabilities and deficiencies of the workers themselves. Training needs may also have to be conducted through *demographic analysis*, which is targeted toward assessing the training needs of specific groups, such as males versus females or the old versus the young. The second step involves establishing training objectives, while the third step focuses on employee training methods. The various training methods can be broken down into two general categories: on-site methods and off-site methods. Of on-site methods, *on-the-job training* is the most widely used, consisting of putting inexperienced workers into the work site under the direction of an experienced teacher-worker. *Apprenticeship* is a much more long-term on-site method, combining classroom training with supervised on-the-job training. *Vestibule training* sets up a model training area adjacent to the actual work site, using professional trainers and hands-on experience. *Job rotation* is a training technique designed to broaden workers' experience by rotating employees among various jobs.

Off-site methods include the common *seminar* method and *audiovisual instruction* that provides graphic depictions of work activities. A technique that uses aspects of both audiovisual technology and concepts of social learning theory is *behavior modeling training*, a method of exposing trainees to videotapes of models engaged in appropriate work behaviors and then having them practice the observed behaviors. *Simulation techniques* involve classroom replications of actual work stations. *Programmed instruction* is a form of self-paced training in which workers can learn at their own pace. A modern, sophisticated version of programmed instruction is *computer-assisted instruction (CAI)*.

Several specific methods and techniques used in management training include *problem-solving case studies*, *role playing*, and *management games*, which all involve simulations of actual management situations. *Conferences*, where participants share ideas or solve shared management problems, are another management training method. *Mentoring* is a management training program in which an inexperienced worker is assigned to an experienced mentor who serves as a role model.

Once training programs have been implemented, the evaluation of their effectiveness is very important. The first step in evaluation is to determine criteria of training effectiveness. Four types are typically used: *reaction criteria*, *learning criteria*, *behavioral criteria*, and *results criteria*. Once the criteria are established, basic research methods and design should be used to evaluate the training programs. The *pretest-posttest design* is a common but inadequate means of assessing a program in which measures of criteria are collected both before and after a training intervention, allowing for a comparison of changes in learning or work behaviors. However, this method is inadequate because of the lack of a good comparison group. Better evaluation designs use both a training group and a comparison, or control, group that is not subjected to the training program. A very complex and sophisticated evaluation design is the *Solomon four-group design*, which uses two training groups and two control groups.

Finally, employee diversity and certain legal issues must be considered in the design and implementation of training programs. In our increasingly diverse workforce, workers should be trained for sensitivity to members of other cultures and to eliminate instances of sexual harassment. Training or educational prerequisites and the training programs themselves must not unfairly discriminate on the basis of ethnicity, age, sex, or disability.

Study Questions and Exercises

1. Consider the basic learning theories: classical conditioning, operant conditioning, modeling or social learning, and cognitive theories. How is each involved in the type of learning that takes place in work organizations? How do they relate to learning in college classrooms?

2. Consider a work organization that you have had some contact with, either one in which you were employed or in which a friend or relative is working. Based on your knowledge, how might a training needs assessment be conducted? Consider all four levels of assessment: organizational, task, person, and demographic analysis.

3. Compare and contrast the advantages and disadvantages of on-site versus off-site training methods.

4. Consider the various designs for evaluating personnel training programs. Although the more complex and sophisticated designs usually

provide better evaluation, what are some of the difficulties of conducting an assessment in actual work organizations?

5. Review the discussion of EEO issues in personnel training. What are the
various ways that training programs could discriminate against members
of protected groups (ethnic minorities, women, people with disabilities,
the elderly)?

Suggested Readings

Goldstein, I. L. (1992). *Training in organizations: Needs assessment, development, and evaluation* (3rd ed.). Monterey, CA: Brooks/Cole. *A classic textbook containing just about everything that you would want to know about
personnel training.*

Ford, J.K., Kozlowski, S.W.J., Kraiger, K., Salas, E., & Teachout, M.S.
(Eds.) (1997). *Improving training effectiveness in organizations.* Hillsdale, NJ:
Lawrence Erlbaum.

Quinones, M.A., & Ehrenstein, A. (Eds.), (1997). *Training for a rapidly
changing workplace: Applications of psychological research.* Washington, DC:
American Psychological Association.

*These two edited volumes represent a good cross-section of research on em-
ployee training and development by leading scholars in the field.*

EVALUATING EMPLOYEE PERFORMANCE

This chapter looks at how employees' job performance is measured and appraised in organizations. Because job performance is such an important outcome variable in I/O psychology, it is important to understand the measurement issues concerning this factor. For example, when reviewing studies that discuss influences on job performance, you should investigate how performance was operationally defined and measured. Were objective or subjective criteria used? How accurate or inaccurate might the assessments of performance be? How can performance assessments and appraisals be improved?

In addition, this is the last chapter in our discussion of personnel processes. Performance appraisals are often used as the crucial outcome for other personnel procedures, such as determining the effectiveness of an employee screening, testing, and/or selection program. Appraisals of employee job performance are also involved in determining the effectiveness of employee training programs. By now, you should see how these various personnel processes fit together.

INSIDE
TIPS

Job Performance and Performance Appraisals

Once a job applicant has been hired and trained, the next logical step in the personnel process is evaluating the new worker's performance. The evaluation of employees' job performance is a vital personnel function and of critical importance to the organization.

In this chapter, we will consider the very important variable of job performance in the context of assessments and evaluations. We will discuss the importance of performance appraisals, procedures for appraising performance, and the difficulties encountered in attempting to appraise performance. We will also look at research on performance appraisals and assessment, and discuss the legal concerns in performance appraisals.

Purposes of Performance Appraisals

performance appraisals
the formalized means of assessing worker performance in comparison to certain established organizational standards

In work organizations, measurement of performance typically takes place in the context of formalized **performance appraisals**, which measure worker performance in comparison to certain predetermined standards. Performance appraisals serve many purposes for the individual worker, for the worker's supervisor, and for the organization as a whole (Cleveland, Murphy, & Williams, 1989).

For the worker, performance appraisals are linked to career advancement. Performance appraisals function as the foundation for pay increases and promotions, provide feedback to help improve performance and recognize weaknesses, and offer information about the attainment of work goals. Work supervisors use performance appraisals to make personnel decisions such as promotions, demotions, pay raises, and firings, and to give workers constructive feedback to improve work performance. Moreover, the formal performance appraisal procedure facilitates organizational communication by helping to encourage interaction between workers and supervisors. For the organization, performance appraisals provide a means of assessing the productivity of individuals and work units (see Table 6.1).

Performance assessments can also serve as a basis for evaluating the effectiveness of organizational programs or changes, such as changes in work design or systems, supervisors, or working conditions. As we saw in Chapter 4, the measurement of performance serves as our criterion measure to determine if employee screening and selection procedures are working. In other words, by assessing new workers' performance at some point after they are hired, organizations can determine if the predictors of job performance do indeed predict success on the job. Measurement of performance is also important in determining the effectiveness of employee training programs, and information from performance appraisals can also play a role in determining the training needs of organizational members, as we saw in Chapter 5.

TABLE 6.1

The Many Purposes of Performance Appraisals

For the Worker:

means of reinforcement (praise, pay raises)
career advancement (promotions, increased responsibility)
information about work goal attainment
source of feedback to improve performance

For the Supervisor:

basis for making personnel decisions (promotions, firings, etc.)
assessment of workers' goal attainment
opportunity to provide constructive feedback to workers
opportunity to interact with subordinates

For the Organization:

assessment of productivity of individuals and work units
validation of personnel selection and placement methods
means for recognizing and motivating workers
source of information for personnel training needs
evaluation of the effectiveness of organizational interventions (e.g., training programs, system changes, etc.)

The Measurement of Job Performance

As we have seen, job performance is one of the most important work outcomes. It is the variable in organizations that is most often measured and that is given the most attention. This makes sense, since the success or failure of an organization depends on the performance of its employees.

There are many ways to measure job performance. Yet, as we saw in our discussion of personnel selection in Chapter 4, I/O psychologists typically refer to measures of job performance as performance criteria (Austin & Villanova, 1992). **Performance criteria** are the means of determining successful or unsuccessful performance. As we saw in Chapter 3, performance criteria are one of the products that arise from a detailed job analysis, for once the specific elements of a job are known, it is easier to develop the means to assess levels of successful or unsuccessful performance.

performance criteria
measures used to determine successful and unsuccessful job performance

STOP AND REVIEW

Describe nine purposes of performance appraisals.

OBJECTIVE VS. SUBJECTIVE PERFORMANCE CRITERIA

One important categorization of job performance assessments is to distinguish between *objective* and *subjective* measures of job performance. Objective and subjective performance criteria are also sometimes referred to as

objective performance criteria
measures of job performance that are easily quantified

"hard" and "soft" performance criteria, respectively (Smith, 1976). **Objective performance criteria** involve the measurement of some easily quantifiable aspects of job performance, such as the number of units produced, the dollar amount of sales, or the time needed to process some information. For example, an objective criterion for an assembly-line worker might be the number of products assembled. For an insurance claims adjuster, the average amount of time it takes to process a claim might be an objective measure of performance (see Table 6.2). Such criteria are often referred to as measures of productivity.

subjective performance criteria
measures of job performance that typically consist of ratings or judgments of performance

Subjective performance criteria consist of judgments or ratings made by some knowledgeable individual, such as a worker's supervisor or coworker. These criteria are often used when objective criteria are unavailable, difficult to assess, or inappropriate. For example, it is usually inappropriate to use objective performance criteria to assess a manager's job, since it is difficult to specify the exact behaviors that indicate successful managerial performance. Instead subjective criteria, such as subordinate or superior ratings, are used.

Objective performance criteria offer two main advantages. First, because objective criteria typically involve counts of output or the timing of

TABLE 6.2

Examples of Objective Job Performance Criteria

Job Title	Measure
Typist	Lines per week
Logger	Cords (of wood) cut; weight of wood legally hauled
Keypuncher	Number of characters; number of errors
Service representative	Errors in processing customer orders
Toll collector	Dollar accuracy/axle accuracy
Clerk	Errors per 100 documents checked; number of documents processed
Wood harvester	Number of cords delivered
Tree planter	Bags of tree seedlings planted
Skateboard maker	Number produced; number rejected
Sewing machine operator	Minutes per operation
Dentist	Errors in reading radiographs
Inspector	Errors detected in finished product
Tool/die maker	Dies produced
Helicopter pilot	Deviations from proper instrument readings
Bank teller	Number of shortages; number of overages
Air traffic controller	Speed of movement of aircraft through the system; correction of pilot error; errors in positioning aircraft for final approach; errors in aircraft separation

Source: F. J. Landy and J. L. Farr, *The Measurement of Work Performance: Methods, Theory, and Applications* (New York: Academic Press, 1983).

tasks, they are less prone to bias and distortion than subjective performance ratings. Second, objective criteria are usually more directly tied to "bottom line" assessments of an organization's success, such as the number of products assembled or dollar sales figures. It is often more difficult to determine the links between subjective criteria and bottom line outcomes.

As mentioned, it is often difficult, if not impossible, to obtain objective performance criteria for certain jobs, such as graphic artist, copy writer, and executive vice president. Jobs such as these may best be assessed through ratings or judgments. Another drawback of objective assessments is that they may focus too much on specific, quantifiable outcomes. Because many jobs are complex, looking at only one or two objective measures of performance may not capture the total picture of performance. Some aspects of job performance such as work quality, worker initiative, and work effort are difficult to assess objectively. For example, a salesperson might have high dollar sales figures, but may be so pushy and manipulative that customers are unlikely to return to the store. Likewise, a machinist may have relatively low output rates because he spends a great deal of time teaching new workers valuable work techniques and helping coworkers solve performance problems. In many cases, collecting objective performance data is time-consuming and costly (although see On the Cutting Edge). By contrast, subjective performance criteria are usually easy and relatively inexpensive to obtain and thus may be the preferred method of assessment for many organizations. Moreover, subjective performance criteria can be used to assess variables that could not be measured objectively, such as employee motivation or "team spirit."

Regardless of the criteria used to evaluate performance of a job, there are a number of important criterion concerns or issues that have implications for conducting accurate performance appraisals (Bernardin & Beatty, 1984). A primary issue is whether the criteria identified in the job analysis relate to the true nature of the job. A particular concern here is **criterion relevance**: the notion that the means of appraising performance is indeed pertinent to job success, as identified in the job analysis. A performance appraisal should cover only the specific KSAOs needed to perform a job successfully. For example, the performance criteria for a bookkeeper should deal with knowledge of accounting procedures, mathematical skills, and producing work that is neat and error-free, not with personal appearance or oral communication skills—factors that are clearly not relevant to the effective performance of a bookkeeper's job. However, for a public relations representative, personal appearance and communication skills may be relevant performance criteria.

A related concern is **criterion contamination**: the extent to which performance appraisals contain elements that detract from the accurate assessment of job effectiveness—elements that should not be included in the performance assessment. A common source of criterion contamination stems from appraiser biases. For example, a supervisor may give an employee an overly positive performance appraisal because the employee has a reputation of past work success or because the employee was a

criterion relevance the extent to which the means of appraising performance is pertinent to job success

criterion contamination the extent to which performance appraisals contain elements that detract from the accurate assessment of job effectiveness

Compare and contrast objective and subjective performance criteria and give examples of each.

criterion deficiency
the degree to which a criterion falls short of measuring job performance

criterion usefulness
the extent to which a performance criterion is usable in appraising a particular job

graduate of a prestigious university. Criterion contamination can also result from extraneous factors that contribute to a worker's apparent success or failure in a job. For instance, a sales manager may receive a poor performance appraisal because of low sales levels, even though the poor sales actually result from the fact that the manager supervises a young, inexperienced sales force.

It is unlikely that any criterion will capture job performance perfectly; every criterion of job performance may fall short of measuring performance to some extent. **Criterion deficiency** describes the degree to which a criterion falls short of measuring job performance perfectly. Criterion deficiency occurs when the measurement of the performance criteria is incomplete. An important goal of performance appraisals is to choose criteria that optimize the assessment of job success, thereby keeping criterion deficiency to a minimum.

A final concern is **criterion usefulness**, or the extent to which a performance criterion is usable in appraising a particular job in an organization. To be useful, a criterion should be relatively easy and cost-effective to measure and should be seen as relevant by the appraiser, the employee whose performance is being appraised, and the management of the organization.

ON THE CUTTING EDGE

The Boss Is Watching: Electronic Monitoring of Employee Performance

Obtaining hard, objective measures of job performance has often been a difficult and time-consuming process, requiring direct observation and the tallying of employee work behaviors by managers. However, in recent years, as more and more workers go "on-line," using computers to perform many activities, it is becoming easier and easier for organizations to obtain objective measures of employee productivity (Aiello, 1993; Botan, 1996). This is especially true when a number of individual terminals are tied into a central computer or phone system. This makes it relatively easy for employers to monitor employees' e-mail and voice mail messages. In addition, employers are increasingly using videotape surveillance to keep tabs on employee performance. A recent survey of nearly one thousand U.S. employers found that more than 35 percent of them used electronic surveillance of employee performance (Silverstein, 1997).

Various computer programs allow an employer to monitor directly the amount and type of computer activities that each employee is engaged in throughout the day. This is particularly true for jobs involving information processing, and for service jobs in which all customer activities are recorded on computer files. For example, employees in the collections department of a credit card company must maintain computer-

At some companies employees using computer terminals are monitored directly through the computer network—a practice that raises questions about workers' rights to privacy.

ON THE CUTTING EDGE (*continued*)

ized records of phone calls, correspondence, and other activity for all accounts. The computerized monitoring system allows supervisors to note the number and length of calls to each account as well as the amount of money collected. Supervisors receive a detailed weekly report of employee computer activities that give a good indication of how the workers spent their time. A hard measure of employee performance is obtained from the amount of money collected from each account.

In some companies and some jobs, this kind of monitoring system is not new. For years, retail employees have had their sales activities monitored through cash register records (Botan, 1996). What is new, however, is the computer's ability to record a number of work-related activities for several employees simultaneously and to present this information quickly in some summary form. Supervisors are usually given several kinds of breakdowns, providing detailed listings of each employee's activities and making comparisons among employees.

While computerized monitoring can lead to more objective assessments of employee performance, workers have raised certain objections. Some have argued that computer monitoring focuses only on those behaviors that are easily quan-

tified, such as time engaged in a particular activity or dollar sales figures, but ignores measures of quality. Another important consideration is the protection of employees' rights to privacy (Botan, 1996). There is some question as to when employer monitoring of work activities begins to infringe on the employees' freedom to conduct work activities in a manner they see fit (Chalykoff & Kochan, 1989). A related problem is that employee creativity and innovation in work methods may be stifled if the workers know that work activities are being monitored.

Recent research has begun to investigate the effects of computerized monitoring on employee performance with controlled experiments (e.g., Aiello & Kolb, 1995; Stanton & Barnes-Farrell, 1996). Much of this research suggests that giving employees feedback about the performance monitoring, and allowing workers a "voice" in the performance monitoring program through having workers participate in setting their performance goals, alleviates many of the "negatives" associated with computerized monitoring (Aiello & Shao, 1993; Nebeker & Tatum, 1993). In any case, computerized monitoring is here to stay and, as systems become more sophisticated, is likely to increase even more in the future.

SOURCES OF PERFORMANCE RATINGS

Because performance ratings play such an important role in performance assessment in organizations, a great deal of research in personnel processes has focused on the process and methods of rating performance. Before we examine the various methods of rating job performance, we need to consider *who*

STOP AND REVIEW

Define four important criterion concerns in performance appraisals.

How would the performance of this artisan best be assessed?

is doing the rating. In the vast majority of cases, it is the immediate supervisor who rates the performance of subordinates (Jacobs, 1986). However, performance appraisals can also be made by a worker's peers, by subordinates, by the worker himself/herself, or even by customers evaluating the performance of a service worker. The obvious advantage of getting these different perspectives on performance assessment is that each type of appraiser—supervisor, self, peer, subordinate, and customer—may see a different aspect of the worker's performance, and thus may offer unique perspectives. Moreover, multiple perspective performance appraisals have increased reliability (there are more raters evaluating the same performance behaviors), and an increased sense of fairness and greater acceptance by the worker being evaluated (Harris & Schaubroeck, 1988).

Supervisor appraisals

By far, most performance appraisals are done by supervisors. In fact, conducting regular appraisals of employee performance is considered one of the most important supervisory functions. Supervisor performance appraisals are so common because supervisors are usually quite knowledgeable about the job requirements, because supervisors are often in a position to provide rewards for effective performance (and suggestions for improvement for substandard performance), and because supervisors typically have a great deal of contact with supervisees. This is probably why research has consistently demonstrated that supervisory ratings have higher reliability than either peer or subordinate ratings of performance (Conway & Huffcutt, 1996; Viswesvaran, Ones & Schmidt, 1996). Still, supervisors may have a limited perspective on employees' performance, so appraisals from other organizational members are important.

Self-appraisals

Self-appraisals of performance have been used by many companies, usually in conjunction with supervisor appraisals. Although there is evidence that self-appraisals correlate slightly with supervisor performance appraisals, self-appraisals tend to be more lenient and to focus more on effort exerted rather than on performance accomplishments (Wohlers, Hall, & London, 1993; Wohlers & London, 1989). Quite often, there are large discrepancies between how supervisors rate performance and the worker's self-rating (Furnham & Stringfield, 1994). It has been suggested that part of the discrepancy between self- and supervisor appraisals can be overcome if both the worker and the supervisor are thoroughly trained to understand how the performance rating system works (Schrader & Steiner, 1996; Williams & Levy, 1992). One advantage of appraisal discrepancies, however, may be that they highlight differences in supervisor and worker perceptions, and can lead to an open dialogue between supervisor and subordinate (Campbell & Lee, 1988). Self-appraisals of performance are also useful in encouraging workers to be committed to performance-related goals (Riggio & Cole, 1992).

While studies of U.S. workers have found that self-appraisals tend to be more lenient than supervisor performance ratings, a study of Chinese workers found that their appraisals showed a "modesty bias." That is, Chinese workers gave themselves lower ratings of job performance than did their supervisors (Farh, Dobbins, & Cheng, 1991). In comparison to U.S. workers, the self-appraisals of Chinese workers were substantially lower on average, indicating that the accuracy of self-appraisals and their discrepancy from supervisor ratings may need to be evaluated with culture taken into account.

Peer appraisals

Although the actual use of peer ratings of performance is quite rare, evidence indicates that there is good agreement between performance ratings made by peers and those made by supervisors (Conway & Huffcutt, 1996; Harris & Schaubroeck, 1988; Vance, MacCallum, Coovert, & Hedge, 1988). This makes sense since both supervisors and peers have the opportunity to directly observe workers on the job. One obvious problem with peer ratings of performance is the potential for conflict among employees who are evaluating each other, a particular problem when peers are competing for scarce job rewards (DeNisi, Randolph, & Blencoe, 1983; McEvoy & Buller, 1987).

With the increased emphasis on coordinated work teams, peer appraisals of performance may be of greater importance in the future. Moreover, research shows that supervisors tend to give some weight to peer appraisals, and will incorporate them into their own supervisory appraisals (Makiney & Levy, 1997).

Subordinate appraisals

Subordinate ratings are most commonly used to assess the effectiveness of persons in supervisory or leadership positions. Research on subordinate appraisals indicates considerable agreement with supervisor ratings (Mount, 1984; Riggio & Cole, 1992). Subordinate ratings may be particularly important because they provide a different, meaningful perspective on a supervisor's performance—the perspective of the persons being supervised—and because there is evidence that ratings of supervisors may be associated with subordinate job satisfaction (Mount, 1984; Riggio & Cole, 1992).

In general, supervisors and managers have been found to support the use of subordinate appraisals. In one study, it was found that supervisors were supportive of subordinate appraisals as a useful and positive source of data, except in situations when they are used as a basis for determining salary (Bernardin, Dahmus, & Redmon, 1993). The most positive attitudes expressed toward subordinate appraisals were from supervisory employees who received appraisal feedback from both subordinates and supervisors at the same time. Attitudes toward the use of subordinate appraisals were less positive and more cautious, however, when subordinate appraisal feedback was given to supervisors with no other sources of appraisal data. Thus, these findings suggest that how subordinate appraisals are used influences their effectiveness.

Customer appraisals

Another form of performance rating for employees working in customer service positions is ratings made by customers. Although customer ratings are not usually considered a method of performance appraisal, they can offer an interesting perspective on whether certain types of workers (salespersons, waitpersons, telephone operators) are doing a good job. Customer evaluations of an individual employee's performance are most appropriate when the employee and customer have a significant, ongoing relationship, such as customers evaluating a supplier, a sales representative, a real estate agent, a stockbroker, or the like. Interestingly, there is evidence that organizations that strongly encourage customer service, and those that train their employees in customer service delivery, tend to receive more favorable evaluations from customers (Johnson, 1996; Schneider & Bowen, 1995).

360-degree feedback

360-degree feedback
a method of gathering performance appraisals from a worker's supervisors, subordinates, peers, customers, and other relevant parties

An innovation that is gathering increased attention is the use of all levels of appraisals in what is commonly called **360-degree feedback** (London & Beatty, 1993; Waldman, Atwater, & Antonioni, 1998). In 360-degree feedback programs, performance ratings are gathered from supervisors, subordinates, peers, customers, and suppliers (if applicable). The obvious advantages of 360-degree feedback include improved reliability of measurement because of the multiple evaluations, the inclusion of more diverse perspectives on the employee's performance, the involvement of more organizational members in the evaluation and feedback process, and improved organizational communication. While 360-degree feedback programs may have distinct advantages, including enhanced development and improved performance of employees (London & Smither, 1995; Tornow, 1993), the costs of such detailed assessments of worker performance may be prohibitive. In addition, there have been recent calls for more research to demonstrate the advantages of 360-degree evaluations over less comprehensive and costly performance appraisal programs (Borman, 1998; Dunnette, 1993; Greguras & Robie, 1997).

Methods of Rating Performance

When it comes to subjectively evaluating employee performance, there are a variety of rating methods that can be used. We will review some of the more common methods. These methods can be classified into two general categories, those that can be termed "comparative methods" and those that can be labeled "individual methods."

COMPARATIVE METHODS

Comparative methods of performance appraisal involve some form of comparison of one worker's performance with the performance of others. These procedures are relatively easy to implement in work organizations, and include *rankings*, *paired comparisons*, and *forced distributions*.

comparative methods
performance appraisal methods involving comparisons of one worker's performance against that of other workers

Rankings

The comparative method of **rankings** requires supervisors to rank order their subordinates from best to worst on specific performance dimensions, or to give an overall comparative ranking on job performance. Although this is a simple and easy technique that supervisors are not likely to find difficult or time-consuming, it has several limitations. First, although ranking separates the best workers from the worst, there are no absolute standards of performance. This is a problem if few or none of the entire group of workers are performing at "acceptable" levels. In this case, being ranked second or third in a group of fifteen is misleading, because even the highest-ranking workers are performing at substandard levels. Conversely, in a group of exceptional workers, those ranked low may actually be outstanding performers in comparison to other employees in the organization or workers in other companies.

rankings
performance appraisal methods involving rank ordering of supervisees from best to worst

Paired comparisons

Another comparative method of performance appraisal uses **paired comparisons**, in which the rater compares each worker with every other worker in the group and then simply has to decide which of the pair is the better performer. Each person's final rank consists of the number of times that individual was chosen as the better of a pair. The drawbacks of this technique are similar to those of the ranking method. However, both these comparative techniques have the advantage of being simple to use and of being applicable to a variety of jobs.

paired comparison
performance appraisal method in which the rater compares each worker with each other worker in the group

Forced distributions

In the comparative method known as **forced distributions**, the rater assigns workers to established categories ranging from poor to outstanding on the basis of comparison with all other workers in the group. Usually, the percentage of employees who can be assigned to any particular category is controlled in order to obtain a fixed distribution of workers along the performance dimension. Most often the distribution is set up to represent a normal distribution (see Figure 6.1). This forced distribution evaluation technique is similar to the procedure used by an instructor who grades on a normal curve, with preassigned percentages of A, B, C, D, and F grades. One possible problem with the forced distribution occurs when there is an abundance of either very good or very poor workers in a supervisor's work

forced distributions
assigning workers to established categories of poor to good performance with fixed limitations on how many employees can be assigned to each category

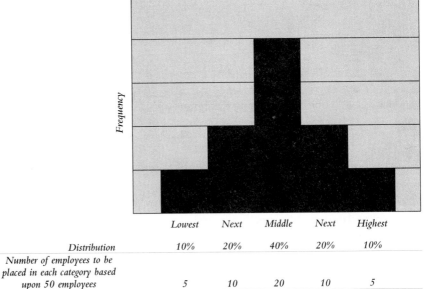

Distribution	Lowest	Next	Middle	Next	Highest
	10%	20%	40%	20%	10%
Number of employees to be placed in each category based upon 50 employees	5	10	20	10	5

FIGURE 6.1

A Forced Distribution Performance Rating Using Five Categories with a Sample of 50 Employees

group. This can create a situation where a supervisor might artificially raise or lower some employees' evaluations to fit them into the predetermined distribution.

Information comparing the performance of one employee to that of others can be used in conjunction with other methods of performance appraisal. For example, a study by Farh and Dobbins (1989) found that when subordinates were presented with information comparing their job performance with that of their peers, their self-ratings of performance were more accurate and there was greater agreement between self-appraisals and appraisals made by supervisors. Thus, while comparative methods may sometimes yield misleading results, the use of comparative information may increase the accuracy and quality of self-appraisals of performance.

INDIVIDUAL METHODS

It is more common for employees to be evaluated using what could be termed "individual methods." **Individual methods** involve evaluating an employee by himself or herself. However, even though ratings are made individually, appraisals using individual methods may still make comparisons of one individual employee's rating with individual ratings of other employees. We will begin our discussion of individual methods with the most widely used method of performance rating: graphic rating scales.

individual methods
performance appraisal methods that evaluate an employee by himself or herself, without explicit reference to other workers

Graphic rating scales

The vast majority of performance appraisals use **graphic rating scales**, which offer predetermined scales to rate the worker on a number of important aspects of the job, such as quality of work, dependability, and ability to get along with coworkers. A graphic rating scale typically has a number of points with either numerical or verbal labels, or both. The verbal labels can be simple one-word descriptors, or they can be quite lengthy and specific (see Figure 6.2). Some graphic rating scales use only verbal end points, or anchors, with numbered rating points between the two anchors.

When graphic rating scales are used in performance assessment, appraisals are usually made on anywhere from seven to twelve key job dimensions, which are derived from the job analysis. Better graphic rating scales define the dimensions and the particular rating categories very clearly and precisely. In other words, it is important that the rater know exactly what aspect of the job is being rated and what the verbal labels mean. For instance, in Figure 6.2 examples *f* and *i* define the job dimension, while example *h* defines the rating categories.

Although good graphic rating scales take some time to develop, often the same basic scales can be used for a number of different jobs by simply switching the relevant job dimensions. However, a common mistake made by many organizations is attempting to develop a "generic" set of performance rating scales for use with all persons and all jobs within the company. Because the relevant job dimensions change drastically from job to job, it is critical that the dimensions being rated are those that actually assess performance of the particular job. The major weakness of graphic rating scales is that they may be prone to certain biased response patterns, such as the tendency to give everyone good or fair ratings. Also, limiting ratings to only a few job dimensions may constrain the appraiser and may not produce a total picture of the worker's job performance.

Behaviorally anchored rating scales

An outgrowth of the critical incidents method of job analysis is the development of **behaviorally anchored rating scales (BARS)**, which attempt to clearly define the scale labels and anchors used in performance ratings (Smith & Kendall, 1963). Rather than having scale labels such as poor, average, or good, BARS have examples of behavioral incidents that reflect poor, average, and good performance in relation to a specific dimension.

Figure 6.3 presents a behaviorally anchored rating scale for appraising the job of Navy recruiter on the dimension of salesmanship skills. Note first the very detailed definition of the job dimension at the top of the scale. On the left are the rating points ranging from 8 to 1. The verbal descriptors to the right of each category give examples of behavioral incidents that would differentiate a recruiter's sales skills, from highest levels to lowest.

As you might imagine, the development of BARS is a lengthy and tedious process. The result, however, is a rating instrument that focuses clearly

graphic ratings scales *performance appraisal methods using a predetermined scale to rate the worker on important job dimensions*

List and define three comparative methods of performance appraisal.

behaviorally anchored ratings scales (BARS) *performance appraisal technique using ratings scales with labels reflecting examples of poor, average, and good behavioral incidents*

(a) Quality   High |_____|___✓___|_____|_____| Low

(b) Quality   High |_____|___✓___|_____|_____| Low
                      5   4   3   2   1

(c) Quality |_____|_____|___✓___|_____|

| Exceptionally high-quality workmanship | Work usually done in a superior way | Quality is average for this job | Work contains frequent flaws | Work is seldom satisfactory |

(d) Quality |_____|_____|_____|___✓___|

| Too many errors | About average | Occasional errors | Almost never makes mistakes |

(e) Quality   5   ④   3   2   1

(f)

Performance factors	Performance grade			
	Consistently superior	Sometimes superior	Consistently average	Consistently unsatisfactory
Quality: Accuracy Economy Neatness	☐	☒	☐	☐

(g) Quality

1 2 3 4 5	6 7 8 9 10	11 12 13 14 15	16 17 18 19 20	21 22 23 24 25
Poor	Below average	Average	Above ☒ average	Excellent

(h) Quality of work

     15   13   ⑪   9   7   5   3   1

| Rejects and errors consistently rare | Work usually OK; errors seldom made | Work passable; needs to be checked often | Frequent errors and scrap; careless |

(i) Quality of work   Judge the amount of scrap; consider the
                         general care and accuracy of work;
                         also consider inspection record.
                         Poor, 1-6; Average, 7-18, Good, 19-25.   20

FIGURE 6.2

Examples of Graphic Rating Scales.
Source: R.M. Guion, *Personnel Testing* (New York: McGraw-Hill, 1965).

Job: *Navy Recruiter*
Job dimension: *Salesmanship skills*

Skillfully persuading prospects to join the navy, using navy benefits and opportunities effectively to sell the navy; closing skills; adapting selling techniques appropriately to different prospects; effectively overcoming objections to joining the navy.

8 *A prospect stated he wanted the nuclear power program or he would not sign up. When he did not qualify, the recruiter did not give up; instead, he talked the young man into electronics by emphasizing the technical training he would receive.*

7 *The recruiter treats objections to join the navy seriously; he works hard to counter the objections with relevent, positive arguments for a navy career.*

6 *When talking to a high school senior, the recruiter mentions names of other seniors from that school who have already enlisted.*

5 *When an applicant qualifies for only one program, the recruiter tries to convey to the applicant that it is a desirable program.*

4 *When a prospect is deciding on which service to enlist in, the recruiter tries to sell the navy by describing navy life at sea and adventures in port.*

3 *During an interview, the recruiter said to the applicant, "I'll try to get you the school you want, but frankly it probably won't be open for another three months, so why don't you take your second choice and leave now."*

2 *The recruiter insisted on showing more brochures and films even though the applicant told him he wanted to sign up right now.*

1 *When a prospect states an objection to being in the navy, the recruiter ends the conversation because he thinks the prospect must not be interested.*

FIGURE 6.3

A Behaviorally Anchored Rating Scale (BARS).
Source: W.C. Borman. "Behavior-Based Rating Scales," in R.A. Berk (Ed.), *Performance Assessment: Methods and Applications* (Baltimore: The Johns Hopkins University Press, 1987), p. 103.

on performance behaviors relevant to a particular job. An appraiser is forced to spend a great deal of time just thinking about what adequate or inadequate performance of a certain job dimension entails, particularly if the rater had a hand in developing the scale. This increased attention to job behaviors helps to overcome some of the general biases and stereotyping that may occur in other performance ratings, for a worker cannot be summarily judged without consideration of how the person's past behavior supports the rating.

Behavioral observation scales

A performance assessment technique that is related to the BARS is the use of **behavioral observation scales (BOS)**. With this method, raters indicate how often the worker has been observed performing key work-related behaviors

behavioral observation scales (BOS) *performance appraisal methods that require appraisers to recall how often a worker has been observed performing key work behaviors*

(Latham & Wexley, 1977). While BARS focus on expectations that a worker would be able to perform specific behaviors that are typical of certain performance levels, behavioral observation scales concentrate on critical behaviors that were actually performed. Bear in mind that behavioral observation scales do not involve the direct observation and assessment of performance behaviors, but rather the recollections of the observers, who may be biased or selective in what they remember. One recent study compared behavioral observation scale and graphic rating scale assessments of performance and showed that employees preferred the BOS method (Tziner, Kopelman, & Livneh, 1993).

Checklists

checklists

performance appraisal methods using a series of statements about job performance

Another individual method of performance rating is the use of **checklists**, which consist of a series of statements about performance in a particular job. The statements are derived from a job analysis and can reflect either positive or negative aspects of performance (see Figure 6.4). The rater's task is to check off the statements that apply to the worker being evaluated. Each of the statements is given a numerical value reflecting the degree of effective performance associated with it. The numerical values assigned to the checked items are then summed to give an overall appraisal of the worker's performance.

Instructions: *Below you will find a list of behavioral items. Read each item and decide whether it describes the person being evaluated. If you feel the item does describe the person, place a check mark in the space provided. If the item does not describe the person, leave the space next to the item blank.*

1 *Regularly sets vague and unrealistic program goals*

2 *Is concerned only with the immediate problems of the day and sees very little beyond the day-to-day*

3 *Develops work schedules that allow for completion of projects provided no major problems are encountered.*

4 *Is aware of needs and trends in area of responsibility and plans accordingly*

5 *Follows up on projects to ensure that intermediate goals are achieved*

6 *Looks for new markets and studies potential declines in current markets*

7 *Anticipates and plans for replacement of key personnel in the event of corporate relocation*

FIGURE 6.4

A Checklist Rating Scale for a Project Manager.
Source: R.R. Jacobs, "Numerical Rating Scales," in R.A. Berk (Ed.), *Performance Assessments: Methods and Applications* (Baltimore: The Johns Hopkins University Press, 1987), pp. 82–99.
Note: This is only a portion of the checklist. Scores are derived based on the number of items checked and the scale values of those items.

A variation of checklist rating is the forced-choice scale, developed in an attempt to overcome the rater's tendency to give generally positive or negative performance appraisals. While using the forced-choice technique the rater is unaware of how positive an appraisal is being made. This format presents groups of descriptive statements from which the rater must select the one that is either most or least descriptive of the worker. The statements carry different values that are later added to form the overall performance appraisal.

While checklists are easy to use and provide detailed appraisals of performance that are focused on job-related behaviors, they do have some drawbacks. The development of such techniques is expensive and time-consuming, requiring the generation of applicable work-related statements and the assignment of accurate performance values. Also, checklists may limit the focus of a performance appraisal, since the rater must choose among a finite set of statements that might not capture all aspects of an individual's performance of a particular job.

Narratives

A relatively simple form of individual performance evaluation is the use of **narratives**, which are open-ended, written accounts of the worker's performance or listings of specific examples of performance strengths and weaknesses. The advantage of narratives is that appraisers have the freedom to describe performance in their own words and to emphasize elements that they feel are important. Their major drawback is that they offer no quantification of performance, which makes it very difficult to compare workers' performance. An additional problem with narratives is that the worker may misinterpret the meaning of the report. For example, an appraiser may write that the worker is doing a "fair job, " meaning that some improvement is needed, but the worker may interpret the word "fair" to mean "adequate" or "good," and may thus believe that no improvement is necessary.

narratives
open-ended written accounts of a worker's performance used in performance appraisals

We have seen that there are quite a number of methods for rating employee job performance, but what works best? All forms of ratings suffer from the same limitation: They are subjective, and thus prone to the unique perspective and biases of the person doing the rating. No one method of rating performance has emerged as superior to the others. However, a key issue is the focus of the rater's attention on actual job performance (see DeNisi & Peters, 1996). Therefore, methods that focus raters on performance-related job behaviors—the BARS and BOS methods—should theoretically improve rater accuracy.

Problems and Pitfalls in Performance Appraisal

Despite the various performance appraisal tools designed to help obtain more objective assessments, the appraisal evaluation process remains very subjective. Because appraisers selectively observe on-the-job performance and rate what they believe to be an individual's performance level, their judgments are prone to a number of systematic biases and distortions. A great deal of research has helped uncover some of these problems. Understanding these potential errors in the performance appraisal process can make it easier to develop the means to combat them and to produce better and better appraisals of work performance. We will consider several types of such systematic problems, including leniency/severity errors, halo effects, recency effects, causal attribution errors, and personal biases.

Leniency/severity errors

leniency error
the tendency to give all workers very positive performance appraisals

A **leniency error** in performance ratings occurs when an appraiser tends to judge all workers leniently, routinely giving them very positive appraisals (see Havenstein, 1992). A **severity error** is the exact opposite, and arises when all workers are placed on the low end of performance scales and are thereby given negative appraisals. For the rater making a severity error, no performance ever seems good enough. There is also a **central tendency error**, whereby the appraiser tends always to use the midpoint of the rating scale. All three of these errors lead to the same problem: a short-circuiting of the appraisal process because the rater's tendency to use only one area of the performance scale does not actually discriminate among poor, fair, and outstanding workers (Houston, Raymond, & Svec, 1991). As shown, some techniques, such as the various comparative methods, help combat such response tendency errors.

severity error
the tendency to give all workers very negative performance appraisals

central tendency error
the tendency to give all workers the midpoint rating in performance appraisals

Halo effects

halo effect
an overall positive evaluation of a worker based on one known positive characteristic or action

A **halo effect** in performance appraisal occurs when appraisers make overall positive appraisals of workers on the basis of one known positive characteristic or action (Nisbett & Wilson, 1977). If a particular worker did an outstanding job on a particular task, the supervisor assumes that all of this person's work is also outstanding, regardless of whether it really is. Certain personal characteristics such as physical attractiveness or being labeled a "rising star" may also lead to halo effects (Landy & Sigall, 1974). Research indicates that halo effects occur because raters use the one, salient characteristic as the basis for forming an overall, generally positive or negative impression of the worker's performance (Lance, LaPointe, & Fisicaro, 1994). There is also a "reverse" halo effect, sometimes called the "rusty halo" or "horns" effect (Baron, 1986), in which an overall negative performance appraisal is made on the basis of one instance of failure or one negative characteristic. Because halo effects are such a common source of bias in performance appraisals, a number of rater training programs have been developed to try to control for them (Ivancevich, 1979; McIntyre, Smith, & Hassett, 1984; Pulakos, 1984). Many of these training programs involve simply making raters more aware of the phenomenon of halo effects and helping them to focus on behavioral dimensions of job performance.

Recency effects

Another potential error in performance appraisals is the tendency to give greater weight to recent performance and lesser value to earlier performance; this can be referred to as the **recency effect**. Because performance assessments usually rely on the appraiser's memory of a worker's past performance, there are bound to be problems related to accurate recall. In general, the greater the delay between the performance and the appraisal of work behaviors, the less accurate the appraisal will be (Heneman & Wexley, 1983; Murphy & Balzer, 1986). The lesser value given to earlier performance because of the recency effect may not always be detrimental to accurate performance appraisals, however. Earlier performance by a relatively new employee may reflect the employee's learning period, where mistakes may be more numerous, whereas later performance may reflect the employee's performance once he or she has more completely learned about the job.

recency effect
the tendency to give greater weight to recent performance and lesser weight to earlier performance

Causal attribution errors

The process by which people ascribe cause to events or behaviors is known as **causal attribution**. Research has uncovered a number of systematic biases in causal attribution that have important implications for the accuracy of performance appraisals. Two of these attributional biases are particularly relevant to performance appraisals. The first is the tendency for appraisers to give more extreme appraisals if they believe that the cause of a worker's performance is rooted in effort rather than ability (Knowlton & Mitchell, 1980). That is, if an appraiser feels that particularly high levels of performance were the result of great effort on the part of a worker, that worker will receive a more positive performance appraisal than one whose high levels of performance were perceived as resulting from possession of natural ability or talent. Similarly, a performance failure due to a lack of sufficient effort will be judged more harshly than a failure believed to be caused by lack of ability.

causal attribution
the process by which people assign cause to events or behaviors

The second pertinent bias in causal attribution is called the **actor-observer bias** (Jones & Nisbett, 1972). This bias is founded in the notion that in any event there is an actor—the person performing a behavior—and an observer—the person watching and appraising the event and the actor's behavior. In performance appraisals the worker is the actor and the appraiser is the observer. The bias in causal attribution occurs when the actor and observer are each asked to state the cause of the particular event. In the case of performance appraisals, the event could be a particularly successful or unsuccessful work outcome. The actor tends to overemphasize the role that situational factors, such as luck, task difficulty, and the work environment, played in the result. In contrast, the observer has a tendency to attribute cause to dispositional factors, or personal characteristics of the actor such as ability, effort, and personality. This means that the performance appraiser tends to believe that performance is due primar-

actor-observer bias
the tendency for observers to overattribute cause to characteristics of the actor and the tendency for the actor to overattribute cause to situational characteristics

ily to qualities in the worker and tends to neglect the role that situational factors played in the performance outcome. Therefore, in certain situations of poor work performance, the supervisor may blame the worker, when the failure was actually due to circumstances beyond the control of the worker. On the other side, the worker is prone to overemphasizing situational factors and, in cases of failure, will try to lay the blame elsewhere, for example, by faulting the working conditions or coworkers. The actor-observer bias not only leads to inaccurate perceptions of work performance but is also one of the main reasons that supervisors and subordinates do not always see eye to eye when it comes to performance appraisals (see Applying I/O Psychology).

Personal biases

In addition to the biases and errors that can afflict any appraiser of work performance, the personal biases of any particular appraiser can also distort the accuracy of assessments. The most common personal biases are those based on the worker's sex, race, age, and physical characteristics, including disabilities (Dipboye, 1985; Ferris, Yates, Gilmore, & Rowland, 1985; Kraiger & Ford, 1985; Woehr & Roch, 1996). It has even been found that pregnancy can be a source of negative bias in performance appraisals (Halpert, Wilson, & Hickman, 1993). It is no secret that women, ethnic minorities, older people, and people with disabilities are sometimes discriminated against in performance appraisals, in spite of legislation specifically designed to ensure fairness. However, recent review of research on racial and gender bias in performance appraisal concluded that such bias may be less of a problem than commonly believed (Arvey & Murphy, 1998).

Personal biases are deeply ingrained in individuals and are therefore difficult to overcome. As with other biases, one way to deal with personal biases is to make appraisers more aware of them. Since discrimination in personnel procedures has been outlawed through federal civil rights legisla-

APPLYING I/O PSYCHOLOGY

Combating the Actor-Observer Bias in Performance Appraisals

The actor-observer bias, or the tendency for actors to make situational attributions and for observers to make dispositional attributions, is a particular problem in performance appraisals that can lead to inaccurate assessments and cause rifts between the evaluating supervisor and subordinates. How can this bias be overcome?

One way to try to combat this problem is to create performance rating forms that require the evaluator to take into account the various situa-

APPLYING I/O PSYCHOLOGY *(continued)*

tional factors that may have hampered the employee's performance. Although this strategy can avoid some of the observer bias, there may still be some tendencies toward overattributing cause to dispositional characteristics of the worker. An even better remedy is to change the perspective of the observers/ evaluators by providing them with direct experience with the actor's job. Because much of the actor-observer bias is the result of the differing perspectives of the actor and the observer, putting the observer/appraiser "in the shoes" of the actor/worker can help the observer see conditions as the actor sees them (Mitchell & Kalb, 1982).

A large savings and loan organization has done just that. All supervisors who are responsible for conducting the performance appraisals of customer service representatives—tellers and loan officers—must spend one week during each appraisal period working in customer service. The belief is that because many of these supervisors are far removed from the customer service situation, they are unable to evaluate objectively the pressures that the workers have to deal with, such as difficult or irate customers. Providing appraisers with this direct experience helps them take into account the situational variables that affect employees' performance, thus leading to more accurate assessments.

A common misconception is that the actor-observer bias will be overcome if both supervisor performance appraisals and workers' self-appraisals are obtained. However, if the actor-observer bias is operating, all this will produce is two very discrepant performance appraisals: one from the supervisor, blaming the worker for poor performance, and one from the worker, blaming the situation. Peer evaluations likewise will not be much help, because coworkers are also subject to the actor-observer bias. Peer evaluations will also overattribute cause to characteristics of the person being appraised, because the coworker is also an observer.

tion, most organizations and managers are on the lookout to prevent such biases from leading to discrimination. Ironically, programs designed to protect against personal biases and subsequent discrimination may lead to instances of reverse discrimination, a bias toward favoring a member of a particular underrepresented group over members of the majority group.

The Performance Appraisal Process

In keeping with the trend toward a more cognitive approach to understanding workers and work behavior, as discussed in Chapter 1, research on performance appraisals has focused more on the cognitive processes underlying performance appraisal decisions (Bretz, Milkovich, & Read, 1992; Feldman, 1981; Kravitz & Balzer, 1992). For example, greater attention has been given to the actual cognitive processes by which an evaluator arrives at an overall performance appraisal of a worker. These cognitive approaches to understanding the process of performance appraisals focus on three sets of cognitive operations: (1) how information about the worker's performance is acquired; (2) how the evaluator organizes and stores information about a worker's performance behaviors; and (3) how the evaluator retrieves and translates the stored information in making the actual performance appraisal (Ilgen, Barnes-Farrell, & McKellin, 1993). Thus, performance appraisal research today has broadened its perspective, viewing performance rating as a complex decision-making process (Judge & Ferris, 1993).

Let's look at an example of how a knowledge of cognitive processes can help I/O psychologists improve the performance appraisal process. The results of several studies suggest that evaluators form ongoing, or "on-line," evaluations of others (Murphy, Philbin, & Adams, 1989; Woehr, 1992). That is, evaluators form opinions as they observe behavior day-to-day, rather than just waiting until the time a formal performance rating is required and then forming an opinion based solely on memory. Because evaluation of performance is an ongoing, information processing task, evaluators should be presented with the performance appraisal rating instruments up front, so that they can familiarize themselves with the rating dimensions before they begin to observe and evaluate performance (Woehr, 1992). Having this knowledge of rating dimensions beforehand has been shown to increase the agreement between supervisor ratings and self-ratings of workers' performance (Williams & Levy, 1992). In addition, it may be helpful for evaluators to keep diaries or daily records of individual employee performance. It has been found that using diaries as a means for structuring information in memory increases the accuracy of evaluators' recall. In one study, evaluators who used diaries to record performance information were more accurate in their recall and were also more accurate in their appraisals of worker performance (DeNisi & Peters, 1996; DeNisi, Robbins, & Cafferty, 1989).

The performance appraisal process involves more than just the process of evaluating and rating worker performance. A good performance appraisal should consist of two parts. The first is the performance assessment, or the means of measuring a worker's performance in order to make personnel decisions. This part we have discussed at length. The second part is **performance feedback**, which is the process of providing information to a worker regarding performance level with suggestions for improving future performance. Performance feedback typically occurs in the context of the performance appraisal interview. Here, the supervisor sits down face to face with the worker and provides a detailed analysis of the worker's performance, giving positive, constructive criticism and suggestions and guidelines for improvement. Guidelines for effective feedback are given in Table 6.3. While constructive feedback is critical to a good performance appraisal, more "informal" feedback from supervisor to subordinate should take place regularly, on a day-to-day basis (Farr, 1993).

performance feedback
*the process of giving
information to a worker
about performance level
with suggestions for future
improvement*

TABLE 6.3

Guidelines for Effective Performance Feedback

1. Feedback should be descriptive rather than evaluative.
2. Feedback should be specific rather than general.
3. Feedback should be appropriate, taking into account the needs of the employer, the worker, and the situation.
4. Feedback should be directed toward behavior that the worker can do something about or is able to change.
5. Feedback should be well-timed. More immediate feedback is usually more effective.
6. Feedback should be honest rather than manipulative or self-serving.
7. Feedback should be understood by both parties. If necessary, additional input should be sought to enhance and clarify the feedback process.
8. Feedback should be proactive and coactive. When change in past behavior is required, specific directions for change should be provided. Both parties should agree on the need for change and the remedy.
9. Feedback should not be used as an opportunity to criticize or to find fault with the worker. It should be a natural process in the ongoing superior-subordinate relationship.

Source: T.E. Harris, *Applied Organizational Communication: Perspectives, Principles, and Pragmatics.* (Hillsdale, NJ: Lawrence Erlbaum Associates, 1993).

Because of the importance of performance appraisals, the appraisal process is likely to have some psychological and emotional effects on the worker. It is crucial that the supervisor be aware of this potential impact of the procedure, and be equipped to deal with the worker's possible reactions. Whether the worker perceives the performance appraisal process positively or negatively and how the worker acts on the information provided in the feedback session are in large part determined by how the information is presented by the supervisor (Ilgen, Fisher, & Taylor, 1979; Kluger & DeNisi, 1996). Research has shown that if the appraiser demonstrates support for the worker and welcomes the worker's input and participation in the assessment process, the performance appraisal is usually more effective (Cederblom, 1982; Wexley, 1986). For example, in one study, workers participated in the construction of behaviorally anchored rating scales to appraise their performance. These workers had more favorable perceptions of the appraisal process and were more motivated to try to improve their performance than were workers who did not have a hand in developing their rating instruments (Silverman & Wexley, 1984). Research has also indicated that training programs for appraisers that include training in providing feedback and in dealing with workers' possible reactions to that feedback are effective in improving the entire performance appraisal process (Ivancevich, 1982) (see Up Close for suggestions on how to improve performance appraisals).

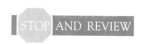

Describe five sources or types of error/bias in performance appraisals.

UP CLOSE

How to Improve Performance Appraisals

Given the pervasiveness of biases and errors in performance appraisals, how can the appraisal process be improved? Research suggests several ways to improve the process.

1. *Improve performance appraisal techniques*—Generally, the more time and energy devoted to the development of detailed, valid instruments for measuring performance, the better the overall quality of the performance appraisal. This means creating different performance appraisal instruments for different job classifications. (You can't, for example, use the same generic rating form for both front-line workers and managerial personnel.) These measures of performance must evolve from detailed job analyses, and should involve relatively straightforward and unambiguous procedures (Yammarino & Waldman, 1993).

2. *Train the* appraisers—Since conducting good performance appraisals is a difficult process, prone to error and potential bias, it is imperative that appraisers be adequately trained. They must be taught how to use the various appraisal instruments and should be instructed to avoid possible errors, such as halo effects and leniency/severity errors (Bernardin & Bulkley, 1981; Hedge & Kavanagh, 1988; Woehr & Huffcutt, 1994). Moreover, evidence suggests that appraisers should be knowledgeable of the performance appraisal methods and procedures up front, before they begin observing workers' performance (Woehr, 1994).

3. *Obtain multiple evaluations*—One way to increase the reliability of performance appraisals is to use multiple ratings, such as more than one supervisor rating or a combination of supervisor ratings, self-appraisals, and peer appraisals. If the results of the multiple appraisals agree with one another, and if all the appraisers are not influenced by a common bias, it is likely that the result will be a very accurate assessment of performance.

4. *Appraise appraisers*—Unfortunately, in many organizations supervisors detest conducting performance appraisals because they view the assessments as a difficult and thankless task—extra work piled onto an already heavy work load. To get supervisors to take performance appraisals seriously, it is important that the task of conducting assessments be considered an integral part of their job. This means that the quality of the supervisors' performance appraisals should be assessed and that the supervisors should also receive feedback about their performance of this crucial task. High-quality appraisals need to be rewarded.

5. *Conduct performance appraisals regularly and often*—Performance appraisals serve not only as tools to assist in personnel decisions, but also as a source of feedback for the worker. Frequent and regular assessments are one of the best ways to help workers learn to overcome problems and improve performance (Cummings & Schwab, 1978).

UP CLOSE (*continued*)

6. *Review and revise performance appraisals*—As jobs change because of technological innovations and organizational restructuring, performance appraisal systems must be constantly updated to deal with the changing nature of the jobs being evaluated.

Legal Concerns in Performance Appraisals

Because performance appraisals are tied to personnel actions such as promotions, demotions, and raises, they are carefully scrutinized in terms of fair employment legislation. Under these legal guidelines, any performance appraisal must be valid. Historically, court cases have ruled that in order to be considered "valid," appraisals must be based on a job analysis and must be validated against the job duties that the workers actually perform (*Albemarle Paper* v. *Moody*, 1975; *United States* v. *City of Chicago*, 1976). Moreover, performance appraisals need to be administered and scored under controlled and standardized conditions (*Brito* v. *Zia Company*, 1973). Specifically, court cases have ruled that appraisers must receive training, or at least written instructions, on how to conduct performance appraisals, that assessments must focus on performance-related behaviors rather than on performance-related personality traits or other dispositional variables, and that appraisals must be reviewed with the employees (Barrett & Kernan, 1987; Feild & Holley, 1982).

Outline five techniques for improving performance appraisals.

Summary

A thorough job analysis is the starting point for measuring and evaluating actual job performance. *Performance appraisals* involve the assessment of worker performance on the basis of predetermined organizational standards. Performance appraisals serve many important purposes, including being the basis for personnel decisions and a means of assessing performance. One way to categorize performance is in terms of *objective* and *subjective* criteria. Objective performance criteria are more quantifiable measurements of performance, such as the number of units produced or dollar sales. Subjective performance criteria typically involve judgments or ratings of performance. Concerns for a performance criterion include: whether it is relevant to job success, called *criterion relevance*; whether the criterion contains elements that detract from the "pure" assessment of performance, termed *criterion contamination*; the degree to which a criterion falls short of perfect assessment of job performance, called *criterion deficiency*; and whether the criterion is usable, called *criterion usefulness*.

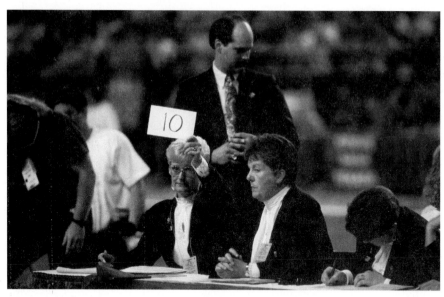

Using multiple evaluators increases the reliability of performance ratings.

Research on ratings of job performance has examined who is making performance ratings. *Self-appraisals* are ratings or evaluations made by the workers themselves. *Peer appraisals* involve coworkers rating each other's performance. In some instances, subordinates may rate the performance of their supervisors. Most common, of course, are supervisory ratings of subordinates' performance. *360-degree feedback* involves getting multiple performance evaluations, from supervisors, peers, subordinates, and customers.

There are a variety of methods for rating performance. *Comparative methods* of appraisal, such as the paired comparison and forced distribution techniques, directly compare one worker's performance with that of other workers. *Individual methods* of appraisal do not make direct comparisons with other workers. Individual methods include *checklists* and forced choice scales, and are easy-to-use methods of appraisal that require the evaluator simply to check off statements characteristic or uncharacteristic of a particular worker's job performance. The most common method of individual performance appraisal involves the use of *graphic rating scales*, whereby an appraiser uses a standardized rating instrument to make a numerical and/or verbal rating of various dimensions of job performance. A specific type of rating technique, the *behaviorally anchored rating scale (BARS)*, uses examples of good and poor behavioral incidents as substitutes for the scale anchors found in traditional rating instruments.

A major problem in rating job performance is caused by systematic biases and errors. *Response tendency errors*, such as *leniency/severity* or *central tendency errors*, lead to consistently good, bad, or average ratings, respectively. *Halo effects* occur when appraisers make overall positive (or negative) performance appraisals because of one known outstanding characteristic or action. There are also errors caused by giving greater weight to more recent performance, known as *recency effects*, and various attribution errors, including the *actor-observer bias*. The latter may lead an appraiser to place greater emphasis on dispositional factors and lesser emphasis on situational factors that may have affected performance.

A good performance appraisal consists of two parts: the performance assessment and *performance feedback*. The feedback should occur in a face-to-face situation in which the supervisor provides constructive information, encouragement, and guidelines for the improvement of the worker's future performance.

Since performance appraisals are important to the worker's livelihood and career advancement, there are considerable legal overtones to the appraisal process. Performance appraisals must be valid procedures, resulting from job analysis, that do not unfairly discriminate against any group of workers.

Study Questions and Exercises

1. Think of a job you have held in the past, or talk to someone you know about his or her current job. Using what you know about the position, try to determine what the relevant performance criteria would be for the job. Develop methods for assessing the performance criteria. Would you measure these criteria objectively or subjectively?

2. Using the job from question 1, design a performance appraisal system for the position. What does it consist of? Who will do the evaluations?

3. What are the advantages and disadvantages of using graphic rating scales versus comparative methods of performance appraisals?

4. In some organizations, performance appraisals are taken too lightly. They receive little attention and are conducted irregularly and infrequently, and there is little motivation for appraisers to do a good job. Why might this occur? Imagine that your task is to convince the management of one of these organizations to improve their performance appraisal system. What would you say to convince them? What components of a good performance appraisal system would you suggest they implement?

Suggested Readings

Arvey, R.D., & Murphy, K.R. (1998). Performance evaluation in work settings. *Annual Review of Psychology, 49*, 141–168. *This article reviews recent research on performance evaluations in work settings, and integrates the recent work with historical research on employee performance evaluations.*

DeNisi, A.S. (1997). *A cognitive approach to performance appraisal: A program of research.* London: Routledge. *This advanced book reviews research exploring cognitive theories of performance appraisal, from one of the leading researchers in the area.*

Mohrman, A.M., Resnick-West, S.M., & Lawler, E.E. (1989). *Designing performance appraisal systems*. San Francisco: Jossey-Bass. *Presents a comprehensive, practitioner-oriented guide to designing appraisal systems.*

Murphy, K.R., & Cleveland, J.N. (1995). *Understanding performance appraisal: Social, organizational and goal-based perspectives*. Thousand Oaks, CA: Sage. *This book reviews research and offers suggestions for developing, implementing, and evaluating performance appraisal systems.*

MOTIVATION

CHAPTER OUTLINE

MOTIVATION WITHIN THE CONTEXT OF INDUSTRIAL/ ORGANIZATIONAL PSYCHOLOGY

INSIDE TIPS

Two areas of I/O psychology involve a tremendous amount of theorizing: motivation and leadership (the topic of leadership will be discussed in Chapter 12). Because both motivation and leadership are extremely complex and important topics in the work world, they are given a great deal of attention by I/O psychologists. This chapter introduces a variety of theories of motivation. Rather than viewing these as isolated models, consider the ways in which they are similar. Some of these similarities are reflected in the grouping of theories into categories, such as need theories and job design theories, as shown in the chapter outline. Other similarities can also help draw related concepts together. For example, the need theories emphasize the satisfaction of basic human needs as a key to motivation, while reinforcement theory argues that motivation is caused by positive reinforcement. However, the satisfaction of human needs can be seen as the experience of a positive reinforcement. By understanding similarities such as these you can begin to synthesize what at first appears to be an overwhelming mass of abstract and unrelated ideas.

Because motivation is presumably behind any work behavior, some of the concepts discussed in this chapter also relate to topics that we have already discussed and that we will consider in upcoming chapters. For example, reinforcement theory is linked to the principles of learning presented in Chapter 5. Certain motivational programs, specifically job enrichment and organizational behavior modification, are also used in organizational development, which is introduced in Chapter 14.

Besides looking for similarities among motivation theories and noticing topics that were previously discussed, pay close attention to the last section of the chapter, which emphasizes that motivation is only one of the many variables that can affect work outcomes. This is an important point because it reminds us to consider the "total picture"—the interrelationships among many organizational variables— when studying work behavior.

Work motivation is one of the most widely researched topics in I/O psychology. If you surveyed managers and asked them to list the most difficult aspects of their jobs, odds are that the majority would mention difficulties in motivating workers as a particular problem. Look around you at work or in school. You will see some people who seem to put more energy and drive into their work, and others who try to get by with minimal effort. When we begin to infer some underlying processes of effort, energy, or drive, we are trying to capture the elusive construct of motivation. Obviously, in any work setting there will be tremendous individual differences in the motivation to work. Why is this the case? What are some of the factors that affect worker motivation? How can we motivate seemingly unmotivated workers?

In this chapter, we will begin by defining motivation. Next, we will examine the various theories of work motivation and see how some of them have been applied in attempts to increase worker motivation. Finally, we will look at how work motivation relates to work performance.

Defining Motivation

motivation
the force that energizes, directs, and sustains behavior

According to one definition (Steers & Porter, 1991), **motivation** is a force that serves three functions: It energizes, or causes people to act; it directs behavior toward the attainment of specific goals; and it sustains the effort expended in reaching those goals.

Since motivation cannot be observed directly, it is very difficult to study. We can only infer motives either by observing goal-directed behavior or by using some psychological measurement technique. Throughout its history, I/O psychology has offered many theories of work motivation. We have already touched on the simplistic models put forth by scientific management and the human relations movement. According to Frederick Taylor, workers are motivated by money and material gains, whereas Elton Mayo stressed the role that interpersonal needs play in motivating workers. Since these early days, more sophisticated theories of motivation have been developed. Some stress the importance of specific needs in determining motivation. Other theories emphasize the connection between work behaviors and outcomes—the influence of attaining rewards and achieving goals. Other theories focus on the role of job design in affecting motivation. Still another category of theories argues that motivation is a rational process and that workers cognitively weigh the advantages and disadvantages of expending work energy. We will review examples of each of these categories of work motivation theories.

Need Theories of Motivation

Several motivation theories assert that people have certain **needs** that are important in determining motivation. Needs involve specific physiological or psychological deficiencies that the organism is driven to satisfy. The need for food and the drive of hunger is a physiological need and drive inherent in all living organisms; the need for human contact is a psychological need. Need theories of motivation propose that motivation is the process of the interaction among various needs and the drives to satisfy those needs. We will first look at some basic need theories, and then examine one need theory, McClelland's achievement motivation theory, in more depth.

needs
physiological or psychological deficiencies that an organism is compelled to fulfill

BASIC NEED THEORIES

Two basic need theories are those proposed by Abraham Maslow and Clayton Alderfer. Both of these theories maintain that there are several different types or categories of needs that play a role in human motivation. Maslow's theory, called the **need hierarchy theory**, proposes that there are five categories of needs, forming a hierarchy from the more basic human needs to more complex, high-order needs (Maslow, 1965, 1970). See Table 7.1 for a description of these needs.

According to Maslow, the lower-order needs (physiological needs, safety needs, and social needs)—what Maslow calls "deficiency needs"—must be satisfied in a step-by-step fashion before an individual can move on to higher-order needs (esteem and self-actualization needs)—what Maslow refers to as "growth needs." Since higher-order needs are unlikely to be satisfied in the typical worker, there is also a constant upward striving that explains why, for example, even successful, high-level executives continue to exhibit considerable motivation.

Building in part on Maslow's theory is Clayton Alderfer's (1972) **ERG theory**, which collapses Maslow's five categories of needs into three: *existence* needs, which are similar to Maslow's basic physiological and safety needs; *relatedness* needs, which stem from social interaction and are analogous to the social needs in Maslow's hierarchy; and *growth* needs, which are

need hierarchy theory
a motivation theory, proposed by Maslow, that arranges needs in a hierarchy from lower, more basic needs to higher-order needs

ERG theory
Alderfer's motivation model that categorizes needs into existence, relatedness, and growth needs

TABLE 7.1

Maslow's Hierarchy of Needs (arranged from lowest to highest order needs)

1. *Physiological needs:* the basic survival needs of food, water, air, sleep, and sex
2. *Safety needs:* the needs for physical safety (need for shelter) and needs related to psychological security
3. *Social needs:* the need to be accepted by others and needs for love, affection, and friendship
4. *Esteem needs:* the needs to be recognized for accomplishments and to be admired and respected by peers
5. *Self-actualization needs:* the needs to reach one's highest potential and to attain a sense of fulfillment; the highest level of needs

the highest-order needs, dealing with needs to develop fully and realize one's potential. Alderfer makes predictions similar to Maslow's, that as each level of need becomes satisfied, the next higher level becomes a strong motivator. However, Alderfer also predicts that frustration will occur when attainment of lower order needs is thwarted, such as a loss of income due to a strike or demotion, leading to an inability to continue to satisfy existence needs.

Although both basic need theories have received a great deal of attention from professionals in psychology, business, and other areas, neither theory has led to any type of useful application or strategy for improving work motivation (Miner, 1983). Although both theories do a good job of describing various types of needs, and of distinguishing the lower- from the higher-order needs, both theories are quite limited. In particular, the predictions made by both theories about need-driven behavior have not held up (Rauschenberger, Schmitt, & Hunter, 1980; Wahba & Bridwell, 1976).

McClelland's Achievement Motivation Theory

achievement motivation theory
McClelland's model of motivation that emphasizes the importance of three needs—achievement, power, and affiliation—in determining worker motivation

A more comprehensive need theory of motivation, and one that deals specifically with work motivation, is David McClelland's **achievement motivation theory** (McClelland, 1961, 1975). This theory states that three needs are central to work motivation: the needs for achievement, power, and affiliation. According to McClelland, people are motivated by different patterns of needs, or motives, terms that he uses interchangeably. The factors that lead to work motivation may differ from person to person, depending on their particular pattern of needs. The three key motives, or needs, in his theory are as follows:

1. *Need for achievement*—the compelling drive to succeed and to get the job done. Individuals with a very high need for achievement are those who love the challenge of work. They are motivated by a desire to get ahead in the job, to solve problems, and to be outstanding work performers.

Need for achievement is also associated with being task-oriented, preferring situations offering moderate levels of risk or difficulty, and desiring feedback about goal attainment.

2. *Need for power*—the need to direct and control the activities of others and to be influential. Individuals with a high need for power are status-oriented and are more motivated by the chance to gain influence and prestige than to solve particular problems personally or reach performance goals. McClelland talks about two sides to the need for power: One is personal power that is used toward personal ends; the other is institutional power, or power that is oriented toward organizational objectives (McClelland, 1970).

3. *Need for affiliation*—the desire to be liked and accepted by others. Individuals motivated by affiliation needs strive for friendship. They are greatly concerned with interpersonal relationships on the job and prefer working with others on a task. They are motivated by cooperative rather than competitive work situations.

This approach emphasizes the differences in these basic needs from person to person. According to McClelland, we all possess more or less of each of these motives, although in each individual a particular need (or needs) tends to predominate. In his earlier theorizing on motivation, McClelland (1961) emphasized the role of need for achievement in determining work motivation (hence the name, "achievement motivation theory"). However, in later analyses, McClelland (1975) stressed the roles that the needs for power and affiliation also play in worker motivation. His theory can also be related to leadership, for he argues that a leader must be aware of and be responsive to the different needs of subordinates in order to motivate workers successfully (see Chapter 12).

To assess an individual's motivational needs, McClelland uses a variation of the **Thematic Apperception Test (TAT)**. Respondents are instructed to study each of a series of fairly ambiguous pictures for a few moments and then "write the story it suggests" (see Figure 7.1). The brief stories are then scored using a standardized procedure that measures the presence of the three basic needs in order to obtain a "motivational profile" for each respondent. The TAT is known as a projective test; that is, respondents project their inner motivational needs into the content of the story they create. One criticism of McClelland's theory concerns the use of the TAT, for its scoring can sometimes be unreliable, with different scorers possibly interpreting the stories differently. Also, there is a tendency for participants who write longer "stories" to be given higher scores on achievement motivation. It is important to note that other measures of motivational needs exist that do not rely on projective techniques (e.g., Spence & Helmreich, 1983; Steers & Braunstein, 1976). Despite the criticisms of McClelland's version of the TAT, and criticisms of the measurement properties of projective tests in general, a recent meta-analysis shows that the TAT is a reasonably good measurement tool (Spangler, 1992).

Thematic Apperception Test (TAT)
a projective test that uses ambiguous pictures to assess psychological motivation

FIGURE 7.1

Sample Item from a Variation of the Thematic Apperception Test (TAT) Used by McClelland

The majority of research on McClelland's theory has focused on the need for achievement (McClelland, 1961; McClelland, Atkinson, Clark, & Lowell, 1953). Evidence indicates that individuals with a high need for achievement attain personal success in their jobs, but only if the type of work that they do fosters personal achievement. That is, there must be a match between the types of outcomes a particular job offers and the specific motivational needs of the person. For example, people who have a great need for achievement might do best in a job in which they are allowed to solve problems, such as a scientist or engineer, or in which there is a direct relation between personal efforts and successful job outcomes, such as a salesperson working on commission. For example, need for achievement tends to be positively correlated with workers' incomes—high achievers made more money than those with a low need for achievement (McClelland & Franz, 1993). However, persons high in need for achievement might be less effective in team situations and they have a tendency to try to accomplish goals by themselves rather than delegate to others or work with them as a unit (a reason why, perhaps, many high-achieving college students prefer individual over group projects and assignments).

Alternatively, those high in the need for affiliation should do best in a job in which they work with others as part of a team, or in occupations that require people skills or the establishing of good interpersonal relationships (e.g., public relations, counseling, coaching). Finally, persons with a high need for power should thrive in jobs that satisfy their needs to be in charge. In fact, research shows that many successful managers are high in the need for power, presumably because much of their job involves directing the activities of others (McClelland & Boyatzis, 1982; McClelland & Burnham, 1976).

The work of McClelland and his associates has led to several applications of the achievement motivation theory toward improving motivation in work settings. One strategy is a program which matches workers' motivational profiles to the requirements of particular jobs in order to place individuals in positions that will best allow them to fulfill their predominant needs (McClelland, 1980). A second application, effective in positions that require a strong need for achievement, is an achievement training program in which individuals are taught to be more achievement-oriented by role playing achievement-oriented actions and strategies, and developing plans for setting achievement-related goals (Miron & McClelland, 1979). (But see Up Close for some potential dangers associated with too much need for achievement.) The achievement motivation theory thus not only has been fairly well tested, but also has led to these useful intervention strategies (Miner, 1983).

Behavior-based Theories of Motivation

The next two motivation theories have been categorized as "behavior-based theories," because each theory focuses on behavioral outcomes as critical to affecting work motivation. These two theories are reinforcement theory and goal-setting theory.

REINFORCEMENT THEORY

Reinforcement theory draws on principles of operant conditioning (mentioned briefly in Chapter 5) and states simply that behavior is motivated by its consequences. A consequence that follows a behavior and serves to increase the motivation to perform that behavior again is a reinforcer. These reinforcers can be of two types. **Positive reinforcers**, more commonly referred to as rewards, are events that are in and of themselves desirable to the person. Receiving praise, money, or a pat on the back are all common positive reinforcers. **Negative reinforcers** are events that lead to the avoidance

reinforcement theory
the theory that behavior is motivated by its consequences

positive reinforcers
desirable events that strengthen the tendency to respond

negative reinforcers
events that strengthen a behavior through the avoidance of an existing negative state

UP CLOSE

What Is a Workaholic?

According to McClelland, the need for achievement is a continuum ranging from very low to very high levels of achievement. Typically, we consider a high achievement level to be positive, but can we ever have *too much* need for achievement? The answer appears to be yes. When an individual's compelling drive to succeed in a job becomes so great that all other areas of life (family, health concerns, and leisure) are given little or no concern, we may label the person a *workaholic* or "achievement-addicted."

According to researchers, the workaholic is not necessarily motivated by money itself or even by power, but by a desire to be "number one" (Machlowitz, 1976). Money is simply a means of keeping score, although many confirmed workaholics are also very wealthy (see Boroson, 1976). The concept of the workaholic is related in many ways to the hard-driving "Type A," or "coronary-prone" behavior pattern, a topic we will discuss in Chapter 9.

Based on interviews with workaholics, Machlowitz has derived fifteen characteristics common to them all. Look over the list and see how you match up to the definition:

1. An ongoing work style
2. A broad view of what a job requires
3. A sense of the scarcity of time
4. The use of lists and time-saving gadgets
5. Long work days
6. Little sleep
7. Quick meals
8. An awareness of what one's own work can accomplish
9. An inability to enjoy idleness
10. Initiative
11. Overlapping of work and leisure
12. A desire to excel
13. A dread of retirement
14. Intense energy
15. An ability to work anywhere (workaholics can always be spotted taking work into the bathroom)

It is interesting to note that many workers and work organizations place a high value on workaholics, and many companies actually encourage workaholism. For example, workaholic bosses may be singled out as role models for younger managers, and workaholic supervisors might encourage and reward similar workaholic behaviors in subordinates. In addition, as more and more companies downsize and eliminate personnel, it may promote workaholism because fewer workers must handle all of the work duties.

STOP AND REVIEW

What are the three needs in McClelland's theory? How are they measured?

of an existing negative state or condition. Being allowed to escape the noise and confusion of a busy work area by taking a short break in a quiet employee lounge, or working hard at a task to avoid the wrath of a watchful supervisor, are negative reinforcement situations. Negative reinforcement increases the motivation to perform the desired behavior again in an effort to keep the aversive negative condition from returning. For example, if a clerical worker feels that being behind schedule is a particularly aversive condition, the individual will be motivated to work hard in order to avoid the unpleasant state of being behind schedule. It is important to reemphasize that both negative and positive reinforcement can increase the motivation to repeat a behavior.

Punishment is the term used to describe any unpleasant consequence that directly follows the performance of a behavior. The effect of punishment is to weaken the tendency to perform the behavior again. Punishment is applied to behaviors that are deemed inappropriate. Receiving a harsh reprimand from your boss for too much socializing on the job and receiving a demotion because of sloppy work are examples of punishment. Reinforcement theory argues that reinforcement is a much better motivational technique than is punishment, since the goal of punishment is to stop unwanted behaviors, while reinforcement is designed to strengthen the motivation to perform a particular desired behavior. In addition, it is important to emphasize that punishment is generally a poor managerial strategy for several reasons: First, the chronic use of punishment can create feelings of hostility and resentment in workers and reduce morale and job satisfaction. Second, punished workers may try to retaliate and "get back" at punitive supervisors. Third, punishment tends only to suppress behavior; once the threat of punishment is taken away, the worker may continue to use the undesirable behavior. Finally, continual use of punishment leads to inefficient supervisors—ones who must spend too much of their time constantly "on watch" to catch workers committing undesirable behaviors and administer the punishment.

punishment
unpleasant consequences that reduce the tendency to respond

Once a particular behavior has been conditioned through repeated reinforcement, removal of the reinforcement will, over time, weaken the motivation to perform that behavior. Eventually, if reinforcement does not occur again, **extinction**, or the elimination of a conditioned response through the withdrawal of reinforcement, will result.

extinction
the elimination of a conditioned response through the withdrawal of reinforcement

In principle, the reinforcement model is fairly simple and obvious. We have seen it in operation all of our lives. Thus far, however, we have presented the reinforcement model in a simplistic form, outlining what is called a continuous reinforcement schedule: Perform a behavior, get a reward. The real work world does not usually operate this way. Reinforcement in the work environment typically takes place on a partial or intermittent reinforcement schedule, which can be of either the interval or ratio type. When interval schedules are used, the reinforcement is based on the passage of time, during which the individual is performing the desired behavior. When ratio schedules are used, reinforcement follows the performance of a number of desired behaviors. Both interval and ratio schedules can be either fixed or variable. Thus there are four reinforcement schedules: fixed interval, variable interval, fixed ratio, and variable ratio. Most typically, in work settings we think of these four types of schedules as representing different schedules of pay.

In the **fixed interval schedule**, the reinforcement occurs after the passage of a specified amount of time. Employees who are paid an hourly or

fixed interval schedule
reinforcement that follows the passage of a specified amount of time

daily wage or a weekly or monthly salary are being reinforced on this schedule, which has two important characteristics. First, the reinforcement is not contingent upon the performance of the desired behavior. Of course, it is assumed that during the intervening time period, people are performing their jobs. However, reinforcement follows regardless of whether the rate of performing job-related behaviors is high or low. Second, the fixed interval schedule is predictable. People always know when a reinforcement is coming.

variable interval schedule
reinforcement that follows the passage of a specified amount of time, with exact time of reinforcement varying

A **variable interval schedule** is a somewhat rare means of work compensation. On these schedules, reinforcement is also determined by the passage of time, but the interval varies. For example, a worker for a small business might be paid on the average of once a month, but the exact time depends on when the owner does the payroll. Bonuses that are given on the bosses' whims are also on a variable interval schedule.

fixed ratio schedule
reinforcement that is contingent on the performance of a fixed number of behaviors

In a **fixed ratio schedule**, reinforcement depends on the performance of a set number of specified behaviors. Examples include workers who are paid for the number of components assembled, baskets of fruit picked, or reports written. This type of fixed ratio payment is commonly referred to as "piece-work." The strength of such a schedule is that reinforcement is contingent upon execution of the desired behavior. Individuals on ratio schedules have high rates of responding in comparison to persons on interval schedules, who are merely "putting in time."

variable ratio schedule
reinforcement that depends on the performance of a specified but varying number of behaviors

A **variable ratio schedule** also involves reinforcement that is contingent upon the performance of behaviors, but the number of responses required for a particular reinforcement varies. An example of a variable ratio schedule is a salesperson on commission, who is required to give a number of sales presentations (the work behavior) to make a sale and receive a commission (the reinforcement). Imagine a door-to-door salesperson who knows that to make a single sale, approximately ten presentations must be made. However, the payoffs will vary. Sometimes the salesperson will make two consecutive sales, and sometimes 20 or 30 presentations will yield only a single sale, but the overall ratio is one in ten. Variable ratio schedules usually lead to very high levels of motivation because the reinforcement is contingent upon performance, and because of the "surprise element": You never know when the next reinforcement is coming. Gambling is reinforced on a variable ratio schedule, which is why it is such an addicting behavior.

A car salesman works on a variable ratio schedule of compensation: His earnings depend on the number of successful sales pitches he makes.

Research indicates that different types of schedules lead to various patterns of responding, and thus have important implications for the use of reinforcement in motivating workers. Generally, evidence suggests that ratio schedules result in higher levels of motivation and subsequent task performance than do fixed interval schedules (Pritchard, Hollenbeck, & DeLeo, 1980; Pritchard, Leonard, Von Bergen, & Kirk, 1976). These findings are important, especially since the majority of U.S. workers are paid on fixed interval reinforcement schedules.

Obviously, reinforcement principles are used informally on a day-to-day basis to motivate workers through compensation systems and other forms of rewards for work outcomes. However, when reinforcement theory is applied formally as a program to increase worker motivation, it most often takes the form of **organizational behavior modification**, in which certain target behaviors are specified, measured, and rewarded. For example, one model of organizational behavior modification takes a four-step approach, involving:

1. *Specifying the desired work behaviors*
2. *Measuring desired performance* of these behaviors using trained observers
3. *Providing frequent positive reinforcement*, including graphs demonstrating individual and group performance of desired behaviors
4. *Evaluation of the program's effectiveness* (Komaki, Coombs, & Schepman, 1991).

Such programs have been used to motivate workers to be more productive, to produce higher quality work, and to cut down on rates of absenteeism, tardiness, and work accidents by rewarding good performance, attendance, and/or safe work behaviors (e.g., Mawhinney, 1992; Merwin, Thomason, & Sanford, 1989). In general, organizational behavior modification has been a successful strategy for enhancing worker motivation (Hamner & Hamner, 1976; Miner, 1983).

Extrinsic versus intrinsic motivation

One limitation to reinforcement theory is that it emphasizes external, or *extrinsic*, rewards. That is, persons are motivated to perform a behavior because they receive some extrinsic reward from the environment. Yet, theorists such as Deci and Ryan (1985) emphasize that people are often motivated by internal, or **intrinsic motivation**. Intrinsic rewards are derived from the worker's sense of accomplishment and competence at performing and mastering work tasks, and from a sense of autonomy or control over one's own work. According to the notion of intrinsic motivation, workers are motivated by challenges at work, with the reward being the satisfaction of meeting the challenge or of a job well done. You have probably experienced firsthand intrinsic motivation at school or work, when you felt the glow of accomplishment with a particularly challenging assignment. Likewise, people who say they love their work because of its challenge and opportunity to "stretch" their skills and abilities are intrinsically motivated workers.

According to intrinsic motivation theorists, it is not enough to offer tangible, extrinsic rewards to workers. To motivate workers intrinsically, jobs need to be set up so that they are interesting and challenging, and so that they call forth workers' creativity and resourcefulness (Deci, 1992). Moreover, relying heavily on extrinsic rewards tends to decrease intrinsic motivation (parents are told, for example, that giving a child money for good grades will lower the child's intrinsic motivation to work hard at school). Another approach used to promote intrinsic motivation at work is to allow workers some control, or autonomy, in deciding how their work should be planned and conducted (Deci, 1972). As we will see as we discuss

organizational behavior modification
the application of conditioning principles to obtain certain work outcomes

intrinsic motivation
the notion that people are motivated by internal rewards

STOP AND REVIEW

Give examples of the four types of reinforcement schedules. How are punishment and negative reinforcement different?

additional theories of motivation, many models of motivation focus on intrinsic rewards as critical for work motivation.

GOAL-SETTING THEORY

goal-setting theory
the motivational theory that emphasizes the setting of specific and challenging performance goals

Goal-setting theory emphasizes the role of specific, challenging performance goals and workers' commitment to those goals as key determinants of motivation. Typically, goal-setting theory is associated with Edwin Locke (1968; Locke & Latham, 1984, 1990a), although theories concerning the establishment of defined performance goals have been around for some time (see, for example, Drucker, 1954; Lewin, 1935). Goal-setting techniques have also been used in nonwork settings to motivate people to lose weight, to exercise regularly, and to study.

Goal-setting theory states that for employees to be motivated, goals must be clear, specific, attainable, and, whenever possible, quantified. General goals, such as urging employees to do their best or to work as quickly as possible, are not as effective as defined, measurable goals. In addition, goal-setting programs may emphasize taking a large, challenging goal and breaking it down into a series of smaller, more easily attained goals. For example, as I sat down to write this textbook, the task seemed overwhelming. It was much easier (and more motivating) to view the book as a series of chapters, tackle each chapter individually, and feel a sense of accomplishment each time the first draft of a chapter was completed. (You may be faced with something similar as you try to study and master the book. It may be less overwhelming to set smaller study "goals" and take it one chapter or section at a time). Difficult or challenging goals will also result in greater levels of motivation, if the goals have been accepted by the workers (Locke, Shaw, Saari, & Latham, 1981). For example, there is evidence that if workers participate in goal setting, as opposed to having supervisors set the goals, there is increased motivation as measured by workers setting higher performance goals than those set by supervisors (Erez & Arad, 1986). Of course, goals should not be so high that they are impossible to achieve (Erez & Zidon, 1984).

Research on goal setting has also stressed the importance of getting workers committed to goals, for without such commitment, it is unlikely that goal setting will be motivating (Locke, Latham, & Erez, 1988; Wofford, Goodwin, & Premack, 1992). A number of strategies have been used to influence employees' commitment to performance goals. These include: the use of extrinsic rewards (e.g., bonuses), the use of peer pressure via setting both individual *and* group goals, and encouragement of intrinsic motivation through providing workers with feedback about goal attainment. In one instance, goal commitment was strengthened through the use of negative reinforcement: Achieving work group goals meant the group would avoid possible layoffs (Latham & Saari, 1982).

As you might imagine, goal-setting theory has generated a great deal of research. Unfortunately, much of this research has been conducted using college students who simulate work behavior in laboratory settings. More recent research, however, is demonstrating the effectiveness of goal-setting techniques in the field. Despite the limitations of some of the goal-setting research, meta-analyses indicate support for the effectiveness of goal-setting as a motivational technique (Mento, Steele & Karren, 1987; Tubbs, 1986; Wofford, Goodwin, & Premack, 1992).

A more recent focus of research on goal setting has tried to discover reasons why goal setting is an effective motivational technique (e.g., Kernan & Lord, 1990; Vance & Colella, 1990). One study found that the setting of specific, challenging goals may stimulate high quality planning on the part of workers. This "planning quality" then contributes to better performance in achieving goals (Smith, Locke, & Barry, 1990). Feedback accompanying goal attainment may also enhance a worker's job performance and ability to become more innovative and creative on the job, through a trial-and-error learning process (Locke & Latham, 1990b). In addition, research has begun to look beyond individual motivation in goal setting, to the effects of setting group goals on group-level or work-team motivation (Crown & Rosse, 1995; Pritchard, Jones, Roth, Stuebing, & Ekeberg, 1988; Weingart, 1992).

While goal-setting theory has stimulated a great deal of research, there has been considerable interest from practitioners in applying goal-setting theory to increase worker motivation. A wide variety of motivational techniques and programs, such as incentive programs and management by objectives, or MBO (which we will discuss in Chapter 14), are consistent with goal-setting theory. Since goal setting is a relatively simple motivational strategy to implement, it has become quite popular.

Job Design Theories of Motivation

The need theories emphasize the role that individual differences in certain types of needs play in determining work motivation. The behavior-based theories focus on behavioral outcomes as the key to motivation. By contrast, two job design theories, Herzberg's two-factor theory and the job characteristics model, stress the structure and design of jobs as key factors in motivating workers. They argue that if jobs are well designed, containing all of the elements that workers require from their jobs to satisfy physical and psychological needs, employees will be motivated.

HERZBERG'S TWO-FACTOR THEORY

Influenced greatly by the human relations school of thought, Frederick Herzberg developed a theory of motivation that highlighted the role of job satisfaction in determining worker motivation (Herzberg, 1966; Herzberg, Mausner, & Snyderman, 1959). He states that the traditional, single-dimension approach to job satisfaction, with its continuum ends ranging from job dissatisfaction to job satisfaction, is wrong, and that job satisfaction and job dissatisfaction are actually two separate and independent dimensions. Herzberg arrived at these conclusions, called the **two-factor theory**, after analyzing the survey responses of many white-collar, professional workers who were asked to describe what made them feel especially good or bad about their jobs. What he found was that the factors clustered into one of two categories. Certain factors, when present, seemed to cause job satisfaction, and Herzberg labeled them **motivators**. Other factors, when absent, tended to cause job dissatisfaction, and he called them **hygienes**. Motivators are factors related to job content; they are inherent in the work itself. The type of work, the level of responsibility associated with the job, and the chances for recognition, advancement, and personal achievement are all motivators. Hygienes are related to the context in which people perform their jobs. Common hygienes include benefits, working conditions (including both physical and social conditions), type of supervision, base salary, and company policies (see Table 7.2).

To illustrate Herzberg's concepts of hygienes and motivators, consider the jobs of high school teacher and paramedic. Neither job is particularly well paid, and the working conditions of the paramedic, with odd hours out in the field working under high pressure to save lives, are not too appealing. In other words, the hygienes in the two jobs are low to moderate. And, as you might expect with reduced hygienes, teachers and paramedics might often voice their dissatisfaction over low pay and poor working conditions. However, the positions of teacher and paramedic have high levels of responsibility, shaping young minds and saving lives, respectively. Moreover, both teachers and paramedics consider themselves to be "professionals," doing work that has value to society. These are the motivators that, according to Herzberg, will lead to job satisfaction and keep levels of motivation high for people in these professions.

Herzberg's theory indicates that if managers are to keep workers happy and motivated, two things must be done. First, to eliminate job dissatisfaction, workers must be provided with the basic hygiene factors. That is, they must be compensated appropriately, treated well, and provided with job security. However, furnishing these hygienes will only prevent dissatisfaction; it will not necessarily motivate workers. To get workers to put greater effort and energy into their jobs, motivators must be present. The work must be important, giving the workers a sense of responsibility, and should provide chances for recognition and upward mobility.

Unfortunately, research has not been very supportive of Herzberg's theory. In particular, the two-factor theory has been criticized on methodological grounds, since subsequent research has not replicated the presence of two distinct factors (Schneider & Locke, 1971). There have also been difficulties in clearly distinguishing hygienes and motivators. For example, salary, which should be a hygiene because it is external to the work itself, may sometimes act as a motivator, since pay can be used to recognize outstanding employees and indicate an individual's status in the organization. It has also been suggested that Herzberg's theory applies more to white-collar than to blue-collar

TABLE 7.2

Profile of Herzberg's Motivators and Hygienes

Motivators	Hygienes
Responsibility	Company policy and administration
Achievement	Supervision
Recognition	Interpersonal relations
Content of work	Working conditions
Advancement	Salary
Growth on job	

workers (Dunnette, Campbell, & Hakel, 1967). As a result, his model is not currently considered to be a viable theory of motivation.

In spite of criticisms and a lack of supportive research, Herzberg's theory helped stimulate the development of an innovative strategy used to increase worker motivation known as job enrichment. We will discuss job enrichment shortly, but first we must consider our second job design theory of motivation: the job characteristics model.

JOB CHARACTERISTICS MODEL

The **job characteristics model** emphasizes the role of certain aspects or characteristics of jobs in influencing work motivation (Hackman & Oldham, 1976, 1980). According to Hackman and Oldham (1976), employees must experience three important psychological states to be motivated: Workers must perceive their work as meaningful, must associate a sense of responsibility with the job, and must have some knowledge of the results of their efforts. Five core job characteristics contribute to a worker's experience of the three psychological states:

1. *Skill variety*—the degree to which a job requires the worker to use a variety of abilities and skills to perform work-related tasks. A job that demands a range of skills is likely to be perceived as challenging and meaningful.

2. *Task identity*—the degree to which a job requires the completion of an entire job or function. The worker needs to see the observable outcome or product of work efforts.

3. *Task significance*—the degree to which a job has a substantial impact on other people within the organization, such as coworkers, or persons outside of the organization, such as consumers.

4. *Autonomy*—the degree to which the job gives the worker freedom and independence to choose how to schedule and carry out the necessary tasks.

STOP AND REVIEW

Under what conditions is goal setting most effective?

job characteristics model
a theory that emphasizes the role that certain aspects of jobs play in influencing work motivation

5. *Feedback*—the degree to which the job allows the worker to receive direct and clear information about the effectiveness of performance.

Skill variety, task identity, and task significance all affect the experience of meaningfulness in work; autonomy influences the sense of responsibility associated with the job and with work outcomes; and feedback influences the worker's experience of work results.

These five core job characteristics can be assessed and then combined into a single *motivating potential score (MPS)* using the following formula:

$$MPS = \frac{\text{skill variety} + \text{task identity} + \text{task significance}}{3} \times \text{autonomy} \times \text{feedback}$$

Hackman and Oldham used this formula to show that motivation is not a simple combination of the five job characteristics. In the formula, skill variety, task identity, and task significance are averaged, which means that jobs can have low levels of one or two of these characteristics which are compensated for by a high score on the third. This average score is then multiplied by the core characteristics of autonomy and feedback. However, if any of the levels of autonomy, feedback, or skill variety plus task identity plus task significance are zero, the MPS will be zero—no motivating potential! For a job to have any motivating potential, it must have both autonomy and feedback and at least one of the other three characteristics.

To summarize the basic job characteristics model, the five core job characteristics influence the three critical psychological states—meaningfulness, responsibility, and knowledge of results—that in turn lead to motivation and certain work outcomes, such as the motivation to work, to improve performance, and to grow on the job (Figure 7.2). Actually, the job characteristics model is more complex. According to Hackman and Oldham, certain "moderators" can affect the success of the model in predicting worker motivation. One such moderator is **growth need strength**, or an individual's need and desire for personal growth and development on the job. In other words, some workers desire jobs that are challenging, responsible, and demanding, while others do not. According to the theory, improving the dimensions of the five core job characteristics should have motivating effects only on those workers who are high in growth need strength. Workers low in this moderator are not likely to be motivated by jobs that offer enriched opportunities for responsibility, autonomy, and accountability.

To validate their theory, Hackman and Oldham (1975) developed a questionnaire to measure the five core characteristics, called the **Job Diagnostic Survey (JDS)**. The JDS and alternative tools, such as the Job Characteristics Inventory (Fried, 1991; Sims, Szilagyi, & Keller, 1976), have stimulated a great deal of research on the job characteristics model. Generally, the results have been favorable (see, for example, Graen, Scandura, & Graen, 1986; Loher, Noe, Moeller, & Fitzgerald, 1985), although there have been some results that are not supportive of the model (Tiegs, Tetrick,

This physical therapist experiences at least two of the psychological states identified by the job characteristics model: she knows her work is meaningful and she sees the results.

growth need strength
the need and desire for personal growth on the job

Job Diagnostic Survey (JDS)
a questionnaire that measures core job characteristics

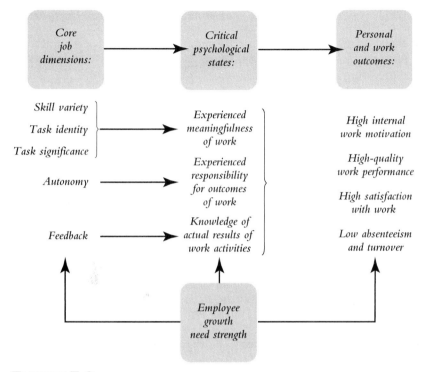

FIGURE 7.2

The Job Characteristics Model of Work Motivation
Source: J.R. Hackman and G.R. Oldham, "Motivation Through the Design of Work: Test of a Theory." *Organizational Behavior and Human Performance, 16* (1979), p. 256.

& Fried, 1992). A meta-analysis of nearly 200 studies of the model found general support for its structure and for its effects on job motivation and related work outcomes (Fried & Ferris, 1987). Most recently, the job characteristics model has been found to predict motivation to come to work, with workers having enriched, "motivating" jobs having better attendance records than workers whose jobs lack the critical job characteristics (Rentsch & Steel, 1998).

One important difficulty with the use of the JDS (and other, similar self-report measures of job characteristics) to test the job characteristics model relates to the old problem with correlation and causality that we discussed in Chapter 2. Research has found a positive correlation between the presence of core job characteristics and employee satisfaction and self-reported motivation. However, because most of this research is based on self-report measures of both job characteristics and job satisfaction/motivation, we cannot be sure of the direction of causality. Is it the presence of motivating job characteristics that causes job satisfaction and motivation, as the job

Define Herzberg's concepts of motivators and hygienes and give examples of each.

characteristics model predicts, or is it the case that motivated, satisfied workers see their jobs as being rich in key job characteristics? Some researchers have criticized the use of self-report measures of job characteristics, advocating instead the use of job analysis methods to determine if jobs have "motivating" job characteristics (Spector, 1992; Spector & Jex, 1991; Taber & Taylor, 1990).

These two job design theories of motivation—Herzberg's theory and the job characteristics model—have led to the development and refinement of a strategy used to motivate workers through job redesign. This intervention strategy is called **job enrichment**, and it involves redesigning jobs in order to give workers greater responsibility in the planning, execution, and evaluation of their work. (Note that job enrichment is not the same as *job enlargement*, because job enrichment raises the level of responsibility associated with a job, while job enlargement does not). When job enrichment is used as a motivational strategy, workers may actually take on some of the tasks that were previously performed by higher-level supervisors, such as allocating work tasks, appraising their own work performance, setting output quotas, and making their own personnel decisions (including hiring, firing, giving raises, and the like). These programs typically include the following elements:

job enrichment
a motivational program that involves redesigning jobs to give workers a greater role in the planning, execution, and evaluation of their work

- Increasing the level of responsibility associated with jobs, as well as the workers' sense of freedom and independence
- Wherever possible, allowing workers to complete an entire task or function
- Providing feedback so that workers can learn to improve their own performance
- Encouraging workers to learn on the job by taking on additional, more challenging tasks, and by improving their expertise in the jobs they perform

As you can see, these elements of job enrichment programs are quite similar to the job characteristics outlined in the Hackman and Oldham model. (For an illustration of job enrichment programs in action, see Applying I/O Psychology.)

Although job enrichment programs have been implemented in quite a few large companies in the United States and Europe, their effectiveness is still in question. Since job enrichment usually takes place at an organizational or departmental level, it is very difficult to conduct a well-controlled evaluation of the effectiveness of the program. Specifically, because the unit of analysis—the participant—is usually the organization or department, it is very difficult to compare the success of various job enrichment programs. Most often, support for or against job enrichment is based on the results of a series of case studies. Although many of these case studies find job enrichment programs to be successful, other case studies illustrate failed job enrichment programs. It is clear, however, that some of these failures may be due more to faulty implementation of the program rather than to any

APPLYING I/O PSYCHOLOGY

Job Enrichment in a Manufacturing and a Service Organization

In 1971, a decision was made to implement a job enrichment program in a Volvo automobile assembly plant in Kalmar, Sweden, that was suffering from extremely high levels of absenteeism and turnover. First, the traditional assembly-line workers were separated into teams with 15 to 25 members. In keeping with the general principles of job enrichment, each team was made responsible for an entire auto component or function (for example, upholstery, transmission assembly, or electrical system wiring). Each team was given the freedom to assign members to work tasks, to set their own output rates, to order supplies, and to inspect their own work, all of which had previously been performed by supervisors. To encourage team spirit, each group was given carpeted break rooms, and job rotation (rotating workers periodically from one task to another) was encouraged to alleviate boredom. The results of the program indicated a significant decline in both absenteeism and turnover along with improved product quality, although there was a slight decline in productivity and the costs of implementing the program were great. It was also discovered that some workers did not adapt well to the enriched jobs and preferred the more traditional assembly line (Goldman, 1976). However, management proclaimed the program a success and implemented the strategy in several other plants (Gyllenhammer, 1977; Walton, 1972).

In another job enrichment program, a large U.S. financial institution decided to introduce job enrichment into their credit and collections department, which serviced the company's credit card account activity, collected on overdue accounts, and dealt with any credit-related difficulties experienced by cardholders, such as changes of address, lost cards, and credit inquiries. In the existing situation, each type of work was handled by a specialist, so that an inquiry on a single account might be handled by several workers. This often led to confusion and to frustration on the part of cardholders, who felt as if they were being passed from worker to worker for even simple service requests. On the employee side, jobs were repetitive and monotonous, which led to high rates of absenteeism and turnover.

The job enrichment program involved dividing the department into two distinct operating units, each composed of a number of two-member teams. One unit dealt solely with actions on current accounts, the other unit only with past due accounts. Rather than assigning work based on the type of task that needed to be performed, each team was now given complete responsibility for certain accounts. This restructuring increased the level of responsibility required of each worker and reduced the routine nature of the jobs. Also, workers were able to receive feedback about their work since they dealt with an action on an account from start to finish. Nine months after the implementation of the job enrichment program, productivity had increased without any increase in staff, collection of past due accounts was more efficient, absenteeism was down 33 percent, and the nine-month turnover rate was zero (Yorks, 1979).

weakness in the concept and theory of job enrichment. For example, failures may result if workers or management do not support the program, or if jobs are not truly enriched because the level of worker responsibility is not increased. In addition, the idea from the job characteristics model that workers vary in growth need strength indicates that some workers (those high in growth need) will benefit and be motivated by enriched jobs, and some will not. Thus, levels of growth need strength in the workforce may also play a role in the success or failure of job enrichment. In conclusion, the most that we can say is that job enrichment is an innovative strategy to increase employee motivation by redesigning jobs. Its ultimate success or failure is still in question (Miner, 1983).

Rational Theories of Motivation

This category, labeled "rational theories of motivation," presents theories that are consistent with the trend toward greater understanding of the cognitive processes that affect work behavior. In this section, we will present two theories that view workers as rational beings who cognitively assess personal costs and benefits before taking action: equity theory and VIE theory.

EQUITY THEORY OF MOTIVATION

Equity theory states that workers are motivated by a desire to be treated equitably or fairly. If workers perceive that they are receiving fair treatment, their motivation to work will be maintained and steady performance can be expected. If, on the other hand, they feel that there is inequitable treatment, their motivation will be channeled into some strategy that will try to reduce the inequity.

Equity theory, first proposed by J. Stacey Adams (1965), has become quite popular. According to this theory, the worker brings **inputs** to the job, such as experience, education and qualifications, energy, and effort, and expects to receive certain **outcomes**, such as pay, fringe benefits, recognition, and interesting and challenging work, each in equivalent proportions. To determine whether the situation is equitable, workers make some social comparisons between their own input-outcome ratio and those of **comparison others**, who can be coworkers, people with a similar job or occupation, or the workers' own experiences. It must be stressed that equity theory is based on workers' *perceptions* of equity/inequity. In certain instances, workers may perceive that an inequity exists when there is not one, but equity theory's predictions are still valid because they operate on worker perceptions.

According to equity theory, lack of motivation is caused by two types of perceived inequity. **Underpayment inequity** results when workers feel that they are receiving fewer outcomes from the job in ratio to inputs. Imagine that you have been working at a particular job for over a year. A new employee has just been hired to do the same type of job. This person is about

STOP AND REVIEW

According to the MPS, which job characteristics are most important in motivating workers?

equity theory
a theory that workers are motivated to reduce perceived inequities between work inputs and outcomes

inputs
elements that a worker invests in a job, such as experience and effort

outcomes
those things that a worker expects to receive from a job, such as pay and recognition

comparison others
persons used as a basis for comparison in making judgments of equity/inequity

underpayment inequity
worker's perception that inputs are greater than outcomes

your age and has about the same background and level of education. However, your new coworker has much less work experience than you. Now imagine that you find out that this new employee is making $1.50 per hour more than you are. Equity theory predicts that you would experience underpayment inequity and would be motivated to try to balance the situation by doing one of the following:

- *Increasing outcomes*—You could confront your boss and ask for a raise, or find some other way to get greater outcomes from your job, perhaps even through padding your expense account or taking home office supplies (see Greenberg, 1990).
- *Decreasing inputs*—You might decide that you need to limit your work production or quality of work commensurate with your "poor" pay.
- *Changing the comparison other*—If you find out that the new employee is actually the boss's daughter, she is clearly not a similar comparison other.
- *Leaving the situation*—You might decide that the situation is so inequitable that you are no longer motivated to work there.

Now imagine that you are on the receiving end of that extra $1.50 per hour. In other words, compared to your comparison others, you are receiving greater outcomes from your average-level inputs. This is referred to as **overpayment inequity**, which also creates an imbalance. In this case, equity theory predicts that you might try doing one of the following:

overpayment inequity worker's perception that outcomes are greater than inputs

- *Increasing inputs*—You might work harder to try to even up the input-outcome ratio.
- *Decreasing outcomes*—You might ask for a cut in pay, although this is extremely unlikely.
- *Changing comparison others*—An overpaid worker might change comparison others to persons of higher work status and ability. For example, "Obviously my boss sees my potential. I am paid more because she is grooming me for a management position."
- *Distorting the situation*—A distortion of the perception of inputs or outcomes might occur. For example, "My work is of higher quality and therefore deserves more pay than the work of others."

It is this last outcome, the possibility of psychological distortions of the situation, that weakens the predictive power of this very rational theory of motivation. Equity theory has difficulty predicting behavior when people act nonrationally, as they sometimes do.

While most of the research on equity theory has used pay as the primary outcome of a job, other factors may constitute outcomes. For example, one study found that workers would raise their inputs in response to receiving a high-status job title (Greenberg & Ornstein, 1983). In other words, the prestige associated with the title served as compensation, even though there was no raise in pay. There was one catch, however; the workers had to perceive the higher job title as having been earned. An unearned promotion led to feelings of overpayment inequity.

Although equity theory has been well-researched, the majority of these studies have been conducted in laboratory settings (Greenberg, 1982; Mowday, 1979; although see Bretz & Thomas, 1992; Carrell, 1978; Martin & Peterson, 1987). As you might imagine, there is greater support for equity theory predictions in the underpayment inequity than in the overpayment inequity condition (Campbell & Pritchard, 1976; Pritchard, Dunnette, & Jorgenson, 1972). Recent research has also examined the role of individual differences as moderators of equity (King, Miles, & Day, 1993). In particular, this research has focused on the construct of *equity sensitivity*. It has been suggested that individuals vary in their concern over the equity of input-outcome ratios. In other words, some people are quite sensitive to equity ratios and prefer balance, while others may be less concerned with equitable relationships, and still other individuals may prefer to have either an outcome advantage or input advantage, preferring to be overcompensated or undercompensated for their work (see Huseman, Hatfield, & Miles, 1987; Miles, Hatfield, & Huseman, 1989). In spite of the voluminous research, no particular applications have been developed directly from the equity theory. As Miner (1983, p. 48) states, "The theory has tremendous potential insofar as applications are concerned, but these have not been realized, even though the theory itself has stood the test of research well."

EXPECTANCY (VIE) THEORY OF MOTIVATION

expectancy theory
a rational theory of motivation that states that workers weigh expected costs and benefits of particular courses before they are motivated to take action

valence
the desirability of an outcome to an individual

instrumentality
the perceived relationship between the performance of a particular behavior and the likelihood of receiving a particular outcome

expectancy
the perceived relationship between the individual's effort and performance of a behavior

One of the most popular motivation theories is **expectancy theory**, which is also known as *VIE theory*, referring to three of the theory's core components: valence, instrumentality, and expectancy. Expectancy theory is most often associated with Vroom (1964), although there have been some later refinements and modifications of the theory (Graen, 1969; Porter & Lawler, 1968). Like equity theory, expectancy theory assumes that workers are rational, decision-making persons whose behavior will be guided by an analysis of the potential costs and benefits of a particular course of action. Also like equity theory, expectancy theory focuses on the particular outcomes associated with a job, which refer not only to pay, but also to any number of factors, positive or negative, that are the potential results of work behavior. For example, positive outcomes include benefits, recognition, and job satisfaction, and negative outcomes include reprimands, demotions, and firings.

As mentioned, the three core components of expectancy theory are: **valence**, which refers to the desirability (or undesirability) of a particular outcome to an individual; **instrumentality**, which is the perceived relationship between the performance of a particular behavior and the likelihood that a certain outcome will result—in other words, the link between one outcome (the worker's behavior) and another outcome (obtaining recognition or a pay raise, for example); **expectancy**, which is the perceived rela-

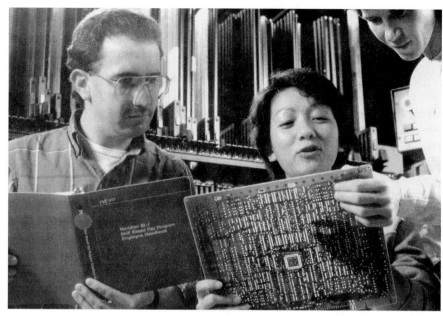

Expectancy theory favors a clear connection between performance and rewards, as in the case of this employee who earns a raise by demonstrating a new skill.

tionship between the individual's effort and performance of the behavior. Both the expectancy and the instrumentality components are represented as probabilities (for example, "If I expend x amount of effort, I will probably complete y amount of work."—the expectancy component; "If I complete y amount of work, I will likely get promoted"—the instrumentality component). Expectancy theory states that the motivation to perform a particular behavior depends on a number of factors: whether the outcome of the behavior is desirable (valence), whether the individual has the ability, skills, or energy to get the job done (expectancy), and whether the performance of the behavior will indeed lead to the expected outcome (instrumentality). In research and applications of expectancy theory, each of the components is measured, and a complex predictive formula is derived.

Consider as an example the use of expectancy theory in studying how students might be motivated, or not motivated, to perform exceptionally well in college courses. For this student, the particular outcome will be acceptance into a prestigious graduate (Ph.D.) program in psychology. First, consider the valence of the outcome. While it may be a very desirable outcome for some (positively valent), it is not for others (negative or neutral valence). Therefore, only those students who view being admitted to a graduate program as desirable are going to be motivated to do well in school in order to achieve this particular outcome. (Note: This does not mean that there are not other reasons for doing well in school, nor that good grades are the only requirements for admission to graduate school.) For those who desire the graduate career, the next component to consider is expectancy. Given what you know about your own abilities, study habits, and effort, what is the probability that you will actually be able to achieve the required grades? Here you might consider your willingness to sacrifice some of your social life in order to study more, as well as considering your past academic performance. Should you say, "Yes, I have the 'right stuff' to get the job done," it is likely that you will be highly motivated. For those individuals unwilling to expend the time and energy required, motivation will be much less. Finally, what about instrumentality? It is well-known that there are many more qualified applicants to graduate programs than there are openings. Therefore, the probability of actually achieving the desired outcome, even if you perform at the required level, is less than certain. It is here that motivation might also potentially break down. Some people might believe that the odds are so poor that working overtime to get good grades is simply not worth it. Others might figure that the odds are not so bad, and thus the *force* of their motivation, in expectancy theory terms, will remain strong.

At work, expectancy theory might be applied using promotions, the performance of special work projects, or avoidance of a supervisor's displeasure as potential outcomes. For example, if an employee's goal is to avoid her supervisor's criticism (which is negatively valent), she might consider the expectancy ("Can I perform the job flawlessly to avoid my supervisor's displeasure?") and the instrumentality ("Even if I do an error-free job, will my supervisor still voice some displeasure?") of that goal before being motivated even to try to avoid having the boss become displeased. If the supervisor is someone who never believes that an employee's performance is good enough, it is unlikely that the employee will exhibit much motivation to avoid her or his displeasure, because it is perceived as inevitable.

Expectancy theory illustrates the notion that motivation is a complex phenomenon, affected by a number of variables. This theory looks at factors such as individual goals, the links between effort and performance (expectancy), the links between performance and outcomes (instrumentality), and how outcomes serve to satisfy individual goals (valence). It is one of the most complicated yet thorough models of work motivation. The theory has generated a considerable amount of research, with evidence both supporting (Matsui, Kagawa, Nagamatsu, & Ohtsuka, 1977; Muchinsky, 1977) and criticizing certain aspects of the theory (Pinder, 1984; Stahl & Harrell, 1981; Van Eerde & Thierry, 1996). In addition, researchers have noted problems in the measurement of the VIE components of valence, instrumentality, and expectancy in several studies (Schmidt, 1973; Schwab, Olian-Gottlieb, & Heneman, 1979; Wanous, Keon, & Latack, 1983). Expectancy theory continues to be a popular rational model for understanding work motivation. Although there is no single agreed-upon strategy for its application, it does lead to many practical suggestions for guiding managers in their attempts to motivate workers, including the following:

- Managers should try to define work outcomes—potential rewards and costs associated with performance—clearly to all workers.
- The relationships between performance and rewards should also be made clear. Workers need to know that if they achieve certain goals, rewards are sure to follow.
- Any performance-related goal should be within the reach of the employee involved.

In sum, both expectancy theory and equity theory are based on rational models of motivation. They assume that individuals are constantly aware of important elements in their work environment and that motivation is determined by a conscious processing of the information received. The problem is that some people may simply be more rational than others in their usual approaches to work. The effectiveness of these rational models of motivation is also weakened by the fact that in some situations, individuals, regardless of their usual rational approach, may behave in a nonrational manner (for example, when workers become so upset that they impulsively quit their job without considering the implications). Moreover, there is some evidence that even when people are using rational means to evaluate a particular situation, individuals vary in the ways that they process information (see Zedeck, 1977).

Comparing, Contrasting, and Combining the Different Motivation Theories

Work motivation is an important topic. The importance of the construct is reflected in the many theories that have been constructed to try to "capture" motivational processes and predict when workers will and will not be motivated. In reviewing the various motivational models it is important to examine the ways in which the theories are similar and how they are different. (See Table 7.3 for a summary of the motivation theories we have discussed).

The early need theories of motivation, those of Maslow and Alderfer, are primarily descriptive models that explain that people's motivation is rooted in different levels of needs. Reinforcement theory, on the other hand, focuses on the role of the environment in "drawing out" a person's motivation. Need theories can be viewed as the "push" from within, while reinforcement represents the "pull" from without. Yet, more complex versions of need theories, like McClelland's, go beyond the simple categorization of needs. In McClelland's model, the needs for achievement, power, and affiliation interact with how a worker views the job and the work environment. For example, someone with a high need for achievement will be concerned with how the job can meet her achievement-related goals. Someone with high power needs will seek out ways to direct others' activities. In other words, there is an interaction between needs from within the individual and what the work environment, external to the person, has to

TABLE 7.3

Summary of Theories of Motivation

Theory	Elements/Components	Applications
Need Theories		
Maslow's Need Hierarchy	Levels of needs arranged in a hierarchy from lower to higher order needs	(no direct intervention programs)
Alderfer's ERG Theory	Three levels of needs: existence, relatedness, growth	
Behavior-Based Theories		
Reinforcement Theory	Consequences of behavior: reinforcers and punishment	Organizational behavior modification
Goal-Setting Theory	Setting of challenging goals and commitment to goals	Various goal-setting programs (e.g., MBO)
Job Design Theories		
Herzberg's Two-Factor Theory	Jobs must provide hygienes and motivators	Job enrichment
Job Characteristics Model	Jobs must provide five key job characteristics	Job enrichment
Rational Theories		
Equity Theory	Inputs = outcomes; emphasizes drive to reduce inequities	(various applications but no agreed-upon intervention programs)
Expectancy (VIE) Theory	Valence, instrumentality, expectancy	

offer. Of course, the fact that workers evaluate how their needs can be achieved suggests that rational, cognitive factors also come into play. Thus, there is some overlap between McClelland's need theory and aspects of the rational models of motivation.

Similar connections can be made between the behavior-based theories of motivation and the rational models. For example, the notion of intrinsic rewards suggests that workers think rationally about their accomplishments, and the setting and achieving of performance goals is an important component of both goal-setting theories and the VIE model of motivation (see Mento, Locke, & Klein, 1992; Tubbs, Boehne, & Dahl, 1993). In fact, in the past several years, motivation researchers such as Locke and Latham (1990b) have started combining elements of different motivation models to develop a new theory of motivation. This new model combines aspects of goal setting, equity and expectancy theory, and the job characteristics model. Their new theory is called the *high performance cycle*. This model states that if challenging work-related goals are combined with a high expectancy for success, motivation and high levels of work performance will result, if the following conditions are met: (1) the worker has the knowledge, skills, and ability to do the job; (2) the worker is committed to the goals; (3) the worker is given feedback about goal attainment; and (4) nothing in the work environment hinders the worker's performance (such as uncooperative coworkers, or inadequate work tools). Models such as the high performance cycle, which draw on the best elements of earlier motivational models, illustrate the value of an extensive understanding of earlier theories and research results.

On the Cutting Edge

Is There a Limit to Worker Motivation, or Is Continuous Improvement Possible?

An interesting question is, "Can you have too much motivation?" In other words, is there a limit to how motivated workers can be? In the past decade, there has been a great deal of interest in the notion of concepts such as *Total Quality Management (TQM)* and the *Continuous Improvement Process* (see Deming, 1982, 1986). These concepts are closely aligned with the Japanese concept of "Kaizen" which has received a great deal of attention as a motivational technique aimed at improving manufacturing quality in Japan and other industrialized nations. The approach characterized by TQM and Kaizen emphasizes that workers must have a continuous drive toward constant improvement in the quality of products and services. Yet, when considering the notion of *continuous* improvement, the issue raised is whether there is a "ceiling" to worker motivation toward continuous improvement. A study was designed to address this issue (Sama, Kopelman, & Manning, 1994).

In this study, nearly 200 medical transcriptionists were divided into a treatment group and a comparison (control) group. Transcriptionists were paid piece rate: their pay was directly related to the number of pages they transcribed. Moreover, these medical transcriptionists were already in an elite group of high producers, since their average rate of work was over 200 percent greater than the industry average. Transcriptionists in the treatment group were put through a program that provided them with detailed information about their production rates and the number of pages produced. The idea behind the study was that these workers were already highly motivated, top producers who were paid directly for their output. Therefore, the feedback they were given should serve to motivate them even more. This was indeed the case, as treatment group transcriptionists improved their output rates by 18.5 percent during the feedback intervention. The feedback program was stopped for a few

ON THE CUTTING EDGE (*continued*)

months and then a second intervention was introduced. Here, the treatment participants attended a meeting where the value of the feedback program was discussed. The workers agreed to participate in another round of the feedback program. This time, transcriptionists in the feedback program improved even more, to 22 percent above their original output rates (there was no significant improvement in comparison participants during these two time periods). These results suggest that motivation, and continuous improvement, are indeed possible. Informal evidence from highly motivated, high-producing workers also supports this conclusion. Many good producers seem to continue to improve their work output and quality over time. There seems to be no end to the motivational capacity of the best workers.

The Relationship Between Motivation and Performance

Motivation is central to any discussion of work behavior because it is believed that it has a direct link to good work performance. In other words, it is assumed that the motivated worker is the productive worker.

Yet this may not always be true, since many other factors can affect productivity independent of the effects of worker motivation, as the high performance cycle suggests. Furthermore, having highly motivated workers does not automatically lead to high levels of productivity. The work world is much more complex than that. As mentioned at the beginning of the chapter, many managers consider motivation to be the primary problem when they see low levels of productivity. However, a manager must approach a productivity problem as a social scientist would. Before pointing the finger at worker motivation, a detailed assessment of all of the other variables that could affect productivity must first be undertaken. These variables can be divided into four categories: systems and technology variables, individual difference variables, group dynamics variables, and organizational variables.

SYSTEMS AND TECHNOLOGY VARIABLES

Regardless of the level of motivation, if workers are forced to work with inadequate work systems, procedures, tools, and equipment, productivity will suffer. Poor tools and systems will affect work productivity independent of employee motivation. This is often seen in the low agricultural production

Lack of technology, not motivational problems, often limits Third World agricultural production.

of some Third World countries. A common mistake is to assume that these disadvantaged nations suffer from a lack of worker motivation. A more reasonable (and accurate) explanation is that they lack the appropriate agricultural technology to be as productive as other countries. You may see this in your own life, when having access to a word processor increases your term paper productivity and efficiency without any significant change in your motivational level. We will look in more detail at the role that systems and technology play in determining work performance in Chapter 15.

INDIVIDUAL DIFFERENCE VARIABLES

A variety of factors within the individual can affect work productivity regardless of motivation. For example, lacking the basic talents or skills to get the job done will hamper productivity even in the most motivated worker. Perhaps the *least* productive workers in any work setting are also the *most* motivated: new employees. At least initially, the novice employee is energized and determined to make a good impression on the boss. Unfortunately, a total lack of knowledge about the job makes this person inefficient and unproductive, in spite of high motivation. Other workers, because of a lack of basic abilities or education, or perhaps because of being placed in a job that is incompatible with their own interests and talents, may be particularly unproductive. What may appear on the surface to be a motivational problem is actually a problem of individual abilities. We have already

Explain the three components of the expectancy theory of motivation.

touched on some of these individual factors that affect performance when we looked at personnel screening, selection, and placement.

GROUP DYNAMICS VARIABLES

Rather than working by themselves, most workers are a part of a larger unit. For the group to be efficient and productive, individual efforts must be coordinated. While most members may be highly motivated, group productivity can be poor if one or two key members are not good team workers. In these situations, the influence of motivation on productivity becomes secondary to certain group dynamics variables.

Group dynamics can also affect productivity apart from motivation when rate setting occurs, which is when a work group develops an informal rule to restrict output. A particular rate is set, far below the group's potential output level, and pressure is exerted to keep members from exceeding the rate. Output rates are set by workers in the first place because workers do not want to be forced to meet what they regard as high production rates set by superiors (but which may in fact be realistic production goals). Although individual workers may be highly motivated, they usually will adhere to the group rule to avoid being ostracized. We will discuss the group processes that come into play in affecting work performance in Chapter 11.

ORGANIZATIONAL VARIABLES

The productivity of an organization requires the concerted and coordinated efforts of a number of work units. High levels of motivation and output in one department may be offset by lower levels in another department. Organizational politics and conflict may also affect the coordination among groups, thus lowering productivity in spite of relatively high levels of motivation in the work force. We will look at the effects of such variables as organizational politics and conflict in upcoming chapters.

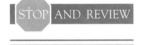

As you can see, the role of motivation in affecting work outcomes is important, but limited. The world of work is extremely complex. Focusing on a single variable, such as motivation, while ignoring others leads to a narrow and limited view of work behavior. Yet, motivation is an important topic, one of the most widely researched in I/O psychology. However, it is only one piece of the puzzle that contributes to our greater understanding of the individual in the work place.

How can technology and group variables affect worker motivation?

Summary

Motivation is the force that energizes, directs, and sustains behavior. The many theories of work motivation can be classified as need theories, behavior-based theories, job design theories, and rational theories. Maslow's and Alderfer's basic need theories propose that *needs* are arranged in a hierarchy from the lowest, most basic needs, to higher-order needs such as the need for esteem or self-actualization. McClelland's *achievement motivation theory* proposes that the three needs important in work motivation are needs for achievement, power, and affiliation, which can be measured with a projective test known as the *Thematic Apperception Test*. Unlike Maslow's and Alderfer's need theories, McClelland's theory has been used extensively in work settings to encourage worker motivation.

Behavior-based theories include both reinforcement and goal-setting approaches to motivation. *Reinforcement theory* stresses the role that *reinforcers* and *punishments* play in motivation. Reinforcement theory is evident in the various schedules used to reward workers. The theory is applied to increase motivation through *organizational behavior modification* programs. *Goal-setting theory* emphasizes setting challenging goals for workers, and getting workers committed to those goals as the keys to motivation.

Job design theories of motivation stress the structure and design of jobs as key factors in motivating workers. Herzberg's *two-factor theory* focuses on job satisfaction and dissatisfaction as two independent dimensions important in determining motivation. *Motivators* are factors related to job content that, when present, lead to job satisfaction. *Hygienes* are elements related to job context that, when absent, cause job dissatisfaction. According to Herzberg, the presence of hygienes will prevent job dissatisfaction, but motivators are needed for employee job satisfaction and hence motivation. Hackman and Oldham have proposed the *job characteristics model*, another job design theory of motivation, which states that five core job characteristics influence three critical psychological states that in turn lead to motivation. This model can be affected by certain moderators, including *growth need strength*, the notion that certain workers feel a need to grow on their jobs. Workers must be high in growth need strength if programs such as job enrichment are indeed going to produce motivation. *Job enrichment*, which involves redesigning jobs in order to give workers greater responsibility in the planning, execution, and evaluation of their work, is the application that grew out of the job design models of motivation.

Rational theories of motivation emphasize the role that cognition plays in determining worker motivation. *Equity theory* states that workers are motivated to keep their work *inputs* in proportion to their *outcomes*. According to equity theory, workers are motivated to reduce perceived inequities. This perception of equity/inequity is determined by comparing the worker's input-outcome ratio to similar *comparison others*. *Expectancy theory* (with its three core components of *valence, instrumentality,* and *expectancy*) is a complex model which states that motivation is dependent on expectations concerning effort-performance-outcome relationships.

The most recent approaches to motivation involve combinations of elements from earlier motivation models, indicating that motivation is indeed a complex construct. Yet, in spite of the importance given to worker motivation in determining work performance, numerous variables related to systems and technology, individual differences, group dynamics, and organizational factors may all affect work performance directly, without regard to worker motivation. Thus, while motivation is important, it is only one determinant of work behavior.

Study Questions and Exercises

1. Motivation is an abstract concept, one that cannot be directly observed. Using your knowledge of research methods, list some of the methodological issues/problems that motivation researchers must face.

2. Some theories of motivation have led to successful strategies for enhancing work motivation, whereas others have not. What are some of the factors that distinguish the more successful theories from the less successful?

3. Apply each of the various theories to describing/explaining your own level of motivation at school or at work. Which model gives the best explanation for your personal motivation?

4. Basic need theories, goal-setting theory and reinforcement theory are very general models of work motivation. What are the strengths and weaknesses of such general theories?

5. How would you design a program to improve motivation for a group of low-achieving high school students? What would the elements of the program be? What theories would you use?

Suggested Readings

Harder, J.W. (1991). Equity theory versus expectancy theory: The case of major league baseball free agents. *Journal of Applied Psychology, 76,* 458–64. *For you baseball fans, this is an interesting study that applied both equity and expectancy theories to performance of free agent major league baseball players. A nice example of using existing, "real world" data to study motivation.*

Lawler, E.E. (1994). *Motivation in work organizations.* San Francisco: Jossey-Bass. *This 20-year-old practioner-oriented overview of work motivation has been recently reissued in paperback.*

Steers, R. M., & Porter, L. W. (Eds.). (1991). *Motivation and work behavior* (5th ed.). New York: McGraw-Hill. *A classic and very detail-oriented text covering theories and research relating to work motivation.*

CHAPTER EIGHT

JOB SATISFACTION, WORK ATTENDANCE, AND QUALITY OF WORK LIFE

CHAPTER OUTLINE

Job Satisfaction
Defining Job Satisfaction
The Measurement of Job Satisfaction
Job Satisfaction and Job Performance

Organizational Commitment
Organizational Commitment and Job Satisfaction

Job Satisfaction, Organizational Commitment, and Employee Attendance

Employee Absenteeism
Employee Turnover

Increasing Job Satisfaction
Changes in job structure • Changes in pay structure • Benefit programs

Quality of Work Life

Summary

JOB SATISFACTION, EMPLOYEE ATTENDANCE, AND QUALITY OF WORK LIFE

INSIDE TIPS

If someone were to ask us about job satisfaction at any given point, we would probably report some positive feelings of satisfaction with some aspects of our jobs as well as indicating some aspects of the job with which we were dissatisfied. This chapter more than any other pulls together a number of issues and topics from I/O psychology. For example, the discussion of job satisfaction will look at the links between job satisfaction and productivity. This is really an issue of motivation, similar to those examined in Chapter 7. Recall that in Herzberg's two-factor theory, motivation, and hence productivity, were caused by job satisfaction resulting from increased worker responsibility. This chapter also deals with some measurement issues that were introduced in Chapter 2. Because job satisfaction is an abstract and elusive concept, it presents a number of measurement problems. Much of the difficulty that I/O psychologists have had in studying this phenomenon has involved the complexity of measuring job satisfaction adequately. The discussion of the quality of work life issues in this chapter will emphasize the importance of proper work conditions and employee well-being, which will be covered in depth in Chapter 16. This topic also involves issues relating to group decision-making processes presented in Chapter 11 and crosses over into some of the issues important for organizational change and development discussed in Chapter 14. For example, many techniques designed to enhance the quality of work life involve allowing employees a greater voice in decision making, while programs for organizational development are often implemented as a way of enhancing the quality of work life. In short, it is impossible to carve I/O psychology into separate, isolated areas of specialization because there is a great deal of integration and overlap of topics. Keep this in mind as you try to understand the "big picture" of the field.

Seventy years ago, the only compensation that most workers received from their jobs was a paycheck. As time went on, this changed as workers began to demand and receive more from their jobs. Today's workers receive a variety of forms of compensation, including health care, retirement, and numerous other benefits and programs. However, one thing that the workers of two generations ago and today's workers have in common is that their jobs constitute a major part of their lives, and are one of the greatest sources of personal pleasure and pain. While jobs can be satisfying in some regards, with positive feelings of accomplishment and purpose, they can also be sources of negative feelings. Such negative feelings may, in turn, affect worker attitudes toward their organization as a whole. In short, nearly all jobs produce some feelings of satisfaction in workers, and also create some negative feelings.

In this chapter we will examine job satisfaction as it relates to organizational commitment, absenteeism and turnover. We will look closely at these three work-related constructs and see how they are associated with each other and with job satisfaction. We will also focus on some of the programs and techniques designed to increase job satisfaction. Finally, we will see how job satisfaction, organizational commitment, and related constructs may affect employees' quality of work life.

Job Satisfaction

In this section, we will define job satisfaction and discuss how it is measured and how it relates to job performance. We will also define organizational commitment and look at the relationship between organizational commitment and job satisfaction.

DEFINING JOB SATISFACTION

Although enlightened management is concerned with worker feelings and attitudes, the most important outcome variables for management are typically the crucial bottom-line variables of job performance/productivity, work quality, and, to a lesser extent, employee absenteeism and turnover. These are the variables that translate directly into dollars and cents for the organization. From the workers' perspective, the most important outcome variable is likely to be job satisfaction. Yet, there is increasing evidence that attitudes about one's job, including job satisfaction, are critically important to the functioning of work organizations (Pratkanis & Turner, 1994; Spector, 1997).

Job satisfaction consists of the feelings and attitudes one has about one's job. All aspects of a particular job, good and bad, positive and negative, are likely to contribute to the development of feelings of satisfaction (or dissatisfaction). As seen in Chapter 2, job satisfaction, along with productivity, quality, absenteeism, and turnover, is one of the key dependent variables commonly considered (and measured) in research in I/O psychology. There are two approaches to conceptualizing job satisfaction. The first is the *global approach,* which considers overall job satisfaction. This way of looking at job satisfaction simply asks if the employee is satisfied overall, using a yes-no response or a single rating scale. The second is the *facet approach,* which considers job satisfaction to be composed of feelings and attitudes about a number of different elements, or facets, of the job. For example, overall, global satisfaction may be a composite of numerous factors: satisfaction with pay, the type of work itself, working conditions, the type of supervision, company policies and procedures, relations with coworkers, and opportunities for promotion and advancement. In contrast, the facet approach considers each of these aspects individually.

There has been considerable discussion over which approach is better (Highhouse & Becker, 1993). Proponents of the global approach argue that it is overall satisfaction with a job that is important and that such complete satisfaction is more than the sum of satisfaction with separate job facets (Scarpello & Campbell, 1983; Schneider, 1985). Moreover, recent evidence suggests that even single-item measures of job satisfaction work reasonably well for assessing job satisfaction (Wanous, Reichers, & Hudy, 1997). On the other hand, advocates of the facet approach maintain that this view provides better, more detailed assessments of job satisfaction. According to the facet approach, a person might be satisfied with one area of their job, such as pay, but dissatisfied with another area, such as the quality of interactions with supervisors and coworkers. Moreover, there may be tremendous variation in how highly individual workers value certain facets of job satisfaction (Rice, Gentile, & McFarlin, 1991). For example, satisfaction with pay may be an important element of job satisfaction for one worker, but not for another. In addition, some facets may not apply to all types of jobs. For instance, CEOs of companies and self-employed professionals are not affected by opportunities for promotion—a facet that may be an important contributor to job satisfaction of lower-level managers in large organizations.

Proponents of the facet definition argue that it helps to indicate specific areas of dissatisfaction that can be targeted for improvement (Locke, 1976; Smith, Kendall, & Hulin, 1969). Still others believe there are advantages to

job satisfaction
the positive and negative feelings and attitudes about one's job.

using both types of measurement approaches based on findings that indicate that each approach offers interesting and important information (Ironson, Smith, Brannick, Gibson, & Paul, 1989). Overall, much of the psychological research on the topic utilizes the facet approach in the measurement of job satisfaction.

THE MEASUREMENT OF JOB SATISFACTION

Regardless of the approach, when considering the measurement of job satisfaction, it is important to bear in mind the difficulties encountered in attempting to define the factors that may influence satisfaction, as well as the difficulties inherent in trying to measure any attitude.

As mentioned above, most instruments designed from the facet approach measure satisfaction with such things as pay, working conditions, and relationships with supervisors and coworkers. However, other variables such as preemployment expectations, individual personality characteristics, and the fit between the organization or job and the employee may also affect worker satisfaction (Ostroff, 1993). Satisfaction with career choice and the employee's career progression can also contribute to job satisfaction (Scarpello & Vandenberg, 1992). Current research has suggested that elements of job satisfaction may be deeply rooted in the individual workers. These researchers have suggested that there may be genetic "predispositions" to be satisfied or dissatisfied with one's job (see On the Cutting Edge).

Describe the two approaches to conceptualizing job satisfaction.

ON THE CUTTING EDGE

Personality, Genetics, and Job Satisfaction

Can job satisfaction be a reality for all workers? And, how much can the organization do toward increasing or maintaining job satisfaction for its workers? Although the organization can do much to foster job satisfaction, the factors that cause job satisfaction are not entirely under the control of the organization. Workers can influence their own levels of job satisfaction through such actions as performing their jobs well and maintaining good attendance at work. Even if we could set up the ideal workplace, would this lead all workers to enjoy high levels of job satisfaction? Recent research on the influences of personality and genetic factors on job satisfaction suggest that the answer is "no."

For example, workers who score high on personal alienation—indicating deep-set tendencies toward feeling isolated, lonely, and powerless—do not seem to be as affected by interventions designed to increase workers' job satisfaction as are workers scoring low on this personality characteristic (Efraty & Sirgy, 1990). Moreover, personality differences may mean that workers will find different "sources" of job satsifaction in the workplace. For instance, workers with low self-esteem

On the Cutting Edge (continued)

appear to find more satisfaction in jobs in which expectations of performance are clear (i.e., there are clear guidelines for performance), whereas job satisfaction in persons with higher self-esteem is not as affected by knowledge of performance expectations (Pierce, Gardner, Dunham & Cummings, 1993). Indications are that workers' personalities may vary in terms of the amount of job satisfaction they are able to achieve, and under what conditions they are best able to achieve it. In fact, it has been argued that dispositional factors may be responsible for the fact that surveys of U.S. workers during both good and bad economic times seem to show approximately the same percentages of satisfied and dissatisfied workers (Staw & Ross, 1985). In other words, although economic conditions fluctuate, the distribution of different personality types in the workforce remains relatively stable.

Perhaps more interesting is the finding that genetic factors present at birth can influence a worker's job satisfaction. Studies examining the genetic and environmental components of job satisfaction using identical twins who were reared apart in different homes found a higher correlation in the twin adults' job satis-

faction than would be found between persons in the general population (Arvey, Bouchard, Segal, & Abraham, 1989; Keller, Bouchard, Arvey, Segal, & Dawis, 1992). In other words, despite the fact that the identical twins were raised in totally different environments, and likely were in completely different job environments, the twins' levels of job satisfaction were quite similar. Although this is not conclusive evidence of a "genetic predisposition" toward job satisfaction, even critics of this research believe that the idea is deserving of further research efforts (Croponzano & James, 1990; Gutek & Winter, 1992).

Of course, such findings do not suggest that organizations have no responsibility in helping workers to achieve job satisfaction. What these findings do suggest is that job satisfaction may not be completely determined by characteristics of the organization or of the job. While organizations must provide an environment where employees can meet their job-related needs, they cannot guarantee that every worker will achieve the same level of satisfaction. Likewise, workers should not place the entire responsibility for their own job satisfaction on the employer.

While there may be a variety of factors that contribute to job satisfaction for most workers (e.g., working conditions, relationships at work, etc.), as mentioned before, the connection between such factors and job satisfaction may not be a direct link. Job satisfaction may be mediated by the perceptions of individual workers (Gardner & Pierce, 1998; Mathieu, Hofmann, & Farr, 1993). This is because different employees may perceive the same job differently, and it is those individual perceptions that determine whether or not an employee is satisfied with the job. For instance, improving the working environment may affect satisfaction for some employees, but not for others, because not everyone is dissatisfied with the environment.

Another major obstacle in the measurement of job satisfaction is the same obstacle encountered in the measurement of any attitude—the necessary reliance upon respondents' self-reports. Recall that problems with self-report measures include the fact that workers may (intentionally or unintentionally) fail to report their true feelings. Strategies for measuring job satisfaction have included interviews, group meetings, and a variety of structured, pencil-and-paper methods, such as rating scales or questionnaires. The obvious advantages of using a rating scale or questionnaire, instead of a face-to-face meeting, are the reduced time invested in the administration of the instrument, and the fact that anonymity of responses can often be maintained (particularly if large numbers of employees are being surveyed). Such anonymity may help to ensure that worker responses are more candid than they might be in a face-to-face interview. That is, some workers, fearing retaliation from management, may not give an accurate representation of their levels of job satisfaction in an interview or a meeting, and may try to present an overly positive picture of their feelings.

On the other hand, meetings or interviews can provide richer information because the interviewer can ask follow-up questions or request futher elaboration or clarification of an answer. In addition, response biases (e.g., tendencies for all or most employees to give overly positive or negative responses), and ambiguous items that employees may interpret differently, may seriously damage the validity of a pencil-and-paper job satisfaction measure. Another problem with survey instruments is *context effects* (Harrison & McLaughlin, 1993). Context effects occur when a neutral item is responded to negatively or positively, simply because it is grouped with other items that are worded negatively or positively. Finally, even well-designed, standardized instruments may become outdated and require periodic revisions due to changes in technology and work roles (Roznowski, 1989). In summary, no matter which type of measurement is selected, careful thought and planning must go into the development and administration of job satisfaction measures.

In spite of the complexities, many organizations develop their own interviews, scales, or surveys which are used to measure employee job satisfaction. While such in-house techniques can be designed to assess satisfaction with specific issues relevant to each company's employees, their results may be difficult to interpret. First, these measures may not be reliable or valid. To construct measures that are reliable and valid, one must have a rather extensive background in survey development and measurement techniques. Moreover, it takes quite a bit of research to establish the reliability and validity of a job satisfaction measure. Many organizations don't have the employees with the skills needed to construct such measures. Second, it is very difficult to know what a particular rating or score means without being able to compare it to some standard. For example, if employees indicate relatively low levels of satisfaction with salary on some scale, does this mean that they are actually dissatisfied with the money they make? They may merely be stating a desire for more money—a desire shared by most employees of most organizations.

Because of these problems in creating and interpreting in-house job satisfaction measures, many companies are using standardized, published surveys. Besides being cost-effective, a major advantage of using such standardized measures is that they provide normative data that permit the comparison of ratings with those from similar groups of workers in other companies who have completed the survey. This allows the organization to know whether the job satisfaction levels of its employees are low, high, or in the "normal" range, as compared to other workers in other organizations. As demonstrated above in the comparison of levels of satisfaction with salary, if a company simply assumes its employees' ratings are low (when, in fact, they are average when compared to the norm), management may spend time and resources on a problem that doesn't exist.

The ability to compare scores from standardized job satisfaction measures which have been obtained from different groups of workers in different companies also allows researchers to investigate the various organizational factors that cause job satisfaction and dissatisfaction. In other words, if different questionnaires were used for all studies, researchers could not be sure that the studies were measuring and comparing the same things.

Two of the most widely used standardized surveys of job satisfaction are the **Minnesota Satisfaction Questionnaire (MSQ)** and the **Job Descriptive Index (JDI)**. The Minnesota Satisfaction Questionnaire (Weiss, Dawis, England, & Lofquist, 1967) is a multiple-item rating scale that asks workers to rate their levels of satisfaction/dissatisfaction with 20 job facets, including supervisor's competence, working conditions, compensation, task variety, level of job responsibility, and chances for advancement. Ratings are marked on a scale from "very dissatisfied" to "neutral" to "very satisfied." Sample items from the MSQ are presented in Figure 8.1.

The Job Descriptive Index (Smith, Kendall, & Hulin, 1969) is briefer than the MSQ, and measures satisfaction with five job facets: the job itself, supervision, pay, promotions, and coworkers. Within each of the five facets are a list of words or short phrases. Respondents indicate whether the word or phrase describes their job, using the answers "yes," "no," and "undecided." Each of the words or phrases has a numerical value that reflects how well it describes a typically satisfying job. Items checked within each scale are summed, yielding five satisfaction scores which reflect the five facets of job satisfaction. In the past it was suggested that the five scales could be summed into a total score of overall job satisfaction. However, one study indicates that such a total score is not the best overall measure, and suggests the use of a global assessment instrument called the Job In General (or JIG scale) as an accompaniment to the five JDI scales (Ironson, et al., 1989).

Since its development in the 1960s, the JDI has become the most widely used standardized measure of job satisfaction (Roznowski, 1989). Moreover, the JDI was revised and improved in the mid–1980s by replacing

Minnesota Satisfaction Questionnaire (MSQ)
a self-report measure of job satisfaction that breaks satisfaction down into 20 job facets

Job Descriptive Index (JDI)
a self-report job satisfaction rating scale measuring five job facets

On my present job, this is how I feel about	Very Dissatisfied	Dissatisfied	Neutral	Satisfied	Very Satisfied
1 Being able to keep busy all the time	1	2	3	4	5
2 The chance to work alone on the job	1	2	3	4	5
3 The chance to do different things from time to time	1	2	3	4	5
4 The chance to be somebody in the community	1	2	3	4	5
5 The way my boss handles his/her workers	1	2	3	4	5
6 The competence of my supervisor in making decisions	1	2	3	4	5
7 The way my job provides for steady employment	1	2	3	4	5
8 My pay and the amount of work I do	1	2	3	4	5
9 The chances for advancement on this job	1	2	3	4	5
10 The working conditions	1	2	3	4	5
11 The way my co-workers get along with each other	1	2	3	4	5
12 The feeling of accomplishment I get from the job	1	2	3	4	5

FIGURE 8.1

Sample Items from the Minnesota Satisfaction Questionaire.
Source: Adapted from D.J. Weiss, R.V. Dawis, G.W. England, and L.H. Lofquist, *Manual for the Minnesota Satisfaction Questionnaire: Minnesota Studies in Vocational Rehabilitation* (Mineapolis: University of Minnesota, Vocational Psychology Research, 1967).

some of the older scale items with improved items (Smith, Kendall, & Hulin, 1987). Figure 8.2 presents sample items from the JDI.

Both the MSQ and the JDI have been widely researched, and both have established relatively high levels of reliability and validity (Smith et al., 1969, 1987; Weiss et al., 1967). One obvious difference between the two measures is the number of job satisfaction facets measured: The JDI measures five facets, the MSQ assesses 20. An important question is how many or how few facets are needed to measure job satisfaction adequately. One study suggested that some of the JDI facets could be split into two parts. For example, the satisfaction with supervision scale could be split into satisfac-

Think of your present work. What is it like most of the time? In the blank beside each word given below, write

_Y_ for "Yes" if it describes your work
_N_ for "No" if it does NOT describe it
_?_ if you cannot decide

Work on present job

____ Routine

____ Satisfying

____ Good

Think of the pay you get now. How well does each of the following words describe your present pay? In the blank beside each word, put

_Y_ if it describes your pay
_N_ if it does NOT describe it
_?_ if you cannot decide

Present pay

____ Income adequate for normal expenses

____ Insecure

____ Less that I deserve

Think of the opportunities for promotion that you have now. How well does each of the following words describe these? In the blank beside each word, put

_Y_ for "Yes" if it describes your opportunities for promotion
_N_ for "No" if it does NOT describe them
_?_ if you cannot decide

Opportunities for promotion

____ Dead-end job

____ Unfair promotion policy

____ Regular promotions

Think of the kind of supervision that you get on your job. How well does each of the following words describe this supervision? In the blank beside each word below put

_Y_ if it describes the supervision you get on your job
_N_ if it does NOT describe it
_?_ if you cannot decide

Supervision on present job

____ Impolite

____ Praises good work

____ Doesn't supervise enough

Think of the majority of the people that you work with now or the people you meet in connection with your work. How well does each of the following words describe these people? In the blank beside each word below, put

_Y_ if it describes the people you work with
_N_ if it does NOT describe them
_?_ if you cannot decide

People on your present job

____ Boring

____ Responsible

____ Intelligent

Think of your job in general. All in all, what is it like most of the time? In the blank beside each word below, write

_Y_ for "Yes" if it describes your job
_N_ for "No" if it does NOT describe it
_?_ if you cannot decide

Job in general

____ Undesirable

____ Better than most

____ Rotten

FIGURE 8.2

Sample Items from the Job Descriptive Index, Revised. (Each Scale is Presented on a Separate Page.)
Source: P.C. Smith, L.M. Kendall, and C.L. Hulin, "Job Descriptive Index," from *The Measurement of Satisfaction in Work and Retirement,* (rev. ed.) (Bowling Green, OH: Bowling Green State University, 1985).
Note: The Job Descriptive Index is copyrighted by Bowling Green State University. The complete forms, scoring key, instructions, and norms can be obtained from Dr. Patricia C. Smith, Department of Psychology, Bowling Green State University, Bowling Green, OH 43403.

tion with the supervisor's ability, and satisfaction with the supervisor's interpersonal skills (Yeager, 1981). Other evidence indicates that some of the 20 MSQ scales are highly correlated with one another, and thus could be collapsed into fewer facets (Gillet & Schwab, 1975). One may conclude from these viewpoints that there is no consensus on what constitutes the ideal or best measurement of job satisfaction. However, most researchers do agree that a valid, reliable and standardized instrument will provide the most accurate assessment.

UP CLOSE

Job Satisfaction at the International Level

As you read this chapter, you will become more aware of some of the aspects of work that are related to job satisfaction for workers. However, the large majority of these studies are done in the U.S. As with research in all areas of psychology, we cannot conclude that the results of studies conducted with workers within the United States will generalize to workers in other countries and cultures. For example, you probably find that good relationships with your coworkers and supervisors add to the satisfaction that you find in your job. Are such personal relationships at work as important to workers throughout the world as they appear to be with American workers? And, what other aspects of work add to job satisfaction for workers outside of the U.S.?

One study conducted in Japan found that supportive supervision, as well as support from coworkers, was positively correlated with workers' job satisfaction (Kumara & Koichi, 1989). According to this study, support from coworkers and supervisors was especially important to employees who did not feel positive about the work they performed (e.g., those who found their jobs unpleasant, very difficult, or stressful). These workers in "unfulfilling" jobs depended on good interpersonal relationships to feel satisfied, similar

to findings of studies conducted using U.S. workers.

Along with having good social relationships at work, many U.S. workers prefer to have a variety of tasks to do, and to have some autonomy in performing those tasks. Similarly, workers in Australia (Hopkins, 1990), Canada (Baba & Jamal, 1991), and the Netherlands (Efraty & Sirgy, 1990) appear to be more satisfied with jobs that offer diverse tasks and independence. These facets of the job may also account for the findings in the U.S. and in other developed nations which show that older workers, and those holding higher-level jobs, experience more satisfaction than very young workers and those in blue-collar positions (Gamst & Otten, 1992; Gattiker & Howg, 1990; Kravitz, Linn, & Shapiro, 1990). In fact, one comparison of white-collar workers in the U.S. and India found remarkable similarity in the factors that contributed to these workers' job satisfaction (Takalkar & Coovert, 1994).

Obviously, the international findings discussed here are mostly based on studies of workers in developed countries, where workers enjoy a certain level of job security, adequate pay, and good working conditions. Whether or not workers in more underdeveloped nations would look to such things as task variety and auton-

UP CLOSE (*continued*)

omy for sources of job satisfaction has not yet been determined. Perhaps workers in underdeveloped nations have different sources of satisfaction, which are possibly related to more basic survival needs (e.g., pay) than workers in more developed nations. However, one would expect that as these nations develop and gain economic strength, workers the world over will look to their jobs to fulfill higher-level needs, such as support from coworkers, recognition, and the opportunity to control their own work behaviors and reach their highest potential.

JOB SATISFACTION AND JOB PERFORMANCE

As you recall from our discussion of the human relations movement, Mayo and his colleagues proposed that there was a relationship between one aspect of job satisfaction—employee satisfaction with social relationships at work—and work productivity. Moreover, the job design theories of motivation discussed in Chapter 7—Herzberg's two-factor theory and the job characteristics model—are as much theories of job satisfaction as they are of motivation. Both theories emphasize that satisfaction with the job is a key to determining motivation. While this idea that the "happy worker is the productive worker" might seem to make sense, research studying the links between job satisfaction and performance has shown inconsistent results. Early research reviews concluded that there were no positive relationships between the two factors (Locke, 1976; Vroom, 1964). In fact, the causal relationship may actually be more the other way around: Good job performance leads to (causes) job satisfaction!

A model suggested by Porter and Lawler (1968) clarifies how this process might operate. According to them, job satisfaction and performance are not directly linked. Instead, effective job performance leads to job-related rewards, such as pay increases, promotions, or a sense of accomplishment. If the process for offering these rewards is perceived as fair, receiving these rewards leads to job satisfaction and also to higher and higher levels of performance. This creates a situation in which job satisfaction and job performance are actually independent of one another, but are linked because both are affected by job-related rewards (see Figure 8.3). Interestingly, the **Porter-Lawler model** builds on the equity theory of motivation discussed in Chapter 7, since notions of equity—fairness in job-related inputs and outcomes—are central to the argument. Specifically, motivation to perform the job and the satisfaction derived from the job are both caused by the relationship between what an individual puts into the job and what is received from the job in terms of rewards. In other words, both motivation and job satisfaction come from the perceived equitable relationship between the employee's inputs to the job and the job outcomes.

Compare and contrast the MSQ and the JDI.

Porter-Lawler model
a theory where the relationship between job satisfaction and performance is mediated by work-related rewards

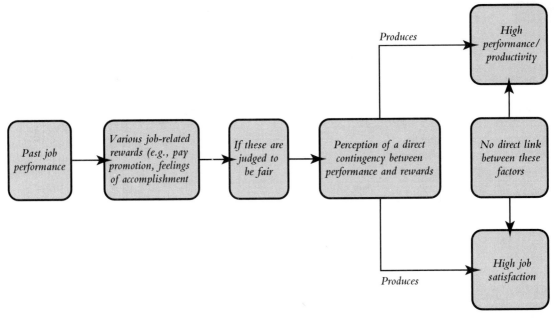

FIGURE 8.3

The Porter-Lawler Model of the Job Performance-Job Satisfaction Relationship
Source: L.W. Porter and E.E. Lawler, *Managerial Attitudes and Performance* (Homewood, IL: Dorsey Press, 1968), as adapted by R.A. Baron in *Behavior in Organizations: Understanding and Managing the Human Side of Work*, 2nd ed. (Boston: Allyn & Bacon, 1986).

Some researchers emphasize that the perception of fairness or justice in pay is the most important part of this link between performance and job satisfaction (Miceli, 1993). That is, "relative deprivation" (a discrepancy between a worker's expectations and rewards) and perceived fairness of pay may mediate the relationship between performance and job satisfaction, regardless of the actual rewards obtained. For example, if highly paid workers do not perceive their pay to be fair, or to meet their expectations, their satisfaction is likely to be negatively affected.

A number of attempts have been made to study the job satisfaction-performance relationship. Meta-analyses of dozens of studies examining this relationship indicate that there is a slight positive relationship between the two factors (Iaffaldano & Muchinsky, 1985; Petty, McGee, & Cavender, 1984). Although a positive relationship was found between job satisfaction and job performance, it was weaker than one might expect, given the popularly held belief that the two are closely tied. Why is the relationship not stronger? One reason is that the relationship may be quite complex, and may be moderated by a number of variables, such as the types of jobs being performed, the conditions under which people work, the rewards and recognitions workers receive, and the personal characteristics of the workers. For example, in jobs that require creative skills and ingenuity, a worker who has high levels of job satisfaction may indeed be more productive. However, for dull, routine jobs, levels of satisfaction may not have a direct effect on productivity. Moreover, we may get weaker results if we examine the relationship between overall job satisfaction and general job performance than if we look at the links between satisfaction with certain facets of the job and specific types of performance. For example, satisfaction with the type of work one performs may be related to job performance, but satisfaction with a company's benefit program may not be related to performance.

In summary, both job satisfaction and job performance are important but complex work outcomes. There is some evidence that these two variables are linked, but the relationship is not very strong. This weak link is likely due to the multitude of variables that can moderate the relationship.

Organizational Commitment

Just as there are different operational definitions of job satisfaction, so too are there different definitions of the construct of *organizational commitment*. For example, is it an attitude, a behavior, or both? Previously, organizational commitment, also referred to as company loyalty, was associated with an acceptance of the organization's goals and values, a willingness to exert effort on behalf of the organization, and a desire to remain with the organization (Porter, Steers, Mowday, & Boulian, 1974). This definition encompasses both attitudes and behaviors. More recently, the concept of organizational commitment has been taken to imply worker *attitudes*, such as those just mentioned, while the concept of *organizational citizenship behaviors* (OCB) refers to commitment-related behaviors (Organ, 1990). (We will discuss OCB more fully in Chapter 11.) For example, there is a negative correlation between the attitude of organizational commitment and the behavior of quitting a job. Organizational commitment is similar to job satisfaction, since both involve feelings about the work situation. However, because organizational commitment deals specifically with workers' attitudes about the organization, it may be more directly linked to employee attendance variables such as absenteeism and turnover than is job satisfaction. A good definition of **organizational commitment** is that it is the worker's attitudes about the entire work organization.

The most widely used organizational commitment measure is a 15-item self-report instrument called the Organizational Commitment Questionnaire (OCQ), which is presented in Figure 8.4.

ORGANIZATIONAL COMMITMENT AND JOB SATISFACTION

The concepts of job satisfaction and organizational commitment are closely related, although distinct. Research indicates a fairly high positive correlation between the two factors (Arnold & Feldman, 1982; O'Driscoll, Ilgen, &

STOP AND REVIEW

Describe the Porter-Lawler model.

organizational commitment
a worker's feelings and attitudes about the entire work organization

Instructions: *Listed below are a series of statements that represent possible feelings that individuals might have about the company or organization for which they work. With respect to your own feelings about the particular organization for which you are now working (company name), please indicate the degree of your agreement or disagreement with each statement by checking one of the seven alternatives below each statement.*★

1   *I am willing to put in a great deal of effort beyond that normally expected in order to help this organization be successful.*

2   *I talk up this organization to my friends as a great organization to work for.*

3   *I feel very little loyalty to this organization. (R)*

4   *I would accept almost any type of job assignment in order to keep working for this organization.*

5   *I find that my values and the organization's values are very similar.*

6   *I am proud to tell others that I am part of this organization.*

7   *I could just as well be working for a different organization as long as the type of work was similar. (R)*

8   *This organization really inspires the very best in me in the way of job performance.*

9   *It would take very little change in my present circumstances to cause me to leave this organization. (R)*

10   *I am extremely glad that I chose this organization to work for over others I was considering at the time I joined.*

11   *There's not too much to be gained by sticking with this organization indefinitely. (R)*

12   *Often, I find it difficult to agree with this organization's policies on important matters relating to its employees. (R)*

13   *I really care about the fate of this organization.*

14   *For me this is the best of all possible organizations for which to work.*

15   *Deciding to work for this organization was a definite mistake on my part. (R)*

★*Responses to each item are measured on a 7-point scale with scale point anchors labeled: (1) strongly disagree;   (2) moderately disagree;   (3) slightly disagree;   (4) neither disagree nor agree;   (5) slightly agree;   (6) moderately agree;   (7) strongly agree. An "R" denotes a negatively phrased and reverse-scored item.*

FIGURE 8.4

Organizational Commitment Questionnaire (OCQ).
Source: R.T. Mowday, R. Steers, and L.W. Porter, "The Measure of Organizational Commitment," *Journal of Vocational Behavior*, 14 (1979), p. 228.

Hildreth, 1992; Stumpf & Hartman, 1984). Part of this high positive correlation may be due to the fact that workers may possibly respond positively to both job satisfaction and organizational commitment measures, due to a positive response bias, or workers may have a desire to avoid *cognitive dissonance*. Cognitive dissonance is an unpleasant state of perceived self-inconsistency (Festinger, 1957). Workers thus avoid cognitive dissonance by convincing themselves that they are satisfied simply because they are loyal to the organization ("I have stayed with this company through thick and thin, therefore I must like my job."). While it is conceivable that a worker could be quite satisfied with a job but have low feelings of commitment to the organization, or vice versa, the feelings tend to be positively related. Studies show mixed results as to the direction of influence between these two constructs. For example, O'Driscoll and colleagues (1992) found that job satisfaction may directly affect organizational commitment, while other studies indicate that organizational commitment leads to job satisfaction (Becker & Billings, 1993; Vandenberg & Lance, 1992).

Both organizational commitment and job satisfaction are most likely affected by numerous factors, including the type and variety of work, the autonomy involved in the job, the level of responsibility associated with the job, the quality of the social relationships at work, compensation, and the chances for promotion and advancement in the company. However, there appears to be some consensus that organizational values influence organizational commitment, whereas perceived equity of rewards influences job satisfaction. That is, perceived fairness in rewards influences job satisfaction, whereas perceived congruence between organizational and employee values, and between organizational values and actions, tends to influence organizational commitment (Vandenberg & Lance, 1992). Organizational commitment also tends to be weakened by the perceived chances of finding a job with another company (Bateman & Strasser, 1984; Rusbult & Farrell, 1983). For instance, if highly skilled worker Carol could easily find a job with another company, but her friend Kim had difficulty finding her current job, Carol will likely have a lower level of organizational commitment than Kim. In addition, there appear to be positive correlations between organizational commitment and age, education, and time on the job, such that older and more educated workers, and those with longer tenure with the company, tend to be more committed to the organization (Becker & Billings, 1993; Lee, Ashford, Walsh, & Mowday, 1992).

Throughout the 1990s, many organizations found it necessary to reduce the size of their workforces by laying off or terminating workers. Thousands of people at a time can lose their jobs when a major corporation reduces the number of people it employs. Such actions, called *downsizing*, can have an impact on the workers who are retained, as well as on those who lose their jobs. For many of the remaining employees, feelings of organizational commitment and job satisfaction can decline following downsizing, especially if the employees are close to those who were laid off, or if they feel that their own jobs may be in jeopardy. However, studies show that explanations from management giving the reasons for the layoffs can have positive effects on the remaining workforce, and there is some evidence that the overall work effort of employees may actually increase following downsizing (Taylor & Giannantonio, 1993).

As you might imagine, maintaining job satisfaction and organizational commitment is a challenge to both employers and employees—a challenge that becomes even more difficult during trying economic times. Yet, organizations must be concerned with both employee job satisfaction and organizational commitment if they are to maintain a high quality, loyal workforce.

Job Satisfaction, Organizational Commitment, and Employee Attendance

As previously mentioned, employee attendance variables such as absenteeism and turnover are associated with both job satisfaction and organizational commitment. Employees who have positive feelings about their jobs and work organizations should be less likely to be absent from work and to leave for a job elsewhere than those with negative attitudes about their jobs. However, before considering these relationships, we must consider how employee attendance variables are defined and measured (Hackett & Guion, 1985; Johns, 1994a; Lee, 1989).

EMPLOYEE ABSENTEEISM

Both absenteeism and turnover can be categorized into voluntary and involuntary forms. Voluntary absenteeism is when employees miss work because they want to do something else. Calling in sick to take a three-day weekend or taking a day off to run errands or to go shopping are examples of voluntary absenteeism. Involuntary absenteeism occurs when the employee has a legitimate excuse for missing work, typically illness. Because involuntary absenteeism is inevitable, the organization must be prepared to accept a certain amount of such absences. It is voluntary absenteeism, however, that the organization would like to eliminate. Of course, it is very difficult to distinguish voluntary from involuntary absenteeism, since most employees are unlikely to admit that they were voluntarily absent (Dalton & Mesch, 1994; Hammer & Landau, 1981). One way that researchers have operationalized the measurement of voluntary and involuntary absenteeism is to use absence frequency (the number of days absent) as a measure of voluntary absenteeism, and absence length (the number of consecutive days absent) as an assessment of involuntary absenteeism (Atkin & Goodman, 1984). However, this is a very crude measure. It is important to note that voluntary absenteeism is likely to be more strongly associated with employee job satisfaction; involuntary absenteeism is beyond the control of the employee (Sagie, 1998).

Research examining the relationship between job satisfaction and employee absenteeism has produced conflicting findings. Sometimes, there is a slight negative relationship between the two (with higher levels of job satisfaction associated with lower rates of absenteeism; Ostroff, 1993), and sometimes no significant relationship at all is found (Ilgen & Hollenback, 1977; Porter & Steers, 1973). A meta-analysis of a number of studies indicates that job satisfaction and absenteeism are indeed negatively correlated but that the relationship between the two is not very strong (Scott & Taylor, 1985). One reason the relationship is not as strong as one might think stems from problems in measuring absenteeism which cause voluntary and involuntary absenteeism to be lumped together in most of these studies. In other words, there may be a significant negative correlation between job satisfaction and voluntary absenteeism, but no significant relationship between job satisfaction and involuntary absenteeism due to illness. According to one recent study, there is an association between voluntary absence and job satisfaction; however, this study concluded that rather than job satisfaction causing the absenteeism, it was really the absenteeism that was leading to lower job satisfaction (Tharenou, 1993). Perhaps to avoid cognitive dissonance, workers who voluntarily missed work rationalized that if they were choosing to be absent, they must not have been very satisfied with their jobs.

Another problem might be that even though workers are satisfied with their jobs, they may find certain nonwork activities (for example, taking an extra day of vacation or attending a ball game) more interesting or more important (Youngblood, 1984). Employees may also be absent because of factors beyond their control, such as health, transportation, or child care problems. Additionally, individual absenteeism may be affected by coworkers' absenteeism rates and by the organization's policy and "climate" toward absenteeism (Johns, 1994b; Gellatly, 1995; Markham & McKee, 1995). For example, if coworkers are frequently absent, or if management has a lenient policy that is tolerant of absences, employees might be inclined to miss work regardless of how satisfied or dissatisfied they are with their jobs (Haccoun & Jeanrie, 1995).

Finally, while the construct of absenteeism may apear quite simple, it, like other behaviors, is probably more complicated than it appears to be on the surface. Some of this complexity may be illustrated by studies indicating a negative correlation between age and voluntary absenteeism, and a positive correlation between age and involuntary absenteeism (Hackett, 1990). In other words, younger workers tend to voluntarily miss work, while older workers tend to miss work because they are more frequently ill.

While it may seem apparent that absenteeism, especially voluntary absenteeism, would be related to turnover (i.e., workers who have a lot of unexcused absences don't last long on the job), researchers hold conflicting views of this relationship. Some researchers have concluded that there is a positive relationship between absenteeism and turnover, while others have concluded that no such relationship exists. A meta-analysis of 17 separate studies showed a relationship between absenteeism and turnover. Moreover, the relationship was not mediated by type of absenteeism. In other words, turnover did not appear to be more related to voluntary absenteeism than to involuntary absenteeism (Mitra, Jenkins, & Gupta, 1992).

EMPLOYEE TURNOVER

As with absenteeism, there are difficulties in defining and measuring turnover (Campion, 1991). Involuntary turnover occurs when an employee is fired or laid off. A certain amount of involuntary turnover is likely to be considered inevitable and possibly even beneficial. Firing workers who are not performing at desirable levels can be viewed as a positive, "weeding" process (Mobley, 1982). Layoffs often occur for financial reasons, and thus are likely to be beyond the control of management. Most voluntary turnover takes place when a competent and capable employee leaves to work elsewhere. It is this turnover that is costly to the organization, because losing a valued employee means reduced organizational productivity and increased expenses associated with hiring and training a replacement. According to one school of thought, voluntary turnover is likely to be influenced by lack of job satisfaction and organizational commitment, while involuntary turnover is not. As with absenteeism, research that does not distinguish between voluntary and involuntary turnover may not find the expected relationships between employee attitudes and turnover simply because the two types of turnover are lumped together. Interestingly, some researchers note that there are also problems in categorizing turnover as either voluntary or involuntary since some poor workers may not be fired but may *voluntarily* choose to leave the organization, which is likely to be glad to see them go. However, this means that voluntary turnover might be further classified as either dysfunctional or functional, depending on whether it has negative or beneficial outcomes for the organization (Dalton, Krackhardt, & Porter, 1981).

Both job satisfaction and organizational commitment have been investigated as predictors of employee turnover. Some studies indicate that low levels of job satisfaction are related to higher rates of turnover (Jenkins, 1993; Mobley, Griffeth, Hand, & Meglino, 1979; Mowday, Koberg, & McArthur, 1984), while others indicate that low levels of job commitment are predictive of employee turnover (Koslowsky, 1991; Shore, Newton, & Thornton, 1990; Steers, 1977). Williams and Hazer (1986) demonstrated that organizational commitment develops from job satisfaction and in turn influences an employee's decision to remain with or leave the organization. However, while organizational commitment appears to be a predictor of turnover, one of the best predictors of employee turnover is absenteeism, particularly the rate of absences in the years immediately before the employee leaves (Mitra, Jenkins, & Gupta, 1992; Waters & Roach, 1979).

Since voluntary turnover can be costly to an organization, it is important to understand some of the reasons why good performers may leave their jobs (Lee & Maurer, 1997). Recently, it was found that productive, valuable employees who do not receive work-related rewards, such as promotions and pay raises, are likely candidates for leaving their jobs (Trevor, Gerhardt, & Boudreau, 1997). Studies also indicate that perceived lack of influence or power within the organization can cause workers to seek employment elsewhere, especially if they feel positive about the other job opportunities available to them (Buchko, 1992; Lee & Mitchell, 1994; Schminke, 1993). As stated earlier, both job satisfaction and organizational commitment are associated with turnover, and this need for workers to feel that they have some influence within the organization may help explain this association. That is, those workers who have such influence are probably more satisfied with their jobs and thus more committed to the organization (Dwyer, 1991). This may also help explain the reason that giving workers a sense of power over their jobs, or allowing them to participate in decision-making processes, is associated with higher levels of job satisfaction, as we shall see later in this chapter.

In summary, when examining the relationships between job satisfaction and other outcome variables such as absenteeism and turnover, it is important to consider the type of absenteeism and turnover being measured. Voluntary absenteeism and turnover are most likely to be affected by employee attitudes. Unfortunately, many studies do not distinguish between voluntary and involuntary absenteeism and turnover, which leads to a possible "watering down" of any observed effects. Moreover, cause and effect relationships often cannot be assumed. In fact, some studies indicate that the relationships are reciprocal, with each variable sometimes being the "cause" and at other times being the "effect."

Increasing Job Satisfaction

As we have seen, job satisfaction is considered important by organizations because it is most likely linked to costly absenteeism and turnover. It is also important to the employee because it reflects a critical work outcome: feelings of fulfillment from the job and the work setting. Because of its significance, organizations have implemented a number of programs and techniques in an effort to increase satisfaction. These programs take many forms. Some change the structure of work, others alter the methods of worker compensation, and still others offer innovative fringe benefit plans and packages. We will examine some of these techniques.

Changes in job structure

Three techniques have been used to try to increase employee satisfaction by changing the structure of jobs. The first technique, **job rotation**, which was introduced in Chapter 5, involves moving workers from one specialized job to another. While job rotation can be used to train workers in a variety of tasks, it can also be used to alleviate the monotony and boredom associated with performing the same work day in and day out. For example, an employee in a retail store may move from maintenance and clean-up duties to stocking merchandise to bagging merchandise on a weekly basis. A receptionist in a large organization might rotate from greeting visitors and answering telephones to simple clerical duties such as filing and photocopying.

Job enlargement is the practice of allowing workers to take on additional, varied tasks in an effort to make them feel that they are more valuable members of the organization. For example, a custodian who is responsible for the cleaning and upkeep of several rooms might progressively have his job enlarged until his duties involve the maintenance of an entire floor. Job enlargement is tricky to implement since it means that workers are required to do additional work, which some might perceive as negative. However, if used correctly, job enlargement can positively affect

job rotation
the systematic movement of workers from one type of task to another to alleviate boredom and monotony (as well as training workers on different tasks; see Chapter 5)

job enlargement
the expansion of a job to include additional, more varied work tasks

Job rotation in a department store makes one employee a stock hauler, a cashier, and a salesperson in turn.

job satisfaction by giving an employee a greater sense of accomplishment and improving valuable work skills. One study of enlarged jobs found that they led to greater employee satisfaction, improved employee initiative, and better customer service than persons in nonenlarged jobs. However, enlarged jobs carried the "costs" of requiring more skilled, more highly trained, and more costly (higher paid) workers than those performing nonenlarged jobs (Campion & McClelland, 1991).

Job enrichment, which we studied in depth in Chapter 7, can also be used to increase job satisfaction. Recall that job enrichment involves raising the level of responsibility associated with a particular job by allowing workers a greater voice in the planning, execution, and evaluation of their own activities. For example, in one such program assembly-line workers were divided into teams, each of which was given many of the responsibilities that were previously held by front-line supervisors, including ordering supplies, setting output rates, creating quality control inspection systems, and even appraising their own performance. This independence and increased responsibility can go a long way toward increasing motivation and job satisfaction for many workers. While job enrichment and job enlargement seem somewhat similar because both require more work from employees, job enrichment raises the level of tasks, while job enlargement does not raise the level of responsibility associated with the work.

Changes in pay structure

According to some researchers, the perception of fairness in pay is associated with greater job satisfaction (Witt & Nye, 1992). And, while the relationship between pay and job satisfaction is not always a direct, positive one, there is some evidence that employees who are compensated well are less likely to search for jobs elsewhere (Cotton & Tuttle, 1986; Trevor, Gerhardt, & Boudreau, 1997). While most innovative compensation programs are introduced primarily in an effort to improve job performance, many changes also increase levels of job satisfaction.

One innovative compensation program is **knowledge-based pay** (also known as *skill-based pay*), which involves paying employees an hourly rate based on their knowledge and skills rather than on the particular job to which they are assigned (Lawler, Mohrman, & Ledford, 1992). In other words, workers are paid for the level of the job that they are able to perform rather than for the level of the position that they hold. For knowledge-based pay programs to be cost-effective, it is imperative that employees be assigned to jobs that match the levels of their skills and knowledge. Research indicates that workers are more satisfied in organizations that use this system than in those that use conventional pay plans, and there is also evidence that they are more productive and concerned with quality (Murray & Gerhart, 1998). Particularly satisfied are those who receive knowledge-based pay and who also have high levels of ability and motivation (Tosi & Tosi, 1987).

knowledge-based pay
a system of compensation in which workers are paid based on their knowledge and skills rather than on their positions in the organization

The Porter-Lawler model (see Figure 8.3) suggested that job performance leads to job satisfaction by way of increased rewards, one of the most important of which is pay. If this is the case, then a system of compensation based directly on performance should be an effective strategy for increasing job satisfaction. One such pay-for-performance system is **merit pay**, a plan in which the amount of compensation is directly a function of an employee's performance. In merit pay plans, workers receive a financial bonus based on their individual output. While sensible in theory, such systems do not work well in practice for a number of reasons. First and perhaps most important, difficulties in the objective assessment of performance mean that it is often impossible to distinguish the truly good performers from the more average performers. This leads to unfairness in the distribution of merit pay and subsequent employee dissatisfaction. Second, most merit pay systems emphasize individual goals, which may hurt the organization's overall performance and disrupt group harmony, especially if jobs require groups to collaborate for the production of a product. Finally, in many such plans the amount of merit compensation is quite small in proportion to base salaries. In other words, the merit pay is simply not viewed as a strong incentive to work harder (Balkin & Gomez-Mejia, 1987; see also Pearce, Stevenson, & Perry, 1985). Research has suggested that a merit pay raise needs to be at least 7 percent to have significant impact on employee attitudes and motivation (Mitra, Gupta, & Jenkins, 1997).

merit pay
a compensation system in which employees receive a base rate and additional pay based on performance

Describe three techniques for changing job structure.

Another strategy for the implementation of pay-for-performance systems is to make pay contingent on effective group performance, a technique termed **gainsharing** (Lawler, 1987). If a work group or department reaches a certain performance goal, all members of the unit receive a bonus. Since the level of productivity among workers usually varies, the gainsharing program

gainsharing
a compensation system based on effective group performance

As part of a gainsharing system, this team of auto mechanics competes with other teams for monthly bonuses.

must be viewed as being fair to all involved. For example, individuals involved in experimental investigations decided that the most fair plan was to set a minimum amount that could be received by any worker, and then base additional pay on each worker's level of productivity. Thus, the low producers received some base compensation, but they found that greater pay would result only if they increased production. The high producers, on the other hand, were well-rewarded for their efforts (Cooper, Dyck, & Frohlich, 1992). Gainsharing may not be appropriate for all organizations or for all groups of workers. Therefore, implementation of a gainsharing program must be based on careful planning and a thorough knowledge of the groups of workers involved (Andrews, Neumann, Grossnickle, Wuensch, & Cope, 1990; Cappelli & Chauvin, 1991; Graham-Moore & Ross, 1990). One important consideration is that a failed attempt at a major change in pay structure, such as a gainsharing plan, could lead to massive worker dissatisfaction (Collins, 1995).

profit sharing
a plan where all employees receive a small share of an organization's profits

A more common plan is **profit sharing**, in which all employees receive a small share of the organization's profits (Rosen, Klein, & Young, 1986). One drawback to profit-sharing programs is that it is difficult for employees to see how their individual performances have an impact on the company's total output. Also, there is typically quite a long delay between reaching performance goals and receiving individual shares of the company's profits (see Applying I/O Psychology).

APPLYING I/O PSYCHOLOGY

Increasing Job Satisfaction and Organizational Commitment Through Employee Ownership

Although the concept of **employee ownership** of organizations either entirely or in part is not new, the number of companies which have implemented some such program has increased dramatically (Pendleton, McDonald, Robinson, & Wilson, 1995). Tales of the quick success of employee-owned companies such as Southwest Airlines, United Airlines, and Wheeling Steel are becoming legendary. Employee ownership can take one of two forms: direct ownership or employee stock ownership. In direct ownership, the employees are the sole owners of the organization. In employee stock ownership programs, which are the more common of the two, stock options are considered part of a benefit package whereby employees acquire shares of company stock over time. Each employee eventually becomes a company stockholder and has voting rights in certain company decisions. Proponents of these programs claim that although they are expensive, the costs are offset by savings created by increased employee organizational commitment, productivity, work quality, and job satisfaction, and decreases in rates of absenteeism and turnover (Buchko, 1992). The basic rationale is that employees will become more committed to an organization of which they are part owners.

Research on the success of employee ownership programs is somewhat inconsistent, and results show that employee ownership does not necessarily lead to increased job satisfaction or organizational commitment (Oliver, 1990). Other research indicates that if employee ownership

employee ownership *ownership of all or part of an organization by its workers, typically through stock purchases*

Well, getting your own airline feels even better.

Come meet the 54,000 new owners of United. Come fly the friendly skies.

✈ UNITED AIRLINES

In 1994, United Airlines became an employee-owned company.

APPLYING I/O PSYCHOLOGY (*continued*)

is going to increase organizational commitment, certain criteria must be met, the most obvious being that the program must be financially rewarding to employees (French & Rosenstein, 1984). Moreover, higher-level employees may have more positive reactions to employee ownership programs than do lower-level workers (Wichman, 1994). One investigation further qualified the conditions required for the success of employee ownership programs. Examining 37 employee stock ownership companies, the study found that rates of employee organizational commitment and satisfaction were highest when the companies made substantial financial contributions to the employee stock purchases, when management was highly committed to the program, and when there was a great deal of communication about the program (Klein, 1987). In addition, the Oliver (1990) study found that the rewards of employee ownership will only have a positive impact on the workers if they place a high value on those rewards. For example, if a worker values the work for its own merits, the worker would likely feel about the same level of satisfaction whether she was working for an employee-owned company or not.

It will likely be some time before we know the actual impact of employee ownership programs on organizational commitment and other important outcome variables. However, it is clear that these programs are becoming quite popular and will likely continue to increase in numbers.

Benefit programs

Perhaps the most common way for employers to try to increase employees' job satisfaction and organizational commitment is through various benefit programs. Benefit programs can include flexible working hours, a variety of health care options, different retirement plans, profit sharing, career development programs, health promotion programs, and employee-sponsored child care. This last program has the potential of becoming one of the most popular and sought-after benefits, and may have the extra advantage of helping to decrease absenteeism caused by employees' occasional inability to find adequate child care (Milkovich & Gomez, 1976). Interestingly, however, studies of the effects of employee-sponsored, on-site child care programs have found that although they increase worker job satisfaction, the expected reductions in absenteeism rates have been small (Goff, Mount, & Jamison, 1990; Kossek & Nichol, 1992).

Growing in popularity are flexible, or "cafeteria style" benefit plans, where employees choose from a number of options. Lawler (1971) long ago argued that allowing employees to choose their own benefits led to increases in job satisfaction and ensured that the benefits suited each employee's unique needs. A recent study demonstrated, however, that it is important that em-

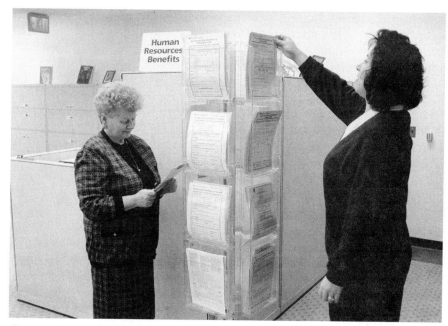

Some employers allow workers to choose among benefits "cafeteria style."

ployees receive adequate information and guidance regarding the characteristics of the various benefit programs, to help them make an informed choice of benefits that best suit their needs, and to avoid dissatisfaction caused by making incorrect choices (Sturman, Hannon, & Milkovich, 1996).

It is important to bear in mind that the costs of employee benefits are rising rapidly—more than doubling in the past 50 years from about 20 percent of payroll costs to more than 40 percent today. As a result, organizations often reduce benefit programs as a cost-saving strategy during times of economic downturn. Yet, organizations must be aware of the potential damaging effects of such cuts in benefits on employee job satisfaction and morale.

The effectiveness of programs designed to increase job satisfaction depends on various factors. While most of the techniques intended to increase job satisfaction do indeed appear to do so, there is less evidence that these programs then lead to changes in other important outcome variables such as productivity, work quality, absenteeism, and ultimately turnover. If a company implements a program aimed at increasing employee job satisfaction, and if management is perceived by employees to be taking positive steps toward the improvement of the workplace, job satisfaction will likely improve immediately after the introduction of the program. However, it may be unclear whether the program actually caused the increase or if it is really a sort of Hawthorne effect, in which employees' positive expectations about management's good intentions lead to increases in satisfaction, merely because

List and define four
alternative pay structure
techniques.

something was done. Regardless of the reason for measured improvements following the implementation of some satisfaction-enhancing program, the increases may tend to disappear over time as some of the novelty wears off, which long-term follow-up evaluations would reveal.

Quality of Work Life

Job satisfaction is an important influence on an employee's quality of work life. For example, a worker who feels a great deal of job satisfaction and very little job distress is apt to have a high quality of work life. On the other hand, an employee who feels little satisfaction and feels a great deal of pressure at work will usually have a low quality of work life.

I/O psychologists, management professionals, organizational decision makers, and the government have become increasingly concerned with workers' quality of work life (QWL). **Quality of work life** is determined by the compensation and benefits which workers receive, by their chances to participate and advance in the organization, by job security, by the type of work, by the characteristics of the organization, and by the quality of interactions among various organizational members. In short, quality of work life is the state of all aspects of life at work. More recently, research on employee satisfaction has gone beyond the narrow focus on work, and has explored the relationships between satisfaction with work and and overall life satisfaction, general health, and well-being (Adams, King, & King, 1996; Beehr & McGrath, 1992).

In the 1970s, a quality-of-work-life movement was begun in the United States, having three interrelated goals: (1) to assess the quality of work life in the U.S. by comparing and contrasting the current quality with that of the past and with that of other industrialized nations, (2) to develop strategies aimed at enhancing the quality of work life for all workers, and (3) to maintain high rates of productivity and organizational effectiveness through the greater participation of workers in organizational processes (Davis & Cherns, 1975; Stein, 1983). This movement aspires to achieve these goals while still improving organizational outcomes. Evidence indicates that enhancing quality of work life can lead to such positive organizational outcomes as increased productivity and quality, and decreased absenteeism and turnover (Efraty & Sirgy, 1990; Herrick & Maccoby, 1975).

Because quality of work life is so complex, made up of a number of interrelated factors, it is very difficult to conceptualize and measure (Lawler, 1982). One comprehensive conceptual model proposes that quality of work life is composed of many categories which cover nearly all aspects of working life, including compensation, working conditions, workers' rights, and the opportunity to grow and develop on the job (Walton, 1975; see Table 8.1). However, obtaining the detailed measurements of quality of work life suggested by the Walton model would be extremely difficult and costly. Lawler (1982) suggests that a simpler way for organizations to get some indication of

quality of work life
the evaluative state of all aspects of work

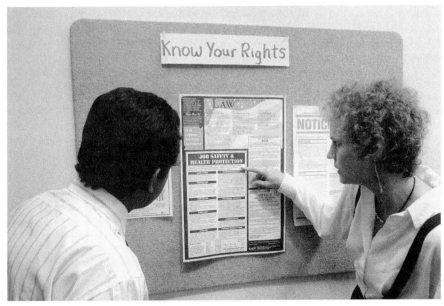

Employer concern with worker rights contributes to a high quality of work life.

TABLE 8.1

The Important Features of Quality of Work Life

1. Adequate and fair compensation
2. Safe and healthy working conditions
3. Opportunity to use and develop worker capabilities (maximizing the use of workers' knowledge, skills, and abilities; allowing workers control and autonomy over their jobs)
4. Opportunity for continued growth and security (job security; opportunities for promotion and advancement; opportunities to grow on the job)
5. Social environment of the workplace (good interpersonal relationships among workers; sense of community in the work organization)
6. Protection of workers' rights (protection against unfair employment decisions; equal opportunity for all workers)
7. Balance of work and nonwork life (adequate work schedules and work demands [for example, not allowing work requirements to interfere with family life]; concern with how work stress affects nonwork life and vice versa)
8. Organizational social responsibility (ethical organizational operations and policies, such as waste disposal, employment practices, and marketing techniques)

Source: R.E. Walton, "Criteria for Quality of Working Life," in L.E. Davis and A.B. Cherns (Eds.), *The Quality of Working Life*, Vol. 1 (New York: Free Press 1975), pp. 91–104.

quality of work life is to regularly measure absenteeism, turnover, accident rates, employee satisfaction levels, and dollars spent in employee training and development—variables that are presumed to be related to quality of work life. Regardless of how quality of work life is conceptualized and measured, it is clearly an important organizational issue that is likely to remain so.

The goals of having a high quality of work life and of maintaining high organizational productivity seem on the surface to be somewhat incompatible. The maintenance of work life quality is an expensive burden on the organization's budget. Adequate and fair wages, benefit programs, and safety and health programs are all quite costly. Is it possible to keep these elements at high levels and have sufficient additional resources to cover basic organizational operating expenses? Quality of work life advocates say "yes." In fact, they maintain that it is more costly for organizations not to maintain a high quality of work life. Inadequate compensation, lack of opportunity for advancement, and a poor social environment lead to job dissatisfaction and high rates of employee turnover, with the accompanying costs associated with the loss and replacement of good workers. An inefficient use of worker skills and a lack of concern with levels of work stress have a direct negative impact on productivity. Unsafe work conditions lead to workplace accidents and losses due to absenteeism. Furthermore, organizations that ignore workers' rights and issues of social responsibility face costly lawsuits and the costs of bad publicity. Maintaining a high quality of work life for employees is expensive, but in the long run it should lead to a more effective and productive organization.

A topic related to the quality of work life in a company is the company's image. With the increasing emphasis on employee rights and welfare, and with concerns over the environment, many organizations have given greater attention to the "corporate image" that they project to the general public and to their own employees. Given the choice, most people would probably think twice before accepting a position with an organization perceived to give only "lip service" to employee welfare, or one known to contribute heavily to environmental pollution. Further, there are indications that job satisfaction may be associated with employees' perceptions of the organization's concern about its workers, as well as the organization's concern with corporate and social issues (Gordon, Anderson, & Bruning, 1992). Thus, it is in the organization's own interest to be concerned with creating a valid, high quality of work life for its employees.

Organizations have used a variety of techniques to improve quality of work life. While some of the enhancements involve such straightforward changes as paying fair market wages for jobs or passing legislation to protect workers' rights (for example, the rights associated with equal employment opportunity and fair personnel decisions), I/O psychologists have been involved in improving quality of work life through programs that encourage greater employee participation in organizational processes (Lawler, 1986). Some of these participative programs include the development of work teams, which are groups of employees collaborating on a project; the use of quality circles, a technique involving having workers meet in groups to solve quality-related production problems; and the use of employee surveys for obtaining input about company operations and policies. We will examine these methods in detail in Chapter 14 as part of our discussion of organizational development. Another participative technique is the introduction of job enrichment, a program mentioned earlier, as a method of increasing job satisfaction through heightened job responsibility. Other participative strategies for enhancing quality of work life involve allowing workers some flexibility in arranging their own work schedules, which we will discuss in Chapter 16.

The concept of quality of work life and the quality-of-work-life movement help to shed light on some of the facets of work that are important to all employees and to their job satisfaction. The quality-of-work-life movement, which is spearheaded by I/O psychologists, also illustrates two important objectives of I/O psychology: to improve the physical and social environment at work in an effort to enhance worker well-being, satisfaction, and work life quality; and to improve organizational outcomes, such as increased productivity, work quality, and reduced absenteeism and turnover, through increasing employee participation in, and commitment to, organizational processes.

What is the quality-of-work-life movement?

Summary

Job satisfaction, which involves the positive feelings and attitudes one has about a job, can be conceptualized in overall, or global, terms, or in terms of specific components or facets, and can be measured through interviews or with self-report instruments. The most widely used self-report measures are the *Minnesota Satisfaction Questionnaire (MSQ)* and the *Job Descriptive Index (JDI)*. Research indicates that there is a slight positive relationship between job satisfaction and job performance, although the link may be moderated by a third variable, such as the receipt of work rewards. Job satisfaction is positively correlated with *organizational commitment*, or employees' feelings and attitudes about the entire work organization.

Both job satisfaction and organizational commitment tend to be negatively correlated with voluntary employee absenteeism. However, the relationships are complex and difficult to decipher, partly due to the difficulty involved in distinguishing voluntary absenteeism from involuntary absenteeism. Job satisfaction and organizational commitment are also related to voluntary employee turnover.

Programs designed to increase job satisfaction include changes in job structure through techniques such as *job rotation*, *job enlargement*, and *job enrichment*. Other satisfaction-enhancing techniques suggest changing the pay structure by using methods such as *knowledge-based pay*, pay-for-performance programs like *merit pay*, *gainsharing*, or *profit sharing*, which are sometimes contingent on effective group performance. Still other methods of improving satisfaction involve increasing job-related benefits.

Both job satisfaction and organizational commitment are incorporated into the notion of *quality of work life*, which encompasses all aspects of life at work. The quality-of-work-life movement in the U.S. has been involved in the assessment and enhancement of work life quality, and in the improvement of productivity and organizational performance through the increased participation of employees in organizational processes.

Study Questions and Exercises

1. What are some of the difficulties in the measurement of employee job satisfaction? How might I/O psychologists try to deal with these problems?
2. How does job satisfaction relate to the important "bottom-line," outcome variables of performance, absenteeism, and turnover?
3. What would a good, comprehensive program to increase job satisfaction contain? What elements would you include in each?
4. In what ways has the quality of work life of U.S. workers changed over the past 60 years? What sorts of changes do you expect to see in the future?

Suggested Readings

Cranny, C.J., Smith, P.C., & Stone, E.F. (1992). *Job satisfaction: How people feel about their jobs and how it affects their performance.* New York: Macmillan.

Spector, P.E. (1997). *Job satisfaction: Application, assessment, causes, and consequences.* Thousand Oaks, CA: Sage. *Two very readable overviews of the effects of job satisfaction on work behavior.*

DeMatteo, J.S., Eby, L.T., & Sundstrom, E. (1998). Team-based rewards: Current empirical evidence and directions for future research. *Research in Organizational Behavior, 20,* 141–183. *An up-to-date, comprehensive review of research on the use of group- or team-based reward and compensation systems.*

Welbourne, T.M., & Gomez Mejia, L.R. (1995) Gainsharing: A critical review and a future research agenda. *Journal of Management, 21,* 59–609. *A detailed, high-level review of research on gainsharing. Particularly interesting and relevant are the discussions of how gainsharing relates to various motivational theories, including expectancy, need, and equity theories.*

WORKER STRESS

CHAPTER OUTLINE

Life stress is a topic with which most of us will be familiar because it is discussed often in the popular press and media. However, this chapter deals with worker stress: the stress that occurs at work and affects work behavior. So be careful not to confuse what you have heard from the media about life stress and what you read in this chapter. For instance, a common misconception is that all stress is bad. As you will find out, a little bit of stress can be motivating and challenging. Yet, it is the negative type of stress that gets most of the attention. Another misconception is that the strategies used in dealing with stress in everyday life will also work in dealing with worker stress. This is not always the case. For example, some stressors can be alleviated by organizational changes, and are therefore under the control of management, while others must be addressed by the individual worker. In addition, some of the techniques for dealing with stress in the workplace are not so much stress reduction techniques as they are simply good management and human resource practices.

Social scientists have had a great deal of difficulty in precisely defining and measuring stress. Be aware of this. Some of the concepts in this chapter are quite abstract and are initially difficult to understand.

This chapter fits well with the previous one (Chapter 8) that focused on worker satisfaction. In some ways, satisfaction and stress can be opposite sides of

INSIDE TIPS

the coin. Jobs can create a great deal of satisfaction, contributing to a sense of well-being and "worth." At the same time, however, jobs can subject us to uncomfortable (and potentially harmful) stress.

As we saw in the previous chapter, most workers feel some sense of purpose and accomplishment about their jobs, which can be very rewarding and self-satisfying. However, work can also be a tremendous burden. Deadlines, work overload, and difficult bosses or coworkers can all place considerable pressure and strain on workers. Thus, jobs and the work environment commonly produce stress, which workers must learn to deal with. In this section, we will define worker stress, see how it affects work behavior, look at how it is measured, examine ways that the individual worker can attempt to cope with it, and consider strategies that organizations can use to try to decrease stress.

Defining Worker Stress

The construct of stress is quite complex. So much so, in fact, that researchers cannot agree on a single definition for stress (Kahn & Boysiere, 1992). Consequently, there are at least eight different definitions (models) for stress (Ivancevich & Matteson, 1980).

According to the early stress researcher, Hans Selye (1976), stress is primarily a physiological reaction to certain threatening environmental events. From Selye's perspective, worker stress would simply refer to the stress caused by events in the work environment. Psychologist John French and his colleagues (French, Rogers, & Cobb, 1974; French, Caplan, & Harrison, 1982), say that worker stress results from a lack of "fit" between a person's skills and abilities and the demands of the job and the workplace. In other words, a worker who is totally unqualified for a particular job should feel a tremendous amount of stress. For example, imagine a worker with no previous computer experience applying for and being hired as a "communication specialist," only to find out that the job requires a thorough knowledge of various computer networking systems. Lazarus (1991; Lazarus & Folkman, 1984), in his "transactional" view of worker stress, sees stress as resulting from the worker's perception that a certain environmental event is a threat or a challenge. From Lazarus' perspective, you and I might interpret the same event very differently—I might find it stressful, you might view it as totally harmless (or perhaps even as pleasantly challenging!).

In order to arrive at a definition of worker stress for our purposes, we need to look at what these three different approaches to stress have in common. All three definitions view worker stress as an interaction between the person and some environmental event, or **stressor**. In addition, all of the definitions emphasize that there are some important reactions to the stressful event. These reactions can be either physiological or psychological in nature, or both. Therefore, we will define **worker stress** as physiological

stressor
an environmental event that is perceived by an individual to be threatening

worker stress
the physiological and/or psychological reactions to events that are perceived to be threatening or taxing

and/or psychological reactions to an event that is perceived to be threatening or taxing.

Although we most often think of stress as an unpleasant state, it can have both negative and positive aspects. For example, imagine that you have been working for several years as an assistant manager for a large company and find out that you have just received a promotion to department manager, a position you have been trying to obtain for some time. With your new position come feelings of stress. Some of these are negative, such as the stress that will result from: having to work many overtime hours without additional compensation; being required to make formal presentations regularly to your peers and superiors (and having your presentations critically evaluated by them); and taking on the responsibility to take the criticism for any problems occurring in your department. On the other hand, there are many positive reactions associated with the promotion, including feelings of accomplishment, anticipation, pride, and challenge. Like the negative aspects, these positive responses also induce physiological and psychological reactions in the body. Some stress researchers distinguish the negative stress, termed *distress*, from the positive kind of stress, called *eustress* (see, for example, Golembiewski, Munzenrider, & Stevenson, 1986; Shanahan & Mortimer, 1996).

We are all likely familiar with the physiological reactions to stress. They include signs of arousal such as increased heart and respiratory rates, elevated blood pressure, and profuse sweating. The psychological reactions to stress include feeling anxiety, fear, frustration, and despair, as well as appraising or evaluating the stressful event and its impact, thinking about the stressful experience, and mentally preparing to take steps to try to deal with the stress.

In many ways, stress is a perceptual process. An event that one individual perceives to be stressful may not be labeled as such by someone else. For example, making a formal presentation in front of a large audience may be perceived as extremely stressful for the average college student, but may be perceived as energizing (and perhaps fun) by a person who is accustomed to public speaking. Because stress may cause a variety of reactions and feelings, and because perceptions of stress may vary from person to person, stress has not been particularly easy to define, and it is very difficult to measure. We will deal with methods of measuring stress shortly.

In the past two decades, there has been a tremendous amount of interest in worker stress. In addition, companies and managers have become more and more concerned with the effects of stress on workers and on important "bottom-line" variables, such as productivity, absenteeism, and turnover. Why all of the interest in worker stress? The most obvious reason is that too much stress can cause illness. Stress-related illnesses include ulcers, hypertension and coronary heart disease, migraines, asthma attacks, and colitis. If worker stress leads to stress-related illnesses, rates of absenteeism can increase. At the psychological level, stress can cause mental strain, feelings of fatigue, anxiety, and depression that can reduce worker productivity and quality of work. If a job becomes too stressful, a worker may be compelled to quit and find a less stressful position. Thus, worker stress may influence turnover as well.

Managers and workers may also be concerned about stress at a more personal level. Worker stress can be, in many ways, the flip side of job satisfaction. While job satisfaction represents the "positives" associated with work, stress is a way of conceptualizing the "negatives" associated with jobs—the pressures, the strains, the conflicts. No doubt, much of the interest in worker stress results from the fact that managers, business owners, and all other sorts of workers experience stress on a day-to-day basis.

Sources of Worker Stress

situational stress
stress arising from certain conditions that exist in the work environment, or in the worker's personal life

Generally, stress can arise from either the environment (situational stress) or from an individual's personal characteristics (dispositional stress). **Situational stress** can come from all aspects of our lives. We are subjected to a wide range of stressors, at home, at school, and in our interpersonal relationships, as well as the stressors we encounter at work. No doubt, all of these various sources of stress accumulate and add to our overall stress levels. That is, stress at home can spill over to work situations, and vice versa. Most stress researchers realize this and emphasize that when studying stress it is important to look at the broad picture of an individual's total stress, rather than focusing narrowly on stress derived from work (Bhagat, Allie, & Ford, 1991; Frone, Russell, & Cooper, 1991; Greenhaus & Parasuraman, 1986).

For our purposes, however, we will focus primarily on the stress that comes from workplace sources. We will first examine stressful occupations, and then focus on the elements of jobs and of work organizations that can cause worker stress. Finally, we will look at how worker stress can result from characteristics of the workers themselves, as we examine individual sources of worker stress, or what we might call *dispositional stress*.

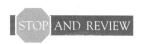

Discuss why worker stress is difficult to define.

STRESSFUL OCCUPATIONS

It is generally believed that certain occupations, such as air traffic controllers, physicians and other health care providers, police officers, and firefighters, are particularly stressful. In recent years, there has been increased attention to postal workers' stress, following highly publicized cases of postal workers attacking and killing coworkers. (In fact, this has led to a new slang term, "going postal."). Is it true that certain occupations are particularly stress-prone? There is some evidence to suggest this. For example, a study of air traffic controllers indicated that they did indeed experience high levels of work-related stress (Mohler, 1983). Medical doctors also report high levels of worker stress (Krakowski, 1982; Roeske, 1981). Similarly, studies of dentists suggest that dentistry is a high-stress occupation (Cooper, Mallinger, & Kahn, 1978; DiMatteo, Shugars, & Hays, 1993). High-level managers and business executives are also believed to hold extremely stressful jobs. Yet, there is research evidence that is inconsistent with commonly held stereotypes about which occupations are most stressful. For example, one might guess that physicians, who have the ultimate responsibility for patient care, would experience higher levels of stress than nurses, who have lower levels of responsibility. But this is not the case. A study comparing physicians, pharmacists, and nurses showed that nurses had the highest levels of stress among the three occupations (Wolfgang, 1988). Another common notion is that police officers' and firefighters' jobs are particularly stressful because of the physical dangers involved. However, some studies suggest that rather than causing stress, the excitement and challenge of dealing with physical danger may actually be motivating and "enriching" to many police officers and firefighters (Jermier, Gaines, & McIntosh, 1989; Riggio & Cole, 1995). Interestingly, studies of police officers suggest that they suffer from the same sources of stress, such as increased responsibilities and workloads, and difficulties with coworkers, as persons in other occupations (Brown, Cooper, & Kircaldy, 1996). In sum, trying to determine levels of worker stress merely by looking at a person's occupation or job title may not be very accurate.

Research on these and other stereotypically stressful occupations has begun to discover exactly why these jobs are characterized as stressful. For instance, air traffic controllers' jobs are stressful because of the heavy workloads, the constant fear of causing accidents, equipment problems, and poor

Dangerous work conditions are a common source of stress on the job, as in the case of firefighters who risk their lives daily.

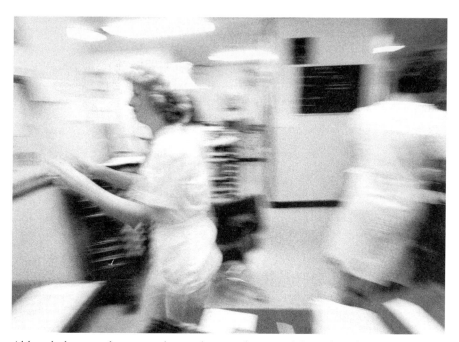

Although they are often seen as having fewer work responsibilities than physicians, nurses often experience very high levels of work stress.

working environments (Shouksmith & Burrough, 1988). The primary sources of dentists' occupational stress come from difficult patients, heavy workloads, and the dentists' own concern that their patients hold negative views about them and about dentists in general (Coster, Carstens, & Harris, 1987; DiMatteo, et al., 1993).

Rather than focusing only on high-stress occupations, it makes sense to examine those sources of worker stress that are common to all kinds of jobs, even those that are not typically considered high-stress jobs. Such sources of stress can be divided into two general categories: organizational and individual. Organizational sources of stress come from the work environment and can be broken down into two subcategories: stress derived from work tasks and stress resulting from work roles. Individual sources of stress include a person's history of exposure to stress as well as certain stress-related personality characteristics and behavioral patterns. For example, there is evidence that certain personality traits make people more prone to stress (and stress-related illnesses), and some characteristics seem to make people more resistant to stress and its negative outcomes.

ORGANIZATIONAL SOURCES OF WORK STRESS: SITUATIONAL STRESSORS

A great deal of worker stress is caused by stressors in the environment of the work organization. Some of this organizational stress is caused by the work tasks themselves—the physical and psychological demands of performing a job. Organizational stress may also be caused by work roles since work organizations are complex social systems in which a worker must interact with many people. Therefore, the work relationships of various kinds that must be created and maintained for a worker to perform the job adequately can also lead to stress. These two types of situational stress—work task and work role stressors—can often be alleviated by management actions.

Work task stressors

work overload

a common source of stress resulting when a job requires excessive speed, output, or concentration

Work overload—A common work task source of stress is **work overload**, which results when the job requires excessive work speed, output, or concentration. Work overload is widely believed to be one of the greatest sources of work stress. Research on work overload indicates that it is related to physiological indicators of stress, such as elevated serum cholesterol and increased heart rate (Caplan & Jones, 1975; Cobb & Rose, 1973); to psychological measures of stress (Spector, 1987; Spector, Dwyer, & Jex, 1988); and to lower quality of work and job dissatisfaction (Kirmeyer & Dougherty, 1988). In fact, work overload has been reported as a common source of stress for jobs as diverse as clerical workers, soldiers, air traffic controllers, and health care workers (Bliese & Halverson, 1996; Carayon, 1994; Iverson, Olekalns, & Erwin, 1998; Shouksmith & Burrough, 1988).

underutilization

a source of stress resulting from workers feeling that their knowledge, skills, or energy are not being fully used

Underutilization—While work overload can cause stress, having too little to do—**underutilization**—can also be stressful (French & Caplan, 1972;

Ganster, Fusilier, & Mayes, 1986). Underutilization may also occur when workers feel that the job does not use their work-related knowledge, skills, or abilities, or when jobs are boring and monotonous (Melamed, Ben-Avi, Luz, & Green, 1995). Some college graduates in low-level clerical or customer service positions may feel some stress due to underutilization of their knowledge and skills (see French, Caplan, & Harrison, 1972).

Work role stressors

Job ambiguity—A potential source of work role stress is **job ambiguity**, which occurs when aspects of a job, such as tasks and requirements, are not clearly outlined. When workers are unsure of their responsibilities and duties, stress can result (Beehr, 1985; Jackson & Schuler, 1985). Job ambiguity is also sometimes referred to as "job uncertainty." However, job uncertainty may better refer to the uncertainty caused by a lack of regular performance feedback concerning how well or how poorly workers are doing their jobs. Research suggests that supervisors can play an important part in reducing job uncertainty for subordinates by clarifying job roles and duties (Schaubroeck, Ganster, Sime, & Ditman, 1993). Findings that job uncertainty can have negative influences on job satisfaction highlights the importance of the supervisor's role in alleviating uncertainty and its accompanying stress (O'Driscoll & Beehr, 1994).

> job ambiguity
> *a source of stress resulting from a lack of clearly defined jobs and/or work tasks*

Attentive supervisors may play an important part in reducing job uncertainty, thus reducing job stress.

Conflict between roles can also occur and can become an additional source of stress (Greenhaus & Beutell, 1985). For instance, a worker's job may require excessive overtime that conflicts with the worker's family roles of spouse and parent. Or, having to play different roles at work simultaneously can cause stress. We will discuss roles and role conflict in more depth in Chapter 11.

Lack of control—Another important source of work stress results from workers sensing that they have little control over the work environment and over their own work behavior. Stress resulting from this feeling of **lack of control** is particularly common in lower-level jobs or in highly structured organizations. Jobs that are so constrained and rule-driven that employees are unable to have any sort of input in work decisions and procedures are likely to be stress inducing, particularly for those workers who want to have some input (see Dwyer & Ganster, 1991; Karasek, 1979). Research indicates that providing workers with a sense of control over their work environment, through techniques such as giving them a voice in decision-making processes or allowing them to plan their own work tasks, reduces work stress and increases job satisfaction (Jackson, 1983; Jimmieson & Terry, 1998). On the other hand, there are some studies that suggest that a sense of a lack of control over one's job may not be stressful for many workers (see Carayon, 1993). It may be the case that different types of workers are more or less concerned with having sense of control over their jobs (recall our discussion in Chapter 7 on the Job Characteristics Model and individual differences in workers' desire for autonomy). In fact, research has found that certain personality characteristics may determine whether or not an individual is

> lack of control
> *a feeling of having little input or effect on the job and/or work environment; typically results in stress*

stressed by a perceived lack of job control (Ivancevich, Matteson, & Preston, 1982).

ON THE CUTTING EDGE

Technostress

The increased use of computerized work systems in today's high-tech "information age" has undoubtedly changed many jobs. Many workers, from entry-level employees to top-level executives, are likely to spend large parts of their days in front of computer screens, or interacting with other sorts of sophisticated computerized systems. The technological revolution has helped reduce some of the aversive aspects of jobs. For example, fewer of today's workers have to deal with such stressors as monotonous or repetitive procedures, since computers can handle much of this boring, repetitive work. Yet, jobs today are still stress-ridden. Modern technology, while alleviating some sources of job stress, has actually increased others, or perhaps created new sources of stress. What are some of the stressors associated with the information age, and which workers are most likely to be affected?

Sethi, Caro, and Schuler (1987) refer to stress related to high technology as "technostress." Technostress is defined as the stress resulting from uncertainty caused by technological changes. For example, a few decades ago workers could learn a trade or profession and their jobs were unlikely to change dramatically over their careers. Many of today's workers, however, are faced with jobs that change almost continually as the technological aspects of the jobs change. Moreover, job uncertainty may become a stressor for workers whose jobs suddenly become computerized, or for those workers who fear that their jobs may be in jeopardy, as more and more of their job functions become computerized.

One study looked at the implementation of sophisticated new technologies, such as the conversion to computer-aided design (CAD) systems, in seven companies in Austria. It was found that implementation of the new technology led to large increases in employee stress, with employees who were not included in the planning and implementation process experiencing the highest levels of stress (Korunka, Weiss, & Karetta, 1993).

Technology-related stress may also result from a high workload coupled with low utilization of skills, a lack of control over the work, and lack of supervisory support (Carayon, 1994). Such factors are often associated with jobs that involve sitting in front of a computer screen while inputting information for hours at a time, with little or no knowledge of the end use of the data, and little control over workload, work priorities, or task diversity. Carayon (1994) found that low-level jobs such as data processor are more stressful than supervisory or professional jobs, primarily due to these technology-related sources of stress, a result that was also found in the Austrian study (i.e., Korunka, Weiss, & Karetta, 1993). Other studies have found that lack of autonomy and

ON THE CUTTING EDGE (continued)

control over such matters as sched- uling work tasks can lead to anxiety (Perrewe & Ganster, 1989), depres- sion, illness, and certain types of substance abuse (Karasek, 1979).

There is no doubt that the infor- mation age will continue, and that technological change will be an ongo- ing characteristic of the workplace. Since technostress is likely to remain, it is important that organizations de- velop strategies to help workers deal with negative stress, no matter what the source.

Physical work conditions—Physical conditions in the work environment are another organizational source contributing to worker stress (Frese & Zapf, 1988). Jobs that must be performed under extreme temperatures, loud noise, or poor lighting or ventilation can be quite stressful. Dangerous jobs that place workers at risk of loss of health, life, or limb are an additional source of work stress. We will discuss these physical conditions of the work environment and work safety further in Chapter 16.

Interpersonal stress—One of the greatest sources of work stress results from difficulties in interpersonal relationships on the job. Such **interper- sonal stress** is one type of stress that nearly every worker encounters. Inter- personal stress stems from difficulties in developing and maintaining relationships with other people in the work setting. Having a harsh, critical boss with a punitive management style would likely be stressful for just about anyone. Interpersonal stress can also result when coworkers are placed in some sort of conflict situation. Imagine, for example, that two employees are both being considered for an important promotion. A great deal of stress may be generated if the two individuals must work together while both are competing for the same honor. There is also evidence that organizational politics, and struggles over power, can be important sources of stress in the workplace (Ferris, Frink, Gilmore, & Kacmar, 1994). We will discuss power and politics in depth in Chapter 13. Whatever its causes, the inability to get along with other workers is one of the most common sources of stress in the workplace (Matteson & Ivancevich, 1982).

Organizational change—A final organizational source of stress is change. People tend to grow accustomed to certain work procedures and certain work structures and they resist change. Most of us prefer things to remain stable and predictable. Such stability in our working environments seems comforting and reassuring. Therefore, it should not be surprising that major changes in a work organization tend to cause stress (Leiter & Harvie, 1998). Some common change situations that lead to worker stress include: com- pany reorganizations, mergers of one company with another or acquisitions of one organization by another, changes in work systems and work technol- ogy, changes in company policy, and managerial or personnel changes (see

interpersonal stress
stress arising from difficulties with others in the workplace

TABLE 9.1

Characteristics of Jobs that Cause Worker Stress

Work overload (for example, time pressures and too much work)
Underutilization of worker knowledge, skills, ability, or energy
Dangerous work conditions
Responsibility for the health and well-being of others
Difficult or complex work tasks
Unpleasant or uncomfortable physical work conditions
Interpersonal conflict
Decision making
Organizational change
Lack of support from supervisors or coworkers
Lack of control over the work situation
Personal factors (for example, Type A behavior or stress-prone personality)

Table 9.1). For example, research has shown that physiological stress responses are stronger in novel or unfamiliar circumstances that involve a threat or challenge (Rose, 1987). Certainly an event like a companywide reorganization, or a merger or acquisition, would be perceived as threatening and stressful by many employees (Marks & Mirvis, 1998).

INDIVIDUAL SOURCES OF WORK STRESS: DISPOSITIONAL STRESSORS

While a great deal of worker stress is created by factors in the organization or by features of jobs and work tasks, some is caused by characteristics of the workers themselves. We will consider two such individual sources of work stress: the Type A behavior pattern and susceptibility to stress and to stress effects. It is the individual worker—not management—who must work to alleviate these sources of stress.

Type A Behavior Pattern

When many people think of individuals who are extremely stressed in the workplace, they immediately picture the stereotypical hard-driving, competitive executive who seeks a job with a heavy work load and many responsibilities—a person who takes on too much work and never seems to have enough time to do it. Is there any truth to this characterization? Research evidence indicates that there is. Researchers have uncovered the **Type A behavior pattern**, or Type A personality, which is characterized by excessive drive and competitiveness, a sense of urgency and impatience, and underlying hostility (Friedman & Rosenman, 1974; Rosenman, 1978). This behavior pattern is particularly significant because there is evidence that persons who possess the Type A personality are slightly more prone to develop stress-related coronary heart disease, including fatal heart attacks, than persons who do not have the behavior pattern, termed

*Type A behavior pattern
a personality characterized
by excessive drive,
competitiveness,
impatience, and hostility
that has been linked to
greater incidence of
coronary heart disease*

Type Bs (Booth-Kewley & Friedman, 1987; Schauebroeck, Ganster, & Kemmerer, 1994).

An important question is how does the Type A behavior pattern relate to stress and to stress-related heart disease? Early research on Type A behavior hypothesized that it was the Type A's hard-working, competitive drive that caused stress and subsequent heart problems (Rosenman, et al., 1964). Later research, however, suggested that the Type A's underlying hostility, and the lack of appropriate expression of that hostility, is also partly responsible for increased stress reactions in Type As (Dembroski & Costa, 1987; Friedman, Hall, & Harris, 1985; Smith & Pope, 1990). Some of the more recent research on the Type A behavior pattern suggests that it may be a combination of factors—competitiveness, hostility, and impatience—that puts Type As at increased risk for coronary heart disease (e.g., Rosenman, 1990). Other studies suggest that the more global construct of "negative affectivity," or the expression of negative emotions, such as anger, hostility, anxiety, and aggression, is what combines with a Type A personality to increase stress-related health risks (e.g., Chen & Spector, 1991; Ganster, Schaubroeck, Sime, & Mayes, 1991).

Do Type As experience more stress than others? Research into this question has produced mixed results. For example, some studies indicate that Type As are more likely to experience or report high stress than are other personality types under the same workload (Kirmeyer, 1988; Payne, 1988). Other studies show that Type As do not report or experience greater stress, but simply have stronger physiological stress reactions to stressful situations (Ganster, 1986). Perhaps the subjective experience of stress has less negative influence on health than the physiological responses. In other words, Type As may have stronger stress-induced physiological responses that they are not necessarily aware of, and it is these strong physiological responses over time that lead to increased health risks. If this is the case, Type As may simply not realize that their long, intense work style is creating wear and tear on their bodies.

While there are obvious stress-related costs to the Type A behavior pattern, there are also some gains. Studies consistently show that Type As tend to work harder (Byrne & Reinhardt, 1989), work well in high-variety jobs (Lee, Earley, & Hanson, 1988), and that they have higher positions and salaries than Type Bs (Boyd, 1984; Chesney & Rosenman, 1980; Payne, 1988). This aspect of Type A behavior is conceptually related to strong achievement orientation or "workaholism" discussed in the motivation chapter (Chapter 7).

In truth, the Type A behavior pattern is likely not a unitary construct, but a composite of different personality characteristics and behavior patterns (Booth-Kewley & Friedman, 1987; Ganster, Schaubroeck, Sime, & Mayes, 1991; Spector & O'Connell, 1994), or possibly, an interaction between stress and personality (Edwards, Baglioni, & Cooper, 1990). Overall, the one characteristic that many researchers agree is associated with the negative aspects of stress in Type As is that of negative affectivity (whether

List and define five
organizational/situational
sources of worker stress.

it be anxiety, anger, pessimism, or whatever). In other words, perhaps it is not the amount of work undertaken, or aspects of the work situation itself that affect type As, but rather the way they think and feel about the work they do.

UP CLOSE

How to Measure the Type A Behavior Pattern

One of the best known dispositional sources of stress is the Type A behavior pattern, which is characterized by such qualities as aggressiveness, anger, competitiveness, impatience, achievement-striving, and feeling time-pressured (Edwards, Baglioni, & Cooper, 1990). The original method for assessing the Type A behavior pattern was through the use of a structured interview (Friedman & Rosenman, 1974). In this structured interview, questions such as, "Do you take work home with you?" and "Do you eat rapidly?" are asked to determine if the individual has the impatience and competitive drive associated with the Type A behavior pattern. In addition, the interviewer notes certain nonverbal cues, such as hurried speech and abrupt gestures, that are associated with being a Type A.

There are also two popular self-report instruments designed to assess Type A behavior: the Jenkins Activity Survey (JAS; Jenkins, Zyzanski, & Rosenman, 1979), and the Framingham Type A Scale (FTAS; Haynes, Levine, Scotch, Feinleib, & Kannel, 1978). Examples of some of the types of questions asked by the FTAS and JAS are presented below:

FTAS

- Are you hard driving and competitive?
- Are you bossy or dominating?
- Do you have a strong need to excel?
- Are you pressed for time after work?

JAS

- Do you have trouble finding time to get your hair cut?
- Do you feel and act impatient when you have to wait in a line?
- Do you get irritated easily?
- When you were younger, was your temper fiery and hard to control?

As you might imagine, affirmative answers to these questions indicate possession of the Type A behavior pattern. Research on measuring Type As indicates that the structured interview, although time-consuming to administer, is a much better indicator of the Type A behavior pattern than any of the self-report instruments (Friedman, 1990).

Susceptibility/resistance to stress

hardiness

the notion that some people may be more resistant to the health-damaging effects of stress.

Another dispositional source of stress may stem from the fact that some persons are simply more susceptible to stress while others have stress-resistant, hardy personalities. The concept of **hardiness** was outlined by psychologist Suzanne Kobasa (1982), who argued that hardy personality types are resistant to the harmful effects of stress because of their style of dealing with stressful events. Rather than viewing a stressful situation as a threat, they view it as a challenge. Moreover, they also believe that they can control and influence the course of their lives (recall that a sense of lack of control can contribute to stress) and are committed to their jobs. Conversely, a lack of hardiness is associated with higher levels of self-perceived stress, and there is evidence that such "unhardy" or "disease-prone" persons may be more susceptible to stress-related illnesses and depression (Friedman & Booth-Kewley, 1987; Kobasa & Puccetti, 1983). Thus, it may be the case that certain types of workers are more "stress-prone." That is, they are more likely to suffer stress-related physical illness and psychological symptoms (depression, anxiety, etc.) than are more hardy workers.

Research has also identified another characteristic that seems to increase resistance to stress: self-efficacy. **Self-efficacy** is defined as an individual's beliefs in his or her abilities to engage in courses of action that will lead to desired outcomes (Bandura, 1997). In other words, self-efficacy is related to one's sense of competence and effectiveness. There is some evidence that a sense of self-efficacy can have positive effects in reducing stress in the workplace (Saks, 1994; VanYperen, 1998).

self-efficacy
an individual's beliefs in his or her abilities to engage in courses of action that will lead to desired outcomes

Measurement of Worker Stress

Since stress is such a complex phenomenon, and since stress researchers cannot agree on a single definition of stress, you might suspect that the measurement of stress is extremely difficult. For the most part, measurement of stress in general, and of worker stress in particular, is problematic. There have been a number of approaches to measuring stress. We will consider several of these.

Physiological measures

As has been stated, the stress response involves physiological reactions as well as psychological and emotional responses. Therefore, one strategy for measuring stress has focused on measuring signs of physiological arousal and strain that accompany stress. This includes blood pressure monitoring, electrocardiogram (EKG) for monitoring heart rate, or blood tests for monitoring levels of certain hormones and cholesterol in the blood stream. One problem with using such physiological indicators of stress is the amount of variation that can occur from hour to hour, day to day, or person to person (Herd, 1988). Another drawback to the use of such stress tests is the requirement for trained medical personnel, as well as the associated costs for equipment and analysis procedures.

What is the Type A behavior pattern, and how does it relate to worker stress?

Self-report assessments

Another approach to measuring stress, one that is favored by psychologists, is to ask people directly to report on their own perceived stress through various pencil-and-paper rating scales. Most self-report assessments fall into one of two major categories: reports about organizational conditions, or reports about psychological and/or physical states.

Reports on organizational conditions typically contain items that ask about facets of the job such as autonomy, feedback, task identity, task significance, skill variety, complexity, dealing with others, ambiguity and workload (Spector, 1992). For example, questions dealing with workload might include the following (Matteson & Ivancevich, 1987):

- Number of projects/assignments you have
- Amount of time spent in meetings
- Amount of time spent at work
- Number of phone calls and visitors you have during the day

There are several standardized self-report measures of psychological and physiological stress and strain, such as the Stress Diagnostic Survey (SDS; Ivancevich & Matteson, 1980), the Occupational Stress Indicator (OSI; Cooper, Sloan, & Williams, 1988), and the newer Job Stress Survey (JSS; Spielberger & Reheiser, 1994). For example, the SDS measures workers' perceptions of stress in 15 work-related areas, including time pressure, workload, role ambiguity, and supervisory style. The JSS is a 30-item instrument that measures the severity and frequency with which workers experience certain stressful working conditions. These instruments have been used in research or by organizations to quickly gauge employees' stress levels.

Measurement of stressful life events

As was mentioned earlier, situational stress in one area of an individual's life, such as the home or school, can affect stress levels at work (Levi, Frankenhaeuser, & Gardell, 1986; Martin & Schermerhorn, 1983). Particularly important is the worker's experience of traumatic or **stressful life events,** which include negative events such as the death of a spouse or loved one, divorce or separation, major illness, and financial or legal troubles, as well as positive events such as marriage, the birth of a child, and vacations. This approach to measuring stress assumes that such events can bring on stress-related illness and may impair job performance.

Measures have been developed to assess a person's stress history. For example, with one measure that is based on a checklist, individuals total the numerical "stress severity" scores associated with the significant life events that they have experienced in the past year (Holmes & Rahe, 1967; see Table 9.2). This provides a personal life events stress index. Research indicates that this score may predict certain work outcomes such as job performance, absenteeism, and turnover. Persons with high personal stress indexes tend to perform more poorly, have higher absenteeism, and change jobs more frequently than persons who experience fewer stressful life events (Bhagat, 1983; Weiss, Ilgen, & Sharbaugh, 1982). Yet, there has been a great deal of criticism of the stressful life events approach to assessing stress (e.g., Hurrell, Murphy, Sauter, & Cooper, 1988). Much of the criticism is that this approach is too general. Certain life events may affect people very

stressful life events
significant events in a
person's recent history that
can cause stress

TABLE 9.2

The Social Readjustment Rating Scale

Life Event	Stress Value
Death of spouse	100
Divorce	73
Marital separation	65
Jail term	63
Death of close family member	63
Personal injury or illness	53
Marriage	50
Fired at work	47
Marital reconciliation	45
Retirement	45
Change in health of family member	44
Pregnancy	40
Sex difficulties	39
Gain of new family member	39
Business readjustment	39
Change in financial state	38
Death of close friend	37
Change to different line of work	36
Change in number of arguments with spouse	35
Mortgage over $10,000	31
Foreclosure of mortgage or loan	30
Change in responsibilities at work	29
Son or daughter leaving home	29
Trouble with in-laws	29
Outstanding personal achievement	28
Spouse begin or stop work	26
Spouse begin or end school	26
Change in living conditions	25
Revision of personal habits	24
Trouble with boss	23
Change in work hours or conditions	20
Change in residence	20
Change in schools	20
Change in recreation	19
Change in church activities	19
Change in social activities	18
Mortgage or loan less than $10,000	17
Change in sleeping habits	16
Change in number of family get-togethers	15
Change in eating habits	15
Vacation	13
Christmas	12
Minor violations of the law	11

Source: T.H. Holmes and R.H. Rahe, "The Social Readjustment Rating Scale," *Journal of Psychosomatic Research*, 11 (1967), pp. 213–18.

differently. For example, it has been suggested that a simple additive weighting of the Holmes and Rahe "Social Readjustment Rating Scale" does not accurately assess the effect of an additional stressful event when an individual is already experiencing other stressful events (Birnbaum & Sotoodeh, 1991). In addition, assessment of stressful life events may not reveal the impact of day-to-day stressors influencing the individual.

Measurement of person-environment fit

person-environment (P-E) fit
the match between a worker's abilities, needs, and values, and organizational demands, rewards, and values

Person-environment (P-E) fit refers to the match between a worker's abilities, needs, and values, and organizational demands, rewards, and values. P-E fit has been found to have a positive correlation with organizational commitment, and a negative correlation with turnover (Ostroff, 1993; Villanova, Bernardin, Johnson, & Dahmus, 1994). According to the P-E fit approach, a mismatch between the worker and the work organization/environment is believed to be a primary cause of worker stress. For example, imagine a worker who has a high need for job clarification, job structure, and feedback who accepts a job with a small, fast-growing company where jobs are neither well-defined nor structured, and where supervisors have little time for feedback due to constant production demands. In such a case, there would be a poor person-environment fit.

Typically, measurement of person-environment fit involves measuring some characteristics of the worker, such as worker skills and/or abilities, and assessing the work environment and job demands. The discrepancy between these two sets of measures is then calculated as an index of fit (e.g., Edwards & Cooper, 1990). It can be argued, however, that the concept of person-environment fit is overly broad, and that measures that specifically look at "subcategories" of P-E fit—such as person-organization fit, person-job fit, and the extent to which a particular job fits an individual's motivational needs (see Chapter 7)—are needed (see Kristoff, 1996; Medcof & Hausdorf, 1995; Sutherland, Fogarty, & Pithers, 1995).

Effects of Worker Stress

The topic of worker stress and its effects is one of the most rapidly growing research areas in I/O psychology (Kahn & Byosiere, 1992). Much of this interest is due to the very powerful impact that stress can have on workers and work behavior, and most dramatically on employee health. It is believed that more than one-half of all physical illnesses are stress-related. Some common stress-related illnesses are ulcers, colitis, high blood pressure, heart disease, respiratory illnesses, and migraine headaches. Moreover, stress can worsen common colds, flus, and infections, making recovery time longer. It is estimated that these illnesses, attributed in part to work stress, cost billions of dollars annually in health care costs and in employee absenteeism and turnover (Beehr & Bhagat, 1985; Gherman, 1981; Hatfield, 1990).

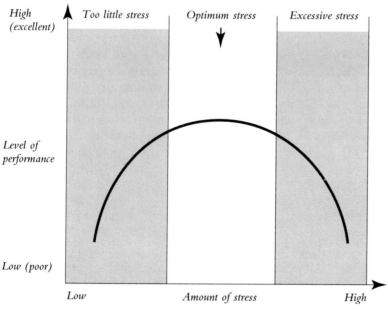

FIGURE 9.1

Relationship Between Performance and Stress.
Source: S. Cohen, "After-effects of Stress on Human Behavior and Social Behavior: A Review of Research and Theory." *Psychological Bulletin* 88 (1980), p. 85.

Worker stress can also have an adverse impact on employees' psychological states. High levels of stress are associated with depression, anxiety, and chronic fatigue. Stress may also contribute to alcoholism and drug abuse in workers, and may influence accident rates on the job (Wolf, 1986; see also Chapter 16). Emotional exhaustion, detachment from coworkers, negative self-evaluations, and lowered self-esteem are also associated with worker stress (Cordes & Dougherty, 1993).

As you might imagine, stress has strong effects on important work outcomes. Stress is believed to cause decreased work performance and increased absenteeism and turnover. However, the relationships between work stress and these key bottom-line variables are quite complex. For example, it has been suggested that the relationship between stress and performance may often take the form of an inverted U (see Figure 9.1), rather than being direct and linear, with greater stress leading to poorer performance. In other words, very low levels of stress (or no stress) and very high levels of stress are associated with poor work performance, while low to moderate levels of stress seem to be related to better performance (Cohen, 1980). This makes sense, since very high levels of stress will interfere with job performance. On the other end, having little or no stress likely means that workers are not being challenged or motivated. In short, a little bit of stress might not be a bad thing. Of course, both stress and job performance are extremely complex variables, and this inverted U relationship may not hold for all types of stressors or for all aspects of job performance (Beehr, 1985).

The effects of work stress on job performance might also be moderated by other variables. For example, one study showed that the effects of stress on the job performance of nurses was moderated by feelings of depression. That is, work stress caused the nurses to be depressed, and the depression led to decreased quality of patient care and problems with relationships with coworkers (Motowidlo, Packard, & Manning, 1986). If stress is caused by an inability to get along with a certain coworker, an employee may try to cope with this situation by avoiding all interactions with the individual. This avoidance strategy may impair the employee's job performance if the coworker has some valuable information that the employee needs to perform his or her job. In this case, it is not the stress that is causing poor job performance, but the coping strategy!

A great deal of evidence suggests that work stress can lead to increased turnover and absenteeism (e.g., Dwyer & Ganster, 1991; Mayes & Ganster, 1988). Gupta and Beehr (1979) found this to be true for a variety of occupations in five organizations. Another study concluded that it was a combination of high levels of work stress and low levels of organizational commitment that predicted voluntary turnover rates for workers in a food processing company (Parasuraman & Alutto, 1984). Further, if stress levels are to blame for certain illnesses, it is a given that stress must be responsible for some absenteeism and some turnover caused by disabling illness.

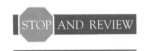

Discuss four ways of measuring worker stress.

JOB BURNOUT

burnout
a syndrome resulting from prolonged exposure to work stress that leads to withdrawal from the organization

Employees exposed to such things as unresolved interpersonal conflicts, lack of clearly defined work tasks and responsibilities, extreme overwork, lack of appropriate rewards, or presence of inappropriate punishment may become victims of **burnout**, a process by which they become less committed to their jobs and begin to withdraw from work. The process of withdrawal may include such reactions as increased tardiness and absenteeism, and decreased work performance and work quality (Gaines & Jermier, 1983; Maslach, 1982; Sutherland & Cooper, 1988).

Burnout usually occurs in three phases. The first phase is *emotional exhaustion* caused by excessive demands placed on the worker. The second phase is *depersonalization*, or the development of a cynical, insensitive attitude toward people (other workers or customers) in the work site. The third phase is marked by feelings of *low personal accomplishment*. Here the burned-out workers feel a sense of frustration and helplessness. They begin to believe that their work efforts fail to produce the desired results, and they may quit trying (Jackson, Schwab, & Schuler, 1986; Lee & Ashforth, 1990). Table 9.3 presents sample items from the Maslach Burnout Inventory Human

Research indicates that job burnout is particularly high in the human service professions, including teachers.

TABLE 9.3

Sample Items from the Maslach Burnout Inventory (MBIHSS)

Respondents answer "how often" they feel the following ways about their jobs, on a 6-point scale, ranging from "Never" (0) to "Every day" (6).

- I feel emotionally drained from my work.
- I feel frustrated by my job.
- Working with people all day is really a strain for me.
- I feel like I'm at the end of my rope.

Reproduced by special permission the Publisher, Consulting Psychologists Press, Inc., Palo Alto, CA 94303 from the *Maslach Burnout Inventory–Human Services Survey* by Christina Maslach and Susan E. Jackson. Copyright 1986 by Consulting Psychologists Press, Inc. All rights reserved. Further reproduction is prohibited without the Publisher's written consent.

Services Survey (MBI; Maslach & Jackson, 1986), an instrument that assesses the three hypothesized components of burnout.

Research has shown that burnout is especially high in human service professions that involve helping others, such as health care providers (physicians, nurses, counselors), teachers, social workers, and policemen (Burke, 1997; Carlson & Thompson, 1995; Cherniss, 1980). A study of nurses found that burnout led to decreased organizational commitment and increased negative interactions with supervisors (Leiter & Maslach, 1988). Similarly, the effects of burnout on teachers include insensitivity toward students, lower tolerance for disruption in the classroom, inadequate preparation for classes, and the feeling that they are no longer able to help students learn (Byrne, 1993). A recent longitudinal study of social welfare workers found that the emotional exhaustion component of Maslach's Burnout Inventory was related to both voluntary turnover and declines in job performance over a one-year period (Wright & Cropanzano, 1998). Although much of the research on burnout focuses on the "helping professions", there is evidence that burnout can occur in many different occupations (Leiter & Schaufeli, 1996; Sonnentag, Brodbeck, Heinbokel, & Stolte, 1994).

It is important to note that there is some debate among researchers about the definition and the complexity of the burnout phenomenon. For instance, researchers have disagreed about the number of components that comprise the burnout syndrome (Evans & Fischer, 1993; Schaufeli & Van Dierendonck, 1993). Yet, burnout is a serious problem and illustrates some of the long-term psychological and behavioral effects of work-related stress.

Coping with Worker Stress

The tremendous variety of strategies and techniques designed to cope with work stress can all be categorized into two general approaches: individual strategies and organizational strategies. Individual strategies are those that can be used by individual employees to try to reduce or eliminate personal stress. Organizational strategies are techniques and programs that organizations can implement to try to reduce stress levels for groups of workers or for the organization as a whole.

Individual coping strategies

individual coping strategies
techniques such as exercise, meditation or cognitive restucturing that can be used to deal with work stress

Individual coping strategies are behavioral or cognitive efforts made in an attempt to manage internal demands and conflicts that have exceeded an individual's usual coping resources (Sethi & Schuler, 1984; Lazarus & Launier, 1978). The most obvious of such techniques are programs developed to improve the individual's physical condition, such as exercise and diet plans. The primary rationale behind such health programs is to make the body more resistant to stress-related illnesses. Some claim that exercise itself may directly reduce the anxiety associated with stress, or that it may have a certain tranquilizing effect on stressed individuals (Jette, 1984). However, it is unclear whether it is the exercise that directly alleviates the physiological symptoms of stress or simply that an individual "feels good" after exercising because of positive psychological factors. For instance, because exercising and keeping physically fit are valued highly by our culture, it may be that physically active persons feel better about themselves and thus psychologically reduce perceived stress. More rigorous evaluation is needed to determine the precise physiological and psychological influences of exercise and diet programs in alleviating stress.

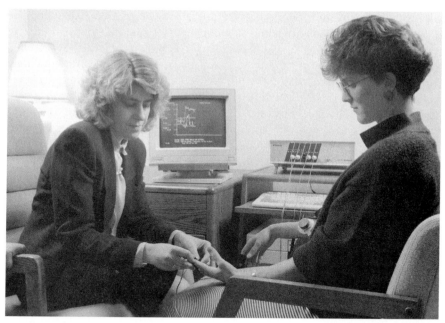

Relaxation techniques such as biofeedback may serve as useful coping strategies, although research questions their effectiveness in the workplace.

Another individual coping strategy is the inducement of states of relaxation to reduce the negative arousal and strain that accompany stress. A variety of techniques have been used to achieve this, including systematic relaxation training, meditation, and biofeedback. In systematic relaxation training individuals are taught how to relax all of the muscles of the body systematically, from the feet to the face. Meditation is a deep relaxed state that is usually brought on by intense concentration upon a single word, idea, or object. Supposedly, meditative states are "free of anxiety, tension, or distress" (Sethi, 1984, p. 145). Biofeedback uses some measure of physiological activity, typically brain waves or muscle tension, that is associated with relaxed states. When the person is in the state of relaxation, the measurement machinery provides some sort of feedback, such as a tone. The individual then learns through practice how to enter into the relaxed, stress-free state. While relaxation, meditation, and biofeedback are intended principally to reduce the physiological arousal associated with stress, they may also induce positive psychological reactions to stress.

While these various methods of coping with stress through relaxation processes are widely touted, there has been very little systematic investigation of their effectiveness. In fact, some findings indicate that such programs are not very effective at all (Ganster, Mayes, Sime, & Tharp, 1982; Sallis,

Johnson, Trevorrow, Hovell, & Kaplan, 1985). Moreover, two popular books on stress and coping do not even mention meditation as a coping strategy (Cooper & Payne, 1988; Perrewe, 1991).

One possible reason why systematic relaxation coping strategies may not be effective is that most of the relaxation techniques require quite a bit of dedication and practice to be used effectively. Not all persons find it easy to induce a deeply relaxed state; others may not be able to adhere to a regular program of systematic relaxation or meditation. Also, many of these programs last only a few hours, which may not be enough time to teach someone difficult relaxation techniques. The timing of the relaxation technique is another problem. Many people would find it difficult (and perhaps inappropriate) to meditate at work, and relaxing before or after work may or may not significantly reduce stress while at work. The same argument can be made for exercise programs—the benefits will only occur if people adhere to their exercise regimens (see Erfurt, Foote, & Heirich, 1992). In short, although any and all of these techniques may be good in theory, they may not function well in practice.

Other individual coping strategies include a variety of techniques to try to fend off work stress through better, more efficient work methods. Courses in time management are often advertised as methods of reducing stress caused by overwork and inefficiency (Schuler & Sethi, 1984; Wratcher & Jones, 1986). For example, learning to approach work tasks systematically by budgeting and assigning parcels of time to specific tasks and by planning ahead to avoid last-minute deadlines may be quite effective in helping reduce stress for some workers. Again, however, these strategies depend on the individual's commitment to the technique, and willingness and ability to use it regularly (Shahani, Weiner, & Streit, 1993). (See Applying I/O Psychology for guidelines on how organizations should implement stress management programs.)

Individuals may also try to cope with stress by removing themselves, temporarily or permanently, from the stressful work situation. It is not uncommon for workers to exchange a stressful job for one that is less stressful (although many do seek more challenging and *more* stressful jobs). While a vacation may temporarily eliminate work stress, certain trips, such as intense tours of eight European countries in seven days, may create a different kind of stress themselves (Lounsbury & Hoopes, 1986). Research indicates that while vacations do indeed reduce work stress and feelings of burnout, the effects are temporary. In fact, levels of stress and burnout are reduced immediately before, during, and immediately after the vacation, but tend to go back to original levels a few weeks after the vacation (Westman & Eden, 1997).

It is interesting to note that workers might use absence from work—voluntarily taking a day off—as a coping strategy. If absence is used as an attempt to cope with a particularly stressful job, then the lost work time must be balanced against the possible gains in terms of the employee's long-term performance and well-being (Hackett & Bycio, 1996).

Finally, cognitive efforts to cope may include cognitive restructuring, which entails changing the way one thinks about stressors (Lazarus, 1991). For example, instead of thinking negative thoughts when faced with a stressor, the individual practices thinking neutral or positive thoughts (i.e., "this is not important," "this is really a challenge"). One study of teachers who used cognitive restructuring found that it reduced their perceptions of stress (Schonfeld, 1990).

Organizational coping strategies

While individual coping strategies are steps that workers themselves can take to alleviate personal stress, **organizational coping strategies** are steps that organizations can take to try to reduce stress levels in the organization for all, or most, employees (Burke, 1993). Since work stress can come from a variety of organizational sources, there are many things that organizations can do to reduce situational stressors in the workplace. These strategies include the following.

Improve the person-job fit—We have already seen that work stress commonly arises when workers are in jobs they dislike or jobs for which they are ill-suited (French & Caplan, 1972). A mismatch between a worker's interests or skills and job requirements can be very stressful. By maximizing the person-job fit through the careful screening, selection, and placement of employees, organizations can alleviate a great deal of this stress.

Improve employee training and orientation programs—Perhaps the most stressed groups of workers in any organization are new employees. Although they are usually highly motivated and want to make a good impression on their new bosses by showing that they are hard-working and competent, their lack of certain job-related skills and knowledge means that new employees are often unable to perform their jobs as well as they would like. This mismatch between expectations and outcomes can be very stressful for new workers. Moreover, they feel a great deal of stress simply because they are in a new and unfamiliar environment in which there is much important information to be learned. Companies can help eliminate some of this stress by ensuring that new workers receive proper job training and orientation to the organization. Not only does this lead to a more capable and productive new workforce, but it also helps to reduce the stress-induced turnover of new employees.

Increase employees' sense of control—We have seen that the lack of a sense of control over one's job can be very stressful. By giving workers a greater feeling of control through participation in work-related decisions, more responsibility, or increased autonomy and independence, organizations can alleviate some of this stress (Caplan, Cobb, French, Harrison, & Pinneau, 1980; Jimmieson & Terry, 1993; Karasek, 1979). Programs such as job enrichment, participative decision making, and systems of delegating authority all help increase employees' sense of control over their jobs and the work environment.

organizational coping strategies
techniques that organizations can use to reduce stress for all or most employees

STOP AND REVIEW

Give three reasons why individual coping strategies may not be effective in alleviating worker stress.

APPLYING I/O PSYCHOLOGY

Designing Effective Work Stress Management Training Programs

A wide range of programs are used to help employees manage work stress. According to two leading researchers, such programs must follow certain guidelines to ensure their effectiveness: They must be systematic; they must teach knowledge, skills, or attitudes that are useful in coping with stress; and their success must be evaluated and documented (Matteson & Ivancevich, 1987; Munz & Kohler, 1997).

The first step in designing a stress management program is the same as in designing any sort of training program: an assessment of training needs. An organizational stress analysis is needed and might include answering such questions as: What are the major producers of stress in the organization? Do these stressors necessarily detract from the accomplishment of organizational goals? (In other words, are they "bad"?) What sort of resources will be committed to the training program?

According to Matteson and Ivancevich, most stress management programs take one of two forms: knowledge acquisition programs or skill training programs. Knowledge acquisition programs provide participants with some information about stress and a number of coping techniques. An outline of a sample four-part stress knowledge acquisition program is presented below:

1. *Overview of stress and its potential consequences (3 hours)*—This might include lecture and readings on facts and myths about stress, the impact of stress on physical and psychological health and on work performance, and potential sources of stress.
2. *Self-analysis: Learning about your personal stress (3 hours)*—This section can include assessments of personal stressors using instruments such as the stressful life events scale or workers' self-reports.
3. *Methods of coping with work stress (3 hours)*—Here various individual coping strategies are presented and perhaps demonstrated.
4. *Developing a personalized coping plan (3 hours)*—In this final part participants work on developing customized programs for managing stress, including setting personal stress management goals and finding means to assess their attainment.

The major advantages of knowledge acquisition programs are that they are relatively inexpensive, do not require a lot of time, and do not place heavy demands on participants. Unfortunately, these "one-shot" training programs may not be as effective as the more involved skill training programs in alleviating work stress.

Skill training programs are designed to improve specific coping skills in areas such as problem solving, time management, communication, social interaction, cognitive coping, or strategies for making changes in life style. An example of a step-by-step problem-solving skill program developed by Wasik (1984) is illustrated next:

APPLYING I/O PSYCHOLOGY (*continued*)

1. Identify problem (What is my problem?)
2. Select goals (What do I want to accomplish by solving the problem?)
3. Generate alternatives (What else can I do?)
4. Review the consequences (What might happen?)
5. Make a decision (What is my decision?)
6. Implement the decision (Did I do what I decided?)
7. Evaluate the decision (Does it work?)

This step-by-step program would be conducted in a series of one- to two-hour sessions over many weeks. Participants learn each of the steps, practice them using role playing, and receive feedback concerning their skill development. They are also encour-age to use the skills to deal with actual work problems and then report back to discuss the success or failure of the strategy. The key to these programs is to practice using and applying the coping strategies to real and simulated stressful situations.

The final stage in any stress management program is to evaluate its effectiveness. Too often, stress management programs are not properly evaluated (Loo, 1994). It has been suggested that an assessment should consider trainees' reactions; how well the program accomplished its immediate objectives; actual behavioral changes; the impact of the program on organizational outcomes such as productivity, absenteeism, morale, and employee health; and the cost effectiveness of the program (Kirkpatrick, 1976).

Eliminate punitive management—It is well known that humans react strongly when they are punished or harassed, particularly if the punishment or harassment is believed to be unfair and undeserved. The very act of being threatened or punished at work can be very stressful. If organizations take steps to eliminate company policies that are perceived to be threatening or punitive, a major source of work stress will also be eliminated. Training supervisors to minimize the use of punishment as a managerial technique will also help control this common source of stress.

Remove hazardous or dangerous work conditions—In some occupations stress results from exposure to hazardous work conditions, such as mechanical danger of loss of limb or life, health-harming chemicals, excessive fatigue, or extreme temperatures. The elimination or reduction of these situations is another way of coping with organizational stress. We will consider dangerous work conditions more fully in Chapter 16.

Provide a supportive, team-oriented work environment—There is considerable research evidence that having supportive colleagues—people who can help deal with stressful work situations—can help reduce worker stress (Fenlason & Beehr, 1994; House, 1981; Lim, 1996). The more organizations can foster good interpersonal relationships among coworkers, and an integrated, highly functioning work team, the more likely that workers will be able to provide support for one another in times of stress (Heaney, Price, & Rafferty, 1995; Unden, 1996). We will look at work group processes and teamwork in more depth in Chapter 11.

Improve communication—Much of the stress at work derives from difficulties in interpersonal relations with supervisors and coworkers. The better the communication among workers, the lower the stress created because of misunderstandings. In addition, stress occurs when workers feel cut off from or uninformed about organizational processes and operations. Proper organizational communication, which will be examined in Chapter 10, can prevent workers from experiencing this stressful sense of isolation.

UP CLOSE

Stress Levels and Stress Sources of Executives Around the World

A common stereotype in the United States is the highly stressed, top-level business executive (Friedman, Hall, & Harris, 1985). Is this characterization accurate, and if so, are high-level managers in other nations similarly stressed? The first question—"are executives highly stressed?"—does not have an easy answer. For example, many executives constantly work under such stressful conditions as work overload, high levels of responsibility, and interrole conflict (e.g., being required to travel extensively on business which interferes with family and person commitments). The finding that executives have a higher rate of certain types of ulcers than certain blue-collar workers attests to the existence of executive stress (Hurrell, Murphy, Sauter, & Cooper, 1988). On the other hand, executives have the benefit of some working conditions that are believed to moderate stress, such as control over the job.

The answer to the question of whether executives worldwide experience similar stressors is also not completely clear. There is some indication, however, that executives in different nations experience different types or sources of stress. For example, executives in less developed countries such as Nigeria and Egypt seem to experience a great deal of stress due to lack of autonomy, while those from more developed countries, such as the U.S., the United Kingdom, and Japan, experience greater stress from work overload (Cooper & Hensman, 1985). One study found that executives in New Zealand experience less job-related stress than executives in nine other countries (McCormich & Cooper, 1988). These researchers mention that this may be due to the more relaxed lifestyle in New Zealand, and the fact that many of these executives worked for rather small organizations.

An interesting study by Kirkcaldy and Cooper (1993) found some evidence that work stress for executives may be modified by preference for leisure activities—and that preferred leisure activities may be related to culture. For example, managers from Germany, who tend to prefer nonaggressive leisure activities, experienced less job stress than British managers, who typically prefer aggressive leisure activities.

Overall, such studies seem to indicate that while executive job stress is universal, the amount of stress experienced, and the sources of the stress, may vary depending on country or culture.

STOP AND REVIEW

List and describe five organizational coping strategies.

Summary

Although there is a great deal of disagreement over definitions of stress, *worker stress* can be defined as physiological or psychological reactions to an event that is perceived to be threatening or taxing. Stress is actually a perception, so there is tremendous individual variation in what one perceives to be stressful. Negative stress, or distress, can cause stress-related illness, and it can affect absenteeism, turnover, and work performance.

Certain occupations, such as air traffic controllers and health care providers, are stereotypically associated with high levels of stress. Worker stress can also come from organizational sources or individual sources, which are commonly classified as *situational* or *dispositional* sources, respectively. Organizational sources may include having too much to do—*work overload*—or too little to do—*underutilization. Job ambiguity,* which occurs when job tasks and responsibilities are not clearly defined; or from inadequate performance feedback or job insecurity; and *interpersonal stress,* which arises from relations with coworkers, are other organizational sources of stress, as are workers' *sense* of a *lack of control* over their jobs and *organizational change.* Individual sources of work stress include the worker's experience of traumatic *life events;* susceptibility to stress, such as the lack of *hardiness,* or resistance to stress-related illnesses; and certain personality characteristics such as the *Type A behavior pattern,* which is the coronary-prone personality.

Attempts to measure stress have included physiological measures, self-report assessments, the measurement of stressful life events, and the match between worker characteristics and the demands of the work situation, referred to as the *person-environment fit* approach. Stress has been shown to be related to certain physical illnesses such as ulcers, high blood pressure, and heart disease. These stress-related illnesses as well as stress itself are tied to rates of employee absenteeism and turnover and to job performance, although the relationship between stress and performance is complex. Long-term stress can lead to *job burnout,* a multi-dimensional construct that relates to one's tendency to withdraw from work.

Strategies for coping with work stress can be divided into *individual coping strategies* and *organizational coping strategies*. Individual strategies include programs of exercise, diet, systematic relaxation training, meditation, biofeedback, time management, work planning, and cognitive coping strategies. Organizational strategies include improving the person-job fit, offering better training and orientation programs, giving workers a sense of control over their jobs, eliminating punitive management styles, removing hazardous work conditions, and improving organizational communication.

Study Questions and Exercises

1. List the sources of stress in your own life. Ask a friend to do the same. Are there important differences in your two lists, or are they quite similar? What are the implications for defining and understanding stress?

2. Consider how the work world will be changing in the next several years. What are the implications for worker stress? Will there be more of it, or less? What are some sources of technology-related stress (technostress) that will increase in the future?

3. Consider the various means of assessing stress. Which seems most accurate, and why?

4. Based on the material in the chapter, design a stress management program for use in an organization.

Suggested Readings

Cartwright, S. & Cooper, C.L. (1997). *Managing workplace stress*. Thousand Oaks, CA: Sage. *A comprehensive treatment of worker stress with practical strategies for dealing with stress-related situations.*

Jex, S.M. (1998). *Stress and job performance: Theory, research and implications for managerial practice*. Thousand Oaks, CA: Sage. *A comprehensive, research-based treatment of the relationship between work stress and job performance from an active researcher in the field.*

Schaufeli, W.B., Maslach, C., & Marek, T. (Eds.). (1993). *Professional burnout: Recent developments in theory and research*. Washington, DC: Taylor & Francis. *An edited book containing a wealth of research on the topic of burnout in a variety of professional occupations.*

COMMUNICATION IN THE WORKPLACE

COMMUNICATION: A COMPLEX PROCESS IN WORK ORGANIZATIONS

INSIDE
TIPS

Communication is a constant process in any work organization. Because organizational communication can take many forms and can occur among any grouping of workers, it is extremely complex and difficult to study. To try to capture communication so that it can be studied, I/O psychologists and other scientists rely heavily on various communication models. This chapter begins with a general model of communication between two persons: sender and receiver. Models of other aspects of communication in the workplace are then presented, including communication networks, which are models of group communication; the organizational chart, which is a model of the formal lines of downward, upward, and lateral communication in an organization; and the grapevine, which represents the informal flow of communication. While these various models describe who communicates with whom, they do not explain the type, content, or quality of the communication. Portions of the chapter concentrate on factors that can contribute to or detract from the effective and accurate flow of communication in work settings.

In contrast to the previous chapters, this chapter is more general. The theories and models tend to represent general aspects of communication, and relatively little new terminology is introduced. The research results and practical applications also tend to be focused more on communication in general rather than on specific aspects, largely because communication is a complex process that we are only beginning to understand fully. Therefore, rather than concentrating on learning new terms or specific theories, think about the complexity of organizational communication and the difficulties encountered in trying to measure and understand this important, ongoing process. Consider the number and types of communication you send and receive each day, the various ways that messages are communicated, and the different settings in which this occurs. The sheer amount of communication you encounter in your daily life should give you an idea of the complexity of organizational communication.

Most of us do not work alone but rather with others in the context of small groups. In large organizations, these groups are in turn members of larger work groups or departments, which in combination make up the work organization. Depending on the size of the organization, our coworkers may number in the tens, hundreds, or even thousands. Much energy in organizations, particularly from the management perspective, involves coordinating the activities of the various members. In the next few chapters, we will examine work behavior in terms of this organizational interaction. We will investigate the dynamics of work groups—how they coordinate activities and make decisions—as well as the very factors that hold them together. We will see how workers differ in terms of their power and status within the organization, paying particular attention to the relationship between those persons designated as leaders and other workers. We will examine the politics within work organizations and the structure of work groups and larger work organizations. However, before we begin to explore these topics, we must understand one of the most basic processes that occurs among workers in organizational settings: communication.

The Communication Process: A Definition and a Model

communication
the passage of information between one person or group to another person or group

Communication can be defined as the transmission of information from one person or group to another person or group. In work settings, communication takes many forms, such as written or spoken orders, informal chatter, electronic messages, printed reports or procedure manuals, discussion among executives in a corporate boardroom, or announcements posted on a bulletin board. Communication is an ongoing process that serves as the lifeblood of the organization. Communication is also extremely complex and can occur in a variety of ways: through the written or spoken word; through nonverbal means such as gestures, nods, or tone of voice; or through a picture or diagram. We can also communicate in a number of contexts, including in face-to-face conversation, over the telephone, in letters or memos, through electronic mail, or in a public address. This complexity, coupled with its al-

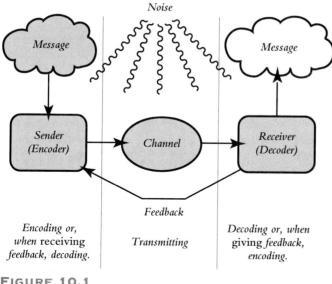

FIGURE 10.1

The Communication Process.

most continuous nature (even our silence can communicate), makes communication very difficult to study.

Communication involves the process of the exchange of information among two or more parties, which is best represented by a simple model of communication between two persons: the *sender* and the *receiver* (see Figure 10.1). The **sender** (also known as the encoder) is the originator of the communication; the **receiver** (also called the *decoder*) is the recipient. Communication begins with some information—a message—that the sender wishes to transmit to a receiver. The sender's task is to take the information and put it into some form in which it can be communicated to the receiver. This process of preparing a message for transmission is referred to as **encoding**, because the sender chooses some sort of shared code as a means of communication. In work settings, this code is usually the shared verbal language, but it might also consist of some common nonverbal code, or "body language."

The next step is for the sender to select a **channel**, the vehicle through which the message will flow from the sender to the receiver. The sender may choose the spoken word, confronting the receiver face-to-face or through the telephone, or the written word, using a memo, or as is becoming increasingly popular, a typed message sent through a computerized mail network. Different methods of communication have various advantages and disadvantages (see Table 10.1). For example, face-to-face or telephone communication is typically quick and convenient, while formal reports or

sender
the originator of a communication, who encodes and transmits a message; also known as the encoder

receiver
the recipient of a communication who decodes the message; also known as the decoder

encoding
the process of preparing a message for transmission by putting it into some form, or code

channel
the vehicle through which a message flows from sender to receiver

TABLE 10.1

Advantages And Disadvantages Of Communication Channels

Channel	Advantages	Disadvantages
Telephone	Verbal Permits questions and answers Convenient Two-way flow Immediate feedback	Less personal No record of conversation Message might be misunderstood Timing may be inconvenient May be impossible to terminate
Face-to-face	Visual Personal contact Can "show" and "explain" Can set the mood Immediate feedback	Timing may be inconvenient Requires spontaneous thinking May not be easy to terminate Power or status of one person may cause pressure
Meetings	Can use visuals Involves several minds at once Two-way flow	Time-consuming Time may be inconvenient One person may dominate the group
Memorandum	Brief Provides a record Can prethink the message Can disseminate widely	No control over receiver Less personal One-way flow Delayed feedback
Formal report	Complete; comprehensive Can organize material at writer's leisure Can disseminate widely	Less personal May require considerable time in reading Language may not be understandable Expensive One-way flow Delayed feedback
Teleconference	Saves time for travel Visual Lessens impact of power/ status Makes users be better prepared	Miss interpersonal contact Not good for initial brainstorming sessions Expensive
Electronic mail	Convenient Messages sent/received at all hours Extremely fast compared to other written messages Can be sent to multiple parties simultaneously	Ease can lead to message "overload" No nonverbal communication Others may be able to get access to messages

Source: P.V. Lewis, *Organizational Communication: The Essence of Effective Management*, 3rd ed.
(New York: John Wiley & Sons, 1987), p. 9.

A channel is any vehicle of communication, such as the spoken word via telephone or the written word via fax machine.

detailed memos can be time-consuming to prepare. However, the more formal, written channels of communication are less likely to be misunderstood or misinterpreted because of their length, detail, and careful preparation. Importantly, the sender must also choose the channel of communication that is appropriate for the situation. For example, personal information is usually conveyed verbally, face-to-face, while an important directive concerning a project deadline might be put in the form of a detailed, typed memo that is distributed to all relevant parties, with follow-up reminders sent as the deadline nears.

In the two-person communication model, the receiver picks up the message and is responsible for **decoding** it, or translating it in an effort to understand the meaning intended by the sender. Of course, in many communications some of the original message—that information drawn from the thought processes of the encoder—will be lost or distorted, either through the encoding process, through transmission, or in decoding. (That is why the second, received "Message" in the communication model is not identical to the original Message.)

Typically, when the receiver has decoded the message, **feedback**, or a response, is transmitted to the sender. The receiver acknowledges receipt of the message and either tells the sender that the message is understood or requests clarification. In the feedback stage of the process, the communication model actually reverses, with the receiver becoming the sender and vice versa. Feedback can be as simple as a nod of the head or as formal as a letter of receipt or the initialing of a memo that is returned to the sender.

decoding
the process of translating a message so that is can be understood

feedback
an acknowledgment that a message has been received and understood

Although this model represents communication as a simple and relatively foolproof process, the effective flow of information from sender to receiver can break down at many points. The sender can have difficulty in encoding the message, making comprehension by the receiver difficult. For example, a supervisor might tell an employee, "I would really like you to try to make this deadline," when what she really means is that the deadline must be met, with no exceptions. On the other side, the receiver may inaccurately decode the message and interpret it in a way wholly different from what the sender had in mind. For example, the employee might interpret the "deadline" statement to mean that the supervisor has now turned entire responsibility for the project over to him, and will no longer be available to help meet the deadline. A poor choice of channel may also result in a breakdown of effective communication. For example, giving a coworker lengthy and detailed instructions about a work task over the telephone rather than in writing may lead to inadequate performance of the job. Furthermore, the work environment may provide any number of distractions that can disrupt the communication process, such as competing conversations, loud machinery, or inconsistent or contradictory messages. Such distractions are collectively called **noise**. Noise may also refer to psychological factors such as biases, perceptual differences, or selective attention, all of which make it difficult for persons to communicate with and to understand one another. For example, psychological noise can occur when the receiver ignores the sender because of a belief that the sender "has nothing important to say."

noise
physical or psychological distractions that disrupt the effective flow of communication

RESEARCH ON THE COMMUNICATION PROCESS

Much of the research on the communication process in work settings has focused on factors that can increase or decrease its effectiveness. Among the factors that can affect the flow of communication from sender to receiver are source factors, channel factors, and audience factors.

Source factors

source factors
characteristics of the sender that influence the effectiveness of a communication.

Source factors are characteristics of the sender—the source of the message—that can facilitate or detract from the effective flow of communication. One such factor is the status of the source, which can affect whether a message is attended to by potential receivers. Generally, the higher the organizational status of the sender, the more likely that the communication will be listened to and acted upon. For example, messages from the president or owner of a company are usually given top priority ("When the boss talks, people listen.").

Another source factor is the credibility, or believability, of the sender. If the source is trusted, it is more likely that the message will receive attention. Variables such as the expertise, knowledge, and reliability of the source (i.e., has this person provided truthful information in the past?)

contribute to the credibility of the sender (O'Reilly & Roberts, 1976). Employees learn which sources can be trusted, and pay closest attention to their messages.

A final source factor is the encoding skills of the sender, or the source's ability to translate an abstract message into some sort of shared code, usually the written or spoken language, so that it can be clearly conveyed to the receiver. In short, these skills include the abilities to speak and write clearly, and to select the appropriate channel for transmitting information. Generally, the better the encoding skills of the sender, the smoother and more effective the flow of communication.

Channel factors

Channel factors, which are positive or negative characteristics related to the vehicle through which the message is communicated, can also influence the effectiveness of the process. Selection of the proper channel can have an important effect on the accurate flow of communication. For example, using a visual device such as a chart or graph, to present complex information on sales and profit figures is likely to be a more effective channel than the spoken word. The channel selected can also affect the impact of the message. For example, a face-to-face reprimand from a supervisor might carry more weight than the same reprimand conveyed over the telephone. Whenever possible, using multiple channels to present complicated information will increase the likelihood that it will be attended to and retained. In the past decade, research in organizational communication has begun to focus on specific types, or "genres" of messages, such as business letters, memos, or group meetings (Yates & Orlikowski, 1992). In one study, it was found that persons higher in the organizational hierarchy had a preference for more formal modes of written communication (word-processed letters and memos), over more informal, handwritten messages (Reinsch & Beswick, 1995). Another study has found that managers are indicating a growing preference for using e-mail to communicate messages, even in situations such as responding to another's telephone message, or when the recipient is in an office just down the hall (Markus, 1994).

Semantic problems are common channel factors that can lead to a breakdown in communication. These difficulties occur because different people may interpret the meanings of certain words differently. For example, if your work supervisor tells you that you are doing a "good" job, you may infer that your performance is well above average. However, if the supervisor defines "good" as work that is barely passable (but really he expects "excellent," "superior," or "outstanding" performance), you may be missing the meaning of the message. Semantic problems may arise through the use of technical language, or **jargon**, the special language that develops within a specific work environment. Jargon is typically filled with abbreviated words, acronyms, special vocabularies, and slang. For example, industrial/organizational psychology could be abbreviated as "I/O Psych," and might be

STOP AND REVIEW

Explain each of the steps in two-person communication.

channel factors
characteristics of the vehicle of transmission of a message that affect communication

jargon
special language developed in connection with certain jobs; also called technical language

BOTTOM LINERS

2-9

"It's important, Miss Harris. Try to remember
who called — the CEO, the CFO or
the CIA ? "

described as the field in which topics such as RJPs, VIE theory, and validity generalization are studied.

While jargon serves the purpose of speeding up communication between those who speak the language, it can create problems when the receiver is not "fluent" in its use. The use of jargon can also create problems when a team of workers is composed of members from different professional disciplines, all of whom may use different jargon (Cooley, 1994). For example, imagine the potential communication breakdowns that occurred during some of the NASA space projects, where decision-making teams were made up of aerospace engineers, military officers, and research scientists, each using their own technical jargon.

ON THE CUTTING EDGE

Communicating in a Diverse, Multicultural Work Environment

The world of work is becoming more and more diverse. The workforce in most organizations is made up of people from various cultural backgrounds, many of whom are nonnative speakers of the dominant language (Maznevski & Peterson, 1997; Orasnu, Fischer, & Davison, 1997). Moreover, many companies are engaged in international business, and interact with workers from a variety of nations and cultures. In the past decade, researchers in the fields of psychology, communication, management, and international business have taken a serious look at intercultural business communication (Granrose & Oskamp, 1997; Limaye & Victor, 1991).

Such cultural diversity has many advantages. Diverse workforces tend to be more creative, more adaptable, and more tolerant of others (Adler, 1991). As you can imagine, however, cultural and language differences can present challenges to the effective flow of communication within organizations. Moreover, cultural differences can threaten a common, shared commitment to organizational goals (Fine, 1991; Granrose, 1997). Culturally based communication differences can also affect the ability of companies from different nations and cultures to work with one another. For example, the communication style of most North American managers tends to be direct and "confrontation-centered." The Japanese business communication style, however, tends to be indirect and "agreement-centered" (Kume, 1985). Such differences can lead to serious communication breakdowns.

Realizing the need to prevent cross-cultural communication breakdown, organizations have taken several steps to facilitate intercultural organizational communication. For example, many organizations have developed multicultural awareness and training programs (Ferdman, 1992; Kossek & Zonia, 1993). In addition, many international businesses have training programs specifically designed for preparing employees for assignments in other countries (see Chapter 5). One model of preparing managers for working with culturally diverse and multinational work groups suggests that general communication competence, proficiency in other languages, an awareness of cultural differences, and an ability to negotiate with people of diverse backgrounds are the keys to success (Tung, 1997). In short, the issues of multicultural and cross-cultural communication are going to be important ones in the world of work as we move into the next century.

The type of channel used to communicate can affect important work-related outcomes, such as job satisfaction. Muchinsky (1977) found that the frequency of face-to-face communication between supervisors and subordinates was positively related to the workers' job satisfaction, while the frequency of written communications was negatively correlated with

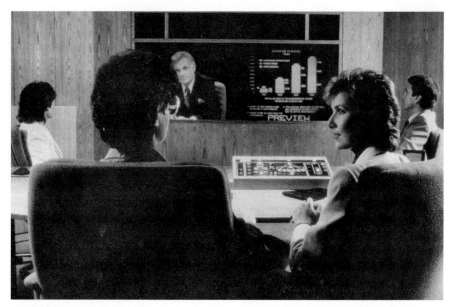

Video conferencing offers instantaneous, face-to-face communication over long distances.

satisfaction. In a more recent study, both frequency of communication from supervisors and the quality of these interactions were related to subordinate job satisfaction (Callan, 1993). The type of channel may also have some influence on work performance and efficiency. For example, a company policy of keeping written documentation of all orders and directives rather than simply relying on spoken orders may decrease the likelihood that workers will forget what they are supposed to be doing, which in turn may have positive effects on the productivity and efficiency of the work unit.

An emerging topic of interest has been the use of computer-mediated meetings, where workers interconnect and hold meetings via computer work stations (Trevino & Webster, 1992; Weisband, 1992). Early research on this communication channel indicated that computer-mediated meetings have the advantages of convenience, with members getting more equal participation in the interaction than occurs in face-to-face meetings. Low-status or shy members may be more willing to share information in computer-mediated meetings. However, the lack of "social dynamics," including the loss of nonverbal cues available in face-to-face interactions, tends to lead members of computer-mediated meetings to engage in more extreme or "risky" decisions. Members communicating via computer may also be more outspoken, and members may engage in "rude" behaviors, including "put-downs" of other participants, since the members do not have to face the disapproving looks of other participants (Kiesler & Sproull, 1992). There may also be some difficulties in coordinating the flow of communication and in taking turns—actually causing electronic meetings to be longer than face-to-face ones (Carey & Kacmar, 1997). However, as video-computer interfaces become more common, this will allow the inclusion of visual representations of group members, and make computer-mediated meetings more similar to face-to-face meetings (Fussell & Benimoff, 1995).

Audience factors

Audience factors are elements related to the receiver, such as the person's attention span and perceptual abilities, which can facilitate or impair the communication process. For example, it is important that training information be presented at a level that matches the audience's ability to perceive and process that information, or much of the communication may be lost. Moreover, it is critical to consider the attention span of the target audience. While all-day classroom training sessions might be appropriate for management trainees who are used to such long sessions, the attention of assembly-line workers might be lost after an hour's lecture because of their unfamiliarity with this format.

The receiver's relationship to the sender can also affect the communication process. For example, if the receiver is subordinate to the sender, the message may be better attended to, since the receiver is supposed to listen to superiors. If, however, the situation is reversed, a message from a lower-ranking organizational member may not receive much attention from a higher-ranking employee.

Finally, the decoding skills of the receiver can influence the effectiveness of communication. Workers vary greatly in their ability to receive, decode, and understand organizational messages. While managers are often considered the source rather than the audience of much organizational communication, research has shown that effective managers have good decoding skills in listening and responding to the needs and concerns of their subordinates (Baron, 1986). In fact, because much of the communication in work settings involves spoken communication, oral decoding skills, often referred to as listening skills, are considered to be the most important decoding skills of all (Hunt, 1980).

Research suggests that "active listening"—where the decoder asks clarifying questions, repeats the encoder's words, and provides feedback ("Yes, I see." "uh-hum," etc.)—has positive effects on the effectiveness of the communication flow, in terms of greater comprehension and mutual understanding, and greater participant satisfaction (Kraut, Lewis, & Swezey, 1982; Rao, 1995).

NONVERBAL COMMUNICATION IN WORK SETTINGS

We commonly think of communication in work settings as taking one of two forms, either written or spoken. However, people can and do use a great deal of **nonverbal communication**, which is sent and received by means other than the written or spoken word. Broadly defined, nonverbal communication can occur through facial expressions, gesture, tone of voice, body movements,

STOP AND REVIEW

List several source and audience factors that affect communication flow.

audience factors *characteristics of the receiver that influence the effectiveness of a communication*

nonverbal communication *messages sent and received through means other than the spoken or written word* posture, style of dress, touching, and the physical distance between sender and receiver (Patterson, 1983). We use nonverbal communication to convey a wide range of feelings and attitudes.

To understand the role of nonverbal communication in work settings, we can examine its use from both the sender's and the receiver's perspective. For the sender, nonverbal communication can be used in three ways. First, nonverbal cues can be substituted for verbal communication. Nodding to show approval, shaking your head in disagreement, or gesturing for a person to come closer or to go away are all ways of sending clear, unspoken messages. In particular, noisy work environments or situations in which coworkers are positioned out of hearing range may necessitate the use of a set of nonverbal signals, which decreases the reliance on verbal communication. The hand signals used by ground crews to guide airline pilots or the gestures used by land surveyors are examples of the use of nonverbal communication.

Nonverbal cues can also be used to enhance verbal messages. We often use our tone of voice, facial expressions, and body movements to emphasize what we are saying. If you want to compliment a subordinate for doing an outstanding job, the words will have greater impact if they are accompanied by an enthusiastic tone of voice and an approving smile. A board member who pounds her fist on the table while voicing disagreement with a proposal is going to command greater attention by including this nonverbal emphasizer.

Nonverbal cues are also important for conveying certain impressions in organizations (Giacalone & Rosenfeld, 1989). For example, it is often important that persons in positions of leadership or authority convey their power and authority nonverbally if they want to get others' attention and be persuasive (Riordan, 1989). Similarly, customer service representatives, such as salespersons or waitpersons, need to convey an image of helpfulness and customer concern if they are to be successful (Grove & Fisk, 1989).

Finally, nonverbal cues can be used to convey underlying feelings. In situations in which a person is restricted in what can be said verbally in order to get the true message across, the verbal message may be accompanied by a nonverbal "disclaimer" (see Mehrabian, 1981). For example, at a new employee orientation, the trainer may verbally praise the company but with her tone of voice she may convey that things are not really going as well as they seem.

From the perspective of a receiver, nonverbal cues serve two important functions. First, they provide additional information. When verbal communication is limited or when the receiver has reason to mistrust the verbal message, the receiver will look to nonverbal cues as a source of more data. This is particularly likely when the receiver feels that the verbal message may be deceptive, although research has shown that people do not read the nonverbal cues of deception very accurately (DePaulo, Stone, & Lassiter, 1985; Kraut, 1980).

Nonverbal cues are also used by receivers in person perception, that is, in making judgments about a person's attitudes, personality, and competence. There is evidence that styles of nonverbal behavior play an important part in person perception (Schneider, Hastorf, & Ellsworth, 1979). This is particularly important in personnel decisions such as hiring. For example, it has been found that persons exhibiting more expressive nonverbal behaviors, such as more smiling and greater eye contact, are more favorably evaluated in hiring interviews than are nonexpressive individuals (Forbes & Jackson, 1980; Gifford, Ng, & Wilkinson, 1985; Imada & Hakel, 1977). However, the relationship between nonverbal cues and interviewing success may be more complex than just simply "more is better" (see Rasmussen, 1984). In other words, rather than looking only at the amount of expressiveness, interviewers or other judges of applicants may look for particular styles of expressive nonverbal behavior which indicate that the person is honest, ambitious, or easy to work with. Other nonverbal cues, such as style of dress, physical attractiveness, and indications of dominance, may likewise play an important role in how people are perceived in work settings (Henley, 1977; Riggio & Throckmorton, 1988). For example, it has been shown that attractively dressed and well-groomed individuals make better first impressions in certain work settings than persons who appear sloppy and unkempt (Arvey & Campion, 1982; Cann, Siegfried, & Pearce, 1981).

Ability to decode subtle nonverbal cues accurately is critically important for work supervisors, not only in helping to understand the subtle messages sent by supervisees, but also in building rapport and in helping the supervisor be responsive to the legitimate needs of workers (Riggio, 1999).

While nonverbal communication sometimes facilitates the flow of communication in work settings, misinterpreting such messages can also lead to considerable confusion and may disrupt work operations. While there are well-known rules and techniques for learning to use appropriate written and spoken language, there are no firm guidelines governing nonverbal communication. Often the misunderstandings that occur in organizational communication, verbal and nonverbal, are related to the inadequate skills of the sender or receiver, or both. While a great deal of attention is paid to trying to improve the verbal and writing skills of employees, less concern is focused on nonverbal communication skills, even though they may represent a great deal of the critical communication that occurs in work settings.

The Flow of Communication in Work Organizations

Just as blood flows through the arteries, giving life to the body, messages flow through communication lines and networks, giving life to the work organization. If you look at the organizational chart of most organizations, you will see positions arranged in a pyramidlike hierarchy. While this hierarchy is most commonly thought of as representing the lines of status and authority within the organization, it also depicts the lines of communication between superiors and subordinates. Formal messages travel back and forth along these routes between the top levels and the lower levels of the organization.

DOWNWARD, UPWARD, AND LATERAL FLOW OF COMMUNICATION

The communication flow in work organizations is usually classified into three types: It can flow downward, through the organizational hierarchy; upward, through the same chain of command; or it can flow laterally, from colleague to colleague. Typically, each type of communication flow takes different forms, and tends to contain different kinds of messages.

Downward communication consists of those messages sent from superiors to subordinates. Most commonly, they are one of several types: (1) instructions or directions concerning job performance, (2) information about organizational procedures and policies, (3) feedback to the subordinate concerning job performance, or (4) information to assist in the coordination of work tasks (Katz & Kahn, 1966). As you might guess, much of the formal communication that occurs in work organizations involves this downward flow, which makes sense, since the top levels are involved in making important decisions that must be communicated to the lower levels.

downward communication messages flowing downward in an organizational hierarchy, usually from superiors to subordinates

While much formal communication in organizations is downward, research indicates that most organizations still do not have enough of this communication. A number of studies have found that workers would like more information from their superiors about work procedures and about what is happening elsewhere in the organization. One reason that downward communication is insufficient in some organizations is that superiors may overestimate the amount of information that their subordinates possess and may underestimate the amount they desire (Likert, 1961). Part of this problem is related to the fact that supervisors tend to overestimate how frequently and how clearly they communicate to subordinates (Callan, 1993).

It also appears that certain types of downward communication may be particularly limited, such as feedback concerning work performance (Baird, 1977). This is especially true in companies that fail to conduct regular performance appraisals. Also, organizations that neglect to provide workers with job descriptions and adequate orientation and training may experience a shortage of downward communication involving proper work procedures and company policies.

Research has shown that the frequency and quality of superior-subordinate communication influences important organizational outcomes (Jablin, 1979). For example, downward communication from supervisors can affect new employees' adjustment to and satisfaction with the work group (Kramer, 1995). Research also suggests that supervisors need to be fair and consistent in their communication with subordinates, or workers can become concerned that supervisors are "playing favorites" (Sias & Jablin, 1995).

upward communication messages flowing upward in an organizational hierarchy, usually taking the form of feedback

Upward communication is the flow of messages from the lower levels of the organization to the upper levels. It most typically consists of information managers need to perform their jobs, such as feedback concerning the status of lower-level operations, which could include reports of production output or information about any problems. The upward communication of feedback is critical for managers, who must use this information to make important work-related decisions. Upward communication can also involve complaints and suggestions for improvement from lower-level workers, and is significant because it gives subordinates some input into the functioning of the organization. Finally, an important form of upward feedback concerns subordinates' evaluations of the particular supervisor's effectiveness as a leader/supervisor (Smither, Wohlers, & London, 1995) (as we saw in Chapter 6 during our discussion of subordinate performance appraisals).

Unfortunately, in many organizations, there is simply not enough upward communication (see Applying I/O Psychology). The upward communication of feedback about problems or difficulties in operations may be restricted, because lower-level workers fear that the negative information might reflect poorly on their abilities, because managers neglect to ask for it, or because subordinates believe that management will not really listen to their suggestions and concerns.

Lateral communication flows between people who are at the same level in the organizational hierarchy, and is particularly important when coworkers must coordinate their activities in order to accomplish a goal. Lateral communication can also occur between two or more departments within an organization. For example, effective lateral communication between the production and quality control departments in a television manufacturing plant can help the two departments to coordinate efforts to find and correct assembly errors. Lateral communication between departments also allows the sharing of news and information, and helps in the development and maintenance of interpersonal relationships on the job (Koehler, Anatol, & Applbaum, 1981). While it can help in coordinating worker activities within or between departments, thereby leading to increased productivity, "unauthorized" lateral communication, such as too much socializing on the job, can detract from effective job performance (Katz & Kahn, 1966).

> **lateral communication**
> *messages between two parties at the same level in an organizational hierarchy*

BARRIERS TO THE EFFECTIVE FLOW OF COMMUNICATION

The upward, downward, and lateral flow of communication within an organization are subject to various types of information distortion that disrupt communication effectiveness by eliminating or changing key aspects of the message, so that the message that should be sent is not the one that the recipient receives. Three types of distortion that often occur in work organizations are filtering, censoring, and exaggeration (Gaines, 1980).

Filtering is the selective presentation of the content of a communication; in other words, certain pieces of information are left out of the message. In downward communication, information is often filtered because it is considered to be unimportant to lower-level employees. Often, messages are sent telling workers *what* to do but not telling why it is being done. Information from upper levels of the organization may also be filtered because management fears the impact of the complete message on workers. For example, management may send a memo to workers about proposed cost-cutting measures, telling them that these actions are needed to increase

> **filtering**
> *the selective presentation of the content of a communication*

APPLYING I/O PSYCHOLOGY

Increasing the Upward Flow of Organizational Communication

Most communication problems in work organizations relate to the insufficient flow of information, which results from a shortage either in downward communication or upward communication. However, since downward communication predominates in most work settings, and since it originates from those who have the most power and control over the organizational environment, attention must be given to increasing the flow of communication from those individuals at the bottom of the organization to those at the top, for a shortage of this communication has been associated with employee dissatisfaction and feelings that management is out of touch with employee needs and concerns. Several strategies that can increase upward communication follow.

Employee Suggestion Systems

There are a variety of procedures by which workers can submit ideas for improving some aspect of company operations. The suggestions are then reviewed by company decision makers, and beneficial ideas are implemented. Usually, suggestions are encouraged by some sort of incentive, such as recognition awards or cash prizes that are either fixed monetary amounts or amounts based on percentages of the savings that the suggestion produces. This form of upward communication can lead to innovations and improvement in company operations, and can increase feelings of lower-level employees that they can indeed have some influence in the organization. One potential problem with suggestion systems is

that employees may use it to voice complaints about conditions that management is unable to change.

Grievance Systems

A related concept is the establishment of formal complaint or grievance procedures. While suggestion systems focus on positive changes, grievances are designed to change existing negative situations, and thus must be handled more delicately in order to protect the employee from the retribution that can result when the complaint concerns mistreatment by someone higher in the organizational hierarchy. Also, to keep communication open and flowing, company officials must acknowledge the receipt of grievances and make it clear what action is to be taken (or why action will not or cannot be taken).

Subordinate Appraisals of Supervisory Performance

As we saw in our discussion of performance appraisals in Chapter 6, upward, subordinate appraisals of managerial performance can provide valuable feedback to improve supervisors' job performance, air the concerns of subordinates, and provide a starting point for the eventual improvement of supervisor-subordinate relationships.

Open-door Policies

The bottom-to-top flow of organizational communication can also be stimulated if upper-level managers establish an open-door policy, which involves setting aside times when employees can go directly to managers and discuss whatever is on their

APPLYING I/O PSYCHOLOGY (*continued*)

minds. This procedure bypasses the intermediate steps in the upward organizational chain, ensuring that important messages do indeed get to the top intact. The obvious drawback to the open-door policy is that a lot of the manager's time may be taken up by dealing with trivial or unimportant employee concerns.

Employee Surveys

Conducting an employee survey is an efficient and quick way to measure employees' attitudes about any aspect of organizational operations in an effort to target particular problem areas or solicit suggestions for improvement. (We discussed employee job satisfaction surveys in Chapter 8.) Because surveys offer the added benefit of anonymity, workers can respond honestly without fear of reprisal from management. As in all methods, feedback from management, either in the form of action taken or justification for not taking action, is critical for the program to operate effectively. Many times, companies will conduct an employee survey, look at the results, and do nothing. If feedback is not given, respondents will begin to see the survey as a waste of time, and future efforts will not be taken seriously.

Participative Decision Making

A number of strategies based on democratic or participative styles of management facilitate the upward flow of communication by involving employees in the process of making important decisions (Harrison, 1985). In participative decision making, employees can submit possible plans and discuss their benefits and drawbacks. They are then allowed to vote on the courses of action the company or work group will take. This strategy covers a wide range of programs and techniques that we will be studying in later chapters. However, any management technique that solicits employee input serves to increase the upward flow of communication.

---

efficiency and productivity. However, the fact that these cost-cutting measures are needed for the company to stay financially solvent is filtered out, because management is afraid that this information might cause workers to anticipate layoffs and thus begin to look for jobs elsewhere. Filtering of content in upward communication can occur if the information is unfavorable and the communicator fears incurring the wrath of the superior. In such cases, the negative information might be altered in order to make it appear less negative. Filtering in lateral communication can occur when two employees feel that they are in competition with one another for important organizational rewards, such as promotions and recognition from superiors. In such cases, workers continue to communicate, but may filter out any important information that is seen as giving the other person a competitive edge.

Censoring is the purposeful omission of information presented to a receiver. While filtering involves the omission of some aspects of the message, in censoring a choice is made not to send a message. Censoring can occur when a sender believes that the receiver does not need the information

censoring
the intentional omission of information from a message or a decision not to transmit particular information

because it is unimportant or would be disruptive to the receiver. Davis (1968) examined the censoring of downward communications in a large manufacturing company. In this study, top management presented middle-level managers with two messages that were to be sent downward. The first message was important and concerned tentative plans for laying off workers. The second message was relatively unimportant, dealing with changes in the parking situation. The results of the study indicated that the middle managers censored the messages as a function of who was receiving the information. The important layoff information was passed on to 94 percent of the foremen, who in turn presented it to only 70 percent of the assistant foremen. The censoring of the unimportant message about the parking changes was even greater, with only 15 percent of the assistant foremen eventually getting the message. In this case, censoring took place primarily when the message was believed to be irrelevant to lower-level workers.

One form of censoring frequently occurs when people are reluctant to transmit bad news. This has been labeled the "MUM effect" (Tesser & Rosen, 1975). The MUM effect can be particularly detrimental to organizational functioning and effectiveness. For example, during the building of the U.S. Air Force's Stealth Bomber, the MUM effect was in operation as officers systematically suppressed bad news about the project's many problems from reaching higher-level officers. As a result, Pentagon officials continued to fund the project, since they were uninformed about the project's many technical problems and errors (Lee, 1993).

Exaggeration is the distortion of information which involves elaborating or overemphasizing certain aspects of the message. To draw attention to a problem, people may exaggerate its magnitude and impact. In downward communication, a supervisor might emphasize that if performance does not improve, subordinates may lose their jobs. In upward communication, workers might present a problem as a crisis in order to get management to react and make some quick decisions. On the other hand, exaggeration may occur through the minimization of an issue, which involves making it seem like less of a problem than it actually is. This can happen, for example, when a worker wants to give the impression of competence and thus says that everything is under control when it is not (see Up Close).

Describe the three directions organizational communication can flow. What form does each typically take?

exaggeration
the distortion of information by elaborating, overestimating, or minimizing parts of the message

UP CLOSE

Why Are Communication Breakdowns So Common in Organizations?

In many ways, the success of an organization depends on the efficient and effective flow of communication among its members. Even in very efficient and productive organizations, however, miscommunication seems to occur almost daily. Why are such breakdowns so common?

One answer is that many informal rules (or norms) in organizations

UP CLOSE (*continued*)

appear to work against open and honest communication. Organizational members learn that it is important to engage in impression management, that is, to present oneself in a favorable light in order to get ahead in the company. It is not considered wise to admit to personal faults or limitations. Likewise, it is seen as important to project an air of self-confidence and competence. This may lead to a worker trying to tackle a very difficult task or problem alone, rather than asking for assistance. As we saw in studying hiring interviews, job applicants are particularly concerned with impression management. The resulting restricted communication may lead to a total mismatch between a worker's skills and abilities and the job requirements.

In competitive organizational settings, an air of mistrust of others may arise. As a result, verbal messages may not be entirely believed, or may be seen as containing underlying alternative meanings ("What was he really saying to me?"). Mistrust is often present in organizations that have a history of not dealing honestly and openly with employees. This lack of trust may lead to limited communication, which is a serious problem for organizations whose lifeblood is the open flow of messages.

Another reason for communication breakdowns is employees' feelings of defensiveness, which often develop when their performance is criticized or questioned. Defensive postures by one participant are often followed by a defensive stance in another (Gibb, 1961). For example, when a work group has failed at some task, one group member might act defensively—"It wasn't my fault"—which then causes others to act in the same way. When employees become overly defensive, a communication breakdown can result. This defensiveness can also stifle employee creativity, as workers become afraid to take chances or to try new things for fear of being criticized.

Organizational communication breakdowns can also be caused by the tendency for people to undercommunicate. Workers generally assume that everyone in the work setting has access to the same information and possesses the same knowledge. Therefore, to avoid redundancy, a communicator may neglect to convey some important information to coworkers, assuming that they already know it. In reality, the other workers may not have the information or may have forgotten it and thus need to be reminded. Supervisors and managers are particularly prone to undercommunication, believing that subordinates do not need to be (or should not be) given certain information. This lack of communication flow can seriously disrupt productivity, and may cause dissatisfaction among workers who feel as if they are left in the dark.

Certain factors increase or decrease the likelihood of distortion taking place in organizational communication. For example, spoken messages are more prone to distortion than are written messages. Regardless of form, a downward-flowing message from a high-status source is less

"All those in favor say 'Aye.'"
"Aye."   *"Aye."*   *"Aye."*
        "Aye."   *"Aye."*

Spoken messages are especially prone to distortion. **Drawing by Ziegler;** © The New Yorker Collection, 1979, Henry Martin from cartoonbank.com. All Rights Reserved.

List and describe four strategies for improving the upward flow of communication in organizations.

likely to be intentionally altered than a communication originating from a low-status member. O'Reilly (1978) studied several factors related to communication distortion, and specifically found a tendency for the greater distortion of upward messages that are unfavorable in content, and less distortion of upward-flowing positive information. He also discovered that low trust in the receiver of a message resulted in a tendency toward distortion, particularly if the information reflected unfavorably on the sender.

COMMUNICATION NETWORKS

In our discussion of the communication model and the downward, upward, and lateral flow of communication, we have been focusing on communication between two individuals, such as superior-to-subordinate or colleague-to-colleague. When we look beyond two-person communication to the linkages among work group, departmental, or organizational members, we are concerned with **communication networks**, which are systems of communication lines linking various senders and receivers.

communication networks
systematic lines of communication among various senders and receivers

The flow of organizational communication is regulated by several factors: the proximity of workers to one another, the rules governing who communicates with whom, the status hierarchy, and other elements of the work situation, such as job assignments and duties (Zahn, 1991). Thus, communication usually follows predictable patterns, or networks. Considerable research has been conducted on these networks and the properties associated with each. Five major types of communication networks have been studied in depth (Shaw, 1978; see Figure 10.2). The first three are termed **centralized networks** because the flow of information is centralized, or directed, through specific members. The next two are called **decentralized networks**, because the communication flow can originate at any point and does not have to be directed through certain central group members. Centralized networks are governed by members' status within the organization; decentralized networks typically are not. Often, decentralized networks are controlled by factors such as proximity of members to one another, or the personal preferences of the sender.

centralized networks
communication networks in which the flow of communication is directed through specific members

decentralized networks
communication networks in which messages can originate at any point and need not be directed through specific group members

Centralized networks

The first centralized communication network, which is known as the *chain*, represents a five-member status hierarchy. A message originates at the top or at the bottom of the chain and works its way upward or downward through the different links. An example might be a message concerning some changes in the formula for payroll deductions. The director of human resources is the source of the message, which is then passed to the payroll manager, who in turn gives the instructions to the assistant payroll manager, who then tells the payroll supervisor. Finally, the payroll supervisor passes the message along to the clerk who will implement the changes. A message that is to go from the clerk to the human resources director must follow the same pattern. As you might guess, the chain is a relatively slow process, but it is direct, with all levels of the hierarchy being made aware of the message since it must pass through each link. A related communication network is the Y (which is actually an upside-down Y). The Y is also a hierarchical

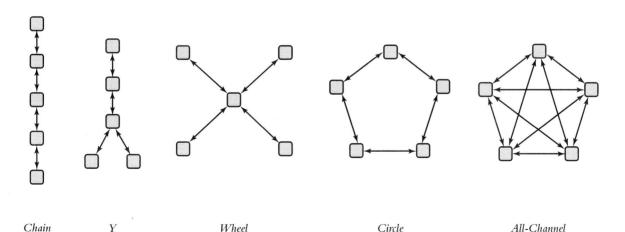

Chain   Y   Wheel   Circle   All-Channel

FIGURE 10.2

Communication Network

network, representing four levels of status within the organization, but its last link involves communication to more than one person. The inverted Y is a model of the communication network typically involved in a traditional, pyramid-shaped organization. The president issues an order to the chief of operations, who then tells the work supervisor. The work supervisor then gathers the bottom-line workers and gives them the order. In the other direction, the front-line supervisor is responsible for gathering information from bottom-line workers that must be sent upward. The chain and the Y networks are very similar in terms of speed of transmission and the formality of who communicates with whom.

The *wheel* network involves two status levels: a higher-status member (usually a work supervisor) and four lower-level members. The higher-status member is the hub, or center, through which all communication must pass. In the wheel network, there are no direct communication links between the lower-level members. An example might be a sales manager and his four salespersons out in the field, each of whom receives instructions directly from the manager, and then sends information about sales activities back to the manager. However, the salespersons do not have any direct contact with one another, only indirect contact as information is relayed through the supervisor.

Decentralized networks

The *circle* network, the first of the two decentralized networks, represents communication between members who are immediately accessible to each other, such as workers positioned side by side on an assembly line. Because any member can initiate a communication and no rules govern the direction in which it is sent, it can be difficult to trace the original source of the message in a circle network. Also, since the message can travel in two directions, the circle network has a fairly quick rate of transmission.

The *all-channel*, or *comcon*, network allows complete freedom among communication links. Any member can freely communicate with any other, and all members are accessible to each other. In all-channel networks, communication can be rapid, and there is maximum opportunity for feedback. Boards of directors, problem-solving task forces, and employees working as a team are examples of these networks.

There has been extensive research on communication networks, most of which has been conducted in laboratory settings. The results of these studies indicate that each of the different networks has different strengths and weaknesses. For example, the centralized networks (the chain, Y, and wheel) are faster and make fewer errors in dealing with simple, repetitive tasks than do decentralized networks. This makes sense because the central person through whom all messages must pass can coordinate group activities because that individual has all of the information needed to perform the simple tasks. Decentralized networks (circle and all-channel), on the other hand, are better at dealing with complex tasks, such as abstract problem solving (Leavitt, 1951; Shaw, 1964). In general, straightforward, repetitive tasks, such as as-

Committees are examples of all-channel communication networks.

sembly or manufacturing work, tend to operate well with a centralized communication network, while creative tasks, such as a group working on a product advertising campaign, are best accomplished using a decentralized network. One reason why centralized networks may have difficulty in solving complex problems is because the central people may be subject to information overload: They may have too much information to deal with efficiently. Because all of the messages cannot be passed on intact to the various network members efficiently and quickly, group performance suffers.

The type of communication network used can also affect the satisfaction of network members. Generally, because of the restrictions on who can initiate communication and on who can communicate with whom, members in centralized networks have lower levels of satisfaction than those in decentralized networks (Shaw, 1964). More specifically, in the centralized networks, the persons holding the central positions tend to have high levels of satisfaction due to their role, whereas the noncentral members have extremely low satisfaction (Bavelas, 1950).

Some of the research on communication networks has been criticized for oversimplifying the communication process. Evidence suggests that the differences in speed and efficiency among the various networks may disappear over time, as the group involved learns to adjust to the required communication patterns (Burgess, 1968). For example, members of decentralized networks may learn to cut down on the amount of member discussion in order to speed up the decision-making process. Because most of the research on communication networks has been conducted in controlled laboratory set-

Define and give examples of
the three barriers to effective
communication.

organigram
*a diagram of an
organization's hierarchy
representing the formal lines
of communication*

grapevine
*the informal communication
network in an organization*

sciogram
*a diagram of the informal
lines of communication
among organizational
members*

tings, there is some concern about whether the results of these studies will generalize to communication networks in actual work settings, although the findings do indeed allow us to model (although simplistically) the communication patterns in work organizations.

FORMAL AND INFORMAL LINES OF COMMUNICATION: THE HIERARCHY VERSUS THE GRAPEVINE

So far we have been discussing the *formal* lines of communication, or how organizational members are supposed to communicate with one another. We have also seen that the official lines of communication in an organization are illustrated in the company's organizational chart, or **organigram**, which is a diagram of the hierarchy. When official messages must be sent up or down the hierarchy, they typically follow the lines shown in the organigram. The formal lines of communication are usually governed by the organizational status or authority of the different members. However, while every organization possesses formal lines of communication each also has informal communication lines, known as the **grapevine**. Just as a real grapevine twists and turns, branching out wherever it pleases, the organizational grapevine can follow any course through a network of organizational members. Throughout the workday, messages are passed from one worker to another along the grapevine. Because much of the daily communication that occurs in work organizations is informal, the organizational grapevine is an important element for I/O psychologists to study.

While formal communication lines are represented by the organigram, the informal lines of communication among work group or organizational members are illustrated by the **sociogram**. In effect, the sociogram is a diagram of the organizational grapevine. Sociograms are used to study the informal contacts and communications occurring among organizational members (see Figure 10.3). In studying informal communication networks, workers are surveyed to determine which other organizational members they typically interact with (Monge & Eisenberg, 1987; Stork & Richards, 1987).

Baird (1977) suggests that three factors determine the pattern of communication links that form the grapevine: friendship, usage, and efficiency. In the informal communication network people pass information on to their friends, which is only natural. We communicate with those people we like and avoid communicating informally with those people we do not like. Friendship is thus perhaps the most important factor that holds the grapevine together. In addition, persons who are used as communication links for other purposes will also be used as links in the grapevine. For example, workers who often come into contact with one another for job-related reasons are more likely to start sharing information informally. Finally, the grapevine sometimes develops because it is easier and more efficient for workers to follow their own informal networks rather than the formal lines of communication. An organizational member who needs to communicate something immediately may try to get the message through via the grapevine rather than by using the slow and cumbersome formal communication lines.

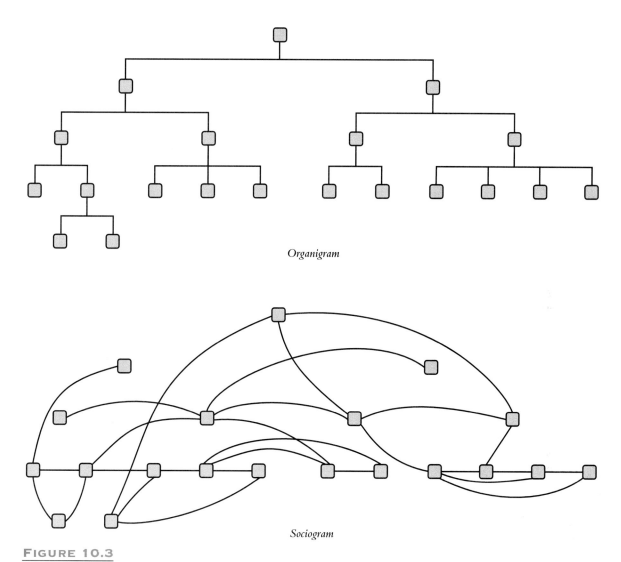

Organigram

Sociogram

FIGURE 10.3

The Organigram versus the Sociogram.

For example, a low-ranking organizational member who wants to get a message to somebody high up in the organizational hierarchy may find it quicker and more efficient to rely on the grapevine to transmit the message, rather than going through the formal organizational channels that involve relaying the message through a successive chain of higher-status managers.

In addition to being a substitute network for formal lines of communication, the grapevine also serves a vital function in maintaining social relationships among workers. Because most formal communication tends to be task-oriented, focusing on jobs and job outcomes, the grapevine helps to meet the social communication needs of workers (which Mayo and his associates in the human relations movement long ago determined were so important to workers). Through informal communication contacts and the subsequent development of strong work friendships, the grapevine can help to bring workers together and encourage them to develop a sense of unity and commitment to the work group and the organization, which can play a big part in reducing absenteeism and turnover rates (Baird, 1977). The grapevine can also help in reiterating important messages which have been sent through formal communication channels. For example, an employee might be reminded through the grapevine of important deadlines or company policies that were originally announced in memos or bulletins. While the grapevine serves many important functions for the smooth operation of the organization, it can also be perceived as having a somewhat negative function: the transmission of rumors.

rumors
information that is presented as fact, but which may actually be true or false

Rumors involve information that is presented as fact, but which may actually be either true or false (Davis, 1972). Rumors are based on such things as employee speculations and wishful thinking. Many managers are concerned about the grapevine and attempt to stifle it, because they believe that it is the source of false rumors that may be damaging to the company and the work force (Mishra, 1990). However, research indicates that this is a myth. The transmission of false rumors via the grapevine is actually relatively rare, and estimates indicate that the grapevine is accurate over 80 percent of the time (Baird, 1977). In comparison, remember that the messages sent through formal communication lines may not always be 100 percent accurate.

A false rumor usually results when organizational members lack information about a topic that concerns them. Thus, when there is a shortage of information transmitted through the formal channels, rumors may be generated by the informal network (Schachter & Burdick, 1955). The best way for a manager to deal with rumor transmission is to be honest and open, providing sufficient information to employees through the formal lines of communication. Also, rather than trying to uproot the grapevine, the effective manager will be aware of it and its importance to the workers, and may even want to be "tapped into" it as another source of information. When false rumors do occur, the best strategy for combatting them may be to provide accurate information through formal channels of communication *and* through the grapevine, if management is tapped into it (Hersey, 1966; Zaremba, 1988).

List the five communication network types and give examples of each.

Organizational Communication and Work Outcomes

The effective flow of communication is crucial to an organization's ability to operate smoothly and productively. While I/O psychologists and organizations themselves believe this to be true, very little research has directly examined the impact of communication on organizational performance (Porter & Roberts, 1976). One comprehensive study looked at the relationships among reported organizational communication effectiveness and five independent measures of organizational performance, including the number of clients served, the costs of operation, and the costs of operation per client served, in 12 district offices of a state social services agency (Snyder & Morris, 1984). Questionnaires administered to over 500 employees assessed perceptions of different types of organizational communication, which included two forms of downward communication—the adequacy of information provided concerning organizational policies and procedures, and the skills of supervisors as communicators; a form of lateral communication—the information exchange within the work group; and one type of downward communication— the feedback given about individual performance. The results indicated that the amount of communication, particularly the lateral communication within work groups, and the communication skills of supervisors were related to more cost-effective organizational performance. In another study, it was found that employees' satisfaction with the amount and quality of organizational communication was positively correlated with measures of worker productivity—those who reported receiving more and better communication were the most productive workers (Clampitt & Downs, 1993). Finally, a laboratory study found that group performance on a manual task—assembling a complex toy—was related to the quality of communication. Specifically, if the groups engaged in high quality "cycles" of communication, including interactions that involved orienting the group to the task, planning how the work would be done, and evaluating the outcomes, then the groups outperformed those who did not have systematic cycles of communication (Tschan, 1995).

While effective communication can lead to bottom-line payoffs in terms of increased productivity, it can also create increased levels of employee satisfaction. Research suggests positive relationships between the amount of upward communication in an organization and feelings of satisfaction in lower-level workers (Koehler, Anatol, & Applebaum, 1981). It has also been demonstrated that employees who receive a great deal of information about the organization in the form of downward communication tend to be more satisfied than those who do not. In fact, even employees who were overloaded with so much downward communication that their job performance was hampered tended to be satisfied with more downward communication (O'Reilly, 1980). Moreover, serving as a communication source is also linked to increased levels of satisfaction (Muchinsky, 1977b).

In addition to job performance and job satisfaction, effective communication may also have an impact on absenteeism and turnover rates. While research has not directly addressed this relationship, one study found that open and supportive downward communication helped one organization retain its "surviving" workers after a companywide downsizing. Moreover, communication seemed to be very important in reducing worker stress and maintaining job satisfaction during the downsizing (Johnson, Bernhagen, Miller, & Allen, 1996).

While it makes sense that organizations with free and open lines of communication would tend to have more satisfied workers, leading to lowered rates of absenteeism and turnover, open communication among workers can also have some drawbacks. For example, researchers who examined the patterns of turnover among workers in three fast food restaurants found that workers tended to quit their jobs in clusters. Most importantly, the clusters tended to be among workers who communicated freely with one another, a phenomenon that has been termed the "snowball effect" (Krackhardt & Porter, 1986).

All in all, when dealing with organizational communication, more is usually better, although there may be a few exceptions, as when workers engage in so much nonwork-related communication or are so deluged with messages and other information that job performance is impaired. Although much evidence indicates that it is usually better to keep communication flowing, open, and honest, some researchers claim that, because of organizational politics, at times organizational members might want to close some communication lines and keep certain types of information to themselves (see, for example, Eisenberg & Witten, 1987).

In summary, it appears that many organizations can benefit from greater amounts of communication and that companies can work to make organizational communication more accurate and effective. Top-level managers need to be aware of employees' needs for information, and must open the flow of downward communication to provide for these needs. On the other hand, there needs to be a greater upward flow of communication in order to make management aware of what is going on at the lower levels of the company and to increase employee participation in and commitment to the organization. It also appears that increased lateral communication plays an important role in the ability of work groups to get the job done, and in the development and maintenance of interpersonal relationships on the job. All of this can lead to more positive outcomes for the individuals, work groups, and organizations involved.

Summary

Communication is crucial for effective organizational performance. The basic communication model begins with the *sender*, who is responsible for *encoding* the message, which involves choosing some mutually understood code for transmitting the message to another person. The sender also selects a vehicle for communication, or the *channel*. The task of the *receiver* is to decode the message in an effort to understand its original meaning. The receiver also sends *feedback* to indicate that the message was received and understood. Any factors that disrupt the effective flow of communication from sender to receiver are referred to as *noise*.

Research on the communication process has examined the factors that can influence communication effectiveness. *Source factors* are variables related to the sender, such as status, credibility, and communication skills, which can influence the effectiveness of communication. *Channel factors* are variables related to the actual communication vehicle that can enhance or detract from the flow of communication from sender to receiver. In verbal communication, semantic problems, or the use of technical language termed *jargon*, can sometimes disrupt the communication flow. *Audience factors*, such as the decoding skills and attention span of the receiver, can also play a role in the communication process.

Nonverbal communication has a subtle but important effect on communication in work settings. It can be used as a substitute for verbal communication, to enhance verbal messages, or to send true feelings. Receivers may also use nonverbal cues as an additional information source or as a means of forming impressions about people.

Communication can flow in three directions through the organizational hierarchy: upward, downward, or laterally. *Downward communication* typically involves messages sent from superiors to subordinates; *upward communication* flows from the lower levels of the organization; and *lateral communication* occurs between persons at the same status level. *Filtering, censoring,* and *exaggeration* are three types of distortion that often disrupt the effective flow of organizational communication.

Much of our knowledge of organizational communication patterns comes from research conducted on *communication networks*, which can be grouped into two types: *centralized*, in which messages move through central members, and *decentralized*, in which communication paths are not directed through specific network members. The formal communication patterns in organizations are represented in the organizational chart, or *organigram*. The informal lines of communication, or *grapevine*, are illustrated in a *sociogram*. The formal lines of communication carry messages that are sanctioned by the organization, whereas the grapevine is an informal network through which messages are passed from worker to worker. Managers are sometimes wary of the grapevine because they see it as a source of *rumors*, although research indicates that the grapevine can be a highly accurate and important information network.

Research suggests that greater and more effective organizational communication is linked to improved levels of performance and job satisfaction. Moreover, there may be links between open, flowing organizational communication and rates of employee absenteeism and turnover.

Study Questions and Exercises

1. List the steps in the basic communication model. Which factors influence the effective flow of communication at each of the steps?
2. In what ways can nonverbal communication affect the interaction between a supervisor and a subordinate? Between two same-status coworkers?

3. Think of an organization with which you have had some contact, such as a work organization, a club or social group, or your college or university. What forms of downward, upward, and lateral communication take place in this organization? How could the flow of each direction of communication be improved?

4. Consider the five types of communication networks. What are the characteristics of each? Can you think of any special work groups that illustrate each network?

5. In what ways will the sources, channels, and audiences of the formal lines of communication and the informal lines of communication (grapevine) in an organization differ?

Suggested Readings

Brislin, R., & Yoshida, T. (1994). *Intercultural communication training: An introduction*. Newbury Park, CA: Sage. *This is a guidebook that shows how training can be done to facilitate intercultural communication—written by a recognized research expert and a practitioner in intercultural issues.*

Management Communication Quarterly and Journal of Business and Technical Communication, both published by Sage Publications, and *The Journal of Business Communication*, published by the Association for Business Communication. *These journals contain articles on the theory and practice of management and business communication. Recent topics include: intercultural communication, computer-mediated communication, and state-of-the-art communication technology.*

Sypher, B.D. (Ed.). (1990). *Case studies in organizational communication*. New York: Guilford. *This edited book provides a series of case studies that illustrate the importance of effective communication in all types of organizations.*

GROUP PROCESSES IN WORK ORGANIZATIONS

GROUP PROCESSES: THE CORE OF ORGANIZATIONS

INSIDE TIPS

This chapter introduces many of the central concepts in the area of psychology known as group dynamics. A knowledge of group dynamics, or the processes by which groups function, is central to understanding how work organizations operate, since they are made up of smaller work groups. This chapter builds on Chapter 10's discussion of workplace communication, for it is communication that holds people together in work groups. This chapter also sets the stage for the next three chapters on organizational processes. In particular, Chapter 12, on leadership, studies a very important ongoing process in work groups: the relationship between the leader and the other members of the group. Chapter 13, which examines influence, power, and politics, continues the discussion of group processes presented in this chapter by considering how these three social processes operate in work groups and larger work organizations. Chapter 14 moves to the next level—the design and structure of work organizations—to explore how work groups link up to form larger organizations.

You may already be familiar with some of the concepts presented in this chapter. For example, conformity, roles, norms, and conflict are central not only in industrial/organizational psychology but in other specialty areas of psychology and in other behavioral sciences. Here, however, we will be applying these concepts specifically to the study of behavior in work settings. Other topics, such as organizational socialization and interorganizational conflict, are more particular to I/O psychology. This chapter represents a blending of some older, traditional concepts with some newer ones.

Many of the issues involved in describing group processes are particularly complex. Specifically, the concept of groupthink, with its many interrelated symptoms, merits attention. The different levels of conflict described in this chapter also have similar-sounding names that can be confusing. An inside tip is to remember that the prefix intra- means "within," while the prefix inter- means "between" or "among." Therefore, intragroup means within a group, whereas intergroup means between groups. Another potential difficulty involves distinguishing between the concept of competition as a motivating process in work groups and the strategy of competition as a means of resolving conflict. At first glance, using the same term to describe two different processes can be confusing, but special attention to these terms should help clarify the situation.

Work organizations are made up of individuals, but typically these individuals are tied together by their membership in particular work groups. A work group might be a department, a job classification, a work team, or an informal group of coworkers who socialize during lunch and after work to discuss work-related problems and issues. Groups are very important to the functioning of work organizations, for the members of a group can pool their talents, energy, and knowledge to perform complex tasks. Work groups also help provide professional identities for members and satisfy human needs for social interaction and the development of interpersonal relationships on the job. Finally, groups help establish rules for proper behavior in the work setting and play a part in determining the courses of action that the work group and the organization will follow. The study of work groups is an important topic in I/O psychology (Sanna & Parks, 1997).

In this chapter, we will examine work groups and their processes. We will begin by defining groups, looking at the different roles within groups, and considering what holds groups together. Next, we will study the processes of cooperation, competition, and conflict, which are regular parts of work group functioning. Finally, we will look at how work groups affect organizational decision making and how group decision making affects organizational outcomes.

Defining Work Groups

group
two or more individuals engaged in social interaction to achieve some goal

A **group** can be defined as two or more individuals, engaged in social interaction, for the purposes of achieving some goal. In work settings this goal is usually work-related, such as producing a product or service. However,

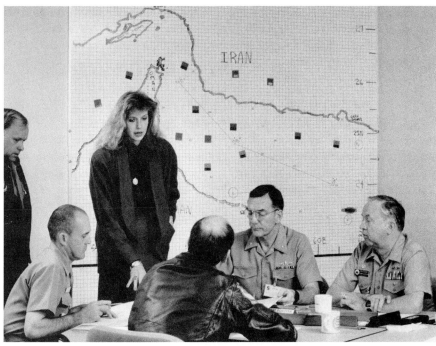

As a civilian analyst, this woman plays a clearly defined role in this military group, identifying tactical problems and possible solutions.

groups at work may form merely to develop and maintain social relationships. Work groups can be either formal—put together by the organization to perform certain tasks and handle specific responsibilities—or informal, developing naturally. Informal work groups might include groups of workers who regularly get together after work to discuss their jobs.

ROLES

Within work groups, members can play various **roles**, or patterns of behavior that are adopted on the basis of expectations about the functions of a particular position. Group roles are important because they help provide some specific plan for behavior. When a worker is playing a particular role within a group, that person usually knows something about the responsibilities and requirements of the role, or the **role expectations**. In most work groups, members are quite aware of the various expectations associated with each of the different positions within the group.

As a work group develops, the various members learn to become responsible for different aspects of its functioning. In other words, members begin to play different roles within the work group. This process whereby group members learn about and take on various defined roles is called **role differentiation**. For example, a new worker who enters a work group may immediately fall into the role of novice worker. However, the person may later

roles
patterns of behavior that are adapted based on expectations about the functions of a position

role expectations
beliefs concerning the responsibilities and requirements of a particular role

role differentiation
the process by which group members learn to perform various roles

develop a reputation for having a good sense of humor and thus begin to play the role of jokester, providing levity when situations get too tense or when boredom sets in.

One important role that is clearly differentiated in most work groups is that of leader. The leader in a formal work group or department plays an important part in directing group activities, being spokesperson for the group, and in deciding which courses of action the group will follow. Because of its significance, we will consider the topic of leadership in great depth in Chapter 12.

The various roles in work groups are often created based on factors such as position or formal job title, status within the group, or the possession of some particular work skill or ability. For example, employees who are designated as assistant supervisor, senior mechanic, or communications specialist perform specific roles and engage in certain behavior consistent with these job titles. While workers can be designated as playing certain usual roles within the work group, they can perform different functional roles at different times. Two early researchers outlined a wide range of work roles, which they grouped into three categories (Benne & Sheats, 1948; see Table 11.1). The first category, *group task roles*, is related to getting the job done. Group task roles are given such titles as information giver, procedural technician, and evaluator-critic. For example, a machinist in a cardboard container factory who outlines the steps necessary for the work group to construct and assemble a new type of box is playing the procedural technician role. The second category of functional roles is *group building and maintenance roles*. These deal with the maintenance of interpersonal relations among group members and include such roles as encourager, harmonizer, and compromiser. A worker who plays an active part in settling an argument between two coworkers may be taking on the harmonizer role. The third category, called *self-centered roles*, involves satisfying personal rather than group goals. Titles of these roles include recognition seeker, aggressor, and help seeker. Employees who look to others for assistance in completing their own work assignments are playing the help-seeker role. The fact that there are so many different roles that members can play in work group functioning illustrates the complexity of the processes that occur daily in work groups.

It is important to mention that sometimes workers are unclear about the requirements of the various roles they are expected to play in the workplace. This can lead to **role ambiguity**, or a sense of uncertainty over the requirements of a particular role an individual is expected to play. Role ambiguity, like job ambiguity (see Chapter 9), is an important source of workplace stress.

In organizations, persons often are expected to play more than one role at a time. In some cases, the behaviors expected of an individual due to one role may not be consistent with the expectations concerning another role. Instances such as these give rise to **role conflict**. Role conflict is quite common, particularly in positions that require workers to be members of different groups simultaneously. For example, imagine that you are the supervisor of a

role ambiguity
a sense of uncertainty over the requirements of a particular role

role conflict
conflict that results when the expectations associated with one role interfere with the expectations concerning another role

TABLE 11.1

The Various Roles Individuals Play in Work Groups

Group Task Roles

Initiator-contributor: Recommends new ideas about, or novel solutions to, a problem
Information seeker: Emphasizes getting facts and other information from others
Opinion seeker: Solicits inputs concerning the attitudes or feelings about ideas under consideration
Information giver: Contributes relevant information to help in decisionmaking
Opinion giver: Provides own opinions and feelings
Elaborator: Clarifies and expands on the points made by others
Coordinator: Integrates information from the group
Orientor: Guides the discussion and keeps it on the topic when the group digresses
Evaluator-critic: Uses some set of standards to evaluate the group's accomplishments
Energizer: Stimulates the group to take action
Procedural technician: Handles routine tasks such as providing materials or supplies
Recorder: Keeps track of the group's activities and takes minutes

Group Building and Maintenance Roles

Encourager: Encourages others' contributions
Harmonizer: Tries to resolve conflicts between group members
Compromiser: Tries to provide conflicting members with a mutually agreeable solution
Gatekeeper: Regulates the flow of communication so that all members can have a say
Standard setter: Sets standards or deadlines for group actions
Group observer: Makes objective observations about the tone of the group interaction
Follower: Accepts the ideas of others and goes along with group majority

Self-Centered Roles

Aggressor: Tries to promote own status within group by attacking others
Blocker: Tries to block all group actions and refuses to go along with group
Recognition seeker: Tries to play up own achievements to get group's attention
Self-confessor: Uses group discussion to deal with personal issues
Playboy: Engages in humor and irrelevant acts to draw attention away from the tasks
Dominator: Attempts to monopolize the group
Help seeker: Attempts to gain sympathy by expressing insecurity or inadequacy
Special interest pleader: Argues incessantly to further own desires

Source: K.D. Benne and P. Sheats, "Functional Roles of Group Members," *Journal of Social Issues, 4* (1948), pp. 41–49.

work group. One of your roles involves holding the group together and protecting the interests of its members. However, you are also a member of the organization's management team, and in this role you are ordered to transfer a very talented and very popular work group member, against her wishes, to another department. Because you cannot satisfy the two incompatible goals of holding the team together while carrying out the organization's plan to transfer the worker, you experience role conflict, another form of stress that can have negative effects on job satisfaction, performance, and mental and physical well-being.

NORMS

norms
rules that groups adopt governing appropriate and inappropriate behavior for members

While work groups contain various members, each playing different roles, all members, regardless of their role, must adhere to certain group rules. **Norms** are the rules that groups adopt to indicate appropriate and inappropriate behavior for members. Group norms can be formalized as written work rules, but are most commonly informal and unrecorded. Norms can govern any work activity, including the speed with which a person should perform a job, proper modes of dress, acceptable topics for group conversation, and even who sits where in the employee lunchroom. According to Feldman (1984), norms develop in a number of ways. They can come from explicit statements made by supervisors or coworkers. For example, a supervisor might tell group members, "No one goes home until the work area is spotlessly clean." This leads to a norm that all workers stop working 15 minutes before quitting time to clean up the work area. Group leaders or powerful group members often play an important role in such norm formation. Norms can also evolve from the group's history. For example, if a certain work procedure leads to a disastrous outcome, the group may place a ban on its use. In other instances, norms may be carried over from past situations. When a member changes groups, norms from the old group may be imported to the new one. For example, a sales supervisor was transferred from the corporate office to a regional sales office. On her first day in the new office, she commented on the casual dress of employees by saying, "At the corporate office, men always wear suits and ties and women always wear skirts or dresses." From the next day on, a new dress code of more formal attire developed.

Describe and define three categories of work roles.

Norms serve many important purposes for groups. First and foremost, they are established to help the group survive. A group must be able to produce enough to ensure the economic success of the group and the organization. Therefore, some norms will develop to facilitate group production. On the other hand, if members feel that production rates are too high and will possibly lead to layoffs, norms to restrict group output (called "rate setting") may arise. Norms can also develop that help commit work group members to producing higher quality products or services, and norms can even develop in organizations and groups that compel workers to be innovative and "entrepreneurial" (Anderson & West, 1998; Russell & Russell, 1992). Norms also help increase the predictability of members' behavior. For example, norms regarding speaking turns and the length of time that one may hold the floor in group meetings may ease the flow of the meetings and avoid embarrassment. Finally, norms provide a sense of identity for the group by giving members a chance to express their shared values and beliefs.

Group norms can govern appropriate work behavior and informal behaviour such as mode of dress.

For example, if an advertising agency believes that they are responsible for setting advertising trends, a norm for producing advertisements that are unique or novel may develop (Feldman, 1984; Katz & Kahn, 1978).

In summary, both roles and norms help provide a structure and plan for group members' behavior. They play an important part in regulating group activities and in helping group members to achieve shared goals.

ORGANIZATIONAL SOCIALIZATION: LEARNING GROUP ROLES AND NORMS

A critical area of research that has received a great deal of attention in the last three decades from I/O psychologists is **organizational socialization**, or the process by which new employees become integrated into work groups. Organizational socialization includes three important processes: (1) the development of specific work skills and abilities, (2) the acquisition of a set of appropriate role behaviors, and (3) adjustment to the work group's norms and values (Feldman, 1981; Schein, 1968). The first process—learning specific work skills and abilities—is the main goal of personnel training, which was discussed in depth in Chapter 5. The other two processes—the acquisition of roles and role behaviors, and the learning of group norms—are of particular interest here. New employees learn about group roles and norms in the same way that they learn new job skills, specifically by observing and imitating the behaviors of others. Newcomers may look to established workers as role models and try to copy their successful work behaviors (Louis, Posner, & Powell, 1983). For example, a novice trial attorney may watch the way that a seasoned senior partner handles herself in court and at firm meetings in order to learn about the expected role behaviors for the firm's successful attorneys. New employees may also learn about group norms by being reinforced for performing appropriate behaviors and being punished for inappropriate actions. A new salesperson in a busy clothing store may learn about norms for appropriate employee dress and the usual procedures for handling impatient customers through receiving a reinforcing smile and nod, or a disapproving frown, from the sales manager.

Typically, organizational socialization occurs in stages, as one moves from being a newcomer to a fully functioning and contributing member of the work group (Wanous, Reichers, & Malik, 1984). One model outlines three stages in the socialization of new employees (Feldman, 1976a, 1976b). The first is *anticipatory socialization*. Here newcomers develop a set of realistic expectations concerning the job and the organization and determine if the organization will provide the right match with their abilities, needs, and values. The second stage in the process is *accommodation*. In this stage, new employees learn about the various roles that work group members play and about their own specific roles in the group. They also begin to "learn the ropes" as they discover important work group norms and standards. In this second stage, the newcomers begin to develop interpersonal relationships with other group members. In the third stage, *role management*, newcomers

organizational socialization
the process by which new employees learn group roles and norms, and develop specific work skills and abilities

make the transition to regular members or insiders, mastering the tasks and roles they must perform. As they move through this stage, they eventually have a thorough knowledge of all facets of work group norms and operations.

Although all new employees are likely to pass through the same stages in the organizational socialization process, research indicates that employees may be socialized at different rates, depending on the characteristics of the workers and of the work environment (Reichers, 1987). For example, workers who are forced to move from an old, established work group or organization to a new setting because of layoffs or geographical moves may have a more difficult time becoming socialized than workers who voluntarily make the move. Research has clearly shown that supervisors and coworkers play an important part in the successful socialization of new employees by establishing positive relationships and mentoring newcomers (Major, Kozlowski, Chao, & Gardner, 1995; Ostroff & Kozlowski, 1993).

Workers can also play an active part in their own socialization (Ashford & Black, 1996; Saks & Ashforth, 1997). For example, newcomer attitudes and willingness to become a part of the new work group can play an important role in how quickly and smoothly socialization occurs. It may also be the case that prior work experience and personality characteristics of workers may affect socialization rates (Adkins, 1995; Ostroff & Kozlowski, 1992).

Organizations can also greatly facilitate the socialization of new employees (Ashforth & Saks, 1996). Good employee orientation and training programs are essential to the process, as are the work group's openness and willingness to welcome new members. One technique for encouraging employee socialization is to link newcomers with established, knowledgeable workers, an approach similar to the mentoring concept discussed in Chapter 5. The more quickly new employees are socialized into the work group and organization, the faster they will become productive and valuable workers. Research also indicates that effective socialization is related to reduced employee turnover, increased organizational commitment, and employee career success (Ashforth, Saks, & Lee, 1998; Feldman, 1989; Nelson, 1987).

Basic Group Processes

Describe the three stages of organizational socialization.

Several basic social processes that occur in all work groups help to hold the groups together, regulate group behavior, coordinate group activities, and stimulate action by group members. In the following section we will consider four of these processes: conformity, cohesiveness, cooperation, and competition. A final group process, conflict, will be considered under a separate heading because of its importance.

CONFORMITY

conformity
the process of adhering to group norms

Conformity is the process of adhering to group norms. Because these norms are so important to a group's identity and activities, groups exert considerable pressure on members to follow them. Violation can result in subtle or overt pressure to comply with the rules, which can take the form of a look of disapproval, verbal criticism, or isolation of the offending individual (giving the person the "silent treatment"). Once the violator conforms to the norm, the pressure is removed and the person is again included in normal group activities. Generally, conformity to norms is very strong, and helps maintain order and uniformity in the group's behavior.

Because pressure to conform to group norms is so strong, we need to consider the circumstances in which an individual might choose to violate a norm. Usually, someone will not conform to a group norm if the individual's goals are different from those of the group. For example, imagine that a manufacturing group has a norm of steady but less than optimal production. If a worker within the group wants to be noticed by management as an exceptionally hard worker who would be a good candidate for a promotion to a supervisory position, that person might break the group's production rate norm. Of course, the group will exert pressure in an effort to get the "rate buster" to conform. Extreme and repeated cases of norm violation may eventually lead to ostracism from the group (Scott, Mitchell, & Birnbaum, 1981). An individual might also resist the pressure to conform to demonstrate that the member believes that the norm is incorrect and should not be followed (Hackman, 1992). Generally, members who have more power and influence in the group, such as the leader, will have a better chance of resisting the group's conformity pressure and persuading the group to change or eliminate the norm. Also, if the violator has a past history of being a "good," conforming member, the nonconformity will be tolerated more and have a better chance of being accepted by the group than if it is done by a member known for repeated norm violations (Feldman, 1984).

GROUP COHESIVENESS

Another basic group process, cohesiveness, is like the social "glue" that holds people together in groups. **Cohesiveness** refers simply to the amount or degree of attraction among group members. It is cohesiveness that explains the team spirit that many work groups possess. It is generally assumed that cohesive groups are more satisfied and more productive than noncohesive groups because their members tend to interact more, participate more fully in group activities, and accept and work toward the groups' goals (Cartwright, 1968; Hare, 1976). In fact, however, while cohesive groups are usually more satisfied than noncohesive groups, the relationship between cohesiveness and productivity is rather weak (Gully, Devine, & Whitney, 1995). That is because typically, for a cohesive group to be productive, the reason for the cohesiveness must be work-related (Evans & Dion, 1991; Klein & Mulvey, 1995). For example, groups with strong work-related norms, such as the willingness to work overtime and a norm of workers taking personal responsibility for doing a good job, had higher group performance than work teams without such strong work-related norms (Langfred, 1998). However, a group may be cohesive yet have as a goal to do as little

cohesiveness
the degree of attraction among group members

Small, equal status work groups tend to be quite cohesive.

work as possible. In this case, cohesiveness is high and group satisfaction may be high, but productivity is likely to be very low (Tziner, 1982).

Because group cohesiveness is theoretically linked to member satisfaction and, under certain circumstances, productivity, there has been considerable research on the factors that increase group cohesiveness. The most important of these factors are the size of the group, the equality of status of members, member stability, member similarity, and the existence of a common threat or enemy.

Generally, the smaller the group, the more cohesive and the more satisfied its members. This makes sense, since small groups offer many more chances to interact with members and to form closer ties than do large groups (Forsyth, 1983). As smaller businesses become larger, gaining more and more employees, cohesiveness often declines. Older workers often lament the strong cohesiveness of the earlier, smaller work group ("In the old days it used to be like a family around here"). Therefore, one way to regain some of the cohesiveness would be to break the large group into smaller work teams.

The more equivalent the status of group members, generally the greater the cohesiveness (Cartwright, 1968). When a status hierarchy exists, the lower-status members may feel resentful of those of higher status, which leads to disharmony. Conversely, the higher-status members may try to use their authority to direct or control the activities of the lower-status members, which can also erode group cohesiveness. Many team approaches, such as job enrichment, attempt to eliminate status differences in groups in order to increase cohesiveness. For example, in many job enrichment programs team members are all given the same work classification and job title.

The stability of group membership can also have positive effects on cohesiveness (Forsyth, 1983). Generally, the more stable the membership, the more time members have to develop strong ties to one another. New members may often disrupt group harmony because they are unaware of group norms and may unwittingly violate them as they try to learn the ropes. Thus, high rates of member turnover and the presence of many new members can be detrimental to group cohesiveness.

Another factor that affects group cohesiveness is the similarity of group members. The more similar the characteristics of the group members, the more cohesive the group is likely to be. If members have similar backgrounds, education, and attitudes, it is reasonable to assume that they will develop closer ties to one another. Years of research on group processes indicate that member similarity is a very powerful force in determining social ties; we tend to be attracted to, and establish close relationships with, persons who are similar to us (Forsyth, 1983; Jackson, Brett, Sessa, Cooper, Julin & Peyronnin, 1991). It is important to emphasize, however, that similarity of group members can limit a group's potential to be creative and to innovate, as similar members may tend to "think alike." Research has emphasized that group member diversity can lead to more creative, innovative, and perhaps more productive work groups (Rogelberg & Rumery, 1996; Watson, Kumar, & Michaelsen, 1993).

The presence of an external threat or enemy can likewise increase the cohesiveness of a work group (Shaw, 1981). When a group perceives itself as under attack, the members tend to pull together. Cohesiveness of this type is often referred to as the **we-they feeling** ("We're the good guys, they're the bad guys"). Often, small, up-and-coming companies will characterize large competitor companies as "threatening" or even "evil," in an effort to increase cohesiveness of workers as they try to overcome the ominous giant company that threatens the smaller company's, and its workers', very existence. The smaller company is hoping that the increased cohesiveness will result in greater productivity as the workers pull together in an effort to beat the competition. Unfortunately, within organizations, this we-they feeling often develops between the workers and management. This can lead to increased cohesiveness within the work group but can be disruptive in coordinated efforts to achieve organizational goals if the workers perceive management as the enemy.

> **we-they feeling**
> *intragroup cohesiveness created by the existence of a common threat, which is typically another group*

In sum, all of these factors tend to increase group cohesiveness, which can in turn be related to improved work outcomes, particularly increased levels of member satisfaction and reduced rates of absenteeism and turnover. Moreover, regardless of the actual relationship between group cohesiveness and group productivity, many managers believe that cohesiveness is critical for work group success. And, if part of the reason for the work group's cohesiveness is task-related, then cohesive groups are usually high-performing groups.

COOPERATION AND COMPETITION IN WORK GROUPS

We have mentioned that the main purpose of work groups is to facilitate the attainment of personal and organizational work goals. This often requires that people work together, coordinating their activities, cooperating with one another, and sometimes helping each other. Yet work groups are also rife with competition as workers try to outperform one another to attain scarce bonuses, raises, and promotions. Competition may also be encouraged when one employee's performance is compared to that of others. Incentive programs are specifically designed to increase motivation by inducing competition—pitting one worker against another. These two seemingly incompatible processes, cooperation and competition, exist simultaneously in all work groups. Because they are such important group processes, we will consider each in depth.

> Name five factors that increase group cohesiveness.

Cooperation

Surprisingly, cooperation in work groups is an understudied topic. Perhaps because work groups are *supposed* to cooperate, it is assumed that mutual cooperation in work settings is the "normal" state of affairs, which it often is. Consider three employees in a bookstore as an example. The employees take turns performing the tasks that their jobs require. At any time, two are at the front desk serving customers. The third worker is opening boxes of books, pricing them, and putting them on the appropriate shelves. The workers are coordinating their efforts in an attempt to meet the organizational goals of selling books and providing good customer service. If one of the workers at the front desk goes on a lunch break, the person stocking shelves moves to the front to help customers. If an employee does not know the answer to a customer's question, he may turn to a more knowledgeable and experienced coworker for assistance. The store employees also coordinate their time off, developing a mutually agreeable vacation schedule.

For the most part, such cooperation among work group members is the rule rather than the exception, chiefly because it is often difficult to achieve work goals alone. As long as workers hold to the same goals, they will usually cooperate with one another. Employees might also go out of their way to help each other because of the **reciprocity rule** (Gouldner, 1960), which is illustrated by the sayings, "One good turn deserves another," and "Do unto others as you would have them do unto you." Thus workers help each other because they believe that when they need assistance, they will be paid back in kind. The reciprocity rule is very strong, and people do indeed tend to reciprocate helping behaviors.

One element that helps increase cooperation among work group members is the degree of **task interdependence**, or the degree to which an individual worker's task performance depends upon the efforts or skills of others (Campion, Medsker, & Higgs, 1993; Wageman & Baker, 1997). Research has shown that task interdependence fosters positive feelings about coworkers and increases cooperative behavior in work groups (van der Vegt, Emans, & van de Vliert, 1998; Wageman & Baker, 1997).

Group members also cooperate because achieving organizational goals can lead to payoffs for the individual workers in terms of raises, bonuses, and promotions. This, in turn, can increase group member satisfaction (Tjosvold, 1998a). Moreover, when work-related rewards are based on effective group performance, such as in the gainsharing programs discussed in Chapter 8, it helps foster cooperation among work group members.

An important question concerns whether cooperative behavior ever occurs without any expected individual or group payoffs. Are workers ever altruistic, acting unselfishly for the good of other workers or of the organization? The answer to the question of whether such altruistic, or *prosocial*, behavior exists in the workplace is "yes."

Bateman and Organ (1983) and Brief and Motowidlo (1986) first defined organizational prosocial behaviors as those that go beyond specific work role requirements. They are behaviors performed to promote the welfare of the work group or the organization. Protecting an organization from unexpected dangers, suggesting methods of organizational improvement without expecting a payoff, undertaking deliberate self-development, preparing oneself for higher levels of organizational responsibility, and speaking favorably about the organization to outsiders are all forms of prosocial behavior. Not only do such actions affect the coordination of efforts among work group members, but there is also evidence that they positively influence job satisfaction (Organ, 1988; Smith, Organ, & Near, 1983).

reciprocity rule
the tendency for persons to pay back those to whom they are indebted for assistance

task interdependence
the degree to which an individual's task performance depends on the efforts or skills or others

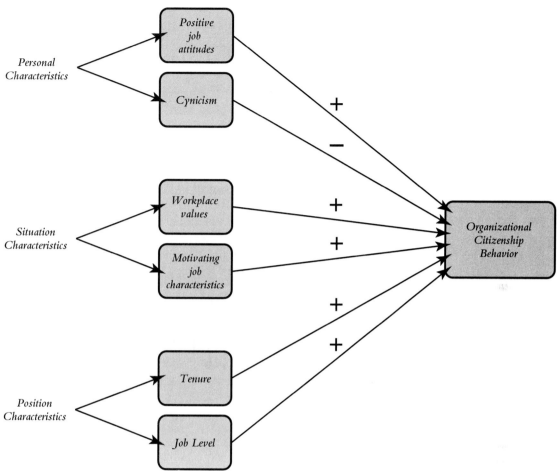

FIGURE 11.1

A Model of Factors Contributing to Organizational Citizenship Behavior (OCB)
Source: L. Van Dyne, J.W. Graham, and R.M. Dienesch, "Organizational Citizenship Behavior, *Academy of Management Journal,* 37 (1994), pp. 765–802.

Researchers have begun to look more broadly at worker behaviors that benefit the organization. This cluster of "pro-organizational" behaviors, which includes organizational prosocial behaviors, has been termed "organizational citizenship behavior" (Graham, 1991; Organ, 1988; Penner, Midili, & Kegelmeyer, 1997; Schnake, 1991). **Organizational citizenship behavior (OCB)** consists of efforts by organizational members that advance or promote the work organization, its image, and its goals. One model of the variables that contribute to increased organizational citizenship behavior is presented in Figure 11.1. As can be seen, this model says that three groups

organizational citizenship behavior
efforts by organizational members that advance or promote the work organization and its goals

of characteristics—personal characteristics, characteristics about the situation, and characteristics of one's position in the organization—all combine to increase the tendency for an employee to engage in organizational citizenship behavior (Van Dyne, Graham, & Dienesch, 1994). For instance, personal factors, such as positive attitudes about one's job and a lack of cynicism, or distrust of others' intentions and motives, lead to greater OCB. Situational characteristics, such as shared workplace values that encourage workers to cooperate with one another also contribute to OCB, as do motivating job characteristics, such as jobs that provide workers with autonomy and meaningful work (recall our discussion of motivating "job characteristics" in Chapter 7). Finally, factors related to one's position in the organization also contribute to increased OCB. For example, workers who have been with the company longer are more predisposed to OCB, as are employees who are higher up in the organizational hierarchy.

ON THE CUTTING EDGE

Organizational Citizenship Behavior: Going Above and Beyond the Call of Duty

The recent era of corporate downsizing, and the increasing complexity of jobs, has meant that there is more to do in the workplace, and fewer people to do it. This has, perhaps, led to the explosion of interest by I/O psychologists in organizational citizenship behavior (OCB), which involves employees who are willing to exceed the formal duties and requirements of the job and volunteer for extra job activities, help out other workers, and display unusually strong dedication to the organization (Organ, 1988; Podsakoff, MacKenzie, & Hui, 1993). An important question is whether OCBs do indeed impact the bottom line of work organizations.

Recent research suggests that employees who "go the extra mile" and exhibit OCB do indeed have work groups and organizations that are more productive and produce higher-quality work than work groups exhibiting low levels of OCB (Podsakoff

& MacKenzie, 1997). Organizational citizenship behavior seems to affect work performance in groups as diverse as salespersons (Podsakoff & MacKenzie, 1994), manufacturing workers (Allen & Rush, 1998), machine crews in a paper mill (Podsakoff, Ahearne, & MacKenzie, 1997), and restaurant crews (Walz & Niehoff, 1996).

Podsakoff and MacKenzie (1997) suggest a number of reasons why OCBs may be related to organizational effectiveness. They include:

- Workers who help new coworkers "learn the ropes" help them to speed up the orientation and socialization process and become more productive employees faster
- Employees who help each other need less managerial supervision, freeing up the managers' time for other important duties
- Employees who have positive attitudes toward one another are more

ON THE CUTTING EDGE (*continued*)

cooperative and avoid destructive conflicts with other workers

- Workers freely and voluntarily meet outside of work times and regularly touch base with one another, improving the flow of organizational communication
- OCBs lead to a positive work environment and help in the recruitment and retention of the best qualified workers
- Workers pick up the slack and "cover" for one another during absences or times of heavy individual workloads

- Employees are more willing to take on new responsibilities or learn new technology or work systems

As can be seen, organizational citizenship behaviors lead to work groups who engage in the best sorts of organizational and personnel processes, and helps explain what separates the top-performing work groups and organizations from those who have substandard levels of performance.

Although the presence of cooperative group members often helps facilitate work performance, there are instances where work group members refuse to cooperate and "pull their load." **Social loafing** is the name given to the phenomenon whereby individuals working in a group put forth less effort than when working alone (Latane, Williams, & Harkins, 1979). Research has shown that social loafing occurs most frequently when workers believe that their individual performance or contribution will not be measured, and when working on simple, additive tasks, rather than complex, interdependent tasks (Comer, 1995; Karau & Williams, 1993). Most recently, however, it was also found that highly cohesive work groups engaged in less social loafing than did less cohesive groups (Karau & Hart, 1998). Another study (Robbins, 1995), found that if group members perceived others as engaging in social loafing, it increased their tendency to loaf—good evidence for the equity theory of motivation (see Chapter 7) ("if they're going to slack off, I'll slack off, too").

social loafing
the phenomenon whereby individuals working in groups exert less effort than when working alone

Competition

Like cooperation, **competition** is also a natural behavior that commonly arises in group dynamics (Tjosvold, 1988). While cooperation involves group members working together toward shared common goals, competition within groups involves members working against one another to achieve individual goals, often at the expense of other members. For example, in a sales competition, all members of a sales group compete with one another but only one can be named top salesperson. Most work groups are rife with competition as members struggle to get ahead. One study by Campbell and Furrer (1995), found evidence that the introduction of competition in a

competition
the process whereby group members are pitted against one another to achieve individual goals

work situation where goals were already set actually led to a *decrease* in performance, so managers should be cautious in their use of competition as a motivational strategy, as we will see shortly in our discussion of conflict.

Because both cooperation and competition are very natural human processes, they often both exist side by side in work groups, and work organizations and work culture actually encourage both. The very fact that work organizations exist indicates that there must be some advantage in having workers cooperate by pooling their efforts to perform some complex tasks. At the same time, the compensation systems adopted by U.S. organizations, and companies in most Western countries, emphasize the rewarding of individual efforts, which breeds competition. Much of this competition is viewed as healthy because it often motivates people to improve their work performance. Indeed, in the United States and many other industrialized Western nations, being competitive is a highly valued characteristic that is considered imperative for individual and organizational success.

CONFLICT IN WORK GROUPS AND ORGANIZATIONS

conflict
behavior by a person or group intended to inhibit the attainment of goals by another person or group

While competition refers to a motivating state, **conflict** is used to describe competitiveness of individual workers or work groups that becomes exposed. Conflict is behavior by a person or group that is purposely designed to inhibit the attainment of goals by another person or group (Gray & Starke, 1984). There are many typical instances of conflict between members of an organization, such as two delivery persons arguing over who gets to drive the new company truck, union and management representatives in heated negotiations over a new contract, or two applicants competing for a single job. Conflict in work organizations and in other areas of everyday life is indeed a common state of affairs.

The key element in the definition of conflict is that the conflicting parties have incompatible goals (Tjosvold, 1998b). Thus, both delivery persons cannot drive the same truck, the union cannot attain its goals unless management is willing to give up some of its goals, and two people cannot hold the same job. Because in extreme cases conflict can lead to a variety of negative behaviors, such as shouting, name calling, and acts of aggression, and perhaps because there is often a "loser" in conflict outcomes, it is commonly believed that conflict is bad. However, this is not necessarily true. Conflict is a natural process that occurs in all work groups and organizations. It can have negative, destructive consequences, but it can also be constructive and lead to positive outcomes for work groups and organizations (Rahim, 1985, 1986; Wall & Callister, 1995). Generally, the only way to be certain when conflict is bad or good is to examine whether it has positive or negative consequences for the conflicting parties and for the work group or organization as a whole. Although the consequences of conflict are very important, we must first examine the different levels of conflict that occur in organizations and the potential sources of conflict.

Levels of conflict

Conflict can occur at four levels within a work organization: intraindividual conflict, interindividual conflict, intragroup conflict, and intergroup conflict. At the larger level, interorganizational conflict can occur between work organizations. We typically think of conflict as occurring between two people or two groups. However, the first level of conflict, **intraindividual conflict**, occurs when one person is faced with two sets of incompatible goals. This is what happens when someone is in role conflict: The goals associated with one of the individual's roles conflicts with the goals of another. In such cases, the two roles represent the two conflicting parties. For example, the business owner who hires her son is going to be faced with serious internal conflict when dealing with him as a work employee. Her roles as mother and as work superior may come into conflict.

Conflict between two people, or **interindividual conflict**, is quite common in work groups and organizations. Two persons vying for the same promotion could create interindividual conflict, because the person who gets the promotion would block the other from attaining the goal. A disagreement between two machinists over a particular work procedure is also interindividual conflict. Many interpersonal problems that arise on the job stem from such conflict (Martin & Bergmann, 1996).

The next level of conflict, **intragroup conflict**, occurs between one person or faction within a group and the other group members. An individual who violates a group norm is creating intragroup conflict, as are members of a work group who disagree over the course of action for the group. Assume, for example, that a legal firm is trying to decide how to conduct their billing operations. Some of the attorneys favor hiring someone in-house who will handle billing, while others believe that billing should be contracted with an outside agency. Until the group settles on one of the plans, the firm will experience high levels of intragroup conflict.

When two groups are in conflict with each other, **intergroup conflict** exists. Such conflict occurs annually in many organizations when departments are asked to submit their budget requests for the upcoming year. Usually, the sum of the requests greatly exceeds the total amount of money available, which creates a great deal of intergroup conflict as each department tries to achieve its budgetary goals at the expense of those of the others (Greenberg, 1987). Some departments within an organization experience ongoing intergroup conflict because of incompatible goals. A classic example of this occurs between the production department and the quality control department in a manufacturing organization. The production group is concerned with meeting certain output quotas, usually expressed as number of components produced. Quality control's goal, on the other hand, is to only pass those components that meet certain specifications and standards. Each time the quality control inspectors reject a component, they interfere with the goal attainment of the production department, leading to ongoing intergroup conflict.

intraindividual conflict
conflict that occurs when an individual is faced with two sets of incompatible goals

interindividual conflict
conflict that occurs when two people are striving to attain their own goals, thus blocking the other's achievement

intragoup conflict
conflict that arises when a person or faction within a group attempts to achieve a goal that interferes with the group's goal attainment

intergroup conflict
conflict that occurs between two groups trying to attain their respective goals

interorganizational conflict
conflict between organizations with incompatible goals

Compare and contrast competition and conflict.

While each of these four levels of conflict takes place *within* a particular organization, **interorganizational conflict** occurs *between* organizations. Businesses that are fighting over the same consumer market are likely to engage in interorganizational conflict as each organization tries to achieve its sales goals at the expense of those of the other. Most businesspersons would agree that, for the most part, interorganizational conflict is a good thing; it is the cornerstone of the free enterprise system. It is the competitive marketplace, spurred on by interorganizational conflict, that helps organizations compete to provide better goods and services for consumers.

Sources of conflict

Conflict in work groups and organizations comes from many sources. Sometimes it is caused by the organizational structure. For example, status differences are a common source of conflict. Sometimes conflict results because of simple disagreements between two parties over the appropriate work behavior or course of action. Although it would be difficult to list all potential sources of conflict, we will examine some of the more common causes.

A scarcity of important resources—money, materials, tools, and supplies—is perhaps the most common source of conflict in work organizations (Greenberg & Baron, 1997). It is a rare organization that has enough resources to satisfy the needs of all of its members. When members are forced to compete with one another for these resources, conflict usually follows.

Individuals and work groups usually must rely on the activities of other persons and groups to get their own jobs done. Therefore, individual and group interdependence is an important source of conflict (Victor & Blackburn, 1987). Generally, the greater the interdependence of work activities, the greater the potential for conflict (Walton & Dutton, 1969). For example, in the airline industry, flight crews must depend on the maintenance crews, luggage handlers, and passenger boarding personnel to do their jobs in servicing and loading the aircraft before they can do their job. Intergroup conflict can result if one group does not feel that another is doing its job. If the flight crew feels that the luggage handlers are too slow, causing delays in takeoff, the fact that the flight crew may be blamed for the delays creates a potential conflict situation. The strong interdependence among all workers on an assembly line also opens up the door for intragroup conflict, because the ability of any single person to perform the job correctly is governed by how others further up the line performed theirs. If an assembled product is rejected and it is another person's fault, the individual's work is also rejected.

We have seen that the we-they feeling plays a large role in fostering group cohesiveness; nothing can draw a group together better than having a common enemy to fight. However, a problem occurs when the "enemy" is within your own organization. This is what often causes the conflict in wage negotiations between workers and managers. The workers ask for a wage increase, while management, in an effort to keep costs down, rejects the request. What commonly results is that each group views the other as an enemy blocking its goal attainment. Although the common enemy helps

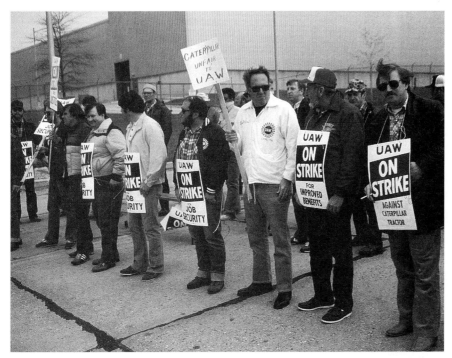

Most organizational conflict occurs behind the scenes, but in extreme instances the dispute becomes public.

draw the members together within their respective groups, it also tends to draw the two groups further and further away from each other. Thus while the we-they feeling can increase group cohesiveness, it may also cause intergroup conflict.

One of the most common sources of conflict is not related to the availability of resources, the structure of the organization, or the formation of work groups, but rather results from the fact that certain individuals simply do not get along with each other (Labianca, Brass, & Gray, 1998). This important source of conflict thus comes from *interpersonal* sources. Two organizational members who dislike each other may refuse to cooperate. This sort of interpersonal conflict can be very disruptive to the larger work group and the organization in general, especially if the problem is between two powerful people, such as two department heads who may turn their subordinates against members of the other department. What was once a conflict between two persons can thus escalate into conflict between two groups.

Research evidence also suggests that some people are more conflict-prone than others. Differences in personality and temperament mean that certain persons may be likely to engage in conflict. Indeed, studies have shown that some people try to stir up interindividual conflict because of their desire to gain at others' expense (McClintock, Messick, Kuhlman, & Campos, 1973; see also Knight & Dubro, 1984).

A final characteristic that can be a potential source of conflict is age. A good deal of evidence indicates that younger workers are more conflict-prone than older workers, presumably because they have less to lose and more to gain from the outcomes of conflict situations (Robbins, 1974).

Conflict outcomes

It has been stated that conflict in work settings can produce both positive and negative outcomes. Attention is usually given to how conflict affects the important organizational outcomes of job performance or productivity, job satisfaction, and employee attendance. Thus, conflict is most often labeled as positive or negative from the standpoint of the organization. First, we will examine the positive outcomes of conflict.

A primary question is how conflict within a work group or organization relates to performance. One way that conflict can indirectly affect performance is by increasing the motivation and energy level of group members. A little bit of conflict seems to energize members, which in turn may increase their motivation to perform their jobs. The complete absence of conflict in work groups can cause workers to become complacent and unmotivated. (It can also be very dull.)

Another positive outcome of conflict is that it can stimulate creativity and innovation (James, Chen, & Goldberg, 1992). When people challenge the existing system, a form of conflict results. But out of this type of conflict come new, and often better, ideas. For example, in many groups, workers continue to use the same old "tried and true" work procedures. When a worker suggests a new, improved method, there may be some initial conflict as members resist having to learn a new technique. However, if the new procedure is effective, group productivity may increase. Thus, although people tend to resist changes, when change is for the better, the organization and its members benefit.

Another performance-related positive outcome of conflict occurs when conflict improves the quality of decisions (Cosier & Dalton, 1990). Giving all members of a group some input into the decision-making process leads to conflict because the group must consider a wide range of opposing views and opinions. Conflict occurs as each member tries to be heard and pushes for what he or she thinks is right. The positive result of all of this, however, is that decisions made are usually of high quality, being the result of a very critical process. (We will return to a discussion of group decision-making processes later in this chapter.)

In Chapters 8 and 10, we saw that employees who feel that they have an active role in affecting group or organizational processes tend to be more satisfied than those who have no influence. Being able to communicate freely with coworkers, having a voice in decision making, and being allowed to make suggestions or criticize group or organizational operations are all ways in which workers can have some impact on group processes. Although some conflict is likely to arise every time workers are allowed to introduce their own opinions, the fact that they can take part in this positive, productive type of conflict is associated with greater group member satisfaction. Therefore, some forms of conflict can be directly associated with member satisfaction and commitment to the work group.

Among the various negative outcomes of conflict, one of the most obvious is the reduction of group cohesiveness. While a little bit of conflict can energize group members, too much can erode cohesiveness and, in extremes, diminish the members' abilities to work with each other. This may contribute to increased voluntary absenteeism and eventually employee turnover.

Conflict can also hamper effective group performance when it retards communication. People who are in conflict may avoid communicating with each other, making it difficult to work together. Conflict can also be destructive to group member satisfaction when conflicting parties begin to send misleading or deceptive messages to one another or when false and disparaging rumors are started. Evidence also suggests that when a great deal of interpersonal conflict occurs among work group members, supervisors may begin to avoid allowing subordinates to participate in decision making processes, thus shutting down this type of communication, presumably in an effort to avoid further conflict (Fodor, 1976). Conflict is especially damaging to performance when it allows group goals to become secondary to the infighting. Sometimes members direct so much energy to the conflict situation that they neglect to perform their jobs. When winning the conflict becomes more important than reaching work-related goals, the outcomes are negative for the individuals and for the organization (Robbins, 1979).

In summary, neither too much nor too little conflict is beneficial for the work group members and the organization. This means that there must be some optimal level of conflict. Because conflict is so pervasive in work groups and organizations, it would be very difficult to assess whether all forms of conflict were at their optimal levels at any given time. However, at times the conflict has obviously gone too far, becoming detrimental to the operations of the work group as a whole. Likewise, at other times the work group has become too complacent and needs some conflict to get the members more active and involved. Since some excess or shortage of conflict is inevitably going to exist, the smart thing to do at all times in all work groups is to learn to manage conflict.

Managing conflict

To manage conflict—to keep it at an optimal level—one of two things must be done. If the conflict becomes too great, leading to severe negative outcomes, it must be resolved. If, on the other hand, the level of conflict is too low, conflict stimulation is needed.

There is little doubt that too much conflict can have devastating consequences on the work group and the organization. Therefore, a great deal of attention has been given to the development and application of various conflict resolution strategies, which can be of two types. Individual conflict resolution strategies are those that the conflicting parties can use themselves to try to resolve the conflict; managerial conflict resolution strategies are steps that managers or other third parties can take to encourage conflict resolution. Thomas (1976, 1992) has identified five individual conflict resolution strategies:

competition
a conflict resolution strategy of persisting in a conflict until one party attains personal goals at the expense of the other's

accommodation
a conflict resolution strategy of making a sacrifice to resolve a conflict

compromise
a conflict resolution strategy in which both parties give up some part of their goals

collaboration
a conflict resolution strategy in which the parties cooperate to reach a solution that satisfies both

avoidance
withdrawing from or avoiding a conflict situation

1. *Competition*—Persisting in the conflict until one party's goals are achieved at the expense of those of the other. This can be labeled a win-lose strategy: One party wins, the other loses.
2. *Accommodation*—Giving in or acting in a self-sacrificing manner to resolve the conflict. This is a lose-win strategy. Often, this strategy of appeasement is done to cut losses, or in an effort to save the relationship between the conflicting parties.
3. *Compromise*—Each party must give up something. This is a lose-lose strategy. Compromise is typical in bargaining situations. For example, in union-management negotiations, management may offer a $.50-an-hour raise, while the union wants a $1.50 raise. They compromise at $1.00, but neither group has achieved its complete goal. They have each lost something from their original position—a lose-lose outcome. Compromise is not an appropriate strategy if both parties cannot afford to yield part of their goals (Harris, 1993).
4. *Collaboration*—The parties try to cooperate and reach a mutually beneficial solution. This is a win-win situation. Unfortunately, this is not always possible, particularly when the conflict is over scarce resources and there is not enough to satisfy both parties' needs. It has been suggested that if both parties work at it, many conflicts can be resolved collaboratively (Ury, Brett, & Goldberg, 1988).
5. *Avoidance*—Suppressing the conflict, not allowing it to come into the open, or simply withdrawing from the situation. While this strategy avoids open conflict, the differences between the two parties still exist and will likely continue to affect their ability to work with one another. Avoidance can be appropriate if the timing for open conflict is not right, or if the conflicting parties need a "cooling-off" period.

While the two conflicting parties can take such steps to try to resolve their differences, managers, because of their status and power in the organization, can play a major role in resolving conflict between subordinates (Blake, Shepard, & Mouton, 1964; Pinkley, Brittain, Neale, & Northcraft, 1995; Sheppard, 1974). Managers may try to force an end to the conflict by deciding in favor of one or the other parties. While this may end the conflict, resentment may be built up in the losing person that may surface later in actions against the manager or the coworker (van de Vliert, Euwema, & Huismans, 1995). Managers can also act as arbitrators or mediators to resolve conflict in a way that may satisfy both parties. For example, in a furniture factory, two workers were constantly fighting over a particular tool that

Compromise and collaboration are just two strategies that can be used to resolve a conflict situation.

each occasionally needed to perform their jobs. When one worker needed the tool, it always seemed that the other person had it, which led to constant arguments. When the shop manager became aware of the problem, he instantly resolved it by simply purchasing another tool. In other circumstances, outside consultants or arbitrators may be called in specifically to resolve internal conflicts in organizations (Thomas, 1992).

One managerial conflict resolution strategy, outlined in a series of studies by Sherif and his colleagues (Sherif, Harvey, White, Hood, & Sherif, 1961), deals with resolving intragroup conflict by stimulating intragroup cohesiveness through the introduction of a common, **superordinate goal** that is attractive to both parties. When a group is split over some minor issue, introducing a more important superordinate goal may draw the two

superordinate goal
a goal that two conflicting parties are willing to work to attain

sides together as they strive to attain the common end. For example, commissioned salespersons in the men's clothing section of a large chain department store were constantly fighting over who would be the first to grab a customer who walked into the area. The manager helped to resolve much of this conflict by introducing a bonus program that pitted the department's overall sales against those of men's departments in other stores. By focusing on pooled sales figures, the employees became oriented toward beating the other stores rather than beating each other.

Managers can also help resolve conflict in group decision making (Conlon & Ross, 1993). For example, they may use their authority to call an issue to a vote, which means that the majority of workers will win the conflict situation. However, there may be a disgruntled minority of losers, who may then carry on the conflict by refusing to follow the elected plan or by some other means. The manager will need to deal with this residual conflict if it is deemed serious enough to require resolution.

The key to successful conflict resolution from the managerial perspective is to maintain a broad perspective, trying to find a workable solution and considering the potential side effects, such as disgruntled losers, that may result from the resolution process (see Applying I/O Psychology).

In certain situations, such as when group members appear to have become complacent and disinterested in work activities, managers may feel that some specific types of conflict are needed. A number of strategies can be used to stimulate conflict. One tactic is simply to ask for it. Asking employees for their suggestions or for complaints about the organization and its policies may lead to some conflict as employees critically evaluate the organization and management. However, it is hoped that this type of conflict will lead to constructive change and improvement. When top management feels that work groups have become *too* cohesive, to the detriment of the groups' energy and motivational levels, they may decide to break up that cohesiveness and inject a little stimulating conflict by making personnel changes such as bringing in new employees or rotating workers to different departments or work sites. Restaurant and retail chains use this strategy when they rotate managers among stores.

Sales or performance competition programs are another way of stimulating some positive group conflict. The key to a successful competition program, however, is to ensure that members do not engage in dysfunctional behaviors, such as sabotaging others' work activities, in an effort to win the competition. Ideally, a good program should allow all participants to achieve a goal. For example, a bonus should be given to each employee who reaches a certain performance level, instead of only to the top performer.

A widely used conflict stimulation strategy that can often lead to positive outcomes is to move from centralized decision-making procedures to a group decision-making process, in which all group members have a say in certain work-related issues. Although this automatically increases conflict by allowing each worker to state his or her opinion and argue for a particular course of action, it is presumed that this type of conflict will yield positive

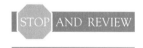

Define the five individual conflict resolution strategies.

results because it allows for consideration of a wider range of plans and greater critiquing of the various possible decisions.

APPLYING I/O PSYCHOLOGY

Reducing Management-Union Conflict

A common type of intergroup conflict in large work organizations exists between management and unions. The behavioral scientists Blake, Mouton, and Sloma (1964) outline a case in which such conflict was reduced through a two-day workshop designed to refocus the two groups' efforts on common work-related goals. The company was a large electronics manufacturing plant with over 4,000 employees. Because there was a history of disagreement between management and the labor union, one of the most difficult tasks for the behavioral scientists was to get both sides to agree to the "experiment." Finally, however, they agreed that the hostility between the two groups was so high that something needed to be done.

The scientists believed that the key to reducing conflict was to get the two groups to increase their understanding of each other and to see that in many ways, they had compatible rather than competing goals.

The workshop designed to achieve this mutual awareness was broken down into eight phases, as follows:

In the first few phases, the management and union representatives wrote down their images of themselves, particularly in their relationship with the other group, and their images of the other side. These images were exchanged, and heated discussion ensued. In these early discussions, the two groups continued their intense conflict. For example, one manager said, "I can't even talk with these union officials. I just 'see red' and clam up every time I see one of them coming." Eventually, however, as the groups moved through the middle phases of the workshop, they began to gain insight into each other's positions and some of the misunderstandings began to disappear. This was helped along by the fifth phase in which both groups' task was to try to discover why the conflict had become what it was. In the discussion that followed, the two

Phase	Activity	Time (hours)
1	Orientation; purposes of workshop explained	½
2	Intragroup development of own images and images of other group	5
3	Exchange of images across groups	1
4	Clarification of images	2
5	Intragroup diagnosis of present relationship	4
6	Exchange of diagnoses across groups	3
7	Consolidation of key issues and sources of friction	2
8	Planning of next steps to be taken	1

sides began to find that they had some common goals:

> *The employee relations manager, who had been listening intently all this time, stood up with a look of disbelief on his face. He didn't seem to realize he was on his feet. "Do you mean to say you people are really interested in production?" He had listened to the union say this for two days, but he had just "heard" it for the first time. His next question was a simple one, but it triggered an hour-long discussion. He asked, "What could management do to use people*

more effectively?" (Blake, Mouton, & Sloma, 1964, p. 189)

By finding that they shared common goals, the two groups set an agenda to work together not only to reduce the management-union conflict further but also to develop some cooperative strategies for dealing with work-related problems. From this workshop arose a plan of action for creating better lines of communication between the two groups and for implementing strategies that would increase plant efficiency and productivity for the benefit of all.

Group Decision-making Processes

One of the most important processes in work groups is group decision making, which includes establishing group goals, choosing among various courses of action, selecting new members, and determining standards of appropriate behavior. The processes by which groups make these decisions have been of interest to I/O psychologists for many years.

Groups can make work-related decisions in a number of ways. The simplest and most straightforward strategy, known as **autocratic decision making**, is when the group leader makes decisions alone, using only the information that the leader possesses. The major advantage of autocratic decision making is that it is fast. Decisions are made quickly by the leader and are then expected to be carried out by group members. However, because the decision is made based only on what the leader knows, the quality of the decision may suffer. For example, suppose a leader of a group of accountants has to decide which accounting software to order. If the leader actually knows which program is the best for the group, there will be no drawback to the autocratic approach. If, however, the leader cannot make an informed choice, the decision may be faulty. In this case, input from the group members would be helpful. A variation on the strict autocratic decision making approach occurs when the leader solicits information from group members to assist in reaching a decision, but still holds the final say. This is sometimes referred to as *consultative decision making*. In the software decision, soliciting input from group members about which systems they favor might lead to a higher quality decision.

autocratic decision making
a process by which group decisions are made by the leader alone, based on information the leader possesses

A very different strategy is **democratic decision making**, in which all group members are allowed to discuss the decision and then vote on a particular course of action. Typically, democratic decision making is based on majority rule. One advantage of this approach is that decisions are made using the pooled knowledge and experience of all of the group members. Moreover, because all members have a chance to voice an opinion or suggest a different course of action, a greater number of alternatives are considered. Also, because group members have a role in the decision making, they are more likely to follow the chosen course.

democratic decision making
a strategy by which decisions are made by the group members based on majority-rule voting

The most obvious drawback to democratic decision making is that it is time-consuming. Because it encourages conflict, it can also be inefficient. While the democratic, majority-rule approach results in a satisfied majority who will back the decision, there may be a disgruntled minority who resist its implementation.

A strategy that overcomes some of the weaknesses of democratic decision making is to make decisions based on **consensus**, which means that all group members have agreed on the chosen course of action. Because consensus decision making is especially time-consuming, it is usually used only for very important decisions. For example, juries use this strategy because the decision affects the freedom and future of the accused. Some company executive boards may strive for a consensus when making major decisions about changes in the direction of the organization or in organizational structure or company policy. As you might imagine, the outcome of consensus decision making is usually a high-quality, highly critiqued decision, backed by all members of the group. The obvious drawback is the tremendous amount of time it may take for the group to reach a consensus. In fact, in many situations, arriving at a consensus may be impossible, particularly if one or more group members is strongly resistant to the majority's decision (the courtroom analogy would be a "hung" jury).

consensus
decision making based on 100 percent member agreement

EFFECTIVENESS OF GROUP DECISION MAKING

In recent years, organizations have been turning more and more to group strategies for making important work-related decisions. Part of this is fueled by beliefs in the inherent advantages of group over individual decision making. However, while group decision making has many positive aspects, it also has some drawbacks (see Table 11.2). The key is to know not only *how* group-made decisions can be more effective than those made by individuals, but also *when* group decision making is superior.

As mentioned, the major advantage of group decision making is that it offers increased knowledge and experience on which to base the decision. But do groups actually make better decisions than individuals? Research does give the edge to group decision making, *on the average*. The average group will make a higher-quality decision than the average individual. However, some research indicates that the best decision-making individual—one who possesses all the information needed to make a high-quality decision—will

TABLE 11.2

Advantages and Disadvantages of Group Decision Making

Advantages	Disadvantages
Works from a broad knowledge base	Slow (can be a problem in crisis situations)
Decision is accepted by members	Creates intragroup conflict
Decision is highly critiqued	Potential for groupthink and group polarization
Aspects of the problem can be divided among group members	Certain members, such as leaders, may dominate the decision making process

be able to perform as well as or better than a group (Hill, 1982; Miner, 1984). In other circumstances, groups may arrive at decisions that are superior to even those made by the group's best decision maker (Michaelson, Watson, & Black, 1989). Moreover, certain members, such as a group leader or respected individual, may have more influence in affecting the outcome and may be able to sway a group toward accepting a particular course of action. If the influential member is not knowledgeable or well-informed about the alternatives, however, the group may be led to make a poor decision.

We have also seen that group decision making tends to be slower than individual decision making, which can be a problem in situations such as an emergency or crisis. At these times, it may be better for an individual to take charge and make decisions for the group (Tjosvold, 1984a). However, if a problem is complex and multifaceted, with many steps required to arrive at a decision, a group may make the decision faster than an individual, because the various aspects of the problem can be divided among group members.

Perhaps the strongest argument in support of group decision making is that it tends to lead to increased member satisfaction and greater member commitment to the course of action than does individual decision making. But what happens if the group-made decision is a bad one? Research indicates that when this occurs, members may increase their commitment to the poor decision (Bazerman, Giuliano, & Appleman, 1984). If the poor decision was made by an individual, group members will not be as committed and may be more likely to see its faults and try another course of action.

■ UP CLOSE

What Is Brainstorming, and Does It Work?

brainstorming

a group process generating creative ideas or solutions through a noncritical and nonjudgmental process

In the 1950s an advertising executive developed a technique to encourage groups to come up with creative ideas (Osborn, 1957). The technique, termed **brainstorming**, involved six to ten group members throwing out ideas in a noncritical and nonjudgmental atmosphere as a means of try-

Up Close (*continued*)

ing to generate as many creative ideas or solutions to a problem as possible. Since its invention, brainstorming has become very popular, and tremendous claims have been made regarding its success.

The basic rules in brainstorming sessions are: (1) No idea is too far out; (2) criticism of any idea is not allowed; (3) the more ideas the better; and (4) members should try to build on each other's ideas. The technique has been widely used in a variety of businesses, but does it work? Evidence from nearly 40 years of research indicates that, despite its popularity, brainstorming is not as effective as its proponents might lead one to believe (see, for example, Bouchard, Barsaloux, & Drauden, 1974; Taylor, Block, & Berry, 1958; Yetton & Bottger, 1982). The problem is that in spite of the rules, group dynamics are too powerful; the creativity of people in the brainstorming groups is often inhibited (Brown & Paulus, 1996; Diehl & Stroebe, 1987). Research indicates that individuals are equal to or better than the brainstorming groups in generating creative ideas. What is extremely interesting, however, is that members of brainstorming groups firmly believe that the group brainstorming was more productive than individual brainstorming, both in terms of the number and the quality of the ideas generated (Paulus & Dzindolet, 1993). The moral is that just because a technique sounds logical or is popular, this does not necessarily mean that it will work.

On a more positive note, a new, seemingly more effective version of brainstorming has been developed. This new "electronic brainstorming" uses computers to have members exchange ideas via computer networks (Gallupe, Bastianutti, & Cooper, 1991). These electronic brainstorming groups seem to work well, presumably because many of the group processes that hinder the group's ability to generate good ideas present in face-to-face groups (e.g., fear that others are negatively evaluating one's ideas; "free-riding" members who allow other members to do the work), are absent in the electronic brainstorming groups (Cooper, Gallupe, Pollard, & Cadsby, 1998; Dennis & Valacich, 1993).

In summary, although group decision making has certain limitations, it offers many advantages over individual decision making, particularly in improving the quality of decisions and in increasing the commitment to decisions once they are made. Recent trends toward encouraging greater involvement of workers in organizational processes mean that group decision making is likely to increase in the future (see Up Close).

GROUP DECISION-MAKING GONE AWRY: GROUPTHINK AND GROUP POLARIZATION

When making important work decisions, particularly those that have a major impact on the work procedures or working lives of group members, group decision making may be preferred over decision making by high-ranking members of the organization. This is done in an effort to increase the amount of relevant information available and to encourage member commitment to the eventually chosen course. However, psychologists have discovered two situations in which the usual advantages of group decision making may not be forthcoming: One is known as groupthink, and the other is termed group polarization.

Groupthink

Groups generally arrive at high-quality decisions because the alternative courses of action have been subjected to critical evaluation. This is particularly true in consensus decision making, since even one dissenting member can argue against a plan favored by all the rest. There is, however, an exception to this rule. A complex set of circumstances can sometimes occur in consensus decision making that retards the critical evaluation process. What results is a complete backfiring of the normal, critical decision making that results in a premature, hasty, and often catastrophic decision. This situation is termed **groupthink**. Groupthink is a syndrome that occurs in highly cohesive decision-making groups, where a norm develops to arrive at an early consensus, thereby reducing the effectiveness of the group's ability to make high-quality, critical decisions.

groupthink
a syndrome characterized by a concurrence-seeking tendency that overrides the ability of a cohesive group to make critical decisions

The concept of groupthink was researched by psychologist Irving Janis (1972, 1982; Janis & Mann, 1977). According to Janis, groupthink usually occurs only in highly cohesive groups in which the members' desire to maintain cohesiveness overrides the sometimes uncomfortable and disruptive process of critical decision making. A course of action is laid out on the table, and without it being adequately critiqued, the members rapidly move toward a consensus to adopt the plan. Despite Janis's assertion that groupthink usually only occurs in highly cohesive groups, research suggests that it is groups whose cohesiveness is "relationship-based" who are more prone to groupthink than groups whose cohesiveness is "task-based," or related to the decision-making and performance goals of the group (Bernthal & Insko, 1993).

In developing his theory of groupthink, Janis studied a number of poor decisions made by high-level decision-making groups, such as U.S. presidential administrations and boards of directors of large companies, the consequences of which were so bad that Janis labeled the outcomes "fiascoes." Janis investigated a number of historical fiascoes, such as the Kennedy administration's failed Bay of Pigs invasion, the Truman administration's decision to cross the thirty-eighth parallel in the Korean War, and the Johnson administration's decision to escalate the Vietnam War. He also studied catastrophic business decisions, such as the decision to market the drug Thalidomide, which led to thousands of birth deformities; the Buffalo Mining Company's decision about dam construction, which caused the deaths of 125 people; and the Ford Motor Company's decision to market the Edsel, one of the greatest failures in U.S. automotive history (Wheeler & Janis, 1980). More recently, researchers have studied NASA's catastrophic decision to launch the *Challenger* space shuttle, and decisions made in the Iran-

Contra affair during the Reagan administration (Esser, 1998). By studying the decision-making processes in each early case of groupthink, Janis noticed certain similarities that he has termed the "symptoms of groupthink"—specific group factors that work toward preventing the critical evaluation usually present in decision-making groups (see Table 11.3).

To understand how the symptoms of groupthink interfere with critical decision making processes, consider the following example. A board of directors of an international air freight service must decide whether the company should enter a cost-cutting war with their competitors. The board begins its decision making meeting with the chairperson's loaded question, "Should we enter into this foolish price war, or just keep rates the way they are?" By labeling the price war as "foolish," the chairperson has already indicated her preferred course of action: Keep the rates as they are. Normally, the critical decision-making process would involve a great deal of discussion about the relative strengths and weaknesses of the various alternatives, and the decision that would result should be of high quality. However, in groupthink situations this does not occur. The symptoms of groupthink, themselves manifestations of such basic group processes as cohesiveness, stereotyped and rationalized views, and conformity, can counteract the critical evaluations that should be made. If groupthink does indeed occur, the consequences may be devastating, particularly because the group believes that the chosen action is the result of a critical and well-conducted decision-making process, when it is not.

Describe the advantages and disadvantages of group decision making.

TABLE 11.3

The Eight Symptoms of Groupthink

1. *Illusion of invulnerability*—The highly cohesive decision-making group members see themselves as powerful and invincible. Their attraction to and faith in the group leads them to ignore the potential disastrous outcomes of their decision.

2. *Illusion of morality*—Members believe in the moral correctness of the group and its decision; related to the first symptom. Derived from the we-they feeling, members view themselves as the "good guys" and the opposition as bad or evil.

3. *Shared negative stereotypes*—Members have common beliefs that minimize the risks involved in a decision or belittle any opposing viewpoints.

4. *Collective rationalizations*—The members explain away any negative information that runs counter to the group decision.

5. *Self-censorship*—Members suppress their own doubts or criticisms concerning the decision.

6. *Illusion of unanimity*—Members mistakenly believe that the decision is a consensus. Since dissenting viewpoints are not being voiced, it is assumed that silence indicates support.

7. *Direct conformity pressure*—When an opposing view or a doubt is expressed, pressure is applied to get the dissenter to concur with the decision.

8. *Mindguards*—Some members play the role of protecting or insulating the group from any opposing opinions or negative information.

If groupthink takes place at the air freight company, the board of directors would likely manifest three symptoms—the *illusion of invulnerability*, the *illusion of morality*, and the presence of *shared negative stereotypes*—that result from the we-they feeling that is typically present in highly cohesive groups. The members believe that they and their organization are powerful and good. Negative stereotypes about nonmembers or other groups (the enemy) also stem from the we-they feeling. Examples of these three symptoms might be seen in the board members' statements that they believe the group and the company are invulnerable ("We're the number one company in this business") and morally good ("We always provide the best possible service to our customers"). Other comments suggest that they hold shared negative stereotypes about the competition ("With their inept management and poor equipment, they will never be able to offer the kind of service that we do"). These three groupthink symptoms thus begin a tendency toward seeking concurrence, as the members strive to stick together and agree with one another (Janis, 1972).

Additional groupthink symptoms—*collective rationalizations* of opposing viewpoints, a tendency for members to engage in *self-censorship*, and the *illusion of unanimity*—lead the group to arrive at a premature consensus. Suppose that one of the board members suggests an alternative to the plan to keep rates as they are that the board is moving toward adopting. The dissenter wants to keep rates the same while starting an advertising campaign that tells customers, "You get what you pay for," thus emphasizing the company's higher quality of service. Collective rationalizations of members immediately put down the alternative plan ("People never listen to advertisements anyway," and "That will cost us more than lowering our rates!"). Other board members may see the merit in the alternative plan, but since it appears that most of the others, because of their silence, do not like it, they engage in self-censorship and keep their opinions to themselves. The fact that no one speaks up leads to the illusion of unanimity, the misconception that everybody is for the original plan.

If dissenters do speak up, two additional groupthink symptoms operate to stifle the critical decision-making process even further. *Direct conformity pressure* might be applied to force dissenters to keep their opinions to themselves and not break up the group's agreement. Some members may even play the role of *mindguards*, by taking it upon themselves to keep dissenting opinions from reaching the ears of the group leader and other members. The member advocating the advertisement plan, for example, might be told by a self-appointed mindguard to not bring the plan up again, "for the good of the group."

Janis believes that groupthink can be combated by breaking up some of the cohesiveness of the group through the interjection of productive conflict. This might involve using strategies such as bringing in outsiders to offer different viewpoints or having some members play the role of critical evaluators—"devil's advocates"—who are highly critical of any plan of action that is brought before the group (Schweiger, Sandberg, & Ragan,

1986). Also, because groupthink is partly brought on by a sense of time urgency, if the group begins with the idea that they need to come up with the best possible decision, regardless of how long it takes, groupthink may be avoided. More recently, t'Hart (1998) suggests that holding individual group members accountable and reducing pressures to conform will help combat groupthink.

Group polarization

The quality of group decisions may also be adversely affected by **group polarization**, or the tendency for groups to make decisions that are more extreme than those made by individuals (Myers & Lamm, 1976). Early research found evidence of the effects of group polarization when decisions carried a high degree of risk. In these studies, individuals were asked to make a decision between an attractive but risky course of action and one that was less attractive but also less risky. After making the decision, the respondents were put into groups and asked to come up with a group decision. It was found that the groups tended to make riskier decisions than the average individual (Wallach, Kogan, and Bem, 1962). This effect became known as the "risky shift," and was the topic of much research and theorizing. It had major implications for the making of important decisions in business and government, since it suggested that group decisions might be more dangerous than decisions made by individuals. However, subsequent research began to challenge these early findings, failing to find a risky shift in some decision-making groups and occasionally finding evidence of a *cautious* shift. What we now know is that group discussion often leads individuals to become more extreme in their opinions. The attitudes and opinions of individuals who favor an idea tend to become even more positive after group discussion, whereas those who do not favor an idea tend to develop opinions that are even more negative (Isenberg, 1986; Lamm, 1988).

How does group polarization relate to decisions made in work situations, and why does it occur? Imagine that a company must choose which of several new products it should introduce. Some of the products are costly to develop and market, but if successful could bring large profits. Other products are less costly but will lead to smaller financial gains. An individual who makes the decision might choose to introduce a product of medium-level risk and payoff. However, if the person is put into a group that is leaning toward marketing a risky product, the group's decision would be more extreme than the individual's. If, on the other hand, the group is leaning toward the side of caution, the group might shift to a more cautious choice than the typical individual would choose.

Two explanations for group polarization have been offered. The first is that in the group, the individual is presented with persuasive arguments by other members that bolster the individual's original positive or negative stance on an issue. After hearing others in the group argue for a decision that coincides with the individual's opinion, he or she becomes more certain that his or her opinion is correct, and there is a tendency for the group

group polarization
the tendency for groups to make decisions that are more extreme than those made by individuals

List and define six symptoms of groupthink.

as a whole to become more extreme in its final decision. The other explanation is that individuals adopt the values of the group. If the group presents a positive opinion on an issue, the individuals go along with the group, becoming even more positive (or negative) about an idea than they would be alone. Individuals may support the viewpoint of the group in order to demonstrate that they endorse the group's values.

Regardless of why it occurs, the fact that some group decisions may be more extreme than those of individuals is a reason for some concern, particularly when a decision involves risks that may compromise the goals of the group, or when extremely cautious decisions inhibit the attainment of group goals.

Despite the persistence of group polarization, there are potential safeguards that may minimize its effect on decision making. Evidence has indicated that groups composed of individuals who all initially agree on an issue, before any group discussion has taken place, tend to make decisions that are the most extreme. That is, these decisions tend to be even more extreme than decisions made by groups composed of members who do not initially agree with one another (Williams & Taormina, 1992). Thus, when groups include members who have varying original opinions on an issue, the decisions made by those groups may be more resistant to the effects of group polarization, and thus less extreme. The presence of even a single dissenting member in a group may help to combat group polarization, just as a "devil's advocate" can help combat groupthink.

Summary

A *group* is two or more individuals, engaged in social interaction to achieve some goal. Within work groups, members play various *roles*, which are patterns of behavior adopted based on *expectations* held about the function of a position. Work groups also develop *norms*, or rules to help govern member behavior. The process of *organizational socialization* refers to the integration of individuals into work groups and organizations through learning work procedures, work roles, and organizational and group norms.

Certain basic processes occur in all work groups. One is *conformity*, the process of adhering to and following group norms. Another basic process, *cohesiveness*, is the degree of attraction among group members. A number of factors, such as group size, member status, member stability, and member similarity can influence group cohesiveness.

Two common yet opposing forces that are evident in all groups are cooperation and competition. *Cooperation* is critical to coordinating the activities of work group members. However, *social loafing* can occur when workers in groups put in less effort than they would when working alone. *Competition* can lead to *conflict*, which is behavior by one party that is designed to inhibit the goal attainment of another party. Conflict can occur at a number of levels within work organizations, taking the form of *intra-*

individual, interindividual, intragroup, intergroup, or *interorganizational conflict.* It can arise from various sources, most notably from a scarcity of desired resources and from individual and group interdependence. The effect of conflict can be both positive and negative; it is positive when it motivates workers or stimulates them to be creative or innovative, and negative when it disrupts group work activities and social relationships. Managing conflict involves regulating the level of conflict, resolving it when it is negative and stimulating it when it is positive or productive. A number of conflict resolution and conflict stimulation strategies are used in organizations.

An important function in work groups is group decision making, which has several advantages and disadvantages over individual decision making. While group decision making is slow and conflict-ridden, it can lead to high-quality decisions and greater member satisfaction with and commitment to the decision. A type of breakdown in the effectiveness of decision making groups is termed *groupthink,* which is a concurrence-seeking tendency that overrides the ability of a cohesive group to make critical decisions. *Group polarization* is the tendency for groups to make more extreme decisions, either more risky or more cautious, than individuals.

Study Questions and Exercises

1. Consider a work or social group of which you are a member. What are the various roles that members play? What roles have you played? What are some of the norms that are particular to this group?
2. In what ways can group cohesiveness facilitate goal attainment in work groups? How might cohesiveness hinder goal attainment?
3. List the levels of conflict that occur in work groups. Give specific examples from your own life to illustrate each.
4. Discuss the ways in which cohesiveness and conflict can be seen as opposite forces in work groups.
5. What are some of the potential positive and negative outcomes of conflict? Using a work or social group with which you have had contact, think of examples of conflict that led to negative outcomes. How might these situations have been managed to reduce their negative impact?
6. Consider the eight symptoms of groupthink. What steps can decision-making groups take to try to avoid each of them?

Suggested Readings

Forsyth, D.R. (1990). *Group dynamics* (2nd ed). Monterey, CA: Brooks/Cole. *This older textbook provides a comprehensive overview of the basics of group processes.*

Group Dynamics: Theory Research and Practice. Begun in 1997, *this new journal focuses on research in group processes, much of which has to deal with work groups.*

Wall, J.A., & Callister, R.R. (1995). Conflict and its management. *Journal of Management 21* , 515–558. *This article reveiws the literature on organizational conflict and includes listings of the causes and consequences of group conflict.*

Zander, A. (1994). *Making groups effective* (2nd ed.). San Francisco: Jossey-Bass. *A guide to work group dynamics by a late, leading researcher in the field.*

LEADERSHIP

UNDERSTANDING LEADERSHIP THEORIES

INSIDE TIPS

This chapter presents some of the many theories of leadership in work organizations in more or less chronological order, beginning with the earliest (and simplest) theories and progressing to the more current (and complex) models. While each of these theories takes a somewhat different perspective in examining work group leadership, you will find common threads. Specifically, most of the more recent models build on the behavioral theories of leadership, which focus on the behaviors displayed by effective leaders. The behavioral theories' dichotomy of leader behavior—task-oriented and relationship-oriented—is used as a starting point for developing more complex theories. Later theories of leadership, called contingency theories, look at the interaction of leader behavior and situational circumstances. All of these theories involve some measurement of leader characteristics or behavior coupled with some measurement of the leadership situation.

Because of their complex analysis of specific situations, contingency theories provide useful approaches to improving leader effectiveness. However, the interventions suggested will depend on the theories' assumptions about leader behavior.

As you will see, the contingency theories have one of two orientations: Leader behavior is considered to be either relatively fixed, as characterized by Fiedler's model, or flexible. These two opposing views lead to very different strategies for applying the theories. If leader behavior is viewed as fixed, the situation must be changed to fit the leader if leader effectiveness is to be improved. If leader behavior is seen as flexible, leaders can be trained to fit situational requirements better.

The theories of leadership introduced in this chapter are directly related to topics discussed previously and also provide a background for upcoming chapters. Specifically, the topic of leadership follows the discussion of group processes in Chapter 11, as the relationship between leaders and other members of the work group is itself an important group process. Leadership and the leadership role are also linked to organizational communication (Chapter 10), particularly the downward flow of communication in organizations. Finally, this chapter will link up with the discussion of influence, power, and politics in Chapter 13, for it is clear that the most influential and powerful members of work groups are usually the leaders.

What Is Leadership?

In Chapter 11 we saw that individuals play various roles in work groups and organizations. One of these roles is that of leader, which in many groups is viewed as the key position. Rightly or wrongly, many people believe that the success or failure of a particular group is largely dependent on the leader and the type of leadership demonstrated. The importance placed on leadership has made it a major topic in politics, the military, and work organizations. Organizations spend millions of dollars annually trying to select managerial personnel who possess the qualities necessary to be effective leaders of work groups. Millions more are spent on training employees to be more effective leaders and to develop important leadership characteristics. Before we can study the qualities of leaders, however, we must first define and understand leadership.

DEFINING LEADERSHIP

There are a great number of definitions of leadership, but most of these definitions involve the leader using his or her influence to assist groups in attaining goals (Yukl & Van Fleet, 1992). Therefore, for our purposes, we will define **leadership** as the ability to direct a group toward the attainment of goals. Often, the leader of a work group is the person who holds a particular position or title, such as supervisor, manager, vice president, or leadperson. But there are such things as *informal* leaders. Thus, a work group leader can be a person with no official title or status. These informal leaders emerge because they have some characteristics that the group members value.

Regardless of whether a leader holds a formal leadership role, or emerges informally, a true leader should move followers toward the attainment of goals. Consequently, the fact that a manager or supervisor holds a position

leadership
ability to guide a group toward the achievement of goals

of responsibility does not necessarily make that person a true leader. Of course, in work organizations, a powerful position or title can provide a strong starting point for a person to become an effective leader, but a position or title alone will not make an effective leader. Therefore, our definition deals with *effective* leadership. We may all know (or have worked under) managers who were not effective leaders. They may actually have done nothing to help the group achieve work goals, or they may have even hindered the group's work. Such leaders are "leaders" in name only. This chapter will concentrate on theories of effective leadership.

There has been a long history of research on and theorizing about leadership. Leadership theories tend to build on one another, with later theories using components of earlier models and expanding on or using them in new ways. The discussion will begin with the earliest theories, which are known as universalist theories because they were attempts to uncover the universal characteristics of effective leaders. The second category consists of the behavioral theories, which focus on the behaviors of effective leaders. The largest category contains the more complex contingency theories, which examine the interaction between leader characteristics and elements of the work situation. Throughout the discussion, relevant research and applications of the theories will also be presented. In particular, we will compare and contrast the various theories. Finally, we will discuss how leadership theories can be used to improve the effectiveness of leadership in work organizations.

Universalist Theories Of Leadership

Universalist theories of leadership search for the one key characteristic or a cluster of key characteristics held by effective leaders, arguing that leaders with these traits will be successful regardless of the situation. Universalist theories represent the earliest and simplest approaches to the study of leadership. We will briefly discuss two of these theories, the great man/woman theory, and the trait theory.

GREAT MAN/WOMAN THEORY

The **great man/woman theory,** which is much older than any of the formal social science disciplines, reflects the adage that "great leaders are born, not made." Rather than being a formal theory, this theory is a belief that personal qualities and abilities make certain great persons natural leaders. Proponents of the great man/woman theory would state that if important historical leaders such as Julius Caesar, Alexander the Great, or Joan of Arc were alive today, they would again rise to positions of leadership because of their natural abilities. Of course this is mere speculation, and there is little evidence to support the theory, but this does not mean that people do not still believe in it. The fact that in certain countries the relatives of great leaders are also put into positions of power may indicate that there is some general faith in this notion of inborn leadership ability.

Does the fact that generations of Kennedys have held leadership positions suggest a belief in the great man theory?

universalist theories
theories that look for the major characteristics common to all effective leaders

great man/woman theory
a universalist theory of leadership that maintains that great leaders are born, not made

TRAIT THEORY

traits
enduring attributes associated with an individual's make-up or personality

trait theory
attempts to discover the traits shared by all effective leaders

In the early part of this century, psychologists made many attempts to isolate the specific **traits,** or consistent and enduring physical and personality attributes that are associated with leader success. The **trait theory** of leadership refers to several of these investigations. Much of this research involved identifying certain physical characteristics, including height, appearance, and energy level; other characteristics, such as intelligence; and personality traits, like extroversion, dominance, or achievement, that were associated with effective leaders (Hollander, 1985; Yukl, 1981). It was presumed, for example, that those who were more intelligent, extroverted, or dominant would be more likely to do well as leaders. Unfortunately, the results of these early studies were inconclusive, and showed no solid evidence of any single trait common to all effective leaders (Hollander, 1985; Stogdill, 1948).

Since the 1980s, however, there has been a resurgence of interest in leadership traits (Kenny & Zaccaro, 1983; Lord, DeVader, & Alliger, 1986; Zaccaro, Foti, & Kenny, 1991). This modern research has focused not on single, unidimensional personality traits, but on more complex "constellations" of leader characteristics, such as *flexibility*, *charisma*, or *social intelligence*. For example, Kenny and Zaccaro (1983, p. 678) describe flexibility as "the ability to perceive the needs and goals of a constituency and to adjust one's personal approach to group action accordingly." As such, leader flexibility may not be a single trait but instead a very complex set of abilities to perceive and understand social situations, to communicate effectively, and to act wisely in a variety of social settings (Marlowe, 1986; Riggio, 1986) that might be better termed "social intelligence" or "social competence" (Hollander, 1978). Certain characteristics, such as a leader's flexibility or social intelligence, may be significant in predicting leader success, although these key leader qualities are probably more complex and multifaceted than those investigated in early leadership research (Riggio & Murphy, 2000).

The major problem with the original trait approach to leadership was that it was too general. It is unlikely that any one trait will be associated with effective leadership in all situations, with all kinds of tasks, and among all groups of followers. The world of work, with the variety of workers and work settings, is much too complex and diverse for any one type of leader to be universally successful. On the other hand, complex constellations of leader characteristics, such as "flexibility" or "charisma", may be related to leader effectiveness, but these complex leader characteristics involve the leader adapting his or her behavior to the leadership situation. We will examine this approach of looking at the *interaction* of leader characteristics and the leadership situation in later theories of leadership.

Behavioral Theories Of Leadership

The general failure of the universalist theories to isolate the characteristics associated with leader effectiveness led to a change in focus. Rather than trying to measure characteristics in the leader's orientation or personality, researchers began to examine the actual behavior of effective leaders to determine what kinds of behavior led to success. In the late 1940s and throughout the 1950s, two research projects, one conducted at Ohio State University and the other at the University of Michigan, investigated the behaviors exhibited by effective leaders. Both projects arrived at some very similar conclusions concerning leaders, their behavior, and effective leadership. Theories based on these studies and focusing on the particular behaviors that related to effective leadership are called **behavioral theories of leadership.**

OHIO STATE LEADERSHIP STUDIES

Using self-reports and detailed observations of leader behavior from both the leaders themselves and their subordinates, researchers at Ohio State University accumulated a list of hundreds of leader behaviors. Using a statistical process called factor analysis, they found that these hundreds of behaviors could all be narrowed into two general categories: initiating structure and consideration (Halpin & Winer, 1957). (Recall from the Statistical Appendix that factor analysis examines how variables are related to each other and clusters them together to form meaningful categories, or factors.) **Initiating structure** includes leader activities that define and organize, or *structure*, the work situation, such as assigning specific tasks, defining work group roles, meeting deadlines, making task-related decisions, and maintaining standards of work performance. **Consideration** describes behaviors that show a genuine concern for the feelings, attitudes, and needs of subordinates by developing rapport with them and showing them mutual respect and trust. Such activities include asking subordinates for their opinions and input, showing concern for the feelings of workers, encouraging communication from and between subordinates, bolstering workers' self-confidence and job satisfaction, and implementing their suggestions.

The Ohio State researchers concluded that these two dimensions, initiating structure and consideration, were independent of each other. That is, a leader's score on one did not relate to the score on the other. This means that *both* categories of leader behavior are associated with effective leadership but that they do not necessarily coexist. In other words, some effective leaders are high on initiating structure alone, others display only consideration behaviors, and still others exhibit both.

A great deal of research has been conducted to test the soundness of the initiating structure and consideration dimensions. Generally, the results show that most leader behavior can indeed be grouped into one of the two categories (Bass, 1981, 1990; Fleishman & Harris, 1962; Schriesheim & Kerr, 1974; Stogdill & Coons, 1957). Additional studies have looked at how the two categories are related to the important outcome variables of work performance and job satisfaction (Kerr & Schriesheim, 1974; Yukl, 1971). Initiating structure has been found to be correlated with effective work performance but also with lower group member job satisfaction and corresponding increases in turnover. On the other hand, consideration leader

behavioral theories of leadership
theories derived from studies at Ohio State and Michigan that focus on the behaviors common to effective leaders

initiating structure
leader behaviors that define, organize, and structure the work situation

consideration
leader behaviors that show a concern for the feeling, attitudes, and needs of followers

Discuss the limitations of universalist theories of leadership.

behaviors tend to be positively related to job satisfaction but may be unrelated to or even negatively correlated with work productivity (Bass, 1981; Locke & Schweiger, 1978). However, these results are inconsistent. For example, one study found that the size of the work group affected the relationships between initiating structure and consideration leader behaviors and member satisfaction. Initiating structure was positively related to satisfaction in large groups but negatively related in small groups. The opposite relationships held for leader consideration: positively correlated with satisfaction in small groups and negatively related in large ones (Schriesheim & Murphy, 1976). The inconsistencies probably arise because the effectiveness of specific leader behaviors is likely to be dependent on a number of other factors that serve as moderating variables that can determine whether a particular behavior will be related to a certain outcome, such as group performance or satisfaction, in a given situation. For instance, in the example above the size of the work group is the moderating variable, affecting the relationship between leader behavior and specific work outcomes.

While the Ohio State behavioral approach stimulated a great deal of research on effective leader behaviors, it, like the universalist theories, is too simplistic. The Ohio State investigations leave us with two categories of leader behavior, both of which may or may not be related to certain indicators of leader effectiveness. While the results had the positive effect of stimulating research on leader behaviors, it is clear that the Ohio State studies fall short when it comes to making firm predictions about the relationships between leader behaviors and specific work outcomes in all types of working situations.

UNIVERSITY OF MICHIGAN LEADERSHIP STUDIES

At about the same time as the Ohio State studies were being conducted, researchers at the University of Michigan were also focusing on the behaviors characteristic of effective leaders and came up with quite similar results. Studying leaders in a number of large industrial organizations, the Michigan researchers found that successful leaders tended to exhibit patterns of behavior that were labeled task-oriented, sometimes also called "production-oriented," and relationship-oriented, also referred to as "employee-oriented" (Kahn & Katz, 1960). **Task-oriented behaviors** are concentrated on performing the job that the work group faces and are thus similar to those of the initiating structure factor. The leader is concerned with setting work standards, supervising the job, and meeting production goals. **Relationship-oriented behaviors** include showing concern for employees' well-being and involving them in decision-making processes. The primary difference between the Ohio State and Michigan studies was that the Michigan results tended to consider relationship-oriented leader behaviors to be more effective than task-oriented behaviors (Likert, 1967). One of the most famous Michigan studies examined the behavior of leaders in a large insurance company. The findings indicated that both task-oriented and relationship-

task-oriented behaviors
leader behaviors focused on the work task

relationship-oriented behaviors
leader behaviors focused on maintaining interpersonal relationships on the job

oriented leadership behavior patterns were positively related to work group performance. However, subordinates of relationship-oriented leaders tended to be more satisfied and had lower turnover rates than employees who were managed by task-oriented leaders (Morse & Reimer, 1956; see also Up Close: How to Be an Effective Leader).

EVALUATION OF THE BEHAVIORAL THEORIES OF LEADERSHIP

While initiating structure (task orientation) and consideration (relationship orientation) seem to be reliable dimensions describing leader behavior, the behavioral approach has one major shortcoming: The two dimensions represent very different types of leader behavior, yet both have been linked to effective management (Bass, 1981; Morse & Reimer, 1956). If we believe the universalist contention that there is one set of effective leader characteristics or one best leadership style, such divergent leader behaviors simply cannot represent a single, effective leader. The most likely explanation is that other variables, particularly those related to the type of tasks or the characteristics of the work group, determine whether certain leadership behaviors will be effective. In other words, a task-oriented leader might be effective in certain situations under specific circumstances, while a relationship-oriented leader might be effective in another situation.

APPLYING I/O PSYCHOLOGY

The Leadership Grid®: The Marketing of Leadership Theory

One of the more successful and widespread applications of leadership theory to the business world is known as the **Leadership Grid** (formerly known as the Managerial Grid; Blake & Mouton, 1985; Blake & McCanse, 1991). This leadership intervention program encompasses two core dimensions—people emphasis and production emphasis. These are attitudinal in character and are to be distinguished from the behavioral dimensions identified in the research originating with the Ohio State and Michigan studies. The basic premise of the Leadership Grid is that the best leaders are those who show both high concern for the task and production and high concern for people. Each leader is rated on two nine-point scales, the first assessing the leader's production orientation, the second measuring the leader's people orientation. The best leader receives a score of 9,9, meaning someone high in both production and people orientation (labeled a "team manager"); the worst leader receives a 1,1 rating, meaning someone low in both production and people orientation (labeled an "impoverished manager"; see the accompanying diagram). By stating that there is one best leadership style (the 9,9 leader), the Leadership Grid takes a universalist approach, which is a departure from the results of the Ohio State studies indicating that either task/production orientation or relationship/people orientation could

Leadership Grid
an application of the findings from the behavioral theories of leadership that stresses that effective leaders should be both task-oriented and relationship-oriented

be related to leader effectiveness (see Figure 12.1)

The Leadership Grid has been criticized primarily because of its universalist approach. Most researchers advocate that there is no one best leadership style and that effective leadership depends on how the leader's style fits with the particular work situation. In spite of some criticisms, the Leadership Grid has had significant impact. According to the authors, the program has "boosted productivity and profits for thousands of corporations worldwide"; they claim that Leadership Grid training has been provided to nearly half a million leaders and managers. In fact, the program has been so well packaged that its name is a registered trademark.

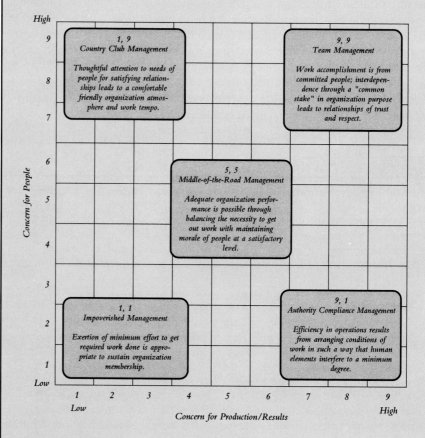

FIGURE 12.1

Leadership Grid
Source: Robert R. Blake and Anne Adams McCanse, *Leadership Dilemmas—Grid Solutions* (Houston, TX: Gulf, 1991).

APPLYING I/O PSYCHOLOGY (*continued*)

Most of these praises, however, are based on the testimonials of client organizations who have used (and paid for) the Leadership Grid. There has been little systematic research on the theory behind the grid by persons other than its authors, although Tjosvold (1984b) found that leaders who were task-oriented and who demonstrated a relationship orientation by expressing leader warmth led groups that were more productive than those led by leaders who lacked both of these orientations—but this is a far cry from conclusive support for the Leadership Grid.

Contingency Theories Of Leadership

The next stage in the evolution of leadership theories produced **contingency theories,** which examine the interaction of characteristics of the leader and the situation, stating that effective leadership depends on the proper match between the two. Many of the contingency theories do, however, build on the behavioral theories, using the leader behavior dichotomies—task-oriented/initiating structure and relationship-oriented/consideration—as a starting point. However, contingency theories recognize no one best style of leadership behavior. Rather, leader effectiveness depends, or is *contingent* upon, the interaction of leader behavior and the situation. We will examine four of the more popular contingency theories of leadership: Fiedler's contingency model, the path-goal theory, the decision-making model, and the leader-member exchange model.

contingency theories
theories that look at the interaction of characteristics of both the leader and the situation

STOP AND REVIEW

Compare and contrast the findings of the Ohio State and Michigan behavioral studies of leadership.

FIEDLER'S CONTINGENCY MODEL

The leadership theory proposed by psychologist Fred Fiedler (1967) is so well-known that it is often simply referred to as *the* contingency model. But, as outlined, the term "contingency model" actually specifies a certain category of theory. **Fiedler's contingency model** argues that effective leadership depends on a match between a leader's behavioral style and the degree to which the work situation gives control and influence to the leader. In other words, the leader's style of behavior must fit with the amount of control and power the leader will have in the work situation.

Building on the Ohio State and Michigan behavioral approaches, Fiedler's theory divides leaders based on their primary motivation—task-oriented or relationship-oriented—which he sees as relatively fixed and stable. According to Fiedler, certain leaders may be primarily concerned with getting the job done (task-oriented), although they are also concerned with

Fiedler's contingency model
a leadership theory that maintains that effective leadership depends on a match between the leader's style and the degree to which the work situation gives control and influence to the leader

maintaining good group relations. Other leaders focus primarily on relationships and give "secondary" concern to the task. In other words, leaders differ on which motivation takes precedence in most situations. A task-oriented leader will attend less to the group, and the relationship-oriented leader will tend to focus on the group at the expense of the task.

To measure a leader's orientation, Fiedler developed a self-report measure referred to as the **LPC** measure, which stands for **least preferred coworker.** The LPC requires leaders to rate the person with whom they had worked least well—"the person with whom you had the most difficulty in getting a job done." These ratings are done using bipolar adjective rating scales, such as pleasant/unpleasant and friendly/unfriendly (see Figure 12.2). The LPC is scored by summing the ratings on the scales. This total score indicates whether a person is a task-oriented or relationship-oriented leader. Persons scoring relatively low on the LPC measure, giving their least preferred coworkers very harsh ratings, are task-oriented leaders. Individuals who rate their least preferred coworker somewhat leniently, leading to relatively high LPC scores, are considered to be relationship-oriented. Scores from normative populations help determine what are low and high LPC scores. The rationale behind this scoring system is that task-oriented leaders will be very critical of a poor worker because they value task success. A relationship-oriented leader, on the other hand, values interpersonal relationships and is likely to rate the least preferred coworker more leniently (Rice, 1978). According to Fiedler, task-oriented leaders with low LPC scores link a worker's poor performance with undesirable personality characteristics, while relationship-oriented leaders with high LPC scores can separate the least preferred coworker's personality from the individual's work performance (Fiedler, 1967).

Determining a leader's task or relationship orientation with the LPC is only the first part of Fiedler's contingency model. The next step is defining characteristics of the work situation to find the proper match between leadership style and the situation. The characteristics of a work situation are defined using three variables—leader-member relations, task structure, and position power—that combine to create circumstances that are either very favorable, very unfavorable, or neither favorable nor unfavorable for the leader.

Leader-member relations is the relationship between the leader and followers—in other words, how well liked, respected, and trusted the leader is by subordinates. According to Fiedler, this dimension can be measured on a scale involving good and poor ratings by having group members indicate their loyalty for and acceptance of the leader.

The second dimension, **task structure,** assesses how well a job is structured by considering such factors as whether the group's output can be easily evaluated, whether the group has well-defined goals, and whether clear procedures for reaching those goals exist. Tasks can be defined as "structured" or "unstructured."

The third dimension that Fiedler uses to define the situation is **position power,** or the leader's authority over subordinates, which is usually defined as the leader's ability to hire, fire, discipline, and reward. Position power is

---

least preferred coworker (LPC)
a measure that assesses leaders' task or relationship orientation by having them rate their most difficult fellow worker

leader-member relations
the quality of the relationship between leader and followers

task structure
an assessment of how well elements of the work task are structured

position power
a leader's authority to punish or reward followers

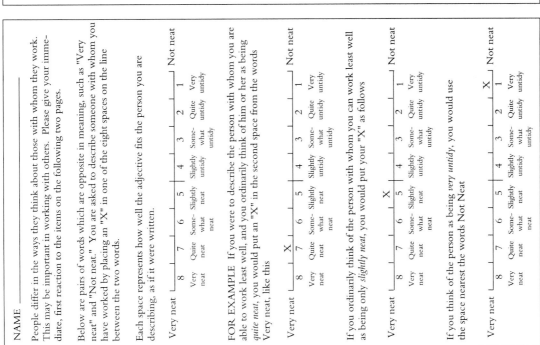

FIGURE 12.2

Least Preferred Co-worker (LPC) Measure
Source: F.E. Fiedler. *A Theory of Leadership Effectiveness* (New York: McGraw-Hill, 1967),
pp 40–41.

According to Fiedler, leader-member relations reflect the respect workers have for their leader.

assessed as either strong or weak. It is usually easy to determine position power, because it is clearly outlined in company policies.

Recall that according to Fiedler's contingency model, the key to effective leadership is the leader's control and influence in a specific situation. Obviously, the situation that is going to be most favorable for the leader is one in which the leader-member relations are good, the task is structured, and the leader has strong position power. The least favorable situation for the leader is one where leader-member relations are poor, the task is unstructured, and the leader has weak position power. Research indicates that task-oriented leaders with low LPC scores are most effective in situations that are either highly favorable or highly unfavorable for the leader—the two extremes of the continuum. Relationship-oriented leaders are more effective in "middle situations" in which the leader's control and influence are neither low nor high.

According to Fiedler, task-oriented leaders with low LPC scores are successful in very unfavorable situations because their take-charge style puts some structure into the circumstances and may encourage the group to perform the job. In other words, in an extremely unfavorable situation, the task-oriented leader has nothing to lose. Taking a firm hand and focusing on task performance and task-related goals may produce results, which is what is needed in such a crisis. At these times followers might walk all over a relationship-oriented leader. In very favorable situations, groups are already likely to be productive because the task is straightforward and structured, relations between leader and members are good, and the leader has the power to reward for good performance. According to Fiedler (1967), in these settings low-LPC leaders actually shift from their dominant, task-oriented style and focus more on relationship-oriented behaviors, which is an effective strategy. Although it may seem that high-LPC, relationship-oriented leaders would be more effective in very favorable situations, such persons are actually less effective than low-LPC leaders because, according to Fiedler, they retreat from the dominant, relationship-oriented style and actually become task-oriented.

Relationship-oriented leaders are more successful when their situational control and influence are neither very high nor low. In these "middle" circumstances, it is important that leaders be well-equipped to deal with the interpersonal conflicts that inevitably arise. This is the specialty of the high-LPC, relationship-oriented leaders. Because such situations may lack one of the three situational variables, a leader who shows increased concern for workers and allows them to voice opinions may increase group member satisfaction levels and even job performance. By contrast, being task-oriented in these situations may be counterproductive, alienating members and decreasing levels of satisfaction, because the leader appears to care only about the task. Fiedler also argues that high-LPC leaders may be more cognitively complex, or better able to deal with complex situations. Situations that are neither clearly favorable nor clearly unfavorable for the leader are complex and are best handled by such a person.

Figure 12.3 is a graphic representation of the predictions made by the Fiedler model. The graph shows that task-oriented leaders (solid line) have higher group performance when in very favorable or very unfavorable situations. Relationship-oriented leaders (dotted line) lead higher-performing groups in situations of moderate favorability.

Although some studies have failed to find the predictions made by Fiedler's theory (Vecchio, 1977), others have generally supported the model (Peters, Hartke, & Pohlmann, 1985; Strube & Garcia, 1981). However, the predictions hold up better in laboratory studies than in studies conducted in actual work settings (Peters, Hartke, & Pohlmann, 1985). Critics have focused primarily on the use of the LPC measure, arguing that it is not clear exactly what it measures since it only infers a leader's orientation from feelings about a coworker rather than directly assessing task and relationship orientation (Ashour, 1973; Schriesheim, Bannister, & Money, 1979). Another criticism concerns individuals who score near the middle of the LPC scale. In fact, one researcher divided the ratings into high, low, *and* middle scores and found that the middle-LPC leaders seemed to be effective in a range of situations (Kennedy, 1982). Another weakness in Fiedler's predictions concerns the assessment of situations, for it is not clear how actual work situations would break down in terms of their favorableness for the leader. In other words, we do not know how many real-world situations would be favorable or very unfavorable for the leader and thus demand a task-oriented leader. Nor do we know how many situations are moderately favorable for the leader or what distinctions there are between moderately favorable situations (i.e., are there "low moderate" and "high moderate" favorable situations?).

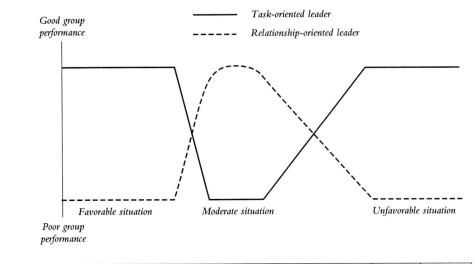

Good group
performance

———— Task-oriented leader

- - - - - Relationship-oriented leader

Poor group
performance

Leader-member relations	Good	Good	Good	Good	Poor	Poor	Poor	Poor
Task structure	Struc-tured	Struc-tured	Unstruc-tured	Unstruc-tured	Struc-tured	Struc-tured	Unstruc-tured	Unstruc-tured
Position power	Strong	Weak	Strong	Weak	Strong	Weak	Strong	Weak

FIGURE 12.3

Fiedler's Contingency Model Predictions

In spite of these criticisms, the Fiedler contingency model is important for many reasons. First, it was the first highly visible leadership theory to present the contingency approach. Second, its detailed attention to the situation emphasized the importance of both situation and leader characteristics in determining leader effectiveness. Third, Fiedler's model stimulated a great deal of research, including tests of its predictions and attempts to improve on the model, and inspired the formulation of alternative contingency theories. Finally, it also led to the development of a program by Fiedler and his colleagues (Fiedler & Chemers, 1984) to apply his theory to actual leadership situations. Known as Leader Match, their program consists of a workbook containing an LPC measure, leadership problems that the leader must analyze and solve, directions on how to assess elements of the leader's situation, guidelines for changing elements of the situation, and suggestions for helping subordinates improve performance. Basically, Leader Match teaches managers to recognize their own leadership orientation using the LPC and then trains them to recognize those situations in which they are most likely to succeed. If a mismatch is discovered between the leader's orientation and the work situation, suggestions are made for changing one or more of the three situational variables to provide a more appropriate fit. For example, if a low-LPC, task-oriented leader is in a situation of moderate favorability in which leader-member relations are fair, the task is unstructured, but position power is strong, an attempt might be made either to improve leader-member relations or to make the group work task more structured to increase the favorability of the situation and thus make it more compatible with the leader. The Leader Match program holds that it is more effective to change the situation, or to fit certain types of leaders to appropriate situations, than it is to try to change the leader's style of behavior.

Leader Match has been widely used. Fiedler claims that is has been used by more than 40,000 managers. Although the program has been shown to be quite successful in increasing managers' leadership effectiveness (Leister, Borden, & Fiedler, 1977), it is not without its critics, who argue that at times Leader Match does not follow the predictions made by the theory (Jago & Ragan, 1986; Kabanoff, 1981).

In sum, Fiedler's contingency model was one of the first detailed theories of leadership. It makes certain predictions about the situations in which certain types of leaders will be effective, and has been a straightforward and widely used intervention for improving leader effectiveness (Ayman, Chemers, & Fiedler, 1995).

Define the three situational characteristics in Fiedler's contingency model.

THE PATH-GOAL THEORY

Expanding on the definition of leadership presented at the start of this chapter, the **path-goal theory** states that a leader's job is to help the work group attain the goals that they desire (House, 1971; House & Mitchell, 1974). The leader is accordingly seen as a facilitator, or guide, who helps the group overcome the various barriers and roadblocks they may encounter on the way to achieving their goals. Usually these goals involve increasing worker motivation to perform the job and attempting to gain increases in worker satisfaction. As is reflected in its emphasis on worker motivation, the expectancy theory of motivation (see Chapter 7) was used as the foundation for the path-goal theory (Yukl, 1998).

To help the group reach its goals, the leader may adopt one of four categories of behavior—directive, achievement-oriented, supportive, and participative—the selection of which depends on the characteristics of the situation. **Directive behavior** provides instructions and suggestions for getting the job done. Examples include giving workers specific guidelines and procedures, setting up schedules and work rules, and coordinating work group activities. **Achievement-oriented behavior** focuses on specific work outcomes and may involve setting challenging goals for the group and measuring and encouraging improvements in performance. **Supportive behavior** concentrates on the interpersonal relations among group members by showing concern for workers' well-being and providing a

path-goal theory
states that a leader's job is to help the work group achieve their desired goals

directive behavior
leader behavior that provides instructions and suggestions for performing a job

achievement-oriented behavior
leader behavior concentrated on particular work outcomes

supportive behavior
leader behavior focusing on interpersonal relationships and showing concern for workers' well-being

friendly work environment. Finally, **participative behavior** encourages members to take an active role in work-group planning and decision making through actions such as soliciting information from workers about how to do the job and asking for opinions and suggestions. These four types of leader behaviors outlined in the path-goal theory offer a more detailed breakdown of the initiating structure (task-oriented) and consideration (relationship-oriented) behaviors: Directive and achievement-oriented behaviors are two kinds of initiating structure behavior, while the supportive and participative behaviors are two kinds of consideration behaviors.

The choice of leader behavior is contingent on the type of work task and the characteristics of the followers. For example, if a task is routine and easy to understand and if the work group is made up of experienced, self-motivated individuals, the directive style of leadership would probably not be needed since followers can perform the job without much supervision. Instead, supportive behavior might be called for to maintain a harmonious work setting, or participative behavior may be necessary to encourage employees to suggest ways to improve work procedures and the work environment. On the other hand, if the task is fairly complex and the workers are somewhat inexperienced, a directive style might be appropriate.

The results of research on the path-goal theory have been mixed (House, 1996). While there has been some support for the model (Downey, Sheridan, & Slocum, 1976; House & Dessler, 1974; Wofford & Liska, 1993), its general approach and its inability to make specific and precise predictions in actual work settings have been criticized (Schriesheim & Kerr, 1977; Yukl, 1989). While the theory does offer some idea of how leaders must change their behavior to fit the situation, the biggest disappointment is that it has not led to a specific type of intervention for use on the job (Miner, 1983). On the positive side, like Fiedler's contingency model, the path-goal theory offers a rather detailed assessment of the situation in an effort to relate the leader's behavior to the characteristics of a specific situation. It also goes a step beyond the simple dichotomy of task orientation and relationship orientation in defining leader behavior.

THE DECISION-MAKING MODEL

As seen in Chapter 11, one of the major tasks of a work group leader is to preside over important work-related decisions. Vroom and his colleagues (Vroom & Jago, 1988; Vroom & Yetton, 1973) have developed a contingency theory of leadership called the **decision-making model** that is based on the premise that leaders are basically decision makers. This theory is somewhat unique in that it not only makes predictions about proper leader behavior in making decisions but also actually gives "prescriptions" for the decision maker to follow. The decision-making theory holds that a leader can make work decisions using a number of strategies, ranging from acting alone (purely autocratic decision making) to arriving at a decision on the basis of group consensus (completely participative decision making). In the latter type of decision making the leader is just another group member. The five decision-making styles used in the decision-making model are presented in Table 12.1.

To define the decision-making situation, the theory provides a series of yes-no work-related questions that a leader must ask before adopting a particular strategy. For example, the first question is whether or not a high-quality decision is needed. If the leader answers "yes," it is likely that a more participative style is needed; if the answer is "no," it is likely that a more autocratic style is appropriate. Of course, the decision making style chosen is a composite of all questions. The decision-making model presents a decision tree framework for the leader to follow, with each of the seven questions representing a choice point that eventually leads to the correct behavior for the decision that needs to be made (see Figure 12.4). Consider, for example, the manager of the parts department of an automobile dealer who must purchase a computerized inventory system for the department. A number of systems are available, each with its own advantages and drawbacks. The leader answers each of the questions on the decision tree as follows:

a. Yes, there is a need for quality—a computer system that will work best in our department.

b. No, the leader doesn't have enough information to make a quality decision alone.

c. No, the problem is not structured, because there is no clear-cut way to decide among the various systems.

d. Yes, subordinates will be using the system and need to accept it.

e. No, if subordinates did not like the computer system they might avoid using it.

f. Yes, workers do share organizational goals (they want a computer system that will do the job).

g. Not applicable.

This framework suggests that the leader should use a group strategy to arrive at a consensus. Since the department is small and the workers are involved in their jobs, they can contribute a great deal to the decision-making process, and it is critical that they accept the decision.

Research has largely supported this decision-making model (Field, 1982; Margerison & Glube, 1979; Paul & Ebadi, 1989). For example, a study found that the effective strategies used by actual managers to solve important work-related decisions were consistent with the theory's prescriptions (Vroom and Jago, 1978). Because of the normative nature of the model, it is also a unique combination of theory and application. As a contingency model, it is effective because it considers how a leader's individual behavior fits with the dynamics of a specific situation. Moreover, it provides a very detailed definition of the situation, as outlined by the decision-related questions. The major problem with the model is its complexity, which may make it difficult for managers to understand and to learn to use.

STOP AND REVIEW

What are the four leader behaviors central to the path-goal theory?

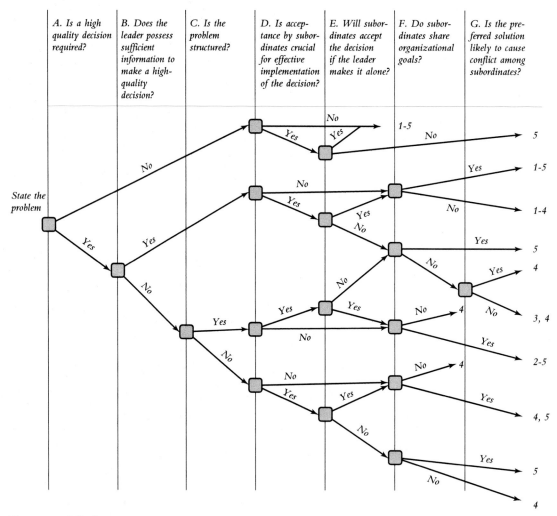

FIGURE 12.4

Decision Tree Flow Chart (Table 12.1)

(In fact, revisions to the decision-making theory have further refined it, and made it even more complex and precise than what is presented in Figure 12.4 (Vroom & Jago, 1995). This occurs to theories in general: As they get closer to modeling real world complexity, they may also become harder to apply. There is a general tendency for people to look for relatively simple solutions to problems. Thus, while complex contingency models, such as the decision-making model, might be sound and accurate, they may not be widely used or accepted in actual work settings due to their complex nature.

TABLE 12.1

Five Decision-Making Strategies: The Model

Decision Making Strategy	Process
1. Autocratic decision I	The leader makes the decision alone, using information available only to the leader.
2. Autocratic decision II	The leader obtains information from subordinates and then makes the decision alone.
3. Consultative decision I	The leader shares the problem with relevant subordinates and gets their ideas and input individually, but makes the decision alone.
4. Consultative decision II	The leader shares the problem with subordinates as a group, gets their collective input, but makes the decision alone.
5. Group decision	The leader shares the problem with subordinates as a group and together they make a consensus decision.

Source: V.H. Vroom and P.W. Yetton, *Leadership and Decision-Making* (Pittsburgh: University of Pittsburgh Press, 1973), p. 13.

UP CLOSE

How to Be an Effective Leader

It is very likely that sometime in the near future you will find yourself in a leadership role. You may serve as a formal manager of a work group, you may be elected to serve as a leader of a club or civic organization, or you may be appointed head of some work task force. In any case, the research on leadership as well as other findings that we have studied in the areas of communication and group dynamics can help you to do a better job. Of course, as you should know by now, there is no one best way to lead. There are, however, some general principles that you can follow to increase your chances of success:

Become a More Effective Communicator

It has been estimated that as much as 80 percent of a manager's job involves communication (Mintzberg, 1973). As we saw in Chapter 10, communication is essential for the effective functioning of work groups and organizations. The better the channels of communication between the leader and followers, the more likely it is that the two will be able to cooperate to get the task done. It is particularly important to listen to subordinates and be sensitive to their needs and concerns. In fact, effective listening may be a leader's

UP CLOSE (*continued*)

most important skill (Harris, 1993). The leader who steals away behind closed doors will be unable to meet these needs, which may lead to breakdowns in productivity and in work group satisfaction.

Be Both Task-Oriented and Relationship-Oriented

As the research indicates, both task-oriented and relationship-oriented behaviors are related to leader effectiveness (Bass, 1990). Therefore, leaders who are able to display concern for both the task and the people are more likely to be successful. Gaining insight into your own leader behavior patterns will help you to realize if you have a deficit in either area.

Give Careful Attention to Decision Making

One of the leader's most important tasks is decision making. As we have seen, in addition to reaching a good and workable solution, the process itself is also important. For example, involving subordinates in the decision can increase their levels of satisfaction but usually also leads to slower decision making. The decision-making leadership model emphasizes flexibility—adapting the leader's decision-making style to the situation. Certain decisions may call for more autocratic decision making; others demand a participative approach. Being able to determine what process to use in what situation is the key. However, since evidence indicates that subordinates are generally satisfied with participative decision making, when in doubt it may be wise to use this style.

Remember that Leadership is a Two-Way Street

While leaders influence their followers, followers also influence their leaders. A leader can be truly effective only if that person has the support of followers (Meindl, 1990; Palich & Hom, 1992). An effective leader knows what his or her own needs are and works to satisfy those needs, but the effective leader is also in tune with, and responsive to, the needs of followers.

Learn to Delegate

Effective leaders learn to delegate certain challenging and responsible tasks to subordinates, which often not only develops their work skills and abilities, thus making them more valuable to the leader and to the organization, but also gives the leader more time to work on other duties, leading to higher levels of productivity. Hughes, Ginnett, and Curphy (1996) provide guidelines for effective delegation. These include choosing what to delegate, and to whom; making the assignment clear and specific; allowing subordinate autonomy, but monitoring performance (after all, the leader is ultimately responsible that the task is completed); and "giving credit, not blame."

Monitor Subordinates' Performance, Set Challenging Goals, and Give Constructive Feedback

Field studies of work groups from a variety of settings indicates that effective leaders keep tabs on what work group members are doing, and provide constructive feedback to help subordinates improve performance and correct errors (Komaki,

UP CLOSE (continued)

1986; Komaki, Desselles, & Bowman, 1989). In addition, effective leaders use effective goal setting to motivate followers (see Chapter 7), to help monitor performance, and to provide a forum for providing constructive feedback.

Be Flexible

Effective leadership means doing the right thing in the right situation. Effective leaders are thus flexible or adaptable. One way to be more flexible is to step back and objectively analyze a situation before you act. Leaders should also be objective about their own feelings, behaviors, attitudes, and biases, and how they may negatively affect leadership ability. Sometimes, leaders fall into comfortable patterns of behavior, using the same leadership style in all situations simply because it is easier than adapting behavior to fit the situation. However, it is the objective, adaptable leaders who are successful.

THE LEADER-MEMBER EXCHANGE MODEL

The previous contingency models of leadership, including Fiedler's model and the path-goal theory, fit the leader's behavior to various characteristics of the work situation. Fiedler's model also considers the amount of power a leader has in a given situation, while the decision-making theory weighs a variety of characteristics related to a situation. The **leader-member exchange model (LMX)** takes a different approach and considers that effective leadership is determined by the quality of the interaction between the leader and a particular work group member (Dansereau, Graen, & Haga, 1975; Graen & Uhl-Bien, 1995). According to this theory, the worker *is* the situation. Basically, the model (which was formerly called the vertical dyad linkage model) states that the types of one-on-one, or dyadic, relationships that develop between the leader and each follower will be somewhat different. In any work group, the leader tends to develop better relationships with a few subordinates (the in-group), while the rest receive less attention or concern from the leader (the out-group). The character of the leader-member exchange can range from low quality, in which the leader has a negative image of the subordinate and the subordinate does not respect or trust the leader, to high quality, in which the leader has a positive view of the worker and the worker feels that the leader is supportive and provides encouragement. Of course, such differences affect important outcomes such as work performance, employee loyalty and attendance, and job satisfaction (Graen, Novak, & Sommerkamp, 1982; Klein & Kim, 1998; Kozlowski & Doherty, 1989; Liden & Maslyn, 1998; Wayne & Ferris, 1990).

The notion that leaders develop different types and quality of relationships with subordinates makes sense. For example, the president of a large company may have to interact with a number of department managers.

leader-member exchange model (LMX)
a theory that effective leadership is determined by the quality of the interaction between the leader and particular group members

Describe the strengths and weaknesses of the decision-making theory of leadership.

Some of them may be the trusted advisers with whom the president interacts quite frequently and to whom he gives an important role in establishing company policy. The president's relationships with other managers may not be close at all, and they may in fact have very little actual contact with the president. Naturally, and as the LMX model predicts, the motivation to perform and the levels of satisfaction of the in-group managers are likely to be high, while the out-group managers may not be very motivated or satisfied.

The authors of the LMX claim that their approach is an improvement over other leadership theories because previous models assume that leaders act in a relatively uniform way toward all subordinates. Because these traditional approaches look only at typical, or average, leader behavior and ignore the nontypical behavior displayed in very good or very poor leader-member exchanges, a focus on specific leader-member relations will lead to better predictions of the effects of that leader behavior on work outcomes (Dansereau et al., 1975; Graen, 1976; see also Vecchio, 1982). In other words, rather than looking at how the leader's behavior influences a particular outcome in subordinates, the LMX approach generally emphasizes how a leader's particular behavior with particular subordinates—both in-group and out-group members—affects their specific job outcomes.

The leader-member exchange model is quite popular and has generated a considerable amount of research. A number of improvements have been made to the theory, including improvements in measuring in-group/out-group membership and the quality of leader-member exchanges (Duchon, Green, & Taber, 1986; Fairhurst, 1993; Graen & Scandura, 1985; Liden & Maslyn, 1998; Phillips & Bedeian, 1994).

The strategy for applying LMX to improving leader effectiveness seems relatively straightforward: Improve the quality of leader-member relationships. Initial tests of leadership training programs aimed at this goal have been encouraging. For example, in one study of 83 computer-processing employees of a large service organization, a program that trained leaders to listen and communicate their expectations to subordinates led to a 19 percent increase in work group productivity and significant increases in subordinates' job satisfaction (Scandura & Graen, 1984). In another study, the quality of leader-member exchanges between supervisors and newly hired employees in the newcomers' first five days on the job predicted the quality of leader-member exchanges at six months, indicating the importance of developing good quality supervisor-subordinate interactions early on (Liden, Wayne, & Stilwell, 1993).

Additional Leadership Theories

While contingency theories of leadership focus on the interaction between a leader's behavior or style and elements of the situation, other leadership theorists have focused on the truly "exceptional" leaders. For example, when we think of exceptional leaders throughout history and the truly great leaders of today, they seem to do more than simply adapt their behavior to the situation. These leaders seem to have the ability to inspire or "energize" followers toward organizational goals. They are often able to "transform" groups of workers into highly effective teams. Great leaders, in effect, inspire followers to become leaders themselves. We will briefly examine two additional theories of leadership that deal with these exceptional types of leaders: charismatic leadership theory and transformational leadership.

CHARISMATIC LEADERSHIP THEORY

We can all think of great political and social leaders who possessed charisma—Winston Churchill, Martin Luther King, Jr., Eleanor Roosevelt, John F. Kennedy, Mahatma Gandhi. There are also charismatic business leaders who seem to inspire and captivate their employees—Lee Iacocca, Steve Jobs. **Charismatic leadership theory** focuses on such exceptional leaders and tries to identify and define the characteristics that these leaders possess that inspire followers to identify with and to be devoted to them, and also outlines the nature of the relationship charismatic leaders have with followers (Klein & House, 1995; Trice & Beyer, 1986; Weierter, 1997). According to House (1977), charismatic leaders have the ability to communicate shared group goals, and they convey confidence in their own abilities as well as those of their followers. Elements of the situation also come into play, however, since charismatic leaders are often most effective in situations where goals are unclear and environmental conditions are uncertain or unstable, presumably because charismatic leaders are able to provide some vision of where the group should be headed (House & Singh, 1987).

charismatic leadership theory
states that leaders possess some exceptional characteristics that cause followers to be loyal and inspired

There is some speculation that the "exceptional" characteristics or qualities of charismatic leaders are related to the possession of exceptionally high social skills, and an ability to relate to (and inspire) followers at a deep, emotional level (Hogan, Raskin, & Fazzini, 1990; Riggio, 1987). Conger and Kanungo (1987, 1998) propose that the key characteristics of charismatic leaders include sensitivity to followers and the situation/environment, ability to inspire, and a desire to change the status quo. It has also been suggested that follower characteristics, such as identification with the leader, susceptibility to the leader's emotional messages, and a willingness to follow, are components of charismatic leadership. Thus, charismatic leadership is indeed an interaction of leader, follower, and situation, as shown in Figure 12.5.

An interesting study applied charismatic leadership theory to the effectiveness of U.S. presidents (House, Spangler, & Woycke, 1991). In this study, the charisma of all U.S. presidents from Washington to Reagan were rated using historical documents. It was found that the more charismatic the president, the more effective he was in dealing with the economy and with domestic affairs—those factors that most directly impact the followers.

Leader Characteristics

Communication of: vision and goals
self-confidence
confidence in followers
Ability to inspire
Desire to change, innovate, and take risks
Sensitivity to followers and situations

Follower Characteristics

Situational Circumstances

Identification with leaders
Emotional Susceptibility
Desire for change and growth

Conditions of uncertainty, ambiguity
or crisis
Opportunities for growth, change,
or innovation

FIGURE 12.5

Charismatic Leadership Theory Is an Interaction Among Leader Characteristics, Follower Characteristics, and Elements of the Situation.

TRANSACTIONAL VERSUS TRANSFORMATIONAL LEADERSHIP

transactional leadership
leadership based on some transaction, such as exchanging money for work

transformational leadership
focuses on the leader's ability to provide shared values and a vision for the future for the work group

Another prominent leadership theory distinguishes between transactional and transformational leadership (Burns, 1978). **Transactional leadership** occurs when the relationship between leader and followers is based on some sort of exchange or "transaction," such as exchanging money or praise for work, or exchanging leader consideration behaviors for employee loyalty and commitment. **Transformational leadership** involves the leader changing the values, beliefs and attitudes of followers. In other words, in transactional approaches the leader and followers can be seen as involved in an implicit or explicit agreement whereby followers devote time and energy to pursuing organizational goals, and the leader, in exchange, provides rewards and job security. The transformational leader, however, inspires followers by providing a vision of where the group is headed, and developing a work culture that stimulates high-performance activities (Bass, 1990). Transformational leaders are viewed as responsible for performance beyond ordinary expectations as they transmit a sense of mission, stimulate workers' learning experiences, and inspire new and creative ways of thinking (Hater & Bass, 1988). To provide a better understanding of transformational leadership, Table 12.2 presents six categories of behavior associated with transformational leaders.

Recent years have seen an explosion of research interest on both charismatic and transformational leadership. A meta-analysis of more than 20 studies found that transformational leadership was superior to transactional leadership in fostering work group effectiveness (Lowe, Kroeck, & Sivasubramaniam, 1996). Moreover, the positive effects of transformational leader-

TABLE 12.2

Behaviors Associated with Transformational Leaders

1. *Identifying and articulating a vision*—The transformational leader develops, conveys, and inspires followers with an exciting vision of the work unit's future.
2. *Providing an appropriate model*—The leader sets an example by adhering to behaviors and expressing attitudes that are consistent with the unit's values. In other words, the leader "practices what the leader preaches."
3. *Fostering the acceptance of group goals*—The leader promotes cooperation among group members in working toward common goals.
4. *Maintaining high performance expectations*—The leader encourages excellence and spurs followers to high levels of performance and work quality.
5. *Providing individualized support*—The leader indicates respect for followers and concern for their personal feelings and needs.
6. *Providing intellectual stimulation*—The leader challenges followers to reexamine their assumptions about their work and to rethink ways that the work can be performed.

Source: P.M. Podsakof, S.B. MacKenzie, R.H. Moorman, and R. Fetter, (1990) "Transformational Leader Behaviors and Their Effects on Followers' Trust in Leader, Satisfaction, and Organizational Citizenship Behaviors." *Leadership Quarterly,* 1, pp. 107–42.

ship on group performance hold for groups as varied as student leaders in laboratory experiments (Kirkpatrick & Locke, 1996; Sosik, Avolio, & Kahai, 1997), nursing supervisors (Bycio, Hackett, & Allen, 1995), and German bank managers (Geyer & Steyrer, 1998).

Comparing And Contrasting Theories Of Leadership

Table 12.3 presents a summary of the various leadership theories we have reviewed. The early universalist theories of leadership were limited because they were too simplistic—leadership is too complex a phenomenon to be captured in terms of a single characteristic, or group of leader characteristics. The behavioral theories of leadership suggested that two very different sets of leader behaviors—task-oriented and person-oriented—were associated with effective leadership. But this perspective too was limited because different leader behaviors will be more or less successful depending on characteristics of the leadership situation. This brought us to the more modern leadership theories, the contingency models.

Each of the contingency theories of leadership presents a different way of examining leader effectiveness by focusing on the leader-situation interaction. To understand better the perspectives that these theories take in predicting leader effectiveness, we need to compare the various models.

TABLE 12.3

Summary of Leadership Theories

Theory	Elements/Components	Applications
Universalist Theories		
Great Man/Woman Theory	Effective leaders are born, not made	(no direct intervention programs)
Trait Theory	Searching for traits common to all effective leaders	(no direct intervention programs)
Behavioral Theories		
Ohio State Studies	Two leader behaviors: Initiating Structure and Consideration	(no direct intervention)
U. of Michigan Studies	Two leader behaviors: Task-oriented and Relationship-oriented	Leadership Grid
Contingency Theories		
Fiedler's Contingency Theory	Leader style must be matched to situational characteristics	Leader Match
Path-goal Theory	Leader must play roles to help groups attain goals	(no specific interventions)
Decision-making Model	Leader asks situation-related questions before choosing decision-making style	Model contains its own application
Leader-Member Exchange	Focuses on quality of leader-member relationship	Leadership training
Additional Theories		
Transformational Leadership	Leader inspires and provides a "vision" for followers	Leadership training
Charismatic Leadership	Followers are drawn to "exceptional" characteristics possessed by leader	Leadership training

One obvious difference among the contingency theories is how they view the leader's primary task. For example, Fiedler's model sees the leader as determining the course the work group should take; the path-goal theory considers the leader as merely a facilitator who helps the group achieve its goals; the decision-making model sees the leader's main job as work-related decision making; and the leader-member exchange theory focuses on the leader's role with subordinates. The models also differ in how they define effective leadership. In Fiedler's contingency model, in contrast to the other models, the leader's style is seen as relatively fixed and unchangeable. Thus, the leader must seek out or create situations that are compatible with the leader's behavioral orientation. All of the other contingency models assume that leaders are more flexible and require leaders to change their behavior in accordance with the situation. For example, according to the decision-making model, a leader should be participative and democratic in dealing with decision making in one situation, and be more autocratic and directive in another. Likewise, according to the path-goal theory, a leader may change roles from time to time to meet the varying goals of the work group. As we shall see, this notion of the flexibility or stability of leader behavior is very important to the application of leadership theory.

Finally, charismatic and transformational leadership theories seem to, at the same time, combine and move beyond both the trait approaches and the contingency approaches to leadership. That is, these newer approaches to leadership focus on characteristics of the leader, and how these extraordinary leader characteristics interact with situational elements, including the attitudes, beliefs, and loyalty of the followers. The charismatic and transformational leadership theories, however, go a step beyond contingency models because in these newer models, the leader's behavior is more than just a simple adjusting or adapting to situational constraints.

Applications Of Leadership Theories

The various leadership theories suggest several possible interventions for improving leaders' effectiveness. For example, Fiedler's Leader Match program offers suggestions for changing a work situation to fit with the leader's behavioral orientation; the decision-making theory prescribes the appropriate decision-making strategy for any situation; and the leader-member exchange model advocates teaching leaders to be more attentive and responsive to group members. The most common suggestion by far is trying to change the leader's behavior. Spurred by this, tremendous energy and resources have gone into programs to train leaders. From the other perspective, some effort has also gone into ways of redesigning jobs to fit particular leaders' styles. It should be noted that these approaches apply equally to male and female leaders; research has shown essentially no difference between the sexes in behavioral orientation (see Up Close: Are There Differences Between Male and Female Leaders?).

■ UP CLOSE

Are There Differences Between Male and Female Leaders?

There is considerable evidence of discrimination against women in gaining leadership positions in work organizations (Van Nostrand, 1993).

Furthermore, when women do attain such positions, they may discover ongoing discrimination in terms of how they are treated and in the

UP CLOSE (*continued*)

Research indicates few differences in how effectively men and women lead

distribution of rewards (Larwood & Wood, 1977; Nieva & Gutek, 1981). Moreover, the career advancement rates of women managers, and their pay rates, lag significantly behind their male counterparts (Stroh, Brett, & Reilly, 1992). While discrimination in work settings certainly exists, are there any actual differences in the effectiveness of female and male leaders or even in female and male leadership behaviors?

No appreciable differences have been found in the effectiveness of female and male leaders and virtually no differences in their leadership behaviors (Bass, 1981; Rice, Instone, & Adams, 1984). Research indicates that males and females are equally effective as leaders. When differences are seen in leader performance, they occur only in those leadership roles that are either highly "masculine" or highly "feminine." Not surprisingly, in these specific instances, male leaders perform slightly better in masculine leader roles and females are slightly better in feminine leader roles (Eagly,

Karau, & Makhijani, 1995). Regarding differences in leader behaviors, one review of 17 studies found that male and female leaders exhibit equal amounts of task-oriented and relationship-oriented leader behaviors (Dobbins & Platz, 1986). The few relatively insignificant sex differences that do emerge in some studies seem to be limited to research on leadership in simulated laboratory settings with college students or manager trainees role playing leader situations. These small differences do not appear in studies of actual leaders.

It thus appears that the belief that female and male leaders behave differently is largely a myth. As Nieva and Gutek (1981, p. 81) wrote, "contrary to popular beliefs, female leaders are not more emotional and suggestible, or less decisive, aggressive, and objective than male leaders. Also contrary to notions about sex specialization in leadership styles, women leaders appear to behave in similar fashion to their male colleagues."

LEADERSHIP TRAINING

Leadership training programs take a number of forms, although most follow two general approaches. The first approach teaches leaders diagnostic skills, that is, how to assess a situation in order to determine the type of leader behavior that will work best. The assumption is that a leader who knows the particular behavior that a situation requires will be able to adjust behavior accordingly. The path-goal and decision-making theories emphasize such diagnosis. The path-goal theory requires leaders to determine the goal expectations of the work group, while the decision-making model asks the leader to perform a detailed assessment of a situation before adopting a decision-making strategy.

The second approach teaches leaders specific skills or behaviors that they lack. For example, such programs might train task-oriented leaders to be more relationship-oriented or train transactional leaders to become more transformational (Barling, Weber, & Kelloway, 1996). Probably a combination of both approaches—teaching diagnostic skills plus increasing the leader's behavioral repertoire—is likely to be most effective.

Organizations invest a great deal of time and money in programs designed to train their leaders to be more effective. While research indicates that many of these programs are successful (Burke & Day, 1986; Latham, 1988), a number of factors must be considered to maximize the chances of such effectiveness.

First, as in all types of training programs, training needs must be determined (see Chapter 5). In leadership training it is important to identify the specific behaviors or diagnostic skills that the trainee lacks. A second, related concern is the leader trainee's openness and acceptance of the training program. If leaders are to be successful in a program that involves a substantial change in behavior, they must see the merit in learning new leadership behaviors and perhaps abandoning past leadership behaviors. This is a problem in many training programs in which managers are "forced" to attend and the program may fail because of resistance from the participants. Third, the more time and energy invested in the program, the more successful it is likely to be. Changing the behavior of practicing managers is neither quick nor easy, for old leadership patterns have likely become deeply ingrained. A two-hour program is not likely to have much impact.

Another important consideration is whether the particular leadership behaviors taught in the training program will be accepted in the work group and organization. In many cases, when the leaders try to use their newly acquired leadership behaviors in the work environment, they meet with resistance from both supervisees and colleagues. The new behaviors may be incompatible with the usual operating procedures within the organization or the work group, and the new leadership style may not fit the expectations of group members. For example, a training program that taught police sergeants to replace task-oriented, authoritarian styles with participative behaviors was a spectacular failure. Although the sergeants accepted the change, it was met with considerable resistance by their subordinates, who felt that the program had made their leaders "soft," a condition that they perceived as dangerous in the life-and-death situations that police officers often face. Thus for leadership training to be effective, the organization must accept and support the new leader behavior.

Finally, sound evaluations of leadership training programs must be conducted routinely to determine whether the programs are indeed successful. Such evaluations include measuring the effects of leadership training programs on organizational outcomes such as work group productivity, work quality, and member satisfaction. Training programs that deal with these various concerns can improve the quality of leadership in work groups and organizations.

ON THE CUTTING EDGE

Transcultural Leadership: Training Leaders For The 21st Century

The increasing internationalization of business, with multinational organizations routinely doing business worldwide, coupled with the increasing diversity of the workforce, means that leaders today and in the future must be specially trained for a more complex work world (Adler, 1986, 1991; Bass, 1990; Simons, Vazquez, & Harris, 1993). It was predicted that by the year 2000, a majority of large work organizations would routinely do business with companies based in other countries. As global diversity increases, so does the cultural diversity of the workforce. For instance, it is estimated that by 2010, fewer than 10 percent of North Americans entering the workforce will be white males. Women and members of ethnic minority groups will be the majority of workers of the future.

One model of leadership training (Conger, 1993) suggests that future leaders will need, among other things, the following areas of training:

- *Global awareness*—Leaders will need to be knowledgeable of worldwide issues that may affect the organization and the organizations and organizational members it must interact with.

- *Capability of managing highly decentralized organizations*—As more and more work is done in independently functioning work teams, leaders will need to play more of a "coaching" or "consultant" role, than the traditional authority role of "boss."

- *Sensitivity to diversity issues*—Leaders will be looked to as "diversity experts," so they must be able to deal effectively with groups that have different values and world views.

- *Interpersonal skills*—The changing and expanding role of work group leaders (e.g., from "bosses" to "coaches") will require them to become more interpersonally skilled.

- *Community-building skills*—Effective leaders of the future will have to build work groups into cooperating, interdependent "communi-

ON THE CUTTING EDGE (*continued*)

ties" of workers. The leader will need to build group cohesiveness and commitment to goals. More and more, group members will turn to leaders for the "vision" of where the work group and the organization is going.

It appears that once again, leader flexibility is called for. Leaders of the future will be required to be "culturally" flexible and adaptable if they are going to be effective in leading diverse work groups in an increasingly complex world of work.

JOB REDESIGN AND SUBSTITUTES FOR LEADERSHIP

Certain critics, such as Fiedler, suggest that leadership training may be ineffective and a waste of organizational resources. Because Fiedler believes that a leader's orientation is inflexible, he argues that organizations should concentrate on changing the job to fit the leader rather than vice versa (Fiedler, 1965). The most obvious example of this approach is his Leader Match program, which offers suggestions for altering the work situation to fit the leader's predominantly task-oriented or relationship-oriented pattern, usually by increasing or decreasing task structure or position power. The main problem with this approach is that many work situations may be unchangeable. In such cases, Fiedler (1973) suggests that it may be easier to transfer the leader to a situation that is more compatible with the leader's orientation than to try to alter the leader's behavioral orientation. However, changing the situation to fit the leader's style may prove to be quite successful.

Research in redesigning jobs indicates that in certain instances leaders may be unnecessary, leading to a search for "substitutes for leadership" (Hackman, 1990; Kerr & Jermier, 1978; Podsakoff & MacKenzie, 1997). For example, a group that is cohesive and has very structured norms for operation may have no need for a leader. Examples of such leaderless groups include some of the job enrichment teams mentioned in Chapter 7, in which all members have equal status and authority, as well as groups of professionals such as physicians or real estate agents who all have high levels of ability, experience, training, and knowledge. In addition, a leader would be redundant in a situation in which the task is well-structured and routine and the work is intrinsically satisfying to workers, since there would be no need for direction or for encouragement. Finally, it has been suggested that a form of self-leadership, or self-management, might substitute for the traditional supervision provided by a formal leader (Manz, 1986; Manz & Sims, 1980; Vanderslice, 1988). However, while some work groups may be able to operate well without formal leaders, such groups probably represent a small proportion of work groups. It is likely that leaders will remain an important part of most work groups.

Describe three applications of leadership theories.

What are the five needs for transcultural leaders outlined by Conger (1993)?

Summary

Leadership is the ability to direct a group toward the attainment of goals. Leadership theories can be divided into three categories: *universalist theories*, *behavioral theories*, and *contingency theories*. The *great man/woman theory*, a universalist theory, holds that some people are natural, born leaders. The *trait theory* specifies certain personality *traits*, or characteristics that are common to all effective leaders. These universalist theories suffer from the facts that they are simplistic and that they focus on individual leader characteristics.

The behavioral theories of leadership are typified by studies conducted at Ohio State and Michigan that looked directly at leader behavior, rather than at inferred leader characteristics. Two dimensions of leader behavior emerged: *initiating structure* (also called *task-oriented behaviors*), which focuses on work task production, and *consideration* (also known as *relationship-oriented behaviors*), which emphasizes interpersonal relationships among workers. The *Leadership Grid* is an application of the findings from the behavioral theories—a program that stresses both task-oriented and relationship-oriented behaviors as the keys to leader success.

The most popular theories of leadership are the *contingency theories*. *Fiedler's contingency model* states that effective leadership depends on a match between the leader's style and the favorableness of the work situation. Leader style is assessed through the *least preferred coworker (LPC)* measure. Task-oriented leaders are most effective in either very favorable or very unfavorable situations, while relationship-oriented leaders do better in moderately favorable situations. The favorability of situations in Fiedler's model is determined by three variables: *leader-member relations*, *task structure*, and the leader's *position power*. The *path-goal theory* asserts that the leader is a facilitator who chooses the type of behavior that will most help the work group to achieve their goals. According to the path-goal theory, the leader can adopt four types of leader behavior: *directive*, *achievement-oriented*, *supportive*, or *participative*. The *decision-making model* sees the leader's main role as making work-related decisions. This prescriptive model contains a decision tree framework for the leader to follow to decide the appropriate decision-making strategy (ranging from autocratic to democratic) to use in a particular situation. The *leader-member exchange model* examines the quality of the relationship between the leader and each subordinate, which leads to a more precise determination of work outcomes. Finally, *transformational* and *charismatic* leadership theories focus on exceptional characteristics or qualities that leaders possess that inspire loyalty in followers and motivate them to achieve extraordinary goals.

The application of leadership theories involves one of two strategies: instituting leadership training programs or redesigning the job to fit the leader. The majority of the theories advocate leadership training, either by teaching specific leader behaviors (for example, task-oriented or relationship-oriented) or by training leaders to diagnose situations that call for task-oriented or relationship-oriented behaviors. Job redesign usually involves changing characteristics of the situation to fit the leader's typical style or orientation. However, work situations that are amenable to such job redesigns may be limited. In other situations, particularly where roles and procedures are well-defined, substitutes for leadership, such as self-managing work teams, may be appropriate.

Study Questions And Exercises

1. Discuss the limitations of the universalist leadership theories. Why do you suppose they had, and continue to have, such popular appeal?
2. Consider the distinction between task-oriented (initiating structure) and relationship-oriented (consideration) leader behaviors. List the role that they play in each of the various contingency theories.
3. Think of a leader of a work or social group whom you have known. How would you characterize this person's leadership style or orientation? What theory of leadership best describes and explains this person's leadership situation?
4. All contingency theories of leadership measure some characteristics of both the leader and the work situation. How do the different theories—Fiedler's, path-goal, decision-making, leader-member exchange—define characteristics of the work situation?
5. Design a leadership training program for leaders of student organizations. Keep in mind the program characteristics that will maximize the effectiveness of the training program.

Suggested Readings

Bass, B.M. (1990). *Stogdill's handbook of leadership: Theory, research, and managerial applications* (3rd. ed.). New York: Free Press. *A classic, comprehensive review of theory and research on leadership from the earliest days through the late 1980s. An excellent resource with well over 5,000 references to research articles relating to leadership.*

Chemers, M.M. (1997). *An integrative theory of leadership.* Mahwah, NJ: Lawrence Erlbaum Associates. *An interesting book that reviews leadership theories and research and presents an overall theoretical framework for understanding leadership.*

Conger, J.A. & Kanungo, R.N. (1998). *Charismatic leadership in organizations.* Thousand Oaks, CA: Sage. *A thorough review of research on charismatic leadership featuring the authors' own theory and work in the area.*

Simons, G.F., Vazquez, C., & Harris, P.R. (1993). *Transcultural leadership: Empowering the diverse workforce.* Houston, TX: Gulf Publishing. *An excellent "workbook" and guide for helping train managers in cultural sensitivity and workplace diversity—complete with training exercises.*

INFLUENCE, POWER, AND POLITICS

INSIDE TIPS

DEFINING AND DIFFERENTIATING INFLUENCE, POWER, AND POLITICS

This chapter presents and discusses three topics: influence, power, and organizational politics. While each is a distinct concept, they are also three facets of the same general process, for all involve one party trying to affect the behavior of another. However, it is important to be able to distinguish among the three. Influence is an informal process by which an individual uses personal skills and abilities to affect the behavior of others. Power is more formal in nature and can come from a position held in an organization or from the possession of important work resources or work-related abilities. Most research on power looks specifically at types of power, which are commonly called power bases. Politics, which is self-serving behavior, is the most difficult concept to distinguish, partly because both influence and the use of power can be labeled political behaviors if they are self-serving. Thus, certain forms of influence and uses of power can be subsets of the category of political behavior, depending on how they are used. This is an important point that will help in understanding how the three concepts are different and similar.

Because the study of influence, power, and politics in work organizations is relatively new, there is less theory and less terminology in this chapter than in many of the others. However, this does not mean that these topics are less important. Indeed, influence, power, and politics are extremely significant and pervasive processes in all work groups and organizations. Power and influence in particular are important aspects of leadership (see Chapter 12), because leaders use their power and influence to help work groups attain their goals. Influence, power, and politics are also important factors in group processes, which we discussed in Chapter 11. For example, conformity to group norms will occur only if the group can influence members to follow the rules. Also, managers can use their power and authority to help resolve conflicts among group members. Furthermore, group decision making, by its very nature, is a political process. Finally, because certain forms of power are linked to the very structure of the organizational hierarchy, our discussion in this chapter will provide some groundwork for examining organizational structure in Chapter 14.

In Chapters 11 and 12 we examined important processes and relationships that occur in work groups. In this chapter we will continue to study key group processes, specifically influence, power, and politics, which are the forces by which individuals and work groups affect the behavior of other persons and groups.

Work organizations are filled with individuals who are trying to succeed, but simply being a dedicated, hard-working employee is usually not enough. People advance in organizations partly due to their talents and energy, but also because they have the ability to gain influence and power over others. As an individual moves up the ladder, authority and power typically increase. However, two managers at the same level in a company may not be equal in terms of their power and influence. For example, one may be more powerful because she is well-liked and respected by subordinates and superiors, and because she understands the politics of the company and knows how to "play the game."

Although influence, power, and politics are ongoing processes in the day-to-day life of any work organization, with important implications for organizational performance and employee satisfaction, these topics have only recently been studied in depth by social scientists (Pfeffer, 1981, 1992). The concepts of influence, power, and politics are also closely intertwined with the topics of group processes and leadership that were discussed earlier. For example, individuals in work groups use influence and power to affect and alter the behavior of other members. Leaders also use their power and influence to achieve group goals. Moreover, they must often act politically to gain and hold their powerful leadership positions, and individuals may also engage in politics to improve their positions in organizations. Influence, power, and politics likewise play major roles in group decision-making processes. For example, a powerful, influential member can have an important impact in deciding the courses of action a group will take. Democratic decision making, by its very nature, involves political behaviors, such as lobbying for and voting on particular plans. Moreover, because influence, power, and politics affect the behavior of others, they can help determine the amount of conflict and coordination within work groups.

Defining Influence, Power, and Politics

In one sense, influence, power, and politics are similar, because all three involve getting others to do something. There are, however, some important differences among them.

influence
the ability to use social forces to affect the behavior of others

Influence can be viewed as a form of social control or social power. It is an individual's ability to get another person to perform a certain action. Usually, influence is exerted by using informal strategies such as persuasion, peer pressure, or compliance techniques. For example, an individual might use persuasive influence in trying to obtain a loan from a friend or when attempting to persuade a coworker to help complete a work task. Peer pressure influence might take the form of a worker's plea to a colleague to break a company rule because "everybody does it." Influence might also involve the use of compliance techniques. For example, an executive might use flattery or the offer of a favor to get a clerical word processor to work overtime to finish producing a report. In this definition, the term might be called "social influence," which is a more restricted usage than the more general notion of influence, which is defined as any process of affecting behavioral change in others (Allen & Porter, 1983).

power
the use of some aspect of a work relationship to compel another to perform a certain action despite resistance

Power in the work place is a more formal process that can be defined as the use of some aspect of a work relationship to force or compel another person to perform a certain action despite resistance. For example, a company president can give an order to a vice president and expect it to be carried out because of the power associated with the status relationship. A safety inspector may be able to demand that operators shut down a piece of machinery that has a potentially dangerous malfunction by virtue of the person's position as an acknowledged safety expert. While influence resides primarily in the individual, power usually derives from the relationship between two parties. For example, a coworker might use persuasion skills—a form of influence—to try to get an unmotivated worker to increase work output by appealing to the worker to "pull his own weight." However, a supervisor, by virtue of the status relationship that gives the person authority over the worker, can use power to order the worker to improve productivity or face the consequences. Thus, power resides in the relationship between parties or in their positions, rather than in the individuals themselves.

organizational politics
self-serving actions designed to affect the behavior of others to achieve personal goals

Organizational politics is a very different process that involves any actions taken to influence the behavior of others to reach personal goals. The one thing that distinguishes political behaviors from power and influence is the fact that organizational politics are *always* self-serving, while power and influence are not necessarily self-serving.

The following example shows how a person might use influence power and politics to achieve a certain outcome: Marilyn James has a problem. The vacation schedules at her company, Mackenzie Electronics, have been set up for several months. However, she has just found out that her husband's vacation will come two weeks earlier than they had anticipated. She now needs to exchange her vacation time with Dan Gibbons, who will be taking his vacation during the two weeks she needs. Marilyn could use influence by trying to persuade Dan to change his plans; she might promise to do him a favor, or she might simply make an appeal to Dan's generous nature and willingness to help. Marilyn would be using power if she ordered a change in the vacation schedule, which she could do because she is assistant manager of the marketing department and Dan is a newcomer, far down in the departmental hierarchy. Finally, she might use politics to get what she wants. Marilyn could encourage the marketing director to assign an important project to Dan, saying, "He's a real hard worker, and he deserves to handle this assignment." The project would require that Dan make a formal presentation on August 24, right in the middle of his vacation. Later, when Dan mentions that he needs to trade vacation times to work on the assignment, Marilyn would be ready to jump right in and offer to switch. In short, Marilyn could use any one of these methods—influence, power, or politics—to affect Dan's behavior.

Influence, power, and politics are pervasive processes in all work organizations that involve efforts by some organizational members to control the actions of others. However, the means exerted in using each process are quite different and thus will be examined separately.

Influence: The Use of Social Control

People often attempt to persuade, cajole, convince, or induce others to provide assistance, change an opinion, offer support, or engage in a certain behavior in both work organizations and in everyday social life. A study by Kipnis, Schmidt, and Wilkinson (1980) attempted to classify the various influence tactics used in the workplace by having 165 lower-level managers write essays describing incidents in which they influenced either their superiors, coworkers, or subordinates. The 370 tactics were put into eight categories: assertiveness, ingratiation, rationality, sanctions, exchanges, upward appeals, blocking, and coalitions (see Table 13.1; it is important to note that this classification includes behaviors that, by our definitions, would include *both* influence and power tactics). Subsequent research has supported the existence of these categories of influence/power tactics (Schriesheim & Hinkin, 1990; Yukl & Falbe, 1990).

In addition to trying to influence others by being assertive or by using logical arguments, one might also employ **ingratiation** by increasing one's personal appeal through such tactics as doing favors, praising, or flattering another (Kumar & Beyerlein, 1991). Other categories of influence include offering exchanges of favors or threatening the other person with negative

ingratiation
influencing others by increasing one's personal appeal to them

TABLE 13.1

Categories of Influence Tactics

Assertiveness

Making orders or demands
Setting deadlines and making sure they are met
Emphasizing rules that require compliance

Ingratiation

Using praise or making the other person feel important
Showing a need for the other person's help
Being polite and/or friendly

Rationality

Using logic to convince someone else
Writing a detailed justification of a plan
Presenting information to support a request along with the request

Sanctions

Withholding salary increases
Threatening to fire someone or to give a poor performance evaluation
Promising or giving a salary increase

Exchanges

Offering an exchange of favors
Reminding another of past favors
Offering to make some personal sacrifice in exchange for a favor

Upward appeals

Obtaining the support of superiors
Sending the target person to see superiors
Filing a report about the target person to superiors

Blocking

Threatening to stop working with the other person
Ignoring the other person or withdrawing friendship
Engaging in a work slowdown

Coalitions

Obtaining coworkers' support of a request
Making a request at a formal conference
Obtaining subordinates' support of a request

Source: D. Kipnis, S.M. Schmidt, and I. Wilkinson, "Intraorganizational Influence Tactics: Explorations in Getting One's Way," *Journal of Applied Psychology,* 65 (1980), pp. 445–48.

sanctions, such as a demotion or firing. The final three categories of influence are making appeals to persons higher in the status hierarchy; engaging in behaviors that block, interfere with, or prohibit the others' work activities; or building coalitions by getting the support of coworkers or subordinates.

The Kipnis et al. study found that the choice of influence tactic was determined by the situation, the status of the individuals involved, and other characteristics of the organization such as size and whether or not the organization was unionized. For example, higher-status persons were more likely to use assertiveness or sanctions, while lower-status individuals used rational appeals to influence superiors. Coworkers commonly employed ingratiation and exchange when attempting to influence one another and to obtain personal favors, while rational and coalition tactics were often used to institute changes in the work task or in the work context. Interestingly, there were no sex differences in the use of the various influence tactics. Men and women seem to use the same tactics in the same ways (see also Driskell, Olmstead, & Salas, 1993).

Other studies have found that subordinates use different upward influence tactics with superiors, depending on whether they were seeking personal goals, such as a pay raise or promotion, or organizational goals, such as gaining the supervisor's approval of a new, more efficient work procedure. When seeking personal goals, subordinates tended to use tactics such as ingratiation. When seeking organizational goals, they favored strategies such as upward appeals and rational persuasion to try to influence superiors (Ansari & Kapoor, 1987; Schmidt & Kipnis, 1984). Moreover, subordinates' influence tactics varied depending on whether the superior was autocratic and task-oriented, or participative and relationship-oriented. Subordinates tended to use ingratiation, blocking, and upward appeal techniques with autocratic managers but rational persuasion strategies with participative superiors (Ansari & Kapoor, 1987). Studies of supervisors' influence tactics found that rational persuasion was a very effective managerial influence strategy, while pressure tactics, such as threats, were least effective. Additionally, the influence tactics of ingratiation and exchange were moderately effective in influencing both subordinates and other managers (Yukl & Tracey, 1992).

Like individuals, groups will also use a wide variety of tactics to exert influence. For example, groups tend to use influence to get members to conform to group norms. As we saw in Chapter 11, if a member is in violation of a group norm, pressure will be exerted in the form of criticism, isolation (the "silent treatment"), or, in extreme cases, expulsion. Such pressure to conform is a very common and very important influence process in work groups and organizations (Feldman, 1984; Moscovici, 1985; see Up Close).

Describe the eight categories of influence tactics and give examples of each.

Power: A Major Force in Work Organizations

Power, in contrast to influence, is a more formal force in work organizations that derives from an individual's role or position or from some specific characteristics of the individual, such as work-related expertise or admirable leadership qualities. Whereas influence depends on the skill of the influencer in affecting another person at a particular place or time, power is a consistent force that is likely to work across situations and time. In organizations, power is a fairly stable capacity or potential that can consistently affect the behavior of others, as long as the power remains with the individual (Hocker & Wilmot, 1985). In other words, the use of influence strategies to affect the behavior of others is sometimes successful, but the use of power is *almost always* successful.

UP CLOSE

How to Resist Social Influence Tactics

Social psychologist Robert Cialdini (1993) has discussed the various uses of social influence tactics by "compliance professionals," such as salespersons, advertisers, and con artists, who are those people whose job it is to get others to do something. Using the technique of participant observation, he infiltrated such groups by posing as a door-to-door vacuum cleaner salesman, a car dealer, and a telephone fundraiser. Through his research, Cialdini was able to identify the most frequently used influence tactics. Three of the more common strategies are the *reciprocity rule,* the *rule of commitment and consistency,* and the *scarcity principle.* With the reciprocity rule, a "favor" is done to get something in return. The rule of commitment and consistency is used in getting people to commit to a small initial request and then hitting them with a larger request. The most infamous example of this is the "foot-in-the-door" tactic used by salespersons or people seeking donations. The compliance professional might begin with the question, "You are concerned about the plight of the whales, aren't you?" Answering af-

firmatively commits you to agreeing with the next question: "Then you would like to make a donation to the Save the Whales Fund, wouldn't you?" The scarcity principle is used to create the illusion of a limited supply, as is done by advertisements that read, "Act now, supply is limited."

A fourth influence tactic identified by Cialdini seems to involve the use of guilt in getting individuals to comply with requests. This additional tactic, called the "door-in-the-face" technique, is a two-step compliance technique that is like using the "foot-in-the-door" tactic in reverse. In using the door-in-the-face, the influencer prefaces the real request with a first request that is so large that it is certain to be rejected. For example, an influencer who wants to borrow ten dollars from a friend will start out asking for a loan of a hundred dollars. When the exorbitant request is denied, the second request for ten dollars is made, and it seems reasonable by contrast, making the friend more likely to grant the ten-dollar loan than he or she would have if the smaller request had been made alone.

UP CLOSE (continued)

Finally, Cialdini also emphasizes the importance of *liking* in influence attempts—we are more easily influenced by people we like, and what better way for influence "peddlers" to get you to like them but by ingratiation. Research has demonstrated that ingratiation is not only used by salespersons, but is often used in the workplace by supervisors to influence supervisees (Aguinis, Nesler, Hosoda, & Tedeschi, 1994), and by subordinates to try to influence the promotion process (Thacker & Wayne, 1995).

As you can see, all of the tactics of influence mentioned by Cialdini can be used by coworkers or bosses to influence people to do what they might not otherwise do. For example, reciprocity is often invoked by management after workers are given a cost-of-living raise. Workers, feeling as if management has just done them a favor, may be more compliant than usual, even though the raise was tied to some factor other than management's generosity. A com-

pany may try to use the commitment and consistency rule to increase company loyalty and cut down on voluntary turnover. For example, each month the company might hold a contest in which employees submit essays about why the company is a great place to work. Winning essays could be published in the company newsletter. This may make it tougher for employees to consider leaving for work elsewhere as they have made such a public act of loyalty. An organization might employ the scarcity principle in performance incentive programs by encouraging employees to work hard to obtain one of a very few scarce rewards.

Cialdini maintains that the best way to combat unethical use of influence tactics is to be able to recognize them. By understanding that people are trying to use these strategies to take unfair advantage of you, you may be able to resist them simply by seeing such obvious exploitation attempts for what they really are.

Psychologist Robert Cialdini studied the influence tactics used by professional salespersons.

POWER SOURCES

Power can take many forms and is derived from a variety of sources that are of two main types (Yukl & Falbe, 1991). Most often, power comes from the organization. **Organizational power** comes from an individual's position in the organization and from the control over important organizational resources conveyed by that position. These organizational resources can be tangible, such as money, work assignments, or office space, or more intangible, such as information or communication access to other people. **Individual power** is derived from personal characteristics, such as particular expertise or leadership ability, that are of value to the organization and its members.

organizational power
power derived from a person's position in an organization and from control over important resources afforded by that position

individual power
power derived from personal characteristics that are of value to the organization, such as particular expertise or leadership ability

Astley and Sachdeva (1984) outline three important sources of organizational power. One is the *hierarchical structure* of the organization. Power derived from the status hierarchy is inherent in one's position in the organization. Workers lower in the hierarchy often obey their superiors simply because they believe that their higher position gives them the right to exercise power (Astley & Zajac, 1991). Organizational power can also result from *control of important resources* such as money, fringe benefits, knowledge, and work-related expertise. Finally, organizational power can come from being in a position of *network centrality* that is crucial to the flow of information. Persons in such positions may have access to information that others do not possess and may develop social relationships with important individuals or groups within the organization. For example, an executive's secretary may have low levels of power due to ranking in the organizational hierarchy and little control over resources, but may still be powerful because of a position of network centrality that involves contact with important people and information.

French and Raven (1959) looked at different types of power that they called **power bases**, which are the sources of a person's power over others in the organization. They specify five important power bases: coercive power, reward power, legitimate power, expert power, and referent power.

Coercive power is the ability to punish or to threaten to punish others. For example, threatening to fine, demote, or fire someone are all means of exercising coercive power, as is assigning a person to an aversive work task. An individual may possess coercive power by holding a position in the organization that allows the person to punish others. However, any individual, regardless of position, can use coercive power by threatening to harm someone either physically or psychologically with tactics such as damaging a reputation by spreading false rumors.

We have seen that the use of coercive power, with its punishment and threats of punishment, carries certain risks since it may create anger and resentment in the subject. Coercive power must be exercised carefully, with awareness of the potential strengths and weaknesses of punitive strategies. For example, while coercive threats may get quick action, the threatened person may try to retaliate later. Raven (1992) says that if a leader is to use coercive power effectively, the leader must be ready and willing to follow through on threats, regardless of the costs involved. Moreover, the leader who uses coercive power must be ready to maintain surveillance over the target, to ensure that the target is behaving appropriately. Thus, to be used effectively, coercive power can put a drain on the manager who uses it, since the manager must constantly watch subordinates to apply sanctions quickly when undesirable work behaviors occur.

In many ways, **reward power** is the opposite of coercive power, for while coercive power is the ability to do harm, reward power is the ability to give something positive, such as money, praise, promotions, and interesting or challenging work assignments. The ability to reward others is a very com-

power bases
sources of power possessed by individuals in organizations

coercive power
the use of punishment or the threat of punishment to affect the behavior of others

Name and describe three influence tactics identified by Cialdini.

reward power
power that results from having the ability to offer something positive, such as money or praise

mon source of power in work organizations, where it often derives from having control over the resources that others value. Having the ability to administer pay raises, bonuses, promotions, or coveted work tasks can be an extremely strong power base.

Legitimate power involves the formal rights or authority that an individual possesses by virtue of a position in an organization. Titles such as manager, shift supervisor, director, or vice president are all bases for legitimate power. When employees carry out a request simply because "the boss" asked them to do it, they are responding to such power. In work organizations legitimate power is typically combined with the reward and coercive power bases. That is, most persons with legitimate authority also have the power to reward or punish subordinates. These three power bases are usually, although not always, tied together. There can be some rare instances in which persons are given some formal position that is not accompanied by reward and coercive power—a position of power in name only. Such is the case of the vice president for public affairs in a relatively small insurance company. The organizational chart for this company reveals that this vice president probably lacks much reward or coercive power to back up his legitimate title because he is the sole employee in the department, with no subordinates! Yet, there is good evidence that workers respond well to persons who possess legitimate power (Hinkin & Schriesheim, 1994; Yukl & Falbe, 1991), perhaps because most individuals are taught from an early age to respect those in authority.

Expert power is one of the strongest power bases an individual can possess, since it results from the possession of some special work-related knowledge, skill, or expertise. Such power is becoming even more important in today's work settings because of the increasing sophistication of technology. The advancing computerization and automation of many types of work tasks means that the people who have the knowledge and expertise to design, operate, and maintain this sophisticated technology are going to be very important—and very powerful—in the organization. For instance, the possession of expertise was found to be strongly related to supervisors awarding subordinates pay raises (Bartol & Martin, 1990). Expert power is also the source of power behind many health care professionals. For example, you are willing to take the advice of a physician because you believe that this individual has some special knowledge concerning your health.

A very different type of power base is **referent power**, which develops because an individual is respected, admired, and liked by others. Because the person is liked or admired, workers respond to the person's wishes in an effort to please the person and to gain favor. The most dramatic illustration of referent power is the charismatic political leader who can spur an entire population to action merely because of their admiration and respect for that person (see Chapter 12). Certain leaders in work settings may also have a strong referent power base and thus be very influential in controlling the activities of others.

legitimate power
the formal rights or authority accompanying a position in an organization

expert power
power derived from having certain work-related knowledge or skill

referent power
power resulting from the fact that an individual is respected, admired, and liked by others

To be effective, members of a race car pit crew must be high in expert power.

Name and describe the five French and Raven power bases.

Because of the renewed interest in studying organizational power, researchers have developed a number of scales to measure the different French and Raven power bases (Hinkin & Schriescheim, 1989; Schriescheim, Hinkin, & Podsakoff, 1991). One such instrument is presented in Table 13.2, and is designed to be administered to workers to assess which power bases are used by their supervisors.

In sum, the different power bases indicate that power can indeed take many forms and arise from many sources. For example, expert power and referent power reside within the individual and thus are forms of individual power. More often than not, legitimate, reward, and coercive power are derived from organizational rather than personal sources and thus are types of organizational power. As you might expect, the various power bases can combine to further increase an individual's power in an organization. At the same time, possession of certain power bases, coupled with the effective use of influence tactics (e.g., assertiveness, ingratiation, upward appeals, etc.) can even further increase the power an individual wields in a group or organization (Brass & Burkhardt, 1993). A great deal of research has been conducted on power dynamics, or on how the different power bases operate in work settings and how they affect work outcomes. Let's explore power dynamics in work organizations.

POWER DYNAMICS IN WORK ORGANIZATIONS

Despite its importance (Bacharach & Lawler, 1980), the topic of power in work settings has only been studied in depth by behavioral scientists since the 1970s (Gandz & Murray, 1980). This research, although limited, has uncovered certain findings concerning the dynamics of power in work organizations. For example, researchers have investigated such issues as the distribution of power in work organizations, the attempts of organizational members to increase power, power and dependency relationships, and the effects of power on important organizational outcomes—specifically job performance and satisfaction.

Differences in power distribution

We know that power, because of its many forms, is unevenly distributed in work settings. Usually, organizations are arranged in a power hierarchy, with people at the upper levels possessing great power and those at the bottom having relatively little power. However, individual differences in the expert and referent power bases ensure that no two people, even those at the same status level, have exactly equal power. Therefore, although persons high in the hierarchy tend to possess more power than those at lower levels, even a low-ranking member can wield considerable power because of personal sources of power, such as expert power and referent power.

McClelland (1975) and others (Winter, 1973), have shown that people place different values on the gain and use of power, with some people being high in the need for power and others having a low need for power (see

TABLE 13.2

A Measure of Power Bases

Instructions: Below is a list of statements which may be used in describing behaviors that supervisors in work organizations can direct toward their subordinates. First, carefully read each descriptive statement, thinking in terms of your supervisor. Then decide to what extent you agree that your supervisor could do this to you. Mark the number which most closely represents how you feel. Use the following numbers for your answers:

(5) = strongly agree
(4) = agree
(3) = neither agree nor disagree
(2) = disagree
(1) = strongly disagree

My supervisor can . . .

(Reward Power)
  increase my pay level.
  influence my getting a pay raise.
  provide me with special benefits.
  influence my getting a promotion.

(Coercive Power)
  give me undesirable job assignments.
  make my work difficult for me.
  make things unpleasant here.
  make being at work distasteful.

(Legitimate Power)
  make me feel that I have commitments to meet.
  make me feel like I should satisfy my job requirements.
  give me the feeling I have responsibilities to fulfill.
  make me recognize that I have tasks to accomplish.

(Expert Power)
  give me good technical suggestions.
  share with me his/her considerable experience and/or training.
  provide me with sound job-related advice.
  provide me with needed technical knowledge.

(Referent Power)
  make me feel valued.
  make me feel like he/she approves of me.
  make me feel personally accepted.
  make me feel important.

Source: T.R. Hinkin and C.A. Schriesheim, *Journal of Applied Psychology, 74* (1989), pp. 561–67. (American Psychological Association).

Low-ranking members of organizations can gain power through forming coalitions

Chapter 7). Thus, organizations may have some individuals who are "power hungry" and others who have little interest in gaining much power. However, although people may differ in their needs for power, once individuals have obtained power, they are usually reluctant to give it up (Kipnis, 1976). Perhaps this is what underlies the common notion that power can be "intoxicating" or "addicting." This makes sense, since it is power that enables organizational members to satisfy their various work-related goals. Does possession of power "corrupt"? Recent evidence suggests that when people are given more power, they may tend to behave in self-serving ways (Mitchell, Hopper, Daniels, Falvy, & Ferris, 1998).

Ways to increase power

One way for an organizational member to increase power is to gain work-related expertise or knowledge (Mechanic, 1962). Learning to solve complex problems, being able to operate or repair sophisticated machinery, and knowing complicated procedures are all linked to an expert power base. Low-power individuals may also increase their organizational power by developing a relationship with a higher-ranking member (Bartol & Martin, 1988). Protégés often benefit from their association with a mentor, leading to greater organizational status and power (see Chapter 5). In fact, it has been shown that networking within the organization, and even simply possessing the knowledge of important social networks in the organization, are related to an individual's possession of power (Krackhardt, 1990).

Low-ranking members may also gain power by forming a **coalition**, which involves a group of workers banding together to achieve common goals. A coalition can be a very powerful force because of its ability to slow or shut down organizational operations. A group of low-level workers acting together as a unit can become very powerful by sheer virtue of their numbers. In other words, a few workers may be easily replaced, but an entire line of workers cannot. A strong coalition can be created when employees join a union, which can exercise its power by threatening to strike or by actually striking. Generally, the larger the coalition, the greater its power. There can indeed be "power in numbers."

coalition

a group of individuals who band together to combine their power

Power and dependency relationships

When a nonreciprocal dependency relationship exists such that party A is dependent on party B, but B is not dependent on A, B will have power over A (Blalock, 1989). In work settings, it is very common for certain individuals or groups to depend on others for certain resources needed to do a job. If the dependency does not go both ways, the individuals or groups who control the scarce resources will have power over the have-nots (Hickson, Hinings, Less, Schneck, & Pennings, 1971). Workers who have a great deal of expertise often have such power because those without the expert knowledge must rely on them to perform their jobs correctly. Because expert power is based in the individual, the dependent party sometimes has higher status than the expert. For example, in the military, commissioned officers attain their positions by attending officer training school. Although they have more formal education than noncommissioned officers, they have virtually no on-the-job experience. Thus, when junior lieutenants receive their first assignments, they quickly find out who holds the expert power—the noncommissioned officers, especially the master sergeants, who have many years of experience. A dependency relationship develops. A lieutenant who does not learn to get along with the master sergeants is in trouble and will be unable to command effectively because of a shortage of expert knowledge. Similar situations exist in business when a new manager may have to rely on the expertise of a long-time employee in order to get the job done.

Businesses strive to avoid dependency relationships on the organizational level. For example, a company will try hard not to have to rely on a single supplier for needed materials because such sole dependency gives the supplier power over the company. One famous fast-food chain has eliminated most dependency relationships by controlling the supply within the company. This restaurant chain owns their own cattle ranches to supply meat, farms to supply grain products, and even paper mills to make bags and containers. The resulting independence allows the company to increase its power over competitors who may be hurt if, for example, their meat suppliers go on strike.

Power and work outcomes

The possession and use of power bases can be directly related to important organizational outcomes such as performance and job satisfaction. For example, expert power is generally related to effective job performance (Bachman, Bowers, & Marcus, 1968), because expert power is based on knowing how to do the job. Referent power, on the other hand, is consistently linked to member satisfaction with the person wielding the power (Carson, Carson, & Roe, 1993). This should not be surprising, because referent power results from the subjects' willingness to submit to the power of someone they admire and respect. In contrast, coercive power tends to decrease the attractiveness of the power wielder and may lead to decreased job satisfaction in work group members. Moreover, the use of coercive power may erode the individual's referent power base. In other words, we lose respect for people who consistently punish or threaten us. In practice, the exercise of coercive power more often involves threats of punishment rather than actual punishment. While drastic threats can be effective means for gaining compliance, the person who makes such threats runs the risk of having someone "call their bluff" and refuse to comply. The exerciser is now faced with a dilemma: If the person does not follow through with the punishment, some coercive power will be lost because the subject learns that it is an empty threat. On the other hand, the exerciser who administers the punishment risks infuriating, or in the case of threats of dismissal, losing the employee. In many instances, the use of coercive power is a no-win situation. While it may be used to threaten workers into higher levels of performance, satisfaction is likely to decrease, and the organization may lose in the long run through increases in voluntary absenteeism and turnover in the dissatisfied work force. It is probably for these reasons that studies of practicing managers indicate that coercive power is the least used of the five power bases (e.g., Stahelski, Frost, & Patch, 1989).

The power corollary

power corollary
the concept that for every exercise of power, there is a tendency for the subject to react with a return power play

One aspect of power dynamics is known as the **power corollary** (Robbins, 1979), which states that for every use of power, there is a tendency for a corollary use of power—a return power play by the subject ("for every action there is a reaction"). In other words, when people are the subject of an obvious power play, they tend to try to assert their own power. According to French and Raven (1959), this is why it is important to possess a legitimate power base when exercising other power bases, particularly coercive power, for the combination will limit the form a corollary use of power can take. For example, if a coworker tries to use coercive tactics on you, you might respond in kind, with threats of your own. However, if the person using coercive power is your supervisor, your response options are limited. In other words, it is unlikely that you will directly threaten someone who has legitimate authority.

Power and leadership

The concepts of power and leadership are closely intertwined. Leaders use their power to help followers attain desired goals. Ideally, to be effective, a leader should possess a number of power bases. Having high levels of all five would be ideal (although it may often be rare), because the various power bases often complement one another (Raven, Schwarzwald, & Koslowsky, 1998). As we have seen, legitimate power tends to validate the use of reward and coercive power. Expert power should also exist in legitimate power positions, because the most qualified persons are usually the supervisors. If the work group is committed to doing a good job, and if they have a leader who is high in legitimate and reward power and who has the expert power to lead a group to high levels of productivity, the leader is likely to develop a strong referent power base as well. Conversely, because of their strong admiration for a leader with referent power, followers may also assume the leader has expertise (Podsakoff & Schriesheim, 1985).

Looking back to some of the concepts of leadership presented in Chapter 12, we can see the importance of power in leader effectiveness. Power is either explicitly or implicitly a crucial part of some of the contingency theories of leadership. For example, the decision-making model views leaders as possessing the power to make major work-related decisions alone or to delegate some of the decision-making power to subordinates. Decision-making power can be a form of legitimate power. The leader-member exchange model focuses on the quality of leader-member relations as a key to effective leadership. Referent power is important here because the quality of leader-member relations may depend on the leader's referent power. Perhaps the leadership

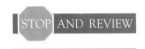

Outline three strategies for increasing power in organizations.

theory that is most strongly linked to notions of power and specific power bases is Fiedler's (1967) contingency model. According to Fiedler, a leader is effective when the leader's style—task-oriented or relationship-oriented—matches the leader's power and control in a given situation. Recall that Fiedler outlines three dimensions for defining the leadership situation: position power, leader-member relations, and task structure. Two of these are strongly linked to certain power bases. Position power deals with the leader's power to reward and punish subordinates. It actually refers to a combination of the three types of organizational power: legitimate, reward, and coercive power. Leader-member relations refers to the quality of the relationship between leader and followers, which represents the leader's referent power. In short, power is a key element in theories of leadership because the role of leader, by its very nature, must be accompanied by some form of power over followers (see Applying I/O Psychology).

APPLYING I/O PSYCHOLOGY

The Empowerment Process: A Key to Organizational Success

A major focus of research in the past two decades has centered on the notion of **empowerment,** which is the process by which organizational members are able to increase their sense of power and personal control in the work environment. Workers can be empowered by managers or other persons in authority positions, or by increasing important work-related skills or responsibilities. While a manager can empower subordinates by giving them some decision-making power or assigning some legitimate power, workers can also be empowered when conditions in the work environment that make them feel powerless are removed. Individual workers can also become empowered by developing a sense of *self-efficacy*, which is, as we saw in Chapter 9, a belief in one's abilities to engage in courses of action that will lead to desired outcomes (Bandura, 1997; Conger & Kanungo, 1988). Other ways in which leaders can empower workers include the following:

Express confidence in subordinates' abilities and hold high expectations concerning their performance—Considerable evidence suggests that supervisors who have high expectations about their work group's performance may subtly communicate these feelings to the workers and thus positively influence their behavior (Eden & Shani, 1982).

Allow workers to participate in decision-making processes—Workers who share in decision making are more committed to the chosen courses of action (see Chapter 11).

Allow workers some freedom and autonomy in how they perform their jobs—For example, let workers be creative or innovative in work methods. The job enrichment programs discussed in Chapter 7 can empower workers by giving them increased responsibility over how their jobs are performed and evaluated.

Set inspirational and/or meaningful goals—Again, there is considerable evidence that goal setting is an

empowerment
the process by which organizational members can increase their sense of power and personal control in the work setting

■■■   APPLYING I/O PSYCHOLOGY (*continued*)

important motivational strategy (see Chapter 7). Also, according to the path-goal theory of leadership (see Chapter 12), setting meaningful goals is one of the important moves that leaders can make to help work groups become more effective.

Use managerial power in a wise and positive manner, such as limiting the use of coercive tactics—Our discussion of the use of different power bases emphasized that coercive power can lead to dissatisfaction in the targets of the power and a reduction in the power user's referent power base. By contrast, reward, expert, and referent power bases allow workers greater choice and flexibility in following the power user. They can decide to strive for the reward or can choose to follow someone who is knowledgeable or admired. These are generally more effective strategies for achieving positive work group outcomes.

The empowerment process can have very positive effects on organizational outcomes. For example, empowering workers can help lessen the impact of demoralizing organiza-

tional changes. If workers feel that they have some sort of personal control over aspects of the work environment, and if they have had a say in some of the organizational changes, they can more easily adapt to and accept the changes (Greenberger & Strasser, 1986). Empowered workers may also be better able to deal with certain types of organizational stress (Spreitzer, 1996), particularly stress that results from a sense of lack of control or from job uncertainty (see Chapter 9). There is considerable evidence that empowerment and feelings of self-efficacy play an important role in motivating workers to achieve challenging work-related goals (Gist, 1987), especially if they have a hand in setting the goals and feel that the goals are within reach. In addition, empowered workers are more likely to persist at a task in spite of difficult organizational or environmental obstacles (Block, 1987; Conger & Kanungo, 1988). Finally, empowerment may be related to future career development and career success of workers (London, 1993).

Organizational Politics

The use of politics occurs daily at all levels of all organizations (Schein, 1977). For example, a qualified individual is passed over for a promotion that goes to a coworker who is clearly less qualified; organizational members say that it was a political decision. Two office workers who have a history of never getting along suddenly file a joint formal complaint about a mutually disliked supervisor; observers explain that their collaboration is due to office politics. A junior-level manager gives up a planned weekend trip to stay at home and take care of the boss's dog while the executive is out of town. The manager's motivation? Obviously political. Anyone who has had the chance to observe the operations of an organization has seen organizational politics in action.

Although the study of organizational politics is relatively new in industrial/organizational psychology, it is very important because politics in organizations is common (Ferris & Kacmar, 1992), occurs at all levels, and can have serious effects on job performance, satisfaction, and turnover (Ferris & King, 1991; Madison, Allen, Porter, Renwick, & Mayes, 1980; Mayes, 1995). However, before we begin to explore the effects of organizational politics, we must start by clearly defining the term.

DEFINING ORGANIZATIONAL POLITICS

Earlier definitions stated that organizational politics involved the self-serving, or selfish, use of power or influence to achieve desired outcomes. This covers a very wide range of behaviors; in fact, just about any behavior can be interpreted as being political. Typically, the types of political behaviors in which we are interested involve the use of power or influence that is not part of one's position or role within the organization (Mayes & Allen, 1977). Because political behaviors are not "sanctioned" by the organization, it is assumed that organizational politics are bad or harmful to the organization's functioning, but this is not always true. Although a worker may act politically to satisfy selfish goals, using means that are not considered to be acceptable organizational procedures, the outcome might actually be favorable to the organization. In other words, political behaviors sometime lead to successful organizational outcomes. Such behavior might be called **functional politics**—behaviors that assist the organization in attaining its goals. On the other hand, political behavior that inhibits the attainment of organizational goals is **dysfunctional politics**. The same political behavior may be either functional or dysfunctional, depending on how it affects the goals of the organization. For example, a salesman may use high-pressure tactics to make a sale, despite an organizational policy that frowns on such techniques. However, if the sale is made and the customer is satisfied, the tactics are functional, because the goals of both the salesperson and the organization have been met. However, if the salesperson uses the unapproved techniques and makes the sale, but the customer is unhappy with being subjected to high-pressure tactics and vows never to buy another of the company's products, the political behavior can be termed dysfunctional. The salesperson's goals have been met, but the organization's goal of keeping customers happy and loyal has been thwarted. It is not always easy to distinguish between functional and dysfunctional political behavior, because the difference between the two often depends on looking at the broad picture of how the behavior affects the organization and its goals (Cavanagh, Moberg, & Velasquez, 1981).

Ideally, if political behavior is going to occur in organizations (and it is), it should be functional. However, in any organization some of the political behavior will be functional and some will be dysfunctional. Figure 13.1 shows how political behavior that operates in the individual's self-interest can sometimes overlap with the organization's goals. The political behavior

functional politics
political behaviors that help the organization to attain its goals

dysfunctional politics
political behaviors that detract from the organization's ability to attain its goals

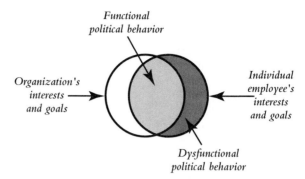

Functional
political behavior

Organization's
interests
and goals

Individual
employee's
interests
and goals

Dysfunctional
political behavior

FIGURE 13.1

Political Behavior
Source: S.P. Robbins, *Organizational Behavior: Concepts and Controversies* (Englewood Cliffs, NJ: Prentice-Hall, 1979), p. 404.

that satisfies the goals of both is functional; the behavior that satisfies the goals of the individual but not those of the organization is dysfunctional.

While some of the political behavior that takes place in government and work organizations is dysfunctional, oriented toward achieving personal goals to the detriment of organizational goals, much political behavior is actually functional, helping both the individual and the organization achieve respective goals. However, it is the dysfunctional politics that often gain the most attention, because they sometimes violate the organization's codes of ethical and moral behavior. For example, in one organization, reporting negative information about another worker to management might be considered a breach of ethics, while in another organization such political behavior might be more accepted. In one company, management might view workers' unionization as an acceptable political practice, while the management of a rival organization might see it as mutiny.

Research has examined how organizational politics is perceived by workers and groups of employees. For example, Ferris, Russ, and Fandt (1989), suggested that for some workers, organizational politics is seen as a significant source of stress. Other workers seem to truly enjoy engaging in organizational politics. While lower-level employees may view politics as an additional burden, managers tend to view organizational politics as "part of the job" (Ferris, Frink, Galang, Zhou, Kacmar, & Howard, 1996). Employees at different levels of the organization also seem to perceive politics differently. One study found that top-level managers and lower-level employees believed that there was less politicking going on in their organizations than did managers at the middle levels (Parker, Dipboye, & Jackson, 1995).

TYPES OF POLITICAL BEHAVIORS

Political behavior was defined as any self-serving behavior. This means that politics includes many different types of behaviors. To better understand organizational politics, it is important to have some scheme for classifying political behaviors. Farrell and Petersen (1982) have suggested that political behaviors can be grouped along three dimensions: internal-external, lateral-vertical, and legitimate-illegitimate.

The internal-external dimension refers to whether political behavior involves only members of the organization, or if it extends beyond the boundaries of the organization to include outside people and resources. Examples of external political behaviors would be bringing a lawsuit against an organization or organizational member, consulting with members of competitor organizations, or leaking secret company information to the press. The lateral-vertical dimension concerns whether the political behavior occurs between members of the same status within the organization, or if it crosses vertical status levels. Political behaviors involving superiors and subordinates would be an example of vertical politics, while two coworkers campaigning for the same promotion are engaging in lateral politics. If a subordinate bypasses the typical chain of command and goes to someone higher in the organization to complain about an immediate supervisor, this is vertical politics. Several coworkers of the same status who form a coalition are engaging in lateral politics. The third dimension is whether a particular political behavior is legitimate or illegitimate. This legitimate-illegitimate dimension concerns whether the behavior is "normal everyday" politics, or some extreme form of political behavior that violates the generally accepted "rules of the game." As mentioned, organizations and work groups establish their own codes of what is appropriate, or legitimate, and what is unacceptable, or illegitimate. Illegitimate political behavior is most likely to be used by alienated members of the organization who feel that they have no other alternatives and nothing to lose, such as a worker who is about to be fired. For example, slowing down work output—rate setting—may be a legitimate form of political behavior in many organizations, whereas sabotage, such as purposely breaking an important piece of work equipment, will always be considered illegitimate.

Interestingly, the distinction between whether a particular political behavior is legitimate or illegitimate, acceptable or unacceptable, or good or bad, is in large part a value judgment. The same type of behavior may be considered unacceptable in one situation, but acceptable when performed in another.

It is also true that political behaviors performed by certain organizational members might be approved, while the same behavior from other workers may be disapproved. For example, political behaviors are usually considered a way of life at the top levels of an organization, while such behaviors among the lower-level members are often labeled subversive and potentially dangerous to the organization. The perspective of the person making the judgment also affects whether a political behavior is considered acceptable or unacceptable. What one person considers to be a perfectly reasonable action, another may consider to be dirty politics. Moreover, actions that many might agree are reasonable political behaviors can, if taken to extremes, lead to very negative and very dysfunctional ends. For example, forming coalitions can be seen as a good way for low-ranking members to gain some collective power and influence within the organization. However,

TABLE 13.3

Organizational Political Behaviors: The Good, The Bad, and The Ugly

Good	Bad	Ugly
Forming coalitions	Striking	Rioting
Blame placing (pointing out who is legitimately at fault)	Passing the buck (avoiding personal blame)	Scapegoating (blaming an individual who is likely not at fault)
Image building (making yourself look good by emphasizing your positive attributes)	Discrediting others (pointing out others' faults so that you look good in comparison)	Mudslinging (bringing up negative and possibly false information about another person)
Making demands and bargaining	Blackmailing	Sabotaging
Limiting communication	Withholding information	Lying
Refusing to comply	Stalling	"Stonewalling"
Forming alliances	Displaying favoritism	"Brown-nosing"

The same basic political behavior, which may initially be seen as "good" or acceptable, can be misused or can be seen as being misused, and can thus be labeled "bad." Certain political behaviors can be taken to extremes that can be very disruptive to the organization and its functioning.

management may perceive such coalitions as precursors to negative outcomes such as work stoppages and striking. At extremes, striking workers may engage in activities to disrupt organizational operations by forming picket lines to keep "scab" workers out, destroying company property, and rioting. The same basic process can thus be perceived as either good or bad depending on the timing, the circumstances, and the people involved (see Table 13.3, and On the Cutting Edge).

One particular political behavior that has received a great deal of attention is termed "whistleblowing." **Whistleblowing** is when employees convey criticisms about their organization's policies and practices to persons or authorities outside the organization (Perry, 1998). (Note that in Farrell and Petersen's scheme, whistleblowing is external political behavior.) Typically, whistleblowers believe that the organization's practices are illegal, immoral, or illegitimate, regardless of whether the criticisms are indeed valid (Near & Miceli, 1985, 1995). Well-known instances of whistleblowing include employees of chemical companies who have reported instances of dumping of hazardous waste, a Federal Aviation Administration employee who exposed improprieties in the FAAs investigation of the Valujet crash, and exposures of the criminal activities of politicians by members of their office staffs.

whistleblowing
political behavior whereby an employee criticizes company policies and practices to persons outside the organization

ON THE CUTTING EDGE

Politics and Influence Tactics Used in Union Organizing Campaigns

When employees in a U.S. company become interested in unionizing, the federal government, under the auspices of the National Labor Relations Act, requires that elections be held in order to determine if a majority of company employees favor joining the union. This is clearly a political process, because both the employees and the employers are interested in maximizing their own self-interests. Employers will often oppose the formation of employee unions because unions may impose restrictions on the organization's employment practices, and may cost the organization money by pushing for increased wages and benefits. Some employers so strongly oppose unions that they may commit unfair labor practices to try to reduce the number of employee votes in favor of the union—practices for which they suffer only limited penalties enforced under the National Labor Relations Act (Cooke, 1985).

A study by Peterson, Lee, and Finnegan (1992) examined the politics involved in union organizing campaigns, and how the influence tactics used by employers and by union officials affect these campaigns. This study found that the political behaviors most frequently exhibited by employers during union organizing campaigns were quite "ugly" (see Table 13.3), including such activities as spreading rumors about plant closings and about loss of jobs, as well as the hir-ing of consultants whose expertise is using questionable or illegal "union-busting" tactics. The frequency of these ugly political behaviors by employers was found to be higher when the employer was victorious and the union lost the election.

At the same time, union officials were found to use "bad" political behaviors, such as distributing hand-bills to the public aimed at discrediting employers, and attacking employers' financial sources. However, union officials were also found to have engaged in "good" political behaviors, such as communicating and meeting with employees to inform them of union benefits, and forming alliances with other unions.

The results of the Peterson et al. study indicated that "bad" or "ugly" political tactics often backfired on the user. Although rumors about plant closings spread by employers often helped employers win elections, other employer political actions, such as intentionally delaying elections and shifting work and jobs to other facilities, actually hurt the employers' chances of winning the electings. On the other side, the union tactics of handbilling and boycotting work were negatively related to union victories, while more positive political behaviors, such as forming alliances with community leaders, helped the union win. The overall findings seem to indicate that playing "clean" by using "good" political tactics is a better strategy in the long run than dirty politicking.

Whistleblowing is a particularly complicated form of organizational politics. The whistleblower may face an ethical dilemma between doing what he or she believes to be right and hurting a company toward which the worker may feel a sense of loyalty and commitment by exposing the company to possible fines, sanctions, and costs. Moreover, there is the possibility that the organization will retaliate against the whistleblower. For this reason, in the U.S., there are laws that partially protect whistleblowers. Of course, disgruntled employees may file false complaints as a way of getting back at the company that they feel has wronged them.

Not surprisingly, it has been found that employees in organizations that have policies encouraging whistleblowing, and workers whose supervisors support their whistleblowing, have greater instances of reporting inappropriate company practices to external agencies. In addition, workers who have strong values are more likely to whistleblow (Sims & Keenan, 1998).

Whistleblowing is only one type of organizational politics, but it is one that receives a great deal of attention because it involves parties outside of the organization (often the press or consumer protection agencies), and because of the ethical and loyalty implications of whistleblowing. Interestingly, many organizational political behaviors, like whistleblowing, are labeled using slang terminology (see Table 13.3).

Distinguish between functional and dysfunctional political behavior and give examples of each.

CAUSES OF ORGANIZATIONAL POLITICS

Organizational politics are attempts by organizational members to use their influence and power to achieve personal goals, such as increased pay and career advancement. Often, in order to achieve these goals, workers must engage in certain types of political behaviors. To understand organizational politics, which is an inevitable, ongoing process with important implications for the operations of work organizations, we need to explore the factors that contribute to increasing the incidence of political behaviors in work organizations. These include such things as competition for power and scarce resources, difficulties in measuring important work outcomes, compensation for worker inadequacies, and increased group decision making.

Competition for power and resources

When resources such as money, promotions, and status are scarce, people may try to exercise their power to obtain what they need to satisfy their goals (Parker, Dipboye, & Jackson, 1995). The scarcer the resources and the more difficult they are to obtain due to "red tape" or arbitrary allocation procedures, the greater the potential that organizational members will act politically to get what they want. For example, an individual who forms a strong relationship with someone in the organization who has control over distributing important resources may be able to get a larger share of the resources (and to get them more quickly). In a publishing company, a manager noticed that new computers were often distributed first to persons who were friendly with the departmental manager rather than to those who needed them most. In a city government, an employee saw that the incidence of political behaviors increased whenever the city obtained a large state or federal grant, as each department lobbied for a greater share of the money. Generally, competition for power resources increases the incidence of organizational politics.

Subjective performance appraisals

When job performance is not measured objectively, it means that performance may be unrelated to career success. When personnel decisions, such as pay raises and promotions, are based on poorly defined or poorly measured subjective criteria, workers may resort to political tactics such as forming alliances, discrediting others, and lobbying in order to gain favor with the appraisers and get ahead. This can be extremely dysfunctional for the organization since the best workers may not be recognized and encouraged for their efforts. Even worse, poor performers who are good politicians will occasionally be placed in positions of responsibility.

When criteria other than performance, such as dressing a certain way or espousing company philosophy, are overemphasized in personnel decisions, workers may make efforts to look good rather than to perform well. When managers make comments like, "He looks like a real company man," they are likely giving weight to factors that are unrelated to good work performance. This is another reason that sound and objective performance appraisals are a necessity (see Chapter 6).

Delay in measurement of work outcomes

In many jobs, particularly white-collar positions, workers are faced with a variety of tasks. Some tasks see immediate results, while with others the results may not be observed for a long time. A problem occurs when management wants periodic appraisals of workers' performance. Workers who are involved in long-term activities may be at a disadvantage over those engaged in "quick-and-dirty" tasks, particularly if existing performance appraisal methods do not take into account performance on long-term tasks. This means that workers faced with long-term jobs may be faced with two choices: focus their energy into short-term tasks, or engage in political behaviors to convince management that they are indeed good workers. Either case can be dysfunctional for the organization, since it directs effort away from the long-term tasks, which are often very important to the organization.

University professors are subject to this delay in measurement with their research activities. Although both longitudinal and field research projects are valuable, they often require a great deal of time, often even several years to complete. Meanwhile, professors are under pressure to "publish or perish." This leads many to abandon valuable long-term projects for simpler laboratory studies in which the results, and the subsequent publications, appear more quickly.

Compensation for inadequacies

When jobs are ambiguous and workers do not know how to perform them correctly, there is the potential for dysfunctional political behavior as the workers try to look as if they know what they are doing. Defining jobs and work procedures clearly and effectively orienting new employees eliminate much of this problem and reduce the likelihood that workers will engage in political behaviors to compensate for being confused or inadequately trained.

According to one management theory, there is a tendency for members in an organizational hierarchy to be continually promoted upward, until they reach a level at which they have exceeded their abilities to perform the job well. This has been labeled the "Peter principle" (Peter & Hull, 1969), which basically states that employees will eventually rise to their level of incompetency. If this is true—and it probably is more true for some employees than for others—then these workers who have "peaked out" must engage in organizational politics in order to maintain their positions and to make further upward progress. This practice is obviously very dysfunctional for the organization.

In certain instances, workers may engage in politics to cover up another's inadequacies. This might occur if a worker, out of pity, helps and covers up for someone who does not have the skills to perform a job. In other instances, subordinates may protect a leader who is incompetent because of strong positive feelings for that person. However, covering up for a leader who is under legitimate attack is a form of dysfunctional politics. While subordinates may feel that they are being loyal to their boss, having a poor leader can be very harmful for the organization.

Lack of cooperation and interdependence

Work groups that are not highly interdependent, that do not have a strong norm for cooperation, or that do not support one another tend to engage in greater levels of political behavior than groups who are cooperative, interdependent, and supportive. In fact, the results of one study suggested that work groups could be defined along a continuum, with highly politicized groups at one end, and supportive, cooperative groups at the other end (Randall, Cropanzano, Bormann, & Birjulin, 1999).

Increased group decision making

The more that group decision-making procedures are used in organizations, the greater is the potential for politics. Group decision making is basically a political process, with members lobbying for certain courses of action and engaging in a variety of exchanges of favors and support to obtain certain outcomes. For the most part, group decision making, when properly regulated, leads to functional outcomes. However, if the process begins to break down, so that high-quality decisions are not being accepted because of opponents' political savvy and power, the results can be dysfunctional. In extremes, group members may begin to focus more and more energy into the political process, ignoring the implementation of decisions, which is also dysfunctional.

CONSEQUENCES OF ORGANIZATIONAL POLITICS

Because organizational politics can be functional or dysfunctional—either helping or hindering the organization from achieving its performance-related goals—connections between politics and productivity are not straightforward. Clearly, if too much dysfunctional politicking is occurring in an organization, it will have a negative effect on work group productivity. In extreme cases, employees may spend so much time politicking that they spend little time doing their work. However, at least one study suggests that organizational politics are positively related to work performance if workers and supervisors share similar goals (Witt, 1998).

The relationship between organizational politics and job satisfaction is a bit clearer. Research has shown a fairly consistent negative relationship between political behaviors and job satisfaction (Cropanzano, Howes, Grandey, & Toth, 1997; Ferris et al., 1996; Gandz & Murray, 1980; Larwood, Wright, Desrochers, & Dahir, 1998; Parker, Dipboye, & Jackson, 1995). In addition, organizational politics is negatively related to organizational commitment and to the incidence of organizational citizenship behaviors (Ferris & Kacmar, 1992; Randall et al., 1999; Shore & Wayne, 1993; Witt, 1998). Finally, organizational politics may be positively related to both absenteeism and turnover, as workers in highly political work environments get tired of the "political games" and call in sick, or begin to look for work elsewhere (Cropanzano et al., 1997; Ferris et al., 1993; Gilmore, Ferris, Dulebohn, & Harrell-Cook, 1996).

MANAGING ORGANIZATIONAL POLITICS

It is clear that politics can be stimulated by a number of factors in work organizations and that political behaviors take many forms. An important concern is how to manage organizational politics. In many ways, the management of organizational politics is much like the management of conflict that was discussed in Chapter 11: The first step is simply to know when it occurs. Learning the causes of political behavior—particularly factors that are likely to lead to dysfunctional political behavior, such as inappropriate performance measures, inadequate job descriptions and procedures, or poor training for new employees—can help to ensure that conditions do not encourage too much political behavior. On the other hand, a certain amount of politics is natural, and may even lead to functional outcomes for the organization. Group decision-making processes, workers' critiques of established work procedures and suggestions for alternatives and improvements, and competition among workers may all result in functional political behaviors and improved organizational outcomes.

One model suggests five strategies for managing organizational politics (Mayes, 1995):

1. *Remove ambiguity and uncertainty*—Written job descriptions and procedures manuals can help clarify jobs and organizational procedures and help eliminate some dysfunctional politicking.

2. *Provide "slack" resources*—Giving managers slightly more than minimal resources (i.e., discretionary funds, extra positions) means that they will not have to trade political favors in order to meet goals.

3. *Create a positive organizational climate*—From the top levels of the organization down, executives and managers should encourage a climate that discourages negative political behavior. If top-level management is engaging in dysfunctional political behavior, lower-level workers will follow their example, and vice versa.

4. *Clarify personnel selection and appraisal processes*—All personnel decisions should be made devoid of politics.

5. *Reward performance, not politics*—Workers should not be able to succeed in the organization through politics alone.

A Contingency Approach to Organizational Power and Politics

The use and effectiveness of organizational power and politics depends on a number of factors. We have seen that individuals vary in their tendencies, abilities, and willingness to use power and politics. Research continues to explore individual differences in the desire and ability to use organizational power and politics (e.g., Kirchmeyer, 1990). We also know that the ability to use power effectively is related to the characteristics of those who are the subject(s) of the power play (Yukl, Guinan, Sottolano, 1995). Moreover, organizations and work groups differ in the extent to which they will allow certain types of power and political maneuvering by members (e.g., Near, Dworkin & Miceli, 1993). All of this indicates that power and politics in work organizations are extremely complex phenomena that are best explained and understood through a contingency approach, which looks at the interaction of characteristics of the individual or group and factors related to the situation in which the individual or group is behaving.

Researchers have attempted to put power and politics into contingency frameworks. Gray and Ariss (1985) propose that politics vary across the stages of an organization's "life cycle." That is, the political behaviors observed in a very new organization (termed the "birth and early growth stage") are very different than those occurring in a more "mature," established organization. According to this model, appropriate political behaviors are critical for success in managing an organization effectively. The manager must be able to adapt political strategies to those appropriate to the organization and its particular life-cycle stage (see also Mintzberg, 1984; Salancik & Pfeffer, 1977). For example, in the earliest stages of an organization, the manager is actually the entrepreneur who founded the organization. At this point, the manager should wield absolute power, controlling and distributing resources as the manager sees fit. The entrepreneur-manager also controls decision-making power, and aligns the organization's goals with the manager's self-interest. In other words, the organization is created in the image and likeness of the manager. As the organization moves toward maturity, the manager will switch to more of a "bargaining" political strategy of exchanging resources for favors.

In another contingency approach, Cobb (1984), building on the work of Porter, Allen, & Angle (1981), proposes an "episodic model of power" that examines power episodes, or the use of power in actual work settings (see Figure 13.2). The episodic model includes consideration of aspects of the exerciser, or agent, of power and the subject, or target, as well as elements of the power situation. For example, in trying to understand the use of power, this model looks at three factors related to the agent of power. The first, *psychological orientation,* is the motivation to use power. The second, *political skills,* is the agent's understanding of organizational politics and her or his ability to act politically. Finally, *personal power base* is the amount and type(s) of power a person possesses. The model also considers two factors related to the target of power: the *readiness* to act and the *ability*

Factors Considered in Cobb's Episodic Model of Power

FIGURE 13.2

"Factors Considered in Cobb's 'An Episodic Model of Power: Toward an Integration of Theory and Research'" by A.T. Cobb in *Academy of Management Review,* Vol. 9, 1984, pp. 482–493. Reprinted by permission of the Academy of Management.

to act. Readiness is defined as the extent to which the target is inclined to act in a manner consistent with the agent's desires. Ability is whether the target can indeed perform the act the agent desires. Finally, this model looks at the power situation, examining whether the "power episode" occurs in the context of the formal organization, the informal organization, or in both. If the power episode is a formal situation, the agent's legitimate power and authority will likely play a greater role in influencing the target than will the agent's political skills. However, if the situation is informal, the agent's influence skills may be more important than legitimate power bases. This model thus attempts to integrate the scattered research on power in organizations in order to offer a broad and complex approach to understanding power dynamics.

In sum, the topics of power and politics in organizations are still fairly new, although they have been the focus of a great deal of research in the past several years. The contingency models briefly presented here represent future directions in the study of organizational power processes.

Name and define the three power agent factors that affect the use of power in the episodic model of power (Cobb).

Summary

Influence, power, and politics are important processes in work groups and organizations. *Influence* is the use of informal social strategies to get another to perform specific actions. *Power* is the use of some aspect of a social relationship to compel another to perform an action despite resistance. *Organizational politics* is the use of power to achieve selfish, or self-serving, goals. A wide variety of influence tactics are commonly employed in work organizations. One such strategy, *ingratiation*, occurs when an individual tries to influence others by increasing personal appeal through doing favors or through flattery.

There are five major *power bases*, or sources of power: *coercive power*, which involves the use or threat of punishment; *reward power*, which is the ability to give organizational rewards to others; *legitimate power*, which involves the formal rights and authorities that accompany a position; *expert power*, which derives from an individual's work-related knowledge, skill, or expertise; and *referent power*, which comes from the fact that an individual is respected and admired by others. Research indicates that the various power bases have different effects on important organizational outcomes, such as work performance and job satisfaction.

Organizational political behaviors can be divided into two categories. The first, *functional politics*, is political behavior on the part of an organizational member that helps the organization to attain its goals. The second, *dysfunctional politics*, inhibits the organization's goal attainment. Organizational politics arise from a variety of sources, including competition for power and resources, subjective performance appraisals, delay in measurement of work outcomes, compensation for inadequacies, and increased group decision making. Research has attempted to categorize political behaviors and recognize conditions under which they are likely to occur. One goal of management is to try to eliminate dysfunctional political behavior by eliminating conditions that give rise to it. The most recent approaches to studying organizational power and politics take a contingency approach, examining the interaction of individual power characteristics, the target of the power play, and the situational context.

Study Questions and Exercises

1. In what ways are influence, power, and organizational politics different? In what ways are they similar?
2. Consider the five power bases described by French and Raven (1959). Give examples of how a manager might use each to increase work group productivity.
3. Recall some instances in which you observed power used in a work or social group. Which power bases were used in each case? How effective were they in influencing others' behavior?
4. What is the distinction between functional and dysfunctional political behavior? Give examples of each.
5. List some of the potential causes of political behaviors.

Suggested Readings

Cialdini, R.B. (1993). *Influence: Science and practice* (3rd ed.). Glenview, IL: Scott, Foresman. *An enjoyable explanation of how social influence is used by compliance professionals to affect the behavior of others.*

Cropanzano, R., & Kacmar, M.K. (Eds.), (1995). *Organizational politics, justice, and support: Managing the social climate of the workplace.* Westport, CT: Quorum Books. *An edited book of research articles on organizational politics, justice in the workplace, and related topics.*

Kramer, R.M., & Neale, M.A. (Eds.) (1998). *Power and influence in organizations.* Thousand Oaks, CA: Sage. *An edited book of research articles on organizational influence, power, and politics by leading researchers in their respective areas.*

Miceli, M.P., & Near, J.P. (1992). *Blowing the whistle: The organizational and legal implications for companies and employees.* New York: MacMillan. *An interesting and detailed account of one important type of political behavior affecting important organizational outcomes.*

CHAPTER FOURTEEN

ORGANIZATIONAL STRUCTURE, CULTURE, AND DEVELOPMENT

INSIDE TIPS

ORGANIZATIONAL STRUCTURE, CULTURE, AND DEVELOPMENT: UNIFYING CONCEPTS IN INDUSTRIAL/ORGANIZATIONAL PSYCHOLOGY

In this chapter, we view organizations at their most general level: looking at how the organization, as a whole, can affect the behavior of the typical worker. Take organizational structure, for example. In rigid, rule-driven, traditional organizations, it is likely that employees will be expected to adhere closely to strict company regulations and policies. By contrast, in nontraditional organizations, there is a lack of rigid structure and rules, which means that workers will have quite a bit of freedom and are expected to take on responsibility and to demonstrate initiative. Knowing about the structure and culture of an organization can help us to understand and analyze the work behavior that occurs within the organization.

Although this chapter focuses on the organization as a whole, the concepts of organizational structure and culture have been touched on previously. For example, in Chapter 10, we saw that the organizational chart, or organigram, illustrates the lines of formal communication within an organization, or the organization's communication structure. In this chapter we will focus more on the organization's authority structure, since the organizational chart also represents the formal lines of status and authority. The general concept of authority was also discussed in Chapter 13 when the topic of legitimate power was introduced. There are strong ties between the concept of power and the structure of organizations because organizations can be viewed as power structures. The concept of organizational culture has been hinted at in several previous chapters. Organizational culture is connected to workers' feelings about their jobs and their organization— recall Chapter 8 and the discussions of job satisfaction and organizational commitment. In addition, the group processes chapter (Chapter 11) explored the elements that contribute to an organization's total "culture."

The field of organizational development (OD), which is introduced in this chapter, emphasizes that organizations must take steps to keep up with the changing world around them. Organizational development is an eclectic area of I/O psychology, for it draws on many theories and applications from a variety of topics within the broader field, and uses them to help organizations change. For example, to be most effective, OD consultants should be strongly grounded in social science research methods (Chapter 2). They use survey instruments, interviews, and observational techniques to diagnose organizational problems. Many OD programs use interventions that try to heighten employee motivation (Chapter 7), reduce stress (Chapter 9), or improve employee job satisfaction and organizational commitment (Chapter 8). Others focus on improving communication in the work setting (Chapter 10) or improving the quality of leader-follower relations (Chapters 11 and 12). In short, in this chapter many of the theoretical topics presented earlier are pulled together into applications that take the form of OD interventions designed to try to help complex organizations deal with complex issues and problems.

So far, we have studied work behavior at a number of levels. We looked at work behavior at the individual level, examining the processes by which individual workers are selected and assigned to jobs, trained, and evaluated, and the internal processes that affect the behavior of individual workers, including the factors that influence worker motivation, job satisfaction, and stress. We have also explored work behavior at the group level. It is now time to look at work behavior from a larger perspective: the *organizational* level. This larger perspective will allow an exploration of how the structure, dynamics, and culture of the organization itself can affect the behavior of its work groups and individuals.

We will begin by studying the structure of organizations, or how they are designed and operate. We will consider how factors both inside and outside of the organization affect its structure, focusing on how different structures affect behavior within the organization. We will then look at how organizations develop their own individual cultures, that can influence nearly all aspects of behavior at work. Finally, we will look at how organizations can change and develop to meet the demands placed on them from both within and without. In particular, we will study some of the various techniques used to help organizations change in order to become more effective and to become better places to work.

Organizational Structure

organizational structure refers to the arrangement of positions in an organization and the authority and responsibility relationships among them

Organizational structure refers to the arrangement of positions in an organization and the authority and responsibility relationships among them. This means that every organization is made up of persons holding particular positions, or playing certain roles in an organization. The organization's structure is then determined by the interrelationships among the responsibilities of these various positions or roles. Consider, for example, a simple mail-order business that has three positions. The first is the director of operations, who has authority over the other two positions. The director's responsibilities include selecting and acquiring the products that will be offered through the business and handling the organization's finances. The second position is the marketing specialist, whose responsibilities consist of designing the advertisements for the organization's products and placing the ads in various publications. In terms of authority, the marketing specialist is subordinate to the director but superior to the third position: the shipping clerk.

The clerk's responsibilities are solely to package and mail orders. In this very small organization, positions and responsibilities are clearly defined, and the responsibilities are linked in such a way that all functions of the company are handled smoothly and efficiently.

Of course, most work organizations are extremely complex, made up of dozens, hundreds, or thousands of workers. Each has an arrangement of positions and responsibilities that is in some way unique. There are a number of different dimensions of organizational structure. For example, organizations can be classified under a general continuum of structure that ranges from the very formal and traditional to the completely informal and nontraditional. Organizations can also be classified by their size or the "shape" of their organizational hierarchy. We will begin our discussion by examining some of the dimensions upon which organizations can be structured.

Dimensions of Organizational Structure

TRADITIONAL VERSUS NONTRADITIONAL ORGANIZATIONAL STRUCTURES

Traditional organizations have formally defined roles for their members, are very rule-driven, and are stable and resistant to change. Jobs and lines of status and authority tend to be clearly defined in traditional structures, which means that much of the work behavior tends to be regulated and kept within organizational guidelines and standards.

Nontraditional organizational structures are characterized by less formalized work roles and procedures. As a result, they tend to be rather flexible and adaptable, without the rigid status hierarchy characteristic of more traditional structures. Generally, nontraditional organizations have fewer employees than the traditional structures and nontraditional structures may also occur as a small organization that is a subunit of a larger, more traditionally structured organization. For example, an organization that manufactures state-of-the-art jet airliners may be made up of a nontraditional organizational unit that is responsible for designing new aircraft and a traditional organizational unit that is charged with producing dozens of the new jets.

Traditional organizational structures arose around the turn of the century, when advancements in technology had led to the growth of manufacturing organizations and the increase in their output. As these manufacturing organizations became larger and larger, there was greater need for establishing rules to coordinate the various activities of the growing numbers of workers in each organization. These traditional structures began to replace the small, family-type manufacturing organizations, and today many work organizations, such as major manufacturers and service organizations—including banks, the Internal Revenue Service, the department of motor vehicles, and your college or university administration—are traditional organizational structures.

Nontraditional structures are often organized around a particular project or product line and are responsible for all aspects of the job. Motion picture production crews are an example of a nontraditional structure. Film crews contain a number of types of experts and professionals—camerapersons, actors/actresses, lighting specialists, editors—who work together, pooling their knowledge and talents to produce a creative, quality product. Nontraditional structures have also been set up in hospitals and health care agencies, financial institutions, and government (Burns, 1989; Burns & Wholey, 1993; Kolodny, 1979). Nontraditional organizations typically have four important characteristics: (1) high flexibility and adaptability, (2) collaboration among workers, (3) less emphasis on organizational status, and (4) group decision making. We will look at examples of traditional and nontraditional organizational structures a bit later.

CHAIN OF COMMAND AND SPAN OF CONTROL

Traditional organizational structures are characterized by an authority hierarchy that is represented in the organizational chart, or organigram. The organigram depicts graphically the various levels of status or authority in a traditional organization and the number of workers that report to each position of authority. The **chain of command** is the number of authority levels in a particular organization. The chain of command follows the lines of authority and status vertically through the organization. The **span of control** is the number of workers who must report to a single supervisor. An organization

chain of command
the number of authority levels in an organization

span of control
the number of workers who must report to a single supervisor

Tall organization

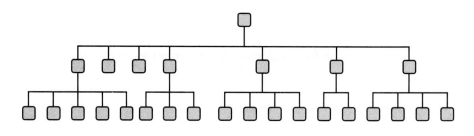

Flat organization

FIGURE 14.1

Tall and Flat Organizational Structures

with a wide span of control has many workers reporting to each supervisor; an organization with a narrow span has few subordinates reporting to each superior. Based on these dimensions of chain of command and span of control, traditional organizations are often described as being either "tall" or "flat" in structure (see Figure 14.1). A tall organizational structure has a long chain of command—many authority levels—and a narrow span of control. A flat organizational structure has a short chain of command but a wide span of control. It is important to note that both dimensions are more descriptive of traditional rather than nontraditional structures. Very nontraditional organizations may have a very small chain of command or none at all, because they deemphasize authority levels.

An organization's shape, either tall or flat, can have important implications for worklife in the organization. For example, in tall organizational structures, workers at the bottom levels may feel cut off from those above, because they are separated by many levels of middle-ranking superiors. On the positive side, tall organizations may offer lower-level employees many different promotional opportunities throughout their careers. Another advantage of such structures is that there is usually adequate supervision because the span of control is narrow; each supervisor is only responsible for a few employees. However, tall organizational structures can become "top heavy" with administrators and managers, because the ratio of line workers to supervisors is very low. Conversely, in a flat structure few levels separate top-level managers from bottom level workers, possibly leading to greater interaction between the top and bottom of the organization. However, flat structures offer few promotional opportunities to workers, and supervision may not always be adequate, because many workers report to the same supervisor.

Although there has been considerable research on how the two types of structures, tall and flat, affect important outcomes such as productivity and worker satisfaction, the results have been inconclusive. It does not appear that one type of structure is better than the other (Gray & Starke, 1984). It is more likely that the shape of the organization follows from its functions and goals. For example, flat organizational structures may be more common when the task is routine or repetitive, thus requiring a large number of workers who need minimal supervision. Organizations with complex and multifaceted goals or products may have taller structures, with different levels handling the various aspects of the company's goals.

FUNCTIONAL VERSUS DIVISIONAL STRUCTURE

Organizations can also be structured by either functions or divisions. **Functional structure** divides the organization into departments based on the functions or tasks performed. For example, a manufacturing firm may be made up of a production department, sales department, and finance department. An amusement park might be divided into operations, publicity, and maintenance.

Divisional structure is based on types of products or customers. Each division may perform the same range of functions, but those functions only serve the goals of the particular division. In other words, each division operates almost as if it were a separate organization. For example, a computer manufacturer may have three types of computers—a "super" multiuse computer designed for large businesses or educational institutions, a small business computer, and a home or personal computer—each of which is represented by a separate division. Within each division are people who handle manufacturing, marketing, and financing, but only for their particular product. Figure 14.2 provides examples of organizations structured by function and division.

functional structure
an organizational structure that divides the organization into departments based on the functions or tasks they perform

divisional structure
an organizational structure that divides the organization according to types of products or customers

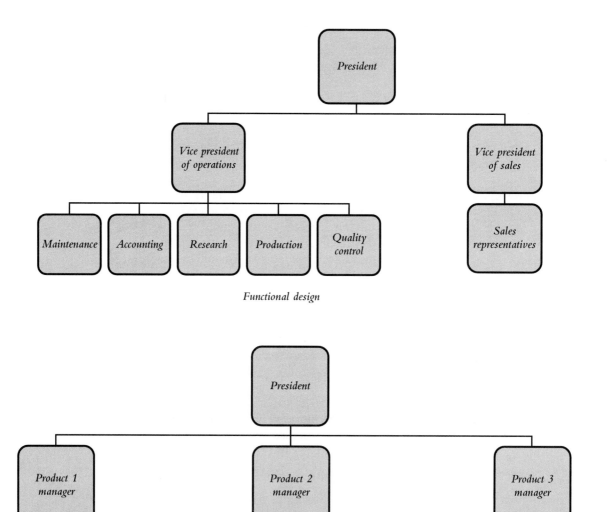

Functional design

Divisional design

FIGURE 14.2

Functional and Divisional Organizational Design

A primary advantage of functional structure is that it creates job specialists, such as experts in marketing or finance, and eliminates duplication of functions. One disadvantage of functional structure is that workers may become overly focused on their own department and area of specialization, and this may breed interdepartmental rivalry and conflict. Another disadvantage is that work must move from one large department to another to be completed, which may decrease productivity, particularly when work is lost in the shuffle or when one department is particularly slow in accomplishing its functions, thereby creating a bottleneck.

Divisional structure has positive and negative aspects as well. One advantage is that the company can easily expand products or services merely by adding a new division. Also, since each division operates as a separate entity, with its own production goals and profit picture, there is greater accountability. It is easy to determine which units are performing at exceptional or substandard levels. One of the major drawbacks to divisional structure concerns the duplication of areas of expertise, since each division contains its own departments for production, sales, research, and other functions. Another potential weakness is that workers with similar skills and expertise may not be able to benefit from professional interaction with each other because they are housed in different divisions.

CENTRALIZED VERSUS DECENTRALIZED STRUCTURE

Another dimension of organizational structure deals with how important work-related decisions are made, which can be either centralized or decentralized. **Centralization** is the degree to which decision-making authority is concentrated at the top of the organizational hierarchy (Fry & Slocum, 1984). In highly centralized organizations, the decision-making power is firmly held by the top levels of the organization. **Decentralization** is the process of taking the decision-making power out of the hands of the top level and distributing some of it to lower levels.

For example, a chain of ice cream parlors could have either a very centralized or a very decentralized structure. In the centralized structure, top-level executives in the corporate office would control all of the decision-making. They would decide what flavors of ice cream should appear in the stores each month, the number of personnel each store can hire, and how the advertising budget for each store will be spent. In contrast, if the same chain had a decentralized structure, each of the store managers would be allowed to make decisions concerning the selection of ice cream flavors, advertising, and personnel. The centralized organization has the advantage of uniformity, which means that each store should operate with some average level of quality and efficiency. However, this structure may limit the ability of individual stores to adjust to special circumstances. For example, one store manager in the centralized chain may complain that his store has special personnel and advertising needs that the corporate decision-makers do not consider. In the decentralized

centralization
the degree to which decision-making power rests at the upper levels of the organizational hierarchy

decentralization
the process of taking the decision-making authority away from the top levels of the organization and distributing it to lower levels.

company, each store can make its own decisions, but this could backfire if the store managers make poor or uninformed decisions.

Examples of Traditional and Nontraditional Organizational Structures

TRADITIONAL ORGANIZATIONAL STRUCTURES

The bureaucracy

bureaucracy
a traditional organizational structure typified by a well-defined authority hierarchy and strict rules governing work behavior

Max Weber, a German sociologist, defined the characteristics of a bureaucracy.

The prototypical traditional organizational structure is the **bureaucracy**, which is characterized by a well-defined authority hierarchy with strict rules for governing work behavior. The bureaucratic organization is often represented as a pyramid, with the few members with highest status on the top, leading directly down to the many bottom-level workers who carry out the organization's goal of producing goods or services. The bureaucratic model was developed around the turn of the century by the German sociologist Max Weber, who formulated a theory of organizational structure that was based on formality and authority (Weber, 1947). Weber believed the bureaucracy established order in the work setting and increased productivity by reducing inefficiencies in organizational operations. According to him, a true bureaucratic organization should possess six characteristics outlined in Table 14.1: the division or specialization of labor, a well-defined authority hierarchy, formal rules and procedures, impersonality, merit-based employment decisions, and an emphasis on written records.

Manufacturing organizations and those providing simple customer service are the most likely candidates for bureaucratic structure, which, with its emphasis on job specialization, tends to lead to greater productivity when

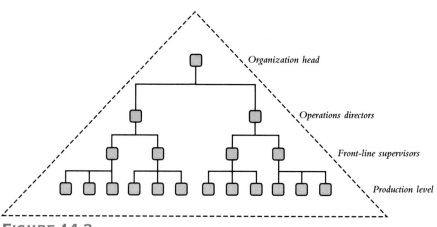

FIGURE 14.3

A Bureaucratic Organization is Arranged Like a Pyramid with Decreasing Authority Levels Leading Down to the Production Line.

the manufacturing of goods or the delivery of services is routine. Many of the organizations you deal with on a daily basis, such as the post office, supermarkets, department stores, and fast-food restaurants, are built on the bureaucratic model. And, contrary to popular notions, these bureaucracies are usually efficient organizations. However, the formal nature of the bureaucratic organization, with inflexible rules that stifle individual creativity and initiative, may lead to dissatisfied employees (Adler & Borys, 1996). The bureaucratic model may restrict an organization's ability to grow and innovate.

The line-staff organizational structure

As organizations grew in complexity, a variation of the traditional bureaucratic model began to emerge. This structure was designated the **line-staff organizational structure** (see Figure 14.4). This traditional structure is made up of two groups of employees, each with different goals. The first group is the **line**, or those workers who are directly engaged in the tasks that accomplish the primary goals of the organization. For example, in manufacturing organizations, line employees are the ones making products on the

STOP AND REVIEW

Define three dimensions used to classify organizational structures.

line-staff organizational structure
a traditional organizational structure composed of one group of employees who achieve the goals of the organization (the line), and another group who support the line (staff)

line
employees in an organization who are engaged directly in tasks that accomplish its goals

TABLE 14.1

Six Characteristics of a Bureaucratic Organization

Specialization of labor—The complex goals or outputs of the organization are broken down into separate jobs with simple, routine, and well-defined tasks. In this way, each person becomes a specialized expert at performing a certain task.

A well-defined authority hierarchy—Bureaucracies are characterized by a pyramid-type arrangement in which each lower position is controlled and supervised by the next higher level. Every position is under the direct supervision of someone higher up, so that there is no confusion about who reports to whom (see Figure 14.3).

Formal rules and procedures—In a bureaucracy there are strict rules and regulations to ensure uniformity and to regulate work behavior. Because of these extensive rules and procedures, there should never be any doubt about what a particular worker is supposed to be doing. Everyone's job is well defined, and procedures for coordinating activities with other workers should be clearly established.

Impersonality—In bureaucracies, behavior is based on logical rather than emotional thinking. This means that personal preferences and emotional factors do not have a place in any work-related decisions. For example, a true bureaucratic service organization would never give preferential treatment to one customer over another.

Employment decisions based on merit—Hiring and promotion decisions are based on who is best qualified for the job rather than on the personal preferences of those making the personnel decisions. In a true bureaucracy, people who are effective workers should be the only ones advancing to higher-level positions.

Emphasis on written records—To ensure uniformity of action, and fair and equitable treatment of employees, bureaucracies keep meticulous records of past decisions and actions. All behaviors occurring in the organization are recorded, which contributes to the image of bureaucrats as compulsive "paper-shufflers."

To many people, modern bureaucracies seem overly large and impersonal, with a dismaying amount of paperwork and "red tape"

staff
specialized employee positions designed to support the line

assembly lines or shop floors. In service organizations, line workers are involved in the distribution of services to customers. The second group of employees is designated as the **staff**, which consists of specialized positions designed to support the line. In today's complex organizations, many organizational members hold staff positions that have very little to do directly with the primary goals of the organization. For example, in a computer assembly plant, many employees' jobs involve functions that have nothing to do with assembling computers, such as bookkeeping, plant maintenance, public relations, marketing research and maintaining employee records (Nossiter, 1979).

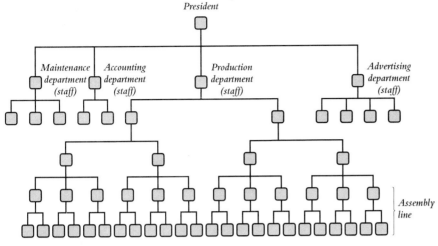

FIGURE 14.4

Line-staff Organizational Structure. In a manufacturing organization, the line is represented by production line workers. The staff consists of specialized positions or departments designed to support the line.

NONTRADITIONAL ORGANIZATIONAL STRUCTURES

The team organization

The **team organization** typifies the nontraditional organization structure. In team organizations, workers have broadly defined jobs, not the narrowly specialized positions common to traditionally structured organizations. Workers in a team structure thus know a great deal about the product or goals of the organization and tend to possess a variety of work-related skills. This enables both the workers and the organization to adopt new technology readily, to take on new projects, and to develop innovative work strategies. A second characteristic of team organizations is the collaboration among workers. Rather than each worker independently contributing a "piece" to the final product, as in a traditional organization, employees in team organizations share skills and resources, working collaboratively to get the job done. Because of this tendency to work together, a great deal of communication in the form of meetings, problem-solving groups, and conferences goes on in team organizations (Ford & Randolph, 1992).

Team organizations also place much less emphasis on organizational status than do traditional structures. Although team organizations may have a formal project leader and supervisors or managers, these workers do not typically possess the "ultimate" authority that leaders or managers have in traditional organizations. Each worker is viewed as a knowledgeable and skilled

team organization
a nontraditional organizational structure consisting of a team of members organized around a particular project or product

Film crews, with many different specialists working together, are an example of a team organization.

professional who is expected to be self-motivated and committed to the goals of the organization.

A final characteristic of team organizations is the tendency toward group decision making. Team members have considerable input into organizational decision making (Randolph & Posner, 1992). Often team organizations make important decisions by consensus. This increase in group decision making means that there is bound to be a great deal of conflict in team organizations (Barker, Tjosvold, & Andrews, 1988). However, this intragroup conflict is usually turned to productive, functional outcomes. The lack of both hierarchy and formally designated roles means that the structure of a team organization is radically different from the pyramidal shape of traditional organizations (see Figure 14.5).

The project task force

Another type of nontraditional organizational structure, which usually only occurs in the context of larger, more traditional organizations, is the **project task force**. Typically, a project task force is a temporary, nontraditional organization of members from different departments or positions within a traditional structure who are assembled to complete a specific job or project. Traditional lines of status or authority do not usually operate in such a task force, whose structure is more like a "temporary" team organization (Ford & Randolph, 1992). All members are viewed as professionals who will contribute collaboratively to the group's output. As in team organizations, deci-

List and define the six characteristics of a bureaucracy.

project task force
a nontraditional organization of workers who are assembled temporarily to complete a specific job or project

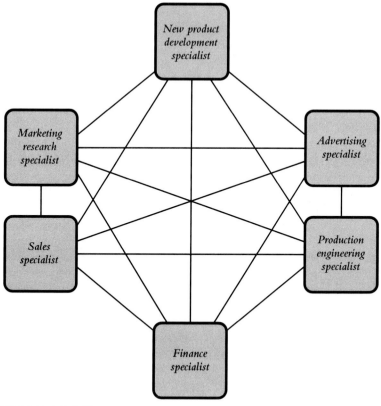

FIGURE 14.5

A Simple Team Organizational Structure

sions are made through democratic or consensus decision making, and members are expected to take on responsibility and be self-motivated.

A project task force might be created in an organization that is suddenly faced with hosting the annual two-day conference of executives from all of the divisions and affiliates. A task force is put together to handle all facets of the meeting, including obtaining space, arranging accommodations for out-of-town participants, assembling the program, mailing information, and conducting the sessions. In creating the task force, persons with varied skills and expertise are selected, including budgeting specialists to handle finances, graphic artists to produce designs for printed programs, and clerical workers to deal with correspondence. All members work together until the task is completed and then return to their original positions. Some companies may even have standing task forces that, like volunteer fire departments, assemble ready for action whenever special projects arise.

The matrix organization: A hybrid of traditional and nontraditional designs

matrix organization
an organizational design that blends functional and product structures

The **matrix organization** is an organizational design that is structured both by product and function simultaneously. This offers the best of both traditional and nontraditional designs. In matrix organizations, workers have two reporting lines: one to a functional manager, a person responsible for the worker's area of expertise (i.e., engineering, marketing, etc.), and one to a product manager, who is responsible for the particular product being produced (see Figure 14.6). In manufacturing, matrix organizations are designed to adapt rapidly to changing conditions. They are characterized by high flexibility and adaptability (Larson & Gobeli, 1987).

Matrix organizations will not work well with all types of tasks or workers. They tend to be best suited for projects and products that require creativity and innovation, but are less well suited for routine tasks that can be easily broken down into specialized components. Routine tasks are better handled in more traditional organizational structures. Matrix organizations tend to have high levels of performance in dealing with complex, creative work products (Ford & Randolph, 1992). Also, because of the amount of interaction among members in matrix structures, and the high levels of responsibility they possess, matrix organizations usually have greater worker communication and job satisfaction. The drawbacks to matrix organizations are obvious: reporting to two bosses simultaneously can cause confusion and potentially disruptive conflict.

CONTINGENCY MODELS OF ORGANIZATIONAL STRUCTURE

It is clear that no one type of structure is appropriate for all work organizations. Organizations differ on many factors, including the number and type of goods or services they produce, their size, their customers, their employees, and the environment in which they reside. All these factors can help determine which structure is "best" for an organization. Many theorists argue that organizational structure should be addressed with contingency models. Recall that these models look at the interaction of characteristics of the individual—in this case, the organization—and characteristics of the situation—in this case, the setting in which the organization operates. We will briefly consider three contingency models of organizational structure, two focusing on how structure adjusts to fit with characteristics of work technology and one considering how structure is made to fit aspects of the external environment.

Compare and contrast traditional and nontraditional organizational structures and give examples of each.

Organizational structure and work technology

One of the earliest contingency models of organizational structure was proposed by sociologist Joan Woodward (1965). Focusing solely on manufacturing organizations, Woodward stated that for maximal performance organizational structure needed to match the type of production technology. Woodward classified manufacturers into three types: small-batch produc-

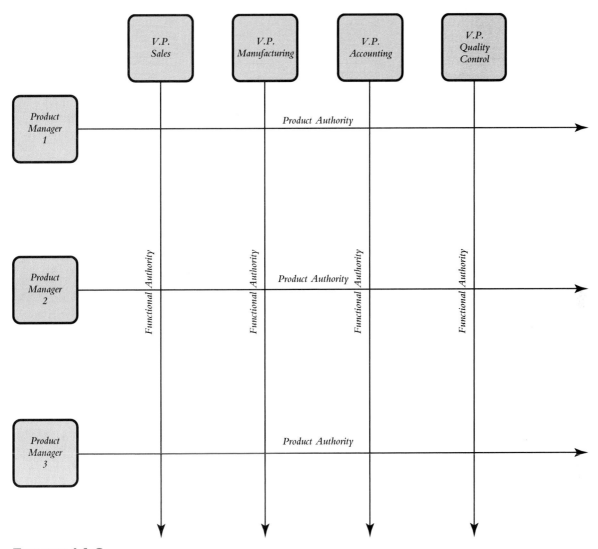

FIGURE 14.6

A Matrix Organization is a Hybrid of Functional and Product Designs

tion, mass production, and continuous-process production. According to Woodward's model, producers of small batches of specialty products, such as specialized electronic components or construction equipment, required a span of control that was moderate in size, with about 20 to 30 workers reporting to a supervisor, and a short chain of command. Mass-production organizations, referred to as "large batch" companies, such as automobile assemblers and manufacturers of household appliances required a large span of control (40 to 50 workers per supervisor), and a fairly long chain of command, with several levels in the organizational hierarchy. Finally, continuous-process manufacturing, such as producing chemicals or refining oil, required a small span of control and a very long chain of command.

When organizational structures fit the level of technological complexity, the organizations were productive. When there was a mismatch between technological complexity and the appropriate structures designated by Woodward's model, productivity suffered (Woodward, 1965; Zwerman, 1970).

The one obvious limitation to Woodward's structural contingency model is that it deals only with manufacturing organizations. A theory proposed by Perrow (1970) looked at the relationship between technology and structure in all types of organizations. Rather than focusing solely on production technology, Perrow examined what he called "information technology," which refers to all aspects of jobs, including the equipment and tools used, the decision-making procedures followed, and the information and expertise needed. Perrow classified work-related technology along two dimensions: whether the technology was analyzable or unanalyzable, and whether the work contained few or many exceptional work situations requiring creative problem solving. Analyzable/nonanalyzable work refers to whether the technology can be broken down into simple, objective steps or procedures. Work with few exceptions is predictable and straightforward—presenting few novel problems. Work with many exceptions has unfamiliar problems turning up often in the work process.

The interaction of these two technology dimensions leads to Perrow's model of four categories of organizational technology: routine, engineering, craft, and nonroutine (see Figure 14.7). Routine technology consists of analyzable work tasks with few exceptions; examples are assembly-line production or the work of grocery store clerks. Engineering technology consists of analyzable tasks with many exceptions; examples are the work of lawyers or civil engineers, which involves tasks that are analyzable but ones that also present workers with novel problems that need to be solved. The lawyer dealing with unique legal cases or an engineer encountering problems in constructing a specific bridge are examples. Craft technology uses technology that is unanalyzable, with no discrete steps, and has few exceptions; examples include the jobs of a skilled woodcarver and a social worker. Both of these jobs involve specialized experience and knowledge, but both present workers with similar types of problems. Finally, nonroutine technology is represented by the work of scientific researchers or professional artists and musicians in which there are no clearly defined steps to follow, yet there are many unique problems to be solved.

According to Perrow's model, the structure of the organization adjusts to the technology. For example, organizations with routine technology tend to be formal, highly rule-driven, and centralized in structure. Nonroutine technology leads to a less formal, more flexible structure, such as a team or matrix organization. The craft and engineering technologies tend to result

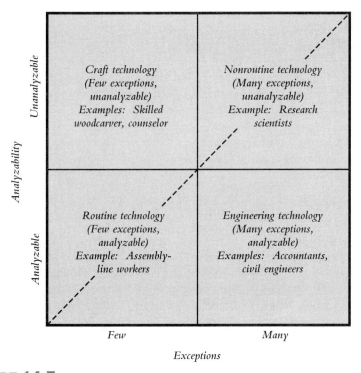

FIGURE 14.7

Perrow's Contingency Model of Organizational Structure

in structures that are neither completely traditional nor completely nontraditional but rather a combination of both (Lynch, 1974; Van de Ven & Delbecq, 1974; Withey, Daft, & Cooper, 1983).

Both Woodward's and Perrow's contingency models emphasize that organizational structure must adjust to fit the technology used by the organization. Woodward's theory focused on the different forms of technology used in manufacturing organizations, while Perrow's model expanded the definition of technology to look at all forms of organizations.

ON THE CUTTING EDGE

The Role of Organizational Structure in Computer-Aided Manufacturing

Since the 1980s, there have been profound advances made in manufacturing technology. The greatest impact has been in the area of computer-aided manufacturing (CAM). More and more, product manufacturing is being controlled and monitored by sophisticated computer systems. The

ON THE CUTTING EDGE (continued)

changeover to CAM has led to significant organizational restructuring for the purposes of adapting and better integrating state-of-the-art production techniques (Shaiken, 1984).

In a study of nearly 200 U.S. metal-working factories, the impact of CAM technology on organizational structure was explored (Dean, Yoon, & Susman, 1992). Of particular concern was how CAM impacted the decentralization of decision making and the formalization of rules in the organizations. It was found that the use of CAM technology led to increased decentralization, as production workers took on greater responsibility for making important work-related decisions. A great deal of the increased decision-making being done by lower-level workers was related to the increased flexibility offered by CAM technology. Specifically, it was found that the computers could be more quickly and easily reprogrammed by lower-level personnel, rather than going through the time-consuming process of going up the chain of command to make reprogramming decisions. Yet, with this increase in decentralization came an increase in the development of rules governing production-related decisions in the factories. The greater decision making of production workers seemed to increase the adoption of specific rules to govern the computer-related decisions they were now shouldered with.

Organizational structure and the external environment

While it is clear that the structure of an organization can be greatly affected by the technology used (David, Pearce, & Randolph, 1989), the organization is also affected by *external* factors: elements in the outside world that exert some influence on the work organization, affecting its operations and its structure (Bluedorn, 1993). Some common environmental factors that have an impact on work organizations include economic forces, competitors, consumer demand, the supply of raw materials, the supply of human resources, and government regulations. Lawrence and Lorsch (1967) have developed a contingency model of organizational structure that looks at how structure must adapt to fit changing environmental conditions. They assert that two processes determine a company's ability to keep up with external changes: differentiation and integration. **Differentiation** is the complexity of the organizational structure: the number of units, the various orientations and philosophies of the managers, and the goals and interests of the organization's members. **Integration** is the amount and quality of collaboration among the various units of the organization. As the external environment becomes more complex and turbulent, the organization must increase its differentiation and integration to match its internal complexity to the external complexity.

differentiation
the complexity of an organization's structure which is based on the number of units, the orientations of managers, and the goals and interests of members

integration
the amount and quality of collaboration among the divisions of an organization

Because performing artists face many unique problems with no clearly defined steps to follow, they require a non-routine technology.

For example, in today's marketplace, a manufacturer of photocopiers must be highly differentiated, with a number of departments designed to meet certain organizational goals. The engineering and research and development departments must keep up with the latest technology in developing improved office and home copier machines, the advertising department must be able to develop eyecatching and convincing ads to rival those of the competition, the sales department must maintain high sales rates, and the service department must provide courteous and efficient service to customers. As environmental conditions change, with consumers demanding better-quality photocopiers and the competition continuing to present new product lines and new advertising and sales campaigns, the organization with its various departments must innovate in order to survive. The organizational complexity must increase to meet more complex environmental demands. This means that there must be good integration among the various departments, so that they are able to work together to achieve shared goals. Therefore, the organization must use a great deal of its resources to make sure that the various departments are well-integrated, for it would do no good to have the best copiers on the market if the servicing of the machines is so poor that it drives away customers.

The Lawrence and Lorsch model makes us aware of the effect of the external environment on the organization, its structure, and its ability to meet its goals. Organizations today exist in a constantly changing world. The work organization that fails to keep up with evolving consumer trends, technology, and industrial developments may have a tough time surviving. This notion that organizations can be structured to adapt to environmental changes is a central tenet of the area of behavioral science known as *organizational development*. We will discuss organizational development later. However, now that we have some understanding of the *formal* structure of organizations, and how that formal structure impacts work behavior, we need to look at the impact of the *informal* organization on workers. We represent these informal "forces" of the organization as aspects of *organizational culture*.

Organizational Culture

organizational culture
the shared values, beliefs, assumptions, and patterns of behavior within an organization

While organizations have a formal structure, there are also "informal" forces that operate to shape the organization and behavior within the organization. A popular approach to viewing these informal aspects of the organization is to refer to them collectively as the "organizational culture." **Organizational culture** can be defined as the shared values, beliefs, assumptions, and patterns of behavior within an organization (Ott, 1989). In many ways, organizational culture is somewhat akin to the organization's "personality" (Kilman, Saxton, & Serpa, 1985). It is differences in organizational culture that cause two companies—similar in most important ways, such as company size, goods produced, and regional location—to "feel" completely different to workers and visitors (Schein, 1992).

Organizational culture develops from many sources. For example, organizations develop certain assumptions and norms governing behavior through a history of experience concerning what seems to "work" and what doesn't work for the organization. Shared norms, values, and goals contribute greatly to an organization's culture (O'Reilly & Chatman, 1996). The technology used in the organization, the markets it sells its products and/or services to, and the organization's competition all influence organizational culture. Organizational culture can also be affected by the societal culture in which the organization is located, and by the makeup of its workers. Finally, the organizational culture can be shaped by the personalities of the companies' founders and their most dominant early leaders, as with companies like Hewlett-Packard, IBM, and J.C. Penney (Schneider, Brief, & Guzzo, 1996).

It has been suggested that organizations vary in terms of the strength and influence of their organizational cultures, with some organizations having strong, dominant cultures, and other companies having weaker cultures (O'Reilly, 1989). It has also been suggested that having a strong organizational culture can be beneficial to companies who provide services since it is crucial that representatives of service organizations provide a strong sense of company identity to customers (Chatman & Jehn, 1994). In other words, it is important that customers of service organizations understand what the company "stands for."

Organizational culture can, by its very nature, serve as a force that guides behavior within the organization. However, organizational culture can oftentimes make an organization resistant to change and innovation (Hilton, 1997; Schein, 1996). By understanding and assessing an organization's culture, it becomes easier to predict organizational behavior under different circumstances (Hofstede, Neuijen, Ohayr, & Sanders, 1990; Ott, 1989). For example, one study found that organizations with strong cultural values that involved flexibility, openness, and responsiveness were more likely to grow, expand and innovate, while organizations whose culture valued consistency and adherence to the company's mission were more productive and profitable (Denison & Mishra, 1995).

One method for assessing organizational culture developed by O'Reilly, Chatman, and Caldwell (1991) is called the *Organizational Culture Profile* (OCP). In measuring organizational culture using the OCP, organizational representatives sort 54 "value statements" describing such things as organizational attitudes toward quality, risk taking, and the respect the organization gives to workers into meaningful categories to provide a descriptive profile of the organization. Recent research using the OCP in a number of different companies indicated that important dimensions of organizational culture include the company's concern with innovation, stability, orientation towards people, orientation towards producing results, and team orientation (Chatman & Jehn, 1994).

The study of organizational culture is an increasingly popular approach for I/O psychologists studying organizations at a global level. Organizational culture is intertwined with the topics of job satisfaction (Chapter 8) and group processes (Chapter 11) covered earlier.

Give two examples of contingency models of organizational structure.

Organizational Development

In recent years, many organizations have had to cease operating because they were unable to change to keep up with the times. Companies that did not use the latest marketing or production techniques lost out to competitors who took advantage of such state-of-the-art technology. Retail stores that were unable to keep pace with changing consumer tastes have gone out of business. Furthermore, organizations have to adapt not only to external conditions but also to internal factors (Burke & Litwin, 1992). For example, as new generations of workers enter the workforce with different types of skills and different ideas about what they want from their jobs, the organization must adjust to utilize their skills and to meet their demands. Otherwise, the better workers will leave the organization, or disgruntled employees may be able to slow down productivity through costly work stoppages and strikes. In addition, the recent trend towards downsizing means that many organizations must produce more with fewer organizational members. In short, the ability to change is critical to an organization's survival (Greenwood & Hinings, 1996; Levinson, 1994).

organizational development (OD)

the process of assisting organizations in preparing for and managing change

The study of organizational change is an important topic. In addition to studying organizational change processes, social scientists have made use of certain interventions to help organizations prepare for and manage organizational change (Porras & Robertson, 1992). The specific specialty area concerned with helping organizations develop, adapt, and innovate is known as **organizational development (OD)**. Organizational development often involves altering the organization's work structure or influencing workers' attitudes or behavior to help the organization to adapt to fluctuating external and internal conditions.

OD typically takes place in a series of phases. The first phase is usually a diagnosis of the organization to identify significant problems. In the next phase, appropriate interventions are chosen to try to deal with the problems. The third phase is the implementation of the interventions, or OD techniques. Finally, the results of the interventions are evaluated (Burke, 1987). Organizational development does not involve one single theory or approach, but rather a variety of orientations and methods for helping organizations manage change.

Organizational development is both a general philosophy about the nature of modern organizations as well as a discipline that studies ways to help organizations be more effective. Most OD programs are oriented toward long-term organizational improvement rather than focused on solving immediate problems. In fact, most OD practitioners believe that their role is not to solve the organization's problems but to help improve the organization's ability to solve its own problems. Typically, employees of all levels collaborate in the development and implementation of the OD program. Moreover, many OD programs use team approaches to deal with problems at the group or organizational level, rather than focusing on problems associated with individual workers (see Up Close). One goal of such programs is to help the organization become aware of its own operations and problems (Friedlander, 1980). Often, this is done by opening up organizational communication channels and increasing members' involvement in the planning and execution of work activities (Monge, Cozzens, & Contractor, 1992). The rationale is that workers who are more involved in and who have a better understanding of important organizational processes will be more committed to helping the organization to achieve its goals (French, 1969).

What are three sources of organizational culture?

UP CLOSE

How to Develop Effective Work Teams

Many innovative strategies for improving work performance involve the development and use of work teams. If work teams or committees are to be effective in solving organizational problems, certain criteria must be met. Care must be taken to select appropriate participants for problem-solving teams and to ensure that certain procedures are followed.

UP CLOSE (*continued*)

Galbraith (1973, 1977) has developed a set of rules for making high-level, decision making work teams effective:

1. *Team members should perceive their participation as important and personally rewarding*—To build commitment to the team, members must view their work as beneficial. One way to do this is to offer some sort of formal rewards for contributions to the team.

2. *The work team should include some persons of organizational power who will be responsible for helping to implement any decisions made by the group*—If a team is to develop innovative strategies, it is important that these efforts are implemented. It is important to have some managers with organizational power as part of the work team to make sure that team suggestions are listened to and implemented.

3. *Team members should have knowledge and information relevant to the decision*—In any problem-solving work team, it is critical that members have job-related knowledge relevant to the decisions that are being made. This involves including lower-level workers who have first-hand experience with the job.

4. *Team members should have the authority to commit their respective departments to the decision*—The work team participants must be able to commit valuable resources (human and otherwise) to help in the suc-

cessful implementation of the strategies developed by the team.

5. *Team members should represent and inform nonteam workers*—If the problem-solving work team or committee is a select group of a larger body of workers, it is crucial that the team members inform nonteam members about the committee tasks and decisions.

6. *The influence of team members on decisions should be based on expertise*—This is especially important when members come from various levels in the organization. Work-related decisions should be based on relevant knowledge, not on organizational politics.

7. *Work team conflict should be managed to maximize the problem-solving process*—The conflict that arises in problem-solving committees should be functional and help to develop a high-level and highly critiqued course of action. It is important that such conflict be controlled to avoid dysfunctional outcomes.

8. *Team members should have good interpersonal skills and adequate leadership*—The success of a work team is going to be directly related to the smooth flow of communication among members. The better their interpersonal skills, the better the group's ability to reach high-quality decisions. It is also important for the team leader to take an appropriate but not too dominant role to facilitate team interaction and to help resolve nonproductive conflicts.

Organizational development is an applied, practice-oriented area of the behavioral sciences. The OD practitioner is oriented toward helping the organization design and implement a program for dealing with change-related

change agent
name for an OD practitioner, referring to the person's role as a catalyst who helps organizations through the process of change

action research
an OD methodological model that applies social science research methods to collecting relevant organizational data that are used for solving organizational problems

problems. The OD practitioner is often referred to as a **change agent**, one who coaches or guides the organization in developing problem-solving strategies. The change agent, however, is not a problem solver. The change agent works with the various levels of the organization, developing or deciding on problem-solving techniques. The change agent is a behavioral scientist, often an industrial/organizational psychologist, who is expert at assisting organizations in diagnosing problems, and skilled in helping organizational members deal with sensitive situations. The change agent will have some special knowledge of particular OD interventions that may be used to help solve the organization's problems. The change agent also acts as an educator who trains the organization to implement strategies for coping with future problems (Burke, 1987).

Organizational development programs usually follow one of several procedural models, all of which typically use an OD consultant, or change agent, and go through the four phases outlined earlier. One popular OD model is **action research**, which is the process of applying social science research methods to collect relevant data within the organization to study an organization and to help it understand and solve its problems (Aguinis, 1993; Frohman, Sashkin, & Kavanagh, 1976). The application-oriented goal of action research means that it is somewhat different than the traditional hypothesis-testing research discussed in Chapter 2. While hypothesis-testing research attempts to find new knowledge that is applicable to a wide range of organizations, action research tries to solve problems specific to a particular organization. Action research involves some of the same tools used by hypothesis-testing research, namely objective observation and the collection and analysis of research data. However, their goals and scope are quite different, for action research is oriented toward producing some specific result.

The first step in the action research process is data gathering and problem diagnosis. Here, the OD consultant collects data in order to diagnose the problem situation. In the next step, feedback is given as the data, and the OD consultant's interpretation of the data, are presented to the organization's members. The next step is joint action planning. Here the OD consultant and the organizational members design a problem-solving program, which might be one of a variety of OD interventions that we will discuss later. Once the program is implemented, the action research process repeats itself. Now, however, the data gathering is an attempt to determine the effectiveness of the OD program. If it is successful, the organization and the OD consultant might discuss ways to make it a regular part of the organization's operations. If unsuccessful, the program might need some alterations, or a different program might be tried. Figure 14.8 graphically depicts the steps in the action research model.

ORGANIZATIONAL DEVELOPMENT TECHNIQUES

In solving organizational problems, OD programs use a wide variety of established techniques (Fagenson & Burke, 1990), some of which we have already discussed. For example, recall from Chapter 7 that job enrichment is a

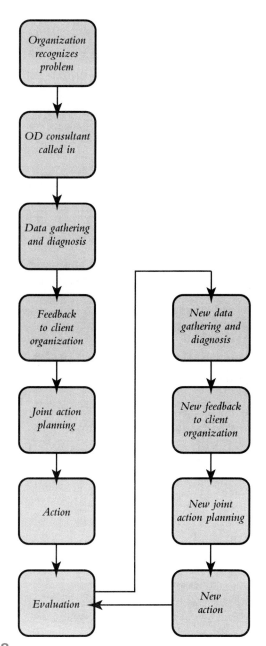

FIGURE 14.8

Steps in the Action Research Process

process of increasing the levels of responsibility associated with jobs to improve worker satisfaction and commitment to the work effort. Although job enrichment was presented in Chapter 7 as a motivational technique, it could also be used in OD efforts because it involves the collaboration of workers in work teams that play an important part in solving change-related problems that may affect the groups' work performance. Organizational behavior modification programs (also presented in Chapter 7), which reinforce desirable work behaviors, can likewise be used as an OD technique. Of the other procedures that have been used by OD practitioners, we will discuss six of the more popular: survey feedback, t-groups, team building, process consultation, management by objectives, and quality circles.

Survey feedback

survey feedback

an OD technique whereby the consultant works with the orgnaization to develop and administer a survey instrument to collect data that are fed back to organizational members and used as the starting point for change

The use of employee surveys is a common OD strategy. **Survey feedback** is the process by which the OD consultant works with the organization to develop a survey instrument to collect data that is then used to solve specific problems or to institute a program for managing change. The survey is usually designed to assess employee attitudes about important work-related issues such as the organization in general, company policies and practices, quality of leadership, and coordination among work units. Once constructed, the survey is distributed either to all workers or to a representative sample. The OD consultant then tabulates the survey data and puts them into a form that will be easily understood by organizational members. Next the results are presented to organizational members. This feedback can be done in a number of ways: in written form, in small or large group discussions, or in a general meeting. Since the survey is merely an assessment tool to indicate which areas of the organization need attention or improvement, the final, crucial step in a survey feedback program involves developing strategies to deal with any problems or concerns that arise from the results. The survey is a starting point for solving organizational problems or for instituting future programs for planned organizational change (Born & Mathieu, 1996).

One of the direct benefits of the survey is that it can increase the upward flow of communication from lower-level workers to management (see Chapter 10). The survey may also have a positive effect on workers' attitudes, as they perceive that management is interested in hearing their views and concerns (Gavin, 1984). This will only occur, however, if steps are taken to address problems. If not, workers may develop negative attitudes about management and the survey process. Finally, the survey results can show workers that they are not alone and that others share their attitudes and concerns.

Outline the methods and terms used in organizational development.

Research indicates that survey feedback is an effective OD technique, if followed by some positive actions (Bowers, 1973; Bowers & Hauser, 1977; Guzzo, Jette, & Katzell, 1985). Surveys have additional advantages as well. They are an efficient way of collecting a large amount of information from a large number of workers. Also, since surveys can be conducted anonymously, lower-level workers feel that they can safely voice their opinions, which can lead to very honest appraisals of work situations. Since it requires considerable training to create valid and reliable employee surveys and to analyze and interpret the results, I/O psychologists or other social science professionals are most often involved in survey feedback programs.

T-groups

The OD strategy known as **t-groups** (also called **sensitivity training**) actually refers to the use of unstructured group interaction to help workers gain insight into their motivations and their behavior patterns in dealing with others. T-groups, which stands for "training groups," consists of small groups of workers who meet in a nonwork setting for an unstructured discussion of their attitudes and beliefs concerning their work, the work environment, and their interactions with supervisors and coworkers. The eventual goals of t-groups are for participants to gain insight concerning their own behavior, to develop greater openness, and to improve skills in understanding and dealing with others. Typically, a professional serves as group leader, although the leader usually plays a nondirective role in merely keeping the goals of the session in everyone's minds and keeping the discussion from getting out of hand. An effective leader will usually prevent problems such as "psychological casualties," which occur when the group targets one or more persons for intense criticism or when participants suffer from airing sensitive personal information in a public forum.

T-groups were very popular in the 1960s and early 1970s, when interest in self-exploration and group encounters was at its height. Although it is not as popular today, this method is still used by some OD practitioners who report very positive results, particularly in improving the communication skills of managers. However, research on the effectiveness of t-groups has been inconclusive. T-groups and related techniques have been shown to be related to improved employee attitudes and increased job satisfaction (Neuman, Edwards, & Raju, 1989; Sundstrom, de Meuse, & Futrell, 1990). While there is some evidence that managers can achieve insight into their behavior and develop interpersonal skills through the process, there is some concern over whether the insights and skills gained from sensitivity training generalize to actual work settings (Campbell & Dunnette, 1968; Mirvis & Berg, 1977). In other words, it is not clear that gaining insight about one's own behavior, and developing communication skills in the "safe" setting of the t-group, will then translate into changes in a worker's behavior in the actual work setting.

Team building

Team building is an OD intervention in which groups of workers meet to discuss ways to improve their performance by identifying strengths and weaknesses in their interaction with one another (Liebowitz & de Meuse, 1982). In some ways, team building is similar to t-groups, although the

t-groups (sensitivity training)
an OD technique that uses unstructured group interaction to assist workers in achieving insight into their own motivations and behavior patterns in dealing with other organizational members

team building
an OD technique in which teams of workers discuss how to improve team performance by analyzing group interaction

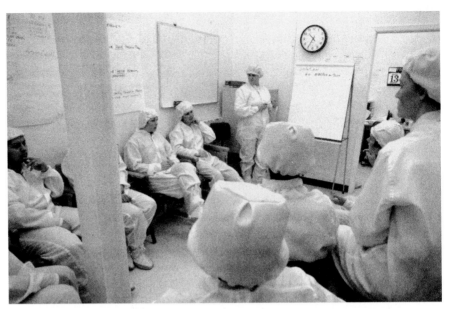

In team building, groups of employees discuss methods of improving their work.

focus is no longer on individual growth and skill development but on improving team functioning and goal attainment. Although some emphasis is put on improving members' abilities to communicate with one another, greater stress is placed on helping the team to achieve performance-related goals.

Team building can use existing groups of workers or construct new work teams. The first session is a diagnostic meeting. The OD consultant serves as moderator, while the team discusses its current level of functioning in an unstructured setting similar to that used in t-groups. Each team member is allowed to present personal views and suggestions for improving the team's performance. Through this process, the group should eventually agree upon strategies for implementing positive changes. Subsequent sessions involve evaluating and "fine-tuning" new procedures or suggesting alternate approaches. One evaluation of various OD techniques found that team building was the technique that had the largest and most consistent positive effects on increasing employee job satisfaction and morale (Neuman, et al., 1989).

Because of its emphasis on the group, rather than the individual, team building does not have the threat of psychological casualties that may exist in t-groups. Also, because team building is focused clearly on performance-related goals, it may be connected to improved job performance (Woodman & Sherwood, 1980).

Process consultation

Process consultation is an OD technique in which a consultant helps a client organization to "perceive, understand, and act upon process events which occur in the client's environment" (Schein, 1969, p. 9). In process consultation, the OD consultant helps the organization to learn how to solve its own problems. In many ways, process consultation epitomizes many of the central themes of organizational development. It uses a change agent, the process consultant, who works as a teacher to assist the client-organization in learning how to use objective methods, such as survey instruments, structured interviews, or the collection of relevant performance data, to diagnose and solve its own problems. The consultant also instructs organizational members in how to implement specific OD problem-solving techniques. The goal is for the organization to become self-reliant by knowing how to deal with change-related problems once the process consultant is gone.

process consultation
an OD technique in which a consultant helps a client-organization study its problems objectively and learn to solve them

To understand the specific steps in process consultation outlined by Schein (1969), we will use the example of a consultant who is working with CDE company, which produces and sells cosmetics. The first step is the *initial contact* with the client-organization, which is usually initiated by someone in the organization who realizes that problems exist and is willing to try to solve them. In the case of CDE, the vice president of sales called in the process consultant, Dr. Io, because of what he considers to be high turnover of sales personnel and managers.

The second step is *developing the contract*. In initial, exploratory meetings, the vice president of sales meets with top decision makers—the other vice presidents and the company president—to determine the problems, explain the consultant's role, and formulate actions to be taken. A formal contract is drawn up to determine matters such as client time and compensation. A "psychological" contract, which includes the expectations and goals of the organization as well as Dr. Io's goals, is also formulated: The company wants to reduce costly turnover, and Dr. Io wants the organization to take steps not only to reduce turnover, but also to ensure that the company can deal with future turnover problems. In addition, she also wants the organization to explore any related problems that the consultation uncovers.

The third step is the *selection of a setting and a method of work*. A site for study is selected collaboratively with the client and is usually a unit near the top of the organization. Those workers who are being observed by the consultant must be made aware of her presence and purpose. Together, Dr. Io and the CDE decision makers choose the largest regional headquarters as the site for study. Because this office is adjacent to corporate headquarters, Dr. Io will have easy contact with the company's top-level executives.

The fourth step is *data gathering and diagnosis*. By using interviews (particularly exit interviews), direct observation, and surveys of employees, Dr. Io tries to obtain an in-depth picture of the organization and its internal processes. She works with certain CDE personnel, instructing them in data collection methods. Through analysis of these data and consultation with relevant CDE personnel and executives, specific problem areas are targeted. The data reveal that turnover is linked to three factors: (1) Salespersons perceive their sales commissions rates to be lower than those in other sales positions; (2) salespersons feel they do not receive enough attention from sales managers; and (3) some salespersons are hired without much experience, and CDE provides little specific training of new personnel.

The next step is the *intervention*. A variety of intervention strategies are used in process consultation. Some are as simple as providing feedback of the consultant's observations to workers. Others may involve counseling work groups or individuals or setting agendas to increase a group's awareness of its own internal processes. In the case of CDE, Dr. Io and company executives jointly decide to develop a "sales force improvement task force," composed of both management personnel and salespersons, who will formulate a proposal to improve the hiring and training procedures for new salespersons. Other goals of the task force will be to conduct a survey of sales commission rates in other companies and to develop a program for improving sales managers' supervision.

The final step in process consultation is the *evaluation of results and disengagement*. According to Schein (1969, p. 123), successful process consultation improves organizational performance by "changing some of the *values* of the organization and by increasing the *interpersonal skills* of key managers." If these goals are met, CDE should see some changes in the organization's perception of the value of the sales force and in the selection, training, and treatment of sales personnel. There will also likely be some improvement in the interpersonal skills of sales managers. The relationship between consultant and client is terminated by mutual agreement. In the case of CDE, Dr. Io may or may not work with the organization in implementing and evaluating the various new programs. Sometimes, a slow disengagement process is used whereby the consultant gradually lessens involvement with the client-organization. This is likely in the case of Dr. Io, since the programs for organizational improvement will probably take a long time to design and implement, and their evaluation will likely initially require her assistance.

Process consultation is a detailed OD program, involving an extensive and long-term relationship between the consultant and the client-organization. Some authors have likened this technique to the psychotherapeutic process in which a therapist works with a client over a long period of time to diagnose and work toward solving the client's problems (Landy, 1989).

Management by objectives (MBO)

management by objectives (MBO)
a goal-setting OD technique in which supervisors and subordinates jointly set performance goals; at the end of the goal period, their attainment is evaluated and new goals are set

Management by objectives, or MBO, is a goal-setting technique that is often used as an OD intervention. In MBO, subordinates work with superiors in jointly setting performance goals. The basic rationales behind the procedure are that work-related goals must be clearly specified and measurable, and that employees should participate in setting them to become committed to their fulfillment. MBO is closely related to the goal-setting techniques of motivation discussed in Chapter 7. Management by objectives can also be used as an alternative to traditional rating methods of performance appraisal, because successful MBO programs must accurately and objectively measure the attainment of performance goals (see Chapter 6). At the end of the goal period—usually three to six months and occasionally twelve months—employees again meet with supervisors and receive feedback concerning the goal attainment. If the goals have not been met, suggestions for improvement are made. If they have been attained, new and perhaps even more challenging goals are set.

The MBO technique actually predates the organizational development movement. Developed in the 1950s by Drucker and his associates (Drucker, 1954), it has been a very popular method for improving worker performance. Unfortunately, MBO has also been widely misused. Often any type of goal setting is labeled MBO, even though it does not follow the MBO model (McConkie, 1979). For MBO to be implemented correctly, the following criteria must be met:

- *Employees must participate in setting personal performance goals*—A potential weakness of MBO goal setting, however, is that workers may take advantage of the freedom they are afforded and set goals that are much too easy and do not represent a motivating challenge. Alternatively, if the supervisor too strongly influences the setting of goals, MBO may not be effective because employees may feel that they have no real voice in the goal-setting process.

- *Feedback concerning goal attainment must be provided*—As in any performance appraisal system, the strength of the appraisal depends on the ability to assess performance objectively. Objective measurement of goal attainment must take place, and this information must be presented to the employees.

- *Guidelines for improvement must be provided*—In the case of the failure to reach goals, supervisors should provide suggestions for improving work performance. Otherwise, employees may become frustrated and unmotivated by their inability to achieve set goals.

- *Goals must be realistic*—They must neither be too high nor too low. If goals are unrealistically high, the workers will be frustrated. If they are too low, the employees are not challenged.

- *The upper levels of the organization must support the program*—Since MBO is a time-consuming process for supervisors, their efforts must be recognized. The best way to do this is to include effective participation in the MBO program as part of the supervisors' own performance goals.

- *Individual, work group, and organizational goals must be equally emphasized*—If jobs involve cooperation with other employees (and most jobs do), overemphasis on individual goals may inhibit the group's ability to work together. Thus, workers must be oriented toward achieving not only their own goals but also those of the group and the organization as a whole.

Management by objectives is one of the most widely used OD techniques, partly because it can be implemented in just about any work organization and with almost any type of job. MBO is also one of the most successful OD programs. A meta-analysis of 70 studies of MBO programs found that there were productivity gains caused by MBO in 68 of the 70 cases (Rodgers & Hunter, 1991).

Quality circles

quality circles
small groups of volunteer employees from the same work area who meet regularly to solve work-related problems

One OD intervention that is typically associated with Japanese management techniques is the concept of **quality circles**, which are small groups of volunteer employees from the same work areas who meet regularly to identify, analyze, and solve product quality problems and other work-related problems (Adam, 1991; Munchus, 1983). In initial quality circle meetings, members are trained in quality control, work on developing communication skills, and learn problem-solving techniques. They then select a particular problem to study and use a variety of methods to gather information pertinent to the issue. Finally, a recommendation is made to management about how to solve the problem. The goal of quality circles is to get employees more involved in their jobs and to increase their feelings of having some control over their work. This increased employee involvement should lead to greater worker satisfaction, work quality (and perhaps productivity), and worker commitment to the organization.

Research indicates that quality circles can indeed lead to increased quality and productivity in both Japanese and American manufacturing organizations, and may also enhance participants' job satisfaction (Barrick & Alexander, 1987; Buch & Spangler, 1990; Marks, Mirvis, Hackett, & Grady, 1986). However, in certain instances U.S. applications of quality circle programs have failed, although analysis suggests that the failures have more to do with poor implementation than with any inherent flaws in the theory underlying quality circles. The failure of quality circle programs, and indeed of other OD programs, can often be traced to a lack of support from management and/or workers, or to poor training and preparation of participants (Tang, Tollison, & Whiteside, 1987, 1991, 1996; Marks, 1986). Moreover, there is evidence that unless quality circles are maintained and fully integrated into the organizational system, their effectiveness will diminish in a year or two (Ledford, Lawler, & Mohrman, 1988).

Other "quality-oriented" programs include total quality management (TQM) and the implementation of continuous improvement work processes (Omachonu & Ross, 1994; Teboul, 1991; Waldman, 1994). The success of all quality enhancement programs involves some fundamental changes in organizational climate and culture in order to get workers committed to improving quality of output. Yet, this is very important because many organizations have found that unless they produce high-quality products or services they cannot compete in the increasingly competitive global market.

APPLYING I/O PSYCHOLOGY

An Organizational Development Program "Develops" at Polaroid

Several years ago, at one of Polaroid's film manufacturing plants near Boston, employees were becoming increasingly frustrated and angry with the treatment they were getting from management (see Albrecht, 1983). The main problem was their dissatisfaction with a plant manager who was considered to be an "oppressive, inconsiderate tyrant" with little concern for workers' needs or concerns. The situation had gone so far that an employee complaint was delivered to the division vice president, asking that the plant manager be replaced or reoriented. An OD consulting team was called in. The OD consultants used interviews, questionnaires, and reviews of the plant's performance to gather relevant data. Interestingly, the plant was one of the most productive Polaroid facilities. According to questionnaire and interview results, employees' dissatisfaction centered on the issue of trust in management.

Working with workers at all levels, the OD consultants, together with Polaroid employees, developed a set of strategies, including sending the plant manager to a leadership training program, conducting communica-tion and problem-solving workshops for various supervisors and key employees, and holding regular meetings between the plant manager and various employee groups.

As a result of the OD program, employees' satisfaction and the social climate in the organization improved greatly. More important, the program's benefits extended to other problems identified during the diagnosis, including improvements in the relationship between managers and hourly workers, the establishment of quality-of-work-life focus groups, and the development of joint productivity-improvement projects that were Polaroid's version of quality circles.

Not only did the OD intervention work to solve immediate problems at this specific Polaroid plant, but the OD diagnosis and assessment uncovered other potential problems that were addressed in subsequent programs. Thus, the first OD intervention led to subsequent OD interventions in other areas of the plant. Furthermore, the success of the OD program in this plant led to the use of OD techniques in other plants within the company.

THE EFFECTIVENESS OF ORGANIZATIONAL DEVELOPMENT

A variety of techniques have been used as interventions in organizational development programs. However, the important question is, "Does OD work?" There is no firm answer to this question. A number of factors make it difficult to ascertain the effectiveness of OD programs. One difficulty concerns the variety of OD techniques that can be used as part of OD programs. Some of these techniques may simply be better than others. For example, evidence suggests that MBO and survey feedback are moderately success-ful (Kondrasuk, 1981; Miner, 1983), whereas there has been some ques-tion about the effectiveness of t-groups (Odiorne, 1963; Miner, 1983). A second reason lies in the nature of the organization that conducts the OD program. What works in one organization may not be effective in another because of differences in the attitudes of organizational members or in the workers' and management's commitment to OD efforts. Another con-cern is the abilities of the OD consultants overseeing the intervention—some OD consultants may simply do a better job than others (O'Driscoll & Eubanks, 1993). Furthermore, determining the effectiveness of organi-zational development is hard because of difficulties in conducting good evaluation research. Because OD interventions usually take place on a large scale, often involving an entire organization, much of the evidence for their effectiveness is based on case studies. The unit of measure-ment—the "participant" in the evaluation of an OD program—is the or-ganization. It is very difficult to combine the results of a specific OD strategy with those of the same method used in other companies because the circumstances may be very different. This often leaves us with only a series of case studies as evidence for the effectiveness of OD programs (see Applying I/O Psychology).

Overall, the results of evaluations of organizational development pro-grams are mixed. There have been some reports of glowing successes, and other reports of failures (French & Bell, 1990; Woodman & Pasmore, 1987). Bass (1983) proposes that the positive effects may be greater in job satisfaction and organizational commitment than in increased organiza-tional productivity. Moreover, he suggests that many of the successes of OD programs may be long-term changes that do not show up for months or years, long after the evaluation of the OD program is completed. Until more rigorous evaluation research of OD programs is routinely conducted, it will be very difficult to draw firm conclusions about their effectiveness. However, organizational development remains quite popular, largely be-cause its underlying theory—that organizations must adapt to keep up with the rapid changes in the world at large—makes sense.

List and describe five organizational development techniques.

Summary

Organizational structure is the arrangement of positions in an organization and the relationships among them. Organizational structures can be gener-ally classified into traditional and nontraditional forms. Traditional organi-zational structures tend to be stable and rule-driven, while nontraditional structures are characterized by their flexibility, adaptability, and lack of for-mal authority lines. Important dimensions of organizational structure are the number of authority levels in an organization, or *chain of command,* and the number of workers reporting to a single work supervisor, or the *span of control.* Organizations can also be divided by the kinds of tasks performed—a *functional structure*—or by the types of products produced or customers served—a *divisional structure*. Decision-making power can either be concentrated at the top levels of the organization (*centralization*), or dispersed throughout the organization (*decentralization*).

The *bureaucracy* and the *line-staff organization* typify the traditional structure. The bureaucracy is a structure based on authority relationships among organizational members that operate through a system of formal rules and procedures. The line-staff organization is a formal structure in which the *line* executes organizational objectives, while the *staff* is designed to support the line. Nontraditional organizational structures are exemplified by the *team organization*, a permanent team of competent workers designed for maximizing organizational adaptability, and by the *project task force*, a more temporary structure. A *matrix organization* is a combination of both product and functional organizational designs. The most recent approaches to organizational structure are contingency models whereby the most effective type of structure depends on the fit between structure and the external or internal environment of the work organization.

Organizational culture refers to the shared values, beliefs, assumptions and patterns of behavior in organizations. Organizational culture derives from many sources, can be stronger in some organizations than in others, and has important influences on organizational behavior.

Organizational development (OD) is the process of preparing for and managing change in organizations. OD programs use a consultant who is commonly called a *change agent*. OD programs usually occur in phases. One model for such a program is *action research*, which involves collecting data, diagnosing organizational problems, and developing strategies to take action to solve them. A variety of interventions are used in OD programs, including *survey feedback*, a technique of using data about organizational members' feelings and concerns as the basis for planned change; *t-groups*, a process of increasing workers' awareness of their own and other members' behavior; *team building*, the development of teams of workers to focus on ways to improve group performance; *process consultation*, a long-term method of helping an organization to develop problem-solving strategies; *management by objectives (MBO)*, a goal-setting technique designed to increase worker commitment to the attainment of personal and organizational goals; and *quality circles*, which are groups of employees who meet regularly to discuss quality-related work problems. Evaluation of OD programs indicates that they can be effective for improving certain aspects of organizational effectiveness, although neither their implementation nor their evaluation is easy.

Study Questions and Exercises

1. Consider an organization with which you have had some contact. Describe the structure of this organization using the dimensions of traditional-nontraditional, functional-divisional, and centralized-decentralized. If you have access to the organization's chart, describe its chain of command and span of control.

2. Based on what you know about traditional and nontraditional organizational structures, contrast the work life of the typical worker in a traditional organization with that of a worker in a nontraditional organization.

3. Compare and contrast the contingency models of organizational structure.

4. Describe the organizational culture of a company or firm you are familiar with. What are some of the sources of this company's organizational culture?

5. Consider a common problem in classrooms, such as a difficulty in communication between professor and students or an unclear grading policy. How might an OD consultant solve this problem? What OD techniques might be used?

6. Drawing on your knowledge of research methods, what are the difficulties in evaluating the success of OD programs?

Suggested Readings

Banner, D.K. (1994). *Designing effective organizations: Traditional and transformational views.* Newbury Park, CA: Sage. *A rather comprehensive overview of organizational structure, including such topics as organizational culture, conflict, and power, and how it interfaces with an organization's structure.*

Harrison, M.I. (1994). *Diagnosing organizations: Methods, models, and processes.* (2nd ed.). Newbury Park, CA: Sage. *A practitioner-oriented, OD book that presents techniques for gathering and analyzing data for organizational assessment, diagnosis, and planning for interventions.*

Howard, A. (Ed.) (1994). *Diagnosis for organizational change: Methods and models.* New York: Guilford. *This edited volume, sponsored by the Society for Industrial-Organizational Psychology (SIOP), presents developments in diagnosis for OD interventions.*

HUMAN FACTORS IN WORK DESIGN

HUMAN FACTORS: SEEING THE BIG PICTURE

In this chapter we will begin to look at the relationship between the worker, the work task, and the work environment. Much of the study of the worker and the work task is the specialty area known as human factors. As you will see, the material presented here is quite different from that of previous chapters. In this chapter there is much less theorizing than in many of the previous chapters covering other areas of I/O psychology, because human factors is more "problem-focused." In other words, human factors psychologists are often concerned with solving specific problems, such as reducing errors in a particular work system or improving efficiency in the performance of some work task.

However, this chapter does have important links to other sections and chapters. For instance, while one major goal of personnel psychology is to find the right person for the job, and the goal of training is to "create" the right person for the job, the goal of human factors is to create the right job for the person. Most important, since human factors psychologists study workers and their jobs, the topics of job analysis and job performance (Chapters 3 and 6) are central. When human factors psychologists study jobs, they typically begin with a job analysis to obtain detailed knowledge of the work tasks. This is the starting point for designing work

INSIDE TIPS

machinery, equipment, and environments to be compatible with the people using them. Of course, human factors psychologists have considerable influence on the training of workers to operate complex machine systems efficiently (Chapter 5). Finally, this chapter fits together with Chapter 16, with the present chapter concentrating on the worker-machine relationship, which is known as the operator-machine system, and the next chapter emphasizing the relationship between the worker and the conditions of work.

While some of the basic principles and procedures of human factors introduced in this chapter may appear to be commonsensical, don't be fooled, for they are actually much more complex. Principles of human factors are based on a thorough understanding of human capabilities and limitations (such as perceptual processes and cognitive and physical abilities), the technical capabilities of machines, and the relationship between the two.

The key to success in human factors psychology is the same as that in other areas of I/O psychology: a solid grounding in basic research methodology. Using established principles and knowledge, the human factors professional strives to improve and innovate. These new developments in technology or procedures are then thoroughly and systematically tested before they are ever put into operation. Human factors psychologists spend a great deal of time testing and evaluating what works and what does not in a particular operator-machine system.

The world of work is getting increasingly complex. Advances in technology, the downsizing of workforces, and increased globalization and diversity of organizations means that many jobs are more sophisticated and more complex than ever before. In order to do these jobs, and to do them efficiently, workers, technology, and work systems and environments must be thoroughly integrated. Nearly every job has been touched by today's increasingly sophisticated technology, while many jobs have been completely transformed by it. Because of the increasing complexity and sophisitication of tools, machines, and work systems, the area within the broad field of I/O psychology that is concerned with issues such as the design and operations of these complex work systems and work environments—human factors—is becoming more and more important and influential.

Human Factors

human factors

a specialty area of I/O psychology concerned with designing tools, machines, work systems, and workplaces to fit workers

Psychologists have played an important role in the design and development of complex work machines, systems, and environments. This specialty area is called **human factors**. Also known as ergonomics or engineering psychology, human factors is concerned with designing tools, machines, work systems, and workplaces to provide an optimal fit between characteristics of work machinery and environments and the skills and abilities of workers. Machine systems and work environments are designed to try to increase efficiency by making the machines more compatible with human capabilities and limitations. Additional goals of human factors are to help train workers to use the machines and systems that have been designed and to protect their safety and comfort while they interact with the machine work system. This latter concern will be discussed more fully in Chapter 16.

Human factors draws on research and information from a number of areas of psychology, including the study of sensation and perception, psychophysiology, and cognitive psychology. It also interacts with other disciplines, particularly engineering and architecture, to try to improve work systems and environments. Although research is an important emphasis of human factors psychology, human factors is a very applications-oriented discipline, often focused on solving particular work-related problems (Howell, 1994).

The earliest roots of human factors psychology lie in the work of Frederick Taylor and his followers (see Chapter 1). Recall that Taylor and his followers used principles of scientific management to devise more efficient ways of performing jobs. While the methods used by modern human factors psychologists are light years ahead of Taylor's time-and-motion studies, some of the methods used by human factors psychologists still follow Taylor's rule of breaking down complex jobs into their basic components. However, the job of a computer systems analyst or an air traffic controller is much more complex than the simple mechanical jobs studied by the Taylorists.

One important distinction between the scientific management approach and human factors is that Taylor and his followers focused primarily on the work task, rather than the worker. Human factors places a much stronger emphasis on the worker—on how human abilities and limitations fit into the broader picture of the worker and the job (Howell, 1992). Moreover, human factors focuses on other human needs such as worker safety and comfort, along with trying to improve the efficiency and productivity of workers and their jobs (Wickens, Gordon, Liu, 1998). In the past 30 years, human factors has played a significant and an increasing role in the design of equipment, machinery, work environments, and products in industries as diverse as the military, aerospace, automotives, pharmaceuticals, nuclear energy, and computers (Haslegrave & Holmes, 1994; Nickerson, 1992).

Operator-Machine Systems

A topic of central concern for human factors psychologists is the design and improvement of the **operator-machine system**, which is the interaction of one or more persons with one or more tools or devices to perform some task. These systems can be as simple as a worker using a hammer to drive a nail or as complex as an astronaut flying the space shuttle. However, as technology advances, a greater percentage of workers are operating fairly sophisticated machine systems as an everyday part of their jobs. These sophisticated work machines include computers, motorized vehicles, automated and robotic assembly lines, and aircraft.

The human factors psychologist views the operator and the machine as engaged in a two-way interaction. With sophisticated machinery, such as a

operator-machine system
the interaction between workers and tools or devices used to perform a task

Today's work places abound in sophisticated, complex machines.

computer system, this notion is quite appropriate, because the operator receives information from a sophisticated work machine through various machine displays. The operator then processes this information and makes some decisions about what the machine should do. The operator communicates these decisions to the machine by using certain controls—the buttons, levers, knobs, or keyboard that control its functioning. The machine responds to the controls and produces the desired operation. The new operating status of the machine is then communicated to the operator via the machine displays (see Figure 15.1). For example, someone working with a personal computer looks at its display: the video screen. Seeing a blank screen, the operator knows that the power to the machine is off. The operator decides to turn on the computer and activates a control switch that causes the computer to "boot up," ready for operation. This computer operation is communicated to the operator by some message on the video screen and perhaps a flashing cursor that lets the operator know that the computer is waiting for the operator's next command. All of this—machine display output, sensory reception by operator, interpretation, decision making, and operator action—may take only a fraction of a second. Moreover, this process occurs hundreds or even thousands of times in a typical workday as humans and machines engage in ongoing interaction.

To design an operator-machine system, a human factors psychologist often begins with a detailed job analysis, using methods quite similar to those discussed in Chapter 3. A basic starting point is breaking the job down into its component tasks. Decisions are made concerning which tasks the human operator should perform and which the machine should be required to do. In making these decisions, psychologists take into account the respective strengths of both the human operator and the machine system (see Table 15.1). For example, unlike people, machines can perform numerous repetitive actions without fatigue, while humans can judge the quality of an object and solve problems through inductive reasoning, which are beyond the capabilities of even the most sophisticated computer.

Once the various tasks have been allocated to the operator and to the machine, the next step is for the human factors psychologist to coordinate these activities. For operators and machines to coordinate their respective tasks, they must have some way of communicating with each other. As mentioned, the model of an operator-machine system is the interaction between two beings, which psychologists typically speak of in terms of the inputs and outputs of both parties. In an operator-machine system, the machine outputs information concerning operating status via its displays. This information becomes the operator's input. The operator processes this information, makes decisions, and then outputs the decisions by manipulating machine controls. The manipulation of the controls becomes the machine's input, which causes the machine to perform the requested action. We will examine each of the specific elements in this interaction, first focusing on machine displays, then looking at operator information processing and decision making, and finally investigating machine controls.

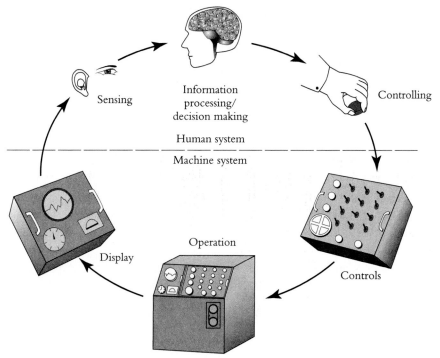

FIGURE 15.1

An Operator-Machine System
Source: A. Chapanis, "Engineering Psychology," from *Man-Machine Engineering,*
Brooks/Cole Publishing Co.; as it appeared in *Handbook of Industrial and Organizational Psychology,* ed. M.D. Dunnette, p. 701, John Wiley and Sons.

TABLE 15.1

Strengths of the Human Operator and the Machine System

Operator Characteristics	Machine Characteristics
Is adaptable/flexible; can handle unexpected events	Does not fatigue; stronger and faster than humans
Can think, be creative, and solve problems	Makes few processing errors
Can easily pull together information from a variety of sources	Can store great amounts of information efficiently
Can learn to correct own mistakes	Can perform several tasks at once
Can perceive and make sense out of ambiguous stimuli	Can perform in a dangerous environment (such as extreme heat, cold, or radiation)
Has low initial costs, high long-term costs (such as salary and benefits)	Has high initial costs, low long-term costs (maintenance)

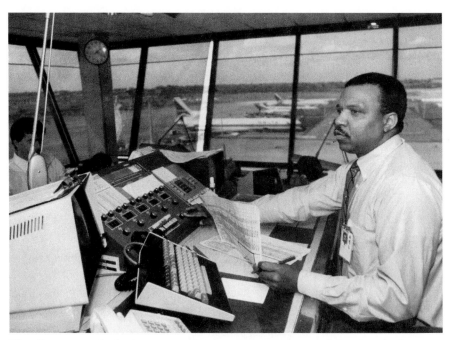

The effectiveness of a display—its speed, accuracy, arrangement, and the type of information it provides—can be crucial to an operator's success, as it is in this air traffic control room.

DISPLAYS

displays
means of communicating information about a machine's operating status to an operator

Machine systems communicate with human operators through a variety of **displays**, or means of communicating information about their operating status to the operator. Some of these displays are visual, such as the radar screen an air traffic controller uses or the lights on your automobile dashboard. Others are auditory: bells, buzzers, and horns that are often used to attract the operator's attention. Tactile displays might include differently shaped knobs to assist in the rapid identification of controls or tiny, raised buttons on the *f* and *j* or *d* and *k* keys of a typewriter to help the operator find the "home row." An example of an olfactory display is the noxious scent mixed with natural gas that warns of possible leaks. Some underground mines in the United States also use a distinguishable odor released into the ventilation system to signal miners to evacuate the mine. Regardless of the type of display, speed and accuracy are often of utmost importance when considering which to use in an efficient operator-machine system. Of the various modes, visual and auditory displays are by far the most common.

List the specific strengths of operators and machines.

Visual displays

Visual displays on machines can be of three types: quantitative, qualitative, and check-reading. **Quantitative displays** are those that give precise numerical values, such as heat gauges, speedometers, and counters. In the past, they have taken a variety of forms, including the circular or "clock-face" displays and the horizontal or vertical scales seen on radios and older stereos. However, with rapid advances in technology, including the development of the LED (light-emitting diode) and LCD (liquid crystal) displays, many of these older, mechanical quantitative displays are being replaced by digital displays. With digital displays, operators generally make more precise readings and fewer reading errors (Sinclair, 1971). However, persons who are trained to read one type of mechanical display may have difficulty quickly reading the digital displays that are replacing many of the older-type quantitative displays. For example, drivers who are used to a semicircular speedometer may have a hard time adapting to digital speed displays.

Qualitative displays provide less precise information to the operator—feedback dealing with certain "qualities" or characteristics of machine operation. For example, the temperature gauge on an automobile or on an automated drillpress may be divided into sections of "cold," "normal," or "hot" operating ranges. Qualitative displays are used when the operator does not need to know precise numerical values. For a truly efficient operator-machine system, it is important to provide the operator with enough information to do the job, but not give *too much* information that might overload the operator or delay response time.

Check-reading displays, which merely tell whether a machine system is on or off, or operating normally or abnormally, provide even less information to the operator. The warning lights on most automobile dashboards that signal low oil pressure or an overheated engine are check-reading displays. They replaced the old quantitative and qualitative gauges, which gave more information than the typical driver needed. After turning on the ignition, the driver merely needs to scan the dashboard display panel; if there are no check-reading displays illuminated, the automobile is safe to drive. Industrial machinery also typically has check-reading displays to tell the operator when something in the system is malfunctioning.

Color coding is often used to enhance visual displays (Chapanis, 1994). For example, a qualitative temperature display might include sections that are red, yellow, and green, to indicate hot, warm and cool operating temperatures respectively. Similarly, check-reading displays often consist of red lights, signifying a "warning" that a system is not operating properly.

In addition to the type of visual display, a human factors psychologist must also be concerned with where displays are located and how they are arranged (Wickens & Carswell, 1995). Consider, for example, the cockpit of a modern jet. The pilot, copilot, and flight engineer are presented with a great number and variety of visual displays that inform them about their altitude, speed, location, and operating status of the aircraft. If displays are

quantitative displays
machine displays that provide precise numerical values

List, in order, the steps (inputs, outputs, etc.) in an operator-machine system.

qualitative displays
machine displays that provide characteristics or "qualities" of machine operation

check-reading displays
displays that indicate whether a machine system is on or off or operating normally or abnormally

not placed so that they can be easily scanned and read, the crew may not receive information that is needed to fly the jet safely. There are some basic rules for the arrangement of visual displays. First, place displays within the line of the operator's sight. If displays are put in places where the operator cannot easily see them, the operator may not receive the information and this may inhibit performance and the efficiency of the operator-machine system. Second, put displays that provide similar or related information next to one another. Third, displays that are to be read sequentially should be placed in reading order, most often left to right or top to bottom. For example, on machinery controlling an automated assembly line, displays that indicate that power is on are placed in a horizontal sequence to the far left of the operator's field of vision. Displays indicating proper hydraulic pressure in each of the line's units are placed next. Gauges that present the speed of line operations are to the immediate right of the pressure gauges, with counters indicating unit production placed to the right of the speed gauges. With a sweep of the head from left to right, the operator can receive all necessary information about the line's operation, from information about whether or not the system is operating to a count of finished products.

A complex type of display that many workers spend a great deal of their workday attending to is the video display terminal (VDT)—the "monitor"— of a computer. In fact, it is estimated that half of all U.S. workers use VDTs at work (Harris, 1993). The size, shape, density, and brightness of alphabet and numerical characters on computer screens can have an important impact on the speed of an individual's work in tasks such as word processing and accounting (Howell, 1992). One series of investigations has indicated that the speed of a proofreader processing text from a VDT improved as the image on the screen more closely approximated the look of words printed on paper (Gould, Alfaro, Finn, Haupt, & Minuto, 1987). The use of VDTs will likely increase even more in the future, since VDTs are replacing many of the mechanical-type machine displays used for industrial purposes.

Auditory displays

Many machine systems have auditory as well as visual displays to communicate information to the human operator. Auditory displays, which most commonly take the form of bells, horns, buzzers, or other sounds designed to get the operator's attention, are used as warning systems because they usually communicate information faster and more efficiently than visual displays. An operator who is not looking at the display might miss a visual warning, while an operator's ears are always open to receive auditory input. Of course, in noisy work environments, there may be a reliance on visual warnings because auditory displays may go unnoticed.

Edworthy (1994) suggests that if auditory warning displays are to be effective, they must be at the appropriate sound and volume level—neither so soft that they go unheeded, nor so loud or "offensive" that workers are tempted to disconnect the warning display. Auditory warning displays also need to be "psychologically appropriate." For example, blaring horns and short bursts of noise are typically perceived as more "urgent" warnings than a single bell-type sound or a single burst of noise.

Recent advancements in auditory communication systems, such as computer-generated, or synthetic, speech, have increased the complexity of auditory information displays from machine systems. For example, many telecommunication systems and certain personal computers use synthetic speech to send messages to system users. While such synthetic speech displays are helpful for the visually impaired or for those who cannot read printed text, for the average operator they may be less efficient than printed displays because the time it takes an operator to receive and process information through the auditory channel may be much greater than the time to process the same information presented in a visual text. In other words, it usually takes longer to listen to a message than to read it. Another problem lies with the quality of computer-generated speech. Synthetic speech is often more difficult to understand than natural speech (Adams, 1989; Paris, Gilson, Thomas, & Silver, 1995).

Human factors psychologists use certain basic rules to determine when visual displays and auditory displays are appropriate for operator-machine systems (see Table 15.2). Generally, visual displays are used when information is lengthy, complex, or abstract, or when a permanent record is needed. Visual displays can include such things as computer printouts or the graphed

TABLE 15.2

Table 15.2
Guidelines for the use of Visual and Auditory Machine Displays

Use Visual Displays When:	Use Auditory Displays When:
The message is complex or abstract.	The message is simple and short.
A permanent record is needed.	The message will not be referred to later.
The environment is too noisy to hear.	The environment is too dark to see.
The operator's attention is focused on displays.	The operator is required to move in all directions.
The message is not particularly urgent.	The message is urgent.
The message deals with location in space (e.g., radar screen).	The message deals with a specific moment (e.g., a gun fired to start a race).
	When continuously changing information is presented (e.g., aircraft flightpath information).
	When the visual system is overloaded.

Source: Adapted from M.S. Sanders and E.J. McCormick, *Human Factors in Engineering and Design,* 7th ed. (New York: McGraw-Hill, 1993).

What are three types of visual displays? Give examples of each.

readouts on medical equipment that provide a detailed, permanent copy of a machine's output. Auditory displays tend to be used when the message is short and simple or urgent. However, if the work environment is too noisy, a visual display will be required, and if the environment does not allow for normal operator vision, an auditory display is needed. Auditory displays will also be used if the operator's visual system is overloaded with too many visual displays.

OPERATOR INFORMATION PROCESSING AND DECISION MAKING

Once the machine displays output information about operating status, it is time for the human part of the system to go to work. The operator receives information through the senses: The eyes receive visual input, the ears take in auditory data. This is often referred to as the *perceptual stage* (Kantowitz, 1989). The operator's attention to the information is an important variable here. If the operator is distracted, inattentive, or overloaded with other stimuli, some of the critical information may not be received. However, the sensory input that does reach the operator must then be classified and interpreted. This is often referred to as the *cognitive stage*. Here, the operator must compare any information provided by a machine display to some cognitively stored information, such as some form of code that is shared by the machine and the operator. For example, an automobile displays speed in terms of miles per hour, a code that every experienced driver can understand. The trained operator will readily classify and interpret these machine displays. The various classifications of information parallel the types of information presented in the display. That is, the information can be *quantitative* or *qualitative*, or give some *status*, or provide a *warning*. Information can also be presented in a more complex code, such as written or spoken language, mathematical formulas, or graphed representations. For example, a certain reading on a gauge may be classified as status information and interpreted as a sign that the machine is functioning at normal capacity. The sound of a bell may be classified as a warning signal and interpreted as indicating that it is time for the operator to change some machine operation. To classify and interpret the incoming information, the operator relies on memory, calling on past experience with the machine system. Through experience and training, the operator has learned the specific language that this particular system uses, which then serves as a reference for interpreting whatever messages the machine displays are outputting.

Once the operator has received the information, the next step is decision making, an extremely complex process in which the operator also relies heavily on memory or training. A variety of decision-making situations can arise in operator-machine interactions. The most basic is whether or not an operator action is needed. For example, if the operator interprets a message about a machine's operational status to mean that all is going smoothly, the decision will be that no operator action is necessary. If, on the other hand, the message is interpreted as a warning of a machine overload, a decision to slow or shut down the machine will be made. A more complex form of operator decision making would involve deciding which of several courses of action should be taken. The operator might rely on memories of how this situation was handled in the past or try to recall what the "normal" procedure is in this instance. When a decision is made, the operator communicates it to the machine by manipulating machine controls. This is called the *action stage* (Kantowitz, 1989).

MACHINE CONTROLS

Controls are the various knobs, switches, buttons, pedals, levers, and the like that are connected to the operation of a machine. The correct type of control is necessary if operator decisions are to be communciated quickly and efficiently to the machine. Controls such as an on-off switch or a forward-reverse lever cause very general changes in machine operations, whereas others, such as a volume dial or a channel/frequency selector on a radio, can be designed to make very precise changes. If operator-machine systems are to be efficient, the design and selection of appropriate controls should follow certain basic principles, as outlined:

controls
mechanical devices that an operator uses to control machine functions

- *Controls should be matched to the operator's body*—Because humans have greater dexterity with their hands than with their feet, controls requiring precision must be hand-operated. To prevent the operator's hands from being overloaded with too many controls, some simple operations can be allocated to foot pedals or switches. An automobile is a good example of how controls can be spread out so that the operator's feet and hands can simultaneously operate different controls.

- *Control movements should mirror the machine actions they produce*—For example, if you turn the steering wheel of an automobile to the left, the car should then turn to the left. This is why people have difficulty learning to drive a forklift forward. Because the steering wheel operates the back rather than the front wheels, when the steering wheel is turned to the left, the front of the forklift turns to the right, and vice versa. Of course, a forklift is designed this way because when it is loaded, the driver will be moving backward. Turned around, the vehicle now follows the "correct" steering pattern: Turn the wheel to the left and the loaded forklift goes left, and vice versa (see Applying I/O Psychology).

- *Related controls should be combined for maximum efficiency*—Two controls that have similar functions should be combined so that in one action, the operator can change the operation of both systems. A simple example is the combined on-off and volume switches on radios. If you turn the volume down completely, you have effectively turned off the radio. Another little turn and a click is heard to indicate that the power has also been shut off (the "click" is an auditory and tactile display). The combined telescopic lens and lens focus on most movie and video cameras is another example. As the camera operator zooms in or out, the focus is automatically changed to keep the image clear.

- *Controls should be clearly marked for rapid identification*—Many industrial accidents have occurred because operators inadvertently operated the wrong controls. To cut down on such errors, controls must be clearly identified as to their use. Many controls are identified with written labels, such as "hot," "cold," "volume," and "tone." However, language barriers and the worldwide distribution of machinery have led to the increasing use of picture-coded controls, such as the light bulb picture on the switch controlling automobile headlights.

On certain sophisticated operator-machine systems, marking controls to be visually recognized may not be enough, since an operator who must quickly operate a variety of controls may not even have time to glance at the control to make sure that the correct one is being operated. Human factors psychologists have thus developed a number of shape-coded controls that can be identified rapidly by touch (see Figure 15.2). Notice that some of these controls are shape-coded to help the operator know immediately which control is being activated (i.e., the landing gear control is shaped like a wheel, and the flap control is shaped like a wing). The operator merely needs to put a hand on the control to know immediately what machine function is regulated by that control. These controls are used in jet fighter

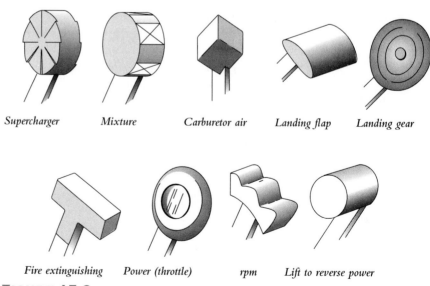

Supercharger   Mixture   Carburetor air   Landing flap   Landing gear

Fire extinguishing   Power (throttle)   rpm   Lift to reverse power

FIGURE 15.2

Tactile-coded Controls: Standardized Shape-coded Knobs for United States Air Force Aircraft
Source: United States Air Force, *Air Force System Command Design Handbook 1–3: Human Factors Engineering,* 1980.

aircraft, where split-second actions can mean the difference between life and death.

- *Placement of controls on similar machine systems should be standardized*— Have you ever borrowed a friend's car? It takes a little while to get oriented to the new machine. You need to find all of the important controls, such as the ignition switch, headlight control, and mirror and seat adjustments. These controls may be placed in very different locations than in your car. Although there is general standardization of some controls, such as the steering wheel and gearshift, there is still some variation in automobile control design and placement. Standardization of controls is especially important when an operator is required to switch back and forth among similar types of machinery.

- *Controls should be adequately spaced and arranged to avoid unintentional activation*—Controls need to be spaced apart from each other so that operating one control does not accidentally activate an adjacent control. Emergency controls should also be clearly labeled and protected either by covering with a shield, by being recessed, or by requiring some force to operate it. This prevents accidental activation that might prove costly or have irreversible results.

APPLYING I/O PSYCHOLOGY

Early Video Games: Problems in the Design of Machine Controls

In the late 1970s, the country was swept by a video game craze. Advances in computerization led to the development of these new entertainment devices. Although the early video games were fairly sophisticated in technical design, they often lacked human factors sophistication, particularly in their controls. These video game "antiques" can thus be analyzed from the standpoint of a human factors psychologist in an effort to spot weaknesses in their operator-machine system design and suggest means of improvement.

One of the very first video arcade games was called Pong. It consisted of two vertical bars of light, which represented the two players' paddles, and a bouncing ball. The object of the game, a video version of Ping Pong, was for the players to hit the ball with the paddles to keep it in play. If one player missed hitting the ball, the opponent received a point. The problem with Pong was that the players' control knobs did not match the functions that they performed. The video paddles were controlled by knobs that were twisted. A clockwise twist made the paddle go up, whereas a counterclockwise twist made it go down (see Figure 15.4). It took players quite a while to learn to control the paddles because the knobs violated the principle that a control should imitate the movement it produces. If

APPLYING I/O PSYCHOLOGY (*continued*)

the Pong paddle controls had been slide switches mounted so that an upward movement on the switch produced an upward movement in the paddle and a downward slide caused a downward movement, there would have been much less operator error.

Asteroids was another early video game. It consisted of a video spaceship (a triangle) that could be rotated to fire at and destroy asteroids before they collided with the ship. Again there was a problem in the control design. The ship was rotated by pressing one of two buttons. Pressing the button on the left caused the spaceship to rotate counterclockwise; pressing the button on the right created a clockwise rotation (see Figure 15.3). Novice operators had trouble pushing the correct button and releasing it at the appropriate time to be able to hit the approaching asteroid targets. Imagine a redesign with a knob (like the ones controlling the paddles on Pong)

that when twisted to the right creates a clockwise rotation and when twisted to the left causes the spaceship to rotate counterclockwise. The game would be made more efficient from the operator's perspective because the control actions would more closely resemble the movements they produced. (Of course if these video games had been made more efficiently, it might have taken the challenge out of them.) Today's video games have more sophisticated controls that produce more complex actions. For the most part, video game controls have been improved following the human factors guidelines for control design. However, it is still possible to find inefficient mismatches between the controls in certain video games and the specific actions they cause. (Interestingly, some of these "antique" video games are back. For example, many personal computers come with a version of Asteroids—including the same poor control functions!).

Pong   *Asteroids*

Down Up   Down Up   Counterclockwise   Clockwise
                          rotation   rotation

FIGURE 15.3

Two Early Video Games, Pong and Asteroids

Keyboard controls

An increasing percentage of jobs today involve processing information. More and more, workers around the world must interact with computer systems, communicating either in some written code, often the workers' language, or in some numeric code. Therefore, the controls that allow workers to enter commands and data into computer systems are becoming increasingly important. The primary control device for most computer systems is some type of alphabetic or numeric keyboard. Much of the information that is entered into a computer system takes the form of alphanumeric characters, such as strings of numerals, words, or alphabetic codes. Generally, the most efficient way to enter this information is through a keyboard. There are three principle arrangements for numeric keyboards. The simplest is the arrangement common to most typewriter keyboards: a simple string of numbers at the top row of the keyboard. A more efficient keyboard arrangement, which is common to calculators and numeric data entry pads, consists of three rows of three digit keys, with the lowest numerals on the bottom row and the zero beneath the third row. Another efficient arrangement, which is typical of push-button telephones, has the numerals in ascending order, with the lowest numerals on the top row (see Figure 15.4).

There are also two types of alphabetic keyboards, although only one is in widespread use. The standard typewriter keyboard, often called the QWERTY keyboard after the arrangement of keys on the first line of letter characters, is clearly the accepted standard. However, as anyone familiar with touch typing can tell, its letter arrangement is not very efficient. For example, vowels, which are very common in English, are scattered throughout the traditional keyboard. Because of these difficulties, more efficient keyboards, such as the Dvorak keyboard (Dvorak, Marrick, Dealey, & Ford, 1936), have been designed (see Figure 15.5). On the Dvorak keyboard, vowels are centrally located on the home row and are all activated by the left hand. The problem, however, is that so many typists have learned the

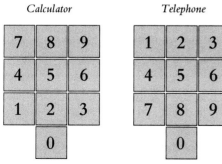

FIGURE 15.4

Common Numeric Keyboards

QWERTY keyboard

Dvorak simplified keyboard

FIGURE 15.5

Alphabetic Keyboards

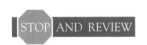

Give five rules for the proper design of machine controls.

QWERTY system that the Dvorak arrangement has never really caught on, even though it is more efficient. For example, with the traditional QWERTY keyboard, only 120 English words can be typed without leaving the home row. With the Dvorak keyboard, over 3,000 words can be typed on the home row keys alone. This may increase typing speed by anywhere from 5 to 20 percent for typists using the Dvorak keyboard (Sanders & McCormick, 1993).

Computer controls

Many workers now operate some form of computer or computer-assisted machinery as part of their jobs. One of the goals of human factors psychologists has been to make computer systems that can be controlled by the novice. These simple-to-operate systems are often described as "user-friendly."

Among the earliest developments designed to make computer systems more efficient and user-friendly was the ability to activate specific computer functions by hitting certain coded keys instead of typing an entire command. For example, some text keys allowed for editing procedures: removing or replacing a single character, an entire word, or a string of characters. Another innovation was the touch screen control, which enabled the user simply to touch some portion of the screen to activate computer functions. For example, a group of boxes with command words appear on the video screen, and a touch on one of the boxes activates that function. Another early computer control development was the joystick, which consisted of a stick attached to a box that could be moved in all directions to position a pointer on the video screen. A very common device that pretty much has replaced the joystick is the mouse, a handheld control with a ball underneath that is rolled on the desktop to move the cursor in any direction on the screen. The trackball used on many laptop computers works on the same principle except that the ball is manipulated directly by the user's fingers. These different types of computer controls can be used for a variety of tasks, from editing text to producing computer drawings. One early study compared four types of computer controls—the mouse, joystick, text keys, and arrow keys (up, down, left, and right)—in a text-editing task (see Figure 15.6). The mouse was found to be the fastest and to have the lowest rate of errors (Card, English, & Burr, 1978). This is the reason that mouse-type and trackball controls have become the standard.

Of course, a number of factors affect the speed and efficiency of interacting with a computer system using different controls. For example, individual differences in users' preference for, and familiarity and experience with, specific controls will influence how well they can be used in performing tasks.

Advanced control systems

Two special and very sophisticated machine control systems are teleoperators and speech-activated controls. These advanced controls are currently in limited operation in certain work situations, but as their technology improves, they may become more widespread. **Teleoperators** are sophisticated control systems that act as an extension of the human operator. Usually teleoperators are used in environments that would be dangerous for humans, such as underwater, in outer space, or in radioactive environments. A common teleoperator system consists of the mechanical arms used for delicate handling of radioactive material. The operator sits in one room, separated by a safety shield from the mechanical arm and radioactive materials in the adjacent room. The operator places his or her hands in a complicated control apparatus while the mechanical arms, with fingerlike prongs, imitate each of the movements of the operator, whose own arms and fingers are harnessed in the control devices. If the operator's left hand makes a pinching motion, the mechanical arm will make a similar motion to grip an object. The operator can watch the process of the mechanical arm either directly through a window or on a television screen.

In dangerous environments, such as outer space, teleoperators allow humans to control the work from a safe distance.

teleoperators
sophisticated control systems that act as an extension of the human operator

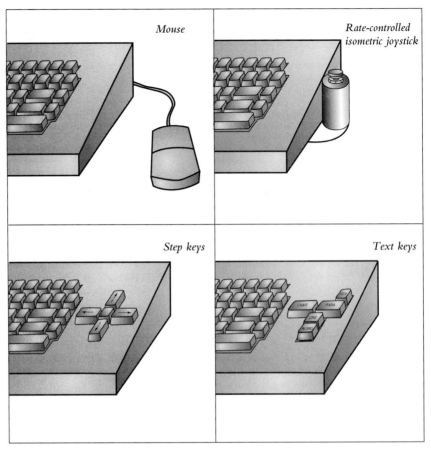

FIGURE 15.6

Computer Controls for Text Editing
Source: S. Card, W. English, and B. Burr, "Evaluation of Mouse, Rate-Controlled Isometric Joystick, Step Keys, and Text Keys for Text Selection on a CRT," *Ergonomics, 21* (1978). Reprinted by permission of Taylor & Francis Ltd., Hampshire, UK.

voice control
machine controls that respond to the spoken words of humans

An even more advanced control system is **voice control**. In sophisticated voice control systems, such as speech-recognition computer systems, the verbal commands of the operator substitute for the keyboard to enter data directly into the system. Although these controls permit the quick entry of information and free the operator's hands for other activities, the current state of speech-activated technology is such that there are some limitations. For instance, each word or command must be programmed into the system, which means that words must be uttered clearly and consistently. To cut down on errors, the operator must learn to use the same speech patterns, pitch, and voice inflections each time a word or command is uttered. Also, extraneous sounds such as coughing, clearing the throat, or stammering will not be recognized and may produce errors in the system operation. Voice control systems need further development before they can be put into everyday work use (it will probably be some time before you and I can actually "speak" to our computers). Currently, however, they are successfully used with certain tasks, such as simple data recording in situations in which the operator's hands are occupied by other activities, such as postal workers who sort packages and enter destinations vocally. Voice controls are also being used more and more to replace telephone operators (Brems, Rabin, & Waggett, 1995). Finally, voice controls are used on a limited basis by individuals with disabilities who are unable to operate manual controls (Noyes, Haigh, & Starr, 1989).

UP CLOSE

Accidents Lead to Increased Attention to Human Factors in Industry

In earlier times, a worker who made a mistake might spoil a piece of work, waste some time, or in extreme cases cause an accident that could injure or kill several workers. Today, however, a worker mistake can lead to dire consequences. Consider, for example, the disasters in the nuclear energy industry—Three Mile Island (TMI) and Chernobyl—or Union Carbide's chemical accident in Bhopal, India. In each of these cases, errors in operator-machine systems led to devastating consequences not only for the workers themselves but also for people in the surrounding communities. Specifically, in each case, operators were unaware of the seriousness of the system malfunctions because warning displays were poorly designed or located, and operators had not been sufficiently trained in dealing with these emergency situations. The Chernobyl nuclear disaster caused many deaths and exposed thousands to deadly radiation. The Bhopal tragedy—the worst industrial crisis in history—resulted in thousands of deaths and injuries to over a quarter of a million

people living around the chemical plant (Morehouse & Subramaniam, 1986). While the TMI incident is classified as a "near disaster," without any direct deaths or injuries, the toll in terms of stress to the nearby residents was considerable (Hartsough & Savitsky, 1984).

The near nuclear meltdown at TMI in March of 1979 has received one of the most extensive investigations into the safety of operations of an industrial plant (Sills, Wolf, & Shelanski, 1982). All of the evidence points to serious human factors flaws in the design and operation of the plant. For example, control panels presented operators with an overwhelming amount of complex information—more than 1,600 gauges and windows that had to be scanned to find where a malfunction was occurring! Moreover, many warning devices were slow to display emergency information and difficult for operators to read (a problem not limited to TMI).

Consider the following excerpt from a government investigation of the TMI incident:

The lack of human factors considerations at the design stage was most evident in TMI's control room. It was poorly designed with problems including: controls located far from instrument displays that showed the condition of the system; cumbersome and inconsistent instruments that often looked identical and were placed side by side, but controlled widely different functions; instrument readings that were difficult to read, obscured by glare or poor lighting or actually hidden from the operators; contradictory systems of lights, levers, or knobs—a red light may mean a valve was open in one plant area and closed in another, or pulling one lever up may have closed a valve, while pulling another lever down may have closed another one. . . . (Comptroller General Report on the Congress of the United States, 1980).

The net result was the near avoidance of a potentially catastrophic nuclear accident. The Chernobyl nuclear accident, on the other hand, was primarily due to poor operator training. Operators at Chernobyl were not informed that a meltdown could occur if plant power was reduced below 25 percent. Moreover, the operators were so poorly trained that their responses to the meltdown situation were too slow and often inappropriate.

It is unfortunate, but it took disasters such as these to force governments and organizations to consider human factors more fully in the design and operations of complex operator-machine systems. In fact, before the TMI accident, there were virtually no human factors psychologists on the staffs of the Nuclear Regulatory Commission (NRC) nor of the firms hired to design, build, and operate nuclear power plants (Cordes, 1983). Since then, considerable attention has been given to human factors issues in the design and operation of American nuclear power plants. The NRC now has dozens of human factors psychologists on staff. Unfortunately, despite these improvements, there is still not enough concern given to human factors in complex plant operations.

Errors in Operator-Machine Systems

Many of the advancements in operator-machine systems are the result of investigations of systematic errors that occur in specific systems. For example, during the 1980s and 1990s there was an alarming increase in airline accidents and near accidents ("near misses"). While much of this was due to the increased volume of air traffic and occasional mechanical malfunctions, such mishaps were frequently said to be due to "human error," the mistakes made by airline pilots or by air traffic controllers. However, such errors are usually not the fault of the human operator alone. Sometimes there is a breakdown in the total system, some mismatch or miscommunication between the machine and the individual operating the machine. Rather than attribute these errors simply to pilot or controller inattention or incompetency, a human factors psychologist may want to examine whether certain mistakes might be caused by faults in the design of the operator-machine systems. For example, perhaps an air traffic controller was overloaded with information, or maybe the system and workload were too complex for a single operator to handle. Maybe information was misread. The pilot may have misread a gauge because it was not placed where he expected it to be on the instrument panel or it was not illuminated enough. Perhaps the pilot tried to correct an initial error, but the system did not respond quickly enough to his adjustment. Whatever the reason for error, the human factors approach to examining such unfortunate instances looks not only at the machine system or the human operator but rather at the interaction of the two (see Up Close: Accidents Lead to Increased Attention to Human Factors in Industry). To study errors in operator-machine systems, some system of categorization is needed. One simple classification examines four types of error that can be investigated in terms of the total operator-machine system (Swain & Guttmann, 1983):

- *Errors of omission*—the failure to do something. An example would be an electrician's failure to shut off the power before working on electrical circuitry. While the worker might be at fault, there could also have been some miscommunication between the operator and the machine system. For example, the power switch may not have been labeled correctly, so that the electrician thought that the power was off when it really wasn't.
- *Errors of commission*—performing an act incorrectly. For example, a worker editing a computer database is presented with the on-screen message, "Hit 'enter' to begin printing." Instead of continuing to edit, the worker strikes the "enter" key and accidentally begins printing the unfinished data.
- *Sequence errors*—performing a task or a step in a task out of order. A sales clerk may make a sequence error when entering a price into the cash register before entering the merchandise identification number.
- *Timing errors*—performing an action either too quickly or too slowly. For example, a worker operating a drill press may activate the press via a foot switch before her hands are removed from the work piece. Better coordination between the operator and the machine system, perhaps by having the press activated by a hand switch, would cut down on such timing errors.

There are basically two approaches to dealing with the human errors that will inevitably occur in the workplace. The first is the personnel approach, which involves selecting only those workers whose skills and abilities are suited to the operation of the machines and equipment needed to perform the job, or developing training programs to teach workers to perform the job safely with a minimum number of errors. (We will discuss safety training programs more fully in Chapter 16.) The second strategy, which is more likely to be used by human factors psychologists, is the design approach. This involves designing equipment, procedures, and environments that reduce the likelihood of errors or the consequences of errors that do occur. This approach should help develop safe and efficient operator-machine systems. Unfortunately, poor design in an operator-machine system is often not discovered until there is a serious accident or breakdown in the system.

The two approaches can work together. That is, some poor designs in equipment and machinery can be overcome by training the operators to take these weaknesses into account and compensate for them. For example, a baker can be taught that when an oven door is opened frequently, the oven's temperature will drop and baking time must be adjusted accordingly, because the temperature gauge does not accurately register the change. However, certain poor machine system designs may not be overcome by training. For example, a trainee learning to be an air traffic controller may be unable to accurately track movement of aircraft as they move across the air traffic radar screen, because the trainee has a perceptual problem that makes it impossible to perform the tracking task. No amount of training can compensate for this weakness.

Automation and Operator-Machine Systems

There is no doubt that operator-machine systems are becoming more complex. Greater sophistication in technology means that machines are being constructed that can do more and more. Tasks that were previously performed by humans are being taken over by sophisticated machine systems. While computers have taken over some of our "thinking" tasks, such as bookkeeping, mathematical calculations, and record keeping, robots and robotic devices have taken over some of the manual tasks. **Robots** are automatic, programmable devices that can carry out tasks that are typically performed by humans. Although humanlike robots, such as C3PO from *Star Wars*, have been made famous in science fiction movies and literature, the industrial robots that are currently in use bear little resemblance to human beings. These industrial robots are used quite extensively in the automobile assembly industry, where they perform tasks such as welding and painting.

Some manufacturing plants, such as oil refineries and chemical plants, are completely automated, with all manufacturing operations carried out by robotic devices. The human operators' jobs are simply to watch the system, making sure that it is operating properly, troubleshooting when problems arise, and taking care of some routine maintenance tasks. While such fully automated factories inevitably replace line workers, the operators of the systems are upgraded; they have high levels of responsibility and the sophisticated skills needed to monitor, control, and maintain the complex machine systems. The situation is thus a trade-off: While workers may lose lower-level positions, the operator positions are enriched.

robots

automatic, programmable devices that can perform tasks typically done by people

List and define four common errors in operator-machine systems.

While the introduction of robots into the workplace is supposed to be a technological breakthrough—because these sophisticated machines can take on monotonous, boring, and physically demanding tasks, thereby freeing the people to perform higher-level and more challenging work operations—not all workers view industrial robots as a blessing. Employee reactions range from the very positive views that robots will improve work quality, efficiency, and safety, to the very negative attitude that they will cause a loss of jobs and will dehumanize the work place.

In one study, researchers looked at the attitudes of workers in a manufacturing plant that was planning to introduce robots into the assembly line. The results indicated that low-skilled workers, such as the assembly-line workers, had negative reactions toward the implementation of robots, perceiving them as a threat to job security. Workers with higher levels of skills, such as plant electricians, reacted more positively toward the robots and perceived robots as providing opportunities to expand their skills (Chao & Kozlowski, 1986). This study points out that it is important to consider employee perceptions and attitudes toward robots in order to prevent possible resistance to implementation of the new technology, as illustrated in the following case in which employees were not notified that a robot was being delivered to the plant. "Before the robot was unpacked it was accidentally dropped. After repairs, the robot was mysteriously moved from its installation site, fed twice the required voltage, and had sand placed in its hydraulic system" (Sullivan, 1982, cited in Chao & Kozlowski, 1986, p. 71).

Robots like this painting arm have taken over many routine manual tasks in industry.

ON THE CUTTING EDGE

Using Robots and Computers to Make Snack Foods

The use of computers and robotic equipment in manufacturing has even been applied to keeping supermarkets and convenience stores stocked with fresh snack food items. For example, several Golden Flake Snack Foods plants in the Southern U.S. have been converted to highly automated computer-aided manufacturing (CAM) systems. To make potato chips, thousands of pounds of potatoes are put into a CAM system that automatically washes, peels, slices, cooks, sorts, seasons, and bags the chips without any human worker directly involved in the process. Computerized scanners even do the visual inspection of the chips, rejecting any chips that are not appealing-looking or cooked adequately.

Yet, Golden Flake has had to go even further in its automation program to compete with snack food giants such as Frito-Lay and Keebler. Golden Flake's delivery trucks have onboard computers to speed up the ordering and delivery process to ensure that its snack foods arrive fresh on store shelves quickly.

Golden Flake is not the only snack maker to make extensive use of computers. Candy manufacturer M&M/Mars Company has been using computers to help design candy

Whenever automated systems are introduced into a company, there is likely to be some resistance from employees, because there is a general tendency to be wary of (and perhaps resist) any changes in usual work operations. Moreover, to introduce new automated systems may require some organizational restructuring, which in itself can cause employee resistance (Dean, Yoon & Susman, 1992; Jackson, Mullarkey, Parker, & Wall, 1994). To ease the transition, certain basic guidelines can be followed to increase worker acceptance of the new technology (Weiner & Curry, 1980):

- *Involve workers in the decision to adopt automation*—Because needs and desires for automation may vary from department to department and from individual to individual, workers should be behind any decisions to automate. To overcome worker resistance to automation, they must be informed of its potential benefits to them, including increased productivity and efficiency, upgraded skills as workers learn to control the sophisticated technology, and the freedom for workers to take on higher-level responsibilities since the machines now handle the repetitive and physically demanding work tasks.

- *Workers must understand how the automated system works*—If workers are to be in ultimate control of the automated system, it is critical that they know how the system works. Workers will be more accepting of the new technology if they understand how it works, and how they themselves fit into the new operator-machine system. This typically involves considerable training and education of operators, leading to an upgrading of workers' skills and job knowledge.

- *The automated system should be designed to be compatible with the human operator*—Any automated system should be designed so that it performs tasks in a way that is similar to the procedures a human operator would use. For example, a computerized filing system should index and retrieve information in a fashion that is compatible with how the operator would perform these operations by hand. This will create greater operator understanding and acceptance of the machine system.

No doubt the future will see even greater increases in the automation of the work place. Therefore, consideration must be given to how automation is introduced to workers and its impact on their work lives. The compatibility of operator and machine must be considered a principal goal if

STOP AND REVIEW

Differentiate between a teleoperator system and a robot system, and give examples of each.

the two components are to work together in an efficient and harmonious relationship.

The Work Environment: Workspace Design

While much of human factors psychology involves the design and improvement of operator-machine systems, psychologists are also concerned with the design and improvement of the larger work environment. A great deal of attention has been given to **workspace design**, the physical layout of individual work stations, and the design and arrangement of space and equipment within factories and offices. Workspaces are designed with considerations of work performance efficiency, operator comfort and safety, operator abilities and limitations, and characteristics of the machines, tools, and products kept firmly in mind. Workspace design considers how individual work stations are designed, and how work stations are linked together to form entire work environments. This section will focus primarily on the design of individual work stations and the equipment used in the station.

There are three categories of individual work stations: seated, standing, and combination, in which the worker must both stand and sit (see Figure 15.7). Seated work stations are most often used when all of the tools, machines, and supplies needed can be placed comfortably within the reach of the seated worker and when the work requires no heavy lifting or forceful movements. Most typically, they are found in fine assembly work, clerical tasks, and writing/word processing. Standing work stations are used when heavy objects are handled, when the worker must reach extensively, and when the worker must frequently move from place to place. They are commonly found in large assembly work, such as automobile factories, and in

workspace design
the design and arrangement of equipment, space, and machinery within a work environment

Workspace design focuses on worker comfort and ease of use.

Sitting work station

Standing work station

Combination work station

FIGURE 15.7

Work Station Designs

packaging and wrapping operations. Combination sitting-standing work stations are set up for work that requires multiple tasks, some best performed seated, others performed best while standing, and when the worker is doing seated work but must repeatedly reach to high or low distances. An example of a sitting-standing job is a draftsperson working with large blueprints or an individual doing layout designs for a newspaper or large advertisement. In combination work stations, workers are often given a high stool to make changing positions easier.

Certain basic principles governing the location and arrangement of equipment, tools, and space should be followed whether designing an individual work station or an entire workspace (McCormick & Sanders, 1993):

Importance principle—The most important functions or operations should take place in a central location. Similarly, crucial displays, such as warning lights, should be directly in front of the operator. For example, a work station for a graphic artist should have a centrally placed drawing table with drawing supplies nearby. An air traffic controller's seated work station should have the radar screen positioned directly in front of the controller, with other important displays surrounding it.

Frequency-of-use principle—Machines, tools, or controls that are used often should be conveniently located. For example, a worker soldering computer circuit boards should have soldering iron and solder on the work table, with frequently used pliers and clamps in holders so that they can be reached without looking up from the work. In office design, workers who play a central coordinating role for other workers, such as a supervisor or a pooled secretary, should be in a central location so that workers have easy access to this person.

Functional principle—Components should be grouped together according to their function. For example, temperature displays and controls should be grouped together. Different machine punch presses should be located together, as should similar types of tools or parts.

Sequence-of-use principle—Items should be placed in the order in which they will be used. Most assembly work follows this principle. Indeed, in an assembly line the product moves from station to station as it approaches completion.

Human factors psychologists have also played an important role in the design of work tools and equipment. One area that has made many advancements in recent years is the human factors specialty of **engineering anthropometry**, which is the measurement of the physical characteristics of the human body and the development of equipment designed to fit the characteristics of the human user (Kroemer, 1983; Wickens et al., 1998). Since body measurements such as stature and arm reach can vary as a function of sex, age, and ethnic populations, certain work equipment, particularly work stations and seats, should be designed to fit the characteristics of the user. A tremendous amount of time and energy has gone into developing functional and comfortable seats for various work stations, including seats for working at computer terminals, and for automobiles and other vehicles. These seats are designed so that the operator is at the proper height and distance to operate the machine, displays are at eye level, and hand and foot controls can be easily reached. Seats are also fashioned so that operators who are seated for long periods do not experience back or leg strain.

engineering anthropometry
the measurement of physical characteristics of the human body and the development of equipment to fit those characteristics

Recent years have seen a great deal of interest in engineering anthropometry, not only in the workplace, but in homes and in schools. One interesting study looked at the effects of ergonomically designed school furniture on the comfort and attitudes of fourth graders. Although the students reported that the new furniture was more comfortable, they did not always sit in the redesigned seats properly—emphasizing the importance of combining appropriate design with instruction in how to use the equipment properly (Linton, Hellsing, Halme, & Akerstedt, 1994).

Thus, not only should workspaces be designed for functional efficiency, but their characteristics must appeal psychologically to the worker (Donald, 1994). That is, the workspace should be reasonably pleasant and comfortable, with adequate space, lighting, and privacy, as we will see in Chapter 16.

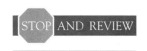

What are four principles of workspace design?

Summary

The area of industrial/organizational psychology called *human factors* deals with the design of tools, machines, work systems, and work places for human use. A great deal of the work of human factors psychologists has involved the development of efficient and productive *operator-machine systems* that coordinate the activities of the worker and the machines and tools the worker uses. In an operator-machine system, the operator and the machine are engaged in two-way interaction, collaborating to perform some work task.

Machine *displays* give the operator information about the machine's operating status in a variety of ways. Visual and auditory displays are the most common. Visual displays, such as gauges, counters, or lights, can provide detailed and complex information to the operator. Auditory displays, such as bells, buzzers, and horns, are most often used as warnings. Once the machine displays have presented data to the operator, the operator must process the information and make some operating decisions, which the operator communicates to the machine through *controls*, or the levers, switches, knobs, or keyboards that are used to input information into the system. A number of principles govern the proper shape, movement, and placement of controls needed for the quick and efficient operation of machine systems.

An important consideration is the reduction of errors in operator-machine systems. Errors that appear to be caused solely by the human operator may actually be due to some lack of coordination between the operator and the machine system. Human factors psychologists take one of two approaches for dealing with such errors. The personnel approach involves the selection of only those individuals who have the skills and expertise to operate the system flawlessly. The design approach is an attempt to create operator-machine systems that minimize the chance for error.

The tremendous advancements in computer technology and the development of *robots*—automatic, programmable devices that can perform human tasks—have led to increased automation of factories and work operations.

Today and in the future, operators will need to be more sophisticated, because they will be overseeing the operations of increasingly complex automated machinery.

Human factors psychologists are also concerned with *workspace design*. A great deal of energy, time, and research have gone into the creation of working environments that are efficient, productive, and comfortable settings for the workers. One related area is *engineering anthropometry*, which is the design of work equipment, such as chairs and tables, to fit the actual physical measurements of the users.

Study Questions and Exercises

1. What are the links between the time-and-motion studies of the scientific management practitioners in the early part of the century and the procedures of human factors professionals of today? How are the two areas different?

2. Consider the configuration of an automobile dashboard, with its various displays and controls. What do you suppose are the reasons behind their placement? Are there any controls or displays that you might change to make the car easier or more efficient to operate? Why or why not?

3. What are the four categories of errors outlined by Swain and Guttman (1983)? How might a counterperson in a fast-food restaurant, working with both a cash register and a soft drink machine, commit each of these errors?

4. In what ways have technological advancements, including machine automation, changed how people work? What factors should be considered before introducing new technology or advanced automated equipment into a work place?

5. Often factors such as status, economics, or personal preferences help determine how a workspace is configured. For example, high-status workers might have work stations near the windows, or lack of funds may lead to the purchase of cheap and uncomfortable office furniture. How might such factors conflict with basic principles of workspace design?

Suggested Readings

Norman, D.A. (1988). *The psychology of everyday things*. New York: Basic Books. *This fascinating book looks at human factors issues in the appliances and things we use everyday.*

Ostrom, L.T. (1994). *Creating the ergonomically sound workplace*. San Francisco: Jossey-Bass. *The first of three volumes on designing the work environment, this book focuses on the "hands-on tools" needed to help create work environments that maximize worker performance.*

Sills, D.L., Wolf, C.P., & Shelanski, V.B. (Eds.). (1982). *Accident at Three Mile Island: The human dimensions*. Boulder, CO: Westview Press. *A detailed analysis of the Three Mile Island nuclear accident with special attention* given to the human factors problems at TMI and other nuclear power plants. A collaborative effort with a variety of social scientists (sociologists, human factors specialists, psychologists, anthropologists, and philosophers) contributing chapters and different perspectives.

Journals that contain articles relating to topics in this chapter include: *Human Factors, Ergonomics, Applied Ergonomics,* and the very specific *International Journal of Aviation Psychology.*

Wickens, C.D., Gordon, S.E., & Liu, Y. (1998). *An introduction to human factors engineering.* New York: Addison Wesley Longman. *A very good introductory human factors text.*

CHAPTER SIXTEEN

WORK CONDITIONS AND WORK SAFETY

CHAPTER OUTLINE

Work Conditions

Physical Conditions of the Work Environment

Illumination • Temperature • Noise • Motion • Pollution •
  Aesthetic factors: Music, color, and scents

Psychological Conditions of the Work Environment

Temporal Conditions of the Work Environment: Work
Schedules

Shift work • Compressed work weeks • Flextime

Work Safety

Dangers in the Work Environment

Dangers in Machine Systems

Dangers in Worker Characteristics and Behavior

Programs to Increase Work Safety

Alcohol and Drug Use in the Workplace

Summary

COMING FULL CIRCLE: THE EFFECTS OF WORK CONDITIONS ON THE WORKER

INSIDE TIPS

With this chapter, we have come full circle. Some of the earliest work in the field of industrial/organizational psychology examined how physical working conditions could affect worker behavior. In this chapter we will look at how physical, psychological, and temporal (work scheduling) conditions of the workplace affect workers.

The topics of work conditions and work safety are related to the human factors issues that we studied in Chapter 15 because an important goal of human factors psychologists is to create a machine or system that is easy and safe for the worker to operate. This chapter, however, expands the discussion of the worker-task relationship to include the context in which workers perform their jobs. In addition, issues of psychological conditions of the work setting, such as privacy and control over the work environment, and work dangers are both connected to the topics of work stress and job satisfaction presented in Chapters 8 and 9. For instance, experiencing crowding or the threat of injury from a work setting can lead to job stress. Similarly, having a sense of control over some aspects of the work environment may promote job satisfaction by making workers feel as if they are an important and influential part of the work organization. Finally, because many work safety programs emphasize safety training, there is a connection between this chapter and Chapter 5, which is devoted to personnel training, for the same issues regarding implementation apply to both forms of training.

The effect of work conditions on work behavior is a longstanding topic in I/O psychology but one that continues to have relevance. Because work conditions have been shown to affect workers' job performance and satisfaction with their jobs, and because extreme work conditions may present life-threatening dangers, the protection and well-being of workers has been and will continue to be an important goal of I/O psychology.

In this chapter, we will continue to explore how factors in the work environment affect work behavior. We will begin by looking at how work conditions influence important outcomes such as work performance and job satisfaction. In particular, we will see how physical conditions, such as lighting, temperature, and noise, and psychological factors, such as feelings of privacy and a sense of control over the job environment, affect worker behavior. We will also examine how temporal factors—work shifts and workweek structures—influence job performance and satisfaction. We will next consider safety in the workplace, outlining specific work-related dangers and safety programs. Finally, we will explore the use and abuse of alcohol and drugs in the workplace and consider programs designed to reduce such abuse at work and improve worker health and well-being.

Work Conditions

Although many workers' ideal might be a comfortable, quiet, and elegant office, complete with the latest in office equipment and technology, in reality people often work under less than perfect conditions. In fact, for some workers the work environment is quite hostile, hampering their ability to get the job done and threatening their health and well-being. Workers exposed to extreme weather conditions, dangerous and noisy machinery, and potentially harmful chemicals all face great difficulty in doing their jobs efficiently. An additional work condition relates to the scheduling of work—the length of workdays and the time of day (or night) during which people work. Industrial/organizational psychologists have long been concerned with the conditions under which people work, particularly the role that the physical work environment plays in affecting worker performance, satisfaction, and health (Oborne & Gruneberg, 1983).

PHYSICAL CONDITIONS OF THE WORK ENVIRONMENT

Among the more obvious factors that can affect the behavior of workers are the physical conditions of the work environment, including the levels of lighting, the usual temperature, the levels of noise, the amounts and types of airborne chemicals and pollutants, and aesthetic features such as the colors of walls and floors and the presence (or absence) of artwork, music, plants, or decorative items. While some of these factors, such as extreme noise, high or low temperature, and very low illumination, can greatly hamper work performance, others, such as music and colors, have more subtle effects on workers.

Illumination

As you may recall, level of illumination was one of the variables manipulated in the classic Hawthorne studies conducted by psychologist Elton Mayo and his associates. In those studies, Mayo was trying to determine the optimal level of lighting for high worker productivity; he discovered instead the Hawthorne Effect. Of course, level of illumination can significantly facilitate or detract from performance of many work tasks. Research generally indicates that increasing the level of illumination tends to improve performance. However, there is a point at which improvement will level off; precisely where this occurs depends on the type of task, particularly the amount of fine visual discrimination demanded (Sanders & McCormick, 1993). It has also been reported that too much lighting can lead to distraction and eye problems in some workers (Nemecek & Grandjean, 1973).

While bright light is necessary for the adequate performance of many work tasks, it is also important to use energy efficiently by not overlighting a work area. The key seems to be to find an optimal level of illumination that is bright enough to aid the performance of a particular job, but that does not use energy inefficiently. Research has led to the development of *Lighting Handbooks* that list appropriate levels of illumination for particular tasks (see, e.g., Kaufman & Christensen, 1984). Also, switching from incandescent to fluorescent lighting provides increased illumination, better light distribution, and considerable energy and dollar savings, which is why many workplaces, schools, and public buildings have fluorescent lights (see Table 16.1).

Lighting can also produce adverse effects, such as the visual fatigue caused by the distracting glare from direct light. Glare can be uncomfortable and dangerous, and can inhibit performance of tasks, as any driver who has tried to control a car while facing into the sun or the headlights of oncoming traffic can testify. Efforts have been made to reduce glare in work settings by the use of light shields, visors, and surfaces that diffuse light, such as wallpaper and flat paint. Such use of indirect lighting not only cuts down on glare but also more uniformly illuminates the work area.

A great deal of energy has also gone into trying to reduce the types of glare and reflections that occur on computer and video display screens. These methods have included the use of etched or frosted screens and screen filters. Persons who work at video display terminals are especially prone to visual fatigue and eyestrain because of the large amounts of time they spend focusing on small, illuminated characters (Dainoff, Happ, & Crane, 1981). Recent advancements in the design of display screens and display characters are attempting to alleviate some of these problems.

TABLE 16.1

Levels Of Illumination Recommended For Certain Work Tasks And Settings

Task	Illuminance (lx)[a]
Living rooms (general lighting)	50
Furnace rooms in glassworks	150
General office work, mainly clerical and typing	500
Motor vehicle assembly	500
Proofreading in printing works	750
Color matching in paint works	1,000
Fine assembly work, such as electronics assembly	1,000
Inspection of hosiery and knitwear	1,500
Inspection and testing shops of detailed work or small instruments	2,000
Jewelry and watchmaking	2,000
Hospital operating rooms	10,000–50,000

[a]lx = lux, a standard measure of illuminance

Source: Chartered Institution of Building Services Engineers, *CIBSE Code for Interior Lighting* (1984).

Temperature

Workers who labor under extreme heat or cold may exhibit some decrease in performance. Realizing this, many offices and factories have installed adequate heating and cooling systems. However, some industrial workplaces still remain too hot in the summer and too cold in the winter (or vice versa, when workplaces are overcooled or overheated). Moreover, it is impossible to escape the heat or cold in certain types of jobs, such as those in steel mills, boiler rooms, and refrigeration plants, or in jobs that require working outside in extreme temperatures, such as construction work and road repair.

Research on the effects of temperature on work performance indicates that when workers are exposed to extreme temperatures—greater than 90°F. or lower than 32°F.—there are some decrements in both manual and cognitive work performance (Kobrick & Fine, 1983). In general, hot and humid conditions tend to increase the demands of heavy physical work, causing excessive fatigue and reducing work output. Prolonged exposure to heat can, in extreme cases, lead to serious injury and even death (Sanders & McCormick, 1993). Extreme cold may impair performance of tasks that require fine hand-motor movements. There is also some evidence that exposure to less extreme temperatures—slightly warm or cool conditions—for prolonged periods may also affect task performance adversely due to worker fatigue or discomfort (Enander, 1984; 1987; Meyer & Rapp, 1995). However, a number of factors, such as workers' adaptation to the extreme temperatures, the duration of exposure to heat or cold, individual differences in the tolerance of extreme temperatures, and the type of clothing worn, make

Some jobs require working under extreme high or low temperatures.

TABLE 16.2

Techniques To Reduce Worker Discomfort Caused By Extreme Temperatures

Heat Discomfort	Cold Discomfort
Decrease the temperature	Raise the temperature
Increase the air velocity	Reduce the air velocity
Reduce the workload	Increase or even out the workload
Adjust the clothing	Increase the amount of clothing insulation
Provide shields against radiant heat	Increase the amount of radiant heat
Reduce the humidity	
Provide intermittent cooling via "personal cooling" gear	

Source: Eastman Kodak Company, *Design for People at Work,* Vol. I (Belmont, CA: Lifetime Learning Publications, 1983), pp. 254–62.

straightforward interpretations of the effects of extreme temperatures on work performance difficult (Bell, 1981; Malchaire, 1995; Vickroy, Shaw, & Fisher, 1982). Moreover, simple measurement of temperature is not easy, since a variety of atmospheric factors can interact with temperature to produce conditions that are more or less extreme in terms of their effects on the human body. For example, raising the humidity in a room that is 79°F. from 50 to 90 percent will increase the feeling of heat discomfort four times (Fanger, 1970). Other factors, such as air velocity and the radiant heat of furnaces, lamps, or the sun, can also affect how temperature is experienced in a particular situation. Table 16.2 presents some typical strategies for reducing worker discomfort caused by extreme temperatures.

Recently, human factors psychologists have begun experimenting with a "personal cooling vest"—a liquid-cooled garment similar to the cooling suits used by NASA astronauts (see Applying I/O Psychology). The results of one series of studies suggest that such personal cooling devices might be useful for workers performing heavy work in extremely hot environments (Constable, Bishop, Nunneley, & Chen, 1994).

Noise

Noise is defined as some unwanted, distracting sound that may interfere with work performance. Individuals perceive noise differently. A sound that is not at all disruptive to one worker may be considered distracting noise to another. Although noise does not have to be loud to be distracting, it is louder noises that are more often considered to be stressful by workers (see Chapter 9). One common way for measuring loudness is to express the sound in terms of **decibels.** The decibel is defined according to a logarithmic scale, thus an increase of ten decibels would result in a tenfold increase in

decibels
a measure of sound loudness

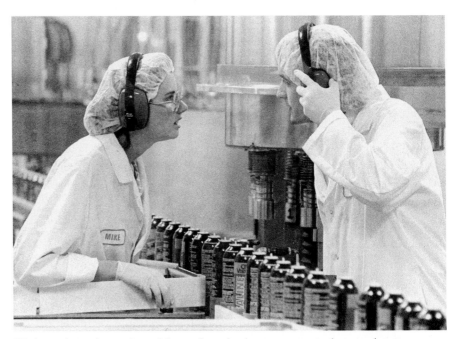

Workers subjected to prolonged doses of very loud noise are required to wear hearing protection.

sound power and a one hundredfold increase in sound pressure. A relatively quiet home or office produces noise of about 40 decibels, the average factory has noise of about 100 decibels, while a rocket launch produces noise of a very loud 180 decibels (see Table 16.3). The threshold of audible sound is somewhere between zero and 10 decibels, depending on the individual's hearing capacity. A whisper has a sound of 20 to 30 decibels, while a sound of 130 decibels will cause pain without the use of protective earwear—the reason why airport ground crews wear protective headwear, since a jet makes a sound of 150 decibels at takeoff (Geldard, 1972). Not only is noise a source of distraction and stress, but repeated or prolonged exposure to loud noises may result in permanent hearing damage or loss (Loeb, 1986).

Research shows that while even low levels of noise can lower the performance of cognitive tasks, there is tremendous individual variation in terms of distractibility. For example, some students have no trouble studying with the TV or radio turned up loud, while others must have absolute quiet to study effectively. Similarly, in one computer manufacturing plant, workers in a "clean room," where air is filtered to eliminate all forms of airborne dust and particles, had to listen to the loud, steady sounds of the air filtration system. It was found that only a certain percentage of workers were able to concentrate on performing the very detailed microassembly of computer components under these conditions of constant noise.

TABLE 16.3

Sounds and Associated Levels of Noise in Decibels

Noise Source	Loudness in Decibels
Quiet home or office	42
Ventilating fan	56
Automobile, 50 feet away	68
Quiet factory area	76
Average factory area	100
Punch press	103
Nail-making machine	111
Pneumatic riveter or hammer	128
Jet airplane at takeoff	150
Rocket at launch	180

On the other hand, noise does not necessarily detract from performance and in some instances may actually enhance performance. Particularly when a worker is performing a simple or boring task, noise may serve as an arousing stimulus to keep the worker aware and attentive (Michael & Bienvenue, 1983). In a summary of research on the effects of environmental noise on cognitive performance, the Environmental Protection Agency (1974) reached the following conclusions:

1. Noise does not generally impair performance unless it exceeds 90 decibels (although there is subsequent evidence that noise levels below 90 decibels can disrupt some complex verbal work tasks [Smith, 1989]).

2. Intermittent or unpredictable noises are more disruptive than steady noises.

3. High-pitched (or high-frequency) noises interfere with performance more than low-frequency noises.

4. Noise is more likely to increase work error rates than to lower rates of performance.

Noise can also interfere with worker-to-worker communication, which can lead to breakdowns in coordinated work activities, reduce the important social interactions in the workplace, and produce worker dissatisfaction with the job and the workplace. There is also some evidence that the breakdown in worker communication due to noise as well as inability to hear feedback from machines is partially responsible for the increased incidence of accidents in noisy industrial settings (Cohen & Weinstein, 1981; Sundstrom, 1986).

Noise seems to be a particular problem in open-plant offices—those with a number of workers in a large room, separated by partitions. While these offices offer the advantage of providing workers with easy access to one another, the constant noise and lack of privacy can distract workers, which may impair job performance. A number of environmental features, including fabric-covered panels, thick carpeting, and acoustical ceilings, have been designed to cut down on noise in open-plan offices and in workspaces generally. Obviously, a goal of human factors psychologists and of workplace architects is to design work environments in such a way to reduce distracting noise levels. This includes designing enclosures that muffle noisy machinery as well as using structural barriers with porous surfaces that absorb noise. Another strategy, when workplace noise is unavoidable, is to provide workers with proper protection (i.e., earplugs or headphones) against noise.

Motion

Some workers conduct their work activities while seated behind the controls of vehicles that move them about on the ground, in the air, and in outer space. The accompanying vibrations, feelings of movement, accelerations, and decelerations (and in outer space, feelings of weightlessness) mean that human factors psychologists must consider motion as a working condition.

The most common motion condition is vibration. All modes of transportation subject occupants to some degree of vibration. Certain machines and tools, such as jackhammers, industrial machinery, and handheld power tools, cause considerable vibrations to operators. What are the effects of continual exposure to vibration? There is some evidence that workers subjected to vibration over long periods may develop problems in their backs, chests, and joints (Grandjean, 1988). Vibrations may also adversely affect task performance, particularly in activities that involve visual tracking and steady hand movements. More common are the subjective effects of vibration, such as the distraction and discomfort caused by vibration and motion, which may lead to feelings of annoyance, disorientation, and motion sickness (Sanders & McCormick, 1987).

Motion is a particular problem in jobs that involve moving at high speeds. Jet pilots and astronauts are subjected to extreme acceleration and deceleration effects that can seriously impair performance. The weightlessness that accompanies working in outer space creates a host of problems, including motion sickness, dizziness, and disorientation, that human factors psychologists are studying intensely, both in actual space flights and in simulated conditions (see Applying I/O Psychology: Dealing with Hostile Work Conditions: Worker Safety and Health in Outer Space).

Pollution

Because of the wide range of chemicals used in industrial workplaces and the variety of substances used in constructing and furnishing working areas, many workers are exposed to a surprising number of potentially harmful substances. Among the many workers who are particularly prone to chemical pollutants are miners, who are exposed to potentially lethal gases; farm workers, who may come into contact with dangerous insecticides or fertilizers; industrial workers, who may have to use toxic chemicals; and even surgical teams, who may be exposed to harmful gases released from anesthetic equipment. While in most of these jobs exposure to the pollutants is a known, job-related risk, many workers may be unaware of the potentially harmful chemicals present in almost any workplace.

Certain building materials used in most offices may contain toxic chemicals. For example, some insulation materials in older buildings contain deadly asbestos. Chemicals used in certain paints and substances intended to make drapes and furniture fire-retardant may give off airborne pollutants. The situation can be particularly dangerous if there is not adequate ventilation. Some work materials, such as cleaning fluids, glues and adhesives, and copying machines (which produce ozone, a chemical that can cause eye and throat irritation), can be dangerous if used in an enclosed area. Although there have been some efforts to remove certain pollutants, such as asbestos, from work environments, a surprising number of harmful substances are not regulated or controlled. For example, recent concerns include the potential cancer-causing effects of insecticides used on fruit crops that may be endangering farm workers, and the potentially harmful effects of certain chemical substances used in the manufacturing of computer components. Moreover, the introduction of new products and substances, such as synthetic plastics, adhesives, and building materials, may mean that we are increasing the variety of possible pollutants in the work environment. We will consider the topic of harmful pollutants more fully in the discussion of work safety.

Evidence of the effects of airborne pollution on job performance is scanty. Most of the research has examined the effects of carbon monoxide and found that exposure has led to decreases in attention, sensorimotor coordination, memory, and problem-solving ability (Evans & Jacobs, 1981). Carbon monoxide pollution may be a particular problem for persons working around automobiles and gasoline-powered machinery, and employees in smoggy and polluted urban centers.

A controversial type of air pollution, one that is a major concern today, is that caused by secondhand cigarette smoke. In recent years, more and more workplaces (as well as public places, restaurants, etc.) are eliminating smoking or confining it to selected locations in an effort both to clean up the air and to ease both the health risks to and the irritation of nonsmokers.

Aesthetic factors: Music, color, and scents

In the 1950s and 1960s strong claims were made for the positive effects of certain kinds of music and certain colors on work performance. Many businesses and industries began to pipe in industrial background music (Muzak, the nondescript instrumental music frequently heard in elevators) or had the walls painted in "motivating" colors. Despite such claims, there is little sound research on the effects of such aesthetic factors on work performance. However, it is possible that factors such as music and an aesthetically pleasing environment may have subtle, but complex, effects on work behavior. There is some evidence that music played in offices and certain office colorings may increase attention to

APPLYING I/O PSYCHOLOGY

Dealing with Hostile Work Conditions: Worker Safety and Health in Outer Space

Outer space, with its extreme temperatures ranging from subfreezing to broiling (literally), exposure to radiation, and a total lack of atmosphere and gravity, is the most hostile work environment imaginable. To allow human beings to live and work in outer space, human factors psychologists have had to develop equipment, clothing, and tools to help astronauts cope with these conditions (Wichman, 1992).

The spacesuits that astronauts wear when working outside of their vehicles provide breathable air and protection against temperature extremes. State-of-the-art insulation materials and a system of circulating liquid help keep them cool or warm, depending on whether they are directly exposed to the superhot rays of the sun or are floating in the frigid shade of the earth. A tinted safety shield over the face protects against the bright, radioactive rays of the sun. However, even with all of this protection, astronauts can only remain in this very hostile environment for an hour or two at a time.

The various life-support systems required for the astronaut simply to survive in space make the spacesuit very bulky, thus greatly restricting the astronaut's movement. While working, care must be taken not to puncture the suit or damage any life-support systems. Therefore, human factors specialists have had to develop various tools specifically designed for use by a space-suited human working in space. Moreover, because of weightlessness, all loose tools and parts must have some means of being attached to the spacesuit so that they do not float away. While the lack of gravity is beneficial because it allows the astronaut to lift and move loads that would be very heavy on earth, it also makes it difficult to get leverage or to provide a stable floor for working on large objects (Wichman & Donaldson, 1996).

Inside the space vehicle are other hazardous and bothersome work conditions. Although sophisticated filtration systems keep the air fresh and clean, a special form of atmospheric pollution still occurs as particles of food, debris, and droplets of water accumulate and float about the interior. Astronaut clean-up chores include the occasional use of a special vacuum to clean the air!

Work stations must be created to fit an astronaut who is maintaining what is called a "zero-gravity neutral" body position rather than a seated or standing position. Standing in a weightless environment is impossible, and remaining seated puts strain on the stomach muscles. However, one of the benefits of designing for a weightless work environment is that both the ceiling and floor can be used as working space.

Astronauts must contend not only with a hostile physical environment but also with a difficult social work environment in a confined space vehicle. Crowding and lack of privacy are always going to be problems in space. Moreover, workspace and living space overlap, and astronauts must live and work together for extended periods. In long-term assignments, such as working in a

APPLYING I/O PSYCHOLOGY (*continued*)

space station for several months, the confined and crowded conditions coupled with a sense of lack of control over much of the environment can be quite stressful (Connors, Harrison, & Summit, 1994). A human factors specialist describes such an assignment as follows:

> *Imagine that you buy a medium-sized motor home, and we put you inside with two to four other people and lock the door. You can look out the windows, but you can't drive. We drive the motor home for you, we refuel it, and we pass food through the door. You're living and working with those same people for 237 days (Reichardt, 1986)*

The boredom of an extended space flight is a problem. Space workers may lose motivation and may make costly and dangerous errors because of inattention or fatigue.

There must be time set aside for diversions, such as movies, TV communication with families on earth, and games. Also, because there is no night and day in space, schedules must be set up to regulate waking and sleep patterns.

Maintaining the physical health of space crews is also a concern. Because of weightlessness, muscles that stay in shape by "wrestling" with earth's gravity may weaken unless they are exercised. The cardiovascular system may also deteriorate for the same reasons. However, exercising is not easy because the astronaut does not have gravity to work against and must be strapped into the exercise apparatus.

In the future, as more and more humans are sent to work in space, psychologists will be challenged to assist in the development of better procedures, equipment, and tools to help deal with the hostile working conditions of outer space.

work tasks, and that most (but not all) employees view music played in offices favorably (Sundstrom, 1986). Office decorations, such as plants and posters, and tidiness also tend to have positive effects on office visitors (Campbell, 1979, Morrow & McElroy, 1981).

Interestingly, one study has investigated the effects of pleasant scents (produced by the use of air fresheners) on worker performance in a simulated work environment (Baron, 1990; Baron & Bronfen, 1994). The results of these experiments indicated that workers set higher performance goals, had more positive work attitudes, and were less prone to conflict when the work area had a pleasant scent. Real estate agents also realize the importance of pleasant smells in creating positive, favorable attitudes in potential buyers. In fact, the author recently looked at a prospective home where he was greeted with a pleasant (and "homey") mixture of aromas. The real estate agent had built a roaring oak fire in the fireplace, had laced the house with fresh potpourri, and was baking chocolate chip cookies in the kitchen!

List six physical conditions of the work setting that can affect work behavior.

It is likely that aesthetic factors affect employees' perceptions of the work environment rather than having any direct effects on their behavior. Individual preferences are of prime importance in determining the effects of aesthetic factors. For example, while many workers may find music in the work setting pleasing, others may find it irritating. Moreover, different types of music may appeal to different workers. In spite of the lack of evidence for the beneficial effects of background music and color on work behavior, millions are spent each year on workplace decorations and music.

PSYCHOLOGICAL CONDITIONS OF THE WORK ENVIRONMENT

Research has shown that the physical layout and design of a work setting, the amount of workspace available, and the types of furnishings can all affect worker behavior by creating various psychological conditions, such as feelings of privacy or crowding, a sense of status and importance, or perceptions of anonymity and unimportance. For example, the layout of a work area can govern the amount of contact and interaction that workers have with one another. Work areas designed to facilitate social interaction typically have positive influences on workers' job satisfaction and performance. However, work areas that are congested and allow too much socializing and too little privacy may be detrimental to important organizational outcomes such as productivity (Canter, 1983).

The amount of workspace allocated to a particular worker and the privacy of that space are also linked to notions of status and importance within the organization. Top-level executives usually have large, private offices, while lowly clerical workers, assemblers, or data processors might be lined up, nearly shoulder to shoulder, in a huge, open room. Research has compared traditional closed-office designs (workers in private office spaces) to open-office designs (workers in a large, open room with partitions). While open-office designs allow ease of interaction among employees and greater opportunity for supervisors to observe and interact with workers, the evidence indicates that workers may sense a lack of privacy and control over their space in such settings (Sutton & Rafaeli, 1987). This may lead to dissatisfaction with the work environment and may negatively affect work behavior (Sundstrom, Burt, & Kamp, 1980). However, the psychological effects of the physical layout of the workspace are complex, and may vary depending on the level of the employees and their status in the organization. For example, lower-level clerical workers may welcome the open-office design because it provides chances to interact informally with coworkers. On the other hand, managers and executive administrators may be dissatisfied with open designs since they lack the status associated with private offices, and afford little privacy and insulation from noisy distractions and interruptions (Werner & Haggard, 1992; Zalesny & Farace, 1987). Moreover, individual differences are also important, since some research indicates that workers' abilities to regulate privacy, by "screening

While open office designs promote communication, they can cause workers to experience a lack of privacy.

out" unwanted interruptions, can reduce the negativity associated with lack of privacy (Fried, 1990; Oldham, 1988; Werner & Haggard, 1992). Previous exposure to different office designs will also likely influence worker satisfaction with the amount of privacy or socialization opportunities provided by open versus closed designs.

Research has shown that physical and psychological conditions of the environment work together to have an important impact on worker behavior and attitudes. One study assessed the effects of four workspace characteristics on the attitudes and behaviors of office workers: (1) the number of workers in an office, which constituted the measure of crowding; (2) the measured seating distance between workers, another index of crowding; (3) the number of enclosures or partitions surrounding each individual work station; and (4) office darkness. The results showed a link between these four variables and rates of employee job dissatisfaction and turnover. When the office was perceived as dark and crowded, and had few partitions, workers tended to be dissatisfied and were more likely to quit than workers who were not exposed to these conditions (Oldham & Fried, 1987).

As we saw when studying stress in Chapter 9, control significantly affects job satisfaction and perceived work stress. Research indicates that giving an employee some sense of control over the work environment goes a long way toward reducing distress and dissatisfaction (Zimring, 1981). This can include control over the amount of openness and privacy in the work-space, over some aspects of the decorating, and if possible over the thermostat.

TEMPORAL CONDITIONS OF THE WORK ENVIRONMENT: WORK SCHEDULES

Industrial/organizational psychologists are concerned not only with the physical and psychological conditions of work but also with the temporal conditions—the time structure of the workday. Although the vast majority of employees work a nine-to-five schedule (give or take an hour on either end and an hour for lunch), more and more people are working on alternative types of schedules (Kogi, 1996). There are some important reasons why nontraditional work schedules exist. First, many production-oriented organizations must operate around the clock to meet the demand for the goods they produce. This necessitates the use of three eight-hour shifts. In addition, many service organizations, such as hotels, hospitals and retirement homes, require an around-the-clock staff, necessitating three eight-hour shifts. Second, over the years stores, restaurants, and other retail operations have extended their hours of operation into the evening, which means that more than one crew of workers is needed. More recently, in the large urban centers, traffic congestion has led to alternative work schedules to allow workers to commute at nonpeak times. Finally, some of the more flexible work schedules have developed in an effort to give workers a greater sense of control over the planning and timing of their workdays. We will examine several types of work schedules and their effects on the worker.

Shift work

shifts

employee schedules designed to alternate work times to keep the workplace in extended or continuous operation

Work **shifts** are any sort of scheduling in which groups of employees alternate working times to keep the workplace in extended or continuous operation. A three-shift day might typically consist of a morning or day shift from 6 A.M. to 2 P.M., an afternoon or "swing" shift from 2 P.M. to 10 P.M., and a night or "graveyard" shift from 10 P.M. to 6 A.M. Shifts may also vary in terms of the days worked. Typically employees work five days and have two days off, although a number of variations are possible. For example, one schedule might be three days on, one day off followed by three on, two off; six on and two off, four on and two off, and so on.

Research indicates that night shifts may disrupt the natural sleep and waking cycles of workers' bodies, often referred to as "circadian rhythms," and may lead to problems such as high rates of stress, fatigue, job dissatisfaction, and performance errors (Monk, Folkard, & Wedderburn, 1996; Zedeck, Jackson, & Marca, 1983). There is also some evidence that work accident rates are higher for workers on late-night shifts (Schweitzer, Muehlbach, & Walsh, 1992). For example, research on nuclear power plant workers found that workers on the night shift had decreased alertness, greater disruptions in sleep patterns, greater health problems, and more family difficulties than workers on the day shift (Smith & Folkard, 1993). Interestingly, one study found that workers who *chose* to work night shifts had fewer difficulties than workers who were involuntarily assigned night shift work (Barton, 1994).

Work performance deficiencies and stress may be particularly problematic when workers are rotated from day to night shifts during a month, which does not allow their bodies to adapt to a regular schedule. Additionally, requesting regular day- or swing-shift employees to switch suddenly to a late-night "graveyard" shift may hamper work performance, at least until these workers get accustomed to working late at night.

What four workspace characteristics were examined by Oldham and Fried (1987)?

Compressed work weeks

Work organizations have also tried **compressed work weeks,** in which the number of workdays is decreased while the number of hours worked per day is increased. Most common are four ten-hour days, although there have been some attempts at scheduling three 12-hour shifts. What are the potential costs and benefits of these compressed work weeks?

On the positive side, the extra day off allows workers time to take care of tasks that need to be done Monday through Friday, such as going to the doctor, dentist, or tax accountant. Usually compressed work weeks include a three-day weekend, which allows workers more free time to take weekend vacations. Both of these benefits cut down on absenteeism, since workers previously might have called in sick to take an extra day of "vacation" or to run errands. An extended shift might also allow a worker to miss peak traffic times. However, a drawback is that working parents might have difficulty finding child care for the extended workday. Also on the negative side, a ten-hour (or 12-hour) workday is more exhausting than the typical eight-hour day (Cunningham, 1989; Ronen & Primps, 1981; Rosa, Colligan, & Lewis, 1989). This fatigue may lead to decreases in work productivity and concern for work quality (although many people say that the extra couple of hours are not necessarily tiring).

For the work organization, the shorter work week can reduce overhead costs when the plant is shut for the fifth day. Company savings are also realized in terms of decreased "start-up" time. Furthermore, certain compressed work schedules, such as 12-hour shifts, are particularly effective for the staffing of organizations that must maintain continuous operation, 24 hours a day, seven days a week (Breaugh, 1983).

Research on the effects of compressed work weeks are inconclusive. The one general finding is that most (although not all) workers are satisfied with the system (Cohen & Gadon, 1978; Di Milia, 1998). Moreover, one study found that workers had more favorable attitudes toward compressed work schedules if they had participated in the decision to implement the schedule change (Latack & Foster, 1985). There is little evidence, however, that compressed work weeks increase overall work performance (Ivancevich & Lyon, 1977).

compressed work weeks *schedules that decrease the number of days in the work week while increasing the number of hours worked per day*

Flextime

flextime

a schedule that commits an employee to working a specified number of hours per week, but offers flexibility in regard to the starting and ending times for each day

Flextime is a scheduling system whereby a worker is committed to a specified number of hours per week (usually 40) but has some flexibility concerning the starting and ending times of any particular workday. Often flextime schedules operate around a certain core of hours during which all workers must be on the job (such as 10 A.M. to 2:30 P.M.). However, the workers can decide when to begin and end the workday as long as they are present during the core period and work an eight-hour day. Some flextime schedules even allow workers to borrow and carry hours from one workday to the next or, in some extremely flexible programs, from one week to another. The only stipulation is that an average of 40 hours per week is maintained.

What are the primary advantages of flextime? For the worker, it affords a sense of freedom and control over planning the working day (Hicks & Klimoski, 1981; Ralston, 1989). Workers can sleep in and begin work later in the morning, as long as they make up the time by staying late. Employees who want to leave work early to do some late-afternoon shopping can arrive early to work that day. Advantages for the company include reduced rates of absenteeism and the virtual elimination of tardiness (Ronen, 1981). Research indicates that flextime programs increase employee satisfaction and morale, and are sometimes but not always positively related to worker productivity (Kim & Campagna, 1981; Narayanan & Nath, 1982; Ralston, Anthony, & Gustafson, 1985; Schein, Mauner, & Novak, 1977).

Obviously, only certain types of companies can institute flextime. It is not possible if a task requires employees to work together, as in assembly-line work, or when there must be some guarantee of minimum staffing, as in a service organization. Also, not all positions are amenable to flextime schedules. For example, in a library, book shelvers and catalogers might be able to work on such schedules, while workers staffing the check-out and information desks may not be able to work on flextime since they have to cover the desks during the hours when the library is open. However, in many organizations, especially in government and civil service, flextime has been quite successful and is very popular with employees (Kirk, 1981; Walker, Fletcher, & McLeod, 1975).

In general, alternative work schedules can be effective when they meet the needs of both the worker and the organization. Careful consideration of the costs and benefits, including the employees' needs and scheduling preferences, should be made before the introduction of any changes (Dunham, Pierce, & Castaneda, 1987).

Work Safety

The conditions of the work environment include more than just physical, psychological, and temporal elements. The work environment can also present many dangers to workers. In extreme situations, these dangers may be seriously health injuring and even life threatening. Each year hundreds of thousands of workers are seriously injured on the job, and tens of thousands are killed or permanently disabled from industrial accidents and hazards in the work environment. The toll in human lives, pain, and suffering is staggering. There are also tremendous economic costs associated with workplace accidents and hazards, including productivity losses, worker compensation, employee health insurance premiums, and medical treatment. Federal agencies estimate that these combined costs total more than $100 billion annually (National Safety Council, 1991). An important goal of organizations and of I/O psychologists is to protect the worker and to reduce health costs by preventing accidents in the workplace and removing health hazards.

In modern times, safety legislation has helped to cut down on the number of work-related accidents and injuries by setting standards for safe and healthful work conditions. The main federal agency involved in administering and enforcing these standards is the **Occupational Safety and Health Administration (OSHA),** established in 1970. Not only is OSHA responsible for establishing safety guidelines, but it also keeps statistics on work-related accidents and injuries. OSHA guidelines and standards include a number of safety rules and regulations for a wide variety of industries that govern such matters as the use of power tools and machinery, the containment and handling of toxic substances, the use of compressed gases, and the handling of flammable materials. OSHA inspectors conduct unannounced inspections of industrial work sites and have the power to issue warnings and citations for safety violations. They may also levy fines for serious or repeated offenses. Unfortunately, in spite of this safety legislation and OSHA's efforts to enforce it, the typical workplace can still be very dangerous. One reason is that OSHA employs only a few hundred inspectors for the millions of workplaces in the United States. It is impossible for these few OSHA inspectors to enforce and maintain safety standards in all of these workplaces. Also, in spite of companies' attempts to maintain safe work environments, accidents and exposure to health-threatening conditions still happen because of the dangers inherent in some jobs. For example, working with heavy equipment and machinery may result in some accidents regardless of the safeguards taken to prevent them.

To understand the dangers in the workplace, it is important to consider their sources. Some of these dangers are caused by conditions of the work environment that may harm workers' health and cause work-related diseases. Other dangers stem from errors in operator-machine system design that can cause industrial accidents, as we saw in Chapter 15. Still other dangers result from the workers themselves—from tendencies to engage in risky or dangerous work behaviors or from fatigue and stress.

DANGERS IN THE WORK ENVIRONMENT

The conditions under which people are required to work can expose them to various dangers. We have already seen that work conditions can vary greatly, from extremely hot to extremely cold, from quiet and bright offices

What are the advantages and disadvantages of compressed work weeks and flextime?

Occupational Safety and Health Administration (OSHA)
the government agency that administers and enforces health and safety standards in work organizations

Some employees, such as those in the hazardous waste industry, need special clothing and equipment because of work place dangers.

to noisy and dim factories. Variables such as inadequate illumination, extremes of temperature, and noise and distractions can lead to accidents and health hazards. For example, workers may experience eye strain and thus be prone to making dangerous errors if levels of illumination are too low or if the glare is too great. Laboring in extremely hot or cold weather can cause harmful increases or decreases in body temperature. Noisy work environments can cause permanent hearing damage unless proper protection is used. Workplace pollution can also increase the incidence of employee health problems (see Table 16.4). For example, workers in the nuclear industry are exposed to cancer-causing radiation; miners are susceptible to a wide variety of respiratory diseases caused by airborne particles; metalworkers come into contact with toxic substances such as mercury, arsenic, and lead; and many workers in a variety of industries work with chemicals that can cause severe burns through explosions, fires, or skin contact. In short, the work environment presents many potential hazards to workers.

An additional source of danger in the workplace stems from a lack of maintenance. Oil or water spills that are not cleaned up can cause workers to

TABLE 16.4

Some Common Occupational Diseases

Disease	Causes	Symptoms	Occupational Victims
Angiosarcoma	Inhaling vinyl chloride	Liver or brain cancer	Plastics workers
Anthrax	Bacteria from animals	Fever, pneumonia	Agricultural workers, ranchers
Asbestosis	Inhaling asbestos	Lung irritation or cancer	Miners, workers exposed to asbestos insulation
Black lung disease	Inhaling coal dust	Lung irritation or cancer, emphysema	Coal miners
Byssinosis	Inhaling cotton dust	Bronchitis, emphysema	Textile workers
Lead poisoning	Exposure to lead	Kidney disease, anemia, birth defects	Metalworkers
Radiation	Exposure to radiation	Thyroid, lung, or bone cancer; leukemia; genetic damage	Medical technicians, nuclear plant workers, uranium miners
Silicosis	Inhaling silica	Bronchitis, emphysema, pneumonia	Miners, quarriers, glassworkers

Source: K.R. Pelletier, *Healthy People in Unhealthy Places: Stress and Fitness at Work.*

slip and injure themselves (Leamon & Murphy, 1995). Piles of boxes or clutter in hallways or exits can lead to accidents or block workers' escape in case of a fire. Worn-out protective gear and malfunctioning safety equipment are other sources of accidents and injuries. For example, protective eye gear that becomes scratched and clouded can dangerously impair a worker's vision.

Work procedures themselves can also cause injury, as when workers are required to lift heavy loads or to remain in unnatural positions or postures for extended periods. For example, major league baseball catchers tend to have shorter careers than outfielders, because catchers spend a great deal of time crouching, and are more prone to injury from batted or thrown balls. It has also been discovered that typists and word processors can get painful wrist and arm injuries caused from maintaining unnatural wrist positions while typing for hours on end.

DANGERS IN MACHINE SYSTEMS

Many complex and sophisticated machine systems present certain dangers to workers. Moving assembly lines, heavy industrial machines that move and rotate, and motor vehicles can all injure workers. Work machinery and equipment can become extremely hot and burn careless operators.

As we saw in Chapter 15, one of the primary concerns of human factors psychologists in the design of operator-machine systems is operator safety. Poor human factors design has been responsible for many industrial accidents and injuries, particularly when machine systems have inadequate safety guards.

Safety guards or shields are especially important features for industrial machinery in order to protect the operator from harm. These safety guards are designed to minimize the chances that an operator's hands or limbs will get caught in moving machinery and protect the operator from flying objects. Booth (1986) lists five common types of dangers that must be guarded against in designing and operating industrial machinery. One is *traps*, components whose movements could trap the operator's limbs, such as a hydraulic press that could crush fingers or rotating gears that could pinch skin. Another danger results from *impact* with moving machines or parts. For example, some industrial equipment moves at high speeds, such as a forklift or a product moving on an elevated conveyor, and could cause injury if the operator gets in the way. A third danger is with *machine part characteristics*, such as machine parts that are sharp, abrasive, hot, cold, or electrically charged. A fourth danger is *entanglement* with moving machine parts that can catch clothing, hair, gloves, and the like. A final machine danger results from the *ejection* of objects from the machine, such as splinters of metal from a grinding wheel.

Besides safety guards, machine systems must have well-designed warning displays that immediately inform the operator of any potential problems. For instance, a worker could be severely burned by escaping steam if a boiler overheats without warning and explodes. Safety control devices, such as emergency shut-off switches, also need to be placed so that they can be

Astronauts must be clearly protected from the most hostile environment imaginable—outer space.

quickly activated. For example, the operator of a metalstamping machine had a hand seriously injured when his sleeve became entangled in the machine feeder and he was unable to reach the emergency shut-off switch.

More and more, machine systems are being designed with safety in mind. Many operator-machine systems today are designed via computers, with safety factors integrated into the design. This is leading to significant reductions in machine system accidents (Mattila, 1996).

In summary, machine systems can be quite dangerous to operators and thus require built-in safeguards. Moreover, workers must be trained to follow proper safety procedures when working with potentially dangerous machinery and equipment to minimize the risk of injury.

DANGERS IN WORKER CHARACTERISTICS AND BEHAVIOR

List and describe five types of dangers associated with industrial machinery.

In some cases it is the worker rather than the environment or the machinery who is primarily responsible for work-related accidents and injury. Inattention, fatigue, and stress as well as other personal variables are all related to the incidence of work accidents.

Lack of job-related experience is often linked to work accidents. An experienced and quick-thinking worker may be able to avert an accident.

Workers who lack insight into machine procedures and work operations may not be able to predict when systems are out of line and an accident is likely. Generally, the more experienced a worker is with a particular task, the less likely he or she is to have an accident, and the more likely he or she is to take safety precautions (Dunbar, 1993). That is why it is important that workers be properly trained, particularly in regard to safety procedures. There is also a tendency for younger workers to have higher accident rates than older workers, due perhaps to lack of maturity and a more carefree or reckless attitude (Sanders & McCormick, 1993).

Because of the role of the individual in accident rates, many early researchers searched for ways to measure **accident proneness,** or the existence of certain personality characteristics that may predispose a person to work accidents (e.g., Hansen, 1989; Shaw & Sichel, 1971). If there is such a thing as accident proneness, industries need only screen out accident-prone individuals from high-risk jobs in order to reduce the number of work-related accidents. Unfortunately, research has been unable to find any firm evidence of accident-prone personality characteristics (McKenna, 1983; Sanders & McCormick, 1993). It thus does not appear that there are certain types of worker personalities that are to blame for the majority of work accidents. There does, however, seem to be individual differences in workers' "pro-safety" attitudes. That is, some workers seem more committed to adhering to safe work behaviors than others, and these workers with positive safety attitudes have fewer work-related accidents (Jones & Wuebker, 1988).

Individuals may interact with other workers, creating a climate that encourages or discourages safe work practices (Hofmann & Stetzer, 1996). Research has investigated the roles that the leader and the social climate of the work group play in influencing accident rates. One study found that a combination of certain leader practices, such as a lack of planning and structuring of work assignments, little concern about whether work groups were coordinating efforts, and leader inexperience, was related to greater incidence of work accidents in their groups than in work groups who had experienced and organized leaders (Butler & Jones, 1979).

Researchers have focused on the notion of a "safety climate" at work. **Safety climate** refers to the positive attitudes workers hold toward promoting safe work behaviors (Coyle, Sleeman, & Adams, 1995). In one study, safety climate was determined by measuring workers' attitudes toward such matters as the perceived importance of safety training programs, management's attitudes toward safety promotion, and the status and importance given to the work group's safety committee and safety officer (Zohar, 1980). It was found that work groups with a safety climate had safer work areas than work groups without such a climate. Clearly, these results indicate that groups and their leaders who consider safety a priority can significantly increase safe work behaviors and reduce work accidents.

As we have seen, accidents can be caused by a number of variables: errors in operator-machine design, work conditions, or worker behavior. Figure 16.1 represents some of the factors that contribute to workplace

accident proneness
personality characteristics believed to predispose a person to work accidents

safety climate
positive attitudes that workers hold toward promoting safe work behaviors

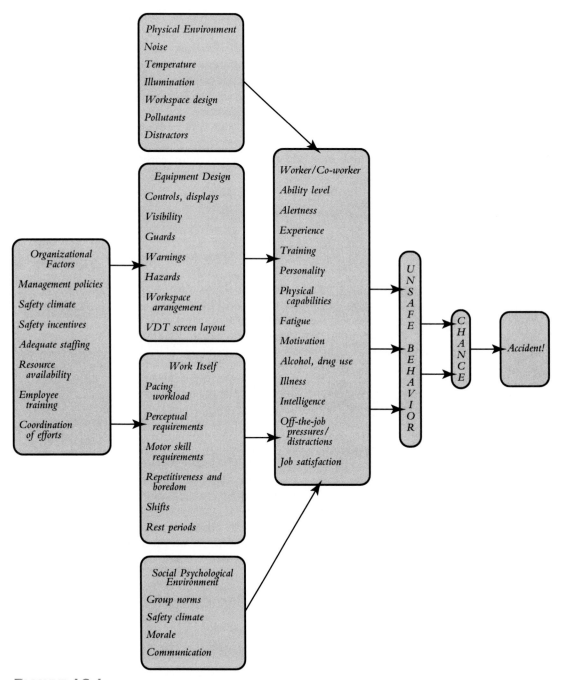

FIGURE 16.1

A Model of Factors Contributing to Workplace Accidents
Source: Adapted from M.S. Sanders and E.J. McCormick, *Human Factors in Engineering and Design,* 7th ed. (New York: McGraw-Hill, 1993).

accidents. Knowing more about the causes of work accidents can help us to develop safety programs to try to prevent them.

PROGRAMS TO INCREASE WORK SAFETY

A variety of programs are designed to increase work safety. Many encourage employees to engage in routine safe work behavior and to follow established safety procedures. Too often, accidents occur because employees disregard proper safety procedures. In fact, it has been estimated that as many as 75 percent of all machinery accidents could have been prevented if proper precautions had been taken (Booth, 1986). These precautions include such practices as wearing protective garb such as goggles to protect eyes from flying debris; following proper procedures, for example, shutting off a machine and/or the electrical current before beginning maintenance operations; or remembering to engage safety guards or locks when machines are not in operation. Such precautions are not taken for a variety of reasons. One is that workers may not be aware of them, usually because of poor employee training. Another reason is the inconvenience of the procedures. For example, workers may not wear protective goggles or hard hats because they are hot and uncomfortable. Others may not bother to shut off power to a machine before working on it or may neglect to raise a safety guard because such procedures inhibit work speed and productivity. Finally, workers may ignore safety procedures because certain work group norms develop that say that following safety procedures indicates that a worker is not "courageous" or "manly" ("*Real* construction workers don't wear hard hats!"). The goal of work safety programs is to try to overcome these impediments and encourage safe work behavior (Hoyos, 1995).

Of the various programs designed to improve work safety, by far the majority have concentrated on employee training and education. Most companies have some formal programs involving lectures or workshops to encourage safe worker behavior. However, although workers may learn about safe and unsafe behaviors, that knowledge may not always translate into safe actions. Workers may still neglect to take proper safety precautions if they are uncomfortable or inconvenient, or cause them to be less productive. Also, unless safety education is an ongoing process, workers may abandon safe procedures out of negligence or in an effort to cut corners. For example, unless safety checks are continually emphasized, employees may begin to ignore routine safety inspection procedures in order to save time and to be able to keep up with backlogged work.

Industrial/organizational psychologists have had considerable success in reducing accident rates by applying organizational behavior modification and goal-setting principles (e.g., Cohen, Smith, & Anger, 1979; Cooper, Phillips, Sutherland, & Makin, 1994; Smith, Anger, & Uslan, 1978). Primarily, these programs involve setting safety goals and providing incentives for reducing the incidence of work-related accidents or rewarding employees for engaging in safe work behaviors or for developing new

Organizational behavior modification programs have been established in companies to reward workers for safe work behaviors.

Outline three reasons why work safety procedures are sometimes not followed by employees.

safety strategies. These programs seem to be effective because they emphasize the positive consequences of engaging in safe behavior—rewards and incentives—rather than the negative consequences, such as inconvenience or decreased productivity and efficiency. In one such program, the accident rates of bus drivers for a large, urban transit authority were reduced by the development of a safety behavior modification program. The program consisted of three components. The first was *performance feedback.* Drivers' daily safety records were posted in the lunchroom for all drivers to see. The second element was a *team competition.* Drivers were put into teams that competed against each other's safety records. The goal was to move the focus of reinforcement contingencies from the individual to the group. Both of these components were designed to develop group norms to encourage safety. The third aspect was *incentives.* Winning drivers and teams received cash or prizes for outstanding safety records. The result was a 25 percent reduction in accident rates. Importantly, the program incentives were paid for by the savings in accident claims (Haynes, Pine, & Fitch, 1982).

In another program, workers in a food manufacturing plant attended a training session at which they received information about safe and unsafe work practices and the reasons why it was important to engage in safe work behaviors. Following the session, departmental safety records were posted. Employees who engaged in safe work behaviors were merely given public recognition by management. The results showed a significant decline in work-related accidents for 25 weeks. When the program was discontinued, the accident rate rose to the earlier high level. The program was finally reinstated, and the accident rate decreased dramatically and remained low for a long-term follow-up period. In fact, the plant that had had the worst safety record of the company's many manufacturing plants went from last to first place following this fairly simple and straightforward safety program (Komaki, Barwick, & Scott, 1978).

These results indicate that monitoring the incidence of unsafe work behaviors, alerting workers to these behaviors, and recognizing safe work behaviors are often enough to reduce work-related accident rates. Companies have tried to reduce accidents and injuries by combining safety training programs, the monitoring of work-related injuries and accidents, and safety incentive programs (see, for example, Reber & Wallin, 1984). Others have set up work safety task forces or committees to develop strategies for keeping the work place safe.

Two additional types of safety training programs are aimed specifically at reducing operator errors in complicated and potentially dangerous operator-machine systems. The first trains workers in problem-solving strategies for dealing with machine emergencies or malfunctions. They are taught to: (1) recognize and define the problem, (2) generate alternative courses of action for solving the problem, (3) evaluate the alternative courses, (4) select and implement the chosen strategy, and (5) evaluate the effectiveness of the strategy for solving the problem. Although this type of problem-solving training has not been widely used in industry, it is expected that this type of training might be effective in helping nuclear power plant operators, air traffic controllers, and others who work with complex machine systems to deal with potential crisis situations.

The second innovative safety program is called *stress inoculation training*, which is designed to keep system operators from panicking when faced with an emergency. The two major components of these programs are helping workers to: (1) prepare cognitively for potential stressful events, such as a malfunction in a nuclear power plant; and (2) learn and rehearse coping strategies for dealing with various types of crises. The goal is to teach workers to ignore the distracting stimuli, such as their own arousal, panicking coworkers, and noise, and focus on the emergency. Stress inoculation training has been used successfully in combat training and may prove useful in helping machine system operators deal with dangerous crisis situations (Spetell & Lebert, 1986).

ON THE CUTTING EDGE

Promoting Worker Health and Well-Being

More and more, organizations are recognizing the value of having a healthy, happy workforce. Healthy workers mean less absenteeism, and there is evidence that suggests that regular exercise cuts down on mortality rates of workers (Paffenburger, Hyde, Wing, & Hsieh, 1986). As the importance of worker health becomes clearer, organizations are putting more resources into employee **health promotion programs**, which typically consist of seminars in healthful living (e.g., proper nutrition, smoking cessation, etc.) and/or fitness and exercise sessions. Some organizations have even set up exercise facilities in the workplace.

In one study of an employees' aerobic exercise fitness program, the participants in the program reported that the program helped in reducing stress, increasing stamina, endurance, and muscle flexibility, and improved their moods at work (Imm, 1990). Another study of fitness programs found an inverse relationship between employee physical fitness and employee medical and disability costs to the organization (Browne, Russell, Morgan, Optenberg, & Clarke, 1984). Additional benefits of employee-sponsored health promotion programs include increased smoking cessation, weight control, and more positive work attitudes (Fielding, 1984; Wilbur, 1983).

Although studies point to the beneficial outcomes of employee fitness programs, there has been little attention given to the most effective ways for organizations to establish and promote these programs. It should be noted that employees who participate more in employee-sponsored health promotion programs tend to be those workers who are already more "fitness-oriented"—interested in weight loss, appearance, and health (Conrad, 1988). One challenging goal is to increase healthful living for those employees who are most at risk—those who are not already inclined toward good health practices.

health promotion programs
a variety of methods for improving the health and well-being of workers through seminars, counseling, and fitness sessions

ALCOHOL AND DRUG USE IN THE WORKPLACE

A growing problem—one that is of increasing concern to businesses and to industrial/organizational psychologists—is employee use and abuse of alcohol and drugs. No doubt a great many industrial accidents occur because of worker intoxication. The combination of alcohol or drugs and heavy machinery or motor vehicles is deadly. Drug and alcohol abuse is also directly responsible for decreased productivity and increased absenteeism and turnover, not to mention all the problems that it can cause in the home life of workers. The costs of all of this are staggering. A conservative estimate is that substance abuse in a company of 1,000 employees costs more than a half million dollars per year in lost work time and productivity (Axel, 1986).

In an effort to combat substance abuse, many companies are developing **employee assistance programs (EAPs),** programs that offer counseling for a variety of employee problems. Of particular concern is counseling for drug and alcohol abuse, although EAPs also help employees to deal with work stress and personal problems that may adversely affect their performance and well-being (Cairo, 1983). Although employee counseling has long been offered by companies, only in the past dozen years have comprehensive EAPs become commonplace in large organizations. This increase is likely due to the growing concern over the devastating consequences of substance abuse in terms of harming worker health and organizational productivity. The majority of large American companies today have some type of formalized employee assistance program.

While industrial/organizational psychologists are greatly concerned about the adverse impact of substance abuse and work stress on employee productivity and well-being, clinical and counseling psychologists, social workers, and drug rehabilitation counselors, rather than I/O psychologists, typically staff EAPs. However, I/O psychologists may have a hand in the design, implementation, and evaluation of EAPs.

Employee assistance programs usually take one of two forms. External programs are those in which the company contracts with an outside agency to provide counseling services for its employees. Internal EAPs offer services at the work site. The advantage of an internal program is its convenience for the employees, although they are expensive to maintain. Usually only large organizations can afford internal EAPs. The main advantages of external programs are the lower costs and the increased employee confidentiality.

In spite of the increasing popularity of employee assistance programs, there has been surprisingly little research on their effectiveness (Weiss, 1987). The problem results partly from the difficulty of evaluating *any* counseling program, because it is not always clear which variables will best determine a program's "success" (Mio & Goishi, 1990). For example, some programs measure success by the number of workers treated, whereas others may use some standard of recovery or "cure." Furthermore, it is difficult to determine how EAP counseling affects bottom-line variables such as employee performance. It is also difficult to determine the effectiveness of

STOP AND REVIEW

What types of work safety programs are most common?

employee assistance programs (EAPs) *counseling provided for a variety of worker problems, particularly drug and alcohol abuse*

EAPs because the large number of external agencies that offer counseling services for businesses usually conduct their own evaluations, and it is unclear how objective and accurate these self-assessments are. Although there are questions about the effectiveness of employee assistance programs in general, it is likely that even a few cases of employee recovery would lead an employer to label an EAP a success because of the severity of drug and alcohol addiction. Moreover, there is some evidence that EAPs do help reduce long-term health care costs for employees (Cummings & Follette, 1976). One critic of substance abuse EAPs argues that they focus primarily on treating alcohol and drug problems after they have reached the problem stage, but give little attention to their prevention (Nathan, 1983). In spite of the uncertainty of the effectiveness of employee assistance programs, it is likely that they will become a mainstay in most work organizations and another service that will be considered an essential part of any employee benefit package.

UP CLOSE

What Will Work Conditions Be Like in the Future?

As we enter into this new century, how will technological changes and the other advancements in work conditions and processes affect the world of work?

Obviously, the biggest change in office technology has been the movement away from printed documents to a paperless, electronic office. With advances in graphics, there will be more pictorial representations of information and less emphasis on written descriptions. For example, rather than telling someone about a new product or piece of equipment, you will be able to show it in graphic detail. With access to numerous databases workers will never have to leave the office to go to a library to research a topic or to examine voluminous company documents and records.

In state-of-the-art offices, receptionists will be replaced by computers who will answer and screen calls, and busy executives will be able to dictate directly into a speech-activated word processor that creates memos or documents instantaneously. Moreover, with increasingly more sophisticated (and smaller) laptop and palmtop computers, and remote communication capabilities, we will never be far from our work and/or our offices. Inside our computers will be "know-bots" that will act like a personal secretary, sorting through and prioritizing our e-mail messages, reminding of us appointments, and reading through articles and correspondence highlighting important points for us (Thach & Woodman, 1994).

The office building of the future may have advanced environmental monitoring and control equipment to allow each individual to control the environmental conditions of the individual workspace. The temperature will remain constantly pleasant,

UP CLOSE (continued)

with humidity controlled, and the air will be filtered to remove all pollutants. The amount and quality of lighting will also be adjusted to suit the worker's needs. More and more workers will also be involved in the design and equipping of their workspaces—creating a physical environment that suits them, as well as choosing the work equipment they prefer. Of course, office furniture and equipment will be more ergonomically designed for comfort and efficiency.

Advances in communication will allow a greater number of workers to telecommute, although it is expected that the majority of workers will still perform their jobs at a central site due to the importance placed on face-to-face social contact in the work setting. However, with "groupware" we will be able to network with work group members to conduct virtual meetings and work on group tasks from our homes. Undoubtedly there will be greater flexibility in work hours, as urban commuting traffic becomes worse and worse. Urban employers will have to allow workers more flexibility in beginning and ending their workdays.

Perhaps the greatest changes in work conditions will occur in factories, where more operations will be performed by computers and robots. As factories become more automated, the worker's job will change from manual tasks to those involving the programming, overseeing, and maintenance of the sophisticated machine systems. The physical environment for factory workers will become more like a comfortable office, with environmentally regulated control rooms. The monitoring and inspection of manufacturing processes will be done remotely through videocameras or sophisticated electronic feedback systems. Safety concerns will be put to rest since the more dangerous operations will be handled by robots or teleoperator systems.

The sweeping changes occurring in the world of work will present challenges to workers and organizations—and the I/O psychologists who study them (Cascio, 1998). However, these changes mean that industrial/organizational psychologists will be even more involved in creating a more productive, harmonious, comfortable, and safe work environment while they help organizations accept and adapt to the rapid and inevitable changes that occur.

Summary

I/O psychologists are greatly concerned with how the physical, psychological, and temporal (or scheduling) conditions of work can affect worker performance, satisfaction, and health. Physical conditions, such as levels of illumination, temperature, noise, motion and vibration, airborne pollutants, and aesthetics, can influence worker behavior. Research indicates that more illumination is positively associated with job performance up to an optimal point, at which increased brightness no longer increases performance, but may detract from it. Because lighting glare can also detract from effective job performance, steps are taken to try to reduce it. Extreme heat or extreme cold can decrease performance, although appropriate clothing can protect against the adverse effects of temperature. While excessive noise can adversely affect job performance, the label of "noise" can be quite subjective. Extremely loud, high-pitched, intermittent, or unpredictable noise may have more negative effects than steady, low-volume noise. In jobs involving transportation of heavy machinery or equipment, motion may adversely affect work performance. The effect of airborne pollution in the workplace is also a particular hazard to performance as well as to worker safety and health. Finally, aesthetic factors, such as the presence of music and certain colors or decorations, may have subtle effects on workers, particularly on satisfaction with the job and the work environment.

The psychological conditions of the work environment that can affect work performance include feelings of privacy or crowding, the status associated with the amount or location of workspace, and the amount of control over the work environment. Industrial/organizational psychologists have also had a hand in influencing the time structure of the typical working day. The effects of various *shifts* (such as day, afternoon, and night) on the productivity and well-being of the worker have received considerable attention. Experiments have also been conducted with *compressed work weeks*, or weeks that are shortened by lengthening each work day, and *flextime*, a scheduling system that gives workers a great deal of control over structuring their own work schedules.

In considering work conditions, a critical concern is safety, for work accidents and injuries are very costly in terms of both the pain and suffering of the victims and the financial losses to the organization. The *Occupational Safety and Health Administration (OSHA)* is the federal agency responsible for establishing safety guidelines in work organizations. However, in spite of OSHA's efforts, workplaces still present many dangers from a variety of sources. Some dangers stem from qualities of the physical work environment, such as inadequate illumination, temperature extremes, or noisy distractions. Lack of workplace maintenance can also lead to accidents and injury. Another major source of danger is the unsafe design of operator-machine systems. Systems with inadequate warning displays, poor placement of controls and displays, and inadequate safety guards can cause serious injury. Finally, accidents may occur because of certain worker characteristics or behaviors. Untrained or inexperienced workers may have more accidents than those who are more expert. Although attempts have been made to distinguish individuals who demonstrate *accident proneness*, or a predisposition to accidents created by certain personality characteristics, no such personality characteristics have yet been identified, although pro-safety attitudes may decrease workplace accidents. Finally, a safety climate where workers hold positive attitudes toward safety can promote safe work behavior.

A variety of programs attempt to increase work safety. Behavior modification programs have been quite successful in reducing accident rates and in increasing attention to safe work behaviors. The monitoring of the incidence of unsafe work behaviors to alert workers to their existence, the recognition of safe work behaviors, emergency problem-solving training, stress inoculation training, and the introduction of incentives for increased work safety have all also been successful strategies.

A growing problem related to worker safety and health is the use and abuse of alcohol and drugs in the workplace. Many companies have created *employee assistance programs (EAPs)* to provide counseling for employees trying to deal with substance abuse. EAPs can be in-house, internal programs or the organization can contract with an outside agency for provision of counseling services. In spite of the tremendous growth and popularity of EAPs, there has been little systematic evaluation of their effectiveness.

Study Questions and Exercises

1. In what occupations are workers exposed to extreme or aversive physical conditions? What are some of the steps that can be taken to help deal with them?

2. Psychologists have attempted to uncover the characteristics that lead to an accident-prone personality. Although there has been no confirmation of such a personality, what personal attributes might be linked to higher accident rates?

3. In spite of federal legislation and agencies such as OSHA, accident rates in industry are still at unacceptably high levels. Based on what you have learned in this course, how can I/O psychologists help to create a safer workplace?

4. Twenty years ago, employee assistance programs in industry were rare. What changes in the attitudes of society and employers have led to their introduction?

Suggested Readings

National Safety Council in Itasca, IL, publishes a number of practitioner-oriented guidebooks for promoting workplace safety and occupational health. These include: *Accident prevention manual for business & industry, Introduction to occupational health and safety, Occupational health and safety in automation and robotics,* as well as brief volumes dealing with protective clothing, noise control, pollution, and workplace vibrations.

Erickson, P.A. (1996). *Practical guide to occupational health and safety.* San Diego, CA: Academic Press. *This book is a practical guide for safety and human resources professionals that covers a number of the important health and safety issues in the workplace.*

GLOSSARY

A

accident proneness personality characteristics believed to predispose a person to work accidents. To date, they have not been uncovered by research.

accommodation a conflict resolution strategy involving one party giving in or making sacrifices to resolve a conflict.

achievement motivation theory McClelland's model of motivation that emphasizes the importance of three needs—achievement, power, and affiliation—in determining worker motivation.

achievement-oriented behavior in the path-goal theory of leadership, leader behavior that is focused on specific work outcomes.

action research a methodological model that applies social science research methods to collect relevant data in an organization and then use the information as the basis for taking action to solve organizational problems.

actor-observer bias in social perception, the tendency for the observer to overattribute cause to characteristics of the actor and the tendency for the actor to overattribute cause to situational characteristics.

adverse impact some form of discrimination against a protected group in personnel actions.

affirmative action voluntary organizational decision to develop policies that attempt to ensure that jobs are made available to qualified persons regardless of sex, age, or ethnic background.

apprenticeship an employee training technique, often lasting several years, that combines on-the-job experience with classroom instruction.

assessment center a detailed, structured assessment of job applicants using a variety of measurements and techniques.

audience factors characteristics of the receiver of information that influence the way the communication is perceived and thus the effectiveness of the communication process.

audiovisual instruction employee training procedures using films, videotapes, audiotapes, or slide presentations.

autocratic decision making a decision-making strategy whereby the leader makes decisions based primarily on information that the leader possesses.

avoidance in conflict situations, a strategy of withdrawing from or avoiding the conflict.

B

behavior modeling training a training method that exposes trainees to role models performing appropriate and inappropriate work behaviors and their outcomes, and then allows them to practice modeling the appropriate behaviors.

behaviorally anchored rating scales (BARS) a performance appraisal method using a rating scale with labels reflecting examples of poor, average, and good behavioral incidents.

behavioral observation scales a performance appraisal method that requires evaluators to recall how often a worker has been observed performing key work behaviors.

behavioral theories of leadership theories derived from studies at Ohio State and the University of

499

Michigan that focus on the behaviors common to effective leaders.

bell-shaped curve a graphic representation of a normal distribution of scores. It is assumed that many variables are normally distributed and thus would be graphed in this form.

biodata background information and personal characteristics that can be used in a systematic fashion in employee screening and selection.

brainstorming when groups generate creative ideas or solutions through a noncritical and non-judgmental process.

bureaucracy Weber's theory that illustrates a traditional organizational structure, characterized by a well-defined authority hierarchy and strict rules governing work behavior.

burnout a syndrome resulting from prolonged exposure to work stress that can lead to decreased performance and eventually withdrawal from the organization. Burnout typically occurs in three phases: emotional exhaustion, depersonalization, and feelings of low personal accomplishment.

C

case study a research investigation involving a one-time assessment of behavior, usually with a single individual, a group, or an organization.

causal attribution the process by which people ascribe cause to events or behaviors.

censoring in the communication process, a purposeful omission of information from a message or a decision not to transmit particular information.

centralization the degree to which decision-making power is concentrated in the top levels of the organizational hierarchy.

centralized networks systematic lines of communication among organizational members by which the flow of information is directed through specific members.

central tendency error the tendency to give all workers the midpoint rating in performance appraisals.

chain of command the authority levels in an organizational hierarchy

change agent an organizational development practitioner or consultant who serves as a catalyst to help organizations through the process of change.

channel in the communication process, the vehicle through which a message flows from a sender to a receiver. Channels may include the written or spoken word, nonverbal communication, pictures, or graphs.

channel factors characteristics of the vehicle of transmission of a message that affect the accuracy and/or perception of the communication.

charismatic leadership theory states that leaders possess some exceptional characteristics that cause followers to be loyal and inspired.

checklists a performance appraisal method consisting of a series of statements about job performance that are checked off by the evaluator.

check-reading displays displays that indicate whether a machine system is on or off, or operating normally or abnormally.

classical conditioning a theory of learning based on the notion that two events, experienced together in space and time, become associated with each other (also called Pavlovian conditioning).

coalition in power dynamics, the uniting of individuals to combine power.

coercive power the use of punishment or the threat of punishment to affect the behavior of others.

cognitive theories of learning a training approach that emphasizes that workers are complex information processors.

cohesiveness the degree of attraction group members feel for one another.

collaboration a conflict resolution strategy whereby the parties cooperate so they can attain their respective goals.

communication the transmission of information from one person or group to another person or group.

communication networks systematic lines of communication linking various senders and receivers.

comparable worth the notion that jobs that require equivalent levels of knowledge and skills should be compensated equally.

comparative methods a performance appraisal method that compares one worker's performance with the performance of others.

comparison others persons who are used as a basis for comparison in making judgments of equity/inequity. A key element in the equity theory of motivation.

compensable factors the job elements or dimensions that are used to determine appropriate compensation.

competition the process whereby group members work against one another to achieve individual goals.

competition (as a conflict resolution strategy) the perpetuation of a conflict situation until one party attains personal goals at the expense of the other party's goal attainment.

compressed work weeks work schedules that shorten the number of days in the work week while increasing the number of hours worked per day.

compromise a conflict resolution strategy whereby both parties give up some part of their goals.

computer-assisted instruction (CAI) programmed instruction using computers to present material and to test trainees.

conference an unstructured management training technique in which participants share ideas, information, and problems; also called a group discussion.

conflict behavior by a person or group that inhibits the attainment of goals by another person or group.

conformity the process of adhering to and following group norms

consensus a decision-making strategy that requires all group members to reach full and complete agreement.

consideration leader behavior that shows a concern for the feelings, attitudes, and needs of subordinates.

content validity in employee screening, a form of validity that is concerned with whether the items in a measurement instrument adequately assess the characteristics necessary to perform the job.

contingency theories theories that look at the interaction of the characteristics or behaviors of individuals (such as leaders) and the qualities of the situation.

control group in an experimental investigation, a comparison group that receives no treatment.

controls the mechanical devices used to operate machine functions.

correlational method the research method that examines the relationship between or among variables as they naturally occur.

correlation coefficient a statistical technique that determines the strength of a relationship between two variables. Expressed as numerical values ranging from $+1.00$ to -1.00.

criterion a measure of job success, typically related to performance.

criterion deficiency the degree to which a criterion falls short of measuring job performance.

criterion-related validity in employee screening, a method of establishing the accuracy of a measurement instrument by determining the relationship between scores on the instrument and some criterion of job success.

criterion usefulness the extent to which a performance criterion is usable in appraising a particular job.

critical incidents technique (CIT) a method of job analysis that uses as its basis instances of particularly successful or unsuccessful job performance.

D

decentralization the process of taking the decision-making power away from the top level of an organization and distributing it to lower levels.

decentralized networks communication networks that allow messages to originate at any point, without having to be directed through certain, central members.

decibels a standardized measure of sound loudness.

decision-making model (Vroom) a theory that matches characteristics of the work decision situation with leader decision-making strategies.

decoding in the communication process, the act of translating a message so that it can be understood.

democratic decision making a decision-making strategy whereby group members are allowed to participate, usually by majority-rule voting.

dependent variable the measured outcome variable in an experimental investigation. Changes in the dependent variable are presumably caused by manipulation of the independent variable.

descriptive statistics arithmetical formulas for summarizing and describing research data. The mean, standard deviation, and frequency distribution of scores are all examples.

Dictionary of Occupational Titles (DOT) a reference guide that classifies and provides job descriptions of over 40,000 jobs.

differentiation the complexity of an organizational structure based on the number of units or departments, the different orientations of managers, and the different goals and interests of members.

directive behavior in the path-goal theory of leadership, leader behavior that provides instructions and suggestions for getting the job done.

displays mechanical means of communicating information about a machine's operating status to an operator.

divisional structure an organizational structure in which divisions are made based on types of products or customers.

downward communication the flow of messages from superiors to subordinates in an organizational hierarchy, usually in the form of orders, directives, or requests for information.

dysfunctional politics political behaviors that detract from an organization's ability to attain its goals.

E

effect size an estimate of the magnitude of a relationship between variables. Used in meta-analysis.

Employee Assistance Programs (EAPs) programs offering counseling for a variety of worker problems, especially drug and alcohol abuse.

employee ownership a concept whereby employees own all or part of an organization, typically through stock purchases.

employee placement the process of assigning workers to jobs.

employee recruitment the process by which organizations attract potential workers to apply for jobs.

employee screening the process of reviewing information about applicants to select individuals for jobs.

employee selection the process of choosing applicants for employment.

employee training planned organizational efforts to facilitate employee learning of job-related knowledge and behavior.

empowerment the process by which organizational members are able to increase their sense of power and personal control in the work environment. Workers can be empowered by managers or may be able to empower themselves through increasing important work-related skills or responsibilities.

encoding in the communication process, the act of preparing a message for transmission by putting it into some recognizable form or code.

engineering anthropometry the measurement of physical characteristics of the human body in order to develop equipment designed to fit those characteristics.

Equal Employment Opportunity Commission (EEOC) the federal agency created to protect against discrimination in employment.

equity theory a motivation theory that states that workers are motivated to reduce perceived inequities between work inputs and outcomes.

ERG theory (existence, relatedness, and growth) Alderfer's motivation model that classifies needs into categories of existence (basic physiological requirements), relatedness (social interaction), and growth (the development of one's full potential).

exaggeration in communication, the distortion of information through the elaboration, overestimation, or minimization of certain aspects of the message.

exceptioning the practice of ignoring pay discrepancies between particular jobs with equivalent duties and responsibilities.

expectancy the perceived relationship between an individual's effort and the performance of a behavior. One of the three components of the expectancy theory of motivation.

expectancy (VIE) theory a rational theory of motivation that states that workers weigh expected costs and benefits of a particular course of action before they are motivated to take action.

experimental method a research design characterized by a high degree of control over the research setting, which allows the determination of cause-and-effect relationships as the researcher manipulates one aspect of the situation and measures its effect on another aspect.

expert power power that results from the possession of some special work knowledge or skill.

external validity whether research results obtained in one setting will generalize to other settings.

extinction the elimination of a conditioned response through the withdrawal of reinforcement.

extraneous variables variables other than the independent variable that may influence the dependent variable.

F

feedback in the communication process, an acknowledgment that a message has been received and understood.

Fiedler's contingency model a leadership theory that maintains that effective leadership depends on a match between the leader's style and the degree to which the work situation gives that person control and influence.

filtering the selective presentation of the content of a communication.

fixed interval schedule a reinforcement schedule in which reinforcement follows the passage of a specified amount of time.

fixed ratio schedule a reinforcement schedule in which reinforcement is contingent on performance of a fixed number of behaviors.

flextime a schedule in which an employee works a specified number of hours per week but has flexibility in the starting and ending times for workdays.

frequency distribution a descriptive statistical technique that arranges scores by categories and often takes a graphic form such as bar graphs or histograms.

functional job analysis (FJA) a job analysis technique that examines the sequence of tasks in a job and the processes by which the worker completes the task.

functional politics political behaviors that assist the organization in attaining its goals.

functional structure an organizational structure that divides the organization into departments based on the functions or tasks they perform.

G

gainsharing a compensation system based on effective group rather than individual performance.

glass ceiling limitations placed on women and minorities which prevent them from advancing into top-level positions in organizations.

goal-setting theory the motivational theory that emphasizes the setting of specific and challenging performance goals.

grapevine the informal communication network in an organization.

graphic rating scale a job evaluation method using a predetermined scale to rate the worker on important job dimensions. Graphic rating scales can take a variety of forms.

great man/woman theory a universalist theory of leadership that maintains that great leaders are born, not made.

group two or more individuals who engage in social interaction to achieve some goal.

group polarization the tendency for groups to make more extreme decisions than individuals.

groupthink a syndrome, proposed by Janis, characterized by a concurrence-seeking tendency that overrides the ability of a cohesive group to make critical decisions.

growth need strength the need and desire for personal growth on the job that is a key element in the job characteristics model.

H

halo effect in social perception, an overall positive evaluation of a person based on one known positive characteristic or action.

hardiness the notion that some people may be more resistant to the health-damaging effects of stress.

Hawthorne effect changes in behavior that occur because participants know that they are being observed, and because of participants' expectations concerning their role as research participants.

health promotion programs a variety of methods for improving the health and well-being of workers through seminars, counseling, and fitness sessions.

human factors the specialty area of I/O psychology focusing on the relationship between the worker and the work task. Human factors is concerned with designing tools, machines, work systems, and workplaces to fit the skills and abilities of the workers who will be using them. Also referred to as engineering psychology and ergonomics.

human relations movement a movement begun by Mayo that emphasizes the influence of social factors on worker performance.

hygienes elements related to job context that, when absent, cause dissatisfaction. A key idea in Herzberg's two-factor theory of motivation.

hypotheses statements used in research methods concerning the supposed relationships between or among variables.

I

independent variable the variable that is manipulated by the experimenter as part of the experimental method of research. The independent variable is the presumed cause of changes in the dependent variable.

individual coping strategies techniques such as exercise or meditation that individuals can use to deal with work stress.

individual methods performance appraisals focusing on evaluating an employee by himself or herself, without making direct comparisons to other employees.

individual power power derived from personal characteristics, such as expertise or leadership ability, that are of value to an organization.

industrial/organizational (I/O) psychology the branch of psychology that studies behavior in work settings and applies psychological principles to change work behavior.

inferential statistics statistical techniques used for analyzing data in order to test research hypotheses.

influence the ability to use social forces, such as persuasiveness, flattery, or manipulation, to affect the behavior of others.

ingratiation influencing others by increasing one's personal appeal by using flattery or doing favors.

initiating structure leader behaviors that define, organize, and structure the work setting.

inputs elements that a worker invests in a job, such as experience, knowledge, and effort. A key factor in the equity theory of motivation.

instrumentality the relationship between performing a behavior and the expected likelihood of receiving a particular outcome. An important factor in the expectancy theory of motivation.

integration the amount and quality of collaboration among the various units or departments within an organization.

integrity tests measures of honest/dishonest attitudes and/or behaviors.

intergroup conflict conflict that results when two groups interfere with one another's goal attainment.

interindividual conflict conflict that arises when two individuals are blocking one another's goal attainment.

internal consistency a common method of establishing the reliability of a test by examining the intercorrelations of the various items.

interorganizational conflict conflict occurring between two organizations with incompatible goals.

interpersonal stress stress that arises from difficulties with relations with others in the workplace.

intragroup conflict conflict that results when a person or faction within a group is attempting to attain a goal and interferes with the group's goal attainment.

intraindividual conflict conflict that occurs when an individual is faced with two sets of incompatible goals and working to attain one goal interferes with the attainment of the other goal.

intrinsic reinforcement the notion that people are motivated by internal rewards, such as a sense of accomplishment, or by challenges at work.

J

jargon specific language developed in connection with certain jobs. Also referred to as technical language.

job ambiguity a source of stress resulting from a lack of clearly defined jobs and/or work tasks; also known as job uncertainty.

job analysis the systematic study of the tasks, duties, and responsibilities of a job and the knowledge, skills, abilities, and other characteristics (KSAOs) needed to perform it.

job characteristics model a theory that emphasizes the role that certain aspects of jobs, or job characteristics, play in influencing work motivation.

job description a detailed account of job tasks, procedures, and responsibilities; requisite tools and equipment; and output.

Job Descriptive Index (JDI) a standardized, self-report job satisfaction rating scale that measures five job facets.

Job Diagnostic Survey (JDS) a questionnaire measure of core job characteristics used in conjunction with the job characteristics model.

job elements method a job analysis method that analyzes jobs in terms of the knowledge, skills, abilities, and other characteristics (KSAOs) required to perform the jobs.

job enlargement expansion of a job to include additional, more varied work tasks to make workers feel that they are more valuable.

job enrichment a program that involves redesigning jobs to give workers greater responsibility in the planning, execution, and evaluation of their work.

job evaluation an assessment of the relative value of jobs to determine appropriate compensation.

job rotation a method of moving workers among a variety of jobs or tasks to increase their breadth of knowledge or to alleviate boredom and monotony.

job satisfaction the positive and negative feelings and attitudes about one's job.

job specification a statement of the human characteristics required to perform a job, such as experience, knowledge, and training.

K

knowledge-based pay a system of compensation whereby workers receive pay based on their knowledge and skills rather than on the positions they hold.

L

lack of control a feeling of having little input or effect on the job and work environment. Research indicates that a sense of lack of control is a significant source of stress.

lateral communication communication between two parties at the same status level in an organizational hierarchy.

leader-member exchange model (LMX) a leadership theory that defines effective leadership by the quality of the interaction between the leader and particular group members.

leader-member relations the quality of the relationship between leader and followers. A key element in Fiedler's contingency model of leadership.

leadership the ability to direct a group toward the attainment of goals.

Leadership Grid an application of the findings from the behavioral theories of leadership that stresses that effective leaders should be both task-oriented and relationship-oriented.

learning a relatively permanent change in behavior, behavior potential, or cognitive structures that occurs as a result of experience.

least preferred coworker (LPC) a measure that assesses a leader's task or relationship orientation by having the leader rate his or her least preferred coworker.

legitimate power an individual's formal rights or authorities that derive from the person's position in an organization.

leniency error the tendency to give all workers very positive ratings in performance appraisals.

line employees directly engaged in tasks that accomplish the primary goals of an organization.

line-staff organizational structure a traditional organizational structure made up of one group of employees—the line—who achieve the goals of the organization, and another group—the staff—who support the line.

M

management by objectives (MBO) a goal-setting organizational development technique in which supervisors and subordinates jointly set performance goals and, at the end of a certain period, evaluate goal attainment and set new goals.

management games a management training technique that uses scaled-down enactments of the operations and management of organizations.

matrix organization an organizational design that blends functional and product structures.

mean a statistical measure of central tendency calculated by taking the sum of scores and dividing by the number of scores. Also referred to as the average.

measures of central tendency present the center point of a distribution of scores. The mean and median are examples.

median a measure of central tendency; the midpoint of a distribution of scores.

mentoring an employee training program in which an inexperienced individual develops a working relationship with an experienced worker who serves as an advisor.

merit pay a compensation system whereby employees receive a base rate and additional pay that is based on individual performance.

meta-analysis a statistical technique that allows the results from several research investigations to be combined and summarized.

Minnesota Satisfaction Questionnaire (MSQ) a standardized, self-report measure of job satisfaction that breaks satisfaction down into 20 job facets.

modeling learning that occurs by observing and imitating the behavior of others.

motivation the force that energizes, directs, and sustains behavior.

motivators elements related to job content that lead to job satisfaction. Used in Herzberg's two-factor theory of motivation.

multiple cutoff an employee selection model that uses a minimum cutoff score on each of several predictors.

multiple hurdle an employee selection model that requires that an acceptance or rejection decision be made at each of several stages in a screening process.

multiple regression model an employee selection method that statistically combines separate predictors to determine how they, in combination, indicate an applicant's potential success at a job.

N

narratives open-ended, written accounts of an employee's performance used in performance appraisal.

need hierarchy theory Maslow's motivation model that arranges needs in a hierarchy from lower, more basic needs to higher-order needs.

needs physiological or psychological deficiencies that an organism is driven to satisfy.

negative reinforcers events that strengthen a behavior through the avoidance of an existing negative state.

noise physical or psychological distractions that can disrupt the flow of communication or cause stress. In extremes, physical noise can cause permanent hearing damage and is a work environment hazard.

nonverbal communication messages sent and received through means other than the spoken or written word.

normal distribution a distribution of scores along a continuum with known properties. The normal distribution is often represented as a bell-shaped curve.

norms rules that groups adopt to govern appropriate and inappropriate behavior for members.

O

objectivity the principle that research methods involve unbiased observations and interpretations of behavior.

obtrusive observation research observation in which the presence of the observer is known to the participants.

Occupational Safety and Health Administration (OSHA) the governmental agency that administers and enforces health and safety standards in work organizations.

on-the-job training an employee training method of placing a worker in the workplace to learn firsthand about a job.

operant conditioning a learning process whereby behaviors are followed by reinforcement or punishment to obtain desired outcomes.

operationalization the process of defining a variable so that it can be measured or manipulated.

operator-machine system the interaction of one or more persons with one or more tools or devices to perform a work task.

organigram a diagram of an organization's hierarchy representing the formal lines of communication within the organization. Also known as an organizational chart.

organizational behavior modification the application of conditioning principles to obtain desired work outcomes.

organizational citizenship behavior efforts by organizational members that advance or promote the work organization and its goals.

organizational commitment employees' feelings and attitudes concerning the entire work organization.

organizational coping strategies techniques and programs that organizations can use to try to reduce stress levels for all or most employees.

organizational culture the shared values, beliefs, assumptions, and patterns of behavior within an organization.

organizational development (OD) the process of assisting organizations to prepare for and manage change.

organizational downsizing a strategy of reducing an organization's workforce for the purpose of improving organizational efficiency and/or competitiveness.

organizational politics self-serving actions used to affect the behavior of others in order to achieve personal goals.

organizational power power derived from a person's position in an organization and from the control over important organizational resources afforded to the person because of the position.

organizational socialization the process by which new employees learn group and organizational roles and norms, and develop specific work skills and abilities.

organizational structure the arrangement of positions in an organization, and the authority and responsibility relationships among the positions.

outcomes in the equity theory of motivation, those things that a worker expects to receive from a job, such as pay and recognition.

overpayment inequity in the equity theory of motivation, workers' perceptions that outcomes are greater than inputs.

P

parallel forms a method of establishing the reliability of a measurement instrument by correlating scores on two different but equivalent versions of the same instrument.

participant observation an unobtrusive observation research method in which the observer becomes a member of the organization or group being studied.

participative behavior in the path-goal theory of leadership, leader behavior that encourages members to take an active role in group planning and decision making.

path-goal theory a leadership theory that states that a leader's job is to help the work group attain their desired goals.

performance appraisals the process of assessing worker performance in comparison to certain predetermined organizational standards.

performance criteria the means of determining successful or unsuccessful job performance, derived from job analysis.

performance feedback the process of providing information to a worker regarding performance level along with suggestions for improvement.

personality tests instruments that measure psychological characteristics of individuals.

person-environment fit the match between a worker's abilities, needs, and values, and organizational demands, rewards, and values.

personnel psychology the subarea of I/O psychology that deals with the study and analysis of people and jobs.

polygraphs tests of honesty that measure physiological reactions, such as heart rate or respiration, presumed to accompany deception; also known as lie detectors.

Porter-Lawler model a theory where the relationship between job satisfaction and performance is mediated by work-related rewards.

Position Analysis Questionnaire (PAQ) a job analysis technique that uses a structured questionnaire to analyze jobs in terms of 187 elements grouped into six categories.

position power a leader's authority to punish or reward subordinates. A key concept in Fiedler's contingency theory of leadership.

positive reinforcers desirable events that follow certain behaviors and strengthen the tendency to perform them again.

posttest only design training evaluation that simply measures training criteria after the completion of a training program.

power the use of some aspect of a work relationship to compel another to perform a certain action despite resistance.

power bases individuals' sources of power in an organization.

power corollary the idea that for every exercise of power, there is a tendency for the subject to react with a "return" power play.

predictor information about applicants that is related to (predictive of) the criterion.

pretest-posttest the evaluation of a training program by comparing criterion measures collected before and after the introduction of the program.

problem-solving case study a management training technique that presents a description of a real or hypothetical organizational problem that trainees attempt to solve.

process consultation an organizational development technique in which a consultant helps a client-organization to study its problems objectively and learn how to solve them.

profit sharing a system whereby employees obtain a share of an organization's profits based on the organization's economic success.

programmed instruction self-paced, individualized training whereby trainees are provided with training materials and can test themselves on how much they have learned.

project task force a nontraditional organizational structure of workers assembled temporarily to complete a specific job or project.

protected groups groups that have been identified as previous targets of employment discrimination, including women, certain ethnic and racial minority groups, the aged, and the disabled.

psychology the scientific study of behavior and mental processes.

punishment unpleasant consequences following the performance of a behavior that reduce the tendency to engage in that behavior in the future.

Q

qualitative data refers to numbers used as labels to categorize people on things. Also referred to as "categorical" or "frequency" data.

qualitative displays machine displays that provide characteristics or "qualities" of machine operation.

quality circles small groups of volunteer employees from the same work areas who meet regularly to solve quality-related work problems.

quality of work life the evaluative state of all aspects of work.

quantitative data numerical representation of a variable. Also known as "measurement" data.

quantitative displays machine displays that provide precise numerical values.

R

random assignment a method of assigning research participants to groups to control for the effects of extraneous variables. Each participant has an equal chance of being assigned to any of the groups.

random sampling selecting research participants from a population so that each individual has an equal probability of being chosen.

realistic job previews (RJPs) an honest presentation of the prospective job and the organization given to applicants.

receiver the recipient of a communication. Also referred to as the decoder, since the receiver decodes the message.

recency effect the tendency in performance appraisals to give greater weight to recent performance and lesser weight to earlier performance.

reciprocity rule the tendency for persons to feel indebted and for them to want to "pay back" others for their assistance.

referent power power resulting from the fact that an individual is respected, admired, and liked by others.

reinforcement theory the theory that behavior is motivated by its consequences.

relationship-oriented behaviors a leader orientation that focuses on maintaining interpersonal relationships on the job.

reliability the stability of a measurement device over time, or the consistency of a measure.

reward power power that results from having the ability to give others something positive, such as money and praise.

robots automatic, programmable devices that can carry out tasks typically performed by humans.

roles patterns of behavior that are adopted based on expectations about the functions of a position.

role ambiguity a sense of uncertainty over the requirements of a particular work-related role.

role conflict conflict that results when the expectations associated with one role interfere with the expectations concerning another role.

role differentiation the process by which group members take on various roles.

role expectations beliefs concerning the responsibilities and requirements of a particular role.

role playing employee training exercises that require trainees to act out situations that often occur at work.

rumors information that is presented as fact but may actually be either true or false.

S

safety climate positive attitudes workers hold toward promoting safe work behaviors.

sampling the selection of a representative group from a larger population for study.

scientific management begun by Taylor, a method of applying scientific principles to improve job productivity and efficiency through procedures such as time-and-motion analyses.

self-efficacy the belief that a person has the abilities and energy to accomplish a particular task or goal.

self-report techniques methods of assessment relying on the reports of research participants concerning their own behavior.

seminars an employee training method in which an expert provides job-related information in a classroom setting.

sender the person who encodes and transmits a communication. Also referred to as the encoder.

severity errors the tendency to give all workers very negative evaluations in performance appraisals.

shifts alternate employee work times scheduled to keep the workplace in extended or continuous operation.

simulation training that replicates job conditions without placing the trainee in the actual work setting.

situational exercises assessment tools that require the performance of tasks that approximate actual work tasks. Often used as part of an assessment center.

situational stress stress arising from certain conditions that exist in the work environment, or in the worker's personal life.

snap judgment arriving at a premature, early overall evaluation of an applicant in a hiring interview.

social learning theory a learning theory that emphasizes observational learning of behavior.

social loafing the phenomenon whereby individuals working in a group put forth less effort than when working alone.

sociogram a diagram of the informal lines of communication among organizational members.

Solomon four-group design a very thorough method of program evaluation using two treatment and two control groups.

source factors in the communication process, characteristics of the sender that influence the effectiveness or accuracy of a message.

span of control the number of workers that must report to a single supervisor in an organization's structural hierarchy.

staff in line-staff organizational structures, specialized employee positions designed to support the line.

standard deviation a measure of variability of scores in a frequency distribution.

statistical significance a method for calculating the probability that a particular research result could have occurred by chance. A statistically significant result is unlikely to have occurred by chance and is thus presumed to have been caused by some other factor, such as an intervention.

stratified sampling selecting research participants based on categories that represent important distinguishing characteristics of a population.

stressful life events significant events in a person's recent history that can cause stress.

stressor an environmental event that causes a stress reaction; perceived by an individual to be threatening.

superordinate goal a goal that both parties in a conflict situation are attracted to and are willing to work to attain.

supportive behavior in the path-goal theory of leadership, leader behavior focusing on interpersonal relationships and showing concern for workers' well-being.

survey a common, self-report measurement technique that asks participants to report on their attitudes, beliefs, or behaviors

survey feedback an organizational development technique in which the consultant works with the organization to develop and administer a survey instrument to collect data about the organization, which are then fed back to organizational members and used as the starting point for change.

T

task interdependence the degree to which a worker's task performance depends on the efforts and skills of others.

task-oriented behavior leader behavior focused on the work task.

task structure an assessment of the amount of structure associated with a group's work task. An important component in Fiedler's contingency theory of leadership.

team building an organizational development technique in which teams of workers meet to discuss ways to improve team performance through improved group interaction and coordination of efforts.

team organization a nontraditional organizational structure consisting of a team of members organized around a particular project or product.

teleoperators sophisticated control systems that act as an extension of the human operator.

test battery a combination of tests that are used together to increase the accuracy of the prediction of job performance.

test-retest reliability a method of determining the reliability of a measurement instrument by administering the same measure to the same individuals at two times, and then correlating the two scores.

test utility the value of a screening test in helping to affect important outcomes, such as dollars gained through its use.

t-groups (sensitivity training) an organizational development technique that uses unstructured group interaction to help workers gain insight into their own motivations and behavior patterns in dealing with other organizational members.

Thematic Apperception Test (TAT) a projective test consisting of ambiguous pictures used to assess psychological motivation.

theory the organization of certain beliefs into a representation of the factors that affect behavior. Also known as a model.

360-degree feedback a performance appraisal system whereby independent evaluations of an employee's performance are gathered from supervisors, peers, subordinates, customers, and others.

time-and-motion studies studies in which work tasks are broken down into simple, component movements and each is timed to develop a more efficient method of performance. Developed by Taylor, time-and-motion studies are an important part of scientific management.

trainee readiness the individual's potential for successful training.

traits consistent and enduring attributes associated with an individual's personality.

trait theory theoretical attempts to discover the characteristics, or traits, shared by all effective leaders.

transactional leadership leadership based on some exchange, such as exchanging money or praise for work.

transfer of training whether what was learned in training is actually applied in the work setting.

transformational leadership focuses on the leader's ability to provide shared values and a vision of the future for the work group.

treatment group the group in an experimental investigation that is subjected to the change in the independent variable.

t-test a test of the statistical significance of the difference between the means of two groups of scores, which is expressed as a numerical value representing the size of the difference between the two means.

two-factor theory Herzberg's motivational theory that proposes that two factors—motivators and hygienes—are important in determining worker satisfaction and motivation.

Type A behavior pattern a pattern of behavior characterized by excessive drive, competitiveness, impatience, and hostility that has been linked to higher incidence of coronary heart disease.

U

underpayment inequity according to equity theory, the situation that exists when workers perceive that their inputs are greater than work outcomes.

underutilization a source of stress that results when workers feel that their knowledge, skills, or energy are not being used fully.

universalist theories leadership theories that look for the key characteristic or group of characteristics common to all effective leaders.

unobtrusive observation research observation in which the presence of the observer is not known to the participants.

upward communication messages flowing upward in an organizational hierarchy, usually taking the form of feedback.

V

valence in the expectancy theory of motivation, the desirability of a particular outcome to an individual.

validity the accuracy of a measurement instrument—whether the instrument measures what it is supposed to measure.

validity generalization the ability of a measurement instrument to predict performance in a job or setting different from the one in which the test was validated.

variability measures that show how scores are distributed in a frequency distribution.

variable interval schedule a schedule of reinforcement in which the reinforcement follows the passage of a specified amount of time, with the exact time of reinforcement varying.

variable ratio schedule a schedule of reinforcement in which the reinforcement is contingent on the performance of a specified but varying number of behaviors.

variables the elements that are measured in research investigations

vestibule training training that uses a separate area adjacent to the work area to simulate the actual work setting.

voice control machine controls that respond to the sounds of human voices.

W

weighted application form a job application form that assigns different values or "weights" to the various information requested

we-they feeling intragroup cohesiveness created when a group is faced by a common threat, typically another group.

whistleblowing political behavior where employees convey criticisms about their organization's policies and practices to persons or authorities outside the organization.

work overload a common source of stress resulting when a job requires excessive speed, output, or concentration.

work samples a job skill test that measures applicants' abilities to perform brief examples of important job tasks.

worker stress the physiological, emotional, and psychological reactions to threatening environmental events.

workspace design the design and arrangement of equipment, space, and machinery in a work environment.

REFERENCES

Ackerman, P.L., & Kanfer, R. (1993). Integrating laboratory and field study for improving selection: Development of a battery for predicting air traffic controller success. *Journal of Applied Psychology, 78*, 413–432.

Adam, E.E. (1991). Quality circle performance. *Journal of Management, 17*, 25–39.

Adams, G.A., King, L.A., & King, D.W. (1996). Relationships of job and family involvement, family social support, and work-family conflict with job and life satisfaction. *Journal of Applied Psychology, 81*, 411–420.

Adams, J.A. (1987). Historical review and appraisal of research on the learning, retention, and transfer of human motor skills. *Psychological Bulletin, 101*, 41–74.

Adams, J.A. (1989). *Human factors engineering.* New York: MacMillan.

Adams, J.S. (1965). Inequity in social exchange. In L. Berkowitz (Ed.), *Advances in experimental social psychology* (Vol. 2), (pp. 267–299). New York: Academic Press.

Adkins, C.E. (1995). Previous work experience and organizational socialization: A longitudinal examination. *Academy of Management Journal, 38*, 839–862.

Adler, N. (1986). Do MBAs want international careers? *International Journal of Intercultural Relations, 10*, 277–300.

Adler, N. (1991). *International dimensions of organizational behavior* (2nd ed.). Boston: PWS-Kent.

Adler, P.S., & Borys, B. (1996). Two types of bureaucracy: Enabling and coercive. *Administrative Science Quarterly, 41*, 61–89.

AFSCME v. State of Washington, 578 F. supp. 846 (W.D. Wash. 1983).

Aguinis, H. (1993). Action research and scientific method: Presumed discrepancies and actual similarities. *Journal of Applied Behavioral Science, 29*, 416–431.

Aguinis, H., Nesler, M.S., Hosoda, M., & Tedeschi, J.T. (1994). The use of influence tactics in persuasion. *The Journal of Social Psychology, 134*, 429–438.

Aiello, J.R. (1993). Computer-based work monitoring: Electronic surveillance and its effects. *Journal of Applied Social Psychology, 23*, 499–507.

Aiello, J.R., & Kolb, K.J. (1995). Electronic performance monitoring and social context: Impact on productivity and stress. *Journal of Applied Psychology, 80*, 339–353.

Aiello, J.R., & Shao, Y. (1993). Electronic performance monitoring and stress: The role of feedback and goal-setting. In M.J. Smith & G. Salvendy (Eds.), *Human computer interaction: Software and hardware interfaces.* (pp. 1011–1016). Amsterdam: Elsevier-Science.

Albermarle Paper v. Moody, 74–389 (1975).

Albrecht, K. (1983). *Organization development: A total systems approach to positive chage in any business organization.* Englewood Cliffs, NJ: Prentice-Hall.

Alderfer, C.P. (1972). *Existence, relatedness, and growth: Human needs in organizational settings.* New York: Free Press.

Allen, R.W., & Porter, L.W. (Eds.). (1983). *Organizational influence processes.* Glenview, IL: Scott, Foresman.

Allen, T.D., & Rush, M.C. (1998). The effects of organizational citizenship behavior on performance judgments: A field study and a laboratory experiment. *Journal of Applied Psychology, 83*, 247–260.

American Psychological Society (1993). Human capital initiative: The changing nature of work. *APS Observer,* October.

Anderson, L., & Wilson, S. (1997). Critical incident technique. In D.L. Whetzel & G.R. Wheaton (Eds.), *Applied measurement methods in industrial psychology* (89–112). Palo Alto, CA: Davies-Black

Anderson, N.R., & West, M.A. (1998). Measuring climate for work group innovation: Development and validation of the team climate inventory. *Journal of Organizational Behavior, 19*, 235–258.

Andrews, M.C., Neumann, D.F., Grossnickle, W.F., Wuensch, K.L., & Cope, J.G. (1990). An experimental study of a gainsharing program. Paper presented at the 98th annual American Psychological Association convention, Boston, MA, August 10, 1990.

Ansari, M.A., & Kapoor, A. (1987). Organizational context and upward influence tactics. *Organizational Behavior and Human Decision Processes, 40*, 39–49.

Argyris, C. (1964). *Integrating the individual and the organization*. New York: Wiley.

Argyris, C. (1980). Some limitations of the case method: Experiences in a management development program. *Academy of Management Review, 5,* 251–298.

Arnold, D.W., & Thiemann, A.J. (1992). To test or not to test: The status of psychological testing with the ADA. *The Industrial-Organizational Psychologist, 29,* 25–27.

Arnold, H.J., & Feldman, D.C. (1982). A multivariate analysis of the determinants of job turnover. *Journal of Applied Psychology, 67,* 350–360.

Arvey, R.D. (1979). *Fairness in selecting employees*. Reading, MA: Addison-Wesley.

Arvey, R.D., & Begalla, M.E. (1975). Analyzing the homemaker job using the Position Analysis Questionnaire (PAQ). *Journal of Applied Psychology, 60,* 513–518.

Arvey, R.D., Bouchard, T.J., Segal, N.L., & Abraham, L.M. (1989). Job satisfaction: Environmental and genetic components. *Journal of Applied Psychology, 74,* 187–192.

Arvey, R.D., & Campion, J.E. (1982). The employment interview: A summary and review of recent research. *Personnel Psychology, 35,* 281–322.

Arvey, R.D., Maxwell, S.E., & Salas, E. (1992). The relative power of training evaluation designs under difficult cost configurations. *Journal of Applied Psychology, 77,* 155–160.

Arvey, R.D., Miller, H.E., Gould, R., & Burch, P. (1987). Interview validity for selecting sales clerks. *Personnel Psychology, 40,* 1–12.

Arvey, R.D., & Murphy, K.R. (1998). Performance evaluation in work settings. *Annual Review of Psychology, 49,* 141–168.

Ashforth, B.E., & Saks, A.M. (1996). Socialization tactics: Longitudinal effects on newcomer adjustment. *Academy of Management Journal, 39,* 149–178.

Ashforth, B.E., Saks, A.M., & Lee, R.T. (1998). Socialization and newcomer adjustment: The role of organizational context. *Human Relations, 51,* 897–926.

Ashford, S.J., & Black, J.S. (1996). Proactivity during organizational entry: The role of desire for control. *Journal of Applied Psychology, 81,* 199–214.

Ashour, A.S. (1973). The contingency model of leadership effectiveness: An evaluation. *Organizational Behavior and Human Performance, 9,* 339–355.

Astley, W.G., & Sachdeva, P.S. (1984). Structural sources of intraorganizational power: A theoretical synthesis. *Academy of Management Review, 9,* 104–113.

Astley, W.G., & Zajac, E.J. (1991). Intraorganizational power and organizational design: Reconciling rational and coalitional models of organization. *Organization Science, 4,* 399–411.

Atkin, R.S., & Goodman, P.S. (1984). Methods of defining and measuring absenteeism. In P.S. Goodman & R.S. Atkin (Eds.), *Absenteeism: New approaches to understanding, measuring, and managing employee absence*. San Francisco: Jossey-Bass.

Austin, J.T., & Villanova, P. (1992). The criterion problem: 1917–1992. *American Psychologist, 77,* 836–874.

Axel, H. (Ed.). (1986). *Corporate strategies for controlling substance abuse*. New York: The Conference Board.

Ayman, R., Chemers, M.M., & Fiedler, F. (1995). The contingency model of leadership effectiveness: Its levels of analysis. *Leadership Quarterly, 6,* 147–167.

Baba, V.V., & Jamal, M. (1991). Routinization of job context and job content as related to employees' quality of working life: A study of Canadian nurses. *Journal of Organizational Behavior, 12,* 379–386.

Bacharach, S.B., & Lawler, E.J. (1980). *Power and politics in organizations: The social psychology of conflict, coalitions, and bargaining*. San Francisco: Jossey-Bass.

Bachman, J.G.. Bowers, D.G., & Marcus, P.M. (1968). Bases of supervisory power: A comparative study in five organizational settings. In A.S. Tannenbaum (Ed.), *Control in organizations* (pp. 229–238). New York: McGraw-Hill.

Baird, J.E. (1977). *The dynamics of organizational communication*. New York: Harper & Row.

Baldwin, T.T., & Ford, J.K. (1988). Transfer of training: A review and directions for future research. *Personnel Psychology, 41,* 63–105.

Baldwin, T.T., Magjuka, R.J., & Loher, B.T. (1991). The perils of participation: Effects of choice of training on trainee motivation and learning. *Personnel Psychology, 44,* 51–65.

Balkin, D.B., & Gomez-Mejia, L.R. (Eds.). (1987). *New perspectives on compensation*. Englewood Cliffs, NJ: Prentice-Hall.

Balzer, W.K., & Howard, A. (1994). 1993 profile of Division 14 members: Noteworthy trends. *The Industrial-Organizational Psychologist, 31,* 95–97.

Bandura, A. (1977). *Social learning theory*. Englewood Cliffs, NJ: Prentice-Hall.

Bandura, A. (1986). *Social foundations of thought and action: A social-cognitive view*. Englewood Cliffs, NJ: Prentice-Hall.

Bandura, A. (1997). *Self-efficacy: The exercise of control*. San Francisco: W.H. Freeman.

Barker, J., Tjosvold, D., & Andrews, R.I. (1988). Conflict approaches of effective and ineffective project managers: A field study in a matrix organization. *Journal of Management Studies, 25,* 167–178.

Barker, L.L., Wahlers, K.J., Watson, K.W., & Kibler, R.J. (1987). *Groups in process: An introduction to small* group communication (3rd ed.). Englewood Cliffs, NJ: Prentice-Hall.

Barling, J., Weber, T., & Kelloway, E.K. (1996). Effects of transformational leadership training on attitudinal and financial outcomes: A field experiment. *Journal of Applied Psychology, 81,* 827–832.

Baron, R.A. (1986). *Behavior in organizations: Understanding and managing the human side of work* (2nd ed.). Boston, MA: Allyn & Bacon.

Baron, R.A. (1990). Environmentally induced positive affect: Its impact on self-efficacy, task performance, negotiation, and conflict. *Journal of Applied Social Psychology, 20,* 368–384.

Baron, R.A., & Bronfen, M.I. (1994). A whiff of reality: Empirical evidence concerning the effects of pleasant fragrances on work-related behavior. *Journal of Applied Social Psychology, 24,* 1179–1203.

Barrett, G.V., & Depinet, R.L. (1991). A reconsideration of testing for competence rather than intelligence. *American Psychologist, 46,* 1012–1024.

Barrett, G.V., & Kernan, M.C. (1987). Performance appraisal and terminations: A review of court decisions since *Brito v. Zia* with implications for personnel practices. *Personnel Psychology, 40,* 489–503.

Barrick, M.R., & Alexander, R.A. (1987). A review of quality circle efficacy and the existence of positive-finding bias. *Personnel Psychology, 40,* 579–592.

Barrick, M.R., & Mount, M.K. (1991). The Big Five personality dimensions and job performance: A meta-analysis. *Personnel Psychology, 44,* 1–26.

Barrick, M.R., & Mount, M.K. (1993). Autonomy as a moderator of the relationship between the Big Five personality dimensions and job performance. *Journal of Applied Psychology, 78,* 111–118.

Barrick, M.R., Mount, M.K., & Strauss, J.P. (1994). Antecedents of involuntary turnover due to reduction in force. *Personnel Psychology, 47,* 515–535.

Bartol, K.M., & Martin, D.C. (1988). Influences on managerial pay allocations: A dependency perspective. *Personnel Psychology, 41,* 361–378.

Bartol, K.M, & Martin, D.C. (1990). When politics pays: Factors influencing managerial compensation decisions. *Personnel Psychology, 43,* 599–614.

Barton, J. (1994). Choosing to work at night: A moderating influence on individual tolerance to shift work. *Journal of Applied Psychology, 79,* 449–454.

Bartram, D., Lindley, P.A., Marshall, L., & Foster, J. (1995). The recruitment and selection of young people by small businesses. *Journal of Occupational Organizational Psychology, 68,* 339–358.

Bass, B.M. (1954). The leaderless group discussion. *Psychological Bulletin, 51,* 465–492.

Bass, B.M. (1981). *Stogdill's handbook of leadership* (rev. and enl. ed.). New York: Free Press.

Bass, B.M. (1983). Issues involved in relations between methodological rigor and reported outcomes in evaluations of organizational development. *Journal of Applied Psychology, 68,* 197–199.

Bass, B.M. (1990). *Bass & Stogdill's handbook of leadership: Theory, research, and managerial applications* (3rd ed.). New York: Free Press.

Bateman, T.S., & Organ, D.W. (1983). Job satisfaction and the good soldier: The relationship between affect and employee "citizenship." *Academy of Management Journal, 26,* 587–595.

Bateman, T.S., & Strasser, S. (1984). A longitudinal analysis of the antecedents of organizational commitment. *Academy of Management Journal, 27,* 95–112.

Baum, H.S. (1989). Organizational politics against organizational culture: A psychoanalytic perspective. *Human Resource Management, 28,* 191–206.

Bavelas, A. (1950). Communication patterns in task-oriented groups. *Journal of Acoustical Society of America, 22,* 725–730.

Bazerman, M.H., Giuliano, T., & Appleman, A. (1984). Escalation of commitment in individual and group decision making. *Organizational Behavior and Human Performance, 33,* 141–152.

Becker, T.E., & Billings, R.S. (1993). Profiles of commitment: An empirical test. *Journal of Organizational Behavior, 14,* 177–190.

Beehr, T.A. (1985). Organizational stress and employee effectiveness: A job characteristics approach. In T.A. Beehr & R.S. Bhagat (Eds.), *Human stress and cognition in organizations: An integrated perspective* (pp. 57–81). New York: John Wiley & Sons.

Beehr, T.A., & Bhagat, R.S. (Eds.). (1985). *Human stress and cognition in organizations: An integrated perspective.* New York: John Wiley & Sons.

Beehr, T.A., & McGrath, J.E. (1992). Social support, occupational stress and anxiety. *Anxiety, Stress, and Coping, 5,* 7–19.

Bell, P.A. (1981). Physiological comfort, performance, and social effects of heat stress. *Journal of Social Issues, 37,* 71–94.

Benne, K.D., & Sheats, P. (1948). Functional roles of group members. *Journal of Social Issues, 4,* 41–49.

Bennett, G.K. (1980). *Bennett Mechanical Comprehension Test.* San Antonio, TX: The Psychological Corporation.

Bennett, G.K. (1981). *Hand-Tool Dexterity Test.* San Antonio, TX: The Psychological Corporation.

Ben-Shakhar, G., Bar-Hillel, M., Bilu, Y., Ben-Abba, E., & Flug, A. (1986). Can graphology predict occupational success? Two empirical studies and some methodological ruminations. *Journal of Applied Psychology, 71*, 645–653.

Berger, M.A. (1983). In defense of the case method: A reply to Argyris. *Academy of Management Review, 8*, 329–333.

Bernardin, H.J., & Beatty, R.W. (1984). *Performance appraisal: Assessing human behavior at work*. Boston, MA: Kent.

Bernardin, H.J., & Bulkley, M.R. (1981). Strategies in rater training. *Academy of Management Review, 6*, 205–242.

Bernardin, H.J., Dahmus, S.A., & Redmon, G. (1993). Attitudes of first-line supervisors toward subordinate appraisals. *Human Resource Management, 32*, 315–324.

Bernthal, P.R., & Insko, C.A. (1993). Cohesiveness without groupthink: The interactive effects of social and task cohesion. *Group and Organization Management, 18*, 66–87.

Berryman-Fink, C. (1985). Male and female managers' views of the communication skills and training needs of women in management. *Public Personnel Management, 14*, 307–313.

Bhagat, R.S. (1983). Effects of stressful life events on individual performance effectiveness and work adjustment processes within organizational settings: A research model. *Academy of Management Review, 8*, 660–671.

Bhagat, R.S. (1985). The role of stressful life events in organizational behavior and human performance. In T.A. Beehr & R.S. Bhagat (Eds.), *Human stress and cognition in organizations: An integrated perspective* (pp. 205–212). New York: John Wiley & Sons.

Bhagat, R.S., Allie, S.M., & Ford, D.L. (1991). Organizational stress, personal life stress, and symptoms of life strains: An inquiry into the moderating role of styles of coping. *Journal of Social Behavior and Personality, 6*, 163–184.

Birnbaum, M.H., & Sotoodeh, Y. (1991). Measurement of stress: Scaling the magnitudes of life changes. *Psychological Science, 2*, 236–243.

Blake, R.R., & McCanse, A.A. (1991). *Leadership dilemmas—Grid solutions*. Houston, TX: Gulf.

Blake, R.R., & Mouton, J.S. (1985). *The managerial grid III*. Houston, TX: Gulf.

Blake, R.R., Mouton, J.S., & Sloma, R.L. (1964). An actual case history of resolving intergroup conflict in union-management relations. In R.R. Blake, H.A. Shepard, & J.S. Mouton, *Managing intergroup conflict in industry* (pp. 155–195). Houston, TX: Gulf.

Blake, R.R., Shepard, H.A., & Mouton, J.S. (1964). *Managing intergroup conflict in industry*. Houston, TX: Gulf.

Blakely, G.L., Blakely, E.H., & Moorman, R.H. (1998). The effects of training on perceptions of sexual harassment allegations. *Journal of Applied Social Psychology, 28*, 71–83.

Blalock, H.M. (1989). *Power and conflict: Toward a general theory*. Newbury Park, CA: Sage.

Bliese, P.D., & Halverson, R.R. (1996). Individual and nomothetic models of job stress: An examination of work hours, cohesion, and well-being. *Journal of Applied Social Psychology, 26*, 1171–1189.

Bliesener, T. (1996). Methodological moderators in validating biographical data in personnel selection. *Journal of Occupational and Organizational Psychology, 69*, 107–120.

Block, P. (1987). *The empowered manager*. San Francisco: Jossey-Bass.

Bluedorn, A.C. (1993). Pilgrim's progress: Trends and convergence in research on organizational size and environment. *Journal of Management, 19*, 163–191.

Booth, R.T. (1986). Machinery hazards. In J. Ridley (Ed.), *Safety at work* (2nd ed., pp. 549–571). London: Butterworth.

Booth, W.S. (1992). The Dictionary of Occupational Titles: A humorous look at cultural artifact. *The Industrial-Organizational Psychologist, 30*, 65–69.

Booth-Kewley, S., & Friedman, H.S. (1989). Psychological predictors of heart disease: A quantitative review. *Psychological Bulletin, 101*, 343–362.

Borman, W.C. (1986). Behavior-based rating scales. In R.A. Berk (Ed.), *Performance assessment: Methods and applications* (pp. 100–120). Baltimore, MD: The Johns Hopkins University Press.

Borman, W.C. (1998). 360° ratings: An analysis of assumptions and a research agenda for evaluating their validity. *Human Resources Management Review, 7*, 299–315.

Born, D.H., & Mathieu, J.E. (1996). Differential effects of survey-guided feedback: The rich get richer and the poor get poorer. *Group & Organization Management, 21*, 388–403.

Boroson, W. (1976, June). The workaholic in you. *Money*, pp. 32–35.

Botan, C. (1996). Communication work and electronic surveillance: A model for predicting panoptic effects. *Communication Monographs, 63*, 293–313.

Bouchard, T.J., Barsaloux, J., & Drauden, G. (1974). Brainstorming procedure, group size, and sex as determinants of the problem-solving effectiveness of groups and individuals. *Journal of Applied Psychology, 59*, 135–138.

Bowers, D.G. (1973). OD techniques and their results in 23 organizations: The Michigan ICL study. *Journal of Applied Behavioral Science, 9*, 21–43.

Bowers, D.G., & Hauser, D.L. (1977). Work group types and intervention effects in organizational development. *Administrative Science Quarterly, 22*, 76–94.

Boyd, D.P. (1984). Type A behavior, financial performance, and organizational growth in small business firms. *Journal of Occupational Psychology, 57,* 137–140.

Brannon, D., Streit, A., & Smyer, M.A. (1992). The psychosocial quality of nursing home work. *Journal of Aging and Health, 4,* 369–389.

Brass, D.J., & Burkhardt, M.E. (1993). Potential power and power use: An investigation of structure and behavior. *Academy of Management Journal, 36,* 441–470.

Braver, M.C.W., & Braver, S.L. (1988). Statistical treatment of the Solomon four-group design: A meta-analytic approach. *Psychological Bulletin, 104,* 150–154.

Bray, D.W., Campbell, R.J., & Grant, D.L. (1974). *Formative years in business: A long-term AT&T study of managerial lives.* New York: John Wiley & Sons.

Breaugh, J.A. (1981). Relationships between recruiting sources and employee performance, absenteeism, and work attitudes. *Academy of Management Journal, 24,* 142–147.

Breaugh, J.A. (1983). The 12-hour work day: Differing employee reactions. *Personnel Psychology, 36,* 277–288.

Brems, D.J., Rabin, M.D., & Waggett, J.L. (1995). Using natural language conventions in the user interface design of automatic speech recognition systems. *Human Factors, 37,* 265–282.

Bretz, R.D., Milkovich, G.T, & Read, W. (1992). The current state of performance appraisal research and practice: Concerns, directions, and implications. *Journal of Management, 18,* 321–352.

Bretz, R.D., & Thomas, S.L. (1992). Perceived equity, motivation, and final-offer arbitration in major league baseball. *Journal of Applied Psychology, 77,* 280–287.

Brief, A.P., & Motowidlo, S.J. (1986). Prosocial organizational behaviors. *Academy of Management Review, 11,* 710–725.

Brito v. Zia Company, 478 F.2d 1200 (1973).

Brodbeck, F.C., Zapf, D., Prumper, J., & Frese, M. (1993). Error handling in office work with computers: A field study. *Journal of Occupational and Organizational Psychology, 66,* 303–317.

Brown, B.B. (1991). Staff changes at EEOC, DOL; Focuses on ADA, 'Glass-ceiling initiative.' *Employment Relations Today,* 107–111.

Brown, J., Cooper, C., & Kirkcaldy, B. (1996). Occupational stress among senior police officers. *British Journal of Psychology, 87,* 31–41.

Brown, V., & Paulus, P.B. (1996). A simple dynamic model of social factors in group brainstorming. *Small Group Research, 27,* 91–114.

Browne, D.W., Russell, M.L., Morgan, J.L., Optenberg, S.A., & Clarke, A.E. (1984). Reduced disability and health care costs in an industrial fitness program. *Journal of Occupational Medicine, 26,* 809–816.

Buch, K., & Spangler, R. (1990). The effects of quality circles on performance and promotions. *Human Relations, 43,* 573–582.

Buchko, A.A. (1992). Employee ownership, attitudes, and turnover: An empirical assessment. *Human Relations, 45,* 711–733.

Buckly, R. (1993). *Job analysis and examination specifications study.* State of California: Department of Real Estate.

Burgess, R. (1968). Communication networks: An experimental reevaluation. *Journal of Experimental Social Psychology, 4,* 324–337.

Burke, M.J. (1992). computerized psychological testing. In N. Schmitt & W.C. Borman (Eds.), *Personnel selection* (pp. 203–239). San Francisco: Jossey-Bass.

Burke, M.J., & Day, R.R. (1986). A cumulative study of the effectiveness of managerial training. *Journal of Applied Psychology, 71,* 232–245.

Burke, R.J. (1993). Organizational-level interventions to reduce occupational stressors. *Work & Stress, 7,* 77–87.

Burke, R.J. (1997). Toward an understanding of psychological burnout among police officers. *International Journal of Stress Management, 4,* 13–27.

Burke, R.J., McKeen, C.A., & McKenna, C. (1993). Correlates of mentoring in organizations: The mentor's perspective. *Psychological Reports, 72,* 883–896.

Burke, W.W. (1987). *Organization development: A normative view.* Reading, MA: Addison-Wesley.

Burke, W.W., & Litwin, G.H. (1992). A causal model of organizational performance and change. *Journal of Management, 18,* 523–545.

Burns, J.M. (1978). *Leadership.* New York: Harper & Row.

Burns, L.R. (1989). Matrix management in hospitals: Testing theories of matrix structure and development. *Administrative Science Quarterly, 34,* 349–368.

Burns, L.R., & Wholey, D.R. (1993). Adoption and abandonment of matrix management programs: Effects of organizational characteristics and interorganizational networks. *Academy of Management Journal, 36,* 106–138.

Bushnell, I.W.R. (1996). A comparison of the validity of handwriting analysis with that of the Cattell 16PF. *International Journal of Selection and Assessment, 4,* 12–17.

Butler, M.C., & Jones, A.P. (1979). Perceived leader behavior, individual characteristics, and injury occurrence in hazardous work environments. *Journal of Applied Psychology, 64,* 299–304.

Bycio, P. (1992). Job performance and absenteeism: A review and meta-analysis. *Human Relations, 45,* 193–220.

Bycio, P., Hackett, R.D., & Allen, J.S. (1995). Further assessments of Bass's (1985) conceptualization of transactional and transformational leadership. *Journal of Applied Psychology, 80,* 468–478.

Byrne, B.M. (1993). The Maslach Burnout Inventory: Testing for factorial validity and invariance across elementary, intermediate, and secondary teachers. *Journal of Occupational and Organizational Psychology, 66,* 197–212

Byrne, D.G., & Reinhardt, M.I. (1989). Work characteristics, occupational achievement, and the Type A behaviour pattern. *Journal of Occupational Psychology, 62,* 123–134.

Cairo, P.C. (1983). Counseling in industry: A selected review of the literature. *Personnel Psychology, 36,* 1–18.

Callan, V.J. (1993). Subordinate-manager communication in different sex dyads: Consequences for job satisfaction. *Journal of Occupational and Organizational Psychology, 66,* 13–27.

Camara, W.J. (1988). Senate approves bill to ban polygraph testing in the workplace. *The Industrial-Organizational Psychologist, 25*(4), 57–58.

Camara, W.J., & Schneider, D.L. (1994). Integrity tests: Facts and unresolved issues. *American Psychologist, 49,* 112–119.

Campbell, D.E. (1979). Interior office design and visitor response. *Journal of Applied Psychology, 64,* 648–653.

Campbell, D.J., & Furrer, D.M. (1995). Goal setting and competition as determinants of task performance. *Journal of Organizational Behavior, 16,* 377–389.

Campbell, D.J., & Lee, C. (1988). Self-appraisal in performance evaluation: Development versus evaluation. *Academy of Management Review, 13,* 302–314.

Campbell, D.T., & Stanley, J.C. (1963). *Experimental and quasi-experimental designs for research.* Chicago: Rand-McNally.

Campbell, J.P., & Dunnette, M.D. (1968). Effectiveness of t-group experiences in management training and development. *Psychological Bulletin, 70,* 73–104.

Campbell, J.P., & Pritchard, R. (1976). Motivation theory in industrial and organizational psychology. In M.D. Dunnette (Ed.), *Handbook of industrial and organizational psychology* (pp. 63–130). Skokie, IL: Rand-McNally.

Campbell, J.P., Dunnette, M.D., Lawler, E.E., & Weick, K.E. (1970). *Managerial behavior, performance, and effectiveness.* New York: McGraw-Hill.

Campion, M.A. (1991). Meaning and measurement of turnover: Comparison of alternative measures and recommendations for research. *Journal of Applied Psychology, 76,* 199–212.

Campion, M.A., Cheraskin, L., & Stevens, M.J. (1994). Career-related antecedents and outcomes of job rotation. *Academy of Management Journal, 37,* 1518–1542.

Campion, M.A., & McClelland, C.L. (1991). Interdisciplinary examination of the costs and benefits of enlarged

jobs: A job design quasi-experiment. *Journal of Applied Psychology, 76,* 186–198.

Campion, M.A., Medsker, G.J., & Higgs, A.C. (1993). Relations between work group characteristics and effectiveness: Implications for designing effective work group. *Personnel Psychology, 46,* 823–850.

Campion, M.A., Pursell, E.D., & Brown, B.K. (1988). Structured interviewing: Raising the psychometric properties of the employment interview. *Personnel Psychology, 41,* 25–42.

Cann, E., Siegfried, W.D., & Pearce, L. (1981). Forced attention to specific applicant qualifications: Impact of physical attractiveness and sex on applicant biases. *Personnel Psychology, 34,* 65–76.

Canter, D. (1983). The physical context of work. In D.J. Oborne & M.M. Gruneberg (Eds.), *The physical environment at work* (pp. 11–38). Chichester, England: John Wiley & Sons.

Caplan, R.D., Cobb, S., French, J.R.P., Harrison, P.V., & Pinneau, S.R. (1980). *Job demands and worker health.* Ann Arbor, MI: University of Michigan Institute for Social Research.

Caplan, R.D., & Jones, K.W. (1975). Effects of workload, role ambiguity, and Type A personality on anxiety, depression, and heart rate. *Journal of Applied Psychology, 60,* 713–719.

Cappelli, P., & Chauvin, K. (1991). An interplant test of the efficiency wage hypothesis. *The Quarterly Journal of Economics, 106,* 769–787.

Carayon, P. (1994). Stressful jobs and non-stressful jobs: A cluster analysis of office jobs. *Ergonomics, 37,* 311–323.

Card, S., English, W., & Burr, B. (1978). Evaluation of mouse, rate-controlled isometric joystick, step keys, and text keys for text selection on a CRT. *Ergonomics, 21,* 601–613.

Carey, J.M., & Kacmar, C.J. (1997). The impact of communication mode and task complexity on small group performance and member satisfaction. *Computers in Human Behavior, 13,* 23–49.

Carlson, B.C., & Thompson, J.A. (1995). Job burnout and job leaving in public school teachers: Implications for stress management. *International Journal of Stress Management, 2,* 15–29.

Carnevale, A.P., Gainer, L.J., & Villet, J. (1990). *Training in America: The organization and strategic role of training.* San Francisco: Jossey-Bass.

Carrell, M.R. (1978). A longitudinal field assessment of employee perceptions of equitable treatment. *Organizational Behavior and Human Performance, 21,* 108–118.

Carroll, S.J., Paine, F.T., & Ivancevich, J.J. (1972). The relative effectiveness of training methods: Expert opinion and research. *Personnel Psychology, 25,* 495–510.

Carson, P.P., Carson, K.D., & Roe, C.W. (1993). Social power bases: A meta-analytic examination of interrelationships and outcomes. *Journal of Applied Social Psychology, 23,* 1150–1169.

Carsten, J.M., & Spector, P.E. (1987). Unemployment, job satisfaction, and employee turnover: A meta-analytic test of the Muchinsky model. *Journal of Applied Psychology, 72,* 374–381.

Cartwright, D. (1968). The nature of group cohesiveness. In D. Cartwright & A. Zander (Eds.), *Group dynamics: Research and theory* (3rd ed., pp. 91–109). New York: Harper & Row.

Cascio, W.F. (1976). Turnover, biographical data, and fair employment practice. *Journal of Applied Psychology, 61,* 576–580.

Cascio, W.F. (1987). *Applied psychology in personnel management* (3rd ed.). Englewood Cliffs, NJ: Prentice-Hall.

Cascio, W.F. (1998). The virtual workplace: A reality now. *The Industrial-Organizational Psychologist, 35,* 32–36.

Cascio, W.F., & Phillips, N.F. (1979). Performance testing: A rose among thorns? *Personnel Psychology, 32,* 751–766.

Cascio, W.F., Alexander, R.A., & Barrett, G.V. (1988). Setting cutoff scores: Legal, psychometric, and professional issues and guidelines. *Personnel Psychology, 41,* 1–24.

Cattell, R.B. (1986). *Sixteen Personality Factors Questionnaire.* Champaign, IL: Institute for Personality and Ability Testing.

Cavanagh, G.F., Moberg, D.J., & Velasquez, M. (1981). The ethics of organizational politics. *Academy of Management Review, 6,* 363–374.

Cederblom, D. (1982). The performance appraisal interview: A review, implications, and suggestions. *Academy of Management Review, 7,* 219–227.

Chalykoff, J., & Kochan, T.A. (1989). Computer-aided monitoring: Its influence on employee job satisfaction and turnover. *Personnel Psychology, 42,* 807–829.

Chan, D., Schmitt, N., DeShon, R.P., Clause, C.S., & Delbridge, K. (1997). Reactions to cognitive ability tests: The relationships between race, test performance, face validity perceptions, and test-taking motivation. *Journal of Applied Psychology, 82,* 300–310.

Chao, G.T., & Kozlowski, S.W.J. (1986). Employee perceptions on the implementation of robotic manufacturing technology. *Journal of Applied Psychology, 71,* 70–76.

Chao, G.T., Walz, P.M., & Gardner, P.D. (1992). Formal and informal mentorships: A comparison on mentoring functions and contrast with nonmentored counterparts. *Personnel Psychology, 45,* 619–636.

Chapanis, A. (1976). Engineering psychology. In M.D. Dunnette (Ed.), *Handbook of industrial and organizational psychology* (pp. 697–744). Chicago: Rand-McNally.

Chapanis, A. (1994). Hazards associated with three signal words and four colours on warning signs. *Ergonomics, 37,* 265–275.

Chatman, J.A., & Jehn, K.A. (1994). Assessing the relationship between industry characteristics and organizational culture: How different can you be? *Academy of Management Journal, 37,* 522–553.

Chen, C.C., Chen, X., & Meindl, J.R. (1998). How can cooperation be fostered? The cultural effects of individualism-collectivism. *Academy of Management Review, 23,* 285–304.

Chen, P.Y., & Spector, P.E. (1991). Negative affectivity as the underlying cause of correlations between stressors and strains. *Journal of Applied Psychology, 76,* 398–407.

Cherniss, C. (1980). *Staff burnout: Job stress in human services.* Beverly Hills, CA: Sage Publications.

Chesney, M.A., & Rosenman, R.H. (1980). Type A behaviour in the work setting. In C.L. Cooper & R. Payne (Eds.), *Current concerns in occupational stress* (pp. 187–212). Chichester, England: John Wiley & Sons.

Cialdini, R.B. (1993). *Influence: Science and practice* (3rd ed.). New York: Harper Collins

Clampitt, P.G., & Downs, C.W. (1993). Employee perceptions of the relationship between communication and productivity: A field study. *The Journal of Business Communication, 30,* 5–28.

Cleveland, J.N., Murphy, K.R., & Williams, R.E. (1989). Multiple uses of performance appraisal: Prevalence and correlates. *Journal of Applied Psychology, 74,* 130–135.

Cobb, A.T. (1984). An episodic model of power: Toward an integration of theory and research. *Academy of Management Review, 9,* 482–493.

Cobb, S., & Rose, R.M. (1973). Hypertension, peptic ulcer, and diabetes in air traffic controllers. *Journal of the American Medical Association, 224,* 489–492.

Cohen, A., Smith, M.J., & Anger, W.K. (1979). Self-protective measures against workplace hazards. *Journal of Safety Research, 11,* 121–131.

Cohen, A.R., & Gadon, H. (1978). *Alternative work schedules: Integrating individual and organizational needs.* Reading, MA: Addison-Wesley.

Cohen, S. (1980). Aftereffects of stress on human behavior and social behavior: A review of research and theory. *Psychological Bulletin, 88,* 82–108.

Cohen, S., & Weinstein, N. (1981). Nonauditory effects of noise on behavior and health. *Journal of Social Issues, 37,* 36–70.

Colarelli, S.M. (1984). Methods of communication and mediating processes in realistic job previews. *Journal of Applied Psychology, 69*, 633–642.

Collins, D. (1995). Death of a gainsharing plan: Power politics and participatory management. *Organizational Dynamics, 24*, 23–38.

Comer, D.R. (1995). A model of social loafing in real work groups. *Human Relations, 48*, 647–667.

Comptroller General Report on the Congress of the United States (1980). *Three-Mile Island: The most studied nuclear accident in history.* Washington, D.C.: U.S. General Accounting Office.

Conger, J.A. (1993). The brave new world of leadership training. *Organizational Dynamics, 21*, 46–58.

Conger, J.A., & Kanungo, R.N. (1987). Toward a behavioral theory of charismatic leadership in organizational settings. *Academy of Management Review, 12*, 637–647.

Conger, J.A., & Kanungo, R.N. (1988). The empowerment process: Integrating theory and practice. *Academy of Management Review, 13*, 471–482.

Conlon, D.E., & Ross, W.H. (1993). The effects of partisan third parties on negotiator behavior and outcome perception. *Journal of Applied Psychology, 78*, 280–290.

Connors, M.M., Harrison, A.A., & Summit, J. (1994). Crew systems: Integrating human and technical subsystems for the exploration of space. *Behavioral Science, 39*, 183–212.

Conrad, P. (1988). Health and fitness at work: A participants' perspective. *Social Science and Medicine, 26*, 545–550.

Constable, S.H., Bishop, P.A., Nunneley, S.A., & Chen, T. (1984). Intermittent microclimate cooling during rest increases work capacity and reduces heat stress. *Ergonomics, 37*, 277–285.

Conway, J.M., & Huffcutt, A.I. (1996, April). Testing assumptions of 360-degree feedback: A meta-analysis of supervisor, peer, subordinate and self-ratings. Paper presented at the 11th annual conference of the Society for Industrial and Organizational Psychology, San Diego, CA.

Conway, J.M., Jako, R.A., & Goodman, D.F. (1995). A meta-analysis of interrater and internal consistency reliability of selection interviews. *Journal of Applied Psychology, 80*, 565–579.

Cook, T.D., Campbell, D.T., & Peraccio, L. (1991). Quasi-experiments. In M.D. Dunnette & L.M. Hough (Eds.), *Handbook of industrial/organizational psychology* (2nd ed., Vol. 2, pp. 4991–5076). Palo Alto, CA: Consulting Psychologists Press.

Cooke, W.N. (1985). The rising toll of discrimination against union activists. *Industrial Relations, 24*, 421–442.

Cooley, E. (1994). Training an interdisciplinary team in communication and decision-making skills. *Small Group Research, 25*, 5–25.

Cooper, C.L., Dyck, B., & Frohlich, N. (1992). Improving the effectiveness of gainsharing: The role of fairness and participation. *Administrative Science Quarterly, 37*, 471–490.

Cooper, C.L., & Hensman, R. (1985). A comparative investigation of executive stress: A ten-nation study. *Stress Medicine, 1*, 295–301.

Cooper, C.L., Mallinger, M., & Kahn, R. (1978). Identifying sources of occupational stress among dentists. *Journal of Occupational Psychology, 51*, 227–234.

Cooper, C.L., & Payne, R. (Eds.) (1988). *Causes, coping and consequences of stress at work.* New York: John Wiley & Sons.

Cooper, C.L., Sloan, S.G., & Williams, S. (1988). *The occupational stress indicator: Management guide.* Oxford: NFER-Nelson.

Cooper, M.D., Phillips, R.A., Sutherland, V.J., & Makin, P.J. (1994). Reducing accidents using goal setting and feedback: A field study. *Journal of Occupational and Organizational Psychology, 67*, 219–240.

Cooper, W.H., Gallupe, R.G., Pollard, S., & Cadsby, J. (1998). Some liberating effects of anonymous electronic brainstorming. *Small Group Research, 29*, 147–178.

Coovert, M. D., Penner, L. A., & MacCallum, R. (1990). Covariance structure modeling in personality and social psychological research. In C. Hendrick & M.S. Clark (Eds.). *Research methods in personality and social psychology* (Vol. 11), 185-216. Newbury Park, CA: Sage.

Cordes, C. (1983). Human factors and nuclear safety: Grudging respect for a growing field. *APA Monitor, 14*, 1, 13–14.

Cordes, C.L., & Dougherty, T.W. (1993). A review and an integration of research on job burnout. *Academy of Management Review, 18*, 621–656.

Cosier, R.A., & Dalton, D.R. (1990). Positive effects of conflict: A field assessment. *The International Journal of Conflict Management, 1*, 81–92.

Costa, P.T. & McCrae, R.R. (1992). *The Revised NEO Personality Inventory (NEO-PI-R) and NEO Five-Factor Inventory (NEO-FFI) professional manual.* Odessa, FL: Psychological Assessment Resources.

Coster, E.A., Carstens, I.L., & Harris, A.M.P. (1987). Patterns of stress among dentists. *Journal of the Dental Association of South Africa, 42*, 389–394.

Cotton, J.L., & Tuttle, J.M. (1986). Employee turnover: A meta-analysis and review with implications for research. *Academy of Management Review, 11*, 55–70.

Coyle, I.R., Sleeman, S.D., & Adams, N. (1995). Safety climate. *Journal of Safety Research, 26*, 247–254.

Craiger, J.P. (1997). Technology, organizations, and work in the 20th century. *The Industrial-Organizational Psychologist, 34,* 89–96.

Crawford, J. (1981). *Crawford Small Parts Dexterity Test.* San Antonio, TX: The Psychological Corporation.

Cropanzano, R., Howes, J.C., Grandey, A.A., & Toth, P. (1997). The relationship of organizational politics and support to work behaviors, attitudes, and stress. *Journal of Organizational Behavior, 18,* 159–180.

Cropanzano, R., & James, K. (1990). Some methodological considerations for the behavioral genetic analysis of work attitudes. *Journal of Applied Psychology, 75,* 433–439.

Crown, D.F., & Rosse, J.G. (1995). Yours, mine, and ours: Facilitating group productivity through the integration of individual and group goals. *Organizational Behavior and Human Decision Processes, 64,* 138–150.

Cummings, L.L., & Schwab, D.P. (1978). Designing appraisal systems for information yield. *California Management Review, 20,* 18–25.

Cummings, N.A., & Follette, W.T. (1976). Brief psychotherapy and medical utilization: An eight-year follow-up. In H. Dorken (Ed.), *The professional psychologist today: New developments in law, health, insurance, and health practice.* San Francisco: Jossey-Bass.

Cunningham, J.B. (1989). A compressed shift schedule: Dealing with some of the problems of shift-work. *Journal of Organizational Behavior, 10,* 231–245.

Dainoff, M.J., Happ, A., & Crane, P. (1981). Visual fatigue and occupational stress in VDT operators. *Human Factors, 23,* 421–438.

Dalton, D.R., & Mesch, D.J. (1991). On the extent and reduction of avoidable absenteeism: An assessment of absence policy provisions. *Journal of Applied Psychology, 76,* 810–817.

Dalton, D.R., Krackhardt, D.M., & Porter, L.W. (1981). Functional turnover: An empirical assessment. *Journal of Applied Psychology, 66,* 716–721.

Dansereau, F., Graen, G., & Haga, B. (1975). A vertical dyad linkage approach to leadership within formal organizations: A longitudinal investigation of the role making process. *Organizational Behavior and Human Performance, 13,* 46–78.

David, F.R., Pearce, J.A., & Randolph, W.A. (1989). Linking technology and structure to enhance group performance. *Journal of Applied Psychology, 74,* 233–241.

Davis, K. (1968). Success of chain-of-command oral communication in a manufacturing management group. *Academy of Management Journal, 11,* 379–387.

Davis, K. (1972). *Human behavior at work.* New York: McGraw-Hill.

Davis, L.E., & Cherns, A.B. (Eds.). (1975). *The quality of working life* (Vols. 1 and 2). New York: Free Press.

Davis, T.R.V., & Luthans, F. (1980). A social learning approach to organizational behavior. *Academy of Management Review, 5,* 281–290.

Dean, J.W., Yoon, S.J., & Susman, G.I. (1992). Advanced manufacturing technology and organization structure: Empowerment or subordination. *Organization Science, 3,* 203–229.

DeAngelis, T. (1994). New tests allow takers to tackle real-life problems. *APA Monitor, 25,* 14–15.

Deci, E.L. (1972). The effects of contingent and noncontingent rewards and controls on intrinsic motivation. *Organizational Behavior and Human Performance, 8,* 212–229.

Deci, E.L. (1992). On the nature and functions of motivation theories. *Psychological Science, 3,* 167–171.

Deci, E.L., & Ryan, R.M. (1985). *Intrinsic motivation and self-determination in human behavior.* New York: Plenum.

Decker, P.J. (1982). The enhancement of behavior modeling training of supervisory skills by the inclusion of retention processes. *Personnel Psychology, 35,* 323–332.

Decker, P.J., & Cornelius, E.T. (1979). A note on recruiting sources and job survival rates. *Journal of Applied Psychology, 64,* 463–464.

Decker, P.J., & Nathan, B.R. (1985). *Behavior modeling training: Principles and applications.* New York: Praeger.

Dembroski, T.M., & Costa, P.T. (1987). Coronary-prone behavior: Components of the Type A pattern and hostility. *Journal of Personality, 55,* 211–236.

Deming, W.E. (1982). *Quality, productivity, and competitive position.* Cambridge: Massachusetts Institute of Technology, Center for Advanced Engineering Study.

Deming, W.E. (1986). *Out of the crisis.* Cambridge: Massachusetts Institute of Technology, Center for Advanced Engineering Study.

DeNisi, A.S., & Peters, L.H. (1996). Organization of information in memory and the performance appraisal process: Evidence from the field. *Journal of Applied Psychology, 81,* 717–737.

DeNisi, A.S., Randolph, W.A., & Blencoe, A.G. (1983). Potential problems with peer ratings. *Academy of Management Journal, 26,* 457–464.

DeNisi, A.S., Robbins, T., & Cafferty, T.P. (1989). Organization of information used for performance appraisals: Role of diary-keeping. *Journal of Applied Psychology, 74,* 124–129.

Denison, D.R., & Mishra, A.K. (1995). Toward a theory of organizational culture and effectiveness. *Organization Science, 6,* 204–223.

Dennis, A.R., & Valacich, J.S. (1993). Computer brainstorms: More heads are better than one. *Journal of Applied Psychology, 78*, 531–537.

DePaulo, B.M., Stone, J.I., & Lassiter, G.D. (1985). Deceiving and detecting deceit. In B.R. Schlenker (Ed.), *The self and social life* (pp. 323–370). New York: McGraw-Hill.

DeWitt, R. (1993). The structural consequences of downsizing. *Organization Science, 4*, 30–40.

Diehl, M., & Stroebe, W. (1987). Productivity loss in brainstorming groups: Toward the solution of a riddle. *Journal of Personality and Social Psychology, 53*, 497–509.

Dienesch, R.M., & Liden, R.C. (1986). Leader-member exchange model of leadership: A critique and futher development. *Academy of Management Review, 11*, 618–634.

DiMatteo, M.R., Shugars, D.A., & Hays, R.D. (1993). Occupational stress, life stress, and mental health among dentists. *Journal of Occupational and Organizational Psychology, 66*, 153–162.

Di Milia, L. (1998). A longitudinal study of the compressed workweek: Comparing sleep on a weekly rotating 8 h system to a faster rotating 12 h system. *International Journal of Industrial Ergonomics, 21*, 199–207.

Dipboye, R.L. (1982). Self-fulfilling prophecies in the selection-recruitment interview. *Academy of Management Review, 7*, 579–587.

Dipboye, R.L. (1985). Some neglected variables in research on discrimination in appraisals. *Academy of Management Review, 10*, 116–127.

Dipboye, R.L. (1989). Threats to the incremental validity of interviewer judgments. In R.W. Eder & G.R. Ferris (Eds.), *The employment interview: Theory, research, and practice* (pp. 45–60). Newbury Park, CA: Sage.

Dipboye, R.L. (1994). Structured and unstructured selection interviews: Beyond the job-fit model. *Research in Personnel and Human Resources Management, 12*, 79–123.

Dipboye, R.L. (1997). Organizational barriers to implementing a rational model of training. In M.A. Quinones & A. Ehrenstein (Eds.), *Training for a rapidly changing workplace: Applications of psychological research* (pp. 31–60). Washington, DC: American Psychological Association.

Dipboye, R.L., Fontenelle, G.A., & Garner, K. (1984). Effects of previewing the application on interview process and outcomes. *Journal of Applied Psychology, 69*, 118–128.

Dobbins, G.H., & Platz, S.J. (1986). Sex differences in leadership: How real are they? *Academy of Management Review, 11*, 118–127.

Dodgson, M. (1993). Organizational learning: A review of some literatures. *Organization Studies, 14*, 375–394.

Donald, I. (1994). The structure of office workers' experience of organizational environments. *Journal of Occupational and Organizational Psychology, 67*, 241–258.

Doppelt, J.E., Hartman, A.D., & Krawchick, F.B. (1986). *Typing Test for Business*. San Antonio, TX: The Psychological Corporation.

Downey, H.K., Sheridan, J.E., & Slocum, J.W. (1976). The path-goal theory of leadership: A longitudinal analysis. *Organizational Behavior and Human Performance, 16*, 156–176.

Driskell, J.E., Olmstead, B., & Salas, E. (1993). Task cues, dominance cues, and influence in task groups. *Journal of Applied Psychology, 78*, 51–60.

Driskell, J.E., Willis, R.P., & Copper, C. (1992). Effect of overlearning on retention. *Journal of Applied Psychology, 77*, 615–622.

Driver, R.W., Buckley, M.R., & Frink, D.D. (1996). Should we write off graphology? *International Journal of Selection and Assessment, 4*, 78–86.

Drucker, P.F. (1954). *The practice of management*. New York: Harper & Row.

Duchon, D., Green, S.G., & Taber, T.D. (1986). Vertical dyad linkage: A longitudinal assessment of antecedents, measures, and consequences. *Journal of Applied Psychology, 71*, 56–60.

Dunbar, E. (1993). The relationship of subjective distress and emergency response experience to the effective use of protective equipment. *Work & Stress, 7*, 365–373.

Dunham, R.B., Pierce, J.L., & Castaneda, M.B. (1987). Alternative work schedules: Two field quasi-experiments. *Personnel Psychology, 40*, 215–242.

Dunnette, M.D. (1990). Blending the science and practice of industrial and organizational psychology: Where are we and where are we going. In M.D. Dunnette & L.M. Hough (Eds.). *Handbook of industrial and organizational psychology* (Vol. 1, 2nd ed., pp. 1–27). Palo Alto, CA: Consulting Psychologists Press.

Dunnette, M.D. (1993). My hammer or your hammer? *Human Resource Management, 32*, 373–384.

Dunnette, M.D., Campbell, J.P., & Hakel, M.D. (1967). Factors contributing to job satisfaction and dissatisfaction in six occupational groups. *Organizational Behavior and Human Performance, 2*, 143–174.

Dvorak, A., Marrick, N., Dealey, W., & Ford, G. (1936). *Typewriting behavior: Psychology applied to teaching and learning typewriter*. New York: American Book.

Dwyer, D.J., & Ganster, D.C. (1991). The effects of job demands and control on employee attendance and satisfaction. *Journal of Organizational Behavior, 12*, 595–608.

Eagly, A.H., Karau, S.J., & Makhijani, M.G. (1995). Gender and the effectiveness of leaders: A meta-analysis. *Psychological Bulletin, 112,* 125–145.

Earley, P.C. (1987). Intercultural training for managers: A comparison of documentary and interpersonal methods. *Academy of Management Journal, 30,* 685–698.

Earley, P.C., & Singh, H. (1995). International and intercultural management research: What's next? *Academy of Management Journal, 38,* 327–340.

Eastman Kodak Company. (1983). *Ergonomic design for people at work* (Vol. 1). Belmont, CA: Lifetime Learning Publications.

Eden, D., & Shani, A.B. (1982). Pygmalion goes to boot camp: Expectancy, leadership, and trainee performance. *Journal of Applied Psychology, 67,* 194–199.

Edwards, J.R., Baglioni, A.J., & Cooper, C.L. (1990a). Stress, Type A, coping, and psychological and physiological symptoms: A multi-sample test of alternative models. *Human Relations, 43,* 919–956.

Edwards, J.R., Baglioni, A.J., & Cooper, C.L. (1990b). Examining the relationships among self-report measures of the Type A behavior pattern: The effects of dimensionality, measurement error, and differences in underlying constructs. *Journal of Applied Psychology, 75,* 440–454.

Edwards, J.R., & Cooper, C.L. (1990). The person-environment fit approach to stress: Recurring problems and some suggested solutions. *Journal of Organizational Behavior, 11,* 293–307.

Edworthy, J. (1994). The design and implementation of non-verbal auditory warnings. *Applied Ergonomics, 25,* 202–210.

Efraty, D., & Sirgy, M.J. (1990). The effects of quality of working life (QWL) on employee behavioral responses. *Social Indicators Research, 22,* 31–47.

Eisenberg, E.M., & Witten, M.G. (1987). Reconsidering openness in organizational communication. *Academy of Management Review, 12,* 418–426.

Enander, A. (1984). Performance and sensory aspects of work in cold environments: A review. *Ergonomics, 27,* 365–378.

Enander, A. (1987). Effects of moderate cold on performance of psychomotor and cognitive tasks. *Ergonomics, 30,* 1431–1445.

Englebrecht, A.S., & Fischer, A.H. (1995). The managerial performance implications of a developmental assessment center process. *Human Relations, 48,* 387–404.

Environmental Protection Agency. (1974). *Information on levels of environmental noise requisite to protect public health and welfare with an adequate margin of safety* (Tech. Rep.). Washington, DC: Environmental Protection Agency.

Equal Employment Opportunity Commission. (1974). *Uniform guidelines on employee selection procedures.* Washington, DC: U.S. Government Printing Office.

Equal Employment Opportunity Commission. (1978). *Uniform guidelines on employee testing procedures.* Washington, DC: U.S. Government Printing Office.

Erez, M., & Arad, R. (1986). Participative goal-setting: Social, motivational, and cognitive factors. *Journal of Applied Psychology, 71,* 591–597.

Erez, M., & Zidon, I. (1984). Effect of goal acceptance on the relationship of goal difficulty to performance. *Journal of Applied Psychology, 69,* 69–78.

Erfurt, J.C., Foote, A., & Heirich, M.A. (1992). The cost-effectiveness of worksite wellness programs for hypertension, weight loss, smoking cessation, and exercise. *Personnel Psychology, 45,* 5–27.

Esposito, M.D. (1992). There's more to writing job descriptions than complying with the ADA. *Employment Relations Today, 19,* 273–281.

Esser, J.K. (1998). Alive and well after 25 years: A review of groupthink research. *Organizational Behavior and Human Decision Processes, 73,* 116–141.

Evans, B.K., & Fischer, D.G. (1993). The nature of burnout: A study of the three-factor model of burnout in human service and non-human service samples. *Journal of Occupational and Organizational Psychology, 66,* 29–38.

Evans, C.R., & Dion, K.L. (1991). Group cohesion and performance: A meta-analysis. *Small Group Research, 22,* 175–186.

Evans, G.W., & Jacobs, S.V. (1981). Air pollution and human behavior. *Journal of Social Issues, 37,* 95–125.

Fagenson, E.A. (1989). The mentor advantage: Perceived career/job experiences of proteges vs. non-proteges. *Journal of Organizational Behavior, 10,* 309–320.

Fagenson, E.A., & Burke, W.W. (1990). The activities of organization development practitioners at the turn of the decade of the 1990s: A study of their predictions. *Group and Organization Studies, 15,* 366–380.

Fairhurst, G.T. (1993). The leader-member exchange patterns of women leaders in industry: A discourse analysis. *Communication Monographs, 60,* 321–351.

Falkenberg, L.E. (1987). Employee fitness programs: Their impact on the employee and the organization. *Academy of Management Review, 12,* 511–522.

Fanger, P.O. (1970). *Thermal comfort, analysis, and applications in environmental engineering.* Copenhagen, Denmark: Danish Technical Press.

Fantuzzo, J.W., Riggio, R.E., Connelly, S., & Dimeff, L.A. (1989). Effects of reciprocal peer tutoring on academic achievement and psychological adjustment: A component analysis. *Journal of Educational Psychology, 81*, 173–177.

Farh, J., & Dobbins, G.H. (1989). Effects of comparative performance information on the accuracy of self-ratings and agreement between self- and supervisor ratings. *Journal of Applied Psychology, 74*, 606–610.

Farh, J., Dobbins, G.H., & Cheng, B. (1991). Cultural relativity in action: A comparison of self-ratings made by Chinese and U.S. workers. *Personnel Psychology, 44*, 129–147.

Farr, J.L. (1993). Informal performance feedback: Seeking and giving. In H. Schuler, J.L. Farr, & M. Smith (Eds.). *Personnel selection and assessment: Individual and organizational perspectives* (pp. 163–180). Hillsdale, NJ: Lawrence Erlbaum.

Farrell, D., & Petersen, J.C. (1982). Patterns of political behavior in organizations. *Academy of Management Review, 7*, 403–412.

Feild, H.S., & Holley, W.H. (1982). The relationship of performance appraisal system characteristics to verdicts in selected employment discrimination cases. *Academy of Management Journal, 25*, 392–406.

Feldman, D.C. (1976a). A contingency theory of socialization. *Administrative Science Quarterly, 21*, 433–454.

Feldman, D.C. (1976b). A practical program for employee socialization. *Organizational Dynamics, 57*, 64–80.

Feldman, D.C. (1981). The multiple socialization of organization members. *Academy of Management Review, 6*, 309–318.

Feldman, D.C. (1984). The development and enforcement of group norms. *Academy of Management Review, 9*, 47–54.

Feldman, D.C. (1989). Socialization, resocialization, and training: Reframing the research agenda. In I.L. Goldstein (Ed.), *Training and development in organizations* (pp. 376–416). San Francisco: Jossey-Bass.

Feldman, D.C., & Klich, N.R. (1991). Impression management and career strategies. In R.A. Giacalone & P. Rosenfeld (Eds.), *Applied impression management: How image-making affects managerial decisions* (pp. 67–80). Newbury Park, CA: Sage.

Feldman, J.M. (1981). Beyond attribution theory: Cognitive processes in performance appraisal. *Journal of Applied Psychology, 66*, 127–148.

Fenlason, K.J., & Beehr, T.A. (1994). Social support and occupational stress: Effects of talking to others. *Journal of Organizational Behavior, 15*, 157–175.

Ferdman, B. (1992). The dynamics of ethnic diversity in organizations: Toward integrative models. In K. Kelly (Ed.), *Issues, theory and research in industrial/organizational psychology* (pp. 339–383). Amsterdam: North Holland.

Ferris, G.R., Brand, J.F., Brand, S., Rowland, K.M., Gilmore, D.C., King, T.R., Kacmar, K.M., & Burton, C.A. (1993). Politics and control in organizations. In E.J. Lawler, B. Markovsky, J. O'Brien, K. Heimer (Eds.), *Advances in group processes* (Vol. 10, pp. 83–111). Greenwich, CT: JAI Press.

Ferris, G.R., Frink, D.D., Gilmore, D.C., & Kacmar, K.M. (1994). Understanding as an antidote for the dysfunctional consequences of organizational politics as a stressor. *Journal of Applied Social Psychology, 24*, 1204–1220.

Ferris, G.R., Frink, D.D., Galang, M.C., Zhou, J., Kacmar, K.M., & Howard, J.L. (1996). Perceptions of organizational politics: Prediction, stress-related implications, and outcomes. *Human Relations, 49*, 233–266.

Ferris, G.R., & Kacmar, K.M. (1992). Perceptions of organizational politics. *Journal of Management, 18*, 93–116.

Ferris, G.R., & King, T.R. (1991). Politics in human resources decisions: A walk on the dark side. *Organizational Dynamics, 20*, 59–71.

Ferris, G.R., Russ, G.S., & Fandt, P.M. (1989). Politics in organizations. In R.A. Giacalone & P. Rosenfeld (Eds.), *Impression management in the organization* (pp. 143–170). Hillsdale, NJ: Lawrence Erlbaum Associates.

Ferris, G.R., Yates, V.L., Gilmore, D.C., & Rowland, K.M. (1985). The influence of subordinate age on performance ratings and causal attributions. *Personnel Psychology, 38*, 545–557.

Festinger, L. (1957). *A theory of cognitive dissonance*. Evanston, IL: Row, Peterson.

Fiedler, F.E. (1965). Engineer the job to fit the manager. *Harvard Business Review, 43*, 115.

Fiedler, F.E. (1967). *A theory of leadership effectiveness*. New York: McGraw-Hill.

Fiedler, F.E. (1973). How do you make leaders more effective? New answers to an old puzzle. *Organizational Dynamics, 54*, 3–18.

Fiedler, F.E., & Chemers, M.M. (1984). *Improving leadership effectiveness: The Leader Match concept* (rev. ed.). New York: John Wiley & Sons.

Field, R.H.G. (1982). A test of the Vroom-Yetton normative model of leadership. *Journal of Applied Psychology, 67*, 523–532.

Fielding, J.E. (1984). *Corporate health management*. Reading, MA: Addison-Wesley.

Fine, M.G. (1991). New voices in the workplace: Research directions in multicultural communication. *The Journal of Business Communication, 23*, 259–275.

Fine, S.A., & Getkate, M. (1995). *Benchmark tasks for job analysis: A guide for Functional Job Analysis (FJA) scales*. Hillsdale, NJ: Lawrence Erlbaum Associates.

Fine, S.A., & Wiley, W.W. (1971). *An introduction to functional job analysis.* Kalamazoo, MI: W.E. Upjohn Institute.

Fisher, B.D., Motowidlo, S., & Werner, S. (1993). Effect of gender and other factors on rank of law professors in colleges of business: Evidence of a glass ceiling. *Journal of Business Ethics, 12,* 771–778.

Fitzgerald, L.F., Drasgow, F., Hulin, C.L., Gelfand, M.J., & Magley, V.J. (1997). Antecedents and consequences of sexual harassment in organizations: A test of an integrated model. *Journal of Applied Psychology, 82,* 578–589.

Flanagan, J.C. (1954). The critical incidents technique. *Psychological Bulletin, 51,* 327–358.

Fleishman, E.A. (1960). *Leader opinion questionnaire.* Chicago: Science Research Associates.

Fleishman, E.A., & Harris, E.F. (1962). Patterns of leadership behavior related to employee grievances and turnover. *Personnel Psychology, 15,* 43–56.

Fodor, E.M. (1976). Group stress, authoritarian style of control, and use of power. *Journal of Applied Psychology, 61,* 313–318.

Forbes, R.J., & Jackson, P.R. (1980). Nonverbal behaviour and the outcome of selection interviews. *Journal of Occupational Psychology, 53,* 65–72.

Ford, J.K., & Noe, R.A. (1987). Self-assessed training needs: The effects of attitudes toward training, managerial level, and function. *Personnel Psychology, 40,* 39–53.

Ford, J.K., Quinones, M.A., Sego, D.J., & Sorra, J.S. (1992). Factors affecting the opportunity to perform trained tasks on the job. *Personnel Psychology, 45,* 511–527.

Ford, R.C., & Randolph, W.A. (1992). Cross-functional structures: A review and integration of matrix organizations and project management. *Journal of Management, 18,* 267–294.

Forsyth, D.R. (1983). *An introduction to group dynamics.* Monterey, CA: Brooks/Cole.

Forsythe, S., Drake, M.F., & Cox, C.E. (1985). Influence of applicant's dress on interviewer's selection decisions. *Journal of Applied Psychology, 70,* 374–378.

Franke, R.H., & Kaul, J.D. (1978). The Hawthorne experiments: First statistical interpretation. *American Sociological Review, 43,* 623–643.

Fredericksen, N. (1962). Factors in in-basket performance. *Psychological Monographs, 76* [Entire issue no. 541].

Freeman, S.J., & Cameron, K.S. (1993). Organizational downsizing: A convergence and reorientation framework. *Organization Science, 4,* 10–29.

French, J.L., & Rosenstein, J. (1984). Employee ownership, work attitudes, and power relationships. *Academy of Management Journal, 27,* 861–869.

French, J.R.P., & Caplan, R.D. (1972). Organizational stress and individual strain. In A.J. Marrow (Ed.), *The failure of success* (pp. 30–66). New York: AMACOM.

French, J.R.P., Caplan, R.D., & Harrison, R.V. (1982). *The mechanisms of job stress and strain.* Chichester, England: Wiley.

French, J.R.P., & Raven, B.H. (1959). The bases of social power. In D. Cartwright (Ed.), *Studies in social power* (pp. 150–167). Ann Arbor, MI: University of Michigan Press.

French, J.R.P., Rogers, W., & Cobb, S. (1974). A model of person-environment fit. In G.V. Coelho, D.A. Hamburgh, & J.E. Adams (Eds.). *Coping and adaptation.* New York: Basic Books.

French, W.L. (1969). Organization development objectives, assumptions, and strategies. *California Management Review, 12,* 23–46.

French, W.L., & Bell, C.H. (1990). *Organization development: Behavioral science interventions for organization improvement* (4th ed.). Englewood Cliffs, NJ: Prentice-Hall.

Frese, M., & Zapf, D. (1988). Methodological issues in the study of work stress: Objective vs. subjective measurement of work stress and the question of longitudinal studies. In C.L. Cooper & R. Payne (Eds.), *Courses, coping and consequences of stress at work.* (pp. 375–411). New York: Wiley.

Fried, Y. (1990). Workspace characteristics, behavioral interferences, and screening ability as joint predictors of employee reactions: An examination of the intensification approach. *Journal of Organizational Behavior, 11,* 267–280.

Fried, Y. (1991). Meta-analytic comparison of the Job Diagnostic Survey and Job Characteristics Inventory as correlates of work satisfaction and performance. *Journal of Applied Psychology, 76,* 690–697.

Fried, Y., & Ferris, G.R. (1987). The validity of the job characteristics model: A review and meta-analysis. *Personnel Psychology, 40,* 287–322.

Friedlander, F. (1980). The facilitation of change in organizations. *Professional Psychology, 11,* 520–530.

Friedman, H.S. (Ed.) (1990). *Personality and disease.* New York: Wiley.

Friedman, H.S., & Booth-Kewley, S. (1987). The "disease-prone personality": A meta-analytic view of the construct. *American Psychologist, 42,* 539–555.

Friedman, H.S., Hall, J.A., & Harris, M.J. (1985). Type A behavior, nonverbal expressive style, and health. *Journal of Personality and Social Psychology, 48,* 1299–1315.

Friedman, M., & Rosenman, R.H. (1974). *Type A behavior and your heart.* New York: Alfred A. Knopf.

Frohman, M.A., Sashkin, M., & Kavanagh, M.J. (1976). Action research as applied to organization development. *Organization and Administrative Sciences, 7,* 129–142.

Frone, M.R., Russell, M., & Cooper, M.L. (1991). Relationship of work and family stressors to psychological distress: The independent moderating influence of social support, mastery, active coping, and self-focused attention. *Journal of Social Behavior and Personality, 6,* 227–250.

Fry, W., & Slocum, J.W. (1984). Technology, structure, and workgroup effectiveness: A test of a contingency model. *Academy of Management Journal, 27,* 221–246.

Furnham, A., & Stringfield, P. (1994). Congruence of self and subordinate ratings of managerial practices as a correlate of supervisor evaluation. *Journal of Occupational and Organizational Psychology, 67,* 57–67.

Fussell, S.R., & Benimoff, N.I. (1995). Social and cognitive processes in interpersonal communication: Implications for advanced telecommunications technologies. *Human Factors, 37,* 228–250.

Gaines, J., & Jermier, J.M. (1983). Emotional exhaustion in a high stress organization. *Academy of Management Journal, 26,* 567–586.

Gaines, J.H. (1980). Upward communication in industry: An experiment. *Human Relations, 33,* 929–942.

Galbraith, J. (1973). *Designing complex organizations.* Reading, MA: Addison-Wesley.

Galbraith, J. (1977). *Organization design.* Reading, MA: Addison-Wesley.

Gallois, C., Callan, V., & Palmer, J.M. (1992). The influence of applicant communication style and interviewer characteristics on hiring decisions. *Journal of Applied Social Psychology, 22,* 1041–1060.

Gallupe, R.B., Bastianutti, L., & Cooper, W.H. (1991). Unblocking brainstorms. *Journal of Applied Psychology, 76,* 137–142.

Gamst, G., & Otten, C.M. (1992). Job satisfaction in high technology and traditional industry: Is there a difference? *The Psychological Record, 42,* 413–425.

Gandz, J., & Murray, U.V. (1980). The experience of workplace politics. *Academy of Management Journal, 23,* 237–251.

Ganster, D.C. (1986). Type A behavior and occupational stress. *Journal of Organizational Behavior Management, 8,* 61–84.

Ganster, D.C., Fusilier, M.R., & Mayes, B.T. (1986). Role of social support in the experience of stress at work. *Journal of Applied Psychology, 71,* 102–110.

Ganster, D.C., Mayes, B.T., Sime, W.E., & Tharp, G.D. (1982). Managing organizational stress: A field experiment. *Journal of Applied Psychology, 67,* 533–542.

Ganster, D.C., Schaubroeck, J., Sime, W.E., & Mayes, B.T. (1991). The nomological validity of the Type A personality among employed adults. *Journal of Applied Psychology, 76,* 143–168.

Gardner, D.G., & Pierce, J.L. (1998). Self-esteem and self-efficacy within the organizational context: An empirical examination. *Group & Organization Management, 23,* 48–70.

Garvin, D.A. (1993). Building a learning organization. *Harvard Business Review, 71,* 78–91.

Gattiker, U.E., & Howg, L. (1990). Information technology and quality of work life: Comparing users with nonusers. *Journal of Business and Psychology, 5,* 237–260.

Gaugler, B.B., Rosenthal, D.B., Thornton, G.C., & Bentson, C. (1987). Meta-analyses of assessment center validity. *Journal of Applied Psychology, 72,* 493–511.

Gavin, J.F. (1984). Survey feedback: The perspectives of science and practice. *Group and Organization Studies, 9,* 29–70.

Geldard, F.A. (1972). *The human senses* (2nd ed.). New York: John Wiley & Sons.

Gellatly, I.R. (1995). Individual and group determinants of employee absenteeism: Test of a causal model. *Journal of Organizational Behavior, 16,* 469–485.

Gerstner, C.R., & Day, D.V. (1997). Meta-analytic review of leader-members exchange theory: Correlates and construct issues. *Journal of Applied Psychology, 82,* 827–844.

Geyer, A.L.J., & Steyrer, J.M. (1998). Transformational leadership and objective performance in banks. *Applied Psychology: An International Review, 47,* 397–420.

Gherman, E.M. (1981). *Stress and the bottom line: A guide to personal well-being and corporate health.* New York: AMACOM.

Ghiselli, E.E. (1973). The validity of aptitude tests in personnel selection. *Personnel Psychology, 26,* 461–477.

Ghorpade, J.V. (1988). *Job analysis: a handbook for the human resource director.* Englewood Cliffs, NJ: Prentice-Hall.

Giacalone, R.A., & Rosenfeld, P. (Eds.). (1989). *Impression management in the organization.* Hillsdale, NJ: Lawrence Erlbaum Associates.

Gibb, J.R. (1961). Defensive communication. *Journal of Communication, 11,* 81–84.

Gifford, R., Ng, C.F., & Wilkinson, M. (1985). Nonverbal cues in the employment interview: Links between applicant qualities and interviewer judg-ments. *Journal of Applied Psychology, 70,* 729–736.

Gilbreth, F.B. (1916). Motion study in surgery. *Canadian Journal of Medicine and Surgery, 1,* 1–10.

Gillet, B., & Schwab, D.P. (1975). Convergent and discriminant validities of corresponding Job Descriptive Index and Minnesota Satisfaction Questionnaire scales. *Journal of Applied Psychology, 60*, 313–317.

Gilmore, D.C., Ferris, G.R., Dulebohn, & Harrell-Cook, G. (1996). Organizational politics and employee attendance. *Group & Organization Management, 21*, 481–494.

Gist, M.E. (1987). Self-efficacy: Implications for organizational behavior and human resource management. *Academy of Management Review, 12*, 472–485.

Gist, M.E., Schwoerer, C., & Rosen, B. (1989). Effects of alternative training methods on self-efficacy and performance in computer software training. *Journal of Applied Psychology, 74*, 884–891.

Goff, S.J., Mount, M.K., & Jamison, R.L. (1990). Employer supported child care, work/family conflict, and absenteeism: A field study. *Personnel Psychology, 43*, 793–809.

Goldman, R.B. (1976). *A work experiment: Six Americans in a Swedish plant*. New York: Ford Foundation.

Goldstein, I.L. (1986). *Training in organizations: Needs assessment, development, and evaluation* (2nd ed.). Monterey, CA: Brooks/Cole.

Goldstein, I.L. (1993). *Training in organizations: Needs assessment, development, and evaluation* (3rd ed.). Monterey, CA: Brooks/Cole.

Goldstein, I.L., & Sorcher, M.A. (1974). *Changing supervisory behavior*. New York: Pergamon.

Golembiewski, R.T., Munzenrider, R.F., & Stevenson, J.G. (1986). *Stress in organizations: Toward a phase model of burnout*. New York: Praeger.

Goodale, J.G. (1989). Effective employment interviewing. In R.W. Eder & G.R. Ferris (Eds.). *The employment interview: Theory, research, and practice* (pp. 307–323). Newbury Park, CA: Sage.

Gordon, W.I., Anderson, C.M., & Bruning, S.D. (1992). Employee perceptions of corporate partnership: An affective-moral quid pro quo. *Employee Responsibilities and Rights Journal, 5*, 75–85.

Gottfredson, L.S. (1986). Societal consequences of the *g* factor in employment. *Journal of Vocational Behavior, 29*, 293–450.

Gough, H.G. (1984). A managerial potential scale for the California Psychological Inventory. *Journal of Applied Psychology, 69*, 233–240.

Gough, H.G. (1985). A work orientation scale for the California Psychological Inventory. *Journal of Applied Psychology, 70*, 505–513.

Gough, H.G. (1987). *California Psychological Inventory*. Palo Alto, CA: Consulting Psychologists Press.

Gould, J.D., Alfaro, L., Finn, R., Haupt, B., & Minuto, A. (1987). Reading from CRT displays can be as fast as reading from paper. *Human Factors, 29*, 497–517.

Gouldner, A.W. (1960). The norm of reciprocity: A preliminary statement. *American Sociological Review, 25*, 161–178.

Graen, G. (1976). Role-making processes within complex organizations. In M.D. Dunnette (Ed.), *Handbook of industrial and organizational psychology* (pp. 1201–1245). Chicago: Rand McNally.

Graen, G., Novak, M., & Sommerkamp, P. (1982). The effects of leader-member exchange and job design on productivity and satisfaction: Testing a dual attachment mode. *Organizational Behavior and Human Performance, 30*, 109–131.

Graen, G., & Scandura, T.A. (1985). *Leader-member exchange scale–17*. Cincinatti, OH: University of Cincinatti.

Graen, G.B. (1969). Instrumentality theory of work motivation: Some experimental results and suggested modifications. *Journal of Applied Psychology Monograph, 53* (Vol. 2, Pt. 2).

Graen, G.B., Scandura, T.A., & Graen, M.R. (1986). A field experimental test of the moderating effects of growth need strength on productivity. *Journal of Applied Psychology, 71*, 484–491.

Graen, G.B., & Uhl-Bien, M. (1995). Relationship-based approach to leadership: Development of leader-member exchange (LMX) theory of leadership over 25 years: Applying a multi-level multi-domain perspective. *Leadership Quarterly, 6*, 219–247.

Graham, J.W. (1991). An essay on organizational citizenship behavior. *Employee Responsibilities and Rights Journal, 4*, 249–270.

Graham-Moore, B., & Ross, T.L. (1990). *Gainsharing: Plans for improving performance*. Washington, D.C.: Bureau of National Affairs.

Grandjean, E. (1988). *Fitting the task to the man* (4th ed.). London: Taylor & Francis.

Granrose, C.S. (1997). Cross-cultural socialization of Asian employees in U.S. organizations. In C.S. Granrose & S. Oskamp (Eds.), *Cross-cultural work groups* (pp. 186–211). Thousand Oaks, CA: Sage.

Granrose, C.S., & Oskamp. S. (Eds.). (1997). *Cross-cultural work groups*. Thousand Oaks, CA: Sage.

Graves, L.M., & Karren, R.J. (1996). The employee selection interview: A fresh look at an old problem. *Human Resource Management, 35*, 163–180.

Gray, B., & Ariss, S.S. (1985). Politics and strategic change across organizational life cycles. *Academy of Management Review, 10*, 707–723.

Gray, J.L., & Starke, F.A. (1984). *Organizational behavior: Concepts and applications* (3rd ed.). Columbus, OH: Charles E. Merrill.

Greenberg, J. (1982). Approaching equity and avoiding inequity in groups and organizations. In J. Greenberg & R.L. Cohen (Eds.), *Equity and justice in social behavior.* New York: Academic Press.

Greenberg, J. (1987). A taxonomy of organizational justice theories. *Academy of Management Review, 12,* 9–22.

Greenberg, J. (1990). Employee theft as a reaction to underpayment inequity: The hidden cost of pay cuts. *Journal of Applied Psychology, 75,* 561–568.

Greenberg, J., & Ornstein, S. (1983). High status job title as compensation for underpayment: A test of equity theory. *Journal of Applied Psychology, 68,* 285–297.

Greenberger, D.B., & Strasser, S. (1986). Development and application of a model of personal control in organizations. *Academy of Management Review, 11,* 164–177.

Greenhalgh, L., Lawrence, A.T., & Sutton, R.I. (1988). Determinants of workforce reduction strategies in declining organizations. *Academy of Management Review, 13,* 241–254.

Greenhaus, J.H., & Beutell, N.J. (1985). Sources of conflict between work and family roles. *Academy of Management Review, 10,* 76–88.

Greenhaus, J.H., & Parasaruman, S. (1986). A work-non-work interactive perspective of stress and its consequences. *Journal of Organizational Behavior Management, 8,* 37–60.

Greenlaw, P.S., & Kohl, J.P. (1993). Now is the time to update salaries and job descriptions. *Journal of Compensation and Benefits, 9,* 61–64.

Greenwood, R., & Hinings, C.R. (1996). Understanding radical organizational change: Bringing together the old and the new institutionalism. *Academy of Management Review, 21,* 1022–1054.

Greguras, G.J., & Robie, C. (1997, April). Reliability of 360-degree feedback ratings. Paper presented at the 12th annual conference of the Society for Industrial and Organizational Psychology, St. Louis, MO.

Griggs v. Duke Power Co. (1971). 401 U.S. 424, 3EPD p8137, 3 FEP Cases 175.

Grove, S.J., & Fisk, R.P. (1989). Impression management in services marketing: A dramaturgical perspective. In C.S. Granrose & S. Oskamp (Eds.), *Cross-cultural work groups* (pp. 427–438). Thousand Oaks, CA: Sage.

Guion, R.M. (1965). *Personnel testing.* New York: McGraw-Hill.

Guion, R.M., & Gibson, W.M. (1988). Personnel selection and placement. *Annual Review of Psychology, 39,* 349–374.

Guion, R.M., & Gottier, R.J. (1965). Validity of personality measures in personnel selection. *Personnel Psychology, 18,* 135–164.

Gully, S.M., Devine, D.J., & Whitney, D.J. (1995). A meta-analysis of cohesion and performance: Effects of level of analysis and task interdependence. *Small Group Research, 26,* 497–520.

Gunn, E. (1995). Mentoring: The democratic version. *Training, 32,* 64–67.

Gupta, N., & Beehr, T.A. (1979). Job stress and employee behaviors. *Organizational Behavior and Human Performance, 23,* 373–387.

Gutek, B.A., & Winter, S.J. (1992). Consistency of job satisfaction across situations: Fact or framing artifact? *Journal of Vocational Behavior, 41,* 61–78.

Gutteridge, T.G. (1986). Organizational career development systems: The state of the practice. In D.T. Hall and Associates, *Career development in organizations* (pp. 50–94). San Francisco: Jossey-Bass.

Guzzo, R.A., Jette, R.D., & Katzell, R.A. (1985). The effects of psychologically based intervention programs on worker productivity: A meta-analysis. *Personnel Psychology, 38,* 275–292.

Gyllenhammer, P. (1977). *People at work.* Reading, MA: Addison-Wesley.

Haccoun, R.R., & Jeanrie, C. (1995). Self reports of work absence as a function of personal attitudes towards absence, and perceptions of the organisation. *Applied Psychology: An International Review, 44,* 155–170.

Hackett, R.D. (1990). Age, tenure, and employee absenteeism. *Human Relations, 43,* 601–619.

Hackett, R.D., & Bycio, P. (1996). An evaluation of employee absenteeism as a coping mechanism among hospital nurses. *Journal of Occupational and Organizational Psychology, 69,* 327–328.

Hackett, R.D., & Guion, R.M. (1985). A reevaluation of the absenteeism-job satisfaction relationship. *Organizational Behavior and Human Decision Processes, 35,* 340–381.

Hackman, J.R. (1990). *Groups that work (and those that don't).* San Francisco: Jossey-Bass.

Hackman, J.R. (1992). Group influences on individuals in organizations. In M.D. Dunnette and L.M. Hough (Eds.), *Handbook of industrial and organizational psychology,* (Vol. 3, 2nd ed., pp. 194–267). Palo Alto, CA: Consulting Psychologists Press.

Hackman, J.R., & Oldham, G.R. (1975). Development of the Job Diagnostic Survey. *Journal of Applied Psychology, 60,* 159–170.

Hackman, J.R., & Oldham, G.R. (1976). Motivation through the design of work: Test of a theory. *Organizational Behavior and Human Performance, 16,* 250–279.

Hackman, J.R., & Oldham, G.R. (1980). *Work redesign.* Reading, MA: Addison-Wesley.

Hakstian, A.R., & Cattell, R.B. (1975–1982). *Comprehensive Ability Battery*. Champaign, IL: Institute for Personality and Ability Testing.

Hall, D.T., & Hall, F.S. (1976). What's new in career management? *Organizational Dynamics, 5*, 62–72.

Hall, D.T., & Parker, V.A. (1993). The role of workplace flexibility in managing diversity. *Organizational Dynamics, 21*, 5–18.

Halpert, J.A., Wilson, M.L., & Hickman, J.L. (1993). Pregnancy as a source of bias in performance appraisals. *Journal of Organizational Behavior, 14*, 649–663.

Halpin, A.W., & Winer, B.J. (1957). A factorial study of the leader behavior descriptions. In R.M. Stogdill & A.E. Coons (Eds.), *Leader behavior: Its description and measurement*. Columbus, OH: Ohio State University Bureau of Business Research.

Hammer, T.H., & Landau, J.C. (1981). Methodological issues in the use of absence data. *Journal of Applied Psychology, 66*, 574–581.

Hamner, W.C., & Hamner, E.P. (1976). Behavior modification on the bottom line. *Organizational Dynamics, 4*, 8–21.

Hansen, C.P. (1989). A causal model of the relationship among accidents, biodata, personality, and cognitive factors. *Journal of Applied Psychology, 74*, 81–90.

Hanson, T.J., & Balestreri-Spero, J.C. (1985). An alternative to interviews. *Personnel Journal, 64*, 114–123.

Harder, J.W. (1991). Equity theory versus expectancy theory: The case of major league baseball free agents. *Journal of Applied Psychology, 76*, 458–64.

Hare, A.P. (1976). *Handbook of small group research* (2nd ed.). New York: Free Press.

Harris, M.M. (1989). Reconsidering the employment interview: A review of recent literature and suggestions for future research. *Personnel Psychology, 42*, 691–726.

Harris, M.M., & Heft, L.L. (1992). Alcohol and drug use in the workplace: Issues, controversies, and directions for future research. *Journal of Management, 18*, 239–266.

Harris, M.M., & Schaubroeck, J. (1988). A meta-analysis of self-supervisor, self-peer, and peer-supervisor ratings. *Personnel Psychology, 41*, 43–62.

Harris, T.E. (1993). *Applied organizational communication: Perspectives, principles, and pragmatics*. Hillsdale, NJ: Lawrence Erlbaum.

Harrison, D.A., Price, K.H., & Bell, M.P. (1998). Beyond relational demography: Time and the effects of surface- and deep-level diversity on work group cohesion. *Academy of Management Journal, 41*, 96–107.

Harrison, D.A., & McLaughlin, M.E. (1993). Cognitive processes in self-report responses: Tests of item context effects in work attitude measures. *Journal of Applied Psychology, 78*, 129–140.

Harrison, J.K. (1992). Individual and combined effects of behavior modeling and the cultural assimilator in cross-cultural management training. *Journal of Applied Psychology, 77*, 952–962.

Harrison, T.M. (1985). Communication and participative decision making: An exploratory study. *Personnel Psychology, 38*, 93–116.

Hartel, C.E.J. (1998). Vantage 2000: Recent advances in diversity research—When diversity has positive outcomes for organizations and when it does not. *The Industrial-Organizational Psychologist, 36*, 57–60.

Hartsough, D.M., & Savitsky, J.C. (1984). Three Mile Island: Psychology and environmental policy at a crossroads. *American Psychologist, 39*, 1113–1122.

Harvey, R.J. (1991). Job analysis. In M.D. Dunnette & L.M. Hough (Eds.), *Handbook of industrial and organizational psychology* (2nd ed., Vol. 2, pp. 71–163). Palo Alto, CA: Consulting Psychologists Press.

Harvey, R.J., Friedman, L., Hakel, M.D., & Cornelius, E.T. (1988). Dimensionality of the Job Element Inventory, a simplified worker-oriented job analysis questionnaire. *Journal of Appllied Psychology, 73*, 639–646.

Harvey, R.J., & Lozada-Larsen, S.R. (1988). Influence of amount of job descriptive information on job analysis rating accuracy. *Journal of Applied Psychology, 73*, 457–461.

Haslegrave, C.M., & Holmes, K. (1994). Integrating ergonomics and engineering in the technical design process. *Ergonomics, 25*, 211–220.

Hater, J.J., & Bass, B.M. (1988). Supervisors' evaluations and subordinates' perceptions of transformational and transactional leadership. *Journal of Applied Psychology, 73*, 695–702.

Hatfield, M.O. (1990). Stress and the American worker. *American Psychologist, 45*, 1162–1164.

Hathaway, S.R., & McKinley, J.C. (1970). *MMPI: Minnesota Multiphasic Personality Inventory*. Minneapolis: University of Minnesota Press.

Havenstein, N.M.A. (1992). An information-processing approach to leniency in performance judgments. *Journal of Applied Psychology, 77*, 485–493.

Haynes, R.S., Pine, R.C., & Fitch, H.G. (1982). Reducing accident rates with organizational behavior modification. *Academy of Management Journal, 25*, 407–416.

Haynes, S.G., Feinleib, M., Levine, S., Scotch, N.A., & Kannel, W.B. (1978). The relationship of psychosocial factors to coronary heart disease in the Framingham study. II. Prevalence of coronary heart disease. *American Journal of Epidemiology, 107*, 384–402.

Heaney, C.A., Price, R.H., & Rafferty, J. (1995). Increasing coping resources at work: A field experiment to increase social support, improve work team functioning, and enhance employee mental health. *Journal of Organizational Behavior, 16,* 335–353.

Hedge, J.W., & Kavanagh, M.J. (1988). Improving the accuracy of performance evaluations: Comparison of three methods of performance appraiser training. *Journal of Applied Psychology, 73,* 68–73.

Heilman, M.E., & Saruwatari, L.R. (1979). When beauty is beastly: The effects of appearance and sex on evaluations of job applicants for managerial and nonmanagerial jobs. *Organizational Behavior and Human Performance, 23,* 360–372.

Heneman, R.L., & Wexley, K.N. (1983). The effects of time delay in rating and amount of information observed in performance rating accuracy. *Academy of Management Journal, 26,* 677–686.

Henley, N.M. (1977). *Body politics: Power, sex, and nonverbal communication.* Englewood Cliffs, NJ: Prentice-Hall.

Herd, J.A. (1988). Physiological indices of job stress. In J.J. Hurrell, L.R. Murphy, S.L., Sauter, & C.L. Cooper (Eds.), *Occupational stress issues and developments in research* (pp. 124–154). Philadelphia: Taylor & Francis.

Herrick, N.Q., & Maccoby, M. (1975). Humanizing work: A priority goal of the 1970's. In L.E. Davis & A.B. Cherns (Eds.), *The quality of working life* (Vol. 1, pp. 63–77). New York: Free Press.

Hersey, R. (1966). Grapevine—Here to stay but not beyond control. *Personnel, 43,* 62–66.

Herzberg, F. (1966). *Work and the nature of man.* Cleveland, OH: World.

Herzberg, F., Mausner, B., & Snyderman, B.B. (1959). *The motivation to work.* New York: John Wiley & Sons.

Hicks, W.D., & Klimoski, R.J. (1981). The impact of flextime on employee attitudes. *Academy of Management Journal, 24,* 333–341.

Hickson, D.J., Hinings, C.R., Less, C.A., Schneck, R.E., & Pennings, J.M. (1971). a strategic contingencies theory of intraorganizational power. *Administrative Science Quarterly, 16,* 216–229.

Highhouse, S., & Becker, A.S. (1993). Facet measures and global job satisfaction. *Journal of Business and Psychology, 8,* 117–127.

Hill, G.W. (1982). Group versus individual performance: Are N+1 heads better than one? *Psychological Bulletin, 89,* 517–539.

Hilton, T.F., & Hertzbach, A. (1997). *Organizational culture reactions to upward feedback.* Washington, DC: Federal Aviation Administration.

Hinkin, T.R., & Schriesheim, C.A. (1989). Development and application of new scales to measure French and Raven (1959) bases of social power. *Journal of Applied Psychology, 74,* 561–567.

Hinkin, T.R., & Schriesheim, C.A. (1994). An examination of subordinate-perceived relationships between leader reward and punishment behavior and leader bases of power. *Human Relations, 47,* 779–800.

Hocker, J.L., & Wilmot, W.W. (1985). *Interpersonal conflict.* (2nd ed.) Dubuque, IA: Brown.

Hoffman, C.C., Nathan, B.R., & Holden, L.M. (1991). A comparison of validation criteria: Objective versus subjective performance measures and self- versus supervisor ratings. *Personnel Psychology, 44,* 601–619.

Hofmann, D.A., & Stetzer, A. (1996). A cross-level investigation of factors influencing unsafe behaviors and accidents. *Personnel Psychology, 49,* 307–339.

Hofstede, G., Neuijen, B., Ohayr, D., & Sanders, G. (1990). Measuring organizational cultures: A qualitative and quantitative study across twenty cases. *Administrative Science Quarterly, 35,* 286–316.

Hogan, R., & Hogan, J. (1985). *Hogan Personnel Selection Series.* Minneapolis: National Computer Systems.

Hogan, R., Raskin, R., & Fazzini, D. (1990). The dark side of charisma. In K.E. Clark & M.B. Clark (Eds.), *Measures of leadership* (pp. 171–184). West Orange, NJ: Leadership Library of America.

Hollander, E.P. (1978). *Leadership dynamics: A practical guide to effective relationships.* New York: Free Press.

Hollander, E.P. (1985). Leadership and power. In G. Lindzey & E. Aronson (Eds.), *The handbook of social psychology* (3rd ed., pp. 485–538). New York: Random House.

Hollenback, J.R. (1990). The past, present, and future of assessment centers. *The Industrial-Organizational Psychologist, 28,* 13–17.

Hollenback, J.R., & Williams, C.R. (1986). Turnover functionality versus turnover frequency: A note on work attitudes and organizational effectiveness. *Journal of Applied Psychology, 71,* 606–611.

Holmes, T.H., & Rahe, R.H. (1967). The Social Readjustment Rating Scale. *Journal of Psychosomatic Research, 11,* 213–218.

Hopkins, A. (1990). Stress, the quality of work, and repetition strain injury in Australia. *Work & Stress, 4,* 129–138.

House, J.S. (1981). *Work stress and social support.* Reading, MA: Addison-Wesley.

House, R.J. (1971). A path-goal theory of leader effectiveness. *Administrative Science Quarterly, 1,* 321–338.

House, R.J. (1977). A 1976 theory of charismatic leadership. In J.G. Hunt & L.L. Larsen (Eds.), *Leadership: The cut-*

ting edge (pp. 189–207). Carbondale, IL: Southern Illinois University Press.

House, R.J. (1996). Path-goal theory of leadership: Lessons, legacy, and a reformulated theory. *Leadership Quarterly, 7*, 323–352.

House, R.J., & Dessler, G. (1974). The path-goal theory of leadership: Some post hoc and a priori tests. In J.G. Hunt & L.L. Larsen (Eds.), *Contingency approaches to leadership* (pp. 29–55). Carbondale, IL: Southern Illinois University Press.

House, R.J., & Mitchell, T. (1974). Path-goal theory of leadership. *Journal of Contemporary Business, 3*, 81–98.

House, R.J., & Singh, J.V. (1987). Organizational behavior: Some new directions for I/O psychology. *Annual Review of Psychology, 38*, 669–718.

House, R.J., Spangler, W.D., & Woycke, J. (1991). Personality and charisma in the U.S. Presidency: A psychological theory of leader effectiveness. *Administrative Science Quarterly, 36*, 364–396.

Houston, W.M., Raymond, M.R., & Svec, J.C. (1991). Adjustments for rater effects in performance assessment. *Applied Psychological Measurement, 15*, 409–421.

Howard, A. (1997). A reassessment of assessment centers: Challenges for the 21st century. In R.E. Riggio & B.T. Mayes (Eds.), *Assessment centers: Research and applications* (pp. 13–52). Corte Madera, CA: Select Press.

Howard, G.S., & Dailey, P.R. (1979). Response-shift bias: A source of contamination of self-report measures. *Journal of Applied Psychology, 64*, 144–150.

Howard, J.L., & Ferris, G.R. (1996). The employment interview context: Social and situational influences on interviewer decisions. *Journal of Applied Social Psychology, 26*, 112–136.

Howell, W.C. (1992). Human factors in the workplace. In M.D. Dunnette & L.M. Hough (Eds.), *Handbook of industrial and organizational psychology* (Vol. 2, 2nd ed., pp. 209–269). Palo Alto, CA: Consulting Psychologists Press.

Howell, W.C. (1994). Human factors and the challenges of the future. *Psychological Science, 5*, 1–7.

Howell, W.C., & Cooke, N.J. (1989). Training the human information processor: A review of cognitive models. In I.L. Goldstein (Ed.), *Training and development in organizations* (pp. 121–182). San Francisco: Jossey-Bass.

Hoyos, C.G. (1995). Occupational safety: Progress in understanding the basic aspects of safe and unsafe behavior. *Applied Psychology: An International Review, 44*, 233–250.

Huffcutt, A.I., & Arthur, W. (1994). Hunter and Hunter (1984) revisited: Interview validity for entry-level jobs. *Journal of Applied Psychology, 79*, 184–190.

Huffcutt, A.I., Roth, P.L., & McDaniel, M.A. (1996). A meta-analytic investigation of cognitive ability in employment interview evaluations: Moderating characteristics and implications for incremental validity. *Journal of Applied Psychology, 81*, 459–473.

Hughes, G.L., & Prien, E.P. (1989). Evaluation of task and job skill linkage judgements used to develop test specifications. *Personnel Psychology, 42*, 283–292.

Hughes, R.L., Ginnett, R.C., & Curphy, G.J. (1996). *Leadership: Enhancing the lessons of experience* (2nd ed.). Chicago: Irwin.

Hunt, G.T. (1980). *Communication skills in the organization.* Englewood Cliffs, NJ: Prentice-Hall.

Hunter, J.E., & Hunter, R.F. (1983). Validity and utility of alternative predictors of job performance. *Psychological Bulletin, 96*, 72–98.

Hunter, J.E., & Schmidt, F.L. (1982). Fitting people to jobs: The impact of personnel selection on national productivity. In M.D. Dunnette & E.A. Fleishman (Eds.), *Human performance and productivity: Human capability assessment* (pp. 233–284). Hillsdale, NJ: Lawrence Erlbaum.

Hurrell, J.J., Murphy, L.R., Sauater, S.L., & Cooper, C.L. (Eds.) (1988). *Occupational stress issues and developments in research.* Philadelphia: Taylor & Francis.

Huseman, R.C., Hatfield, J.D., & Miles, E.W. (1987). A new perspective on equity theory: The equity sensitivity construct. *Academy of Management Review, 12*, 222–234.

Hyland, A.M., & Muchinsky, P.M. (1991). Assessment of the structural validity of Holland's model with job analysis (PAQ) information. *Journal of Applied Psychology, 76*, 75–80.

Iaffaldano, M.T., & Muchinsky, P.M. (1985). Job satisfaction and job performance: A meta-analysis. *Psychological Bulletin, 97*, 251–273.

Ilgen, D.R., Barnes-Farrell, J.L., & McKellin, D.B. (1993). Performance appraisal process research in the 1980s: What has it contributed to appraisals in use? *Organizational Behavior and Human Decision Processes, 54*, 321–368.

Ilgen, D.R., Fisher, C.D., & Taylor, M.S. (1979). Consequences of individual feedback on behavior in organizations. *Journal of Applied Psychology, 64*, 349–371.

Ilgen, D.R., & Hollenback, J.H. (1977). The role of job satisfaction in absence behavior. *Organizational Behavior and Human Performance, 19*, 148–161.

Illuminating Engineering Society. (1977). *IES code for interior lighting.* London: Author.

Imada, A.S., & Hakel, M.D. (1977). Influence of nonverbal communication and rater proximity on impressions and decisions in simulated employment interviews. *Journal of Applied Psychology, 62,* 295–300.

Imm, P.S. (1990). Perceived benefits of participants in an employees' aerobic fitness program. *Perceptual and Motor Skills, 71,* 753–754.

Ingate, M. (1992). ADA: We assume we will still be testing. *The Industrial-Organizational Psychologist, 30,* 35–38.

Ironson, G.H., Smith, P.C., Brannick, M.T., Gibson, W.M., & Paul, K.B. (1989). Construction of a job in general scale: A comparison of global, composite, and specific measures. *Journal of Applied Psychology, 74,* 193–200.

Isenberg, D.J. (1986). Group polarization: A critical review. *Journal of Personality and Social Psychology, 50,* 1141–1151.

Ivancevich, J.M. (1979). Longitudinal study of the effects of rater training on psychometric error in ratings. *Journal of Applied Psychology, 64,* 502–508.

Ivancevich, J.M. (1982). Subordinates' reactions to performance appraisal interviews: A test of feedback and goal-setting techniques. *Journal of Applied Psychology, 67,* 581–587.

Ivancevich, J.M., & Lyon, H.L. (1977). The shortened workweek: A field experiment. *Journal of Applied Psychology, 62,* 34–37.

Ivancevich, J.M., & Mattson, M.T. (1980). *A managerial perspective: Stress and work.* Glenview, IL: Scott-Foresman.

Ivancevich, J.M., Matteson, M.T., & Preston, C. (1982). Occupational stress, Type A behavior, and physical well-being. *Academy of Management Journal, 25,* 373–391.

Iverson, R.D., Olekalns, M., & Erwin, P.J. (1998). Affectivity, organizational stressors, and absenteeism: A causal model of burnout and its consequences. *Journal of Vocational Behavior, 52,* 1–23.

Jablin, F.M. (1979). Superior-subordinate communication: The state of the art. *Psychological Bulletin, 86,* 1201–1222.

Jackson, P.R., Mullarkey, S., Parker, S.K., & Wall, T.D. (1994). Advanced manufacturing systems and the changing nature of work. In P.T. Kidd & W. Karwoski (Eds.), *Advances in agile manufacturing* (pp. 590–593). Amsterdam: IOS Press.

Jackson, S.E. (1983). Participation in decision making as a strategy for reducing job-related strain. *Journal of Applied Psychology, 68,* 3–19.

Jackson, S.E. (Ed.) (1994). *Diversity in the workplace: Human resources initiatives.* New York: Guilford.

Jackson, S.E., Brett, J.F., Sessa, V.I., Cooper, D.M., Julin, J.A., & Peyronnin, K. (1991). Some differences make a difference: Individual dissimilarity and group heterogeneity as correlates of recruitment, promotions, and tenure. *Journal of Applied Psychology, 76,* 675–689.

Jackson, S.E., & Schuler, R.S. (1985). A meta-analysis and conceptual critique of research on role ambiguity and role conflict in work settings. *Organizational Behavior and Human Decision Processes, 36,* 16–78.

Jackson, S.E., Schwab, R.L., & Schuler, R.S. (1986). Toward an understanding of the burnout phenomenon. *Journal of Applied Psychology, 71,* 630–640.

Jacobs, R.R. (1986). Numerical rating scales. In R.A. Berk (Ed.), *Performance assessment: Methods and applications* (pp. 82–99). Baltimore: The Johns Hopkins University Press.

Jago, A.G., & Ragan, J.W. (1986). The trouble with Leader Match is that it doesn't match Fiedler's contingency model. *Journal of Applied Psychology, 71,* 555–559.

James, K., Chen, J., & Goldberg, C. (1992). Organizational conflict and individual creativity. *Journal of Applied Social Psychology, 22,* 545–566.

Janis, I.L. (1972). *Victims of groupthink: A psychological study of foreign-policy decisions and fiascoes.* Boston, MA: Houghton Mifflin.

Janis, I.L. (1982). *Groupthink: Psychological studies of policy decisions and fiascoes.* Boston: Houghton-Mifflin.

Janis, I.L., & Mann, L. (1977). *Decision making: A psychological analysis of conflict, choice, and commitment.* New York: Free Press.

Janz, T. (1982). Initial comparisons of patterned behavior description interviews versus unstructured interviews. *Journal of Applied Psychology, 67,* 577–580.

Jenkins, C.D., Zyzanski, S.J., & Rosenman, R.H. (1979). *Manual for the Jenkins Activity Survey.* New York: Psychological Corporation.

Jenkins, J.M. (1993). Self-monitoring and turnover: The impact of personality on intent to leave. *Journal of Organizational Behavior, 14,* 83–91.

Jermier, J.M., Gaines, J., & McIntosh, N.J. (1989). Reactions to physically dangerous work: A conceptual and empirical analysis. *Journal of Organizational Behavior, 10,* 15–33.

Jette, M. (1984). Stress coping through physical activity. In A.S. Sethi & R.S. Schuler (Eds.), *Handbook of organizational stress coping strategies* (pp. 215–231). Cambridge, MA: Ballinger.

Jimmieson, N.L., & Terry, D.J. (1993). The effects of prediction, understanding, and control: A test of the stress antidote model. *Anxiety, Stress, and Coping, 6,* 179–199.

Jimmieson, N.L., & Terry, D.J. (1998). An experimental study of the effects of work stress, work control, and task information on adjustment. *Applied Psychology: An International Review, 47,* 345–369.

Johns, G. (1994a). How often were you absent? A review of the use of self-reported absence data. *Journal of Applied Psychology, 79,* 574–591.

Johns, G. (1994b). Absenteeism estimates by employees and managers: Divergent perspectives and self-serving perceptions. *Journal of Applied Psychology, 79,* 229–239.

Johnson, J.R., Bernhagen, M.J., Miller, V., & Allen, M. (1996). The role of communication in managing reductions in work force. *Journal of Applied Communication Research, 24,* 139–164.

Johnson, J.W. (1996). Linking employee perceptions of service climate to customer satisfaction. *Personnel Psychology, 49,* 831–851.

Johnston, J.H., Driskell, J.E., & Salas, E. (1997). Vigilant and hypervigilant decision making. *Journal of Applied Psychology, 82,* 614–622.

Jones, E.E., & Nisbett, R.E. (1972). The actor and the observer: Divergent perceptions of the causes of behavior. In E.E. Jones, D.E. Kanouse, H.H. Kelley, R.E. Nisbett, S. Valins, & B. Weiner (Eds.), *Attribution: Perceiving the causes of behavior* (pp. 79–94). Morristown, NJ: General Learning Press.

Jones, J.W., & Wuebker, L.J. (1988). Accident prevention through personnel selection. *Journal of Business and Psychology, 3,* 187–198.

Judd, K., & Gomez-Mejia, L.R. (1987). Comparable worth: A sensible way to end pay discrimination or the "looniest idea since looney tunes." In D.B. Balkin & L.R. Gomez-Mejia (Eds.), *New perspectives on compensation* (pp. 61–79). Englewood Cliffs, NJ: Prentice-Hall.

Judge, T.A., & Ferris, G.R. (1993). Social context of performance evaluation decisions. *Academy of Management Journal, 36,* 80–105.

Kabanoff, B. (1981). A critique of Leader Match and its implications for leadership research. *Personnel Psychology, 34,* 749–764.

Kacmar, K.M., Delery, J.E., & Ferris, G.R. (1992). Differential effectiveness of applicant impression management tactics on employment interview decisions. *Journal of Applied Social Psychology, 22,* 1250–1272.

Kahn, R., & Katz, D. (1960). Leadership practices in relation to productivity and morale. In D. Cartwright & A. Zander (Eds.), *Group dynamics: Research and theory* (2nd ed.). Elmsford, NY: Row, Peterson, & Co.

Kahn, R.L., & Byosiere, P. (1992). Stress in organizations. In M.D. Dunnette & L.M. Hough (Eds.), *Handbook of industrial/organizational psychology* (2nd ed., pp. 571–650). Palo Alto, CA: Consulting Psychologists Press.

Kanfer, R., & Ackerman, P.L. (1989). Motivation and cognitive abilities: An integrative/aptitude-treatment approach to skill acquisition. *Journal of Applied Psychology, 74,* 657–690.

Kantowitz, B.H. (1989). The role of information processing models in system development. *Proceedings of the Human Factors Society* (pp. 1059–1063). Santa Monica, CA: Human Factors Society.

Kaplan, A. (1964). *The conduct of inquiry.* New York: Harper & Row.

Karasek, R. (1979). Job demands, job decision latitude, and marital strain: Implications for job redesign. *Administrative Science Quarterly, 24,* 285–306.

Karau, S.J., & Hart, J.W. (1998). Group cohesiveness and social loafing: Effects of a social interaction manipulation on individual motivation within groups. *Group Dynamics: Theory, Research, and Practice, 2,* 185–191.

Karau, S.J., & Williams, K.D. (1993). Social loafing: A meta-analytic review and theoretical integration. *Journal of Personality and Social Psychology, 65,* 681–706.

Katz, D., & Kahn, R.L. (1966). *The social psychology of organizations.* New York: John Wiley & Sons.

Katz, D., & Kahn, R.L. (1978). *The social psychology of organizations* (2nd ed.). New York: John Wiley & Sons.

Katzell, R.A., & Austin, J.T. (1992). From then to now: The development of industrial-organizational psychology in the United States. *American Psychologist, 77,* 803–835.

Kaufman, J., & Christensen, J. (Eds.). (1984). *IES lighting handbook* (reference vol.). New York: Illuminating Engineering Society of North America.

Keller, L.M., Bouchard, T.J., Arvey, R.D., Segal, N.L., & Dawis, R.V. (1992). Work values: Genetic and environmental issues. *Journal of Applied Psychology, 77,* 79–88.

Kennedy, J.K. (1982). Middle LPC leaders and the contingency model of leadership effectiveness. *Organizational Behavior and Human Performance, 30,* 1–14.

Kenny, D.A., & Zaccaro, S.J. (1983). An estimate of variance due to traits in leadership. *Journal of Applied Psychology, 68,* 678–685.

Kernan, M.C., & Lord, R.G. (1990). Effects of valence, expectancies, and goal-performance discrepancies in single and multiple goal environments. *Journal of Applied Psychology, 75,* 194–203.

Kerr, S., & Jermier, J.M. (1978). Substitutes for leadership: Their meaning and measurement. *Organizational Behavior and Human Performance, 22,* 375–403.

Kerr, S., & Schriesheim, S. (1974). Consideration, initiating structure, and organizational criteria: An update of Korman's 1966 review. *Personnel Psychology, 27,* 555–568.

Keys, B., & Wolfe, J. (1990). The role of management games and simulations in education and research. *Journal of Management, 16,* 307–336.

Kiesler, S., & Sproull, L. (1992). Group decision making and communication technology. *Organizational Behavior and Human Decision Processes, 52,* 96–123.

Kilman, R.H., Saxton, M.J., & Serpa, R. (Eds.). (1985). *Gaining control of the corporate culture*. San Francisco: Jossey-Bass.

Kim, J.S., & Campagna, A.T. (1981). Effects of flextime on employee attendance and performance: A field experiment. *Academy of Management Journal, 24*, 729–741.

King, W.C., Miles, E.W., & Day, D.D. (1993). A test and refinement of the equity sensitivity construct. *Journal of Organizational Behavior, 14*, 301–317.

Kipnis, D. (1976). *The powerholders*. Chicago: The University of Chicago Press.

Kipnis, D., Schmidt, S.M., & Wilkinson, I. (1980). Intraorganizational influence tactics: Explorations in getting one's way. *Journal of Applied Psychology, 65*, 440–452.

Kirkcaldy, B.D., & Cooper, C.L. (1993). The relationship between work stress and leisure style: British and German managers. *Human Relations, 46*, 669–675.

Kirchmeyer, C. (1990). A profile of managers active in office politics. *Basic and Applied Social Psychology, 11*, 339–356.

Kirk, R.J. (1981). *Interim report to the President and Congress: Alternative work schedules experimental program*. Washington, DC: Office of Personnel Management.

Kirkpatrick, D. (1976). Evaluating in-house training programs. *Training and Development Journal, 32*, 6–9.

Kirkpatrick, D.L. (1959–60). Techniques for evaluating training programs. *Journal of the American Society of Training Directors, 13*, 3–9, 21–26; *14*, 13–18, 28–32.

Kirkpatrick, S.A., & Locke, E.A. (1996). Direct and indirect effects of three core charismatic leadership components on performance and attitudes. *Journal of Applied Psychology, 81*, 36–51.

Kirmeyer, S.L., & Dougherty, T.W. (1988). Work load, tension, and coping: Moderating effects of supervisor support. *Personnel Psychology, 41*, 125–139.

Klein, K.J. (1987). Employee stock ownership and employee attitudes: A test of three models. *Journal of Applied Psychology, 72*, 319–332.

Klein, H.J., & Kim, J.S. (1998). A field study of the influence of situational constraints, leader-member exchange, and goal commitment on performance. *Academy of Management Journal, 41*, 88–95.

Klein, H.J., & Mulvey, P.W. (1995). Two investigations of the relationships among group goals, goal commitment, cohesion, and performance. *Organizational Behavior and Human Decision Processes, 61*, 44–53.

Klein, K.J., & House, R.J. (1995). On fire: Charismatic leadership and levels of analysis. *Leadership Quarterly, 6*, 183–198.

Kleinmann, M. (1993). Are rating dimensions in assessment centers transparent for participants? Consequences for criterion and construct validity. *Journal of Applied Psychology, 78*, 988–993.

Klimoski, R., & Brickner, M. (1987). Why do assessment centers work? The puzzle of assessment center validity. *Personnel Psychology, 40*, 243–260.

Klimoski, R.J., & Strickland, W.J. (1977). Assessment centers—Valid or merely prescient? *Personnel Psychology, 30*, 353–361.

Kluger, A.N., & DeNisi, A. (1996). The effects of feedback interventions on performance: A historical review, a meta-analysis, and a preliminary feedback intervention theory. *Psychological Bulletin, 119*, 254–284.

Knight, G.P., & Dubro, A.F. (1984). Cooperative, competitive, and individualistic social values: An individualized regression and clustering approach. *Journal of Personality and Social Psychology, 46*, 98–105.

Knouse, S.B. (1994). Impressions of the resume: The effects of applicant education, experience, and impression management. *Journal of Business and Psychology, 9*, 33–45.

Knowlton, W.A., & Mitchell, T.R. (1980). Effects of causal attributions on a supervisor's evaluation of subordinate performance. *Journal of Applied Psychology, 65*, 459–466.

Kobasa, S.C. (1982). The hardy personality: Toward a social psychology of stress and health. In J. Suls & G. Sanders (Eds.), *The social psychology of health and illness* (pp. 3–32). Hillsdale, NJ: Lawrence Erlbaum.

Kobrick, J.L., & Fine, B.J. (1983). Climate and human performance. In D.J. Oborne & M.M. Gruneberg (Eds.), *The physical environment at work* (pp. 69–107). Chichester, England: John Wiley & Sons.

Koehler, J.W., Anatol, K.W.E., & Applbaum, R.L. (1981). *Organizational communication: Behavioral perspectives* (2nd ed.). New York: Holt, Rinehart and Winston.

Kogi, K. (1996). Improving shift workers' health and tolerance to shiftwork: Recent advances. *Applied Ergonomics, 27*, 5–8.

Kolodny, H.F. (1979). Evolution to a matrix organization. *Academy of Management Review, 4*, 543–553.

Komaki, J.L. (1986). Toward effective supervision: An operant analysis and comparison of managers at work. *Journal of Applied Psychology, 71*, 270–279.

Komaki, J.L., Barwick, K.D., & Scott, L.R. (1978). A behavioral approach to occupational safety: Pinpointing and reinforcing safe performance in a food manufacturing plant. *Journal of Applied Psychology, 63*, 434–445.

Komaki, J.L., Coombs, T., & Schepman, S. (1991). Motivational implications of reinforcement theory. In R.M. Steers & L.W. Porter (Eds.), *Motivation and work behavior* (5th ed., pp. 87–107). New York: McGraw-Hill.

Komaki, J.L., Desselles, M.L., & Bowman, E.D. (1989). Definitely not a breeze: Extending an operant model of effective supervision to teams. *Journal of Applied Psychology, 74*, 522–529.

Kondrasuk, J.N. (1981). Studies in MBO effectiveness. *Academy of Management Review, 6*, 419–430.

Koppes, L.L. (1991). I/O psychology master's-level training: Reality and legitimacy in search of recognition. *The Industrial-Organizational Psychologist, 29*, 59–67.

Korunka, C., Weiss, A., & Karetta, B. (1993). Effects of new technologies with special regard for the implementation process per se. *Journal of Organizational Behavior, 14*, 331–348.

Koslowsky, M. (1991). A longitudinal analysis of job satisfaction, commitment, and intention to leave. *Applied Psychology: An International Review, 40*, 405–415.

Kossek, E.E., & Nichol, V. (1992). The effects of on-site child care on employee attitudes and performance. *Personnel Psychology, 45*, 485–509.

Kossek, E.E., & Zonia, S.C. (1993). Assessing diversity climate: A field study of reactions to employer efforts to promote diversity. *Journal of Organizational Behavior, 14*, 61–81.

Kottke, J.L., & Shultz, K.S. (1997). Using an assessment center as a developmental tool for graduate students: A demonstration. In R.E. Riggio & B.T. Mayes (Eds.), *Assessment centers: Research and applications* (pp. 289–302). Corte Madera, CA: Select Press.

Kozlowski, S.W., & Doherty, M.L. (1989). Integration of climate and leadership: Examination of a neglected issue. *Journal of Applied Psychology, 74*, 546–553.

Kozlowski, S.W.J., & Salas, E. (1997). An organizational systems approach for the implementation and transfer of training. In J.K. Ford (Ed.), *Improving training effectiveness in work organizations* (pp. 247–287). Hillsdale, NJ: Lawrence Erlbaum.

Krackhardt, D. (1990). Assessing the political landscape: Structure, cognition, and power in organizations. *Administrative Science Quarterly, 35*, 342–369.

Krackhardt, D., & Porter, L.W. (1986). The snowball effect: Turnover embedded in communication networks. *Journal of Applied Psychology, 71*, 50–55.

Kraiger, K. (1991). Vantage 2000: Issues in training and opportunity for involvement. *The Industrial-Organizational Psychologist, 28*, 79–81.

Kraiger, K., & Ford, J.K. (1985). A meta-analysis of rat race effects in performance ratings. *Journal of Applied Psychology, 70*, 56–65.

Kraiger, K., Ford, J.K., & Salas, E. (1993). Application of cognitive, skill-based and affective theories of learning outcomes to new methods of training evaluation. *Journal of Applied Phychology, 78*, 311–328.

Kraiger, K., & Jung, K.M. (1997). Linking training objectives to evaluation criteria. In M.A. Quinones & A. Ehrenstein (Eds.), *Training for a rapidly changing workplace: Applications of psychological research* (pp. 151–175). Washington, DC: American Psychological Association.

Krakowski, A.J. (1982). Stress and the practice of medicine II—stressors, stresses & strains. *Psychotherapeutics and Psychosomatics, 38*, 11–23.

Kram, K.E., & Hall, D.T. (1989). Mentoring as an antidote to stress during corporate trauma. *Human Resource Management, 28*, 493–510.

Kramer, M.W. (1995). A longitudinal study of superior-subordinate communication during job transfers. *Human Communication Research, 22*, 39–64.

Krau, E. (1981). Turnover analysis and prediction from a career developmental point of view. *Personnel Psychology, 34*, 771–790.

Kraut, R.E. (1980). Humans as lie detectors: Some second thoughts. *Journal of Communication, 30*, 209–216.

Kraut, R.E., Lewis, H.L., & Swezey, L.W. (1982). Listener responsiveness and the coordination of conversation. *Journal of Personality and Social Psychology, 43*, 781–831.

Kravitz, D.A., & Balzer, W.K. (1992). Context effects in performance appraisal: A methodological critique and empirical study. *Journal of Applied Psychology, 77*, 24–31.

Kravitz, R.L., Linn, L.S., & Shapiro, M.F. (1990). Physician satisfaction under the Ontario health insurance plan. *Medical Care, 28*, 502–512.

Kristoff, A.L. (1996). Person-organization fit: An integrative review of its conceptualizations, measurement, and implications. *Personnel Psychology, 49*, 1–49.

Kroemer, K.H.E. (1983). Engineering anthropometry: Work space and equipment to fit the user. In D.J. Oborne & M.M. Gruneberg (Eds.), *The physical environment at work* (pp. 39–68). Chichester, England: John Wiley & Sons.

Kumar, K., & Beyerlein, M. (1991). Construction and validation of an instrument for measuring ingratiatory behaviors in organizational settings. *Journal of Applied Psychology, 76*, 619–627.

Kumara, U.A., & Koichi, F. (1989). Employee satisfaction and job climate: An empirical study of Japanese manufacturing employees. *Journal of Business and Psychology, 3*, 315–329.

Kume, T. (1985). Managerial attitudes toward decision-making: North American and Japan. In W.B. Gudykunst,

L.P. Stewart, & S. Ting-Toomey (Eds.), *Communication, culture, and organizational processes* (pp. 231–251). Beverly Hills, CA: Sage.

Labianca, G., Brass, D.J., & Gray, B. (1998). Social networks and perceptions of intergroup conflict: The role of negative relationships and third parties. *Academy of Management Journal, 41,* 55–67.

Lamm, H. (1988). Review of our research on group polarization: Eleven experiments on the effects of group discussion on risk acceptance, probability estimation, and negotiations positions. *Psychological Reports, 62,* 807–813.

Lance, C.E., LaPointe, J.A., & Fisicaro, S.A. (1994). Tests of three causal models of halo rater error. *Organizational Behavior and Human Decision Processes, 57,* 83–96.

Landy, F.J. (1985). *Psychology of work behavior* (3rd ed.). Homewood, IL: Dorsey Press.

Landy, F.J. (1989). *Psychology of work behavior* (4th ed.). Pacific Grove, CA: Brooks/Cole.

Landy, F.J. (1993). Job analysis and job evaluation: The respondent's perspective. In H. Schuler, J.L. Farr, & M. Smith (Eds.), *Personnel selection and assessment: Individual and organizational perspectives.* Hillsdale, NJ: Lawrence Erlbaum.

Landy, F.J., & Sigall, H. (1974). Beauty is talent: Task evaluation as a function of the performer's physical attractiveness. *Journal of Personality and Social Psychology, 29,* 299–304.

Langfred, C.W. (1998). Is group cohesiveness a double-edged sword? An investigation of the effects of cohesiveness on performance. *Small Group Research, 29,* 124–143.

Larson, E.W., & Gobeli, D.H. (1987). Matrix management: Contradictions and insights. *California Management Review, 29,* 126–138.

Larwood, L., & Wood, M.M. (1977). *Women in management.* Lexington, MA: Lexington Books.

Larwood, L., Wright, T.A., Desrochers, S., & Dahir, V. (1998). Extending latent role and psychological contract theories to predict intent to turnover and politics in business organizations. *Group & Organization Management, 23,* 100–123.

Latack, J.C., & Foster, L.W. (1985). Implementation of compressed work schedules: Participation and job redesign as critical factors for employee acceptance. *Personnel Psychology, 38,* 75–92.

Latane, B., & Darley, J. (1970). *The unresponsive bystander: Why doesn't he help?* New York: Appleton-Century-Crofts.

Latane, B., Williams, K., & Harkins, S. (1979). Many hands make light the work: The causes and consequences of social loafing. *Journal of Personality and Social Psychology, 37,* 822–832.

Latham, G.P. (1988). Human resource training and development. *Annual Review of Psychology, 39,* 545–582.

Latham, G.P. (1989). The reliability, validity, and practicality of the situational interview. In R.W. Eder & G.R. Ferris (Eds.), *The employment interview: Theory, research, and practice* (pp. 169–182). Newbury Park, CA: Sage.

Latham, G.P., & Saari, L.M. (1979). Application of social-learning theory to training supervisors through behavioral modeling. *Journal of Applied Psychology, 64,* 239–246.

Latham, G.P., & Saari, L.M. (1982). The importance of union acceptance for productivity improvement through goal setting. *Personnel Psychology, 35,* 781–787.

Latham, G.P., & Saari, L.M. (1984). Do people do what they say? Further studies on the situational interview. *Journal of Applied Psychology, 69,* 569–573.

Latham, G.P., Saari, L.M., Pursell, E.D., & Campion, M.A. (1980). The situational interview. *Journal of Applied Psychology, 65,* 422–427.

Latham, G.P., & Wexley, K.N. (1977). Behavioral observation scales for performance appraisal purposes. *Personnel Psychology, 30,* 225–268.

Lau, D.C., & Murnighan, J.K. (1998). Demographic diversity and faultlines: The compositional dynamics of organizational groups. *Academy of Management Review, 23,* 325–340.

Lawler, E.E. (1971). *Pay and organizational effectiveness.* New York: McGraw-Hill.

Lawler, E.E. (1982). Strategies for improving the quality of work life. *American Psychologist, 37,* 486–493.

Lawler, E.E. (1986). *High-involvement management: Participative strategies for improving organizational performance.* San Francisco: Jossey-Bass.

Lawler, E.E. (1987). Paying for performance: Future directions. In D.B. Balkin & L.R. Gomez-Mejia (Eds.), *New perspectives on compensation* (pp. 162–168). Englewood Cliffs, NJ: Prentice-Hall.

Lawler, E.E. (1994). *Motivation in work organizations.* San Francisco: Jossey-Bass.

Lawler, E.E., Mohrman, S.A., & Ledford, G.E. (1992). *Employee involvement and total quality management.* San Francisco: Jossey-Bass.

Lawrence, D.G., Salsburg, B.L., Dawson, J.G., & Fasman, Z.D. (1982). Design and use of weighted application blanks. *Personnel Administrator, 27,* 47–53.

Lawrence, P.R., & Lorsch, J. (1967). *Organization and environment.* Cambridge, MA: Harvard University Press.

Lazarus, R.S. (1991). Psychological stress in the workplace. *Journal of Social Behavior and Personality, 6,* 1–13.

Lazarus, R.S., & Folkman, S. (1984). *Stress, appraisal and coping*. New York: Springer.

Lazarus, R.S., & Launier, R. (1978). Stress-related transactions between person and environment. In L.A. Pervin & M. Lewis (Eds.), *Perspectives in interactional psychology* (pp. 287–327). New York: Plenum.

Leamon, T.B., & Murphy, P.L. (1995). Occupational slips and falls: More than a trivial problem. *Ergonomics, 38,* 487–498.

Leavitt, H.J. (1951). Some effects of certain communication patterns on group performance. *Journal of Abnormal and Social Psychology, 46,* 38–50.

Ledford, G.E., Lawler, E.E., & Mohrman, S.A. (1988). The quality circle and its variations. In J.P. Campbell & R.J. Campbell (Eds.), *Productivity in organizations* (pp. 255–294). San Francisco: Jossey-Bass.

Lee, C., Earley, P.C., & Hanson, L.A. (1988). Are type As better performers? *Journal of Organizational Behavior, 9,* 263–269.

Lee, F. (1993). Being polite and keeping MUM: How bad news is communicated in organizational hierarachies. *Journal of Applied Social Psychology, 23,* 1124–1149.

Lee, R.T., & Ashforth, B.E. (1990). On the meaning of Maslach's three dimensions of burnout. *Journal of Applied Psychology, 75,* 743–747.

Lee, T.W. (1989). The antecedents and prediction of employee attendance. *Journal of Business Issues, 17,* 17–22.

Lee, T.W., Ashford, S.J., Walsh, J.P., & Mowday, R.T. (1992). Commitment propensity, organizational commitment, and voluntary turnover: A longitudinal study of organizational entry processes. *Journal of Management, 18,* 15–32.

Lee, T.W., & Maurer, S.D. (1997). The retention of knowledge workers with the unfolding model of voluntary turnover. *Human Resource Management Review, 7,* 247–275.

Lee, T.W., & Mitchell, T.R. (1994). An alternative approach: The unfolding model of voluntary employee turnover. *Academy of Management Review, 19,* 51–89.

Leibowitz, Z.B., Farren, C., & Kaye, B.L. (1986). *Designing career development systems*. San Francisco: Jossey-Bass.

Leister, A., Borden, D., & Fiedler, F.E. (1977). Validation of contingency model leadership training: Leader Match. *Academy of Management Journal, 20,* 464–470.

Leiter, M.P., & Harvie, P. (1998). Conditions for staff acceptance of organizational change: Burnout as a mediating construct. *Anxiety, Stress, and Coping, 11,* 1–25.

Leiter, M.P., & Maslach, C. (1988). The impact of interpersonal environment on burnout and organizational commitment. *Journal of Organizational Behavior, 9,* 297–308.

Leiter, M.P., & Schaufeli, W.B. (1996). Consistency of the burnout construct across occupations. *Anxiety, Stress, and Coping, 9,* 229–243.

Lengnick-Hall, M.L. (1995). Sexual harassment research: A methodological critique. *Personnel Psychology, 48,* 841–864.

Lester, T. (1993). A woman's place . . . *Management Today, 25,* 46–50.

Levi, L., Frankenhaeuser, M., & Gardell, B. (1986). The characteristics of the workplace and the nature of its social demands. In S.G. Wolf & A.J. Finestone (Eds.), *Occupational stress: Health and performance at work* (pp. 54–67). Littleton, MA: PSG Publishing.

Levine, E.L., Ash, R.A., & Bennet, N. (1980). Exploratory comparative study of four job analysis methods. *Journal of Applied Psychology, 65,* 524–535.

Levine, E.L., Ash, R.A., Hall, H., & Sistrunk, F. (1983). Evaluation of job analysis methods by experienced job analysts. *Academy of Management Journal, 26,* 339–347.

Levinson, H. (1994). Why the behemoths fell: Psychological roots of corporate failure. *American Psychologist, 49,* 428–436.

Lewin, K. (1935). *Dynamic theory of personality*. New York: McGraw-Hill.

Lewis, P.V. (1987). *Organizational communication: The essence of effective management* (3rd ed.). New York: John Wiley & Sons.

Liden, R.C., & Maslyn, J.M. (1998). Multidimensionality of leader-member exchange: An empirical assessment through scale development. *Journal of Management, 24,* 43–72.

Liden, R.C., Wayne, S.J., & Stilwell, D. (1993). A longitudinal study on the early development of leader-member exchanges. *Journal of Applied Psychology, 78,* 662–674.

Liebowitz, S.J., & de Meuse, K.P. (1982). The application of team building. *Human Relations, 16,* 1–18.

Likert, R. (1961). *New patterns of management*. New York: McGraw-Hill.

Likert, R. (1967). *The human organization*. New York: McGraw-Hill.

Lim, V.K.G. (1996). Job insecurity and its outcomes: Moderating effects of work-based and nonwork-based social support. *Human Relations, 49,* 171–194.

Limaye, M.R., & Victor, D.A. (1991). Cross-cultural business communication reasearch: State of the art and hypotheses for the 1990s. *The Journal of Business Communication, 28,* 277–299.

Linton, S.J., Hellsing, A., Halme, T., & Akerstedt, K. (1994). The effects of ergonomically designed school furniture on pupils' attitudes, symptoms, and behaviour. *Applied Ergonomics, 25,* 299–304.

Lissy, W.E. (1993). U.S. female executives see improvements in pay and job status but say they still hit a glass ceiling. *Compensation and Benefits Review, 25*, 9–10.

Locke, E.A. (1968). Toward a theory of task motivation and incentives. *Organizational Behavior and Human Performance, 3*, 157–189.

Locke, E.A. (1976). The nature and causes of job satisfaction. In M.D. Dunnette (Ed.), *Handbook of industrial and organizational psychology* (pp. 1297–1350). Chicago: Rand-McNally.

Locke, E.A., & Latham, G.P. (1984). *Goal setting: A motivational technique that works.* Englewood Cliffs, NJ: Prentice-Hall.

Locke, E.A., & Latham, G.P. (1990a). *A theory of goal setting and task performance.* Englewood Cliffs, NJ: Prentice-Hall.

Locke, E.A., & Latham, G.P. (1990b). Work motivation and satisfaction: Light at the end of the tunnel. *Psychological Science, 1*, 240–246.

Locke, E.A., Latham, G.P., & Erez, M. (1988). The determinants of goal commitment. *Academy of Management Review, 13*, 23–39.

Locke, E.A., & Schweiger, D.M. (1978). Participation in decision making: One more look. In B.M. Staw (Ed.), *Research in organizational behavior* (pp. 265–340). Greenwich, CT: JAI Press.

Locke, E.A., Shaw, K.N., Saari, L.M., & Latham, G.P. (1981). Goal setting and task performance: 1969–1980. *Psychological Bulletin, 90*, 125–152.

Loden, M., & Rosener, J.B. (1991). *Workforce America! Managing employee diversity as a vital resource.* Homewood, IL: Business One Irwin.

Loeb, M. (1986). *Noise and human efficiency.* Chichester, England: John Wiley & Sons.

Loher, B.T., Noe, R.A., Moeller, N.L., & Fitzgerald, M.P. (1985). A meta-analysis of the relation of job characteristics to job satisfaction. *Journal of Applied Psychology, 70*, 280–289.

London, M. (1993). Relationships between career motivation, empowerment, and support for career development. *Journal of Occupational and Organizational Psychology, 66*, 55–69.

London, M., & Bassman, E. (1989). Retraining midcareer workers for the future workplace. In I.L. Goldstein (Ed.), *Training and development in organizations.* San Francisco: Jossey-Bass.

London, M., & Beatty, R.W. (1993). 360-degree feedback as a competitive advantage. *Human Resource Management, 32*, 353–372.

London, M., & Moses, J.L. (1990). The changing roles of the industrial/organizational psychologist: From analyst/technician to change agent/strategist. *The Industrial-Organizational Psychologist, 27*, 17–26.

London, M., & Smither, J.W. (1995). Can multi-source feedback change perceptions of goal accomplishment, self-evaluations, and performance-related outcomes? Theory-based applications and directions for research. *Personnel Psychology, 48*, 803–839.

Loo, R. (1994). The evaluation of stress management services by Canadian organizations. *Journal of Business and Psychology, 9*, 129–136.

Lord, R.G., DeVader, C.L., & Alliger, G.M. (1986). A meta-analysis of the relation between personality traits and leadership perceptions: An application of validity generalization procedures. *Journal of Applied Psychology, 71*, 402–410.

Louis, M.R., Posner, B.Z., & Powell, G.N. (1983). The availability and helpfulness of socialization practices. *Personnel Psychology, 36*, 857–866.

Lounsbury, J.W., & Hoopes, L.L. (1986). A vacation from work: Changes in work and nonwork outcomes. *Journal of Applied Psychology, 71*, 392–401.

Lowe, K.B., Kroeck, K.G., & Sivasubramaniam, N. (1996). Effectiveness correlates of transformational and transactional leadership: A meta-analytic review of the *MLQ* literature. *Leadership Quarterly, 7*, 385–425.

Lowe, R.H., & Wittig, M.A. (Eds.), (1989). Approaching pay equity through comparable worth. *Journal of Social Issues, 45* (Whole issue #4).

Lowry, S.M., Maynard, H.B., & Stegemerten, G.J. (Eds.). (1940). *Time and motion study and formulas for wage incentives* (3rd ed.). New York: McGraw-Hill.

Ludwig, T.D., & Geller, E.S. (1997) Assigned versus participative goal setting and response generalization: Managing injury control among professional pizza deliverers. *Journal of Applied Psychology, 82*, 253–261.

Lynch, B.P. (1974). An empirical assessment of Perrow's technology construct. *Administrative Science Quarterly, 19*, 338–356.

Macan, T.H., & Dipboye, R.L. (1994). The effects of the application on processing of information from the employment interview. *Journal of Applied Social Psychology, 24*, 1291–1314.

Machlowitz, M.M. (1976, October 3). Working the 100-hour week—and loving it. *The New York Times.*

Madison, D.L., Allen, R.W., Porter, L.W., Renwick, P.A., & Mayes, B.T. (1980). Organizational politics: An exploration of managers' perceptions. *Human Relations, 33*, 79–100.

Mael, F.A. (1991). A conceptual rationale for the domain and attributes of biodata items. *Personnel Psychology, 44*, 763–792.

Major, D.A., Kozlowski, S.W.J., Chao, G.T., & Gardner, P.D. (1995). A longitudinal investigation of newcomer expectations, early socialization outcomes, and the moderating effects of role development factors. *Journal of Applied Psychology, 80*, 418–431.

Makiney, J.D., & Levy, P.E. (1997, April). Supervisor's use of self- and peer ratings for appraisal decisions. Paper presented at the 12th annual conference of the Society for Industrial and Organizational Psychology, St. Louis, MO.

Malchaire, J. (1995). Methodology of investigation of hot working conditions in the field. *Ergonomics, 38*, 73–85.

Mann, R.B., & Decker, P.J. (1984). The effect of key behavior distinctiveness on generalization and recall in behavior modeling training. *Academy of Management Journal, 27*, 900–909.

Manz, C.C. (1986). Self-leadership: Toward an expanded theory of self-influence processes in organizations. *Academy of Management Review, 11*, 585–600.

Manz, C.C., & Sims, H.P. (1980). Self-management as a substitute for leadership: A social learning perspective. *Academy of Management Review, 5*, 361–367.

Marcoulides, G.A., Mills, R.B., & Unterbrink, H. (1993). Improving preemployment screening: Drug testing in the workplace. *Journal of Management Issues, 5*, 290–300.

Margerison, C., & Glube, R. (1979). Leadership decision-making: An empirical test of the Vroom and Yetton model. *Journal of Management Studies, 16*, 45–55.

Markham, S.E., & McKee, G.H. (1995). Group absence behavior and standards: A multilevel analysis. *Academy of Management Journal, 38*, 1174–1190.

Marks, M.L. (1986). The question of quality circles. *Psychology Today, 20*, 36–46.

Marks, M.L., & Mirvis, P.H. (1998). *Joining forces: Making one plus one equal three in mergers, acquisitions, and alliances.* San Francisco: Jossey-Bass.

Marks, M.L., Mirvis, P.H., Hackett, E.J., & Grady, J.F. (1986). Employee participation in a quality circle program: Impact on quality of work life, productivity, and absenteeism. *Journal of Applied Psychology, 71*, 61–69.

Markus, M.L. (1994). Electronic mail as the medium of managerial choice. *Organization Science, 5*, 502–527.

Marlowe, H.A. (1986). Social intelligence: Evidence for multidimensionality and construct independence. *Journal of Educational Psychology, 78*, 52–58.

Martin, G.E., & Bergmann, T.J. (1996). The dynamics of behavioural response to conflict in the workplace. *Journal of Occupational and Organizational Psychology, 69*, 377–387.

Martin, J.E., & Peterson, M.M. (1987). Two-tier wage structures: Implications for equity theory. *Academy of Management Journal, 30*, 297–315.

Martin, T.N., & Schermerhorn, J.R. (1983). Work and non-work influences on health: A research agenda using inability to leave as a critical variable. *Academy of Management Review, 8*, 650–659.

Martocchio, J.J. (1993). Employee decisions to enroll in microcomputer training. *Human Resource Development Quarterly, 4*, 51–70.

Martocchio, J.J., & Webster, J. (1992). Effects of feedback and cognitive playfulness on performance in microcomputer software training. *Personnel Psychology, 45*, 553–578.

Marx, R.D. (1982). Relapse prevention for managerial training: A model for maintenance of behavior change. *Academy of Management Review, 7*, 433–441.

Maslach, C. (1982). *Burnout: The cost of caring.* Englewood Cliffs, NJ: Prentice-Hall.

Maslach, C., & Jackson, S.E. (1986). *MBI: Maslach Burnout Inventory.* Palo Alto, CA: Consulting Psychologists Press.

Maslow, A.H. (1965). *Eupsychian management.* Homewood, IL: Richard D. Irwin.

Maslow, A.H. (1970). *Motivation and personality* (2nd ed.). New York: Harper & Row.

Mason, J.C. (1993). Knocking on the glass ceiling. *Management Review, 82*, 5.

Mathieu, J.E., Hofmann, D.A., & Farr, J.L. (1993). Job perception-job satisfaction relations: An empirical comparison of three competing theories. *Organizational Behavior and Human Decision Processes, 56*, 370–387.

Mathieu, J.E., Martineau, J.W., & Tannenbaum, S.I. (1993). Individual and situational influences on the development of self-efficacy: Implications for training effectiveness. *Personnel Psychology, 46*, 125–147.

Mathis, R.L., & Jackson, J.H. (1985). *Personnel: Contemporary perspectives and applications.* St. Paul, MN: West.

Matsui, T., Kagawa, M., Nagamatsu, J., & Ohtsuka, Y. (1977). Validity of expectancy theory as a within-person behavioral choice model for sales activity. *Journal of Applied Psychology, 62*, 764–767.

Matteson, M.T., & Ivancevich, J.M. (1987). *Controlling work stress: Effective human resource and management strategies.* San Francisco: Jossey-Bass.

Mattila, M. (1996). Computer-aided ergonomics and safety: A challenge for integrated ergonomics. *International Journal of Industrial Ergonomics, 17*, 309–314.

Maurer, S.D., & Faye, C. (1988). Effect of situational interviews, conventional structured interviews, and training on interview rating agreement: An experimental analysis. *Personnel Psychology, 41*, 329–344.

Maurer, S.D., Howe, V., & Lee, T.W. (1992). Organizational recruiting as marketing management: An interdisciplinary study of engineering graduates. *Personnel Psychology, 45,* 807–833.

Mawhinney, T.C. (1992). Total quality management and organizational behavior management: An integration for continual improvement. *Journal of Applied Behavior analysis, 25,* 525–543.

May, K. (1998). Work in the 21st century: Recruiting in a tight labor market. *The Industrial-Organizational Psychologist, 36,* 39–41.

Mayes, B.T. (1995). Power and organizational politics. In McGraw-Hill's *Virtual organizational behavior.* New York: McGraw-Hill.

Mayes, B.T., & Allen, R.W. (1977). Toward a definition of organizational politics. *Academy of Management Review, 2,* 672–678.

Mayes, B.T., & Ganster, D.C. (1988). Exit and voice: A test of hypotheses based on fight/flight responses to job stress. *Journal of Organizational Behavior, 9,* 199–216.

Mayo, E. (1933). *The human problems of an industrial civilization.* Cambridge: Harvard University Press.

Maznevski, M., & Peterson, M.F. (1997). Societal values, social interpretation, and multinational teams. In C.S. Granrose & S. Oskamp (Eds.), *Cross-cultural work groups* (pp. 61–89). Thousand Oaks, CA: Sage.

McClelland, D.C. (1961). *The achieving society.* New York: Van Nostrand.

McClelland, D.C. (1970). The two faces of power. *Journal of International Affairs, 24,* 29–47.

McClelland, D.C. (1975). *Power: The inner experience.* New York: Irvington Press.

McClelland, D.C. (1980). Motive dispositions: The merits of operant and respondent measures. In L. Wheeler (Ed.), *Review of personality and social psychology* (Vol. 1, pp. 10–41). Beverly Hills, CA: Sage Press.

McClelland, D.C., Atkinson, J.W., Clark, R.A., & Lowell, E.L. (1953). *The achievement motive.* New York: Appleton-Century-Crofts.

McClelland, D.C., & Boyatzis, R.E. (1982). Leadership motive pattern and long term success in management. *Journal of Applied Psychology, 67,* 737–743.

McClelland, D.C., & Burnham, D.H. (1976). Power is the great motivator. *Harvard Business Review, 54,* 100–111.

McClelland, D.C., & Franz, C.E. (1993). Motivational and other sources of work accomplishments at midlife: A longitudinal study. *Journal of Personality, 60,* 679–707.

McClintock, C.G., Messick, D.M., Kuhlman, D.M., & Campos, F.T. (1973). Motivational bases of choice in three-choice decomposed games. *Journal of Experimental Social Psychology, 9,* 572–590.

McConkie, M.L. (1979). A clarification of the goal setting and appraisal processes in MBO. *Academy of Management Review, 4,* 29–40.

McCormick, E.J. (1979). *Job analysis: Methods and applications.* New York: AMACOM.

McCormick, E.J., Jeanneret, P.R., & Mecham, R.C. (1969). *Position analysis questionnaire.* West Lafayette, IN: Occupational Research Center, Purdue University.

McCormick, E.J., & Cooper, C.L. (1988). Executive stress: Extending the international comparison. *Human Relations, 41,* 65–72.

McEvoy, G.M., & Buller, P.F. (1987). User acceptance of peer appraisals in an industrial setting. *Personnel Psychology, 40,* 785–797.

McEvoy, G.M., & Cascio, W.F. (1985). Strategies for reducing employee turnover: A meta-analysis. *Journal of Applied Psychology, 70,* 342–353.

McGeehee, W., & Thayer, P.W. (1961). *Training in business and industry.* New York: Wiley.

McGill, M.E., & Slocum, J.W. (1993). Unlearning the organization. *Organizational Dynamics, 22,* 67–79.

McIntyre, R.M., Smith, D.E., & Hassett, C.E. (1984). Accuracy of performance ratings as affected by rater training and perceived purpose of rating. *Journal of Applied Psychology, 69,* 147–156.

McKenna, F. (1983). Accident proneness: A conceptual analysis. *Accident Analysis and Prevention, 15,* 65–71.

Mead, A.D., & Drasgow, F. (1993). Equivalence of computerized and paper-and-pencil cognitive ability tests: A meta-analysis. *Psychological Bulletin, 114,* 449–458.

Mechanic, D. (1962). Sources of power of lower participants in complex organizations. *Administrative Science Quarterly, 7,* 349–364.

Medcof, J.W., & Hausdorf, P.A. (1995). Instruments to measure opportunities to satisfy needs, and degree of satisfaction with needs, in the workplace. *Journal of Occupational and Organizational Psychology, 68,* 193–208.

Meehl, P. (1954). *Clinical vs. statistical prediction.* Minneapolis: University of Minnesota Press.

Megargee, E.I., & Carbonell, J.L. (1988). Evaluating leadership with the CPI. In C. Spielberger & J.N. Butcher (Eds.), *Advances in personality assessment* (Vol. 7, pp. 121–139). Hillsdale, NJ: Lawrence Erlbaum.

Meglino, B.M., DeNisi, A.S., & Ravlin, E.C. (1993). Effects of previous job exposure and subsequent job status on the functioning of a realistic job preview. *Personnel Psychology, 46,* 803–822.

Mehrabian, A. (1981). *Silent messages* (2nd ed.). Belmont, CA: Wadsworth.

Meindl, J.R. (1990). On leadership: An alternative to the conventional wisdom. *Research in Organizational Behavior, 12,* 159–203.

Melamed, S., Ben-Avi, I., Luz, J., & Green, M.S. (1995). Objective and subjective work monotony: Effects on job satisfaction, psychological distress, and absenteeism in blue-collar workers. *Journal of Applied Psychology, 80,* 29–42.

Mento, A.J., Locke, E.A., & Klein, H.J. (1992). Relationship of goal level to valence and instrumentality. *Journal of Applied Psychology, 77,* 395–405.

Mento, A.J., Steele, R.P., & Karren, R.J. (1987). A meta-analytic study of the effects of goal-setting on task performance: 1966–1984. *Organizational Behavior and Human Decision Processes, 39,* 52–83.

Merwin, G.A., Thomason, J.A., & Sanford, E.E. (1989). Methodology and content review of organizational behavior management in the private sector: 1978–1986. *Journal of Organizational Behavior Management, 10,* 39–57.

Meyer, H.H., & Raich, M.S. (1983). An objective evaluation of a behavior modeling training program. *Personnel Psychology, 36,* 755–761.

Meyer, J.P., & Rapp, R. (1995). Survey of heat stress in industry. *Ergonomics, 38,* 36–46.

Miceli, M.P. (1993). Justice and pay system satisfaction. In R. Croponzano (Ed.), *Justice in the workplace: Approaching fairness in HRM* (pp. 257–283). Hillsdale, NJ: Lawrence Erlbaum.

Michael, P.L., & Bienvenue, G.R. (1983). Industrial noise and man. In D.J. Oborne & M.M. Gruneberg (Eds.), *The physical environment at work* (pp. 179–209). Chichester, England: John Wiley & Sons.

Michaelson, L.K., Watson, W.E., & Black, R.H. (1989). A realistic test of individual versus group consensus decision making. *Journal of Applied Psychology, 74,* 834–839.

Miles, E.W., Hatfield, J.D., & Huseman, R.C. (1989). The equity sensitivity construct: Potential implications for worker performance. *Journal of Management, 15,* 581–588.

Miles, R.H., & Randolph, W.A. (1985). *The organization game: A simulation: Participant's manual* (2nd ed.). Glenview, IL: Scott, Foresman.

Milkovich, G., & Gomez, L.R. (1976). Child care and selected work behaviors. *Academy of Management Journal, 19,* 111–115.

Milkovich, G.T., & Newman, J.M. (1987). *Compensation* (2nd ed.). Plano, TX: Business Publications.

Milliken, F.J., & Martins, L.L. (1996). Searching for the common threads: Understanding the multiple effects of diversity in organizational groups. *Academy of Management Review, 21,* 402–433.

Miner, F.C. (1984). Group versus individual decision making: An investigation of performance measures, decision strategies, and process losses/gains. *Organizational Behavior and Human Performance, 31,* 112–124.

Miner, J.B. (1983). The unpaved road from theory: Over the mountains to application. In R.H. Kilmann, K.W. Thomas, D.P. Slevin, R. Nath, & S.L. Jerrel (Eds.), *Producing useful knowledge for organizations* (pp. 37–68). New York: Praeger.

Miner, J.B. (1984). The unpaved road over the mountains: From theory to applications. *The Industrial-Organizational Psychologist, 21,* 9–20.

Mintzberg, H. (1973). *The nature of managerial work.* New York: Harper & Row.

Mintzberg, H. (1984). Power and organization life cycles. *Academy of Management Review, 9,* 207–224.

Mio, J.S., & Goishi, C.K. (1989). The employee assistance program: Raising productivity by lifting constraints. In P. Whitney & R.B. Ochman (Eds.), *Psychology and productivity.* New York: Plenum Press.

Miron, D., & McClelland, D.C. (1979). The impact of achievement motivation training on small businesses. *California Management Review, 21,* 13–28.

Mirvis, P.H., & Berg, D.N. (1977). *Failures in organization development and change: Cases and essays for learning.* New York: John Wiley & Sons.

Mishra, J. (1990). Managing the grapevine. *Public Personnel Management, 19,* 213–228.

Mitchell, T.R., Hopper, H., Daniels, D., Falvy, J.G., & Ferris, G.R. (1998). Power, accountability, and inappropriate actions. *Applied Psychology: An International Review, 47,* 497–517.

Mitchell, T.R., & Kalb, L.S. (1982). Effects of job experience on supervisor attributions for a subordinate's poor performance. *Journal of Applied Psychology, 67,* 181–188.

Mitra, A., Gupta, N., & Jenkins, G.D. (1997). A drop in the bucket: When is a pay raise a pay raise? *Journal of Organizational Behavior, 18,* 117–137.

Mitra, A., Jenkins, D., & Gupta, N. (1992). A meta-analytic review of the relationships between absenteeism and turnover. *Journal of Applied Psychology, 77,* 879–889.

Mobley, W.H. (1982). Some unanswered questions in turnover and withdrawal research. *Academy of Management Review, 7,* 111–116.

Mobley, W.H., Griffeth, R.W., Hand, H.H., & Meglino, B.M. (1979). Review and conceptual analysis of the employee turnover process. *Psychological Bulletin, 86,* 493–522.

Mohler, S.R. (1983). The human element in air traffic control: Aeromedical aspects, problems, and prescriptions. *Aviation, Space and Environmental Medicine, 54,* 511–516.

Mohrman, A.M., Resnick-West, S. M., & Lawer, E. E. (1989). *Designing performance appraisal systems.* San Francisco: Jossey-Bass.

Monge, P.R., Cozzens, M.D., & Contractor, N.S. (1992). Communication and motivational predictors of the dynamics of organizational innovation. *Organization Science, 3,* 250–274.

Monge, P.R., & Eisenberg, E.M. (1987). Emergent communication networks. In F. Jablin, L. Putnam, K. Roberts, & L. Porter (Eds.), *Handbook of organizational communication: An interdisciplinary approach.* Beverly Hills, CA: Sage.

Monk, T.H., Folkard, S., & Wedderburn, A.I. (1996). Maintaining safety and high performance on shiftwork. *Applied Ergonomics, 27,* 17–23.

Morehouse, W., & Subramaniam, M.A. (1986). *The Bhopal tragedy: What really happened and what it means for American workers and communities at risk.* New York: Council on International and Public Affairs.

Morgeson, F.P., & Campion, M.A. (1997). Social and cognitive sources of potential inaccuracy in job analysis. *Journal of Applied Psychology, 82,* 627–655.

Moriarty, S.E., & Scheiner, E.C. (1984). A study of close-set text type. *Journal of Applied Psychology, 69,* 700–702.

Morrisby, J.R. (1955). *Mechanical Ability Test.* London: Educational and Industrial Test Services.

Morrison, E.W. (1993). Longitudinal study of the effects of information seeking on newomer socialization. *Journal of Applied Psychology, 78,* 173–183.

Morrow, P.C., & McElroy, J.C. (1981). Interior office design and visitor response: A constructive replication. *Journal of Applied Psychology, 66,* 646–650.

Morse, N.C., & Reimer, E. (1956). The experimental change of a major organizational variable. *Journal of Abnormal and Social Psychology, 52,* 120–129.

Moscovici, S. (1985). Social influence and conformity. In G. Lindzey & E. Aronson (Eds.), *Handbook of social psychology* (3rd ed., pp. 347–412). New York: Random House.

Motowidlo, S.J., Carter, G.W., Dunnette, M.D., Tippins, N., Werner, S., Burnett, J.R., & Vaughan, M.J. (1992). Studies of the structured behavioral interview. *Journal of Applied Psychology, 77,* 571–587.

Motowidlo, S.J., Dunnette, M.D., & Carter, G.W. (1990). An alternative selection procedure: The low-fidelity simulation. *Journal of Applied Psychology, 75,* 640–647.

Motowidlo, S.J., Packard, J.S., & Manning, M.R. (1986). Occupational stress: Its causes and consequences for job performance. *Journal of Applied Psychology, 71,* 618–629.

Mount, M.K. (1984). Supervisor, self- and subordinate ratings of performance and satisfaction with supervision. *Journal of Management, 10,* 305–320.

Mowday, R.T. (1979). Equity theory predictions of behavior in organizations. In R.M. Steers & L.W. Porter (Eds.), *Motivation and work behavior* (2nd ed.). New York: McGraw-Hill.

Mowday, R.T., Koberg, C.S., & McArthur, A.W. (1984). The psychology of the withdrawal process: A cross-validational test of Mobley's intermediate linkages model of turnover in two samples. *Academy of Management Journal, 27,* 79–94.

Mowday, R.T., Steers, R., & Porter, L.W. (1979). The measurement of organizational commitment. *Journal of Vocational Behavior, 14,* 224–247.

Muchinsky, P.M. (1977a). A comparison of within- and across-subjects analyses of the expectancy-valence model for predicting effort. *Academy of Management Journal, 20,* 154–158.

Muchinsky, P.M. (1977b). Organizational communication: Relationships to organizational climate and job satisfaction. *Academy of Management Journal, 20,* 592–607.

Muchinsky, P.M. (1979). The use of reference reports in personnel selection: A review and evaluation. *Journal of Occupational Psychology, 52,* 287–297.

Muchinsky, P.M. (1987). *Psychology applied to work* (2nd ed.). Chicago: Dorsey.

Muchinsky, P.M. (1993). Validation of intelligence and mechanical aptitude tests in selecting employees for manufacturing jobs. *Journal of Business and Psychology, 7,* 373–382.

Mullins, W.C., & Kimbrough, W.W. (1988). Group composition as a determinant of job analysis outcomes. *Journal of Applied Psychology, 73,* 657–664.

Munchus, G. (1983). Employer-employee based quality circles in Japan: Human resource policy implications for American firms. *Academy of Management Review, 8,* 255–261.

Munsterberg, H. (1913). *Psychology and industrial efficiency.* Boston, MA: Houghton Mifflin.

Munz, D.C., & Kohler, J.M. (1997). Do worksite stress management programs attract the employees who need them and are they effective? *International Journal of Stress Management, 4,* 1–11.

Murphy, K. (1998). Trends facing work, work organizations, and I-O psychologists. *The Industrial-Organizational Psychologist, 35,* 95–97.

Murphy, K.R. (1993). *Honesty in the workplace.* Pacific Grove, CA: Brooks/Cole.

Murphy, K.R., & Balzar, W.K. (1986). Systematic distortions in memory-based behavior ratings and performance evaluations: Consequences for rating accuracy. *Journal of Applied Psychology, 71*, 39–44,

Murphy, K.R., Philbin, T.A., & Adams, S.R. (1989). Effect of purpose of observation on accuracy of immediate and delayed performance ratings. *Organizational Behavior and Human Decision Processes, 43*, 336–354.

Murray, B., & Gerhart, B. (1998). An empirical analysis of a skill-based pay program and plant performance outcomes. *Academy of Management Journal, 41*, 68–78.

Myers, D.G., & Lamm, H. (1976). The group polarization phenomenon. *Psychological Bulletin, 83*, 602–627.

Naisbett, J. (1982). *Megatrends: Ten new directions transforming our lives.* New York: Warner.

Narayanan, V.K., & Nath, R. (1982). A field test of some attitudinal and behavioral consequences of flextime. *Journal of Applied Psychology, 67*, 214–218.

Nathan, P.E. (1983). Failures in prevention: Why we can't prevent the devastating effect of alcoholism and drug abuse. *American Psychologist, 38*, 459–467.

National Safety Council (1991). *Accident facts.* Chicago: National Safety Council.

Near, J.P., Dworkin, T.M., & Miceli, M.P. (1993). Explaining the whistle-blowing process: Suggestions from power theory and justice theory. *Organization Science, 4*, 393–411.

Near, J.P., & Miceli, M.P. (1985). Organizational dissidence: The case of whistle-blowing. *Journal of Business Ethics, 4*, 1–16.

Near, J.P., & Miceli, M.P. (1995). Effective whistle-blowing. *Academy of Management Review, 20*, 679–708.

Nebeker, D.M., & Tatum, C. (1993). The effects of computer monitoring, standards, and rewards on work performance, job satisfaction, and stress. *Journal of Applied Social Psychology, 23*, 508–536.

Nelson, D.L. (1987). Organizational socialization: A stress perspective. *Journal of Occupational Behavior, 8*, 311–324.

Nemecek, J., & Grandjean, E. (1973). Results of an ergonomic investigation of large-space offices. *Human Factors, 15*, 111–124.

Neuman, G.A., Edwards, J.E., & Raju, N.S. (1989). Organizational development interventions: A meta-analysis of their effects on satisfaction and other attitudes. *Personnel Psychology, 42*, 461–489.

Nickerson, R.S. (1992). *Looking ahead: Human factors challenges in a changing world.* Hillsdale, NJ: Lawrence Erlbaum.

Nieva, V.F., & Gutek, B.A. (1981). *Women and work: A psychological perspective.* New York: Praeger.

Nisbett, R.D., & Wilson, T.D. (1977). The halo effect: Evidence for unconscious alteration of judgments. *Journal of Personality and Social Psychology, 35*, 250–256.

Noe, R.A. (1986). Trainees' attributes and attitudes: Neglected influences on training effectiveness. *Academy of Management Review, 11*, 736–749.

Noe, R.A. (1988). An investigation of the determinants of successful assigned mentoring relationships. *Personnel Psychology, 41*, 457–479.

Noe, R.A. (1996). Is career management related to employee development and performance? *Journal of Organizational Behavior, 17*, 119–133.

Norman, D.A. (1988). *The psychology of everyday things.* New York: Basic Books.

Normand, J., Salyards, S.D., & Mahoney, J.J. (1990). An evaluation of preemployment drug testing. *Journal of Applied Psychology, 75*, 629–639.

Nossiter, V. (1979). A new approach toward resolving the line and staff dilemma. *Academy of Management Review, 4*, 103–106.

Noyes, J., Haigh, R., & Starr, A. (1989). Automatic speed recognition for disabled people. *Applied Ergonomics, 20*, 293–298.

Oborne, D.J., & Gruneberg, M.M. (Eds.). (1983). *The physical environment at work.* Chichester, England: John Wiley & Sons.

O'Connor, F. (1977). *O'Connor Finger Dexterity Test.* Lafayette, IN: Lafayette Instruments.

Odiorne, G. (1963). The trouble with sensitivity training. *Training Directors Journal, 17*, 12–19.

O'Driscoll, M.P., & Beehr, T.A. (1994). Supervisor behaviors, role stressors and uncertainty as predictors of personal outcomes for subordinates. *Journal of Organizational Behavior, 15*, 141–155.

O'Driscoll, M.P., & Eubanks, J.L. (1993). Behavioral competencies, goal-setting, and OD practitioner effectiveness. *Group & Organization Management, 18*, 308–327.

O'Driscoll, M.P., Ilgen, D.R., & Hildreth, K. (1992). Time devoted to job and off-job activities, interrole conflict and affective experiences. *Journal of Applied Psychology, 77*, 272–279.

Oldham, G.R. (1988). Effects of changes in workspace partitions and spatial density on employee reactions: A quasi-experiment. *Journal of Applied Psychology, 73*, 253–258.

Oldham, G.R., & Fried, Y. (1987). Employee reactions to workspace characteristics. *Journal of Applied Psychology, 72*, 75–80.

Olian, J.D., Carroll, S.J., & Giannantonio, C.M. (1993). Mentor reactions to proteges: An experiment with managers. *Journal of Vocational Behavior, 43*, 266–278.

Oliver, N. (1990). Work rewards, work values, and organizational commitment in an employee-owned firm: Evidence from the U.K. *Human Relations, 43,* 513–526.

Omachonu, V.K., & Ross, J.E. (1994). *Principles of total quality.* Delray Beach, FL: St. Lucie Press.

Ones, D.S., & Viswesvaran, C. (1998). Looking ahead in I-O psychology (If we had a crystal ball. . .). *The Industrial-Organizational Psychologist, 35,* 92–95.

Ones, D.Z., Viswesvaran, C., & Schmidt, F.L. (1993). Comprehensive meta-analysis of integrity test validities: Findings and implications for personnel selection and theories of job performance. *Journal of Applied Psychology, 78,* 679–703.

Orasnu, J., Fischer, U., & Davison, J. (1997). Cross-cultural barriers to effective communication in aviation. In C.S. Granrose & S. Oskamp (Eds.), *Cross-cultural work groups* (pp. 134–162). Thousand Oaks, CA: Sage.

O'Reilly, C.A. (1978). The intentional distortion of information in organizational communication: A laboratory and field approach. *Human Relations, 31,* 173–193.

O'Reilly, C.A. (1980). Individuals and information overload in organizations: Is more necessarily better? *Academy of Management Journal, 23,* 684–696.

O'Reilly, C.A. (1989). Corporations, culture, and commitment: Motivation and social control in organizations. *California Management Review, 31,* 9–25.

O'Reilly, C.A., & Chatman, J.A. (1996). Culture as social control: Corporations, cults, and commitment. *Research in Organizational Behavior, 18,* 157–200.

O'Reilly, C.A., Chatman, J., & Caldwell, D. (1991). People and organizational culture: A Q-sort approach to assessing person-organization fit. *Academy of Management Journal, 34,* 487–516.

O'Reilly, C.A., & Roberts, K.H. (1976). Relationships among components of credibility and communication behaviors in work units. *Journal of Applied Psychology, 61,* 99–102.

Organ, D.W. (1988). *Organizational citizenship behavior: The good soldier syndrome.* Lexington, MA: Lexington.

Organ, D.W. (1990). The motivational basis of organizational citizenship behavior. In B.M. Staw & L.L. Cummings (Eds.), *Research in organizational behavior* (vol. 14, pp. 43–72). Greenwich, CT: JAI Press.

Organ, D.W., & Ryan, K. (1995). A meta-analytic review of attitudinal and dispositional predictors of organizational citizenship behavior. *Personnel Psychology, 48,* 775–802.

Osborn, A.F. (1957). *Applied imagination.* New York: Charles Scribner's Sons.

Ostroff, C. (1993a). Relationships between person-environment congruence and organizational effectiveness. *Group and Organization Management, 18,* 103–122.

Ostroff, C. (1993b). The effects of climate and personal influences on individual behavior and attitudes in organizations. *Organizational Behavior and Human Decision Processes, 56,* 56–90.

Ostroff, C., & Ford, J.K. (1989). Assessing training needs: Critical levels of analysis. In I.L. Goldstein (Ed.), *Training and development in organizations* (pp. 25–62). San Francisco: Jossey-Bass.

Ostroff, C., & Kozlowski, S.W. (1992). Organizational socialization as a learning process: The role of information acquisition. *Personnel Psychology, 45,* 849–874.

Ostroff, C., & Kozlowski, S.W.J. (1993). The role of mentoring in the information gathering processes of newcomers during early organizational socialization. *Journal of Vocational Behavior, 42,* 170–183.

Otis, A.S. (1929). *Self-Administering Test of Mental Ability.* Tarrytown-on-Hudson, NY: World.

Ott, J.S. (1989). *The organizational culture perspective.* Pacific Grove, CA: Brooks/Cole.

Owen, G., & Arnold, B. (1958). *Purdue Blueprint Reading Test.* West Lafayette, IN: Purdue University.

Owens, W.A. (1976). Background data. In M.D. Dunnette (Ed.), *Handbook of industrial and organizational psychology* (pp. 609–644). Chicago: Rand-McNally.

Paffenburger, R.S., Hyde, R.T., Wing, A.L., & Hsieh, C.C. (1986). Physical activity, all-cause mortality, and longevity of college alumni. *New England Journal of Medicine, 314,* 605–613.

Palich, L.E., & Hom, P.W. (1992). The impact of leader power and behavior on leadership perceptions. *Group and Organization Management, 17,* 279–296.

Parasuraman, S., & Alutto, J.A. (1984). Sources and outcomes of stress in organizational settings: Toward the development of a structural model. *Academy of Management Journal, 27,* 330–350.

Paris, C.R., Gilson, R.D., Thomas, M.H., & Silver, N.C. (1995). Effect of synthetic voice intelligibility on speech comprehension. *Human Factors, 37,* 335–340.

Parker, C.P., Dipboye, R.L., & Jackson, S.L. (1995). Perceptions of organizational politics: An investigation of antecedents and consequences. *Journal of Management, 21,* 891–912.

Parsons, H.M. (1974). What happened at Haw-thorne? *Science, 183,* 922–932.

Patterson, M.L. (1983). *Nonverbal behavior: A functional perspective.* New York: Springer-Verlag.

Paul, R.J., & Ebadi, Y.M. (1989). Leadership decision making in a service organization: A field test of the Vroom-Yetton model. *Journal of Occupational and Organizational Psychology, 62,* 201–211.

Paulus, P.B., & Dzindolet, M.T. (1993). Social influence processes in group brainstorming. *Journal of Personality and Social Psychology, 64*, 575–586.

Payne, R.L., Jabri, M.M., & Pearson, A.W. (1988). On the importance of knowing the affective meaning of job demands. *Journal of Organizational Behavior, 9*, 149–158.

Pearce, J.L., Stevenson, W.B., & Perry, J.L. (1985). Managerial compensation based on organizational performance: A time series analysis of the effects of merit pay. *Academy of Management Journal, 28*, 261–278.

Pendleton, A., McDonald, Robinson, A., & Wilson, N. (1995). The impact of employee share ownership plans on employee participation and industrial democracy. *Human Resource Management Journal, 5*, 44–60.

Penner, L.A., Midili, A.R., & Kegelmeyer, J. (1997). Beyond job attitudes: A personality and social psychology perspective on the causes of organizational citizenship behavior. *Human Performance, 10*, 111–131.

Perrewe, P.L. (Ed.) (1991). Handbook of job stress. *Journal of Social Behavior and Personality, 6* (entire special issue).

Perrewe, P.L., & Ganster, D.C. (1989). The impact of job demands and behavioral control on experienced job stress. *Journal of Organizational Behavior, 10*, 213–229.

Perrow, C. (1970). *Organizational analysis: A sociological perspective*. Belmont, CA: Wadsworth.

Perry, N. (1998). Indecent exposures: Theorizing whistleblowing. *Organization Studies, 19*, 235–257.

Peter, L.J., & Hull, R. (1969). *The Peter principle*. New York: William Morrow.

Peters, L.H., Hartke, D.D., & Pohlmann, J.T. (1985). Fiedler's contingency theory of leadership: an application of the meta-analysis procedures of Schmidt and Hunter. *Psychological Bulletin, 97*, 274–285.

Peterson, N.G., & Jeanneret, P.R. (1997). Job analysis: Overview and description of deductive methods. In D.L. Whetzel & G.R. Wheaton (Eds.), *Applied measurement methods in industrial psychology* (pp. 13–50). Palo Alto, CA: Davies-Black.

Peterson, R.B., Lee, T.W., & Finnegan, B. (1992). Strategies and tactics in union organizing campaigns. *Industrial Relations, 31*, 370–381.

Petty, M.M., McGee, G.W., & Cavender, J.W. (1984). A meta-analysis of the relationships between individual job satisfaction and individual performance. *Academy of Management Review, 9*, 712–721.

Pfeiffer, J. (1992). Understanding power in organizations. *California Management Review, 34*, 29–50.

Pfeiffer, J. (1981). *Power in organizations*. Boston, MA: Pitman.

Phillips, A.S., & Bedeian, A.G. (1994). Leader-follower exchange quality: The role of personal and interpersonal attributes. *Academy of Management Journal, 37*, 990–1001.

Pierce, J.L., Gardner, D.G., Dunham, R.B., & Cummings, L.L. (1993). Moderation by organization-based self-esteem of role condition-employee response relationships. *Academy of Management Journal, 36*, 271–286.

Pinder, C. (1984). *Work motivation*. Glenview, IL: Scott-Foresman.

Pinkley, R.L., Brittain, J., Neale, M.A., & Northcraft, G.B. (1995). Managerial third-party dispute intervention: An inductive analysis of intervenor strategy selection. *Journal of Applied Psychology, 80*, 386–402.

Pinzler, I.K., & Ellis, D. (1989). Wage discrimination and comparable worth: A legal perspective. *Journal of Social Issues, 45*, 51–65.

Podsakoff, P.M., Ahearne, M., & MacKenzie, S.B. (1997). Organizational citizenship behavior and the quantity and quality of work group performance. *Journal of Applied Psychology, 82*, 262–270.

Podsakoff, P.M., & MacKenzie, S.B. (1997). Kerr and Jermier's substitutes for leadership model: Background empirical assessment and suggestions for future research. *Leadership Quarterly, 8*, 117–125.

Podsakoff, P.M., & MacKenzie, S.B. (1997). Impact of organizational citizenship behavior on organizational performance: A review and suggestions for future research. *Human Performance, 10*, 133–151.

Podsakoff, P.M., & MacKenzie, S.B. (1994). Organizational citizenship behaviors and sales unit effectiveness. *Journal of Marketing Research, 31*, 351–363.

Podsakoff, P.M., MacKenzie, S.B., & Hui, C. (1993). Organizational citizenship behaviors and managerial evaluations of employee performance: A review and suggestions for future research. *Research in Personnel and Human Resources Management, 11*, 1–40.

Podsakoff, P.M., MacKenzie, S.B., Moorman, R.H., & Fetter, R. (1990). Transformational leader behaviors and their effects on followers' trust in leader, satisfaction, and organizational citizenship behaviors. *Leadership Quarterly, 1*, 107–142.

Podsakoff, P.M., & Schriesheim, C.A. (1985). Field studies of French and Raven's bases of power: Critique, reanalysis, and suggestions for future research. *Psychological Bulletin, 97*, 387–411.

Porras, J.I., & Robertson, P.J. (1992). Organizational development: Theory, practice, and research. In M.D. Dunnette & L.M. Hough (Eds.), *Handbook of industrial and organizational psychology* (Vol. 3, 2nd ed., pp. 719–822). Palo Alto, CA: Consulting Psychologists Press.

Porter, L.W., Allen, R.W., & Angle, H.L. (1981). The politics of upward influence in organizations. In B. Staw

(Ed.), *Research in organizational behavior* (pp. 109–149). Greenwich, CT: JAI Press.

Porter, L.W., & Lawler, E.E. (1968). *Managerial attitudes and performance*. Homewood, IL: Richard D. Irwin.

Porter, L.W., & Roberts, K.H. (1976). Communication in organizations. In M.D. Dunnette (Ed.), *Handbook of industrial and organizational psychology*. Skokie, IL: Rand-McNally.

Porter, L.W., & Steers, R.M. (1973). Organizational, work, and personal factors in employee turnover and absenteeism. *Psychological Bulletin, 80,* 151–176.

Porter, L.W., Steers, R.M., Mowday, R.T., & Boulian, P.V. (1974). Organizational commitment, job satisfaction, and turnover among psychiatric technicians. *Journal of Applied Psychology, 59,* 603–609.

Powell, G.N., & Butterfield, D.A. (1997). Effect of race on promotions to top management in a federal department. *Academy of Management Journal, 40,* 112–128.

Powell, G.N., & Butterfield, D.A. (1994). Investigating the "glass ceiling" phenomenon: An empirical study of actual promotions to top management. *Academy of Management Journal, 37,* 68–86.

Pratkanis, A.R., & Turner, M.E. (1994). Of what value is a job attitude? A socio-cognitive analysis. *Human Relations, 47,* 1545–1576.

Premack, S.L., & Wanous, J.P. (1985). A meta-analysis of realistic job preview experiments. *Journal of Applied Psychology, 70,* 706–719.

Primoff, E. (1975). *How to prepare and conduct job element examinations*. Personnel Research and Development Center, Washington, DC: U.S. Government Printing Office.

Pritchard, R.D., Dunnette, M.D., & Jorgenson, D. (1972). Effects of perceptions of equity on worker motivation and satisfaction. *Journal of Applied Psychology, 56,* 75–94.

Pritchard, R.D., Hollenback, J., & DeLeo, P.J. (1980). The effects of continuous and partial schedules of reinforcement on effort, performance, and satisfaction. *Organizational Behavior and Human Performance, 25,* 336–353.

Pritchard, R.D., Jones, S.D., Roth, P.L., Stuebing, K.K., & Ekeberg, S.E. (1988). Effects of group feedback, goal setting, and incentives on organizational productivity. *Journal of Applied Psychology, 73,* 337–358.

Pritchard, R.D., Leonard, D.W., Von Bergen, C.W., & Kirk, R.J. (1976). The effects of varying schedules of reinforcement on human task performance. *Organizational Behavior and Human Performance, 16,* 205–230.

Psychological Corporation. (1986). *Computer Competence Tests*. San Antonio, TX: The Psychological Corporation.

Pulakos, E.D. (1984). A comparison of rater training programs: Error training and accuracy training. *Journal of Applied Psychology, 69,* 581–588.

Quinones, M.A. (1997). Contextual influences on training effectiveness. In M.A. Quinones & A. Ehrenstein (Eds.), *Training for a rapidly changing workplace: Applications of psychological research* (pp. 177–199). Washington, DC: American Psychological Association.

Rafaeli, A., & Klimoski, R.J. (1983). Predicting sales success through handwriting analysis: an evaluation of the effects of training and handwriting sample content. *Journal of Applied Psychology, 68,* 212–217.

Ragins, B.R. (1989). Barriers to mentoring: The female manager's dilemma. *Human Relations, 42,* 1–22.

Ragins, B.R., & Cotton, J.L. (1993). Gender and willingness to mentor in organizations. *Journal of Management, 19,* 97–116.

Ragins, B.R., & Scandura, T.A. (1993). Expected costs and benefits of being a mentor. Paper presented at 8th annual conference of the Society for Industrial/Organizational Psychology, San Francisco, CA, April.

Rahim, A. (1985). A strategy of managing conflict in complex organizations. *Human Relations, 38,* 81–89.

Rahim, A. (1986). *Managing conflict in organizations*. New York: Praeger.

Ralston, D.A. (1989). The benefits of flextime: Real or imagined? *Journal of Organizational Behavior, 10,* 369–373.

Ralston, D.A., Anthony, W.P., & Gustafson, D.J. (1985). Employees may love flextime, but what does it do to an organization's productivity? *Journal of Applied Psychology, 70,* 272–279.

Randall, M.L., Cropanzano, R., Bormann, C.A., & Birjulin, A. (1999). Organizational politics and organizational support as predictors of work attitudes, job performance, and organizational citizenship behavior. *Journal of Organizational Behavior, 20*.

Randolph, W.A., & Posner, B.Z. (1992). *Getting the job done: Managing project teams and task forces for success*. Englewood Cliffs, NJ: Prentice-Hall.

Rao, V.S. (1995). Effects of teleconferencing technologies: An exploration of comprehension, feedback, satisfaction and role-related differences. *Group Decision and Negotiation, 4,* 251–272.

Rasmussen, J. (1986). *Information processing and human-machine interaction: An approach to cognitive engineering*. New York: North-Holland.

Rasmussen, K.G. (1984). Nonverbal behavior, verbal behavior, resume credentials, and selection interview outcomes. *Journal of Applied Psychology, 69,* 551–556.

Rauschenberger, J., Schmitt, N., & Hunter, J.E. (1980). A test of the need hierarchy concept by a Markov model of change in need strength. *Administrative Science Quarterly, 25,* 654–670.

Raven, B.H. (1992). A power/interaction model of interpersonal influence: French & Raven thirty years later. *Journal of Social Behavior and Personality, 7,* 217–244.

Raven, B.H., Schwarzwald, J., & Koslowsky, M. (1998). Conceptualizing and measuring a power/interaction model of interpersonal influence. *Journal of Applied Social Psychology, 28,* 307–322.

Reber, R.A., & Wallin, J.A. (1984). The effects of training, goal setting, and knowledge of results on safe behavior: A component analysis. *Academy of Management Journal, 27,* 544–560.

Reichardt, T. (1986, January). Sociology on the space station: An interview with B.J. Bluth. *Space World,* pp. 8–10.

Reichers, A.E. (1987). An interactionist perspective on newcomer socialization rates. *Academy of Management Review, 12,* 278–287.

Reilly, R.R., & Chao, G.T. (1982). Validity and fairness of some alternative employee selection procedures. *Personnel Psychology, 35,* 1–62.

Reinsch, N.L., & Beswick, R.W. (1995). Preferences for sending word-processed versus handwritten messages: An exploratory study. *Journal of Business and Technical Communication, 9,* 45–62.

Rentsch, J.R., & Steel, R.P. (1998). Testing the durability of job characteristics as predictors of absenteeism over a six-year period. *Personnel Psychology, 51,* 165–190.

Rice, B. (1982). The Hawthorne defect: Persistence of a flawed theory. *Psychology Today, 16*(2), 70–74.

Rice, R.W. (1978). Construct validity of the least preferred coworker (LPC) score. *Psychological Bulletin, 85,* 1199–1237.

Rice, R.W., Gentile, D.A., & McFarlin, D.B. (1991). Facet importance and job satisfaction. *Journal of Applied Psychology, 76,* 31–39.

Rice, R.W., Instone, D., & Adams, J. (1984). Leader sex, leader success, and leadership process: Two field studies. *Journal of Applied Psychology, 69,* 12–31.

Riggio, R.E. (1999). Interpersonal sensitivity research and organizational psychology: Theoretical and methodological applications. In J.A. Hall & F. Bernieri (Eds.), *Measurement of interpersonal sensitivity.* Mahwah, NJ: Lawrence Erlbaum Associates.

Riggio, R.E. (1986). Assessment of basic social skills. *Journal of Personality and Social Psychology, 51,* 649–660.

Riggio, R.E. (1987). *The charisma quotient.* New York: Dodd-Mead.

Riggio, R.E., Aguirre, M., Mayes, B.T., Belloli, C., & Kubiak, C. (1997). The use of assessment center methods for student outcome assessment. In R.E. Riggio & B.T. Mayes (Eds.), *Assessment centers: Research and applications* (pp. 273–278). Corte Madera, CA: Select Press.

Riggio, R.E., & Cole, E.J. (1992). Agreement between subordinate and superior ratings of supervisory performance and effects on self- and subordinate job satisfaction. *Journal of Occupational and Organizational Psychology, 65,* 151–158.

Riggio, R.E., & Cole, E.J. (1995). *Stress and coping processes in on-duty firefighters.* Paper presented at meeting of the American Psychological Association, Toronto, Canada.

Riggio, R.E., & Murphy, S.E. (Eds.). (2000). *Multiple intelligences and leadership.* Mahwah, NJ: Lawrence Erlbaum.

Riggio, R.E., & Throckmorton, B. (1988). The relative effects of verbal and nonverbal behavior, appearance, and social skills on evaluations made in hiring interviews. *Journal of Applied Social Psychology, 18,* 331–348.

Riordan, C.A. (1989). Images of corporate success. In R.A. Giacalone & P. Rosenfeld (Eds.), *Impression management in the organization* (pp. 87–103). Hillsdale, NJ: Lawrence Erlbaum Associates.

Risher, H. (1984). Job evaluation: Problems and prospects. *Personnel, 61,* 53–66.

Ritchie, R.J., & Moses, J.L. (1983). Assessment center correlates of women's advancement into middle management: A 7-year longitudinal analysis. *Journal of Applied Psychology, 68,* 227–231.

Robbins, S.P. (1974). *Managing organizational conflict: A nontraditional approach.* Englewood Cliffs, NJ: Prentice-Hall.

Robbins, S.P. (1979). *Organizational behavior: Concepts and controversies.* Englewood Cliffs, NJ: Prentice-Hall.

Robbins, T.L. (1995). Social loafing on cognitive tasks: An examination of the "sucker effect." *Journal of Business and Psychology, 9,* 337–342.

Robertson, I.T., & Kinder, A. (1993). Personality and job competencies: The criterion-related validity of some personality variables. *Journal of Occupational and Organizational Psychology, 66,* 225–244.

Roche, G.R. (1979). Much ado about mentors. *Harvard Business Review, 57,* 14–19.

Rock, M.L. (1984). *Handbook of wage and salary administration* (2nd ed.). New York: McGraw-Hill.

Rodgers, R., & Hunter, J.E. (1991). Impact of management by objectives on organizational productivity. *Journal of Applied Psychology, 76,* 322–336.

Roeske, N.C.A. (1981). Stress and the physician. *Psychiatric Annals, 11,* 245–258.

Roethlisberger, F.J., & Dickson, W.J. (1939). *Management and the worker.* Cambridge: Harvard University Press.

Rogelberg, S.G., & Rumery, S.M. (1996). Gender diversity, team decision quality, time on task, and interpersonal cohesion. *Small Group Research, 27,* 79–90.

Ronen, S. (1981). Arrival and departure patterns of public sector employees before and after implementation of flextime. *Personnel Psychology, 34,* 817–822.

Ronen, S. (1989). Training the international asignee. In I.L. Goldstein (Ed.), *Training and development in organizations.* San Francisco: Jossey-Bass.

Ronen, S., & Primps, S.B. (1981). The compressed work week as organizational change: Behavioral and attitudinal outcomes. *Academy of Management Review, 6,* 61–74.

Rosa, R.R., Colligan, M.J., & Lewis, P. (1989). Extended workdays: Effects of 8-hour and 12-hour rotating shift schedules on performance, subjective alertness, sleep patterns, and psychosocial variables. *Work & Stress, 3,* 21–32.

Rose, R.M. (1987). Neuroendocrine effects of work stress. In J.C. Quick, R.S. Bhagat, J.E. Dalton, & J.D. Quick (Eds), *Work stress: Health care systems in the workplace* (pp. 130–147). New York: Praeger.

Rosen, C., Klein, K.J., & Young, K.M. (1986). *Employee ownership in America: The equity solution.* Lexington, MA: Lexington Books.

Rosenman, R.H. (1978). The interview method of assessment of the coronary-prone behavior pattern. In T.M. Dembroski, S.M. Weiss, J.L. Shields, S.G. Haynes, & M. Feinlib (Eds.), *Coronary-prone behavior* (pp. 55–69). New York: Springer-Verlag.

Rosenman, R.H. (1990). Type A Behavior Pattern: A personal overview. *Journal of Social Behavior and Personality, 5,* 1–24.

Rosenman, R.H., Friedman, M., Strauss, R., Warm, M., Kositchek, R., Hahn, W., & Werthessen, N.T. (1964). A predictive study of coronary heart disease: The Western Collaborative Group Study. *Journal of the American Medical Association, 189,* 15–22.

Rosenthal, R. (1991). *Meta-analytic procedures for the social sciences* (2nd ed.). Newbury Park, CA: Sage.

Roth, P.L., BeVier, C.A., Switzer, F.S., & Schippmann, J.S. (1996). Meta-analyzing the relationship between grades and job performance. *Journal of Applied Psychology, 81,* 548–556.

Roth, P.L., & Campion, J.E. (1992). An analysis of the predictive power of the panel interview and pre-employment tests. *Journal of Occupational and Organizational Psychology, 65,* 51–60.

Rothstein, H.R., Schmidt, F.L., Erwin, F.W., Owens, W.A., & Sparks, C.P. (1990). Biographical data in employment selection: Can validities be made generalizable? *Journal of Applied Psychology, 75,* 175–184.

Rothwell, S. (1992). The development of the international manager. *Personnel Management, 24,* 33–35.

Roznowski, M. (1989). Examination of the measurement properties of the Job Descriptive Index with experimental items. *Journal of Applied Psychology, 74,* 805–814.

Rusbult, C.E., & Farrell, D. (1983). A longitudinal test of the investment model: The impact on job satisfaction, job commitment, and turnover on variations in rewards, costs, alternatives, and investments. *Journal of Applied Psychology, 68,* 429–438.

Russell, J.S. (1984). A review of fair employment cases in the field of training. *Personnel Psychology, 37,* 261–276.

Russell, R.D., & Russell, C.J. (1992). An examination of the effects of organizational norms, organizational structure, and environmental uncertainty on entreprenurial strategy. *Journal of Management, 18,* 639–656.

Ryan, A.M., & Sackett, P.R. (1987). Pre-employment honesty testing: Fakeability, reactions of test takers, and company image. *Journal of Business and Psychology, 1,* 248–256.

Rynes, S.L. (1993). When recruitment fails to attract: Individual expectations meet organizational realities in recruitment. In H. Schuler, J.L. Farr, & M. Smith (Eds.), *Personnel selection and assessment: Individual and organizational perspectives* (pp. 27–40). Hillsdale, NJ: Lawrence Erlbaum.

Rynes, S.L. (1989). The employment interview as a recruitment device. In R.W. Eder & G.R. Ferris (Eds.), *The employment interview: Theory, research, and practice* (pp. 127–141). Newbury Park, CA: Sage.

Sackett, P.R., & Mullen, E.J. (1993). Beyond formal experimental design: Towards an expanding view of the training evaluation process. *Personnel Psychology, 46,* 613–627.

Sackett, P.R., & Wanek, J.E. (1996). New developments in the use of measures of honesty, integrity, conscientiousness, dependability, trustworthiness, and reliability for personnel selection. *Personnel Psychology, 49,* 787–829.

Sagie, A. (1998). Employee absenteeism, organizational commitment, and job satisfaction: Another look. *Journal of Vocational Behavior, 52,* 156–171.

Saks, A.M. (1994). A psychological process investigation of the effects of recruitment source and organization information on job survival. *Journal of Organizational Behavior, 15,* 225–244.

Saks, A.M. (1996). The relationship between the amount and helpfulness of entry training and work outcomes. *Human Relations, 49,* 429–451.

Saks, A.M. (1998). Moderating effects of self-efficacy for the relationship between training method and anxiety and stress reactions of newcomers. *Journal of Organizational Behavior, 15,* 639–654.

Saks, A.M., & Ashforth, B.E. (1997). Organizational socialization: Making sense of the past and present as a prologue for the future. *Journal of Vocational Behavior, 51,* 234–279.

Saks, A.M., & Cronshaw, S.F. (1990). A process investigation of realistic job previews: Mediating variables and channels of communication. *Journal of Organizational Behavior, 11,* 221–236.

Salancik, G.R., & Pfeffer, J. (1977). Who gets power and how they hold on to it: A strategic-contingency model of power. *Organizational Dynamics, 5,* 3–21.

Sallis, J.F., Johnson, C.C., Trevorrow, T.R., Hovell, M.F., & Kaplan, R.M. (1985). *Worksite stress management: Anything goes?* Paper presented at the meeting of the American Psychological Association, Los Angeles.

Sama, L.M., Kopelman, R.E., & Manning, R.J. (1994). In search of a ceiling effect on work motivation: Can Kaizen keep performance "risin." *Journal of Social Behavior and Personality, 9,* 231–237.

Sanders, M.S., & McCormick, E.J. (1987). *Human factors in engineering and design* (6th ed.). New York: McGraw-Hill.

Sanders, M.S., & McCormick, E.J. (1993). *Human factors in engineering and design* (7th ed.). New York: McGraw-Hill.

Sanna, L.J., & Parks, C.D. (1997). Group research trends in social and organizational psychology: Whatever happened to intragroup research? *Psychological Science, 8,* 261–267.

Scandura, T.A., & Graen, G.B. (1984). Moderating effects of initial leader-member exchange status on the effects of a leadership intervention. *Journal of Applied Psychology, 69,* 428–436.

Scarpello, V., & Campbell, J.P. (1983). Job satisfaction: Are all the parts there? *Personnel Psychology, 36,* 577–600.

Scarpello, V., & Vandenberg, R.J. (1992). Generalizing the importance of occupational and career views to job satisfaction attitudes. *Journal of Organizational Behavior, 13,* 125–140.

Schachter, S., & Burdick, H. (1955). A field experiment of rumor transmission and distortion. *Journal of Abnormal and Social Psychology, 50,* 363–371.

Schaubroeck, J., Ganster, D.C., & Kemmerer, B.E. (1994). Job compexity, Type A behavior, and cardiovascular disorder: A prospective study. *Academy of Management Journal, 37,* 426–439.

Schaubroeck, J., Ganster, D.C., Sime, W.E., & Ditman, D. (1993). A field experiment testing supervisory role clarification. *Personnel Psychology, 46,* 1–25.

Schaufeli, W.B., & Van Dierendonck, D. (1993). The construct validity of two burnout measures. *Journal of Organizational Behavior, 14,* 631–647.

Schein, E.H. (1968). Organizational socialization and the profession of management. *Industrial Management Review, 34,* 171–176.

Schein, E.H. (1969). *Process consultation: Its role in organization development.* Reading, MA: Addison-Wesley.

Schein, E.H. (1992). *Organizational culture and leadership* (2nd ed.). San Francisco: Jossey-Bass.

Schein, E.H. (1993). On dialogue, culture, and organizational learning. *Organizational Dynamics, 22,* 40–51.

Schein, E.H. (1996). Culture: The missing concept in organization studies. *Administrative Science Quarterly, 41,* 229–240.

Schein, V.E. (1977). Individual power and political behaviors in organizations: An inadequately explored reality. *Academy of Management Review, 2,* 64–72.

Schein, V.E., Mauner, E.H., & Novak, J.F. (1977). Impact of flexible working hours on productivity. *Journal of Applied Psychology, 62,* 46–56.

Schippman, J.S., Prien, E.P., & Katz, J.A. (1990). Reliability and validity of in-basket performance measures. *Personnel Psychology, 43,* 837–859.

Schmidt, F.L. (1973). Implications of a measurement problem for expectancy theory research. *Organizational Behavior and Human Performance, 10,* 243–251.

Schmidt, F.L., & Hunter, J.L. (1977). Development of a general solution to the problem of validity generalization. *Journal of Applied Psychology, 62,* 529–540.

Schmidt, F.L., & Hunter, J.E. (1981). Employment testing: Old theories and new research findings. *American Psychologist, 36,* 1128–1137.

Schmidt, F.L., Hunter, J.E., McKenzie, R.C., & Muldrow, T.W. (1979). Impact of valid selection procedures on work-force productivity. *Journal of Applied Psychology, 64,* 609–626.

Schmidt, F.L., Hunter, J.E., Outerbridge, A.N., & Trattner, M.H. (1986). The economic impact of job selection methods on size, productivity, and payroll costs of the federal work force: An empirically based demonstration. *Personnel Psychology, 39,* 1–29.

Schmidt, F.L., Law, K., Hunter, J.E., Rothstein, H.R., Pearlman, K., & McDaniel, M. (1993). Refinements in validity generalization methods: Implications for the situational specificity hypothesis. *Journal of Applied Psychology, 78,* 3–13.

Schmidt, F.L., & Ones, D.S. (1992). Personnel selection. *Annual Review of Psychology, 43,* 627–670.

Schmidt, R.A., & Bjork, R.A. (1992). New conceptualizations of practice: Common principles in these paradigms suggest new concepts for training. *Psychological Science, 3,* 207–217.

Schmidt, S.M., & Kipnis, D. (1984). Managers' pursuit of individual and organizational goals. *Human Relations, 37,* 781–794.

Schminke, M. (1993). Consequences of power in a simulated job: Understanding the turnover decision. *Journal of Applied Social Psychology, 23,* 52–78.

Schmitt, N. (1976). Social and situational determinants of interview decisions: Implications for the employment interview. *Personnel Psychology, 29,* 79–101.

Schmitt, N., Gilliland, S.W., Landis, R.S., & Devine, D. (1993). Computer-based testing applied to selection of secretarial applicants. *Personnel Psychology, 46,* 149–165.

Schmitt, N., Gooding, R.Z., Noe, R.A., & Kirsch, M. (1984). Meta-analyses of validity studies published between 1964 and 1982 and the investigation of study characteristics. *Personnel Psychology, 37,* 407–422.

Schnake, M.E. (1991). Organizational citizenship: A review, proposed model, and research agenda. *Human Relations, 44,* 735–759.

Schneider, B. (1985). Organizational behavior. *Annual Review of Psychology, 36,* 573–611.

Schneider, B., & Bowen, D.E. (1995). *Winning the service game.* Boston: Harvard Business School Press.

Schneider, B., Brief, A.P., & Guzzo, R.A. (1996). Creating a climate and culture for sustainable organizational change. *Organizational Dynamics, 24,* 6–19.

Schneider, D.J., Hastorf, A.H., & Ellsworth, P.C. (1979). *Person perception.* Reading, MA: Addison-Wesley.

Schneider, J., & Locke, E.A. (1971). A critique of Herzberg's incident classification system and a suggested revision. *Organizational Behavior and Human Performance, 6,* 441–457.

Schonfeld, I.S. (1990). Coping with job-related stress: The case of teachers. *Journal of Occupational Psychology, 63,* 141–149.

Schrader, B.W., & Steiner, D.D. (1996). Common comparison standards: An approach to improving agreement between self and supervisory performance ratings. *Journal of Applied Psychology, 81,* 813–820.

Schriesheim, C.A., Bannister, B.D., & Money, W.H. (1979). Psychometric properties of the LPC scale: An extension of Rice's review. *Academy of Management Review, 4,* 287–290.

Schriesheim, C.A., & Hinkin, T.R. (1990). Influence tactics used by subordinates: A theoretical and empirical analysis and refinement of the Kipnis, Schmidt, and Wilkinsen subscales. *Journal of Applied Psychology, 75,* 246–257.

Schriesheim, C.A., Hinkin, T.R., & Podsakoff, P.M. (1991). Can ipsative and single-item measures produce erroneous results in field studies of French and Raven's (1959) five bases of power? An empirical investigation. *Journal of Applied Psychology, 76,* 106–114.

Schriesheim, C.A., & Kerr, S. (1974). Psychometric properties of the Ohio State leadership scales. *Psychological Bulletin, 81,* 756–765.

Schriesheim, C.A., & Kerr, S. (1977). Theories and measures of leadership: A critical appraisal of current and future directions. In J.G. Hunt & L.L. Larson (Eds.), *Leadership: The cutting edge* (pp. 9–45). Carbondale, IL: Southern Illinois University Press.

Schriesheim, C.A., & Murphy, C.J. (1976). Relationship between leader behavior and subordinate satisfaction and performance: A test of some situational moderators. *Journal of Applied Psychology, 61,* 634–641.

Schuler, R.S., & Sethi, A.S. (1984). Time management and leader communication behavior. In R.S. Schuler & A.S. Sethi (Eds.), *Handbook of organizational stress coping strategies* (pp. 69–87). Cambridge, MA: Ballinger.

Schwab, D.P., Olian-Gottlieb, J.D., & Heneman, H.G. (1979). Between-subjects expectancy theory research: A statistical review of studies predicting effort and performance. *Psychological Bulletin, 86,* 139–147.

Schweiger, D.M., Sandberg, W.R., & Ragan, J.W. (1986). Group approaches for improving strategic decision making: A comparative analysis of dialectical inquiry, devil's advocacy, and consensus. *Academy of Management Journal, 29,* 51–71.

Schweitzer, P.K., Muehlbach, M.J., & Walsh, J.K. (1992). Countermeasures for night work performance deficits: The effect of napping or caffeine on continuous performance at night. *Work & Stress, 6,* 355–365.

Scott, K.D., & Taylor, G.S. (1985). An examination of conflicting findings on the relationship between job satisfaction and absenteeism: A meta-analysis. *Academy of Management Journal, 28,* 599–612.

Scott, W.D. (1908). *The psychology of advertising.* New York: Arno Press.

Scott, W.G., Mitchell, T.R., & Birnbaum, P.H. (1981). *Organizational theory: A structural and behavioral analysis.* Homewood, IL: Richard D. Irwin.

Selye, H. (1976). *The stress of life* (Rev. ed.). New York: McGraw-Hill.

Sethi, A.S. (1984a). Meditation for coping with organizational stress. In A.S. Sethi & R.S. Schuler (Eds.), *Handbook of organizational stress coping strategies* (pp. 145–165). Cambridge, MA: Ballinger.

Sethi, A.S. (1984b). Introduction to organizational stress coping. In A.S. Sethi & R.S. Schuler (Eds.), *Handbook of organizational stress coping strategies* (pp. 1–13). Cambridge, MA: Ballinger.

Sethi, A.S., Caro, D.H.J., & Schuler, R.S. (1987). *Strategic management of technostress in an information society.* Leviston, NY: C.J. Hogrefe.

Sethi, A.S., & Schuler, R.S. (Eds.). (1984). *Handbook of organizational stress coping strategies.* Cambridge, MA: Ballinger.

Shahani, C., Weiner, R., & Streit, M.K. (1993). An investigation of the dispositional nature of the time management construct. *Anxiety, Stress, and Coping, 6,* 231–243.

Shaiken, H. (1984). *Work transformed: Automation and labor in the computer age.* New York: Holt, Rinehart, & Winston.

Shanahan, M.J., & Mortimer, J.T. (1996). Understanding the positive consequences of psychosocial stressors. *Advances in Group Processes, 13,* 189–209.

Shaw, L., & Sichel, H.S. (1971). *Accident-proneness.* Oxford: Pergamon Press.

Shaw, M.E. (1964). Communication networks. In L. Berkowitz (Ed.), *Advances in experimental social psychology* (Vol. 1). New York: Academic Press.

Shaw, M.E. (1978). Communication networks fourteen years later. In L. Berkowitz (Ed.), *Group processes.* New York: Academic Press.

Shaw, M.E. (1981). *Group dynamics: The psychology of small group behavior* (3rd ed.). New York: McGraw-Hill.

Sheppard, B.H. (1974). Third party conflict intervention: A procedural framework. In B.M. Staw & L.L. Cummings (Eds.), *Research in organizational behavior* (Vol. 6, pp. 141–190). Greenwich, CT: JAI Press.

Sherif, M., Harvey, O.J., White, B.J., Hood, W.R., & Sherif, C.W. (1961). *Intergroup conflict and cooperation: The Robbers Cave experiment.* Norman, OK: Institute of Group Relations.

Shore, L.M., Newton, L.A., & Thornton, G.C. (1990). Job and organizational attitudes in relation to employee behavioral intentions. *Journal of Organizational Behavior, 11,* 57–67.

Shore, L.M., & Wayne, S.J. (1993). Commitment and employee behavior: Comparison of affective commitment and continuance commitment with perceived organizational support. *Journal of Applied Psychology, 78,* 774–780.

Shouksmith, G., & Burrough, S. (1988). Job stress factors for New Zealand and Canadian air traffic controllers. *Applied Psychology: An International Review, 37,* 263–270.

Sias, P.M., & Jablin, F.M. (1995). Differential superior-subordinate relations, perceptions of fairness, and coworker communication. *Human Communication Research, 22,* 5–38.

Sills, D.L., Wolf, C.P., & Shelanski, V.B. (Eds.). (1982). *Accident at Three Mile Island: The human dimensions.* Boulder, CO: Westview Press.

Silverman, S.B., & Wexley, K.N. (1984). Reaction of employees to performance appraisal interviews as a function of their participation in rating scale development. *Personnel Psychology, 37,* 703–710.

Silverstein, S. (1997, May 23). Careful—the cubicles have ears. *Los Angeles Times* (B-7).

Simmons, P.O. (1993). The Judd test for Lotus 1–2–3. *HR Magazine, 38,* 33–36.

Simon, S.J., & Werner, J.M. (1996). Computer training through behavior modeling, self-paced, and instructional approaches: A field experiment. *Journal of Applied Psychology, 81,* 648–659.

Simons, G.F., Vazquez, C., & Harris, P.R. (1993). *Transcultural leadership: Empowering the diverse workforce.* Houston, TX: Gulf.

Sims, H.P., Szilagyi, A.D., & Keller, R.T. (1976). The measurement of job characteristics. *Academy of Management Journal, 19,* 195–212.

Sims, R.L., & Keenan, J.P. (1998). Predictors of external whistleblowing: Organizational and intrapersonal variables. *Journal of Business Ethics, 17,* 411–421.

Sinclair, H.J. (1971). Digital versus conventional clocks—A review. *Applied Ergonomics, 2,* 178–181.

Smith, A. (1989). A review of the effects of noise on human performance. *Scandinavian Journal of Psychology, 30,* 185–206.

Smith, C.A., Organ, D.W., & Near, J.P. (1983). Organizational citizenship behavior: Its nature and antecedents. *Journal of Applied Psychology, 68,* 653–663.

Smith, K.G., Locke, E.A., & Barry, D. (1990). Goal setting, planning, and organizational performance: An experimental simulation. *Organizational Behavior and Human Decision Processes, 46,* 118–134.

Smith, L., & Folkard, S. (1993). The impact of shiftwork on personnel at a nuclear power plant: An exploratory survey study. *Work & Stress, 7,* 341–350.

Smith, M. (1994). A theory of the validity of predictors in selection. *Journal of Occupational and Organizational Psychology, 67,* 13–31.

Smith, M.J., Anger, W.K., & Uslan, S.S. (1978). Behavioral modification applied to occupational safety. *Journal of Safety Research, 10,* 87–88.

Smith, P.C. (1976). Behavior, results, and organizational effectiveness: The problem of criteria. In M.D. Dunnette (Ed.), *Handbook of industrial and organizational psychology* (pp. 745–766). Skokie, IL: Rand-McNally.

Smith, P.C., & Kendall, L.M. (1963). Retranslation of expectations: An approach to the construction of unambiguous anchors for rating scales. *Journal of Applied Psychology, 47*, 149–155.

Smith, P.C., Kendall, L.M., & Hulin, C.L. (1969). *The measurement of satisfaction in work and retirement*. Chicago: Rand-McNally.

Smith, P.C., Kendall, L.M., & Hulin, C.L. (1987). The revised JDI: A facelift for an old friend. *The Industrial-Organizational Psychologist, 24*(4), 31–33.

Smith, T.W., & Pope, M.K. (1990). Cynical hostility as a health risk: Current status and future directions. *Journal of Social Behavior and Personality, 5*, 77–88.

Smith-Jentsch, K.A., Jentsch, F.G., Payne, S.C., & Salas, E. (1996). Can pretraining experiences explain individual differences in learning? *Journal of Applied Psychology, 81*, 110–116.

Smither, J.W., Wohlers, A.J., & London, M. (1995). A field study of reactions to normative versus individualized upward feedback. *Group & Organization Management, 20*, 61–89.

Snyder, R.A., & Morris, J.H. (1984). Organizational communication and performance. *Journal of Applied Psychology, 69*, 461–465.

Solomon, R.L. (1949). An extension of control group design. *Psychological Bulletin, 46*, 137–150.

Sonnentag, S., Brodbeck, F.C., Heinbokel, T., & Stolte, W. (1994). Stressor-burnout relationship in software development teams. *Journal of Occupational and Organizational Psychology, 67*, 327–341.

Sorensen, E. (1994). *Comparable worth: Is it a worthy policy?* Princeton, NJ: Princeton University Press.

Sosik, J.J., Avolio, B.J., & Kahai, S.S. (1997). Effects of leadership style and anonymity on group potency and effectiveness in a group decision support system environment. *Journal of Applied Psychology, 82*, 89–103.

Spangler, W. (1992). Validity of questionnaire and TAT measures of acheivement: Two meta-analyses. *Psychological Bulletin, 112*, 140–154.

Spector, P.E. (1987). Interactive effects of perceived control and job stressors on affective reactions and health outcomes for clerical workers. *Work and Stress, 1*, 155–162.

Spector, P.E. (1992). A consideration of the validity and meaning of self-report measures of job conditions. In C.L. Cooper & I.T. Richardson (Eds.), *International review of industrial and organizational psychology* (Vol 7, pp. 123–151). New York: John Wiley & Sons.

Spector, P.E. (1997). *Job satisfaction: Application, assessment, causes, and consequences*. Thousand Oaks, CA: Sage.

Spector, P.E., Dwyer, D.J., & Jex, S.M. (1988). Relation of job stressors to affective, health and performance outcomes: A comparison of multiple data sources. *Journal of Applied Psychology, 73*, 11–19.

Spector, P.E., & Jex, S.M. (1991). Relations of job characteristics from multiple data sources with employee affect, absence, turnover intentions and health. *Journal of Applied Psychology, 76*, 46–53.

Spector, P.E., & O'Connell, B.J. (1994). The contribution of personality traits, negative affectivity, locus of control, and Type A to the subsequent reports of job stressors and job strains. *Journal of Occupational and Organizational Psychology, 67*, 1–11.

Spence, J.T., & Helmreich, R.L. (1983). Achievement-related motives and behaviors. In J.T. Spence (Ed.), *Achievement and achievement motives: Psychological and sociological approaches* (pp. 7–74). San Francisco: Freeman.

Spetell, C.M., & Liebert, R.M. (1986). Training for safety in automated person-machine systems. *American Psychologist, 41*, 545–550.

Spielberger, C.D., & Reheiser, E.C. (1994). The job stress survey: Measuring gender differences in occupational stress. *Journal of Social Behavior and Personality, 9*, 199–218.

Spreitzer, G.M. (1996). Social structural characteristics of psychological empowerment. *Academy of Management Journal, 39*, 483–504.

Stahelski, A.J., Frost, D.E., & Patch, M.E. (1989). Use of socially dependent bases of power: French and Raven's theory applied to workgroup leadership. *Journal of Applied Social Psychology, 19*, 283–297.

Stahl, M.J., & Harrell, A. (1981). Modeling effort decisions with behavioral decision theory: Toward an individual differences model of expectancy theory. *Organizational Behavior and Human Performance, 27*, 303–325.

Stanton, J.M. & Barnes-Farrell, J.L. (1996). Effects of electronic performance monitoring on personal control, task satisfaction, and task performance. *Journal of Applied Psychology, 81*, 738–745.

Staw, B.M., & Ross, J. (1985). Stability in the midst of change: A dispositional approach to job attitudes. *Journal of Applied Psychology, 70*, 469–480.

Stamp, G. (1990). Tokens and glass ceilings: The real issue of minorities in organizations. *Equal Opportunities International, 9*, 9–15.

Steers, R.M. (1977). Antecedents and outcomes of organizational commitment. *Administrative Science Quarterly, 22*, 46–56.

Steers, R.M., & Braunstein, D.N. (1976). A behaviorally based measure of manifest needs in work settings. *Journal of Vocational Behavior, 9*, 251–266.

Steers, R.M., & Porter, L.W. (Eds.). (1983). *Motivation and work behavior* (3rd ed.). New York: McGraw-Hill.

Steers, R.M., & Porter, L.W. (Eds.). (1991). *Motivation and work behavior* (5th ed.) New York: McGraw-Hill.

Stein, B.A. (1983). *Quality of work life in action: Managing for effectiveness*. New York: American Management Association.

Steiner, D.D., Lane, I.M., Dobbins, G.H., Schnur, A., & McConnell, S. (1991). A review of meta-analyses in organizational behavior and human resources management: An empirical assessment. *Educational and Psychological Measurement, 51*(3), 609–626.

Stevens, C.K. (1997). Effects of preinterview beliefs on applicants' reactions to campus interviews. *Academy of Management Journal, 40*, 947–966.

Stevens, C.K. (1998). Antecedents of interview interactions, interviewers' ratings, and applicants' reactions. *Personnel Psychology, 51*, 55–85.

Stogdill, R.M. (1948). Personal factors associated with leadership: A survey of the literature. *Journal of Psychology, 25*, 35–71.

Stogdill, R.M. (1963). *Manual for the leader behavior description questionnaire—Form XII*. Columbus, OH: Ohio State University, Bureau of Business Research.

Stogdill, R.M., & Coons, A.E. (Eds.). (1957). *Leader behavior: Its description and measurement*. Columbus, OH: Ohio State University, Bureau of Business Research.

Stokes, G.S., Mumford, M.D., & Owens, W.A. (Eds.). (1994). *Biodata handbook: Theory, research and use of biographical information in selection and performance prediction*. Palo Alto, CA: Consulting Psychologists Press.

Stork, D., & Richards, W.D. (1992). Nonrespondents in communication network studies. *Group and Organization Management, 17*, 193–209.

Streufert, S., Pogash, R., & Piasecki, M. (1988). Simulation-based assessment of managerial competence: Reliability and validity. *Personnel Psychology, 41*, 537–557.

Stroh, L.K., Brett, J.M., & Reilly, A.H. (1992). All the right stuff: A comparison of female and male managers' career progression. *Journal of Applied Psychology, 77*, 251–260.

Strube, M.J., & Garcia, J.E. (1981). A meta-analytic investigation of Fiedler's contingency model of leader effectiveness. *Psychological Bulletin, 90*, 307–321.

Stumpf, S.A., & Dawley, P.K. (1981). Predicting voluntary and involuntary turnover using absenteeism and performance indices. *Academy of Management Journal, 24*, 148–163.

Stumpf, S.A., & Hartman, K. (1984). Individual exploration to organizational commitment or withdrawal. *Academy of Management Journal, 27*, 308–329.

Sturman, M.C., Hannon, J.M., & Milkovich, G.T. (1996). Computerized decision aids for flexible benefits decisions: The effects of an expert system and decision support system on employee intentions and satisfaction with benefits. *Personnel Psychology, 49*, 883–908.

Sundstrom, E. (1986). *Work places: The psychology of the physical environment in offices and factories*. Cambridge: Cambridge University Press.

Sundstrom, E., DeMeuse, K.P., & Futrell, D. (1990). Work teams: Applications and effectiveness. *American Psychologist, 45*, 120–133.

Sundstrom, E., Burt, R.E., & Kamp, D. (1980). Privacy at work: Architectural correlates of job satisfaction and job performance. *Academy of Management Journal, 23*, 101–117.

Sutherland, L.F., Fogarty, G.J., & Pithers, R.T. (1995). Congruence as a predictor of occupational stress. *Journal of Vocational Behavior, 46*, 292–309.

Sutherland, V.J., & Cooper, C.L. (1988). Sources of work stress. In J.J. Hurrell, L.R. Murphy, S.L., Sauter, & C.L. Cooper (Eds.), *Occupational stress issues and developments in research* (pp. 3–40). Philadelphia: Taylor & Francis.

Sutton, R.I., & D'Aunno, T. (1989). Decreasing organizational size: Untangling the effects of money and people. *Academy of Management Review, 14*, 194–212.

Sutton, R.I., & Rafaeli, A. (1987). Characteristics of work stations as potential occupational stressors. *Academy of Management Journal, 30*, 260–276.

Swain, A., & Guttmann, H. (1983). *Handbook of human reliability analysis with emphasis on nuclear power plant applications*. Washington, DC: Nuclear Regulatory Commission.

Swaroff, P.G., Barclay, L.A., & Bass, A.R. (1985). Recruiting sources: Another look. *Journal of Applied Psychology, 70*, 720–728.

Taber, T.D., & Taylor, E. (1990). A review and evaluation of the psychometric properties of the Job Diagnostic Survey. *Personnel Psychology, 43*, 467–500.

Takalkar, P., & Coovert, M.D. (1994). International replication note: The dimensionality of job satisfaction in India. *Applied Psychology: An International Review, 43*, 415–426.

Tang, T.L., Tollison, P.S., & Whiteside, H.D. (1987). The effect of quality circle initiation on motivation to attend quality circle meetings and on task performance. *Personnel Psychology, 40*, 799–814.

Tang, T.L., Tollison, P.S., & Whiteside, H.D. (1991). Managers' attendance and the effectiveness of small work groups: The case of quality circles. *The Journal of Social Psychology, 131*, 335–344.

Tang, T.L., Tollison, P.S., & Whiteside, H.D. (1996). The case of active and inactive quality circles. *The Journal of Social Psychology, 136*, 57–67.

Tannenbaum, S., & Yukl, G. (1992). Training and development in work organizations. *Annual Review of Psychology, 76*, 759–769.

Tavakolian, H.R. (1993). Break on through to the other side of the glass ceiling. *Equal Opportunities International, 12*, 14–20.

Taylor, D., Block, C., & Berry, P. (1958). Does group participation when using brainstorming facilitate or inhibit creative thinking? *Administrative Science Quarterly, 3*, 23–47.

Taylor, F.W. (1911). *The principles of scientific management.* New York: Harper.

Taylor, M.S., & Bergmann, T.J. (1987). Organizational recruitment activities and applicants' reactions at different stages of the recruitment process. *Personnel Psychology, 40*, 261–285.

Taylor, M.S., & Giannantonio, C.M. (1993). Forming, adapting, and terminating the employment relationship: A review of the literature from individual, organizational, and interactionist perspectives. *Journal of Management, 19*, 461–515.

Taylor, M.S., & Schmidt, D.W. (1983). A process-oriented investigation of recruitment source effectiveness. *Personnel Psychology, 36*, 343–354.

Teboul, J. (1991). *Managing quality dynamics.* Englewood Cliffs, NJ: Prentice-Hall.

Tesser, A., & Rosen, S. (1975). The reluctance to transmit bad news. *Advances in Experimental Social Psychology, 8*, 192–232.

Tett, R.P., Jackson, D.N., & Rothstein, M. (1991). Personality measures as predictors of job performance: A meta-analytic review. *Personnel Psychology, 44*, 703–742.

Thach, L., & Woodman, R.W. (1994). Organizational change and information technology: Managing on the edge of cyberspace. *Organizational Dynamics, 24*, 110–117.

Thacker, R.A., & Wayne, S. (1995). An examination of the relationship between upward influence tactics and assessments of promotability. *Journal of Management, 21*, 739–756.

Tharenou, P. (1993). A test of reciprocal causality for absenteeism. *Journal of Organizational Behavior, 14*, 269–290.

t'Hart, P. (1998). Preventing groupthink revisited: Evaluating and reforming groups in government. *Organizational Behavior and Human Decision Processes, 73*, 306–326.

Thomas, K.W. (1976). Conflict and conflict management. In M. Dunnette (Ed.), *Handbook of industrial and organizational psychology* (pp. 889–936). Chicago: Rand-McNally.

Thomas, K.W. (1992). Conflict and negotiation processes in organizations. In M.D. Dunnette & L.M. Hough (Eds.), *Handbook of industrial and organizational psychology* (2nd ed., Vol 3, pp. 651–717). Palo Alto, CA: Consulting Psychologists Press.

Thorndike, R.L. (1986). The role of general ability in prediction. *Journal of Vocational Behavior, 29*, 332–339.

Thornton, G.C. (1980). Psychometric properties of self-appraisals of job performance. *Personnel Psychology, 33*, 236–271.

Tiegs, R.B., Tetrick, L.E., & Fried, Y. (1992). Growth need strength and context satisfactions as mediators of the relations of the job characteristics model. *Journal of Management, 18*, 575–593.

Tiffin, J. (1968). *Purdue Pegboard.* West Lafayette, IN: Science Research Associates.

Tjosvold, D. (1984a). Effects of crisis orientation on managers' approach to controversy in decision making. *Academy of Management Journal, 27*, 130–138.

Tjosvold, D. (1984b). Effects of leader warmth and directiveness on subordinate performance on a subsequent task. *Journal of Applied Psychology, 69*, 222–232.

Tjosvold, D. (1988). Cooperative and competitive interdependence. *Group & Organization Studies, 13*, 274–289.

Tjosvold, D. (1998a). Making employee involvement work: Cooperative goals and controversy to reduce costs. *Human Relations, 51*, 201–214.

Tjosvold, D. (1998b). Cooperative and competitive goal approach to conflict: Accomplishments and challenges. *Applied Psychology: An International Review, 47*, 285–342.

Tornow, W.W. (1993). Perceptions or reality: Is multiperspective measurement a means or an end? *Human Resource Management, 32*, 221–230.

Tosi, H., & Tosi, L. (1987). What managers need to know about knowledge-based pay. In D.B. Balkin & L.R. Gomez-Mejia (Eds.), *New perspectives on compensation* (pp. 43–48). Englewood Cliffs, NJ: Prentice-Hall.

Tracey, J.B., Tannenbaum, S.I., & Kavanagh, M.J. (1995). Applying trained skills on the job: The importance of the work environment. *Journal of Applied Psychology, 80*, 239–252.

Treiman, D.J., & Hartmann, H.I. (Eds.). (1981). *Women, work and wages.* Washington, DC: National Academy Press.

Trevino, L.K., & Webster, J. (1992). Flow in computer-mediated communication. *Communication Research, 19*, 539–573.

Trevor, C.O., Gerhart, B., & Boudreau, J.W. (1997). Voluntary turnover and job performance: Curvilinearity and the moderating influences of salary growth and promotions. *Journal of Applied Psychology, 82*, 44–61.

Trice, H.M., & Beyer, J.M. (1986). Charisma and its routinization in two social movement organizations. *Research in Organizational Behavior, 8*, 113–164.

Truxillo, D.M., Donahue, L.M., & Sulzer, J.L. (1996). Setting cutoff scores for personnel selection tests: Issues, illustrations, and recommendations. *Human Performance, 9,* 275–295.

Tschan, F. (1995). Communication enhances small group performance if it conforms to task requirements: The concept of ideal communication cycles. *Basic and Applied Social Psychology, 17,* 371–393.

Tubbs, M.E. (1986). Goal setting: A meta-analytic examination of the empirical evidence. *Journal of Applied Psychology, 71,* 474–483.

Tubbs, M.E., Boehne, D.M., & Dahl, J.G. (1993). Expectancy, valence, and motivational force functions in goal-setting research: An empirical test. *Journal of Applied Psychology, 78,* 361–373.

Tucker, F.D. (1985). A study of the training needs of older workers: Implications for human resources development planning. *Public Personnel Management, 14,* 85–95.

Tung, R.L. (1997). International and intranational diversity. In C.S. Granrose & S. Oskamp (Eds.), *Cross-cultural work groups* (pp. 163–185). Thousand Oaks, CA: Sage.

Turban, D.B., Forret, M.L., & Hendrickson, C.L. (1998). Applicant attraction to firms: Influences of organization reputation, job and organizational attributes, and recruiter behaviors. *Journal of Vocational Behavior, 52,* 24–44.

Tziner, A. (1982). Differential effects of group cohesiveness types: A clarifying overview. *Social Behavior and Personality, 10,* 227–239.

Tziner, A., Kopelman, R.E., & Livneh, N. (1993). Effects of performance appraisal format on perceived goal characteristics, appraisal process satisfaction, and changes in related job performance: A field experiment. *The Journal of Psychology, 127,* 281–291.

Tziner, A., Ronen, S., & Hacohen, D. (1993). A four-year validation study of an assessment center in a financial corporation. *Journal of Organizational Behavior, 14,* 225–237.

Unden, A. (1996). Social support at work and its relationship to absenteeism. *Work & Stress, 10,* 46–61.

United States v. City of Chicago. (1977). 549 F.2d 415, *cert. denied,* 434 U.S. 875.

United States Air Force. (1980). *Air Force System Command design handbook 1–3: Human factors engineering* (3rd ed.). Washington, DC: U.S. Air Force.

Ury, W., Brett, J., & Goldberg, S. (1988). *Getting disputes resolved: Designing systems to cut the costs of conflict.* San Francisco: Jossey-Bass.

U.S. Department of Labor. (1977). *Dictionary of occupational titles* (4th ed.). Washington, DC: U.S. Government Printing Office.

Vale, C.D., & Prestwood, J.S. (1987). *Minnesota Clerical Assessment Battery.* San Antonio, TX: The Psychological Corporation.

Vance, R.J., & Colella, A. (1990). Effects of two types of feedback on goal acceptance and personal goals. *Journal of Applied Psychology, 75,* 68–76.

Vance, R.J., Kuhnert, K.W., & Farr, J.L. (1978). Interview judgments: Using external criteria to compare behavioral and graphic scale ratings. *Organizational Behavior and Human Performance, 22,* 279–294.

Vance, R.J., & MacCallum, R.C., Coovert, M.D., & Hedge, J.W. (1988). Construct validity of multiple job performance measures using confirmatory factor analysis. *Journal of Applied Psychology, 73,* 74–80.

Vandaveer, V.V. (1998). As we enter the twenty-first century. *The Industrial-Organizational Psychologist, 35,* 99–102.

Vandenberg, R.J., & Lance, C.E. (1992). Examining the causal order of job satisfaction and organizational commitment. *Journal of Management, 18,* 153–167.

Vanderslice, V.J. (1988). Separating leadership from leaders: An assessment of the effect of leader and follower roles in organizations. *Human Relations, 41,* 677–696.

van der Vegt, G., Emans, B., & van de Vliert, E. (1998). Motivating effects of task and outcome interdependence in work teams. *Group & Organization Management, 23,* 124–143.

Van de Ven, A.H., & Delbecq, A. (1974). A task contingent model of work-unit structure. *Administrative Science Quarterly, 19,* 183–197.

van de Vliert, E., Euwema, M.C., & Huismans, S.E. (1995). Managing conflict with a subordinate or a superior: Effectiveness of conglomerated behavior. *Journal of Applied Psychology, 80,* 271–281.

Van Dyne, L., Graham, J.W., & Dienesch, R.M. (1994). Organizational citizenship behavior: Construct redefinition, measurement, and validation. *Academy of Management Journal, 37,* 765–802.

Van Eerde, W., & Thierry, H. (1996). Vroom's expectancy models and work-related criteria: A meta-analysis. *Journal of Applied Psychology, 81,* 575–586.

Van Nostrand, C.H. (1993). *Gender-responsible leadership.* Newbury Park, CA: Sage.

Van Vianen, A.E.M., & Van Schie, E.C.M. (1995). Assessment of male and female behaviour in the employment interview. *Journal of Community and Applied Psychology, 5,* 243–257.

VanYperen, N.W. (1998). Informational support, equity and burnout: The moderating effect of self-efficacy. *Journal of Occupational and Organizational Psychology, 71,* 29–33.

Vecchio, R.P. (1977). An empirical examination of the validity of Fiedler's model of leadership effectiveness. *Organizational Behavior and Human Performance, 19,* 180–206.

Vecchio, R.P. (1982). A further test of leadership effects due to between-group and within-group variation. *Journal of Applied Psychology, 67,* 200–208.

Vecchio, R.P. (1995). The impact of referral sources on employee attitudes: Evidence from a national sample. *Journal of Management, 21,* 953–965.

Vickroy, S.C., Shaw, J.B., & Fisher, C.D. (1982). Effects of temperature, clothing, and task complexity on task performance and satisfaction. *Journal of Applied Psychology, 67,* 97–102.

Victor, B., & Blackburn, R.S. (1987). Interdependence: An alternative conceptualization. *Academy of Management Review, 12,* 486–498.

Villanova, P., Bernardin, H.J., Johnson, D.L., & Dahmus, S.A. (1994). The validity of a measure of job compatibility in the prediction of job performance and turnover of motion picture theatre personnel. *Personnel Psychology, 47,* 73–90.

Viswesvaran, C., Ones, D.S., & Schmidt, F.L. (1996). Comparative analysis of the reliability of job performance ratings. *Journal of Applied Psychology, 81,* 557–574.

Vroom, V.H. (1964). *Work and motivation.* New York: John Wiley & Sons.

Vroom, V.H., & Jago, A.G. (1978). On the validity of the Vroom-Yetton model. *Journal of Applied Psychology, 63,* 151–162.

Vroom, V.H., & Jago, A.G. (1988). *The new leadership: Managing participation in organizations.* Englewood Cliffs, NJ: Prentice-Hall.

Vroom, V.H., & Jago, A.G. (1995). Situation effects and levels of analysis in the study of leader participation. *Leadership Quarterly, 6,* 169–181.

Vroom, V.H., & Yetton, P.W. (1973). *Leadership and decision-making.* Pittsburgh, PA: University of Pittsburgh Press.

Wageman, R., & Baker, G. (1997). Incentives and cooperation: The joint effects of task and reward interdependence on group performance. *Journal of Organizational Behavior, 18,* 139–158.

Wahba, M.A., & Bridwell, L.T. (1976). Maslow reconsidered: A review of research on the need hierarchy theory. *Organizational Behavior and Human Performance, 15,* 212–240.

Waldman, D.A. (1994). The contributions of total quality management to a theory of work performance. *Academy of Management Review, 19,* 510–536.

Waldman, D.A., Atwater, L.E., & Antonioni, D. (1998). Has 360-degree feedback gone amok? *Academy of Management Executive, 12,* 86–94.

Walker, J., Fletcher, C., & McLeod, D. (1975). Flexible working hours in two British government offices. *Public Personnel Management, 4,* 219.

Wall, J.A., & Callister, R.R. (1995). Conflict and its management. *Journal of Management, 21,* 515–558.

Wall Street Journal (1993, April 2). "More U.S. companies test employees for drug use."

Wallach, M.A., Kogan, N., & Bem, D.J. (1962). Group influence on individual risk taking. *Journal of Abnormal and Social Psychology, 65,* 75–86.

Walton, R.E. (1972). How to counter alienation in the plant. *Harvard Business Review, 50,* 22.

Walton, R.E. (1975). Criteria for quality of working life. In L.E. Davis & A.B. Cherns (Eds.), *The quality of working life* (Vol. 1, pp. 91–104). New York: Free Press.

Walton, R.E., & Dutton, J.M. (1969). The management of interdepartmental conflict: A model and review. *Administrative Science Quarterly, 14,* 73–84.

Walz, S.M., & Niehoff, B.P. (1996). Organizational citizenship behaviors and their effect on organizational effectiveness in limited-menu restaurants. In J.B. Keys & L.N. Dosier (Eds.), *Academy of Management best paper proceedings* (pp. 307–311). Briarcliff Manor, NY: Academy of Management.

Wanous, J.P. (1980). *Organizational entry: Recruitment, selection, and socialization of newcomers.* Reading, MA: Addison-Wesley.

Wanous, J.P. (1989). Installing realistic job previews: Ten tough choices. *Personnel Psychology, 42,* 117–134.

Wanous, J.P. (1992). *Organizational entry: Recruitment, selection, and socialization of newcomers* (2nd ed.). Reading, MA: Addison-Wesley.

Wanous, J.P. (1993). Newcomer orientation programs that facilitate organizational entry. In H. Schuler, J.L. Farr, & M. Smith (Eds.), *Personnel selection and assessment: Individual and organizational perspectives* (pp. 125–139). Hillsdale, NJ: Lawrence Erlbaum.

Wanous, J.P., Keon, T.L., & Latack, J.C. (1983). Expectancy theory and occupational/organizational choices: A review and test. *Organizational Behavior and Human Performance, 32,* 66–86.

Wanous, J.P., Poland, T.D., Premack, S.L., & Davis, K.S. (1992). The effects of met expectations on newcomer attitudes and behaviors: A review and meta-analysis. *Journal of Applied Psychology, 77,* 288–297.

Wanous, J.P., Reichers, A.E., & Hudy, M.J. (1997). Overall job satisfaction: How good are single-item measures? *Journal of Applied Psychology, 82,* 247–252.

Wanous, J.P., Reichers, A.E., & Malik, S.D. (1984). Organizational socialization and group development: Toward an integrative perspective. *Academy of Management Review, 9,* 670–683.

Wanous, J.P., Stumpf, S.A., & Bedrosian, H. (1979). Job survival of new employees. *Personnel Psychology, 32,* 651–662.

Warr, P., & Bunce, D. (1995). Trainee characteristics and the outcomes of open learning. *Personnel Psychology, 48,* 347–375.

Wasik, B. (1984). *Teaching parents effective problem solving: A handbook for professionals.* Chapel Hill, NC: University of North Carolina Press.

Waters, L.K., & Roach, D. (1979). Job satisfaction, behavioral intention, and absenteeism as predictors of turnover. *Personnel Psychology, 32,* 393–397.

Waterworth, J.A., & Thomas, C.M. (1985). Why is synthetic speech harder to remember than natural speech? *Human factors in computing systems proceedings* (pp. 201–206). New York: Association for Computing Machinery.

Watson, W.E., Kumar, K., & Michaelsen, L.K. (1993). Cultural diversity's impact on interaction process and performance: Comparing homogeneous and diverse task groups. *Academy of Management Journal, 36,* 590–602.

Waung, M. (1995). The effects of self-regulatory coping orientation on newcomer adjustment and job survival. *Personnel Psychology, 48,* 633–650.

Wayne, S.J., & Ferris, G.R. (1990). Influence tactics, affect, and exchange quality in supervisor-subordinate interactions: A laboratory and a field study. *Journal of Applied Psychology, 75,* 487–499.

Weber, M. (1947). *The theory of social and economic organizations* (A.M. Henderson & T. Parsons, Trans.). New York: Free Press.

Webster, J., & Martocchio, J.J. (1993). Turning work into play: Implications for microcomputer software training. *Journal of Management, 19,* 127–146.

Webster, J., & Martocchio, J.J. (1995). The differential effects of software training previews on training outcomes. *Journal of Management, 21,* 757–787.

Wechsler, D. (1981). *Wechsler Adult Intelligence Scale-Revised.* New York: The Psychological Corporation.

Weekley, J.A., & Gier, J. A. (1987). Reliability and validity of the situational interview for a sales position. *Journal of Applied Psychology, 72,* 484–487.

Weierter, S.J.M. (1997). Who wants to play "follow the leader?" A theory of charismatic relationships based on routinized charisma and follower characteristics. *Leadership Quarterly, 8,* 171–193.

Weiner, E.L., & Curry, R.E. (1980). Flight deck automation: Promises and problems. *Ergonomics, 23,* 995–1012.

Weingart, L.R. (1992). Impact of group goals, task component complexity, effort, and planning on group performance. *Journal of Applied Psychology, 77,* 682–693.

Weisband, S.P. (1992). Group discussion and first advocacy effects in computer-mediated and face-to-face decision-making groups. *Organizational Behavior and Human Decision Processes, 53,* 352–380.

Weiss, D.J., Dawis, R.V., England, G.W., & Lofquist, L.H. (1967). *Manual for the Minnesota Satisfaction Questionnaire* (Minnesota Studies on Vocational Rehabilitation, Vol. 22). Minneapolis: University of Minnesota Industrial Relations Center.

Weiss, H.M., Ilgen, D.R., & Sharbaugh, M.E. (1982). Effects of life and job stress on information search behaviors of organizational members. *Journal of Applied Psychology, 67,* 60–66.

Weiss, R.M. (1987). Writing under the influence: Science versus fiction in the analysis of corporate alcoholism programs. *Personnel Psychology, 40,* 341–356.

Wellington, A.J. (1993). Changes in the male/female wage gap. *Journal of Human Resources, 28,* 383–411.

Werner, C.M., & Haggard, L.M. (1992). Avoiding intrusions at the office: Privacy regulation on typical and high solitude days. *Basic and Applied Social Psychology, 13,* 181–193.

Westman, M., & Eden, D. (1997). Effects of a respite from work on burnout: Vacation relief and fade-out. *Journal of Applied Psychology, 82,* 516–527.

Wexley, K.N. (1986). Appraisal interview. In R.A. Berk (Ed.), *Performance assessment: Methods and applications* (pp. 167–185). Baltimore, MD: The Johns Hopkins University Press.

Wexley, K.N., & Baldwin, T.T. (1986). Post-training strategies for facilitating positive transfer: An empirical exploration. *Academy of Management Journal, 29,* 503–520.

Wexley, K.N., & Latham, G.P. (1981). *Developing and training human resources in organizations.* Glenview, IL: Scott, Foresman.

Wexley, K.N., & Latham, G.P. (1991). *Developing and training human resources in organizations* (2nd ed.). New York: Harper-Collins.

Wexley, K.N., & McCellin, D.G. (1987). The effects of varying training task difficulty on training transfer. Paper presented at the 95th annual convention of the American Psychological Association, New York.

Wexley, K.N., Sanders, R.E., & Yukl, G.A. (1973). Training interviewers to eliminate contrast effects in employment interviews. *Journal of Applied Psychology, 57,* 233–236.

Wexley, K.N., & Yukl, G.A. (1984). *Organizational behavior and personnel psychology* (Rev. ed.). Homewood, IL: Richard D. Irwin.

Wheaton, G.R., & Whetzel, D.L. (1997). Contexts for developing applied measurement instruments. In D.L. Whetzel, & G.R. Wheaton (Eds.), *Applied measurement methods in industrial psychology* (pp. 1–10). Palo Alto, CA: Davies-Black.

Wheeler, D.D., & Janis, I.L. (1980). *A practical guide for making decisions.* New York: Free Press.

Wichman, A. (1994). Occupational differences in involvement with ownership in an airline employee ownership program. *Human Relations, 47,* 829–846.

Wichman, H. (1992). *Human factors in the design of spacecraft.* Stony Brook, NY: Research Foundation of the State University of New York.

Wichman, H., & Donaldson, S.I. (1996). Remote ergonomic research in space: Spacelab findings and a proposal. *Aviation, Space, and Environmental Medicine, 67,* 171–175.

Wickens, C.D. (1984). *Engineering psychology and human performance.* Columbus, OH: Charles E. Merrill.

Wickens, C.D. (1993). *Engineering psychology and human performance* (2nd ed.), New York: Harper Collins.

Wickens, C.D., & Carswell, C.M. (1995). The proximity compatibility principle: Its psychological foundation and relevance to display design. *Human Factors, 37,* 473–494.

Wickens, C.D., Gordon, S.E., & Liu, Y. (1998). *An introduction to human factors engineering.* New York: Addison Wesley Longman.

Wiesner, W.H., & Cronshaw, S.F. (1988). A meta-analytic investigation of interviewer format and degree of structure on the validity of the employment interview. *Journal of Occupational and Organizational Psychology, 61,* 275–290.

Wilbur, C.S. (1983). The Johnson and Johnson program. *Preventative Medicine, 12,* 672–681.

Williams, C.R., Labig, C.E., & Stone, T.H. (1993). Recruitment sources and posthire outcomes for job applicants and new hires: A test of two hypotheses. *Journal of Applied Psychology, 78,* 163–172.

Williams, J.R., & Levy, P.E. (1992) The effects of perceived system knowledge on the agreement between self-ratings and supervisor ratings. *Personnel Psychology, 45,* 835–847.

Williams, K.Y., & O'Reilly, C.A. (1998). Demography and diversity in organizations: A review of 40 years of research. *Research in Organizational Behavior, 20,* 77–140.

Williams, L.J., & Hazer, J.T. (1986). Antecedents and consequences of satisfaction and commitment in turnover models: A reanalysis using latent variable structural equation methods. *Journal of Applied Psychology, 71,* 219–231.

Williams, S., & Taormina, R.J. (1992). Unanimous versus majority influences on group polarization in business decision making. *The Journal of Social Psychology, 133,* 199–205.

Williamson, L.G., Campion, J.E., Malos, S.B., Roehling, M.V., & Campion, M.A. (1997). Employment interview on trial: Linking interview structure with litigation outcomes. *Journal of Applied Psychology, 82,* 900–912.

Winter, D.G. (1973). *The power motive.* New York: Free Press.

Winters, D., & Latham, G.P. (1996). The effect of learning versus outcome goals on a simple versus a complex task. *Group & Organization Management, 21,* 236–250.

Withey, M., Daft, R.L., & Cooper, W.H. (1983). Measures of Perrow's work unit technology: An empirical assessment and a new scale. *Academy of Management Journal, 26,* 45–63.

Witt, L.A. (1998). Enhancing organizational goal congruence: A solution to organizational politics. *Journal of Applied Psychology, 83,* 666–674.

Witt, L.A., & Nye, L.G. (1992). Gender and the relationship between perceived fairness of pay or promotion and job satisfaction. *Journal of Applied Psychology, 77,* 910–917.

Wittig, M.A., & Berman, S.L. (1992). Wage structure analysis: An empirical approach to pay equity in segregated jobs. *Social Justice Research, 5,* 291–317.

Woehr, D.J. (1992). Performance dimension accessibility: Implications for rating accuracy. *Journal of Organizational Behavior, 13,* 357–367.

Woehr, D.J. (1994). Rater training for performance appraisal: A quantitative review. *Journal of Occupational and Organizational Psychology, 67,* 221–229.

Woehr, D.J., & Huffcutt, A.I. (1994). Rater training for performance appraisal: A quantitative review. *Journal of Occupational and Organizational Psychology, 67,* 189–205.

Woehr, D.J., & Roch, S.G. (1996). Context effects in performance evaluation: The impact of ratee sex and performance level on performance ratings and behavioral recall. *Organizational Behavior and Human Decision Processes, 66,* 31–41.

Wofford, J.C., & Liska, L.Z. (1993). Path-goal theories of leadership: A meta-analysis. *Journal of Management, 19,* 857–874.

Wofford, J.C., Goodwin, V.L., & Premack, S. (1992). Meta-analysis of the antecedents of personal goal level and of the antecedents and consequences of goal commitment. *Journal of Management, 18*(3), 595–615.

Wohlers, A.J., Hall, M., & London, M. (1993). Subordinates rating managers: Organizational and demographic correlates of self-subordinate agreement. *Journal of Occupational and Organizational Psychology, 66*, 263–275.

Wohlers, A.J., & London, M. (1989). Ratings of managerial characteristics: Evaluation difficulty, coworker agreement, and self-awareness. *Personnel Psychology, 42*, 235–261.

Wolf, F.M. (1986). *Meta-analysis: Quantitative methods for research synthesis.* Beverly Hills, CA: Sage Press.

Wolf, S.G. (1986). Common and grave disorders identified with occupational stress. In S.G. Wolf & A.J. Finestone (Eds.), *Occupational stress: Health and performance at work* (pp. 47–53). Littleton, MA: PSG Publishing.

Wolfgang, A.P. (1988). Job stress in the health professions: A study of physicians, nurses, and pharmacists. *Behavioral Medicine, 14,* 43–47.

Wonderlic, E.F. (1983). *Wonderlic Personnel Test.* Northfield, IL: Wonderlic and Associates.

Woodman, R.W., & Pasmore, W.A. (Eds.). (1987). *Research in organizational change and development* (Vol. 1). Greenwich, CT: JAI Press.

Woodman, R.W., & Sherwood, J.J. (1980). Effects of team development intervention: A field experiment. *Journal of Applied Behavioral Science, 16,* 211–227.

Woodward, J. (1965). *Industrial organization: Theory and practice.* London: Oxford University Press.

Wratcher, M.A., & Jones, R.D. (1986). A time management workshop for adult workers. *Journal of College Student Personnel, 27,* 566–567.

Wright, G.E., & Multon, K.D. (1995). Employer's perception of nonverbal communication in job interviews for persons with physical disabilities. *Journal of Vocational Behavior, 47,* 214–227.

Wright, P.M., Lichtenfels, P.A., & Pursell, E.D. (1989). The structured interview: Additional studies and a meta-analysis. *Journal of Occupational and Organizational Psychology, 62,* 191–199.

Wright, T.A., & Cropanzano, R. (1998). Emotional exhaustion as a predictor of job performance and voluntary turnover. *Journal of Applied Psychology, 83,* 486–493.

Yammarino, F.J., & Waldman, D.A. (1993). Performance in relation to job skill importance: A consideration of rater source. *Journal of Applied Psychology, 78,* 242–249.

Yates, J., & Orlikowski, W.J. (1992). Genres of organizational communication: A structrational approach to studying communication and the media. *Academy of Management Review, 17,* 299–326.

Yeager, S.J. (1981). Dimensionality of the Job Descriptive Index. *Academy of Management Journal, 14,* 205–212.

Yetton, P.W., & Bottger, P.C. (1982). Individual versus group problem solving: An empirical test of a best-member strategy. *Organizational Behavior and Human Performance, 29,* 307–321.

Yorks, L. (1979). *Job enrichment revisited.* New York: AMACOM.

Youngblood, S.A. (1984). Work, nonwork, and withdrawal. *Journal of Applied Psychology, 69,* 106–117.

Yukl, G.A. (1971). Toward a behavioral theory of leadership. *Organizational Behavior and Human Performance, 6,* 414–440.

Yukl, G.A. (1981). *Leadership in organizations.* Englewood Cliffs, NJ: Prentice-Hall.

Yukl, G.A. (1989). *Leadership in organizations* (2nd ed.). Englewood Cliffs, NJ: Prentice-Hall.

Yukl, G.A. (1998). *Leadership in organizations* (4th ed.). Englewood Cliffs, NJ: Prentice-Hall.

Yukl, G.A., & Falbe, C.M. (1990). Influence tactics and objectives in upward, downward, and lateral influence attempts. *Journal of Applied Psychology, 75,* 132–140.

Yukl, G.A., & Falbe, C.M. (1991). Importance of different power sources in downward and lateral relations. *Journal of Applied Psychology, 76,* 416–423.

Yukl, G.A., Guinan, P.J., & Sottolano, D. (1995). Influence tactics used for different objectives with subordinates, peers, and superiors. *Group & Organization Management, 20,* 272–296.

Yukl, G.A., & Tracey, J.B. (1992). Consequences of influence tactics used with subordinates, peers, and the boss. *Journal of Applied Psychology, 77,* 525–535.

Yukl, G.A., & VanFleet, D.D. (1992). Theory and research on leadership in organizations. In M.D. Dunnette and L.M. Hough (Eds.), *Handbook of industrial and organizational psychology* (Vol. 3, 2nd ed., pp. 147–197). Palo Alto, CA: Consulting Psychologists Press.

Zaccaaro, S.J., Foti, R.J., & Kenny, D.A. (1991). Self-monitoring and trait-based variance in leadership: An investigation of leader flexibility across multiple group situations. *Journal of Applied Psychology, 76,* 179–185.

Zahn, G.L. (1991). Face-to-face communication in an office setting. *Communication Research, 18,* 737–754.

Zalesny, M.D., & Farace, R.V. (1987). Traditional versus open offices: A comparison of sociotechnical, social relations, and symbolic meaning perspectives. *Academy of Management Journal, 30,* 240–259.

Zaremba, A. (1988, July). Communication: Working with the organizational grapevine. *Personnel Journal,* pp. 83–84.

Zedeck, S. (1977). An information processing model and approach to the study of motivation. *Organizational Behavior and Human Performance, 18,* 47–77.

Zedeck, S., Jackson, S.E., & Marca, E.S. (1983). Shift work schedules and their relationship to health, adaptation, satisfaction, and turnover intention. *Academy of Management Journal, 26,* 297–310.

Zehr, M.A. (1993). Evolution, not revolution. *Foundation News, 34,* 46–47.

Zimring, C.M. (1981). Stress and the designed environment. *Journal of Social Issues, 37,* 145–171.

Zohar, D. (1980). Safety climate in industrial organizations: Theoretical and applied implications. *Journal of Applied Psychology, 65,* 96–102.

Zussman, Y.M. (1983). Learning from the Japanese: Management in a resource-scarce world. *Organizational Dynamics, 11,* 68–80.

Zwerman, W.L. (1970). *New perspectives on organizational theory.* Westport, CT: Greenwood Press.

CREDITS

58 **Table 3.1** "Job Descriptions" from E.J. McCormick, *Job Analysis: Methods and Applications*, p. 63. Copyright © 1979 E.J. McCormick.

59 **Figure 3.1** "Links Between Job Analysis and Personnel Functions" by Jai V. Ghorpade, *Job Analysis: A Handbook for the Human Resource Director*, p. 6, Copyright © 1988. Adapted by permission of Prentice Hall, Inc., Englewood Cliffs, New Jersey.

69 **Figure 3.2** From E.J. McCormick, P.R. Jeanneret, and R.C. Meacham, *Position Analysis Questionnaire*, copyright 1969 by Purdue Research Foundation. West Lafayette, Indiana 47907. Reprinted with permission.

71 **Figure 3.3** "Critical Incidents Interview Form" from "The Critical Incidents Technique" by J.C. Flanagan, in *Psychological Bulletin*, 51, p. 342, 1954. Copyright © 1954 by the American Psychological Association. Reprinted with permission.

74 **Table 3.4** "Job Evaluation" from *Psychology of Work Behavior*, 3/e by Frank J. Landy, Copyright © 1985 by Wadsworth, Inc. Adapted by permission of Brooks/Cole Publishing Company, Pacific Grove, CA 93950.

74 **Table 3.4** Adapted from *Handbook on Wages and Salary Administration*, 2/e, by M.L. Rock. Copyright © 1984. Used with permission of McGraw-Hill Companies., p. 158.

97 **Figure 4.4** "Sample Items" from the Bennett Mechanical Comprehension Test. Copyright 1942, 1967–1970, 1980 by The Psychological Corporation. Reproduced by permission. All rights reserved. "Bennett Mechanical Comprehension Test" and "BMCT" are registered trademarks of The Psychological Corporation.

99 **Figure 4.5** Reproduced by special permission of the Publisher, Consulting Psychologists Press, Inc., Palo Alto, CA 94303 from the *California Psychological Inventory-Form 434* by Harrison G. Gough. Copyright © 1987 by Consulting Psychologists Press, Inc., All rights reserved. Further reproduction is prohibited without the Publisher's written consent.

115 **Figure 4.7** "Multiple Hurdle Model for Police Officer Selection" from *Applied Psychology in Personnel Management*, 3/e by W.F. Cascio, p. 282, Copyright © 1987. Adapted by permission of Prentice Hall, Inc., Englewood Cliffs, New Jersey.

125 **Table 5.1** "Benefits of a Career Development System" from *Designing Career Development Systems* by Leibowitz, Farren, Kaye, 1986, p. 7. Copyright © 1986 by Leibowitz, Farren, Kaye and Jossey-Bass Inc., Publishers. Reprinted by permission.

163 **Table 6.2** "Objective Job Performance Criteria" table from *The Measurement Of Work Performance: Methods, Theory, and Applications*, 1983 by F.L. Landy and J.L. Farr. Reprinted by permission of Academic Press, Inc.

168 **Figure 6.2** "Examples of Graphic Rating Scales" from *Personnel Testing* by R.M. Guion, Copyright © 1965. Reprinted by permission of the author.

169 **Figure 6.3** "Checklist Rating Scale" by R.R. Jacobs in *Performance Assessments: Methods & Applications*, ed. R.A. Berk. The Johns Hopkins University Press, Baltimore/London, 1987, p 82–99.

170 **Figure 6.4** "Behaviorally Anchored Rating Scale (Bars)" from W.C. Borman in *Performance Assessments: Methods and Applications*, ed. R.A. Berk, The Johns Hopkins University Press, Baltimore/London, 1987, p. 103.

177 **Table 6.3** "Guidelines for Effective Performance Feedback" from *Applied Organizational Communication: Perspectives, Principles and Pragmatics*, by T.E. Harris, Copyright © 1993. Reprinted by permission of Lawrence Erlbaum Associates, Inc.

199 **Figure 7.2** "Job Characteristics Model of Work Motivation" by J.R. Hackman and G.R. Oldham, from *Organizational Behavior and Human Decision Processes* (formerly *Organizational Behavior and Human Performance*), Vol. 16, p. 256 (1979). Reprinted by permission of Academic Press, Inc.

222 **Figure 8.1** Sample Items adapted from *The Minnesota Satisfaction Questionnaire*, by D.J. Weiss, G.W. England, and L.H. Lofquist, Copyright © 1977. Reproduced

agement Review, Vol. 9, 1984, pp. 482–493. Reprinted by permission of the Academy of Management.

443 **Figure 15.1** From A. Chapanis, "Engineering Psychology" from *Man-Machine Engineering*, Brooks/Cole Publishing Co.; as it appeared in *Handbook of Industrial and Organizational Psychology*, ed. M.D. Dunnette, p. 701, John Wiley and Sons.

447 **Table 15.2** "Guidelines for the Use of Visual and Auditory Mechanical Displays" from *Human Factors in Engineering and Design*, 7/e by M.S. Sanders and E.J. McCormick, Copyright © 1993. Reprinted by permission of the McGraw-Hill Companies.

450 **Figure 15.2** Tactile-Coded Controls: Standardized Shape-Coded Knobs for USAF Aircraft from *Air Force System Command Design Handbook* 1–3: Human Factors Engineering, 1980.

456 **Figure 15.6** "Computer Controls for Text Editing" adapted from "Evaluation of Mouse, Rate-Controlled Isometric Joystick, Step keys and Text Keys for Text Selection on a CRT" by S. Card, W. English, and B. Burr in *Ergonomics*, Vol. 21, 1978. Reprinted by permission of Taylor & Francis Ltd., Hampshire, UK.

472 **Table 16.1** "Levels of Illumination Recommended for Certain Work Tasks and Settings" adapted from *CIBSE Code for Interior Lighting*, 1984 by permission of The Chartered Institution of Building Services Engineers.

473 **Table 16.2** "Techniques to Reduce Worker Discomfort Caused by Extreme Temperatures" from *Design for People at Work*, Vol. 1, pp. 254–262. Copyright © 1983 Eastman Kodak Company. Reprinted by permission from Eastman Kodak.

486 **Table 16.4** "Some Common Occupational Diseases" from *Healthy People in Unhealthy Places: Stress and Fitness at Work*, by K.R. Pelletier, 1984. Reprinted by permission of Robert Briggs Associates.

490 **Figure 16.1** "Accident Figure" from *Human Factors in Engineering And Design*, 7/e by M.S. Sanders and E.J. McCormick, Copyright © 1993. Reprinted by permission of the McGraw-Hill Companies.

PHOTO CREDITS

Chapter 1

Page 3L © Taro Yamasaki; **3R:** © Taro Yamasaki; **8B:** © UPI Corbis-Bettmann; **8T:** © Stock Montage, Inc.; **10:** © AT&T Archives; **11:** © Adam Bartos; **15:** © Terry Vine/Tony Stone Images

Chapter 2

Page 25: © Charles Harbutt/Actuality Inc.; **35:** Scott, Foresman and Company

Chapter 3

Page 60: © Bob Daemmrich/Stock Boston; **61:** © Frank Siteman/Stock Boston; **66:** © Nancy Lane/The Picture Cube; **75:** Marlette © The Charlotte Observer

Chapter 4

Page 84: © Martha Evanson; **92:** © Tom Sheppard/Tony Stone Images; **101:** © Tim Barnwell/Stock Boston; **105:** Scott, Foresman and Company; **108:** © Bruce Ayres/Tony Stone Images; **111:** © Sidney Harris

Chapter 5

Page 128: © David Wells/The Image Works; **137:** © Greg Pease/Tony Stone Images; **139:** © Michael L. Abramson/Woodfin Camp & Associates; **135:** © Bruce Ayres/Tony Stone Images; **149:** © Mathew Brokoski/Stock Boston

Chapter 6

Page 160: © Rhoda Sidney/The Image Works; **162:** © Susan Van Etten/The Picture Cube; **180:** © John Iocono/Sports Illustrated

Chapter 7

Page 192: © Dennis Brack/Black Star; **198:** © Charles Harbutt/Actuality Inc.; **205:** © John Harding; **211:** © David Hiser/Photographers Aspen

Chapter 8

Page 234L: © Andy Freeberg; **234:** M: © Andy Freeberg; **235R:** © Andy Freeberg; **236:** © James Lukoski; **237:** Courtesy, United Airlines; **239:** Scott, Foresman and Company; **241:** Scott, Foresman and Company

Chapter 9

Page 249T: © Diane Graham-Henry; **249B:** © David Witbeck/The Picture Cube; **251:** © Frank Siteman/The Picture Cube; **263:** © Bob Daemmrich/The Image Works; **265:** © Susan A. Anderson

Chapter 10

Page 277L: © Adam Smith Productions/West Light; **277R:** © Stacey Pick/Uniphoto; **280:** Reprinted by permission: Tribune Media Services; **282:** Courtesy of U.S. Sprint; **292:** © The New Yorker Collection 1982 Ziegler from cartoonbank.com. All Rights Reserved.; **295:** © Sarah Putnam/The Picture Cube

Chapter 11

Page 305: © Chad Slattery; **308:** © Spencer Grant/Stock Boston; **312:** © Charles Gupton/Stock Boston; 321: © Paul Conklin/Uniphoto; **325:** © Skjold/The Image Works

Chapter 12

Page 341B: © UPI/Corbis-Bettmann; **341M:** © Caraballo/Monkmeyer; **341T:** © Cindy Loo/The Picture Cube; **350:** © Jeffrey W. Meyers/Stock Boston; **366L:** © Bruce Ayres/Tony Stone Images; **366R:** © Walter Hodges/Tony Stone Images

Chapter 13

Page 379: © Mimi Forsyth/Monkmeyer; **382:** © Martha Stewart/The Picture Cube; **384:** © David Wells/The Image Works

Chapter 14

410: © Brown Brothers; **412:** Photo copyright 1985 U.S. News & World Report, Inc. Credit: Gary L. Kieffer, U.S. News & World Report; **414:** Don Smetzer/Tony Stone Images; **421:** © Zimbel/Monkmeyer; **430:** © Charles Harbutt/Actuality Inc.

Chapter 15

Page 442: © McConnell NcNamara & Company 1982; **444:** © M. Granitsas/The Image Works; **455:** © NASA; **461:** © McConnell McNamara & Company 1982; **463:** Courtesy Bestar

Chapter 16

472: © Tom Cheek/Stock Boston; **474:** © Bob Daemmrich/The Image Works; **481:** © Rhoda Sydney/The Image Works; **486:** © McConnell McNamara & Company 1982; **488:** © NASA/The Image Works; **492:** © Alan Carey/The Image Works

NAME INDEX

SUBJECT INDEX